Finding Philosophy
in Social Science

MARIO BUNGE

YALE UNIVERSITY PRESS
NEW HAVEN AND LONDON

Published with assistance from the foundation established
in memory of Philip Hamilton McMillan
of the Class of 1894, Yale College.

Designed by Sally Harris, Summer Hill Books.

Set in Galliard type by The Composing Room of Michigan, Inc., Grand Rapids, Michigan.
Printed in the United States of America by Book Crafters, Inc., Chelsea, Michigan.

Library of Congress Cataloging-in-Publication Data

Bunge, Mario Augusto.
Finding philosophy in social science / Mario Bunge.
p.   cm.
Includes bibliographical references and index.
ISBN 0-300-06606-6 (cloth : alk. paper)
1. Social sciences—Philosophy.   I. Title.
H61.B793   1996
300'.1—dc20   96-4399
                                                          CIP

A catalogue record for this book is available
from the British Library.

The paper in this book meets the guidelines for
permanence and durability of the Committee on
Production Guidelines for Book Longevity of the
Council on Library Resources.

10 9 8 7 6 5 4 3 2 1

*To all those interested in social studies, and who either
hate philosophy because they find it irrelevant or obscure, or
love it because they realize that it can bring clarity, depth, unity, and insight*

Contents ::

Preface   xi

Introduction :: *Why Philosophy?*   1
   1 Social Science Includes Some Philosophy   1
   2 Philosophical Controversies in Social Science   4
   3 What Is Social Metatheory About and Up To?   6
   4 Kinds of Philosophy of Social Science   8
   5 Evaluating Philosophies of Social Science   10

PART A :: *From Fact to Theory*

1 :: *Fact*   15
   1 Thing and Property   17
   2 Emergence and System   19
   3 State, Event, Process   23
   4 Pattern   26
   5 Causation   30
   6 Chance and Chaos   36
   7 Phenomenon   41
   8 Social Fact   44

2 :: *Idea*   47
   1 Concept and Proposition   49
   2 Form and Content   53

3 Fuzziness and Exactness   57
4 Formalization   61
5 Ideal Type   66
6 Definition   68
7 Assumption   70
8 Rule   73

3::*Inquiry*   76
1 Approach and Paradigm   79
2 Problem   81
3 Datum   84
4 Hypothesis   90
5 Truth   94
6 Criticism   99
7 Method   101
8 The Problem of Knowledge   104

4::*Systematization*   108
1 Sketch   109
2 Classification   111
3 Theory and Model   113
4 Theoretical Law   119
5 Kinds of Theory   121
6 Reduction   126
7 Reductionism   128
8 Merger   130

PART B::*From Explanation to Justification*

5::*Explanation and Prediction*   135
1 Description   135
2 Explanation   137
3 Logical Form   142
4 Upward and Downward   145
5 Verstehen   150
6 The Role of Verstehen   154
7 Forecast and Hindcast   157
8 Designer Future   164

6::*Empirical Operations*   166
1 Testability   167
2 Indicator   169
3 Social Indicator   172
4 Reality Check   174
5 The Weight of Evidence   180

7::*Science et al.*   184
  1 Basic Science   186
  2 The Unity of Science   191
  3 Applied Science   196
  4 Technology   197
  5 Pseudoscience   205
  6 An Example: The New Sociology of Science   208
  7 Ideology   211
  8 Confusing Science with Ideology   214

8::*Values and Morals*   219
  1 Nature and Roots of Values   219
  2 Utility   222
  3 Morals   225
  4 Freedom   227
  5 Ethics   229
  6 Science, Technology, and Morals   234

PART C::*General Philosophy Problems in Social Science*

9::*Individualism and Holism*   241
  1 Individualism   243
  2 The Case of Rational Choice Theory   248
  3 Individholism and Crypto-Systemism   253
  4 Shortcomings of Individualism   255
  5 Holism   258

10::*Systemism*   264
  1 The Systemic Approach   265
  2 Systemism in Social Science   267
  3 Social System   270
  4 Social Structure and Social Change   274
  5 Micro–Macro Relations   277

11::*Idealism and Materialism*   282
  1 Idealism   285
  2 Contemporary Hermeneutics   290
  3 Phenomenology   293
  4 Ontological Constructivism   295
  5 Materialisms   298

12::*Intuitionism, Empiricism, Pragmatism, and Rationalism*   305
  1 Intuitionism   306
  2 Contemporary Obscurantism   309
  3 Vulgar Empiricism and Crypto-Empiricism   311
  4 Logical Empiricism   316

5 Pragmatism 317
6 Rationalism 320
7 Ratio-Empiricism 322

13::*Subjectivism and Realism* 326
1 Subjectivism 330
2 Conventionalism 332
3 Social Constructivism 335
4 Relativism 338
5 Epistemological Hermeneutics 343
6 Probability: Objective and Subjective 346
7 Objective Study of Subjectivity 351
8 Scientific Realism 353

14::*Between Reason and Fact: Rational Choice Theory* 359
1 Foundations of Rational Choice Theory 361
2 Five Versions of the Rationality Postulate 366
3 Maximizers or Survivors? 370
4 Subjective and Unconscious Rationality? 373
5 Instrumental Rationality 376
6 Explanation by Reasons versus Explanation by Causes 377
7 Evaluation of the Rational Choice Approach 378
8 The Fatal Flaws of Rational Choice Theory 383

APPENDIXES
1 State Space Representation 391
2 Law and Rule 392
3 The Logic of Theory Operationalization 393
4 Utility: A Skeleton in the Closet of Rational Choice Theory 394
5 Futility Theory 397
6 Objective Value 399
7 Utility as a Set 399

References 401
Index of Names 421
Index of Subjects 427

Preface ::

This book has been written for social scientists curious about philosophy, as well as for philosophers interested in social studies. As suggested by its title, it focuses on the philosophy involved in social studies—albeit, usually in a tacit manner. I will argue that all social studies, whether scientific or literary, are crammed with philosophical concepts, such as those of fact, system, process, theory, test, and truth. They also contain or presuppose some philosophical assumptions, such as that societies are (or are not) mere aggregates of individuals, that people can (or cannot) choose and act rationally, and that social facts can (or cannot) be studied scientifically.

Regrettably, most students of society rarely pause to examine the philosophical ideas they adopt. When they do, they often fall under the influence of philosophies that do not match the practice of contemporary social science research. Most of the philosophers who have paid attention to the philosophy in or about social science have held some or all of the following three theses: that there is a clear divide between the social and the natural sciences, there being no mixed or socio-natural sciences; that science and philosophy are mutually disjoint, so cannot learn from one another; that the philosophy of social science is the same as that of the natural sciences—or else that the two are utterly disjoint. I will argue that all three, and many more received opinions, are false.

I will examine some of the key philosophical ideas inherent in the social (and socio-natural) sciences, as well as some of the topical philosophical problems raised by them. Thus I will elucidate the ontological notions of event and causation, the semantic concepts of meaning and truth, the epistemological ideas of hypothesis and indicator, the axiological notions of value and utility, and the ethical concepts of right and duty. I will also wrestle with such classical controversies as individualism versus holism, idealism versus materialism, subjectivism versus realism, rationalism versus empiricism, explanation versus understanding, and nomothetic versus idiographic sciences.

My aim in writing this book has been not only the enjoyment that comes from thinking about such problems, but the wish to be of some service to social scientists, who are sometimes hampered in their empirical work because, as a well-known sociologist put it, "they are confused by logical and philosophical difficulties" (Stinchcombe 1968, vi). I share Einstein's contempt for what he called "intellectual acrobatics"—which, as Hilbert thought, is good only for academic promotion. I believe that the philosopher's duty is to grapple with difficult and interesting conceptual problems, the solutions to which may be of some use to other thinkers or to men and women of action in all walks of life. In particular, I believe that the philosopher of social science has a duty to elucidate the key philosophical concepts, problems, assumptions—hidden as well as explicit—and findings of the social sciences of his time. To accomplish this task, he must become reasonably familiar with the contemporary social science literature. Ideally, he should also try his hand—as I have—at social research, for no amount of reading can replace the experience of original research.

In this book I deal only with some key philosophical ideas that occur throughout the social and socio-natural sciences and technologies. The peculiar problematics of the various special social disciplines are tackled in a companion volume, *Social Science under Debate* (Bunge forthcoming). The latter could equally well have been titled *Looking at Social Science through Philosophy*, just as the present work could well have been titled *Looking at Philosophy through Social Science*.

Finally, two disclaimers: unless stated otherwise, translations are my own; and masculine pronouns are used throughout this book to denote all three sexes.

I am grateful to a number of generous scholars and curious students who, in two dozen countries and over several decades, have asked interesting questions, offered useful information, or engaged me in fruitful debate. I also thank the Humanities and Social Sciences Research Council of Canada for supporting my research over many years. Last, but not least, I am grateful to the editorial staff of Yale University Press, particularly to Jean van Altena, for having cleaned up the manuscript.

Finding Philosophy in Social Science

Introduction :: Why Philosophy?

1 Social Science Includes Some Philosophy

Science and philosophy were hardly distinguishable until the Romantic period. Then they became estranged, but they never really split. Actually, science and philosophy share a number of extremely general key concepts, principles, and even problems. Hence, far from being disjoint, they overlap partially. To prove this claim, I shall exhibit random samples of each category of ideas.

To begin with, consider the following statements, disregarding their truth-value and noting only their constitutive concepts, although an analysis of their negations would in fact yield the same conclusion.

—All societies are concrete systems composed of living beings (rather than, say, either mere agglomerations of individuals or sets of beliefs, values, and norms).

—Some social systems (e.g., families and circles of friends) are natural, whereas others (e.g., business firms and schools) are artificial.

—All social systems are located in space and evolve over time.

—Agency and structure interact: there is neither individual action in an institutional vacuum nor social structure without individual social behavior.

—Every type of society is characterized by, among other things, its own value system and its own system of moral and legal norms.

—Society can—indeed, ought to—be studied in a scientific manner, though not as if it were a natural object, for it is largely artifactual, and people have feelings and thoughts.

—The findings of the scientific study of society are items of testable knowledge about social systems (rather than, say, speculations about individual behavior).
—Description is necessary but insufficient: we should attempt to explain data and, whenever possible, to predict them as well.
—Programmatic hypotheses of the form "Variable y depends upon variable x," as well as statistical correlations, are necessary but insufficient: we should strive to conjecture causal, probabilistic, and mixed mechanisms.
—Some rational choice models involve fuzzy concepts of utility or rationality, and all of them include the controversial hypothesis of maximizing behavior.

It is not hard to identify the philosophical components in the above list. The universal concepts "all" and "some," as well as "and" (or a comma) and "or," are studied in logic; so is "are." And logic is of course part of philosophy as well as of mathematics. The concepts "about" (or "refers to") and "fuzzy" (or "inexact") belong in semantics, a next-door neighbor of logic. The concepts of matter, process, nature, space, time, system, history, society, and artifact are extremely general: they are not the exclusive property of any special science, and they are analyzed and systematized in ontology (or metaphysics), one of the oldest branches of philosophy. The concepts of knowledge, science, model, and testability belong in epistemology (the theory of knowledge), another branch of philosophy. (Each of the words *rationality* and *utility* designate different concepts, some of which are philosophical.) Finally, the concepts of value and norm are studied in value theory and moral philosophy. We have thus shown that philosophy and science—in particular, social science—share some concepts.

I shall next show that social science and philosophy share some principles. Any of the following will do, and so will their denials.
—Social facts are objective and can be known, albeit only partially and gradually.
—Ordinary experience (including intuition and empathy) is necessary but insufficient to understand complex systems such as societies: we also need systematic observation, calculation, and theory.
—Observation should be guided by theory, and, in turn, theory should be tested by data.
—Social science is in need of theories of various ranges: "grand," or maximum-range, theories, middle-range, and narrow-range theories—or philosophical, general, and specific theories, respectively.
—The empirical tests of hypotheses in social science are tests for truth, whereas the tests of social policies are tests for fairness and efficiency.
—The truths about social facts and policies are often only approximate, but they can be improved upon through further research.
—To explain a social fact is to disclose its plausible mechanisms.

—Social science makes use of some biology and some psychology but is not reducible to either.

—The frontiers among the social sciences are artificial and shift over time.

—It is morally wrong to make up data or to publish incomprehensible texts.

These propositions and their denials are philosophico-scientific, because they belong in the philosophy (or metatheory) of social science, and they are supposed to be observed (or violated) by social scientists.

Now let us list a few problems that, in being extremely general and in concerning either society or social studies, are philosophical as well as scientific, all of which are currently the object of spirited controversies.

—Are social facts out there, or are they all constructions of the observer or of the community of social students? (This is part of the ontological and epistemological problem of realism.)

—Are there objective social patterns (laws), or are social facts utterly lawless? (This is part of the ontological problem of lawfulness and the epistemological problem of distinguishing objective patterns from the statements claiming to represent them.)

—What is society? An amorphous collection of individuals, an unanalyzable block, or a system? (This is the individualism–holism–systemism trilemma, an ontological problem with an epistemological counterpart.)

—How do societies change? Under the action of external forces, through their internal dynamics, or both? And as a result of ideas, material factors, or both? (This is part of the philosophy of history.)

—What prevails in society? Solidarity (cooperation) or conflict (competition) or a combination of the two? (This question is relevant to moral and political philosophy.)

—Are people totally free to act, or are they the pawns of historical forces, or neither? (This is part of the ontological and ethical problem of free will.)

—Are the social sciences idiographic (limited to particulars), nomothetic (seeking or using laws), or both? (This is a central problem in the epistemology and methodology of social science.)

—Do social science theories represent social facts in a literal manner, or are they mere metaphors? (This is one of the semantic and epistemological problems concerning fact–idea relations.)

—What impact, positive, nil, or negative, have the various philosophical schools, such as empiricism and idealism, had on social studies? (This is part of the task of identifying and evaluating the philosophies underlying the various schools in social studies.)

—Are the basic social sciences value-free and morally neutral? And how about the social policy sciences? (These problems belong to the ethics of science and technology.)

These problems are situated at the intersection of social science and philosophy. Hence they must be tackled with the help of the tools and findings of both research fields.

I have thus proved that there is some philosophy in social science. (Note, by the way, how easy it is to check weak or particular generalizations—i.e., propositions prefixed by "some." All one has to do is to find at least one example, in contrast to strong or universal generalizations—i.e., propositions starting with "all.")

In other words, there is no frontier between science and philosophy. Consequently, the search for a criterion of demarcation, which has occupied many philosophers, among them the positivist Rudolf Carnap and the rationalist Karl Popper, is in vain. And if such a search is in vain, this suggests that it originates in seriously mistaken conceptions of both science and philosophy. This is one of the reasons why we must find our own way, doing our best to observe the canons of rationality, while at the same time keeping in touch with reality and its scientific exploration.

2 Philosophical Controversies in Social Science

Since social scientists utilize philosophical concepts and principles and pose problems of philosophical interest, they are likely to adopt definite philosophical stands or even to get involved in philosophical controversies. This was the case with Smith, Bentham, Condorcet, Mill, Cournot, Marx, Engels, Jevons, Menger, Marshall, Pareto, Weber, Keynes, Marc Bloch, Braudel, Merton, Samuelson, Myrdal, and Milton Friedman, among others: none of them was philosophically innocent or neutral.

However, most scientists do not bother to examine their philosophies in any depth. A consequence of this philosophical insouciance is inconsistency between theory and practice. Thus Marx praised Hegel's confused dialectics and often adopted Hegel's convoluted style. But because he also engaged in hard-nosed research based on industrial reports, social surveys, and economic, political, and historical data, he did not betray science to Hegalianism (Schumpeter 1950 [1942], 10). Likewise, Weber paid lip service to the idealist philosophy of Dilthey, Windelband, and Rickert but transcended the idiographic–nomothetic dichotomy they preached (Merton, 1987, 13). And, despite his defense of methodological individualism, Weber rarely engaged in micro–macro analysis. As a result, his later work does not differ much from Marx's (Alexander and Giesen 1987, 18). Few scientists have avoided inconsistencies between their sermonizing and their practice. Galileo, Einstein, and Cajal were among the exceptions. Moreover, Einstein warned that in order to find out what science really is, we should watch scientists at work, rather than read what they say about science when philosophizing.

Philosophical controversies in science can be enlightening, constructive, and scholarly—or none of these. An early example of a destructive philosophical controversy in social science was the *Methodenstreit* in the German-speaking world, which started in the 1880s and, to all intents and purposes, is still going on worldwide, albeit in a muted way. This controversy was destructive in opposing two perfectly legitimate, complementary fields of research: namely, economics and economic history. As a result, each of these disciplines was retarded, instead of being enriched by its complement (see Swedberg 1991). Paradoxically, economics won the political battle but lost the intellectual one, because, by gaining independence, it became increasingly remote from economic realities, both past and present.

Other famous controversies have been those between Marxists and their rivals, and between conservative and liberal economists. Unlike the Methodenstreit, these debates had strong ideological components, which the controversies succeeded in exposing. Many further controversies are currently brewing. Some of the main current philosophical debates in and about contemporary social science concern the following questions:

—Are social systems and their structure out there, or are they only in the student's mind? (an aspect of the epistemological problem of realism)

—Is social conflict the engine of history, or is cooperation equally powerful? (part of the ontological problem of the main types of change mechanism)

—Are social classes entities or concepts? (a member of the class of semantic and epistemological problems concerning fact–idea relations)

—Are scientific ideas processes in individual minds (or brains), or social constructions, or do they hover above people? (part of the ontological mind–body problem)

—Can there be true scientific ideas, or only conventions accepted by the scientific community of the day? (another aspect of the epistemological problem of realism)

—Are there laws of history? (part of the philosophy of history)

—Is it possible to study society in exactly the same way as we study nature, or do we have to take into account the perceptions, delusions, interests, intentions, and decisions of the agents? (part of the methodology of social science)

—Can mathematical models of social systems and processes capture the variety and changeability of social life? (part of the semantic and epistemological problem of the relation of mathematics to reality)

—Are all social events predictable? And is predictability (or lack of it) inherent in social reality, or is it merely a matter of knowledge (or ignorance)?

—Can anything be salvaged from the shipwreck of Marxist philosophy, social theory, and ideology? (In particular, does the crisis in Marxism entail that materialism and realism are indefensible?)

Every one of these questions has been answered both positively and negatively at one time or another. We shall tackle them in due course. The point of reciting them at this juncture is not to find out the correct answers, but as a reminder that, contrary to Thomas Kuhn's contention, science, like theology, ideology, philosophy, and politics, is rife with controversy. What *is* true is that scientific controversies can be conducted in a rational manner and can be settled honestly in the light of empirical data and logical argument, as opposed to resorting to rhetorical flourishes, negotiations, or decrees. That is because such controversies are ultimately about truth, not power.

3 What Is Social Metatheory About and Up To?

The philosophy of social science is a branch of the metascience of social science. Other disciplines concerned with social science are the history, sociology, economics, and politics of social science. These additional disciplines supply the philosopher with useful data and may provide him with penetrating insights. However, the social sciences of social science are, in turn, indebted to the philosophy of science for the elucidation of such key concepts as those of quality and quantity, truth and error, testability and test, science and pseudoscience. In other words, although all the sciences of social science interact with one another, the philosophy of social science is logically prior to the social studies of social science.

The philosophy (or metatheory) of social science refers to the ideas and methods that occur in the synchronic and diachronic studies of social facts. It does not refer directly to such facts: it does not dispute the turf of the social scientist. However, it cannot help but refer indirectly to social facts. Indeed, a philosophical discourse about a specific construct of social science, concerning a domain of social facts, is indirectly about the latter. For example, the statement "The hypothesis that all societies are stratified is testable" refers directly to the hypothesis in question, and indirectly to all societies. (In general, formal terms, the reference function $R_1: P \to S$, which maps philosophical constructs into social science ones, and the reference function $R_2: S \to F$, which maps social science constructs into social facts, compose to yield the indirect reference function $R = R_2 \circ R_1: P \to F$.)

Philosophical statements about constructs in the social sciences fall into several classes: (*a*) logical, or about logical form (structure); (*b*) semantical, or concerning meaning or truth; (*c*) epistemological, or about ways in which constructs are formed; (*d*) methodological, or concerning matters of general method and special technique; (*e*) ontological, or about the nature of the referents of the constructs; (*f*) axiological, or concerning the value concepts and value judgments that may occur in social science; and (*g*) ethical, or about the morality of the uses of social studies or policies.

In other words, the philosophy of social science entails the following:

The *logic* of social science analyzes the logical form of concepts, propositions, theories, and inferences in social science, regardless of their content. Thus it asks such questions as: Is concept X well defined, either explicitly or by way of axioms? Does proposition B follow from assumption(s) A? Is theory T internally consistent? What are the analogies and differences between explanation and prediction? How are such and such theories related? What are the structure, power, limits, and functions of the reduction and merger of theories? Is logic androcentric?

The *semantics* of social science explores the concepts of sense, reference, and truth (formal and factual, total and partial) as they occur in social science. Thus it asks: What does such and such a concept, hypothesis, or theory refer to? (i.e., what is it about?) In particular, what is social science about: individuals, ideas, supra-individual forces, or social systems? Does construct A make sense in context B? What is truth? Is truth attainable in social science? Is every truth relative to some culture?

The *epistemology* of social science examines the roles of observation and speculation, intuition and reason, analogy and induction, discovery and invention, in the formation of constructs and methods in social science; the nature and role of *Verstehen* (comprehension or interpretation); the relation between theory and policy; and the power and limits of deduction. Thus it is concerned with questions such as: What can we learn about society by observing individuals? What can we learn about individuals by studying their societies? Is every generalization an induction from data? Are constructs discovered or invented?

The *methodology* of social science looks at the nature of data and hypotheses, the meaning of the expression "interpretation of the data," the role of indicators ("operational definitions"), the modes of empirical validation, the notions of testability, confirmation, and infirmation, and the relations between idiographic and nomothetic studies. Thus it asks: Can social cohesiveness, social inertia, political stability, and the rate of social change be quantitated—and if so how? What are the scopes and roles of quantitation and measurement in social studies? Can there be a general theory of measurement? Is the scientific method exclusive of the "male-stream" and therefore inimical to women?

The *ontology* of social science examines the nature of society, the kinds of social process, the difference between law and rule, the roles of causation and chance, and the nature of planning. Hence it is concerned with questions such as: Are there social systems, or only aggregates of individuals? Are cultures systems of values and norms, or concrete social systems? What is a micro–macro link? What are the engines of history: the environment, biological factors, the economy, politics, culture, or all of these? Are there occasionally leaps in social evolution, or was Marshall right in inscribing the maxim *Natura non facit saltum* on the title page of his classic *Principles of Economics*? Is society a text to be deciphered by hermeneutics or semiotics? Is human history analogous to biological evolution?

The *axiology* of social science investigates the role of values in social science. It asks: Can social science stay clear of values? What kind of value is more relevant to social science: objective, subjective, or both? Are the concepts of poverty and oppression descriptive, valuational, both, or neither? Should social scientists abstain from making value judgments, as Max Weber demanded, or should they declare their values, as Gunnar Myrdal required?

The *ethics* of social science examines the code of conduct of social scientists. Thus it is concerned with questions like: What, if any, is the role of moral norms in the design of economic and social policies? How does one go about proposing a moral justification for them? What are the ethical limits on experimentation in social science? Is social science morally neutral? Is it right for a social scientist to advise an agency intent on destabilizing a foreign government or a company engaged in plundering a country? Is it right for a social scientist to skirt social issues? Is the historian entitled to praise or condemn the actions he studies?

We recognize, then, seven distinct areas in the philosophy of science and, in particular, in the metatheory of social studies. Whereas some metatheoretical problems can be handled by a single branch of the philosophy of science, others require the cooperation of all seven branches. The latter is particularly the case with respect to the following questions: What is basic science? What is sociotechnology? How does social science differ from natural science? Are there sciences straddling the natural–social divide? Is the present fragmentation of the social sciences healthy, and if not, how can it be corrected?

In sum, philosophy is a system of ideas of seven different kinds: it may be pictured as a heptagon. However, this spatial analogy is apt only insofar as it emphasizes the interdependence of the various components of philosophy. It is incorrect as a description of philosophy, which is neither a geometric object nor one that is visualizable. (Many of the diagrams found in the social science literature are merely didactic props.) It would be equally inappropriate to emphasize the systemic character of philosophy at the expense of its analytic component. Indeed, to philosophize is sometimes to analyze ideas—in particular, to subject them to logical, semantical, epistemological, or methodological analysis. Yet, at other times, to philosophize is to build or refine general concepts or conceptual systems (such as classifications and theories). In this regard, philosophy is like theoretical science—in other regards too, as will be argued in due course.

4 Kinds of Philosophy of Social Science

So far I have acted as if there were a single philosophy of social science. But actually, there are as many philosophies of social science as there are philosophical schools. These may be grouped in various ways. In particular, they may be grouped according to logical, epistemological, ontological, or ethical criteria.

From a logical point of view, philosophies can be partitioned into rational and irrational. (Strictly speaking, a school that rejects argument altogether cannot claim any support for its theses and therefore does not rank as a philosophy.) Seen from an epistemological standpoint, philosophies are empiricist or anti-empiricist to various degrees. From an ontological point of view, they can be materialist, spiritualist, or dualist. Seen from an ethical viewpoint, they can be consequentialist or inconsequentialist, egoistic or altruistic, and so on.

Thus, regardless of its many shortcomings, logical positivism is indeed logical, in that it admits and uses logic. By contrast, existentialism is illogical, in that it explicitly rejects logic (and reason generally) and produces plenty of nonsensical sentences, such as "The world worlds." Hegelianism and phenomenology are nearly illogical, in that they employ hermetic lingos and denounce the exact sciences. Positivism is empiricist and, more particularly, phenomenalist, in claiming to keep close to observational data and in distrusting deep hypotheses and theories. In a way, so is phenomenology, in limiting itself to data obtained by introspection or by observation of the *Lebenswelt* or everyday life—but, unlike positivism, phenomenology does not care for empirical tests. Both positivism and phenomenology reject ontology basically for the same reason: namely, their refusal to admit the autonomous existence of an external world. Marxism is not quite logical (in embracing dialectics), not quite empiricist (in adhering to dogmas), and only half-materialist (in splitting society into a material infrastructure and an ideal superstructure). Finally, none of these philosophies includes an ethical theory.

Every one of the philosophical schools just mentioned, as well as several others, has its own philosophy of science. In particular, there are positivist and anti-positivist philosophies of science; some are realist, others anti-realist—for example, conventionalist or pragmatist; some are rationalist, others irrationalist, and so on. This diversity poses the metaphilosophical problem of choosing among the various philosophies of science—or constructing an alternative one.

There are two ways of choosing a philosophy of science. One is to check whether the philosophy under consideration is consistent with one's philosophical or ideological preconceptions: this is the dogmatic procedure. The second way is to check whether it offers faithful descriptions of scientific research, as well as fruitful prescriptions for its conduct: that is, whether it both accounts for science and promotes its advancement. The first way is easier, for it requires no knowledge of science and no overcoming of inertia to rethink one's position. This is why it is the most popular—and the least reliable. Let us see why the second way is preferable: why philosophies can be confirmed or refuted, *pace* Popper (1963, 197).

The philosophy of science is only one of the many philosophies of x, where x is a blank or variable that can stand for mathematics, natural science, social science, technology, medicine, politics, law, morality, art, religion, and so on.

Now, a philosophy of x should match x rather than be at variance with x, for only then will it be able to (a) give an adequate (true) description of x, (b) suggest fruitful avenues for the conduct of inquiry in x, and (c) participate competently and effectively in philosophical controversies in or about x. We call these the *conditions of adequacy and fertility*. A philosophy of x that is totally uncongenial to x or, worse, hostile to x, can be of no help in the development of x. Thus I shall propose the following general metaphilosophical norm: For all x, if x is a field of study, the philosophy of x should match x.

But what does "match" mean in this context? Loosely speaking, a philosophy Px of x matches x if Px shares the "spirit" or "attitude" of x, deals with philosophical issues raised by the actual practice of x, and makes use of scientific findings to construct and check its own hypotheses. Let us now substitute science for x. I submit that a philosophy of science matches science if it depicts faithfully and, to some extent, shares the precision, testability, systematicity, realism, worldliness, and integrity that characterize mature science, refers to contemporary scientific research, and uses some of the latter's findings. A hermetic tirade against the exact sciences and naturalism, such as Husserl's celebrated *Crisis of European Sciences* (1954 [1936]), fails this test.

Ideally, a philosophy of science should be as exact and as scientific as the best science it studies. This was precisely the goal of the Vienna Circle (1926–36), whose members developed logical empiricism (or neo-positivism). Regrettably, this philosophy, though somewhat exact—and so hostile to the obscurities of neo-Thomism, neo-Kantianism, dialectical materialism, phenomenology, and existentialism—was largely unscientific. Indeed, though genuinely interested in contemporary science, and in a few cases working scientists themselves, most members of the Vienna Circle approached science from a narrow empiricist and, to be more precise, inductivist, phenomenalist, and even subjectivist viewpoint. Moreover, the neo-positivists tended to oversimplify philosophical problems, seeing them all as problems of logic, semantics, or methodology—that is, of coherence, meaning, or testability. They rejected metaphysics (ontology) and neglected or underrated value theory and ethics. Hence, while their criticism of woolliness was helpful, their rejection of realism, materialism, and cognitivist ethics was not. In particular, they encouraged behaviorism and subjectivist interpretations of physics, as well as irrationalism in value theory and ethics.

In short, none of the best-known philosophies matches science. No wonder, then, that none of them helps us to understand social science, let alone advance it.

5 Evaluating Philosophies of Social Science

How should a philosophy of social science be evaluated? I submit that the following battery of tests should be used for this purpose.

Relevance. Does it address real problems in contemporary social science, or is it merely an exegesis of worn-out classical texts or an exercise in intellectual (or, worse, anti-intellectualist) gymnastics?

Intelligibility. Can the philosophy in question be understood by any intelligent college student, or is it the property of an esoteric group? Existentialism is at the bottom, and ordinary language (Wittgensteinian) philosophy at the top of the intelligibility scale. Any genuine, relevant, deep philosophy will be way above the bottom but somewhat below the top of this scale. That it should not be at the very top is not because obscurity is inevitable, but because to grasp nontrivial ideas requires some effort: there is no "philosophy without tears" (as Russell called linguistic philosophy).

Exactifiability. Can the basic concepts and propositions of the given philosophy be rendered more precise with the help of logical or mathematical tools, or are they incurably fuzzy, as with Hegel's dialectics, Dilthey's Verstehen, and Heidegger's *Dasein*?

Internal consistency. Is the philosophy under consideration without contradictions? Or, if it contains contradictions, can they be eliminated without destroying it entirely?

External consistency. Is the philosophy in question compatible with the bulk of contemporary science and technology, or at variance with it?

Size and depth. Does the philosophy in question concern itself with miniproblems (e.g., "What did *x* mean by *y*?") and shallow solutions (e.g., with regard to the problem of reality: "To be is to be perceived, or to be measured, or to be talked about, or to occur in a text"), or does it tackle any of the Big Questions in a deep way?

Truth. Does the philosophy at issue match actual scientific research practice, or is it based on a caricature of it?

Universality. Is the philosophy in question universal (cross-cultural), or does it support the views, biases, or interests of a particular sex, ethnic group, social class, nation, religious group, or party?

Fertility. Does the philosophy under consideration solve any philosophical or scientific problems, or at least allow them to be reformulated in a clearer or deeper way? Does it help spot any new problems? Is it of assistance in crossing bridges between adjoining disciplines? Does it criticize any ideas held dogmatically? And does it suggest any promising heterodoxies?

Originality. Does the philosophy in question include any original components: novel approaches, new hypotheses worth investigating, or novel conceptual techniques worth trying out? Or is it a rehash of some obsolete doctrine?

I submit that none of the popular philosophies meets all these conditions, particularly as applied to social science. And some of them, notably phenomenology, existentialism, and their postmodern offspring, fail all these tests. (In the succeeding chapters I will attempt to justify this assertion.) This is why I have endeavored to build a new, science-oriented philosophical system, ex-pounded in the eight volumes of my *Treatise on Basic Philosophy* (1974–89), and why I have written this book and its companion, *Social Science under Debate* (Bunge forthcoming).

In summary, philosophy is of direct relevance to social science because the two fields overlap and because any important advance in either raises problems for the other, as well as supplying tools to solve them. To be sure, scientists do not need philosophers in order to know what they are doing. But sometimes they do need to be shown that what they have done is mistaken or, worse, irrelevant, as a result of paying insufficient attention to philosophy.

   This being the case, it is not wise for social scientists to leave philosophy in the hands of philosophers like Husserl and Wittgenstein, who have never bothered with science, in particular with social studies. And it is downright foolish to seek inspiration in the likes of Heidegger and Derrida, who have written only gibberish, platitudes, or falsities. It would advance the two fields in question if students in each were to take their counterparts in the other more seriously. And it would be even better if social scientists were to engage in serious philosophizing, so as to avoid philosophical blunders, and if philoso-phers were to try their hand at social research, so as to get the hang of it.

PART A :: *From Fact
to Theory*

1 :: *Fact*

The social sciences study social facts such as helping and fighting, marrying and divorcing, hiring and firing, working and stealing, organizing and disorganizing, innovating and resisting innovation, voting and rebelling, invading and repelling invasion, setting up or dismantling organizations, and so on. This makes them *factual* sciences, unlike logic and mathematics, which may be called *formal* sciences, in that they deal with pure "forms"—that is, ideas unrelated to any matters of fact.

So far, there is near consensus in the community of social scientists. But there is no unanimity as to the signification of the expression 'social fact' or even about the humble word *fact*. Indeed, whereas in some cases *fact* denotes an objective occurrence, in others it is used as a synonym for a datum or a particular, true proposition. Thus one often utters sentences of the form "It is a fact that *x*," which in some cases is intended to mean that *x* is indeed the case, and in others that the assertion "*x* is the case" is true. One also meets the expression 'stylized fact,' which actually denotes a simplified representation of a complex fact—hence not a fact at all, but a construct. Yet again, one encounters the expression 'scientific fact,' without any accompanying explanation, despite its ambiguity. Does it mean an actual or possible fact that is or could only be studied by science, or a scientific finding such as an experimental datum or a well-confirmed hypothesis? We are seldom told.

Worse, among the so-called postmoderns, facts, particularly "scientific facts," are sometimes said to be stories (or symbols or metaphors), and at other times social constructions or conventions on a par with road signs and table manners. The latter is, indeed, a major thesis of the constructivist-relativist sociology and philosophy of science and technology. According to this collectivist variety of subjectivism, there is no difference between facts and ideas (or texts). More precisely, all facts are ideas (or texts) shared by a "collective" such as a scientific community. Hence the notions of objectivity and truth are redundant, or even misleading. Scientists would not study facts out there in the hope of coming up with true accounts of them, but would make them up collectively: they would "construct reality." They would even restrict themselves to making "inscriptions" (words, graphs, and the like), and to fighting and negotiating with colleagues (see, e.g., Latour and Woolgar 1979).

This view is very convenient for anyone who cannot be bothered to study science or technology, or to analyze and test any ideas about them, in particular to perform a philosophical analysis of the constructs involved in scientific research, technological design, and policymaking. But it is untenable, for it denies individual creativity and makes a mockery of both the search for truth and any test procedure. The first point is obvious, since upholders of the view explicitly replace discovery and invention with social construction, convention, or even conversation. The second point is evident not only in relation to experimental and technological testing but also in law, in business, and even in ordinary life. The following example should bring the point home.

Fact: John took Mary's gold watch. Datum 1: Mary's report of the fact. Datum 2: John's admission (or else an eyewitness's account of the fact). Hypothesis 1: John borrowed Mary's watch. Hypothesis 2: John stole Mary's watch. Possible direct evidence for H1: John promptly and spontaneously returned the watch. Possible circumstantial evidence for H1: the day he took the watch, John was seen to be acting absent-mindedly. Possible direct evidence for H2: John pawned or sold Mary's watch. Possible circumstantial evidence for H2: John was known to be in debt. The reader may wish to embroider the case with further data suggesting alternative hypotheses or with further pieces of evidence relevant to the given hypotheses. But if he has ever come anywhere near a court of law or a laboratory, he will observe the distinction between fact and datum, as well as between a hypothesis and the data serving as evidence for or against it, for he will realize that justice is critically dependent upon tests for objective truth. (Moral: The just avoid relativism.)

Given the confusion between fact and truth in the popular mind, as well as the current vogue of the constructivist-relativist doctrine, it may be apposite to reexamine the old-fashioned ideas of objective fact and its close relatives: thing, property of a thing, state of a thing, change in a thing, and pattern of being or becoming. I shall adopt what is essentially the standard usage in the sciences, business, and law, where facts are not supposed to be made up, either individually or collectively.

1 Thing and Property

Every fact involves some concrete thing: it is a state of a thing or a change in the state of a thing. (There are neither states nor changes in themselves. Nor are there abstract facts.) A concrete thing can be imperceptible, like an electron or a nation, or tangible, like a table or a person. What is peculiar to all concrete or material things is their changeability. By contrast, conceptual objects, such as numbers and theories, are unchangeable: only the brains that think of them are subject to change; in fact, they change as they think.

Consequently, any collection of objects can be divided into two mutually disjoint subsets: a class of concrete or material things and its complement, a class of constructs. (Note, however, that either subset may be empty.) Consequently, there are no mixed objects—that is, objects composed of both things and ideas. But, of course, there are concrete objects, such as human groups, within which certain ideas "rule" by virtue of being held (thought, believed, and acted upon) by the group members. In addition, there are certain artificial things, such as written words and drawings, which may stand for, or represent, ideas.

The social sciences are interested in things of all kinds: natural and artificial, living and inanimate, persons and social systems. For example, economics and history deal with people and social systems—such as families, business firms, and governments—as well as with natural resources and artifacts. Moreover, since all these things are changeable by virtue of being concrete, they must be studied historically as well as synchronically.

Every real thing possesses several properties. Properties may be grouped in several ways. One important distinction is between intrinsic and relational properties. An *intrinsic* property is one that a thing possesses regardless of other things, even if it is acquired under the action of other things. For example, the age and skills of an individual are intrinsic properties; so are the population and GDP of a society. A *relational* property is one that a thing possesses by virtue of its relation to other things. For example, being married or being employed are relational properties of individuals; likewise the immigration flux and the foreign affairs of a nation are relational properties.

Whereas some properties are essential, others are accidental. An *essential property* of a thing is one that the thing loses if it is transmuted into a thing of a different species, whereas an *accidental property* is one that makes little, if any, difference to any essential properties. For example, division of labor is essential to modern industry and trade, whereas the name of a firm is an accidental property of that firm, so much so that it may be changed at will. The thesis that there are essential properties, called "essentialism," is unpopular in contemporary philosophy—a tacit confession of shallowness.

Essential properties may be divided into *source* properties and *derived* properties; the former determining the latter, but not conversely. For example, teaching (or, rather, learning) is the source property of any school, in that it determines the other (derived) properties of the system, such as having black-boards and issuing report cards. A derived property depends on one or more source properties. Moreover, every property of either kind is lawfully related to at least one other property. Hence there are no stray essential properties: they all come in natural bundles or property systems. By contrast, an accidental property of a thing is not necessarily connected to any other property of the thing: think of proper names.

Any property may be conceptualized or represented by an attribute or predicate, which is a special kind of concept. Intrinsic properties are represented by unary predicates, such as "is populated," whereas relational properties, such as "is more populated than," are conceptualized as binary, ternary, or, in general, n-ary predicates. (A unary predicate may be analyzed as a function mapping a set of things into a set of propositions involving the predicate in question— e.g., the predicate "social mobility" is a function from the collection S of all societies to the collection P of propositions of the form "x is socially mobile," where x is in S. A binary predicate, such as "exchanges," is a function from ordered couples of individuals, firms, or nations to the set of propositions of the form "x exchanges with y." A somewhat finer analysis reveals "exchange" to be a triadic predicate, relating two trading partners to the good they exchange. If the amounts and values of the goods exchanged are added, a fifth-degree predicate results. This confirms the need to distinguish properties from the concepts that represent them. The former are objective, whereas the latter depend on the analyst, the level of analysis he adopts, and the state of his discipline.)

The property–predicate distinction is unnecessary in logic and mathematics, where the words in question are synonymous. Nor does it occur in an idealist world view, where properties ("forms") are self-existing ideas. (These two circumstances help to explain why most philosophers ignore the difference.) But it is indispensable everywhere else, particularly in science and technology, for one and the same property of a concrete thing may now be conceptualized as a certain attribute and, later on, in the light of fresh information or deeper analysis, as a different attribute. Remember the historical changes undergone by the notions of social structure, capital, political power, and culture. Realists assume that society at large took hardly any notice of such conceptual changes occurring in the brains of social scientists.

Another rationale for the property–predicate distinction, one that escapes the anti-realist, is that not all predicates represent properties of real things. In particular, negative predicates, such as "classless," and disjunctive predicates, such as "literate or employed," represent no properties of things, even though they may occur in true discourse about things. For instance, the proposition

"Some people are jobless" is true, but this does not entail that joblessness is a property on a par with that of holding a job. Failing to report regularly to work and not getting a paycheck are nonevents.

A third reason for distinguishing predicates from properties is that whereas the former satisfy a theory (viz., predicate logic), properties satisfy objective laws. Thus, "For all x and all F: If x is an F, then x is an F or x is a G" is a formula of ordinary predicate logic. It states something about predicates and logical implication, but nothing about the world. By contrast, the statement "In every society inequity generates conflict" asserts a causal (not a logical) relation between two properties of a society: namely, inequity and conflict. The logical law does not refer to anything in particular, hence it cannot be put to empirical tests; whereas the sociological generalization refers to actual societies and can be confirmed or refuted by observation. (More on predicates in chap. 2.)

In short, we distinguish a property P of a thing from the attribute, predicate, or function F that represents P; and we bear in mind that one and the same property may be represented by different predicates in alternative analyses or theories. (The distinction may be summarized thus: Whereas the set of all properties constitutes an inf-semilattice, that of all predicates constitutes a Boolean algebra, a much richer formal object.)

Now, even though there are no two exactly identical things, all things share some properties. For example, at a given time all persons have some age or other, and every society has some population or other. Age and population are *general* properties, whereas the particular age of a person and the particular population of a society are *individual* properties. These individual properties are particular numbers: namely, values of the age and population functions, respectively.

In conclusion, every object has properties, some essential, others accidental, some of which can be known and conceptualized as attributes.

2 Emergence and System

A property of a social group is called a *collective* property. Following Lazarsfeld and Menzel (1965), I distinguish three kinds of collective property: aggregate, structural, and global (or emergent). *Aggregate* properties, such as averages, modes, and variances, are statistical artifacts, yet they characterize wholes. *Structural* (or *relational*) properties are properties that individuals or groups possess by virtue of their relations to other units—for example, being a daughter or an employee, a manager or a piece of merchandise. Finally, *global*, or *emergent*, properties are those possessed by wholes regardless of any statistical manipulation of data concerning their components. For example, the territory and population of a nation, as well as the dominant modes of production, the ruling ideology, and the type of government, are global, or emergent, properties of that nation. They emerge along with the system and submerge as it breaks down.

The notions of aggregate property and structural property are unproblematic, but the concept of an emergent property raises some eyebrows. Yet Durkheim (1988 [1895], 81–83) and Piaget (1965, 28), among others, had clear concepts of emergence; so have Coleman (1964, 1990), Boudon (1979), and a few others. (For a definition of the concept, see Bunge 1977*b*; for its history, see Blitz 1992.) Two objections have been raised to the concept of emergence. Individualists object to it because they deny the existence of wholes, such as social systems, with properties of their own. This prevents them from understanding the formation and breakdown of systems. The second objection comes from the rationalist quarter. If "emergence" is wrongly identified—as it often is—with "unexplainable and unpredictable novelty," the rationalist will rightly regard the term as a piece of obscurantism. But "emergence" is an ontological, not an epistemological, category, and so is its dual, "submergence." We then face the dilemma that if we admit emergence but regard it as mysterious, we give up rationality; but if we deny emergence, then we curtail the reach of knowledge and thereby that of rationality. The knot can be cut only by defining "emergence" as an ontological category.

I propose the following definition. *P* is an *emergent* property of a thing *b* if and only if either *b* is a complex thing (system) no component of which possesses *P*, or *b* is an individual that possesses *P* by virtue of being a component of a system (i.e., *b* would not possess *P* if it were independent or isolated). Examples of the former: the structure, cohesiveness, stability, and history of a social system. Examples of the latter: role, civil right, scarcity, and price.

We have just used the concept of a social system. We may as well define it explicitly, not only because it is central to this book, but also to avoid ambiguities, which arise because the expression 'social system' is variously used to denote a social order, a political regime, or a type of government. But before doing so, it will be convenient to introduce a general notion of a system, utilizable in all fields of knowledge. Things and ideas, as well as their properties and changes, tend to come in packages, or systems: there are no strays. To be sure, some ties connecting the parts of a system are weak and thus break easily, resulting in partial isolation, though only in some respects and only temporarily. Strictly speaking, every item, whether concrete or conceptual, is a system or a part of one: this is a postulate of our systemic philosophy.

A *system* is a complex object every part or component of which is connected with other parts of the same object in such a manner that the whole possesses some features that its components lack—that is, emergent properties. A system may be conceptual or concrete but not both. A *conceptual system* is a system composed of concepts linked together by logical or mathematical relations. Classifications and theories are conceptual systems. A *concrete,* or *material, system* is one composed of concrete things linked together by nonconceptual ties, such as physical, chemical, biological, economic, political, or cultural links. Atoms and molecules, cells and organs, families, business firms and nongovernmental organizations, as well as governments and informal social networks, are concrete systems. Concrete systems that stand for or represent other objects, such as languages, texts, and diagrams, may be called *symbolic* or *semiotic*.

Some concrete systems change swiftly, others slowly; some assemble themselves, others are made; some are closed and self-regulated, most are neither; some have shapes (geometric boundaries), others do not—and so on. In line with the conceptual–material (or formal–concrete) dichotomy proposed above, I deny the existence of mixed (half-conceptual, half-material) systems. This is not to deny the existence of concrete systems whose specific function is to transmit or process signals that, when properly encoded and decoded, convey information.

(Our definition of a system differs radically from the two definitions given in the general systems theory literature, in which a system is defined either as a *set* of interrelated elements or as a *relation*. Since sets and relations are abstract objects, they cannot be identical to concrete systems such as molecules and families.)

At any given time a concrete system is characterized by its composition, environment, and structure or organization. The latter is the collection of relations among the parts of the system as well as between these and environmental items. The former constitute the internal, the latter the external, structure of the system. (e.g., the Ministry of the Interior deals with some of the relations between the individual and institutional components of the nation, whereas the Ministry of External Affairs is in charge of international relations.) The structure of a system is its key emergent property. No wonder, then, that the study of social structure and its changes is of central concern to social science.

A *social system* is a system composed of gregarious animals. And a *human social system* is a social system composed of people and their artifacts. Such a system is held together or torn asunder by feelings (e.g., of benevolence or hatred) and beliefs (e.g., norms and ideals), by moral and legal norms, and above all by social actions such as sharing and cooperating, exchanging and informing, discussing and commanding, coercing and rebelling. All such actions are dynamic social relations. They are relations in that they involve two or more individuals. And they are dynamic in being carried out over time, in affecting their relata, and by varying in intensity. Some social actions involve several social relations (E.g., an organizer informs and discusses, cooperates and fights, persuades and cajoles, promises and threatens, rewards and punishes). Despite the enormous variety of social relations, many social scientists have chosen to highlight only one kind, such as those entailing conflict (e.g., Marx), solidarity (e.g., Durkheim), exchange (exchange and rational choice theorists), or communication.

Social systems come in all sizes and degrees of complexity, from the nuclear family to the United Nations. The more complex among them are super-systems—that is, systems the constituents of which are systems—for example, federations, cartels, supermarket chains, governments, and the world system. But the intrasystem bonds are stronger than the intersystem ones; were it not so, the system would not exist or persist.

In the course of this book I shall make repeated use of the following basic assumption, or BEPC model. Every human society, no matter how primitive, is composed of four main interacting, partially intersecting subsystems: the biological, or kinship, system and the economic, the cultural, and the political systems. Some members of a human social system belong to all four subsystems, others to fewer. For example, a solitary immigrant belongs to a kinship system in the society he has left; and an infant is a passive member—sometimes a beneficiary, at others times a victim—of the economy and polity of the society it has been born into.

All formal organizations, such as companies and schools, are social systems, but the converse is not true. For example, a family and a street-corner gang are systems, hence they possess a structure or organization, but they are not formal organizations. A formal organization is a social system that, far from growing spontaneously or by accretion, is set up and governed according to some explicit blueprint or plan: it is organized or shaped deliberately, with a definite goal in view. Thus armies, churches, and government departments are formal organizations. However, an informal group, such as a group of regulars at a particular pub or a street-corner gang, may evolve into a formal organization, such as a club or a criminal band. Conversely, a formal organization may decay into an informal association.

What about social institutions? I submit that the expression 'social institution' is ambiguous. There are two kinds of social institution: namely, the family of social systems of the same kind and the socially accepted practice. For example, 'business' stands for the collection of all business firms; 'the mail,' 'the school,' and 'organized religion' are parallel. By contrast, marriage, education, punishment, and exchange are socially accepted practices regulated by social conventions or norms.

The twin concepts of social system and emergence are at the center of an age-old problem in social science: namely, that of the relation between (individual) agency and (social) structure: which determines which? Those concepts constitute the eye of a storm that has been raging for three centuries in social studies and the philosophy thereof. This is the controversy between individualists and holist. As the reader will doubtless have surmised by now, this book espouses an alternative to both: namely, systemism. Moreover, I shall argue that all creative social scientists have, albeit tacitly, adopted a systemic viewpoint. (More on this in chap. 10 and in Bunge 1979a, 1979b.)

3 State, Event, Process

Every concrete thing, no matter how simple, has a number of properties. It is a tacit philosophical assumption of scientific research that we can get to know only some of these properties, but that we may find further properties if we investigate the thing in question. (The first part of this sentence is a version of fallibilism, the second of meliorism.) Our knowledge about a given thing at a certain time includes a list of its known individual properties at that time. This list represents the *state* of the thing at the time, as known to the student. For example, the state of an economy can be given by listing the values of the relevant economic indicators.

If we know n properties of a thing, we can represent each of them as a mathematical function. The list of n such functions is called a 'state function' for things of that particular kind. In the early stages of a science, when there is a dearth of quantitative variables, we may have to settle for a qualitative description of the state of a system. In such cases a state function will be a list of n qualities, or nonquantitative predicates, such as "agricultural," "preliterate," "traditional," "hierarchical," or "democratic."

In principle, all properties, other than existence, can be quantitated (see chap. 2, secs. 3 and 4). When all the variables of interest have been quantitated, the state function is an n-tuple of numerical functions, such as "area," "population," "birthrate," "life expectancy," and "GDP." The value of the state function for a system at a given time represents the state of the system at that time. For example, the balance sheet of a business firm can be construed as the value of a state function for the firm at a given time. (Caution: Different accountants may come up with different state functions, or balance-sheet formats, for one and the same firm. E.g., some will include the firm's prestige and brand names, others not. In other words, the state of the system may be "perceived" differently by people with different mind-sets or goals.)

When all the relevant properties have been quantitated, the state function determines an n-dimensional abstract space called a 'state space' for things of the kind in question. The instantaneous state of any such thing may be represented as a point in that space. This point may be visualized as the tip of an arrow that originates in the intersection of the n axes. A state space for things of a given kind is the collection of points representing all the possible states of an arbitrary thing of that kind (see Appendix 1).

Note the cautious indefinite article in the phrases 'a state function' and 'a state space.' The reason for this caution surfaced a moment ago, in the discussion of balance sheets. The state of a thing is definite and objective, but it can be conceptualized in different ways. Indeed, there are as many state functions (and spaces), as representations or models of the thing, as we can conceive of. It is not only that we may be forced to alter our models or theories as new research findings come in. Theorists with different backgrounds or perspectives may come up with alternative models compatible with one and the same set of empirical data: one territory, many maps. Still, the choice of representation is neither arbitrary nor merely a matter of taste. Indeed, it is determined by a number of desiderata, among them accuracy, depth, explanatory power, predictive power, heuristic power, ease of interpretation, and computational convenience. (More on this in chap. 4, sec. 4.)

All concrete things are in a state of flux. (This, of course, is a principle shared by most philosophical schools. It cannot be proved, but it underlies the study of change in all factual sciences.) That is, as "time goes by"—as the world unfolds—some of the properties of each thing will change, however slowly. In other words, the state of any concrete thing changes in the course of time. These changes can be represented by the motion of the representative point in a state space. The most advanced sciences have equations for such changes, whereas the less advanced ones have to make do with graphics, tables, or even verbal descriptions. But whatever the degree of sophistication of a science, it employs the concepts of state and change of state.

By definition, an *event* is a change of state. Such change may be merely quantitative, as in the case of growth and decline, or it may be qualitative as well, as in the case of the assembly and breakdown of social systems. A marriage and a change of government are events. But a finer analysis will reveal these as not point events but processes. By definition, a *process*, or *history*, is a sequence of states—for example, the life history of an organism, a family history, or the history of a social organization. An event (or point process) is describable by the ordered couple <initial state, final state>. By contrast, a process involves a path; hence it is described by a sequence of more than two—perhaps infinitely many—states, so by a curve or trajectory in some state space.

Evolution, whether natural or social, is a particularly important, interesting type of process. A process may be said to be *evolutionary* if it involves the emergence and spread of qualitatively new things. Shorter: Evolution involves speciation. The best-known evolutionary processes are of course those of bio-populations and social systems. (Note the difference between evolution and the emergence of novelty. A thing endowed with a new property is the founder of a new kind. But this kind does not count as a species unless the mutant multiplies—by division, sexual reproduction, imitation, or some other mechanism. That is, speciation equals radical novelty plus diffusion. For example, the prototype of a new gadget or a social invention initiates a new kind, but this becomes a new species only if the founder replicates and spreads. This is the difference between invention, a psychological process, and innovation, a social one.)

The general concept of a state logically precedes that of a process: the former helps define the latter. However, the current state of certain complex things depends on their entire past, or at least part of it, so that, in describing it, we must use a specific concept of process. This is the case with all hereditary processes, which occur in systems with "memory," such as plastics, certain alloys (elastic hysteresis), all ferromagnets (magnetic hysteresis), all organisms (DNA and learning), and all social systems (tradition): they all retain traces of their past. (Caution: The "memory" in question has nothing to do with Durkheim's ghostly "collective memory.")

Being changes of state of things, events and processes are representable in state spaces. For example, an event can be represented by an arrow connecting the initial state with the final state; and a process or history can be represented as a string of states, perhaps a continuous trajectory. If things could be only in any of a countable set of states at a particular time, as assumed in automata theory, their changes would be strings of point events. But even the simplest physical thing, such as an electron or a photon, can be in any of an uncountable (hence infinite) set of states and can undergo continuous changes as well as discontinuous ones.

People and social systems change all the time, sometimes undergoing qualitative transformations—that is, acquiring or losing properties. However, for lack of information, such ongoing changes can seldom be fully plotted. For example, the production of a factory is recorded daily, not continuously, and most social and macroeconomic statistics are compiled on a quarterly, or even a yearly, basis. In other words, even while assuming that social changes are continuous, one records them as discontinuous, in the manner of a digital watch. This has a parallel in computer science, where the basic physical processes are known to be continuous, but their idealized models, such as the theory of Turing machines, involve denumerable, sometimes even finite, state spaces.

The concept of change can be used to define that of a concrete, material, or real thing. Indeed, we propose the following definition: "For any x: x is a *concrete* (or *material*, or *real*) thing $=_{df} x$ is changeable." The symbol '$=_{df}$' is read "identical by definition.") In turn, *matter* may be defined as the collection of all material things. We distinguish five major kinds, or levels, of matter: physical, chemical, biological, social, and technical.

Note that our definition of a concrete, or material, thing is strictly objective: it does not include the notion of a knowing subject. Hence a subjectivist has no use for it: he is interested only in what is real for him. Thus Feyerabend (1981, 1. xiii) tells us: "*[W]e decide to regard those things as real which play an important role in the kind of life we prefer.*" This reality criterion may suit the homeless or the playboy, but not the scientist or the technologist. Indeed, in science and technology the attribution of reality is not a matter of choice or life-style, but of objective tests. Thus I regard the aurora borealis and the Club Méditerranée as equally real, because their existence has been well attested, even though neither plays any role in my life.

The import of our definition becomes clearer when we contrast real things with ideal objects, such as numbers and theories, when studied in themselves— that is, independently of the people who think of them. A concrete object, such as a person or a business firm, changes throughout its existence, whereas an ideal object, such as a mathematical figure or a sociological theory, is unchanging. If a construct were to change, it would become a different construct. In sum, I propose the following convention: "For all x: x is *ideal* $=_{df} x$ is unchanging." Caution: I am not asserting the autonomous existence of ideas—far from it. I am just laying down a convention concerning the meaning I shall attribute to the concept "ideal"—or, equivalently, the signification to be attributed to the word *ideal*.

If the first definition is admitted, then *reality*, or the collection of all real things, turns out to be identical with the collection of all changeable things. But note that collections, unlike aggregates and systems, are conceptual, not real. Hence reality, though made up of all real things, is not real itself. (Similarly, motion does not move, language does not speak, and history does not evolve.) However, the membership of a collection or an aggregate, unlike that of a set, is variable over time. Hence the expression 'Reality is changeable' is ambiguous: it can designate either "Every real thing is changeable" or "The collection of real things is changeable." Both are philosophical propositions, and we assert them both.

In sum, every fact proper involves some concrete thing or other, and it consists either in the thing being in a given state or in the thing undergoing a change of state. Moreover, all the objects or referents of factual science, in particular, social science, are changeable and, by the same token, real.

4 Pattern

Patterns are regularities or uniformities. They can be conceptual or real. A mathematical theorem is a conceptual pattern, one that concepts of some kind satisfy. By contrast, a natural or social law is a real pattern, an order among facts, actual or possible. If real or objective, a pattern can be spatial, temporal, or spatiotemporal. It can also be natural, artificial, or mixed; for example, the laws of genetics are natural, legal codes are artificial, and in some societies sex ratios are semi-artificial, in that the natural ratios are distorted by female infanticide. Furthermore, patterns may be manifest, like the tiling of a floor and the formation of a platoon, or they may be imperceptible, like the stages in the manufacture of a good or the stratification of a society.

The thesis that there are objective patterns and that these inhere in the things concerned belongs to scientific realism. The main alternative views regarding patterns are idealism and positivism. According to idealism, patterns are ideas external to things, which things obey or disobey the way a citizen of a country observes or breaks the law of the land. (Subjective idealists profess not to believe in the external world, and objective idealists do not necessarily believe that reality is lawful.) Positivists hold that all laws are descriptions of empirical regularities—whence all hidden patterns escape them. Thus neither idealists nor positivists admit that the formulas we usually call 'laws' represent (more or less accurately) objective patterns. Only realists distinguish between a pattern and its conceptualizations—that is, between a law and the corresponding law statement(s). (More on this in chap. 4, sec. 4.)

I distinguish four kinds of real or objective patterns: law, trend, statistical correlation, and rule, or norm. A *law* is a stable pattern that holds independently of human knowledge or will: it inheres in things. Hence it is discovered, not invented. A law may be spatially and temporally boundless, as is the case with the basic physical laws. Or it may be bounded in space or time, as is the case with biological laws, which came into existence on our planet only about three billion years ago, together with the first terrestrial organisms, and social laws, which have evolved with society. An objective law cannot be violated the way a legal norm can; nor can it be bent as a result of human action. A law is in the nature of things: it is an essential property of things of some kind. Consequently, finding laws—the supreme goal of research in the natural sciences— amounts to discovering the essences of things.

That laws are complex properties of things can be shown in two ways. One is by noting that, far from hovering above things, the latter are supposed to satisfy ("obey") laws. Another procedure is to disclose the referents of any conceptualization of an objective law, i.e., a law statement. Consider the simplest possible example of a law statement. Let the predicates A and B represent two qualitative properties of things of some kind K, and assume that the possession of A implies the possession of B: "For every x of kind K: if x is an A, then x is a B." In standard symbols, $(\forall x)[Kx \Rightarrow (Ax \Rightarrow Bx)]$. Introducing the abbreviation "$L = (A \Rightarrow B)$," the law statement schema can be rewritten thus: $(\forall x)(Kx \Rightarrow Lx)$. In plain words: every thing of kind K has property L—or, equivalently, satisfies law L. It is even possible to define K as the natural class of all the things with property L; i.e., $K = \{x|Lx\}$ (Bunge 1977*b*).

There is no doubt that nature is, so to speak, law-abiding. Whether there are social laws, and if so, which ones hold across all societies and which are peculiar to societies of a certain type, are intriguing philosophico-scientific questions that I will focus on in the companion volume (Bunge forthcoming). Suffice it to say here that not all laws are universal in the sense that they hold everywhere at all times. If one demands, as many people do, that all laws be spatiotemporally universal, then it is clear that social science will never discover any. But physics, chemistry, and biology are in the same boat. The laws of liquids and of solids did not emerge before the planets were formed. Likewise, the laws of chemical reactions do not exist where the temperature is too low or too high for such processes to occur. The case of biological laws is parallel. (See Marshall 1920 [1890], 631.)

Hence there should be no difficulty in admitting the possibility of social laws. Moreover, given that all societies have some features in common, it is likely that there are some universal social laws—for example, "The inertia of a social system is directly proportional to the number of its components and inversely proportional to its cohesiveness," and "Higher culture does not emerge in a society until the basic needs of some of its members have been satisfied." And, given the diversity of social systems, it is conceivable that social laws come in the same variety; moreover, assuming that all social systems have limited "life" spans, their laws must be equally time-bound—for example, "Gatherer-hunter societies are egalitarian," and "In all capitalist societies the likelihood of getting out of unemployment falls as the unemployment rate increases."

A *trend* is a temporary pattern, such as that described by the statement "Capital and technological expertise are becoming increasingly global—not so people and goods." Although a trend presumably results from lawful events, it is not a law itself. People can reverse trends, but not laws. For example, fertility exhibits different patterns in different regions of the world. In some it grows, in others it remains constant, and in still others it declines. Consequently, the shape of any given demographic curve is a trend, not a law. Curves for GDP as a function of time, and income inequality as a function of industrialization are parallel. Trends can change, though not overnight, because some of the effects of yesterday's actions are still felt today: there is such thing as social inertia, whence time lags.

(Although trends are not laws, they may be construed as laws with variable parameters. E.g., every arc of a demographic curve is covered by the same equation, but with different birthrates and migration rates in each period. These values are empirical, not the results of computations based on further law statements. However, one can hope to explain eventually such parameter changes in environmental, economic, political, or cultural terms. For instance, it is well known that birth and death rates decline, though with some time lag, as the standard of living rises.)

A *statistical correlation* is a covariation of two variables, each representing a property of things of some kind. Correlations, whether genuine or spurious, can be positive or negative, direct or indirect (via a third variable), sustained or temporary, strong or weak. Even if strong for a while, a correlation may be spurious—accidental or the product of an artifact, rather than systematic. Such an artifact may occur if only a short period or a selected portion of the total population is studied, or if the sample is not random. For example, a positive correlation between sickness, on the one hand, and level of education, on the other, has been observed. In fact, what happens is that only a fraction of sick people report to health care centers, and those who do are usually better off or better educated than those who do not. When the total population is studied carefully, the inverse correlation is found.

So far, the search for patterns in social science has been mainly a search for statistical correlations. This search has been enormously facilitated by the computer and by a sharp increase in the amount of socially significant information available. But of course, only strong, sustained correlations are of value. They point to possible underlying laws, particularly causal ones. However, there are no techniques for inferring a law from a correlation: all but the simplest laws must first be guessed, then tested (see chap. 3, sec. 4).

Finally, a *rule*, or *norm*, is a social convention set up by people, either spontaneously or deliberately, and in force in some social system or even in an entire society. Every time a social system of a new type emerges, a set of new norms is built into it. These norms regulate the way the system functions: they constitute a sort of operating manual for the system. Unlike laws and trends, norms can be criticized, violated, or even repealed overnight. This is what social reforms and revolutions are all about: changes in certain man-made laws and the social systems they regulate.

Some human activities can be carried out in accordance with explicit rules, but none is fully rule-directed. There is always some tacit know-how, intuition, and judgment. For example, the first rule of scientific method is to start by posing clearly the problem in which one is interested, but there are no rules for finding or stating problems or even for clarifying their formulation. These are largely matters of curiosity, insight, experience, and even taste. (Incidentally, this is the main reason why computers will never replace original thinkers.)

Although norms are made, they cannot be wholly arbitrary if they are to be observed, but must be compatible with the relevant laws. In particular, the norms for setting up or managing a social organization must conform to the laws satisfied by the organization's components. For example, a norm requiring people to abstain from consuming energy or from polluting the environment would stand no chance of being observed. Social life cannot escape natural law. Moreover, it is the declared intention of much progressive public policy and legislation to improve social conditions, so as to make it possible for people to meet the needs inherent in normal biological and psychological patterns.

Sometimes one is told that "Anything is possible." This amounts to the assertion that there are lawless events, such as paranormal phenomena and miracles. The scientific attitude is at variance with this belief: scientists look for patterns in all facts. If they do not find them, they conjecture either that (*a*) for the time being the search for pattern has failed, or (*b*) that they are faced with random events with a very low probability, or (*c*) that they have been looking at strings, or collections, of heterogeneous facts that, though individually lawful, fail to exhibit collective regularities. In short, scientists abide, usually tacitly, by the *principle of lawfulness*. This philosophical postulate can be stated thus: Every fact satisfies some laws or can be analyzed into lawful components.

(The principle of lawfulness can be reformulated in terms of the state space concept, thus. The really possible states of a thing are confined within a box inside the set of all conceivable or logically possible states. This box may be called a *lawful state space* for things of the kind concerned. E.g., in social structure research the instantaneous state of a community may be construed as the distribution of its population among the various occupational groups in the community. If *n* such groups are distinguished, the state space will have *n* axes, and the corresponding lawful occupational state space will be an *n*-dimensional box. See Appendix 1.)

The principle of lawfulness is confirmed every time a new pattern is found, but it cannot be proved conclusively. Nor does it stand refuted every time we fail to find a pattern, for we can always allege that further research is bound to succeed. The principle is an article of scientific faith inherent in every scientific endeavor. It underlies the rule of scientific method that enjoins us to look for patterns in every collection of related facts and encourages us not to give up when we fail to find such patterns.

Lawfulness must not be mistaken for uniformity. The principle of *uniformity* states that the laws are the same throughout the cosmos at all times. In a stronger version it states that the same events recur everywhere. The application of uniformitarianism to social science is obvious: all persons and all social groups—present, past, and future—satisfy the same regularities. If this thesis were true, there would be no evolution and no history. In fact, patterns of individual and collective behavior are changeable, so uniformitarianism is just as false in social studies as it is in natural science.

5 Causation

The notion of causation, or causal relation, is pervasive in all fields of inquiry and action. We use it, for instance, when we say that so and so did such and such, or that one thing leads to another; when we ask whether Protestantism gave rise to capitalism or conversely, or whether poverty originates in ignorance or the other way round. True, there has been much talk about the demise of causation in modern physics, but this has proved to be a false rumor (see

Bunge 1959). What is true is that sometimes causation occurs in combination with chance, as when one computes or measures the probability that a photon will knock off an atomic electron. It is also true that some systems, such as radioactive atoms, self-exciting neurons, and highly original people, have some outputs without external inputs: they escape causation.

One says that event C is *the* cause of event E if, and only if, the occurrence of C is sufficient for that of E (e.g., severe drought causes crop failure, which in turn causes food scarcity). On the other hand, we say that C is *a* cause of E if and only if C is necessary but not sufficient for E (e.g., food scarcity is necessary but not sufficient to raise food prices, and the latter is necessary but not sufficient to cause food riots). A necessary but insufficient cause is often called a *contributory* cause. Most, if not all, social facts have multiple contributory causes.

The causal relation links *events*—not things, properties, or states. That is, only changes can be causally related. For example, in industrialized societies an increase in unemployment always causes an increase in crime. When we say that thing A caused thing B to do C, we mean that a certain event in the thing A (the "agent") generated a change C in the state of the "patient" B (which may be a part of A).

Unlike other relations among events, such as spatiotemporal ones, the causal relation is not external to the relata: every effect is somehow produced by its cause(s). In other words, causation is a mode of event generation. (Causally efficient information flows, such as those running through informal social networks and organizations, ride on physical processes such as sound waves or electromagnetic signals. There is no such thing as information without some material substratum.)

We distinguish two types of causal mechanism: type 1, involving *energy transfer*, as in manual work, and type 2, involving a *triggering signal*, as in giving an order to fire a gun or an employee. In the first case the quantity of energy transferred is critical, whereas in the second a small energy transfer may initiate a process involving a large energy. In other words, in type 2 processes the effect may be "disproportionate" to the cause: that is, a very small cause may trigger a process giving rise to a catastrophic effect. This is the case in unstable systems, such as social systems relying on a strong leader and unpopular governments founded on coercion. In these cases the removal of a single very influential person may cause the breakdown of the entire system. Both types of causal mechanism are found at all levels of reality, but type 2 mechanisms are partic- ularly important at the biological and social levels because organisms and social systems are unstable.

Causal relations can sometimes be exactified with the help of the mathemati- cal concept of a function. However, functional relations do not express causal relations without further ado. Indeed, a functional relation of the form $y = f(x)$

may state only a concomitance or constant conjunction between the properties represented by the variables x and y, such as the population and the area of a nation. The assumption that a given functional relation expresses a causal link is a separate hypothesis. Moreover, a formula such as $y = f(x)$ is not suited to this purpose because, as stated earlier, a causal relation is a relation between events (changes in properties), not properties. However, the formula in question entails $dy = f'(x) \cdot dx$, which may be interpreted in causal terms thus: change dy is proportional to change dx. (E.g., below a certain level, an increase in income causes an increase in consumption.) This is a causal interpretation of the ontologically neutral mathematical formula $y = f(x)$. And such an interpretation is hypothetical—so much so, that an experiment involving a deliberate change dx and the measurement of the corresponding dy may refute the causal hypothesis.

In the social sciences, the search for causation usually starts by looking for a conjunction (or concomitance, correlation, or covariation). Thus, it is well known that highly paid labor is in general more efficient than lowly paid labor. The question is whether high labor power is the cause of high wages, or the other way round. The correct answer to this loaded question is both; that is, it is a case of circular causation (and, in particular, of feed-forward). That is, to hire skilled workers, one must offer high pay, and only well-treated workers will attain the well-being and motivation necessary to work efficiently. Likewise, investment leads ultimately to savings, which in turn favor investment. In general, if two or more social variables are related, they are likely to be *interdependent* rather than unilaterally dependent. For this reason, linear causal chains are the exception rather than the rule in social matters, whereas causal cycles are common.

Mere observation of concomitances or constant conjunctions can suggest false causal links. Take, for instance, the finding that the ratio of increments in the number of mental patients and the number of criminals is roughly constant in all industrial Western societies. A century ago, Darwinists would readily have "concluded" (hypothesized) that mental imbalance is the cause of criminality. Recent work has shown that unemployment is a source of both mental imbalance and criminality. (In self-explanatory symbols, $dC/du = a$, and $dM/du = b$, where a and b are positive real numbers. Dividing the first equation by the second yields $dC/dM = a/b$, which is the empirical finding.) Moral: The constant conjunction of two variables may be a result of two hidden causal links. Corollary: Hume was wrong in equating causation with constant conjunction. Causation satisfies patterns (laws and norms) rather than being arbitrary or capricious. That is, there are causal laws and norms or, at least, patterns with a causal range. However, not all regularities are causal, and not all interconnected events are causally related. Causation is just one mode of determination, along with self-determination (or spontaneity), chance, and purpose (Bunge 1959). Moreover, these four categories often intertwine, particularly in human affairs. (E.g., I may make use of a certain means in order to attain some goal, believing that the given cause has a nonvanishing chance of causing the desired effect.) Because there are several categories of determination, and because these may intertwine, determinism should be construed broadly, rather than in a narrow, causalist fashion.

Behaviorism was the golden age of causality in psychology and sociology. Indeed, the environmentalist or stimulus–response (S–R) schema and the unconditioned reflex do have the properties of causal links, especially since they overlook the internal states of an organism. But of course this oversight leads to faulty results: the internal state, I, of the organism does matter, this being why one and the same stimulus is likely to elicit different responses at different times. In other words, S–R relations are only coarse approximations to S–I–R relations. (If the relation is functional, it will be of the form $f: S \times I \to R$ rather than $g: S \to R$. See Bunge and Ardila 1987.)

In particular, a human being is likely at different times (hence in different states) to perceive or evaluate differently any given (physical or social) stimulus. Likewise, different people are likely to have different perceptions and evaluations of the same external item. In other words, we tend to react to external events according to our own perceptions and evaluations of them, and these are colored by our own experience, interests, and expectations. This makes it difficult—though not impossible—to be objective, particularly in matters that affect us. It also explains in part why science, especially social science, has arrived so very late in human evolution. And it suggests that the scientific study of society is indispensable to understanding social events and keeping them under control.

The state of an organism at a given time depends not only on its environment but also on its history, which is partly recorded in its memory. In humans and other animals the current internal state depends also on the organism's spontaneous mental processes, which are not caused by the immediately preceding environmental stimuli. The higher we climb the ladder of brain functions, the more we find that internal states and stimulus-independent processes matter. Eventually we meet the affective, ideational, and volitional processes that can delay or distort "normal" responses to the point of inhibiting them altogether.

Another aspect of the causal arrow peculiar to intelligent animals is that it may involve expectations. That is, whereas the present state of an unintelligent being is determined only by its past and present circumstances, the present state of an intelligent being is determined partially by its expectations as well. For example, a dog's present behavior depends partly on the meal or the caress that he expects from it. And a businessman's present actions depend in part on his more or less reasonable expectations concerning both his firm and the economy at large. Both behaviors are in part goal seeking.

Some mental processes are self-starting rather than evoked by sensory stimuli. (The underlying neural mechanisms seem to be spontaneous firing and self-assembly of neurons: see Hebb 1949, 1980; Bindra 1976; Bunge 1980.) The spontaneous mental processes are not totally uncaused, of course; but the point is that they are not responses to external stimuli. Because of its increasing concern with mental functions and the corresponding internal neural processes, psychology is rapidly moving away from behaviorism, hence from causalism—though not from determinism in the broad sense.

Both chance and design are always present in human affairs. Were it not for them, we might be able to predict accurately the future of our social systems. However, causation is still a factor to be reckoned with, and it is likely to remain so, because there are causal links which we all count on when doing something or when intending to influence other people. For example, social mobility can be accelerated or slowed down; social cohesion can be strengthened or weakened; economic growth can be increased or decreased; and political participation can be encouraged or discouraged, by making certain events happen and preventing others—that is, by controlling the strategic variables.

This is not to say that we always know the relevant causal relations and can thus tune the relevant variables so as to get the desired effects. In fact, all too often we ignore such variables and the relations among them. This (to be hoped, decreasing) ignorance is not just the price we pay for living in complex societies composed of systems too large to be observable, controllable, and understandable in intuitive terms. It is also the price we pay for having followed Hume, Kant, Comte, and Mach in confining research to the description of observable phenomena—in particular, constant conjunctions and successions—and rejecting as "metaphysical" any attempt to disclose deep causal mechanisms inherent in social systems. However, when censored by any such philosophy, causal thinking merely goes underground. Thus, in distinguishing different kinds of inflation, such as demand and cost inflation, and pointing the finger at automatic markup, wage push, bureaucratism, or militarism, we tacitly point to different causes (hence also kinds) of inflation.

Fortunately, descriptivism is on the way out in social science. Thus, anthropologists and archaeologists look for the possible causes of the rise or decline of primitive and archaic societies; sociologists focus on interaction as the source of both maintenance and change of social systems; economists are interested in discovering the causes of growth and stagnation; historians try to uncover the preconditions and triggers of social movements—as well as the obstacles to change. And in every social science it matters that we ascertain whether, given any two concomitants, one of them is the cause and the other the effect. In sum, causality—though not causal determinism—is back in social science. (For causal analysis in social science, see Blalock and Blalock 1968 and Franck 1994.)

Once a causal relation has been established, if a human being gets hold of it, he can adapt the input to the desired value of the output. For example, industrial output can be altered by graduating the labor force or some other factor of production. Conversely, once a level of industrial output has been chosen, the corresponding input(s) can be determined. This is but one example of the practical importance of causal knowledge.

The preceding refers to one-way causation, which runs forward from cause or input to effect or output. In addition to one-way causation, there is circular causation (or feedback cycle). In this case, part of the output is fed back (later) into the system to either increase its output (feed-forward) or attenuate it (negative feedback). Thus, industrial sociologists have found that wage raises are followed by increases in productivity. But, in turn, the latter can be used by labor unions to demand higher wages.

Some controversies in social science are over causal arrows. For example, does marginality cause criminality, or conversely? Whereas some sociologists may plump for the former hypothesis, others may prefer the latter. But of course both are right, though not over the same stretch of the entire process. Indeed, in most cases people start stealing because they have no other ways of meeting their needs, let alone their wants. But once they have become professional criminals, they find themselves marginalized.

Finally, a word of caution concerning the relation between cause and reason. Radical rationalists, such as Descrates, Spinoza, and Leibniz, equated causes with reasons and demanded that a reason be advanced for whatever exists or happens. Thus Leibniz's most cherished postulate was his principle of sufficient reason, according to which "Nothing happens without a sufficient reason." He conflated the ontological principle of causality with the rule of procedure which demands that we give a reason for, or justify, our beliefs and actions.

Reasons must be distinguished from causes: the former are constructs, whereas the latter are real events; and whereas philosophical explanations invoke reasons, only scientific ones may invoke causes. For example, reasons, but not causes, can be either valid or invalid; and causes, but not reasons, can change the world. However, distinction should not entail detachment. Indeed, causes and reasons join in both thought and action. In fact, from the point of view of physiological psychology the processes of proposing and examining reasons are partly causal (and partly random). And whenever we engage in rational action, we start by advancing reasons for our doing (or refraining from doing), and end up by discussing rationally the outcome of our action. (More in chap. 14, sec. 7.)

Rational action and the rational discussion of it are among the features that distinguish society from nature, and consequently social science from natural science. However, this distinction should not be overdone, for reason is impotent without causation, just as action is likely to be ineffective without reason. This caution is necessary in view of the popularity of rational choice theories, which underrate the power of causation and objective chance.

In short, causation is an important change mechanism. Though not the only one, it is everyone's favorite for being the easiest to understand and control. Chance is quite different and harder to handle, hence it deserves a separate section.

6 Chance and Chaos

In addition to causation there is chance, sometimes combined with causation. But the word *chance* is ambiguous: it denotes both accident (or coincidence) and randomness (e.g., stochastic process). When accidents or coincidences are unique or extremely rare, as is the case with the appearance of the proverbial right man at the right spot at the right time, they do not fit into any patterns. But when they occur repeatedly, as in the cases of automobile accidents and suicides, they do show patterns. These patterns are probabilistic or statistical, such as the bell-shaped curve. In such cases one speaks of randomness and, in particular, of the random distribution of the values of a property.

Randomness can be basic, or irreducible, as in the case of radioactive decay, or it may emerge from the intersection of initially independent causal lines, as in the case of gene (or card) shuffling or the bringing together of people with different life histories, such as those in a freshman class. (The concept of basic chance does not occur in social science.) Randomness can be natural, as in the case of white noise, or artificial, as with random sampling. And in either case it may appear all of a sudden or gradually over time.

A random process is one in which every step (state or event) has a definite objective probability. The probability of each step (state or event) in a random process may or may not depend on that of the preceding event. If it does not, the successive steps are said to be statistically independent; otherwise they are statistically dependent. In the latter case, if m and n label any two successive steps in a process, the probability of n, given m, equals a definite real number p greater than 0 and smaller than 1. In symbols, $P(n|m) = p$, where $P(n|m)$ is called the 'conditional probability' of n, given m. If p varies in the course of time, it is usually assumed that such variation is lawful—that is, that the rate of change of p is a precise function of certain variables.

Randomness, or chance, may inhere in the facts themselves, in our selection of them (i.e., in random sampling), or in both. But it must be there somewhere, in order for us to be justified in using the concept of probability. As a matter of fact, chance lurks everywhere, both in and between things on all levels, from electrons to genes to organisms to societies. Let the following laundry list suffice to make the point: diffusion, contagion, the propagation of rumors, accidental errors of measurement, random sampling, and actuarial tables. Given the ubiquity of chance, one may well suspect that no "deterministic" (better: purely causal) theory can capture all the features of any real object.

The concept of randomness is rendered mathematically precise by the calculus of probability. This is a branch of pure mathematics. But, when used in science or technology, probability gets interpreted in factual terms. (No circularity here: exactification bears on intuitive concepts, whereas factual interpretation bears on formal ones.) Thus, in the equation $P(n|m) = p$ for conditional probability, m and n name either states or events, and the value, p, of the probability equals the intensity of the tendency for the thing concerned to jump from state (or event) m to state (or event) n. If $m = n$, the corresponding probability measures the tendency of the thing being (or staying) in state m. This is the realist interpretation of probability, according to which the latter is an objective magnitude independent of the state of our knowledge. This interpretation, introduced by Poisson in 1837, used by physicists, biologists, and others, and popularized by Popper under the name "propensity theory," is at variance with the subjectivist or Bayesian interpretation, according to which a probability is nothing but a measure of uncertainty. (See chap. 13, sec. 6; Du Pasquier 1926; Bunge 1988a.)

For example, in the probabilistic theory of social mobility, $P(n|m)$ measures the tendency for an arbitrary member of a given society to move from social rung m to rung n, whereas $P(m|m)$ measures a person's tendency to remain in group m. Second example: If the observed death rate at age t in a given population is $m(t)$, then the probability that an individual aged t, picked at random, will die during the interval Δt, is $m(t) \cdot \Delta t$. (Note that in this case the probability is inferred from a rate.) Third example: The life expectancy at age t is the amount of time that an individual aged t, picked at random in the given population, is likely to live from instant t. In all three cases the randomness condition is essential: *no randomness, no probability.* However, randomness may inhere in the things themselves, in our choice of them, or in both.

The phrase "picked at random," which occurs above, tells us that in those particular cases randomness is involved in the sampling process, whether or not the property itself is randomly distributed. In general, a relative frequency or a rate, together with some random choice or randomization procedure, allows us to infer a probability, or to measure it. The psychological concepts of plausibility and uncertainty do not occur in the preceding: in science, probabilities measure real possibilities, not states of knowledge or credences (belief intensities). Psychologists have yet to figure out how to conceptualize and measure credences. And we should know from quantum physics, genetics, and other disciplines, as well as from reflecting upon our own life histories, that chance is often for real, not just a name for our ignorance of real causes. Clearly, the objectivist or realist interpretation of probability is at variance with the subjectivist (or Bayesian) one. Let it suffice now to state that subjectivity has no place in science except as an object of psychological research. (More in chap. 13, sec. 7.)

Nor is probability to be confused with truth. It cannot be said of propositions that they are probable or improbable, because they are not distributed at random. (This is particularly so with the constituents of a hypothetico-deductive system.) What can be said instead is either that a proposition is *partially true* or that it "looks" true—that is, seems *plausible* or *verisimilar* in the light of some body of knowledge. Thus, the proposition that the present world population equals 5 billion is approximately true; that is, it is affected by a small error. And the hypothesis that the world population will continue to grow till the middle of the twenty-first century is plausible or verisimilar, but not probable, since it cannot be assigned a probability.

The concept of truth is logically prior to (more basic than) that of probability. Indeed, we need the former to assess the adequacy of probabilistic statements. (E.g., it is true that, if a and b are mutually independent events, $P(a \ \& \ b) = P(a) \cdot P(b)$.) Hence it is doubly incorrect to try to define truth, particularly approximate truth, in terms of probability, as many philosophers have tried to do. It is incorrect because truth precedes probability, and because only states and events can occur randomly and thus be assigned probabilities. To say of a proposition that it is probable is just as wrong as to attribute to it an area.

The concept of probability does not generalize; nor can it be replaced by that of causation—notwithstanding a popular tradition systematized by Suppes (1970). The reason is that the concept of causation is logically prior to that of conditional probability. Indeed, if in the formula $P(n|m) = p$, m and n name successive, repeatable events, and the later event n depends uniformly on the earlier event m, then m can be called a (contributory) cause, n the corresponding effect, and p the strength of the link between them. If $0 < p < 1$, the occurrence of cause m renders effect n probable (with strength p) rather than necessary. In other words, the concept of conditional probability of an event given that another event has occurred involves the concepts of cause and effect. Some random sequences are more or less weak chains of causes and effects. Markov chains, widely used in social science, constitute a case in point. In fact, in such sequences the probability of each event depends only on the immediately preceding event—a case of very short "memory," or a weak causal link.

There is no such link among the successive flips of a coin: this is a case of pure randomness or statistical independence, involving neither "memory" nor causal dependence.

Another vulgar mistake is the belief that chance and law are mutually exclusive. This belief is false because there are laws of chance. These are of two kinds: general laws found in the theory of probability and special probabilistic law statements found in the various sciences. A well-known example of a general law of chance is the law of large numbers, whereas life expectancy tables are well-known special probabilistic laws. In short, in the real world, chance, or randomness, is a lawful mode of being and becoming.

Probabilities can sometimes be estimated by the corresponding relative frequencies, but the two concepts are different, and neither is definable in terms of the other. For one thing, probabilities are properties of individuals in either populations or sequences of random events. By contrast, frequencies are collective properties, even when no random mechanism is present, as is the case with the frequency of presidential elections. For another, while the concept of frequency is empirical, that of probability is theoretical. In other words, frequencies result from observation, whereas probabilities are posited or calculated.

In simple cases, however, the two concepts are related as follows. First, *given the frequency f_s of events of kind E* in a random sample S of a total population P, the probability of an individual event of kind E picked at random in the population P lies near f_s. Second, *given the probability p* of a random event of type E in a total population P, the long-run frequency of any event of type E in P is close to p. (Caution: Probabilities may be inferred not just from frequencies but from other variables as well, depending on the theory. Thus, as we saw above, in demography and actuarial mathematics some probabilities are inferred from rates. In statistical mechanics they are inferred from certain thermodynamic variables such as energy and temperature, and in quantum mechanics from state functions.)

A last vulgar mistake against which we must guard is the idea that there is a probabilistic *logic* different from ordinary logic. Actually, the logic underlying (presupposed by and used in) the theory of probability is ordinary logic, as can be seen by axiomatizing the theory. Some or all of the premises of probabilistic reasoning are probabilistic, but the reasoning itself, if valid, satisfies ordinary logic rather than being random.

Finally, a word on "chaos theory" is in order. This name is doubly unfortunate. First, there is no unified *theory* of "chaotic" processes, but only a rapidly increasing jumble of intriguing nonlinear, finite-difference or differential equations, mostly easy to write but hard to solve and interpret. (The simplest and most popular of them is the logistic equation $x_{n+1} = rx_n(1 - x_n)$, where n is a natural number, and the tuning parameter r is a real number between 1 and

4. Chaos, or aperiodicity, appears as r increases above 3.) So far, only a few processes satisfying such equations seem to have been found. In fact, chaos theory is still largely a necklace of mathematical gems in search of real-life necks. Second, "chaos" is a misnomer, because the equations are supposed to represent objective, if seemingly irregular, patterns, hence the very opposite of chaotic (lawless or arbitrary) events or processes. "Mock randomness" might be a more adequate name. So much for words.

In recent times chaos has emerged as a serious potential rival of probability because, in the absence of additional information, both chaotic dynamics and randomness can generate any given, seemingly irregular (in particular, aperiodic) evolution. In other words, such data are ambiguous: a time path that looks random to the naked eye may actually result from a chaotic dynamics—that is, one described by nonlinear differential or finite-difference equations. This is a reminder that data do not speak for themselves. It is also a warning against the fashionable tendency to attribute chaotic behavior to a system, such as the polity or the stock market, that exhibits irregularities suggestive of instabilities.

The scientific potential of chaos theory is great, because it can handle endogenous fluctuations and instabilities in systems—that is, instabilities due to structural imbalances, produced, for example, by positive feedbacks, rather than to external shocks. (See, e.g., Glass and Mackey 1988.) It has therefore been suggested that chaos theory should be suitable for representing social crises and even for managing business organizations. However, the currently fashionable talk of chaos in social studies is mostly hand waving. Indeed, such talk rarely includes nonlinear equations interpreted in social science terms. For instance, Rosenau's (1990) much-acclaimed work on "turbulence" in world politics contains no equations; it is totally discursive and revolves around superficial analogies between "flow of action" (e.g., capital "flow") and liquid flow and between political turbulence and fluid turbulence. Likewise, Stacey's (1992) much-praised book on "managing the unknowable," allegedly with the help of chaos theory, is nonmathematical. Moreover, while C. Brown (1994) does write some equations, these involve two key variables—level of public concern and environmental damage—that he fails to define, so the equations are merely ornamental. Word is no substitute for equation, analogy no substitute for theory, and uninterpreted mathematical theory no tool for describing reality. And unless a theory is explicitly formulated and interpreted, it cannot be put to the test, let alone be pronounced true.

Any rigorous talk of social instability requires setting up, analyzing, and testing a mathematical model interpreted in social terms. Such a study includes playing with the tuning parameter(s) involved in the equations to check whether, in fact, cycles of increasing periodicity appear until the behavior of the system becomes chaotic (or apparently patternless) when the parameter(s) go beyond certain values. (Usually such changes in tuning parameter(s) are merely simulated on computers. But they should also be made experimentally.) Moreover, the key state function(s) or time series should be subjected to statistical tests for instability (or rapid exponential growth of any small deviation in the initial values). Yet all such work, though necessary, is insufficient to reach a conclusion of instability, for the latter may be a feature of the model, rather than of its referent. Indeed, instability may depend on such features as the choice of a frame of reference and the way in which the distance between stable and perturbed solutions is defined (Zak 1994). Thus we face an antinomy: no serious talk of instability without equations and no certainty that mathematical instability has a real counterpart.

Finally, the chaos-theoretical model should be compared to its probabilistic rival, to ascertain which of the two fits the data better and has the greater explanatory power. Regrettably, few, if any, chaos-theoretical models in economics take these precautions. Consequently, "the evidence for the existence of chaotic behavior in real economic time series is far from compelling so far" (Baumol and Benhabib 1989). More work is needed to ascertain the role of chaos in society. (See also Brock 1990, and Brock and Dechert 1991.)

Any discussion concerning the instability of social systems or the impredictability of social processes due to chaotic features should therefore be postponed until precise models have been invented and accurate, compelling empirical evidence has been produced. For the time being, it may be more fruitful to regard the observed irregularities as outcomes of either rare coincidences or mutually reinforcing circumstances, such as the occurrence of an economic boom (or bust) together with a political power vacuum, or some other *concours de circonstances*.

In sum, we may have to reckon with chaos as well as chance along with causation. This, far from restricting determinism, can only enrich it. Determinism would be at risk only if both lawfulness and Lucretius's principle—"Nothing from nothing and nothing into nothingness"—were to fail (Bunge 1959).

7 Phenomenon

A *phenomenon* is a perceptual appearance to someone. This is the etymologically correct and philosophical usage of the word. However, in ordinary parlance and in the factual sciences 'phenomenon' is often used (incorrectly) as a synonym for 'fact.' Yet, at the same time, appearance is often contrasted to reality. Thus, the sun appears to be only one foot across; emotion appears to be located in the heart; and some politicians appear to be what they really are not.

Since our powers of perception are limited, phenomenal knowledge is limited: it is only skin-deep. For example, a display of status symbols does not always exhibit the real social relations in which the agent is enmeshed: indeed, it often masks the latter. And graduation ceremonies do not exhibit the inputs (hard work and money) or the outputs (social goods and bads) of the learning process. In other words, the set of appearances is only a small part of the collection of facts. And since different animals are never in the same state and can never adopt exactly the same standpoint, a fact is bound to appear different, if at all, to different animals or to the same animal in different circumstances. In sum, there is no one-to-one correspondence between facts and appearances.

Phenomenalism is the philosophical school which holds that scientists should study only phenomena—that is, appearances. There are two kinds of phenomenalism: ontological and epistemological. *Ontological phenomenalism* is the view that there are only phenomena: that everything is a bundle of appearances to someone, and every change is a human experience. *Epistemological phenomenalism* is the view that only phenomena can be known—whence the question as to whether there are things in themselves, apart from phenomena, is an undecidable question. Obviously, the first kind of phenomenalism implies the second. Mill, Avenarius, Mach, William James in his philosophical phase, the young Carnap, Bohr, and Goodman were ontological as well as epistemological phenomenalists. By contrast, Ptolemy, Hume, Kant, Comte, Lange, Nietzsche, Duhem, and Vaihinger were only epistemological phenomenalists. The latter neither deny nor assert the existence of things in themselves (existing independently of the inquiring subject): they deny only the possibility of getting to know them.

In either version, phenomenalism is at variance with modern science and even with ordinary knowledge. Indeed, phenomena, or perceptual appearances, are only the starting point of factual inquiry. Even in everyday life we distinguish reality from appearance, as in keeping up appearances and trying to find out other people's real circumstances beneath their glitter or their real intentions behind their rhetoric.

Scientific research seeks reality beneath appearance, because the latter is superficial and subject-centered, whereas scientific knowledge aims to be profound and objective. Furthermore, appearance is rather chaotic, depending on the shifting abilities, opportunities, interests, and moods of the observer. Pattern can be found only beneath appearance. And the search for pattern is what scientific research is all about. This search takes us beyond perception, into conception and, particularly, into theory. Sometimes we succeed in explaining appearances in terms of hypotheses that posit imperceptible things or processes. Well-known examples are Copernicus's explanation of the apparent orbits of the planets, the atomistic explanation of the shine of metallic objects, the genetic explanation of some phenotypic features, neurophysiological explanations of overt behavior, psychological explanation of some social behavior, sociological explanation of some economic processes, and economic explanation of some political facts. In sum, phenomenalism is incompatible with science.

The alternative to phenomenalism is *realism,* or the view that there are imperceptible facts and that some of these can be known—though of course not perceptually, but conceptually. There are two kinds of realism: idealist and scientific. *Idealist* (or metaphysical or Platonic) *realism* identifies reality with the totality of eternal ideas and their concrete, but fuzzy, shifting, shadows. The former are assumed to exist forever, in a realm of their own, whereas concrete things are their rough, ephemeral copies. Thus, a circular table top is only a poor copy of a perfect, eternal geometric circle. One trouble with this ingenious ontology is that Plato's realm of ideas is inaccessible; another is that the only ideas we know of occur in some living brains.

By contrast, *scientific realism* identifies reality with the collection of all concrete things—that is, things capable of changing in some respect or other. According to scientific realism, ideas, far from being self-existing, are processes occurring in the brains of some animals. Accordingly, ideation can be studied scientifically, and ideas (or rather the corresponding brain processes) have an impact on social behavior insofar as they guide action. Moreover, not only true ideas but also false ones can have social efficacy. This holds, in particular, for ideas involving the mistaking of appearance for reality. Therefore the scientific realist is interested not only in the study of objective facts but also in the way we perceive them. This is particularly important in the case of social facts, for, ordinarily, we react to the way they appear to us rather than to the way they really are. For example, we do not ask political scientists for whom we should cast our ballot. But political scientists are supposed to see political reality through political rhetoric. So, far from overlooking appearance, the scientist attempts to account for it—in realistic terms of course.

The scientific realist, then, does not confine himself to appearances, but he does not write them off either. On the contrary, he often starts from them and attempts to explain them in terms of imperceptible things and processes. This point is particularly important in social science. As Pareto (1935 [1916], sec. 149) wrote: "Every social phenomenon may be considered under two aspects: as it is in reality, and as it presents itself to the mind of this or that human being. The first aspect we shall call *objective,* the second *subjective.*" Social scientists must take both aspects into account because, when not engaging in scientific research, people react to perceived, or apparent, social stimuli rather than to the stimuli themselves. For example, we may "read" gestures as friendly when actually they are hostile, and conversely.

How are we to choose between Platonic realism and scientific realism? The answer depends on the kind of philosophy we want and the role we wish it to play. If we care only for speculative philosophy and, accordingly, place philosophy in an ivory tower, we may settle for idealist realism, because it takes ideas seriously, it is simple and internally consistent, and it encourages mathematical invention. But if we want philosophy to be of some use in our quest to understand the real world, we should adopt (and enrich) scientific realism, for it postulates the autonomous existence of the external world and admits that we are largely ignorant of it, thus encouraging us to explore it further. (More in chap. 13.)

In sum, we must take appearances (phenomena) seriously, but we must not regard them as unanalyzable, let alone as the bricks the world is built of. Instead, we should try to analyze appearances in terms of real events occurring inside the brain, sometimes spontaneously, at other times caused by events outside it.

8 Social Fact

Most social scientists admit the existence of social facts, as well as that it behooves them to study those facts. However, there is no consensus concerning what such facts are. For instance, sociobiologists regard social facts as natural facts of a special kind, whereas idealists (in particular, hermeneuticists) place them above nature. Again, according to individualists, any item of social behavior, such as waiting in line or nodding to a stranger, is a social fact. But, because they deny the real existence of supra-individual entities with properties of their own, they also deny the legitimacy of the study of collective facts—or, rather, they claim that all such facts are just aggregates of individual actions. By contrast, holists count as social only those facts that occur outside or above individuals, constraining them in some fashion.

I adopt here *emergent materialism,* according to which social facts are supra-biological (in particular, suprapsychological), although they involve biological processes. For example, giving birth, killing, eating, and having an idea are natural facts, whereas christening, murdering, buying food, and communicating ideas are social facts. But, though distinct, the two categories are related through the following principle: Every social fact involves a natural one, but not the converse. For instance, the politological concept of a nation presupposes the geographical concept of territory and the biological concept of population, but not all territories or populations constitute nations.

I also adopt *systemism,* an alternative to both individualism and holism (see sec. 4). Accordingly, I call *social fact* a state or a change of state of a social system; there are no social facts outside or above social systems. For example, the criminalization or decriminalization of behavior of a certain kind is a nationwide social fact. By contrast, a judge's evaluation of someone's behavior as rendering him either guilty or innocent according to the law of the land is a restricted social fact.

In turn, a *social system* may be defined as a system composed of at least two animals of the same species interacting in a manner other than physical, chemical, or biological. Social facts take place in the course of social interactions—such as cooperating or competing, exchanging information or goods, taking part in rituals, or playing games—which contribute to building, maintaining, or altering some social system. They are collective: they involve two or more individuals. By contrast, individual actions are not social facts even when they are socially embedded and their goal is social, as in contributing to a charity, driving a bus, collecting garbage, or shouting a political slogan. To be sure, all social facts and the systems in which they happen exist only by virtue of individual actions. However, social facts have properties of their own: emergent properties. For example, no individual could manufacture a jumbo jet by himself; a public utility delivers goods or services that no single person could supply; and a university produces new knowledge and graduates, tasks that no scholar on his own could carry out.

Even such staunch methodological individualists as Boudon and Bourricaud (1986, xiv) note this explicitly: "Although social facts must be treated as the products of systems or of processes of action or of interaction, they are not reducible to interpersonal relations, but must always be treated as emergent phenomena or, as one may also say, of composition." For example, even though every person working in a business firm performs his job according to a fixed routine that requires hardly any supervision, the business activity as a whole is a social process. Shorter: Far from being mere aggregates of individuals, firms are social systems and, as such, emergents. So are schools and religious groups, clubs and political parties, armies and police forces, and many more.

There are, of course, many kinds of social fact. Nearly every school of social studies emphasizes the importance of facts of certain kinds at the expense of others. For example, idealists emphasize the role of ideas and decisions; diffusionists, that of imitation or borrowing; exchange theorists, that of exchange; geographic determinists, that of environmental constraint; Marxists, that of class struggle; Durkheimians, that of solidarity; rational choice theorists, that of calculated choice. I take the view that, since all these and many other things do happen, the social scientist must study them all. Moreover, in accordance with my view of a social system, I group social facts into the following categories:

—*environmental* in origin, such as famines, migrations, and political changes caused by soil erosion, droughts, or floods;

—*biological* in origin, such as overpopulation caused by a high birthrate in conjunction with agricultural surplus and public health care;

—*economic*, such as the spread or decline of agriculture or industry;

—*political*, such as a change of government or the passing or repealing of welfare legislation;

—*cultural*, such as the introduction or diffusion of writing, new artifacts, works of art, scientific findings, or philosophical ideas.

I shall treat these five categories on an equal footing. I submit that every macrosocial fact is, by definition, one which has all five aspects, even though one of them may be more salient than the others. However, I admit that, in any particular case, a fact of one of the above categories is likely to be at the root of facts of the four remaining kinds. For example, the introduction of a new cultivar or a new agricultural technique may produce a food surplus, which may lead to a sharp increase in population; this in turn is likely to favor urbanization, which is likely to necessitate political reorganization and promote cultural change. The environment, biological processes, the economy, the polity, and the culture take turns in initiating changes in the entire society. This pentagonal view is at variance with five unicausal, or unifactorial, views, those of geographic, biological, economic, political, and cultural determinism. (More in my *Social Science under Debate*, forthcoming.)

In sum, social facts are objective facts involving two or more individuals. Although they originate in individual agency, they occur within or between social systems and have supra-individual features: think of crowding, scarcity, industrialization, or democratization.

The word *fact* designates any and all members of a family of concepts anchored to that of a concrete or material thing: property and state of a thing, event and process in a thing, and a few others, such as phenomenon or appearance to some animal. When a qualitatively new thing is formed, one speaks of the emergence of the thing along with its characteristic features or emergent properties. The emergence of anything new is always accompanied by the submergence of something old.

Facts must be distinguished from the ideas used to describe them, particularly since ideas may be false—that is, they may not match the facts in question. (Caution: Regarded as processes not in themselves, ideas are facts—viz., brain processes.) Regrettably, this distinction is sometimes blurred, as when one says (sloppily) that proposition p is fact, not theory, while intending to say that p is true to fact. However, the examination of propositions and ideas of other kinds belongs in the next chapter.

2 :: *Idea*

The concept of an idea is very broad: it embraces percepts, mental images, memories, concepts, propositions, theories, inferences, problems, proposals, instructions, plans, and more. Most ideas can be expressed in symbols, such as spoken or written words, drawings, or mathematical formulas. All symbols are conventions. One and the same idea can be symbolized in many different ways. In particular, there is no necessary connection between sound and meaning. Therefore, to understand a text or a technical drawing, we need to know the conventional code that pairs symbols with ideas. In particular, understanding a scientific text calls for substantive knowledge as well as linguistic knowledge. This platitude must be stated in order to counter the fashionable claim that literary critics and semioticians are competent to understand the scientific literature.

Ideas can be studied either in themselves or as facts—that is, as mental (or brain) processes as well as social processes. Logicians, mathematicians, and philosophers engage in the first kind of study, whereas psychologists and social scientists are mainly interested in ideas as mental processes. Social scientists are particularly interested in the social conditions that stimulate or inhibit ideation, in the ways in which ideation guides or misguides social action, and in the ways people communicate. In short, they are primarily interested in ideation processes and their social inputs and outputs, whereas logicians, mathematicians, and philosophers are interested only in the end products of such processes, ideas per se. For example, a deductive inference can be studied in any of the following three ways: as a relation between a set of premises and a conclusion, as a brain process, or as a dialogue—a kind of social interaction. These kinds of study are, of course, mutually compatible and, moreover, complementary. Thus, in order to study the ways in which a political idea can stimulate or inhibit a citizen, we must study not only the cognition–emotion–behavior connection: we must understand the idea in question too. However, this dependence is asymmetric, for no psychological, sociological, or historical study is needed to find out the logical form or meaning of a concept, the logical consistency of a set of propositions, or the adequacy (degree of truth) of a scientific hypothesis. In short, the study of ideas in themselves is logically and methodologically prior to the psychology, sociology, and history of ideas. Thus, the sociologist of science or technology who does not understand the ideas guiding the social behavior he observes is wasting his time and ours.

When studying ideas in themselves, it makes no sense to ask where they come from or where they reside. It is only when regarded as processes that these questions make sense. And in this case there are three main alternative answers to the problem of residence. Computer fanatics identify ideas with the symbols that designate them, maintaining that ideas reside in information-processing systems, whether natural, artificial, or perhaps even ghostly. They do not stop to ask who invented the rules or programs for manipulating the symbols concerned, or who created or evaluated the ideas designated by the symbols. Holists hold that ideas dwell either in the "collective mind" or in social groups, in particular in "thought collectives" such as scientific communities. They overlook the fact that only individual brains can think, and they confuse the thinking process with its social determinants. Finally, philosophical materialists agree with physiological psychologists that ideas dwell in brains, and explain new ideas in terms of the self-assembly of new neuronal systems (Hebb 1949; Bindra 1976). They admit that, because individuals live and learn in society, their mental processes are influenced by their social circumstances. However, this is not the place to discuss the ideation process or even the various philosophies of mind. (For this, see Bunge and Ardila 1987.)

In this chapter we will study ideas in themselves. That is, we will feign that ideas can be detached from thinkers and the social systems in which they are embedded. This is not an ontological thesis but a methodological convention, one that will enable us to study the structure, content, and validity of ideas regardless of the persons who happen to think the ideas in question.

The study of ideas in themselves is the task of logic, semantics, mathematics, and philosophy. In the following I will combine all four fields and engage in some exact philosophizing. This is not to say that logic and mathematics are sufficient to study either the world or our knowledge of it. Clarity, rigor, and method, all stressed by the rationalist tradition, are necessary but not sufficient for the success of any cognitive endeavor. Passion, imagination, and intuition—extolled but not investigated by the irrationalist tradition, in particular by the Romantics—are also needed. The creative process is anything but rule-directed: in fact, it is more or less dark, messy, and unruly. But its final product must be precise and orderly if it is to qualify as a piece of scientific, technological, or humanistic knowledge. In sum, in all fields of original research, passion fuels reason, and reason disciplines and expands imagination and cleans up and elaborates intuition (see Bunge 1962*b*).

1 Concept and Proposition

Concepts, such as those of man, work, and implication, are the units of meaning and hence the building blocks of rational discourse. We use concepts to form propositions, just as we analyze complex propositions into simpler ones and these, in turn, into concepts. A proposition or statement "says" something about one or more items: it is an assertion or a denial. Even statements of possibility and of doubt are affirmations. (Note that propositions should not be mistaken for proposals, such as "Let's go.") Propositions are the bearers of testability and untestability, as well as of truth and falsity. That is, only propositions can be tested for truth. Concepts cannot be so tested, because they neither assert nor deny anything. Hence there are no true or false concepts: concepts can only be exact or fuzzy, applicable or inapplicable, fruitful or barren.

In scientific discourse every key concept ought to be elucidated. The innocent-looking "is" is a case in point. In traditional logic, "is," as in "Aristotle is human," was called "the copula," and it was treated as a separate logical concept. Its function was said to be to join, or glue, the predicate (e.g., "human") to the subject (e.g., "Aristotle")—an obvious, yet fuzzy, idea. Mathematical logic distinguishes five different concepts behind the innocent-looking word *is* and its cognates ("are," "were," etc.). They are identity ($=$), as in "1 is the successor of 0"; equality ($:=$), as in "The sine of 90° is 1"; membership ($\in$), as in "This man is a liberal"; class inclusion ($\subseteq$), as in "The social sciences are sciences"; and predication (Px), as in "Silvia is clever."

The "is" of predication comes together with a predicate or attribute, such as fallibility, as in "is fallible." Thus the proposition "Aristotle is human," which can be symbolized as "Ha," breaks down into two concepts, not three. (On the other hand, the equivalent statement "Aristotle belongs to the human species" is indeed made up of three concepts, one of which, "belongs to," was unknown to traditional logic.) This example shows that modern logic scratches the surface of language, to expose the underlying concepts and propositions, if any. (In other words, deep structure equals logical form.)

Whereas linguists and literary critics hear or see terms, phrases, sentences, and discourses (or texts), logicians look for the corresponding concepts, propositions, and systems (e.g., theories) designated by such symbols—and sometimes they find none. For example, Heidegger's sentence "Die Welt weltet" ("The world worlds") is but a meaningless juxtaposition of words on a par with "The brain brains." But at least it is translatable nonsense, which is not the case with plenty of other sentences in his celebrated *Sein und Zeit*. Witness "Zeit ist ursprünglich als Zeitigung der Zeitlichkeit, als welche sie die Konstitution der Sorgestruktur ermöglicht" (Heidegger 1986 [1927], 331). Whoever claims to have translated this sentence into English, or even into intelligible German, deceives himself or others.

Nonlogical concepts can be partitioned into individuals, such as "France"; collections of individuals (sets, classes, or kinds), such as "humankind"; and predicates, such as "works." A predicate can be unary, such as "works"; binary, such as "interacts"; ternary, such as "mediates"; and so on. A unary predicate denotes a property of an individual (simple or complex); a binary predicate denotes a relation between two items, a ternary predicate a relation between three things, and so on. (Actually analysis often shows that predicates are more complex than they appear at first sight. E.g., "trades" looks binary, as in "a trades with b," but it can be analyzed as quaternary, as in "a trades c for d with b.")

Mathematical functions, often called "variables," are a particular kind of relation: they match every member of one class to a single member of another class. More precisely, a *function* from a set A to a set B assigns every element of A one member of B. One writes $f: A \rightarrow B$, and $y = f(x)$, where x is in A and y is the image of x in B under f. A is called the 'domain,' and B the 'co-domain' of f. For example, age is a function from the set of things (in particular, organisms) into positive numbers. If an arbitrary member y of B is a number, or an n-tuple of numbers, one calls it a 'variable.' In general, a dependent variable y may be a function of several independent variables: that is, $y = f(x_1, x_2, \ldots, x_n)$. For example, the quality of life of a society depends upon the average life expectancy in that society, the average number of years spent in school, the average disposable income, and other such collective variables. (But there is still no agreement on the precise form of this dependence, i.e., the exact function.)

The simplest function is of course the constant function, and the next simplest the linear function. The corresponding expressions are: "For all $x, f(x) = a$," and "For all $x, f(x) = a + bx$." Here the constants a and b are numbers of some kind, usually real. (Real numbers are, of course, just as fictitious as any other mathematical objects.) If a so-called constant varies from one run of observations to the next, or from one problem to another, it is called a 'parameter.' For example, birth and death rates are constant for a given population only over a short period of time. We know that both rates decrease as the standard of living rises, but we ignore the exact form of this functional relation. A vague hypothesis of the form "Variable y is a (so far unspecified) function of variable *x*," where *x* and *y* are fairly well known, may be called a "programmatic hypothesis." It is a preliminary finding that may stimulate and guide further research.

In the social sciences, statistical parameters, such as averages, modes, and variances, are particularly important, because they represent properties of aggregates such as communities, social classes, or collections of business firms. Thus, the mode of an income distribution identifies typical wealth-holders; the kurtosis (or sharpness of a peak) measures wealth concentration; and the Gini coefficient measures wealth inequality. All statistical parameters are second-order variables, in that they are calculated from values of first-order variables such as age and income. In other words, the statistical properties of a whole derive from the properties of its individual components. (For instance, if all the households in a community have roughly the same wealth, the corresponding Gini index is near zero; whereas if wealth is concentrated in a few hands, it is near unity.) This statement, which looks philosophically innocuous, suffices to refute the holistic tenet that wholes cannot be understood in terms of their parts. (More in chap. 9.)

From an epistemological or methodological viewpoint there are two kinds of variable and three kinds of function. Variables can represent observable or unobservable properties. And functions may relate observable variables, such as the inputs and outputs of a system; unobservable properties, such as social cohesion or political stability; or unobservable and observable variables, such as intention and action. The functions of the third class bridge theory and data. Some of them function as indicator hypotheses (of which, more in chap. 6, sec. 2).

As we saw a while ago, the relation between predicate and subject is that of predication, or *attribution*. Predicates are attributed to individuals, couples, triples, or, in general, *n*-tuples. (Individuals need not be irreducibly so: some of them may be analyzable into collections.) The result of attributing predicate F to individual b is the proposition Fb, short for "*b* is an F." That of attributing predicate G to the ordered pair $<a,b>$ is the proposition Gab, and that of attributing predicate H to the *n*-tuple $<a,b, \ldots, n>$ is $Hab \cdots n$. In other words, the proposition Fb is the value of the function F at b; likewise, Gab is the value of the function G at $<a, b>$, and so on. In general, a predicate may be construed as a function from individuals into propositions.

The relation between individuals and collections is that of belonging, $\in$. For example, the proposition "Spain is a nation" can be analyzed as "Spain belongs to (is a member of) the class of nations," or $s \in N$ for short. The notion of membership is elucidated in set theory, where it occurs as a primitive (undefined) concept. But of course we use it everywhere. Still, a warning is in place. In mathematics, 'set' is synonymous with 'collection,' and every collection has a fixed membership. Not so in the factual sciences, where one often studies collections with variable membership, such as populations. At any given time a variable collection is a set proper. At a different time it may contain different members—or none.

The relation between predicates and classes is this. Every predicate determines a class called the 'extension' of the predicate. This is the collection of individuals (or couples, triples, etc.) that happen to possess the property designated by the predicate concerned. For example, the extension of the unary predicate "farms," as it occurs in the proposition "Peter farms his land," is the class of farmers. (In obvious symbols, $\mathscr{E}(F) = \{x \in P|\, Fx\}$; i.e., the extension of F is the collection of individuals in the collection P of persons that have the property F.) The extension of the binary predicate "reads" is the collection of ordered pairs <person, text>. (Shorter: $\mathscr{E}(R) = \{<x, y> \in P \times T|\, Rxy\}$, where $P \times T$ is the collection of ordered pairs <person, text>, called the 'Cartesian product' of P by T. Example of a Cartesian product: $[0,1] \times [0,2]$ is a rectangle of base 1 and height 2.) The extension of the ternary predicate "lies between," as in "New York lies between Boston and Philadelphia," is the collection of ordered triples <place, place, place>. And the extension of the quaternary predicate "exchanges," as in "a exchanges b for c with d," is the set of all quadruples <person, commodity, commodity, person>. Some predicates have an empty extension, meaning that they hold truthfully of nothing: for example, "ghost," "collective mind," "manifest destiny." (When the extension of a predicate F is empty, one writes $\mathscr{E}(F) = \varnothing$.)

Another important property of any predicate is its *reference class,* or the collection of items the predicate is about. For example, "social order" refers to entire societies. The concept of reference is particularly important in the social sciences, where spirited controversies over what such sciences are about abound. Individualists hold that the social sciences are about individuals, holists that they refer to social wholes, and systemists that they concern social systems analyzable into interrelated individuals who share an environment. In order to resolve such controversies in a rational way, rather than appeal to authority, we need a theory of reference. Such a theory will be sketched in section 2.

The extension of a predicate must be distinguished from its reference class—a difference unknown to most philosophers. A psychologist who criticizes the notion of a soul for having no real counterpart (i.e., for having an empty extension) refers to the soul while regarding it as a fiction. And a scientist who surmises the existence of an object that has not yet been found assigns the defining predicate(s) a nonempty reference class even while admitting that, so far, the corresponding extension has proved uninhabited.

The main differences between the extension and the reference class of a predicate are these. First, the notion of extension presupposes that of truth, whereas the concept of reference class does not. (Indeed, we only include in the extension of a predicate the items for which it holds.) Second, whereas the extension of a binary predicate is a set of ordered couples (and, in general, that of an *n*-ary predicate a set of *n*-tuples), the corresponding reference class is a set of individuals. Third, whereas the extension function is sensitive to negation, disjunction, conjunction, and the other logical connectives, the reference function is not. For example, the extension of "not stratified" is the complement of that of "stratified" in the class of societies, whereas the reference class of both predicates is the same: namely, the entire set of societies (present, past, and future). Again, the extension of the disjunctive predicate "*P* or *Q*" is the union (logical sum), and that of the conjunctive predicate "*P* and *Q*" is the intersection (logical product), of the extensions of *P* and *Q*. But the reference class of both compound predicates is the same: namely, the union of the partial reference classes. We shall return to reference in the next section.

2 Form and Content

Most social scientists do not hold logic in high esteem: some because they believe that only fact finding is research, and others because they see theorizing as just lining up words. We will not waste words on the latter, but the former should know that contempt for logic may lead to worse than fuzziness and inconsistency: namely, tautology (conceptual platitude). For example, certain political scientists have recently revealed that those who value freedom of speech and participation in decision making tend to support democracy. A dose of logic a day keeps both triteness and nonsense away.

Formal (or mathematical) logic studies the form of concepts, propositions, systems of propositions (in particular, classifications and theories), and deductive arguments. Logic has nothing to say about the content of constructs, which is a matter for semantics. From a logical point of view, propositions can be simple (atomic) or composite (molecular). A proposition containing one or more logical operators, such as "and" and "not," is said to be composite, or molecular—for example, the excluded middle principle: "*A* or not-*A*," or $A \lor \neg A$, for short, where *A* is an arbitrary proposition; and the principle of noncontradiction: "not-(*A* and not-*A*)," or $\neg (A \& \neg A)$ for short. Both laws hold in ordinary, or classical, logic for arbitrary propositions, regardless of what they "say" and whether or not they are true. The same holds for the basic rule of deduction, *modus ponens*: "From *A*, and if *A* then *B*, infer *B*," abbreviated $A, A \Rightarrow B \therefore B$.

The excluded middle and noncontradiction laws are paragons of *tautologies*—that is, propositions that are true by virtue of their form: they hold in ordinary logic regardless of the state of the world. Tautologies are thus radically different from mathematical, chemical, or sociological truths, every one of which depends on the nature of its referents and on the context. (All tautologies are formal truths, but not all formal truths are tautologies. E.g., "12 + 1 = 13" is true in number theory, though not in clock arithmetic, where "12 + 1 = 12"—but it does not belong in logic, which does not refer to numbers.)

Tautologies say nothing in particular about reality. However, we need them to reason correctly and nontrivially about anything. Indeed, logic, the canon of valid reasoning, consists of infinitely many tautologies together with a handful of inference rules. A major use of logic is as a tool for identifying logical platitudes—that is, tautologies—and their negations—that is, contradictions or logical falsities. A logical falsity either includes a self-contradictory predicate or contains a pair of mutually contradictory propositions. "Democratic dictatorship" is an instance of the former, and "Society corrupts and society purifies [in the same respect]" exemplifies the latter. Being logically false, no observation is required to dismiss them. Likewise, the statement that the arrow is and is not at some place at every instant is manifestly contradictory. However, Zeno, instead of rejecting this statement out of hand for being false, took it as proof that change is impossible. By contrast, Hegel and his followers regarded the same statement as proof that things, being changeable, are inherently contradictory—the nucleus of dialectics. Moral: Although logic is insufficient to build philosophies, it suffices to refute some of them.

Not all tautologies are manifest: some are hidden. I shall call these 'crypto-tautologies.' "The content of every dream is either overtly or latently sexual" and "All human action is rational, either objectively or subjectively" are crypto-tautologies for, when analyzed, they are seen to exemplify the law of excluded middle ("A or not-A"). Hence they say nothing about the world and, consequently, are empirically untestable. Similarly, "All cultures at the same stage of development have many characteristics in common" (in an anthropology paper) is tautologous. Indeed, it exemplifies the identity law "$A = A$," since two cultures are defined as being at the same stage of development if they share many characteristics. Likewise, the proposition "The more solidary the group, the less expressions of self-interest predominate" is crypto-tautologous by definition of the word *solidary*. Social studies are littered with such pseudo-hypotheses. Ignore logic at your own risk.

Maximal generality and independence from subject matter are peculiar to logic. No other science has such breadth—or, consequently, such shallowness. This is why logic can be used to analyze all manner of discourse. And this is why such expressions as "logic of choice," "logic of decision," "logic of action," and "situational logic," which occur in social studies, are misguided. Logic does not handle choices, decisions, actions, or social situations any more than it tackles earthquakes or plagues: it is subject-matter-free.

Logic is the basic theory of rational discourse: it is the study of the form of concepts, propositions, theories, and arguments of the deductive kind. It teaches us to tell correct from incorrect arguments, not how to explore the world, let alone how to change it. Pure mathematics is similarly portable across all fields of inquiry in not being committed to any factual subject matter. In short, neither logic nor mathematics is about the world. But, of course, they underlie rational, precise discourses about the world.

A view cannot be discussed rationally if it is recognizedly at variance with logic, for that automatically disqualifies any attempt to argue cogently either in favor of it or against it. (Parallel: the psychoanalytic tactic of interpreting any criticism of psychoanalysis as a case of emotional resistance to it.) This is the case with existentialism, deconstructionism, and the irrationalist strands in feminist theory, environmentalism, and the sociology of science. Why should one believe their theses if they cannot be argued about rationally?

Though necessary, logic is insufficient for the study of reality. It is not enough because, being about form and consequence, it is an a priori science, hence one impregnable to observation, measurement, and experiment. If the social sciences were to dispense with empirical research, they would produce no findings about social life. Yet the economists von Mises (1949) and Debreu (1991) have claimed that their theories are a priori and, consequently, unassailable by empirical evidence—a claim that betrays a basic misunderstanding of the nature of both logic and social science.

Others misuse logic. For example, Milton Friedman (1953), Machlup (1955), and Graaff (1967) have claimed that in economics it does not matter whether the assumptions are true as long as their consequences are. Consider the following reasoning: "All humans are vegetables. All vegetables are mortal. Ergo, all humans are mortal." This argument is formally valid, and its premises cancel each other out, thereby entailing a true conclusion. But what is the point of the exercise, other than to discourage the search for reasonably true theories, as well as the design of economic policies based on such?

So much for the form of ideas. Let us now look at their content or meaning. The word *meaning* is one of the most abused in both ordinary language and social science. Pop philosophy speaks of the meaning of life, whereas exact philosophy assigns meanings only to constructs and their symbols, so life is neither meaningful nor meaningless. In social studies, too, there is careless talk about the meaning of an action, referring to either the goal or the effectiveness of the action. I will steer clear of such equivocations, admitting only constructs as bearers of meaning. And I will analyze meaning as sense (connotation) together with reference (denotation), or as what is being said about what. Let us start with reference.

What does a proposition of the form "b is F," or Fb for short, refer to? Obviously, Fb is about b: it attributes predicate F to individual b. Now, we saw in section 1 that Fb may be construed as the value of the function F at b. But the individual b belongs to one or more collections, such as that of all human beings or all schools. (In particular, the collection may be a singleton; i.e., it may contain a single member. But a singleton $\{a\}$ is not the same as its solitary member a. In any case, the predicate F may be construed as a function mapping a collection D of individuals into the set P of all propositions of the form Fb. In short, $F: D \rightarrow P$. Recall sec. 1.)

We stipulate next that a (unary) predicate F refers to (is about) any and all of the members of its domain D. In other words, the *reference class* of the predicate F equals its domain D, or $\mathfrak{R}(F) = D$ for short. For example, the reference class of the energy concept is the collection of all actual and possible concrete things, and that of poverty is the human species. Note that, since in fact all concrete things possess or exchange energy, the extension and the reference class of "energy" coincide. On the other hand, since not all humans are poor, the extension of "poverty" is included in its reference class.

What about higher-order predicates, such as "cook" (binary), "mediate" (ternary), and "exchange" (quaternary)? To find out their reference classes, we must identify their respective domains. Since it is people (or their proxies) who cook, and since what they cook is food of some kind, the predicate "cook" (C) applies to ordered pairs <person, food>. (In technical terms, the domain of the function C is the Cartesian product of the collection P of people by the collection F of food items. We stipulate that the reference class of C is the union of the factors P and F: that is, $\mathfrak{R}(C) = P \cup F$. In general, the *reference class of an* n-*ary predicate F* with domain $A \times B \times \ldots \times N$ is $\mathfrak{R}(F) = A \cup B \cup \ldots \cup N$.)

We stipulate next that the reference class of a proposition, or any other construct in which predicates occur, is the union of the reference classes of the constituent predicates. For example, the reference class of the proposition "Every firm has some customers" is the union of the collection of firms and the collection of customers. Note that the denial of the given proposition has the same reference class. Likewise, the reference class of "*A* and *B*" is the same as that of "*A* or *B*," "If *A*, then *B*," and the other combinations of *A*, *B*, and their negations by means of logical connectives. In short, the reference function $\mathfrak{R}$ is insensitive to the logical connectives.

Finally, we stipulate that the reference class of a system of propositions, such as a theory, equals the union of the reference classes of all the predicates occurring in the theory. Since, while crafting a theory, one may introduce as many predicates as needed, the task of finding the reference class of the theory looks at first sight open-ended and therefore hopeless. This is, indeed, the case with untidy theories. But if a theory has been axiomatized, one can easily identify the set of basic or defining predicates, which is a small subset of the collection of all the predicates occurring in the theory. This allows one to identify from the beginning the reference class of the theory. The preceding semantic postulates should come in handy when attempting to find out the referents of hypotheses and theories in social science. And they should suffice to lay to rest the quaint hermeneutic dogma that "Words . . . refer *only* to other words" (Bloom 1990, 9).

Let us now move on to the second component of meaning: namely, sense. The sense or content of a construct is what it "says" about its referent(s). But a proposition can also "say" something in an indirect way. For example, since a proposition is "pregnant" with (entails) any number of logical consequences, these must be counted as belonging to its full sense. We call this the 'import' of the proposition. Moreover, unless the proposition happens to be an initial assumption (a postulate or axiom), it makes complete sense only in relation to the propositions that entail (originate) it. We call the generators or logical ancestors of a proposition its 'purport.' Finally, we stipulate that the *full sense* of a proposition is the set of all the propositions it entails or is entailed by—that is, the union of its purport and its import. Caution: Any given formula may have somewhat different senses (or none) in different contexts (e.g., a proposition about the unemployment rate makes no sense in pure mathematics). Hence, when ambiguity threatens, the context should be explicitly indicated.

Having defined the reference and sense of an arbitrary construct, we can now introduce the semantic concept of meaning. We define the *meaning* of a construct as its reference, or denotation, together with its sense, or connotation. In obvious symbols, $\mathcal{M}(c) =_{df} <\mathcal{R}(s), \mathcal{S}(c)>$. (Note that the concept of truth does not occur in this definition.) We further stipulate that every construct has a meaning: that is, both a nonvoid (though possibly indefinite) reference class and a sense (even if known only in part). In turn, we stipulate that a sign or symbol is *significant* provided it either designates a construct proper or denotes an actual or possible fact. Otherwise the sign is nonsignificant.

According to the neo-positivist theory of meaning, a construct is meaningful only if it is verifiable. This convention is usually called the "verifiability theory of meaning." Now, testability is certainly a sufficient condition for the meaningfulness of propositions, but it is not a necessary one. Thus, "The soul survives the body" makes perfect sense in a theological context, even though it is untestable. Moreover, constructs other than propositions have meaning, yet they are not testable and consequently can neither have nor acquire a truth-value. For example, the question "What is monopoly?" and the norm "We must not be greedy" are perfectly meaningful, although they are not propositions and consequently are not testable. Hence we invert the positivist verifiability theory of meaning to read: If a proposition is testable, then it is meaningful. In other words, meaningfulness is necessary for testability. But it is not sufficient, because tests require test means, such as indicators and observation devices of some kind. (In other words, the predicate "is testable" is binary, not unary, in that it occurs in propositions of the form "*p* is testable by means *m*.")

3 Fuzziness and Exactness

Ironically, both intellectual immaturity and intellectual decadence share one trait: namely, conceptual imprecision. Witness the pre-Socratic philosophers, on the one hand, and the Neoplatonists, on the other. But whereas with the former, obscurity was an indicator of novelty, with the latter, it was a sign of exhaustion. In modern times, obscurity in academic circles is a manifestation of a deliberate retreat from reason, and sometimes even a sign of magical thinking if not humbuggery. Whether in philosophy or in social studies, gobbledygook not only betrays weak thinking: sometimes it also serves to intimidate the naive. Hence, unless it is a product of insanity, gobbledygook is intellectually dishonest. It is talk of the crook for the gullible.

Rabelais, one of the grandfathers of modernity, made fun of the obscurities of the schoolmen and the superstitions of his own contemporaries. So did Francis Bacon and Galileo, two of the parents of modernity. Descartes, another parent of modernity, enjoined us to admit only "clear and distinct ideas." The poet and literary critic Boileau said that only that which is conceived clearly can be said clearly. The Enlightenment intensified and popularized the search for clarity and truth and the denunciation of hollow pedantry, joining it to the expansion of civil liberties. It thus prepared the ground for the radical scientific, technological, and political innovations of the subsequent centuries.

The Romantic reaction against the rationalism, scientism, universalism, and liberalism of the Enlightenment exhumed the taste for obscurity and, indeed, for obscurantism. In particular, Kant, Fichte, Hegel, and Schelling succeeded in persuading their readers that obscurity is the seal of gravity and depth. Moreover, Hegel discovered that confusion, contradiction, and paradox become intellectually respectable when dubbed "dialectical." Even while rebelling against Hegel's idealism and engaging in innovative social research, Marx and Engels took on board much of Hegel's obscurity, particularly in philosophical matters. Likewise, although praising and practicing rationality, when writing philosophy. Weber was ambiguous and engaged in neo-Kantian intuitionism. Still, Hegelian and neo-Kantian obscurities are as nothing compared with those of existentialism and its heir, deconstructionism. Typical sentences of these schools are so obscure as to defy translation; or, if preferred, they can be translated in any number of mutually nonequivalent ways. To a large extent, the same can be said of phenomenology, hermeneutics, and the principles of ethnomethodology.

Philosophical obscurantism has often misled social scientists. In fact, social studies contain plenty of vague notions with philosophical associations, such as those of the meaning and interpretation of an action, Verstehen, dialectics, residual category, utility, rational expectation, freedom, totality, functionality, ideology, and culture—to mention just a few. However, most of the technical terms in social science have no obvious philosophical associations, yet they are remarkably vague—for example, 'function,' 'institution,' 'social class' (in particular, 'middle class'), 'social force,' 'social structure,' 'power,' 'state,' 'conceptual framework,' 'theory,' and 'model.' Obviously, any social view hinging on such vague concepts will itself be fuzzy and thus a source of endless barren disputation.

Popper (1962 [1945], 2:19–20) did science a disservice when he asserted that all matters of definition and elucidation (or clarification of meaning) are trivial and the mark of "verbal and empty scholasticism." His erstwhile disciple Feyerabend (1981, 1:ix) went further and praised "fruitful imprecision," presumably because most fruitful ideas are born somewhat fuzzy. This view is particularly harmful in social studies, in which even eminent scholars have, over and over again, used terms such as 'meaning,' 'interpretation,' 'social structure,' and 'social force' without bothering to define them, or even expressions devoid of signification, such as 'das Sein des Daseins.' Verbal imprecision betrays woolliness, and the lack of interest in improving verbal precision fosters obscurity and thereby obscurantism. It also promotes unending, fruitless scholastic disputations about what such and such an author "really meant." This is not to say that clarification of meaning and definition should replace empirical research and theory construction. Rather, the three tasks should go hand in hand, as will be argued in what follows.

A construct will be said to be *exact* if and only if it has a precise meaning; that is, a definite reference and a definite sense. Otherwise it will be called *inexact* or *fuzzy*. For instance, the concepts of market, price, and occupation are fairly exact, whereas those of utility, rationality, and information are not. (Caution: Exactness is unrelated to numerical accuracy. E.g., "$\pi = 3$," though only approximately true, involves exact concepts.)

I just mentioned *utility, rationality,* and *information* as examples of ubiquitous, if fuzzy, words. I shall tackle utility in chapter 8 and rationality in chapter 14. As for *information,* its ambiguity is such that it is being employed in such disparate fields as mathematics, electrical engineering, genetics, psychology, and social studies, in each case with a different signification. In fact, the word can stand for meaning, knowledge, structure of genetic material, signal, message carried by a pulse-coded signal, and communication of knowledge or emotion with the help of conventional signals. Such ambiguity enables one to draw "information flowcharts" without stating exactly what, where, or how whatever is being designated flows. It has also made it possible to translate prebiological psychology into Info-speak.

The information (or communication) fad has invaded social studies, where it has been claimed that "Social systems . . . consist of communications and nothing but communications—not of human beings, not of conscious mental states, not of roles, not even of actions. They produce and reproduce communications by meaningful reference to communications" (Luhmann 1987, 113). This idealistic concept of an unpeopled society is open to the following objections: that communication is a link and, like every relation, does not exist without relata, which in this case happen to be animals such as people; that nothing can be communicated unless there are animals (e.g., people) capable of producing, encoding, and decoding signals that convey messages; and that social science is supposed to deal with real people, not disembodied entities.

Babies cannot handle sharp pencils, but economists and financial analysts are expected to use them. However, imprecision is still a blight of social studies and the humanities. Yet, it is not unavoidable. In fact, imprecision can be reduced through conceptual analysis, mathematization, and theory construction. True, original constructs emerge and grow spontaneously: there are no rules for creating them, any more than for creating works of art. Moreover, constructs are born untidy. But, once formed, they can—nay must—be analyzed in various ways: logically, semantically, or methodologically. And analysis, if pushed far enough, can yield new concepts, more exact than the original intuitive notions. That is, concept analysis, far from being opposed to concept formation, can be made into a part of the latter process.

Inexactness is an obstacle to classification, which is the least we can expect from a systematic study of any collection of objects. Indeed, hopelessly vague predicates, such as "small," "heavy," "heap," "young," and "balding," give rise to fuzzy sets—that is, sets with borderline elements. And a characteristic of a fuzzy set is that it is not disjoint from its complement: thus one and the same thing may be a member of both a certain set and its complement. This makes it impossible to partition collections of things. (On classification, see chap. 4, sec. 2.) Worse, tolerating borderline cases may lead to contradictions, such as "She is poor and rich." Contradictions of this sort can be averted only by either dropping or exactifying the predicates that generate them. To accommodate fuzzy predicates in a special theory (fuzzy logic) is to defeat the very purpose of logic: to keep thought straight.

As for theory construction, it, too, contributes to elucidating concepts and propositions by relating them. Indeed, the full sense of a construct is the set of both its logical ancestors and its progeny: recall section 2. Moreover, a construct belonging to a theory can be analyzed in the light of other constructs of the theory, as well as from the outside—that is, in light of constructs belonging to other theories, particularly logical, semantical, and mathematical ones. Hence, the clearest concepts are those embedded in theories (hypothetico-deductive systems). By the same token, the more isolated a concept, the more vague it is. Witness the central concepts of the pseudosciences—for example, "id," "channeling," and "aura"—alien as they are to the system of the sciences.

Like almost everything else, precision can be faked. The simplest way to do this is to state a definition or a conjecture in ordinary language, then replace words with letters or other symbols and hope that, by some miracle, these symbols will then designate precise concepts, such as numerical functions. For example, we may suppose that happiness (H) is greater, the more needs (N) and wants (W) are met, and the less pain (P) is experienced in the process. A simple equation that seems to express this idea is $H = N \cdot W / P$. The trouble with this formula is, of course, that the independent "variables" are not mathematically defined: they are letters, not concepts. We do not even know what their dimensions, let alone their units, might be. Thus there is no guarantee that the two sides of the equation, so-called, even have the same dimensions. In short, the formula is not well formed. Consequently it has no precise meaning, ergo, it is not empirically testable. We shall say that we have here a case of "pseudoquantitation."

The social studies literature teems with pseudoquantities. For example, it has recently been proposed that we measure the quality of life as the sum of the standard of living, the services received, and the experiences undergone, or $Q = L + S + E$ for short. But, since no hint is given as to how to reckon or measure L, S, and E, we are left with a case of pseudo-exactness. (See Appendix 4 for a more serious offense.) Even Sorokin (1937, 162), one of the founders of contemporary sociology and an early critic of pseudo-exactness, sometimes indulged in the latter. For example, he defined the freedom of an individual as the quotient of the sum of his wishes by the sum of his means for gratifying them. But he did not define wishes and means in a mathematically correct way; he merely "divided" words. In sum his symbols were no more than shorthand for intuitive notions. Of course, had he restricted himself to commodities, he could have reckoned both wishes and means in dollars. But then he would have defined pecuniary power, rather than freedom. (For more on pseudoquantities in social science, see Bunge 1995*c*.)

In conclusion, let me propose the following *Exactness Decalogue:*

E1. Exactification is not just a matter of symbolization, but the replacement of an imprecise idea by a logically and mathematically well-defined construct.

E2. Any intuitive (inexact) but reasonably intelligible idea can be exactified.

E3. Given any exact idea, it is possible to construct an even more exact one.

E4. The best analysis is synthesis—that is, embedding what is being investigated in a theory.

E5. An idea becomes more important, the larger the number of ideas to which it can be related in an exact manner and the more new ideas it suggests.

E6. Never expect a single exact concept, proposition, norm, or theory to solve all your problems.

E7. A good idea, even if somewhat fuzzy, is preferable to an exact but pointless or false one.

E8. Do not use exactification to intimidate or fool people.

E9. Do not pursue exactness for its own sake or at the expense of substance.

E10. Do not crow over any exactification you obtain, for it may prove to fall short of even higher standards of precision—or, worse, it may turn out to be hollow.

4 Formalization

To *formalize* a construct is, of course, to endow it with an exact logical or mathematical form. For example, the concept of the union of sets formalizes the intuitive concept of the "sum" of two or more collections; the concept of semigroup operation formalizes the intuitive concept of concatenation or juxtaposition of individuals such as words; the mathematical concept or probability formalizes that of chance; the intuitive concept of diversity or variability of a feature in a population is exactified by, among other things, the concept of variance; the idea of association between two properties can be formalized by, *inter alia,* the concepts of function and statistical correlation; the intuitive idea of interdependence among the members of a system can be formalized as a matrix, such as Leontief's input–output matrix; an intuitive idea about a process of either growth or decline can be mathematized by a rate equation or by its solution; and so on and so forth. Once such formalizations have been adopted, it is hard to give them up for the fuzzy constructs characteristic of ordinary knowledge and the initial stage of scientific research.

The first two of the above examples involve qualitative mathematics or, to be precise, set theory and semigroup theory. They were intended to puncture the popular myth that all mathematics is quantitative, so that formalization amounts to quantitation. As a matter of fact, mathematics contains a number of nonquantitative theories, such as set theory, abstract algebra, and topology (in particular, graph theory). Moreover, it can be argued that social scientists should make more intensive use of these formal tools before turning to numerical functions and differential equations. Still, many social properties, such as population, population density, production, and price, are intrinsically quantitative, so that an adequate (true), precise representation of them calls for the use of quantitative concepts. Further, every quantitative construct subsumes (is more inclusive than) the corresponding qualitative construct. Thus, "The population of A equals a, with $a > 0$" entails "A is populated." And "The population of A equals a, and that of B equals b, with $a > b$" entails "A is more populated than B." Since quantitative statements are richer pieces of knowledge than the corresponding qualitative ones, why settle for less? Since human groups and what they produce, trade, consume, and waste come in definite, if variable, quantities, why ignore them? Just from obedience to the idealist conceit that man is a spiritual being and that the mental cannot be quantitated, to the elitist thesis that quantity is the opposite of quality, to the intuitionist dogma that precision is the enemy of insight, or to the "feminist theorists" according to whom the quantitative is androcentric?

It is remarkable how many features of the social world can be quantified in terms of time. Thus the degree of integration of a family may be gauged by the time its members spend doing things together; the level of income, by the number of time units of labor needed to buy a food basket; and the level of investment, by the number of years it takes the investor to repay a loan. Energy and money are other favorite basic concepts. On the other hand, the quality of a product or service is often hard to quantitate. So, consequently, are manager performance and organization effectiveness. Still, nobody has proved that these are imponderables. Failure to quantitate is often only one's own failure.

As an example of exactification through quantitation, let us consider the concept of social (economic, cultural, and political) marginality, central to any serious discussion of democracy and distributive justice, yet hitherto handled in an intuitive fashion and therefore ignored by social statistics. Social marginality can be measured as follows. Start with its dual, that of belonging, or participation. If all the members of a social group G are members of a social system S_i, we say that G is included in S_i. If only some members of G are in S_i, we say that the two overlap partially. The size of this overlap is the number of people in the intersection of G and S_i—that is, $|G \cap S_i|$. Dividing this by the number of people in the host group S_i, we obtain the degree of participation of G in S_i:

$$\pi_i(G,S_i) = |G \cap S_i|/|S_i|, \text{ a number between 0 and 1.}$$

If we now take the average of the participation indices for all the social systems in the society S, we end up with an indicator of the overall participation of G in S:

$$\pi(G,S) = (1/n)\,\Sigma\pi_i.$$

Finally, we define marginality as the complement of participation to unity:

$$\mu_i = 1 - \pi_i,\ \mu = 1 - \pi.$$

Every successful quantitation constitutes an advancement in precision. Still, one should not engage in quantity worship, for a deep, fruitful qualitative idea is superior to a trivial, barren quantitative one, and quantitative research is often shallow, though more often for lack of theoretical imagination than for any alleged intrinsic limitation of quantitative tools.

Having praised exactness, let me hasten to warn that it is never sufficient. Indeed, a logical or mathematical formula cannot capture the full sense of a scientific construct. This is because formalization does not provide the reference class of the construct in question, which means that it supplies only part of its meaning. This will be illustrated by a couple of examples. First, the statement that the probability of event E equals 0.2 is mathematically exact but not enlightening unless accompanied by a proposition telling us what kind of an event E is—which is not for mathematicians to say. To discover the full meaning of the proposition, we must place it in its proper context—physical, biological, sociological, and so forth.

Second example: one of the characters in Fielding's *Tom Jones* states that "those masters who promise the most, perform the least." In the absence of further information, this maxim can be formalized in a number of ways, among them $P + A = $ a constant and $P \cdot A = $ a constant, where P designates the number of promises and A the number of corresponding actions. Both these formulas capture the quantitative aspect of the maxim, but neither elucidates the concepts of promise and performance, which could presumably be elucidated in a theory of action. As long as this elucidation is not forthcoming, the above formulas are at best research projects.

Third example: an inverted U curve, corresponding to the formula $P(t) = -at^2 + bt + c$, may formalize a demographic trend representing first the growth, then the decline in population of a given society. Clearly, only the part of the curve falling in the upper quadrants is demographically meaningful; the part in the lower quadrants is demographically meaningless, since it involves negative populations. In this case the semantic convention, according to which $P(t)$ represents the population of the society at time t, performs two functions. It transforms an algebraic formula into a demographic one; and, by restricting the range of the function, it indicates its truth domain.

The point of these examples is to show that mathematical formulas by themselves cannot represent any facts. In order for a mathematical formula to represent a fact, it must be conjoined with one or more *semantic assumptions*—that is, statements identifying the intended referents and the properties of the referents that the predicates are supposed to represent. What holds for a formula holds for the entire mathematical formalism of a theory. A correctly formalized factual theory—for example, one in mathematical economics—consists of a formalism, or mathematical skeleton, plus a set of semantic assumptions. In short, $T \neq F \cup S$. Hence, by altering S, the interpretation of F, one obtains a different T. In other words, one and the same mathematical formalism may be interpreted in different ways. This lack of commitment to any particular matters of fact helps to explain the ubiquity of mathematics.

Outside economics, formalization has never been popular in the social sciences. One of the reasons for this is that, traditionally, most social scientists have come from a humanistic background. A second, related reason is that some of them have been influenced by idealist philosophers who, like Kant and Hegel, believed that mathematics had no place in the so-called human sciences. A third is the influence of traditional empiricism, according to which only data matter.

In recent years three further factors have contributed to the decline of interest in formalization in social science. One is the irrationalist wave generated in the mid-1960s, of which more in chapters 11 and 12. Another is the disappointment caused by the shallowness, or even irrelevance, of many mathematical models in social science. This irrelevance is partly to be blamed on mathematicians who turned to social science and produced a number of unrealistic, if formally sophisticated, models. Some of these models are just intellectual games. A third cause for the decline in mathematical modeling in social studies over the past few decades is the myth that the computer is a substitute for theory—whereas, actually, computing without theory is mere data processing devoid of explanatory power.

Yet formalization, though never sufficient, is always necessary to advance science and technology beyond a preliminary stage. It is necessary because mathematics exactifies, systematizes, and is the most powerful deductive engine. Mathematics is not just a form of shorthand and a tool for compressing and analyzing data—although it certainly does both these things. The main functions of mathematics in factual science and technology are to hone concepts and propositions and suggest new ones, as well as to put ideas together in systems and ferret out their logical consequences.

A by-product of such honing and systematization is enhanced testability. Thus, linear and exponential functions, as well as other monotonically increasing or decreasing functions, not only exactify the vague statement that a certain variable increases or decreases along with another. Such a precise statement calls, in turn, for a much more demanding test, both direct and indirect: direct, in that the given function, rather than any among infinitely many monotonically increasing functions, is in the dock, hence any discrepancy between it and the relevant data will force one to revise the choice of function (or else the data); and indirect, in that confirmation (or refutation) of other formulas in the theory will reinforce (or weaken) the truth claims of the given formula.

Unfortunately mathematics—or, rather, symbolism—has been used not only to advance social science but also to intimidate the innumerate and to pass off vague, untested, or even false assumptions as scientific truths. This is the case with the rational choice models involving undefined utility functions (see chap. 14 and Appendix 4). Any economic theory involving unspecified production functions is in the same boat.

Another case of vacuous or incorrect symbolism is the set of dimensionally inhomogeneous formulas which occur all too often in social science. Thus, a well-known sociologist proposed the formula $Q = a + v$, where Q denotes output per worker, a the average grade of worker on an assembly line, and v the speed of the latter. This is an ill-formed formula because the three variables have different dimensions, so are measured in different kinds of units: it is like adding meters to seconds to obtain grams. (By contrast, the kinematic formula "distance equals velocity times time," $s = vt$ for short, is dimensionally homogeneous because the dimensions of v are LT^{-1}, so vt and s have the same dimensions: $LT^{-1}T = L$.) A formula that is not well formed is even worse than a false formula for, by just negating the latter, one can obtain a true formula.

5   Ideal Type

The formation of scientific concepts and propositions involves idealization (or stylization), which is a form of simplification. Thus, although there are no two identical human beings, we all resemble each other sufficiently to warrant speaking of human beings. In other words, we form the concept of a human species by focusing on certain similarities, among them common descent from hominids, and abstracting from individual differences.

To form a natural kind, one starts by comparing two or more individuals in some regard(s). If individuals a and b posses a common property (or property cluster) P, we say that they are *equivalent* with respect to P, or P-equivalent, and write: $a \sim_P b$. All such individuals constitute an *equivalence class* under P. Thus the P-equivalence class of a, which is also that of b, is designated $[a]_P$. For example, all plumbers, regardless of their competence and honesty, are equivalent insofar as they do plumbing jobs.

A relevant equivalence relation allows one to split any collection into mutually disjoint, homogeneous equivalence classes. For example, the relation "is of the same sex as" splits humankind into three mutually disjoint, complementary classes: M, F, and I (for intersex). This splitting, or *partition*, is indicated thus: $P = H/ \sim = \{M, F, I\}$, equals "The same-sex equivalence relation splits humankind (H) into the male, female and intersex kinds." These three classes are mutually disjoint; that is, $M \cap F = \varnothing$, $M \cap I = \varnothing$, and $F \cap I = \varnothing$. Moreover, there is no fourth sex; that is, the partition is exhaustive: $M \cup F \cup I = H$. We shall use these concepts in the theory of classification (chap. 4, sec. 2).

While some idealizations are fruitful on account of being reasonably true, others are not, because they involve severe distortions. In social science a concept of the first kind is often called an "ideal type" (Menger 1963 [1883]; Weber 1922; von Mises 1949). For instance, "feudal society" is an ideal type because, even in societies where lord–serf relations were dominant, there were also free farmers, craftsmen, traders, and so on. Capitalism is parallel (Dahrendorf 1988, 4). Much the same holds for "slave society," "perfect competition," "political democracy," "bureaucratism," and "militarism," as well as for the three basic ideal types of domination distinguished by Weber: rational, traditional, and charismatic. Real types are "impure"—that is, mixtures of ideal types (Mann 1993).

Ideal types are not vague predicates or, consequently, fuzzy sets. On the contrary, they are well-defined concepts. But they match their real counterparts only approximately. Nor are ideal types peculiar to social science. The regular geometric figures are ideal types for the carpenter, who can produce only approximately circular or square tables. So are ideal gases, frictionless gears, weightless shafts, free electrons, plane waves, and pure substances (except in tiny amounts). So Weber was right to emphasize that the social scientist disregards individual idiosyncrasies: to insist that he focus on shared features and the concomitant central trends. But he was wrong in believing that this procedure is peculiar to social science, for, as a matter of fact, it is employed in all sciences, natural, social, or mixed—which is one point in favor of the thesis of the unity of science.

Another common idealization is the approximation of discontinuous functions, such as population as a function of time, by continuous ones. This approximation is unreasonable for a village but reasonable for a country. On the other hand, the representation of the collection of consumers as an interval of the real line is totally unrealistic, because such an interval is an infinite set and, moreover, a nondenumerable one. Yet it is sometimes employed in economics just because it is pretty and mathematically expedient.

Ideal types are not idle fantasies, but rough conceptual sketches or models of real things, introduced with the sole aim of getting theorizing started. Complications are added only as needed—that is, as discrepancies between model and reality appear and become serious. As science advances, its successive ideal types represent their real referents increasingly accurately. (Actually, this statement is a crypto-tautology [sec. 2], for the progress of science involves, by definition, the replacement of less by more realistic models.) Thus, the *homo oeconomicus* of classical and neoclassical economies is gradually being replaced by a more realistic model that includes emotional, political, and cultural features.

There are a number of misconceptions concerning the nature and function of ideal types. A short while ago we met one of them: namely, the belief that ideal types are peculiar to social science, whereas actually they have been inherent in all the sciences and technologies from their beginnings. A second mistake is the empiricist bias against constructs that do not match the data in every detail—as if accurate theories, representing their referents in all their complexity, could be crafted at one go. This empiricist mistake has a rationalist counterpart: namely, an uncritical trust in any elegant mathematical model. Such trust is rampant in mainstream mathematical economics. For example, many scholars take seriously the so-called von Neumann technology, a model of economic growth that involves the assumption that every production process requires every commodity as an input, an output, or both. (In other words, it is assumed that no cell in the Leontief input–output matrix for an economy is empty.) This assumption is mathematically convenient, but economically unreasonable: it is too far removed from the facts.

The preceding should dispose of the popular misconception, embraced by the "humanist" camp in social studies, that social matters are too complex to be modeled. This notion ignores an important point: that the fact that there are no two things in the world that are identical does not prevent us from grouping things into equivalence classes. It also ignores the fact that, by definition, modeling involves a simplification of the given, which in turn allows one to distinguish the essential from the accidental, the lawful from the idiosyncratic. This point was clearly understood by Ricardo, Marx, and Weber, among others.

6 Definition

One way of elucidating a concept or the sign designating it is to define it. But not all concepts are definable: some must do the job of defining. For example, the concept of identity is taken as undefined, or primitive, and it helps define its dual, that of inequality. The defining, or basic, concepts are said to be *primitive*. As a matter of fact, the most important concepts in any context are the primitive ones, precisely because they help to define all the other concepts in the same context. (But some of the defining concepts in a given context may turn out to be defined in another context: definability is contextual.)

For example, in economics a durable good is defined as a commodity that lasts for an extended period of time. In this case the defining concepts are those of commodity, defined elsewhere in economics, and time, borrowed from physics. Further concepts borrowed by social science from natural science or even philosophy are those of nature, thing, fact, event, system, energy, organism, human being, action, and mental process—to name just a few. In this way social science is indebted to, and even based on, natural science and philosophy. (Recall introduction, sec. 1.) Logic is the only science that is not (logically) based on any other—although it interacts vigorously with mathematics.

As far as logical form is concerned, there are two main kinds of definition: explicit and implicit. *Explicit* definitions are of the form A = $_{df}$B. The symbol =$_{df}$, read "identical by definition," plays only a methodological role: it indicates that A is the defined concept, or *definiendum*, and B the defining one, or *definiens*. From a strictly logical point of view, explicit definitions are identities, as Peano showed long ago—so much so that, from this point of view, A = B is the same as B = A. (By contrast, equalities are not symmetrical. Thus "The number of planets equals 9" is not the same as "9 equals the number of planets." The first proposition can be formalized as |P| := 9, where |P| designates the numerosity of P, and := abbreviates "is equal to.")

In the case of an *implicit* definition, the defined concept (definiendum) cannot be expressed in terms of other concepts: it occurs in combination with other constructs. For example, the concept "if . . . , then" of logical implication, or ⇒, may be defined thus: For any propositions p and q, $p ⇒ q =$ $_{df}$ $p ∨ ¬q$. Similarly, the concept of a social class is definable in context, namely thus: A human group C is a *social class* in a given society S if and only if (a) there is another social group C' in S that either dominates C or is dominated by C in some respect, and (*b*) the members of the dominant group benefit from their membership in it more than those of the dominated group in their own.

Being undefined is not necessarily the same as being fuzzy: only the converse is true. The undefined, or primitive, concepts in a well-constructed theory are defined via axioms—that is, initial propositions. This is done sometimes directly, at other times indirectly. In the former case one constructs an axiomatic definition of the form "*A* is [or is called] an *F* if and only if *A* satisfies the following axioms: . . . ." For example, in the theory of the perfectly competitive market it is possible to define the latter as the social group that satisfies the so-called laws of the market—which, alas, are seldom met in the real world of oligopolies and big governments. In most cases, when laying down an axiomatic definition, one does not single out a given member of the set of primitive concepts, but treats them all on a par by specifying the conditions (axioms) that they must satisfy.

Definitions are stipulations, or conventions, not assumptions. They are true by convention, not by proof or by virtue of empirical evidence. To be sure, the definitions in factual science have real referents: they used to be called "real" definitions, and thus they smack of truths of fact (e.g., social system $=_{df}$ system composed of animals held together by some bonds). Still, even such definitions are conventions. What happens is that we may become so used to employing the defined concepts that we find them "natural." In principle, nothing but practical convenience stands in the way of changing the conventional name for a thing, property, or process. In fact, such changes happen all the time. Thus, in American political lingo, 'working class,' 'state,' and 'reactionary' have been replaced by 'middle class,' 'government,' and 'conservative,' respectively.

Regrettably, the distinction between definition (a convention) and assumption (a fallible assertion) is not always observed. For example, "In a conservative system outflow equals inflow," though sometimes paraded as a law, is actually a disguised definition of 'conservative system.' And many an economist believes that the definition of the productivity of a firm is an economic law. (The formula in question is $E = P/\pi h$, where E designates the number of persons employed, π the productivity, and h the average working hours per week. Solving for π, one realizes that the formula defines π, an unobservable, in terms of measurable quantities.)

Definitions are conventions bearing only on concepts or their symbols, not on facts. We can do many things with concrete things other than define them. If someone says that human nature is "defined" by tool making, language, rationality, or what have you, he must be taken to mean that he regards these properties as peculiar to, or characteristic of, human nature. Moreover, a conjunction of such properties may be used as a *criterion* or *test* for telling humans from nonhumans, much as litmus paper can be used as a test of acidity.

It has been said that definitions, however handy, are in principle dispensable.

But this holds only for logic and mathematics, which deal with exact concepts; and even here it holds only for explicit definitions, not axiomatic definitions, for these introduce new concepts. And definition is important in the factual sciences, particularly the social ones, as a means of enhancing accuracy and thus preparing the ground for theorizing. Still, it is mistaken to believe, as some social scientists and philosophers do, that a theory is just a set of definitions. A theory about X is a set of assumptions about X, not a set of conventions concerning the use of concepts or words.

So much for definitions proper. Finally, a word about persuasive definitions: those whose function is not to elucidate but to mask. Two cases in point are the concepts of rationality and growth employed in mainstream economics. "Rationality" is often defined as self-interest or, more precisely, as utility (or profit) maximization. In this way selfishness is made to look virtuous. Likewise, "economic growth" is often equated with increase in production or consumption, regardless of poverty and unemployment. In this way a conservative government can boast of having helped "the economy" grow even though poverty and unemployment have risen also. Moral: Definitions matter, particularly in fields of knowledge close to ideology. Nevertheless, assumptions matter far more.

7 Assumption

Reasoning leads from one set of propositions (the assumptions) to another (the conclusions). It may be fruitful or barren, transparent or opaque, correct or incorrect, deductive or nondeductive, persuasive or unpersuasive. Only deductive reasoning, regardless of its fruit, is subject to rule: other types of reasoning may be more or less plausible, but never rule-directed, in that they depend on the content and context of the propositions. Every act of correct deductive reasoning starts from some premises and yields some conclusion in conformity with agreed rules of inference. The premises of an argument may be data, definitions, or hypotheses, either tentative or well confirmed. In this section we shall examine assumptions with a factual reference, or *factual assumptions* for short, such as "Automation eliminates jobs."

A first division of the set of factual assumptions is into implicit (or tacit) and explicit. An implicit assumption, or *presupposition*, is a premise which either goes unnoticed or is taken for granted, and in any case in not usually examined. We saw in the Introduction, section 1, that scientific research proceeds on the basis of a number of philosophical presuppositions, such as that we must resort to both reason and experience. In addition to such general presuppositions borrowed from philosophy, every social science employs special presuppositions borrowed from other sciences. For example, all social scientists take the physical principle of conservation of energy for granted, and they all admit the psychological principle that human behavior is in part shaped by environmental stimuli. Most presuppositions surface fully only under the lens of the axiomatizer or the metatheorist. And only when they do surface, can they be subjected to critical scrutiny. Otherwise they may do untold harm.

Explicit factual assumptions come in three major kinds: data, empirical generalizations, and hypotheses. A *datum* is a singular (nongeneral) proposition representing the outcome of a piece of empirical research—an observation, measurement, or experiment (e.g., "The American Revolution occurred in 1776"). An *empirical generalization* is a statement summarizing data and starting with "some," "most," or "all" (e.g., "Most political revolutions have been violent"). Finally, a *factual hypothesis,* whether particular or general, goes beyond the data at hand either in breadth or in depth. That is, it asserts or denies the actual or possible occurrence of facts of a certain kind that, at best, are only partially known (e.g., "All political revolutions have occurred with the connivance of some members of the power against which they were directed").

It may seem odd to call data "assumptions," all the more so since they are often miscalled "facts." But assumptions they are, because in principle they are corrigible. In fact, scrutiny of any set of data may lead to the discovery that some of them are somewhat inaccurate or even totally false—as is often the case in social science. This suggests that, rather than being *given,* as the etymology of the word indicates, data are products of inquiry—and inquiry, like any other human activity, is fallible. But it is also perfectible, since errors in knowledge, unlike some practical errors, are corrigible. Hence a correct methodology will be meliorist as well as fallibilist, rather than either dogmatic or radically skeptic.

From data one may leap to empirical or inductive generalizations, such as "All men are fallible." There is nothing wrong with generalizing from even a few instances. We do it all the time, and it often results in finding objective patterns. What is wrong is to employ such generalizations without further scrutiny, for, after all, many popular superstitions are the product of hasty or untested inductions. Also, it is wrong to believe that induction is the one and only way to legitimate general knowledge. This empiricist thesis, often called 'inductivism,' is wrong because induction results in new propositions but not in new concepts—that is, concepts not occurring in the data base. And the occurrence of such nonempirical concepts is the mark of depth (though not necessarily of truth).

Thus, the leap from the singular propositions $Pa, Pb, \ldots, Pn$ to the empirical generalization "For all x: Px" does not introduce a new predicate save for the nonempirical (logical) prefix "for all." Likewise, every statistical table is built from individual data. To be sure, it may contain new (collective or statistical) predicates, such as "average," "mode," and "variance." But these are constructed from data about individuals. If we want radically new concepts, we must invent them: mere observation, aggregation, or statistical analysis will not supply them. And we do need concepts that do not occur in the data if we wish to explain the latter—for example, in terms of forces, dispositions, probabilities, demand elasticities, business strategies, class conflicts, trends, and so on, none of which is directly observable.

Induction can be mechanized. In fact, computers can be fed any curve-fitting technique. Thus, they can generalize from a set of data, jumping from a set of points (on a plane or in a higher-dimensional space) to a continuous curve (a polynomial in one or more variables). By contrast, there are no rules or methods, in particular algorithms, for inventing problems, concepts, hypotheses, or methods. In particular, there are no self-programming systems except for the human brain. Radical (i.e., noncombinatorial) invention cannot be mechanized: it is the privilege of natural intelligence. Thus, whereas economic statistics is largely inductive, the building of economic concepts and theories calls for inventiveness.

The methodological status of empirical generalizations differs in several respects from that of high-level hypotheses. For one thing, the former are syntheses of known singulars, whereas a hypothesis involves an imaginary expansion of the data base. The more modest hypotheses are interpolations between data or extrapolations from them: they consist in fitting a continuous curve to a set of data, which, however numerous, is finite. Second, unlike empirical generalizations, high-level hypotheses contain, by definition, concepts that do not occur in the data relevant to them, such as those of kinship structure, social cohesion, price elasticity, economic decline, and political legitimacy. Third, whereas empirical generalizations summarize only past findings, high-level hypotheses point to the future, since, if intriguing, they are likely to guide future research—in the first place, research aimed at testing them (e.g., "Social cohesion is proportional to participation"). (We shall return to the matter of hypotheses in chap. 3, sec. 4.)

The initial, or basic, hypotheses of a theory are called its 'axioms' or 'postulates.' Such assumptions, often together with auxiliary assumptions and data, entail any number of theorems. The great advantages of axiomatization are that it exhibits most, if not all, of the premises, thus facilitating their critical examination; and it expedites deduction by facilitating the discovery of new theorems and the eradication of pseudo-theorems.

Regrettably, axioms are often mistaken for either self-evident and indisputable truths or stifling dogmas. For example, whereas the partisans of mainstream economics regard their axioms as unquestionable, some of their critics claim that the main trouble with such economics is that it is cast in an axiomatic format—that is, it proceeds deductively from axioms. But axioms need be neither obvious truths nor paralyzing dogmas. In the factual sciences an axiom is nothing but a hypothesis, hence corrigible, but one which, for some reason such as generality, it is convenient to place at the base of a hypothetico-deductive system or theory. The trouble with mainstream economics is not that some of it has been axiomatized, but that most of its axioms are obsolete (Bunge forthcoming).

8 Rule

We need and make hypotheses at all times and in all walks of life, but they are not enough. We also need rules for handling things, ideas, and symbols. We need, among others, rules for doing things, rules of conduct, and rules for moving from assumptions to conclusions. And we need to be clear about the nature of rules and their grounds, if any. In particular, we need to know whether rules can be true, or only efficient, as well as how to devise relevant and efficient rules—that is, rules that will help us attain our goals.

A *rule* is an instruction for doing something definite with things, processes, or ideas. (In particular, the things or processes may be words, drawings, or sounds.) Some human activities are rule-directed, others not; and even those activities that are rule-bound do not always follow explicit rules: there is such a thing as tacit knowledge. In particular, there are inference rules, but they cover only deduction. Analogy and induction are not subject to rules, because they depend on content. In other words, there are neither analogical nor inductive logics, although much used to be written about these ghosts.

Being instructions, not propositions, rules cannot be true or even false. On the other hand, rules can be relevant (to the goal in view) and efficient to some degree. This is obvious from the general form of the simplest rules, which is: To attain goal G, use means M. An instance of this form of rule will be efficient only if there is a law statement of one of the following forms: "M is followed by G, M causes G, or M makes G likely." (More precisely, "The probability of G given M is significantly greater than 0.") A law statement of any of these kinds will be said to constitute the 'scientific ground' of the rule in question, and the latter will be said to have a 'scientific basis.' If the rule is efficient ("works") but we do not know why, it will be said to be an 'empirical rule,' or a rule of thumb.

We have just laid down a *meta-rule*, or rule about rules, namely:

MR1. Every technological rule should be based on a scientific law statement.

Should a rule thus grounded not be efficient enough, we may try a second one:

MR2. To improve on the efficiency of a technological rule, replace the underlying law statement.

If repeated attempts of this kind fail, we should try a third meta-rule:

MR3. If the given goal proves unattainable, replace it with a different one— either more modest or more ambitious.

One of the main differences between prescientific and scientific technology is that the former employs only empirical rules, whereas modern technology uses mostly rules based on scientific laws. However, there is no one-to-one correspondence between the set of rules and that of laws: first, because many scientific laws (such as those of high energy physics) have yet to find practical application; second, and more important, because every scientific law is the actual or potential basis for *two* technological rules, one for getting something done, the other for avoiding it. In fact, consider the simplest possible law statement: namely, one of the conditional form "If *M*, then *G*." This single statement is the ground for a couple of rules:

R1. In order to get *G*, do *M* (or let *M* happen).

R2. In order to avert the occurrence of *G*, abstain from doing *M* (or prevent *M* from occurring).

We shall say that such rules are mutually dual. Take, for instance, the well-confirmed generalization that unemployment tends to either freeze or depress wages. This proposition may be restated as: "If unemployment rises, wages do not increase." Two rules suggest themselves:

R1. To keep wages down, push unemployment up.

R2. To raise wages, create jobs.

The first rule is recommended by conservatives, who hold that in a healthy economy there is a "natural" rate of unemployment, though they do not say whether it is 2, 4, 6, 8, or 10 percent. The second rule is recommended by everyone else.

This duality of technological rules is the cognitive root of the moral ambivalence of technology, by contrast with the moral univalence of basic science. Indeed, a law statement is descriptive, explanatory, or predictive, hence morally neutral. On the other hand, a technological rule is a prescription for rational action. It may prescribe a morally right or wrong action. Thus, if the goal *G* is morally worthy, and the means *M* employed to attain it is not evil, then the law "If *M*, then *G*" is the ground for the morally right rule "In order to get *G*, do *M*." If, on the other hand, the goal or the means is morally objectionable, the first rule is morally wrong, and we must apply its dual.

Scientific or technological knowledge is not a pile of facts, but a collection of ideas about facts. Hence the disciplines that study ideas in general—in particular, logic and semantics—are relevant to the understanding of science and technology. They teach us, for instance, that, while propositions can be true or false, concepts, proposals, instructions, and rules can be neither. They also teach us that, while definitions are important in refining and relating concepts, only assumptions and their logical consequences can say anything about the real world. Also, logic and semantics help detect and correct conceptual confusion, imprecision, and error. This is why they are disparaged by those who, like the Romantics and their successors, decry rigor, extol "weak thinking," and prefer the story to the research report (see, e.g., Featherstone 1988; Harvey 1989; Agger 1991).

3 :: *Inquiry*

We all want to know certain things, and sometimes we also wish to understand them: this is why we inquire into all manner of things. In some cases we need knowledge in order to solve practical problems; in others we want it to satisfy sheer curiosity. Exclusive focusing on practical needs leads to philosophical pragmatism, whereas exaggerating cognitive wants leads to philosophical idealism. Both trends are present in the sociology and history of knowledge, as well as in philosophy. As with so many other questions, the whole truth is a synthesis of the two extremes. Evidence for this thesis is the variety of types of inquiry people engage in: ordinary, scientific, technological, and humanistic.

We get to know ideas by thinking of them, and concrete things by perceiving, conceiving, or manipulating them. All these are cognitive processes, at least in part, and their outcomes are items of knowledge. In traditional terms, there are three sources of knowledge: perception, conception, and action. (Empiricism acknowledges only the former, rationalism the second, and pragmatism the third.) Divine inspiration and alleged paranormal abilities, such as extrasensory perception, precognition, and telekinesis, have no place in science or technology. On the other hand, scientific study of the claims of the mystic and the paranormal is legitimate, socially important, and occasionally interesting.

The difference between cognition and knowledge is an instance of the process–state distinction (see chap. 1, sec. 3). Cognition, a process, is mainly of interest to neuroscientists, psychologists, ethologists, and social scientists.

Knowledge, an end product of cognition, draws the attention of everyone but is of particular interest to philosophers. (Recall the methodological distinction between ideas as brain processes and ideas in themselves drawn at the start of chap. 2.) But the scientific philosopher and the methodologist are almost as interested in cognition as in knowledge, because the latter must be continually updated, deepened, and expanded.

However, in this chapter we shall focus on the end product rather than the process, even while admitting that in reality there is no knowledge in itself— that is, apart from the cognitive processes occurring in the brains of higher vertebrates. We shall also ignore to a large extent the social inputs and outputs of cognition, which are of particular interest to sociologists and historians of knowledge. Again, this is not because I think it possible for the knowing subject to exist in a social vacuum or outside history, but because someone has got to study the form and content of the product of cognitive processes, and this task has traditionally fallen to philosophers.

Knowledge can be sensorimotor (e.g., walking), perceptual (e.g., hearing a shout as a call), or conceptual (e.g., knowing something about people or about our knowledge of people). But distinction does not entail separation. In fact, knowledge of all three kinds often combines, as in social interaction, bench work, drawing, and writing.

Knowledge can be of self or of other things. But again, knowledge of both kinds may combine, as when we try to guess other people's mental processes by imagining ourselves in their shoes. Knowledge can be by acquaintance (by personal experience) or description (conceptual). For example, I have direct (introspective) knowledge of some of my own mental processes, as well as some scientific knowledge of other people's states of mind. All scientific knowledge is knowledge by description; merely feeling or perceiving something, however strongly or distinctly, does not qualify as scientific knowledge. However, scientific psychologists cannot help using introspection to investigate other people's subjective experience.

Knowledge can be at first or second hand. But since we must always make use of some knowledge garnered by others, the two kinds combine. Knowledge can be tacit, in which case it is called "know-how," or explicit, in which case it is known as "know-that" (or declarative). Being tacit, know-how is hardly analyzable: we can judge it only by its fruits. Still, the professional pursuit of knowledge involves learning some skills that cannot be rendered fully explicit and hence are not found in manuals: they must be learned by imitation or by trial and error. If explicit, knowledge can be private or public. But the sphere of private (or privileged) knowledge is shrinking, as new methods of brain imaging and surveillance are being invented.

Knowledge can be ordinary or specialized. However, today's specialized knowledge may become part of tomorrow's common knowledge. Knowledge can be general (e.g., of patterns) or particular (e.g., of individual facts). But all scientific search for particular knowledge makes use of some general ideas; and once an item of particular knowledge has been acquired, it may spark off a general idea. Knowledge can be of facts or ideas, of natural things or artifacts, of actual human behavior or technical, moral, or legal norms, and so on and so forth. It can range from complete truth to utter falsity, as well as from practical uselessness to usefulness. Finally, the vulgar opposition between knowledge and error is wrong, because much of our knowledge about facts has at best a grain of truth. Error is the dual or complement of truth, not of knowledge.

Nor is knowledge true belief, although it is often defined as such. For one thing, some true knowledge may at first be hardly believable. For another, belief, disbelief, and doubt are mental processes which can be investigated empirically, whereas knowledge in itself is a subject for philosophical inquiry. Furthermore, social psychologists know that sometimes there is a discrepancy between what we actually believe and what we say we believe: at times we lie to others or to ourselves, particularly with regard to moral and social issues. This is why questionnaires, unless framed in an astute fashion, are not fully reliable.

There are no stray beliefs: all beliefs come in clusters, or systems. Belief systems, whether individual or collective, worldly or supernatural, are to be investigated empirically by psychologists and social scientists. The philosopher should abstain from building a priori "logics of belief" (doxastic logics), but he should encourage the scientific investigation of belief systems. He can do so by stressing that, unlike knowledge considered in itself, believing and doubting are mental (or brain) processes. He can also help dispel the holistic belief that social groups hold beliefs. He can do so by noting that believing is a brain process, and that social groups are brainless, so that "Group G holds belief B" should be rewritten "All, or at least most, members of group G hold belief B."

Finally, the philosopher acquainted with a modicum of mathematics and science can criticize the fashionable relativist thesis that there are no universal, or cross-cultural, truths, and that in any event what matters is the beliefs people hold, regardless of whether they are true or false. This belief about beliefs is doubly false. First, scientists are interested in finding out whether certain beliefs are true: this is part of their job description. Second, a false belief may be sustained only as long as it is not put to the test. New situations may arise that put a belief to the test. If the test invalidates the belief, yet people cling to it, they may invent *ad hoc* hypotheses to save it. But this remedy is usually short-lived. For example, a shaman's powers may not be questioned as long as his fellow tribesmen do not come into contact with strangers carrying germs against which they are not immunized—which is what happened during the two centuries following the European conquest of America. When such contagion does occur, and the tribe is all but wiped out, belief in the shaman's healing power is bound to wane. The relativist cannot explain the decline of shamanism because, unlike the disillusioned tribesman, he does not care for truth and does not believe that other people care for truth either. He thus becomes a victim of his own system of false beliefs. (More on relativism in sec. 5 and chap. 13, sec. 4.)

1 Approach and Paradigm

Every inquiry starts with a gap in a body of knowledge—that is, a problem; if successful, it ends with a solution—often called a "finding," even if it was invented rather than found. If somebody finds the solution interesting or useful, it may prompt him to ask new questions, such as how to improve on the given solution. In fact, one of the characteristics of scientific and technological inquiry is that their problem–solution sequences are branching, self-sustaining, and open-ended.

Problems are the starters of research projects, but they do not come out of the blue, and, at least in science and technology, they are not handled in an improvised fashion. Problems emerge in some body of background knowledge, and they are approached in some way or other. The notion of background knowledge is comparatively clear: it is the body of available knowledge found scattered in up-to-date technical reports, specialized journals, and advanced books. On the other hand, the notion of an approach, or way of wrestling with problems, is somewhat fuzzy, so we should elucidate it.

An *approach* may be analyzed as a body, B, of *background knowledge* together with a set P of problems (*problematics*), a set A of *aims*, or goals, and a set M of methods (*methodics*). In short, $\mathcal{A} = <B, P, A, M>$. Every component of this quadruple is to be taken as at a given time. The order of the components is obvious. One always starts with a body of knowledge: it is here that one finds a hole, the second component of our quadruple. Then, one works on the problem with some aim, which may be either cognitive or practical. Finally, the aim determines the method of handling the problem—scientific, technological, or humanistic. Let us glance at the way of approaching scientific problems.

A *scientific approach* is characterized by the following components:

B = the bulk of relevant scientific knowledge and its underlying philosophy;
P = a set of cognitive (rather than practical or moral) problems;
A = gaining objective knowledge about a domain of facts;
M = scientific method plus a collection of special, scrutable techniques.

Let us start by examining the *background knowledge, B*. We require only the bulk, rather than the totality, of antecedent knowledge, because no single person has access to all of it, some of it may be in the dock, and no research project needs more than a comparatively small part of all the available knowledge. B includes the philosophical principles presupposed by scientific research, which were mentioned in the Introduction, section 1, such as those of the existence, lawfulness, and knowability of the external world.

The *problematics* envisaged in a scientific approach is a set of purely cognitive problems: practical problems are peculiar to the technological and moral spheres. For instance, a study of land tenure belongs in science, whereas a rational plan of land reform belongs in social technology.

The *aim* of the scientific approach is to gain new, disinterested, objective knowledge about some real, or putatively real, facts. The first feature, novelty or originality, is of course a matter of degree. We shall discuss it in the next section when dealing with the difference between research and routine problems. The second feature, disinterestedness, distinguishes basic science (and the humanities) from the rest. And the third, objectivity, is peculiar to science and technology, whereas subjectivity is peculiar to art, mysticism, and pseudoscience. An approach is said to be *objective* if it distinguishes the subject (researcher, evaluator, doer) from his object, hence appearance from reality, and refrains from attributing his own characteristics to his object—unless his object of study happens to be someone very much like himself. An objective account includes only propositions or rules open to peer inspection, criticism, and evaluation.

Finally, the *methodics* of a scientific approach is constituted by all the relevant scrutable procedures: that is, all the rule-directed procedures that yield objective knowledge and can be justified theoretically as well as empirically. For example, trial and error (hit or miss) is not a method proper, even though it is occasionally successful. Nor is it enough for a method to "work": we must explain how it "works" before we dub it "scientific." For example, members of the hermeneutic school claim that social matters must be studied exclusively using Verstehen (insight or "interpretation") rather than the scientific method. But since nobody has described that procedure in a clear manner, nobody knows how it works, much less how it could be refined. Hence one is justified in suspecting that if someone who, like Max Weber, claims to use Verstehen comes up with sound findings, he is likely to have engaged in ordinary scientific research aided by learning and flair. (More in chap. 5, secs. 5 and 6.)

Different approaches are likely to lead to different solutions to one and the same problem. For example, the question of human nature receives different answers if approached in a theological, biological, psychological, or sociological fashion, or again in a multidisciplinary one. Another example: The ideological and humanistic approaches to social problems have no place for the construction of precise, adequate models of social systems—a typically scientific task. And a student who adopts the individualist approach will miss the emergent properties of systems, just as the holist is unable—nay, unwilling—to explain the formation and breakdown of systems in terms of the interactions of their components.

A related notion is that of a "thought style," introduced by Fleck (1979

[1935]), which his admirer Kuhn (1962) rechristened "paradigm." This fashionable, if vague, notion may be elucidated as follows. As we saw above, an approach is only a way of "looking" at things—that is, a manner of studying them. If enriched with some specific substantive hypotheses, an approach becomes a paragon, or paradigm, which, if regarded as successful, is adopted again and again (e.g., the rational choice, functionalist, Marxist, and systemic paradigms). The general concept may then be defined as follows: A *paragon*, or *paradigm*, $\mathcal{P}$ is a body, B, of background knowledge together with a set, H, of specific substantive hypotheses, a problematics, P, an aim, A, and a methodics, M; that is, $\mathcal{P} = <B, H, P, A, M>$. A *paradigm shift*, or change in perspective, occurs when a radical change occurs in H, P, or both. Examples: (*a*) classical economics (value is work) → neoclassical economics (value is in the eye of the beholder); (*b*) crime as a sin to be atoned for → crime as antisocial behavior to be prevented or corrected.

Let us take a closer look at the problem of a problem—something usually neglected in the philosophical literature, even though problems are what trigger research.

2 Problem

In science, technology, and philosophy, nothing is obvious, and little is final: almost anything can become the object of a problem. We distinguish practical problems, or issues, from epistemic problems, or problems proper. And we distinguish personal issues from social ones. A personal issue, such as whether to study sociology, concerns an individual person; a social issue, such as poverty or an epidemic, affects a comparatively large number of people. The decision to tackle an issue raises problems, or intellectual challenges, such as how to gather information, refine concepts, test hypotheses, or design policies. Just as the worth of a man of action can be measured by the volume (number and difficulty) of issues he has tackled successfully, so that of a scientist or philosopher can be gauged by the volume of epistemic problems he has spotted and solved.

In every field of human cognition or action we must distinguish between routine and research problems. A routine problem is well posed, its approach is well defined, and its solution can be foreseen, at least in outline, for it requires only existing knowledge and more or less hard work. Schematically, a *routine* problem-solving process is the sequence *formulation—analysis—search—solution—checking of solution*.

A *research* problem is likely to be somewhat fuzzy at the beginning; consequently, so is the approach within which it is worked on. Hence the first difficulty a research problem raises is that of formulating it correctly. Furthermore, its solution cannot be foreseen even in outline, because it requires new knowledge and often poses new problems. Schematically, a research process consists in the sequence raw problem—analysis choice (or invention) of approach—reformulation of the problem within this approach—preliminary search—research plan—search—solution candidate—checking—examination of possible impact on background knowledge—identification of the new problem(s) posed by the solution—. . . .

In every science we can distinguish the following kinds of research problem: *reference* questions, such as, What is social science about: individuals or social systems? *problematics* problems, such as, Is this problem well-posed? *formal background* problems, such as, Does this system of equations have a unique solution? *specific background* problems, such as, Can economists afford to ignore all the other sciences? *fund of knowledge* problems, such as, How reliable are the available data on the increase in child abuse: could it be that more of it is being reported because of an increased openness and sensitivity? *goal* problems, such as, Should all social scientists tackle social issues? *methodological* problems, such as, How can the pace of historical events be measured? *philosophical* problems, such as, What are the ontological and epistemological presuppositions of this theory or that method?

If found interesting, a problem may trigger an inquiry, in particular a research project. There are several kinds of inquiry. Most are of the problem-solving type; they grapple with problems that arise within given frameworks or that can be tackled with known methods (e.g., finding the income distribution in a given community). But not all research problems are of this kind. When a given framework or method is found to be inadequate, the problem of finding an alternative framework or method arises. For example, an economist dissatisfied with neoclassical economics is faced with the problem of building a better theory, one capable of accounting for real socioeconomic issues.

As regards their referents, social science problems are of two kinds: substantive and methodological. *Substantive* problems concern social facts, whereas *methodological* problems are about ways of studying social facts. In principle, every category of social facts raises both substantive and methodological problems. For example, nationalist movements raise problems of description, classification, explanation, and forecast. We want to find out what they are, how they emerge and develop, why they are not declining in an increasingly interdependent world, whether they are likely to subsist, and, if so, for how long. And as we envisage work on any of these problems, we ask ourselves how best to tackle them: whether within political science or in a wider context, in a purely empirical fashion or theoretically, and so on. In practice, many social problems are either ignored or assumed to have been solved, and many hypotheses and methods are taken for granted rather than questioned—as they should be once in a while, since there is little definitive about factual knowledge.

Just as reflection on facts induces substantive and methodological problems, so work on these problems raises metatheoretical (or philosophical) problems. For example, the study of any social fact poses the problem of choosing the most suitable approach: whether individualist, holist, or neither; humanist or scientific; historical, synchronic, or both; sectoral or interdisciplinary, and so on. Any social inquiry is also bound to call for the elucidation of certain key philosophical concepts, such as those of system, process, social issue, rule, truth, theory, evidence, and confirmation. Only those who wear the blinkers characteristic of the narrow specialist (or the classical positivist) can afford to ignore the fact that a careful examination of any social science problem is bound to open a can of metatheoretical worms. But the narrow specialist sees only what he is prepared to see: only the generalist is likely to spot big problems.

Is there any objective way of grading problems in order of difficulty, other than Sherlock Holmes's counting the number of pipes he had to smoke before hitting on the correct solution? A problem becomes more difficult the more variables it involves, the more complex their mutual relations and the less accessible they are, the poorer the relevant antecedent knowledge, and the thicker the philosophical fog surrounding it. Let us look at the latter.

One of the philosophical myths that has hindered the scientific treatment of social problems is the belief that the study of a system, such as a society, is necessarily more difficult than that of its components. This belief is mistaken for two reasons. First, if we decide to take a superficial look at things of interest, our task will be comparatively easy, regardless of their real complexity. Only if we want depth, will we encounter enormously complex problems, even in the study of simple things such as electrons or photons. (By the way, any theory of these things is far more complex than any known social theory.) Second, there are a number of global or systemic regularities that do not occur at the component level. (For instance, the average life span, the average number of children per family, and the ratio of female to male criminals in any society are roughly constant, by comparison with large individual variations.)

Problems can be direct or inverse. An example of a *direct* problem is this: Given the composition, environment, and structure of a system, find out its behavior. The corresponding *inverse* problem is: Given the behavior of a system, "infer" (guess) its composition, environment, and structure. This problem is harder than the former, because different internal mechanisms may produce the same overt behavior: think of mechanical and electronic watches or of differently motivated people performing the same task. As a rule, inverse problems are much harder to solve than their direct counterparts or duals.

Except for some very sophisticated mathematical problems, well-posed direct problems are in principle soluble, if only approximately. By contrast, inverse problems seldom have unique solutions. This is one major reason for the failure—indeed, unwillingness—of behaviorism to explain animal behavior and social systems. (A second major reason is its refusal to look into the source of behavior, i.e., the central nervous system. A third is its anti-theoretical stance.) It is also the major reason for the very low productivity of the Verstehen method, consisting as it does in imagining the motivations—in particular, the passions and interests—that drive people to act as they do. If we know what makes an agent tick, we can explain and predict his behavior. But if we have only his behavior to go on, as is usually the case, we can at best guess his motivations—and, in the absence of privileged information, your guess may be as good as mine. (More in chap. 5, secs. 5 and 6.)

What guides the choice of research problems? Let us limit our discussion to social science. In this field, choice is determined jointly by the state of the discipline—in particular, the open problems noted by others—and the investigator's curiosity, competence, theoretical perspective, and sensitivity to the human predicament. The first factor is obvious from the very definition of a research problem as a gap in our antecedent knowledge. One may certainly think of problems that require a so far nonexisting body of knowledge, but one does not work on them for lack of the necessary knowledge. The second and third factors, curiosity and competence, are even more obvious. Only the fourth and fifth call for comment.

If the investigator's theoretical perspective is narrow or shallow, of if he is indifferent to human misery, he will prefer such safe subjects as Balinese cock-fighting or what is understood, but left unsaid, in a dialogue. If, on the other hand, his theoretical perspective is wide and deep (though not necessarily correct), and if he has a moral sensibility, he is likely to tackle macro-problems such as those of civil liberty (e.g., Mill), social inequality (e.g., Marx), unemployment (e.g., Keynes), racial discrimination (e.g., Myrdal), national dependency (e.g., Prebisch), or development (e.g., Hirschman).

Still, even some of the deepest and most sensitive social thinkers have been blind to major social issues of their time. For example, Mill, Durkheim, Pareto, Weber, and Simmel had nothing to say about sexism, colonialism, or militarism; and Marx, Durkheim, and Weber said nothing important about nationalism, imperialism, racism, or environmental degradation. Hence their writings did not help our understanding of fascism, which was nationalist, racist, colonialist, and sexist as well as militarist. Perhaps they were blinded by serious deficiencies in their theoretical perspectives, particularly regarding so-called social forces.

Finally, are there perennial problems in any field other than mathematics? *This* is one.

3 Datum

There is no *factual* science without empirical data, but there is also no factual *science* without some data filters that allow one to discriminate between relevant and irrelevant information, particularly in our age of information overload. Such filtering devices are philosophy and theory: both tell us the kind of data we ought to collect or produce. In this way they can spare us fruitless toil and the concomitant extra costs. For example, both empiricists and methodological individualists are bound to collect micro-data blindly and in excessive quantities and to analyze them in unnecessary detail, hoping against reason to be able to infer regularities without exerting their imagination.

Having made my case for the relevance of philosophy to data gathering, let me turn to an analysis of the very concept of a datum. A datum, or given, is a particular (as opposed to general) item of knowledge. In mathematics the word *data* designates special assumptions in a problem, such as the values of two sides of a right-angle triangle. In ordinary life many data are precisely that: givens; these are the data of memory, perception, and hearsay. They are not necessarily sought after, and they are usually (though often wrongly) taken to be true. Moreover, in ordinary language 'datum' and 'fact' are often used interchangeably. This usage is incorrect, for data are propositions, not facts. Hence data can be more or less true and, if less than true, are corrigible, whereas facts can be real or imaginary, pleasant or painful, and so on, but neither true nor false.

In factual science all data are *empirical:* they are outcomes of observations, measurements, or experiments on such concrete things as persons or social systems. Consequently they are produced, rather than either given or collected. They are sought and scrutinized: they are a result of research and possibly objects of further investigation. Hence they are subject to error and may be questioned a soon as they are obtained. Just think of the difficulty in obtaining reliable data on the underground economy, the connivance of politicians with big business, the efficiency of social programs, or even such trivial economic variables as actual (as distinct from reported) costs and benefits, particularly in the service sectors. (See Morgenstern 1963 for the specious accuracy of most economic data.)

A major reason for such difficulty is of course that macrosocial facts are not directly observable: they must be accessed via indicators which are not always reliable. (E.g., unemployment figures are aggregations of the partial figures supplied by labor exchanges, which do not include the many unemployed who have stopped looking for work.) Still, in principle, it is possible to refine social data, though in fact some of them are getting more elusive (see Griliches 1994). After all, nuclear and atomic events are far less directly observable than social facts, yet nuclear and atomic physics are way ahead of social science.

Empirical data can be either objective or subjective. The objective kind provide information about the world external to the observer, whereas subjective data provide information about a subject's feelings, perceptions, desires, intentions, and the like. For example, "So-and-so is unemployed" is an objective (though perhaps false) datum, whereas "I feel useless" is a subjective one. Subjective data are inadmissible in the natural sciences, whereas they are admissible—indeed, indispensable—in psychology and social science. For example, we need to know not only whether a given government is honest but also whether it is popularly "perceived" as such. We also need to know whether such "perception" is correct—that is, whether the subjective datum is true. And this calls for further empirical investigation—for example, using a thermometer in the case of the person who says he feels cold and checking on the expenditures of officials under suspicion. All this sounds obvious, but it is sometimes disputed. For example, positivists—in particular behaviorists—reject all subjective data. On the other hand, idealists, such as Hayek (1955) and Leach (*apud* Spaulding 1988, 266), have claimed that all data in social science are subjective. Consequently the former have no access to the subjective sources of deliberate action, whereas the latter stand no chance of conducting scientific research.

Whether objective or subjective, empirical data can be primary or derivative, according as they are obtained at the source or are the result of mathematical (e.g., statistical) processing, as is the case with aggregate data and statistical parameters. For example, the total amount of grain sold by one nation to another over a certain period is a secondary datum obtained by adding up ("aggregating") the sales of the various exporters, whereas the prices of grain per ton are primary data. An information processor will transform these data into the volume of the transaction, a third item of knowledge useful to both parties. If the production, transportation, and transaction costs are added, a seventh useful piece of information can be obtained: namely, the benefit. This set of seven propositions is the minimum needed to be able to claim that one has an adequate knowledge of the grain transaction in question. Five of them are data, and the other two are deduced with the help of two definitions. Counting the latter, our set consists of nine propositions. If the data are processed with the help of a theory cast in mathematical language, the total number of propositions involved may rise to hundreds, and most of them will contain concepts lacking an observational counterpart.

Social scientists get their primary data in a number of ways, such as case studies, questionnaires, surveys, opinion polls, balance sheets, censuses, and media reports. While some of these are micro-data—that is, data concerning individuals or very small social systems—others are macro-data—that is, they are about large social systems. Some macro-data, such as averages and variances, are the results of processing micro-data. Others—namely, some of those concerning the state or change of state of macrosocial systems—are irreducible to micro-data (e.g., "The European Economic Community was born in 1958" and "Economic recessions are becoming increasingly frequent").

Case studies have fallen into disfavor by comparison with statistical studies: they have been discredited for being idiosyncratic and for not being generalizable. However, case studies are an indispensable complement to statistical studies when the latter are hard to come by or when we wish to explain mass behavior in terms of individual characteristics. For example, no statistics on the underground economy can be accurate precisely because of the illegal nature of that economy. Moreover, if we want to explain why the informal sector of the economy has not decreased even during periods of industrial growth, we must interview some of the individuals involved in that sector. Incidentally, one result of such a study is that people who start their own informal (perhaps clandestine) businesses expect to increase their earnings or have grown tired of being told what to do or wish to climb up a rung on the social ladder (Portes and Sassen-Koob 1987).

A second example is this: Statistics show clearly that welfare recipients are likely to be recidivists, and that the more frequently they apply for welfare, the more likely they are to become permanently unemployed. Conservatives use such data to "prove" that workers are naturally lazy and prone to abusing social programs, and so they propose eliminating the latter. Liberals use the same data to "prove" that the unemployed have no opportunity to acquire the new skills demanded by an increasingly sophisticated industry, and so they propose retraining programs. Both explanations and corresponding proposals are consistent with the statistics in question. Only a large number of case studies could explain the given fact. And only experiments involving groups of people (both employed and unemployed) enrolled in retraining programs, as well as corresponding control groups (without retraining), could estimate the efficiency of such programs.

Case studies involve direct observation, questioning, or both. The methodologist will alert us to the pitfalls in each. For example, at first blush the simplest questions to answer are autobiographical—for example, How many jobs have you held over the past ten years, and, Why did you change each time? However, it is common experience that we often have trouble answering such questions. The unreliability of memory casts doubts on all research techniques involving questioning (Bradburn et al. 1987). However, this does not entail that questioning should be abandoned altogether. It merely suggests that the data obtained by these techniques should be checked by alternative techniques.

In addition to primary, or direct, data there are secondary data derived from the former by statistical or other techniques. When data come massively, they may—indeed, must—be subject to computer-assisted statistical analysis in order to find percentages, averages, modes, deviations from the averages, correlation coefficients, and other statistical parameters that characterize a population as a whole. In the advanced sciences, theory determines which are the relevant statistical parameters: they are those that the theory can help us calculate (e.g., in quantum mechanics one typically calculates probabilities of states and events, as well as averages and variances of physical properties). In the less advanced sciences, statistics are usually independent of theory, often for lack of it. Consequently, there is an accumulation of statistical data that have no theoretical counterparts and thus remain unexplained and gather dust.

The way data are displayed is important for their understanding. For example, graphs are more suggestive than tables. However, graphs can be manipulated to mask or enhance certain facts. For example, a logarithmic graph is convenient for curve fitting, but it flattens everything. In particular, it represents multiplication as addition, and exponential growth as linear: it dulls both pain and gain. Therefore, once the curve-fitting task has been accomplished, it is advisable to return to the original variables.

Scientists in the less developed fields of inquiry spend most of their time and energy in what is often called "fact-finding"—that is, gathering or producing data. This task is certainly indispensable, but it should be regarded as a means rather than an end, for facts do not "speak" for themselves. Indeed, in science, data are useful only as inputs to some brain capable of supplying understanding. Besides, as Darwin noted, interesting data can only be collected in the light of interesting hypotheses. And their collection involves methodological sophistication and careful planning (see, e.g., Rossi 1988). Moreover, in this age of massive information processing, it may be pertinent to remember that relevance and reliability are more important than volume and speed.

Data are valued differently by different philosophies of science. *Apriorists,* especially idealists, believe that theories are omnipotent, whereas data are either useless or derivable from theories alone. In particular, apriorists do not cherish unfavorable data. (Recall Hegel's reaction to someone's observation that a theory of his was contradicted by the facts: "So much the worse for the facts.") They would welcome the closing of all laboratories, observatories, and census bureaus. Obviously, apriorists are mistaken. They would have been spared their mistake had they bothered to analyze scientific theories, for all such theories include parameters and constants, such as initial populations or unemployment rates, that must be determined empirically because no theory could possibly calculate them. After all, we do not construct the world.

At the other extreme are data-worshipers, or *naïve empiricists,* who collect and process raw data indiscriminately. Their task has been considerably facilitated by the electronic computer, which is capable of handling masses of data unimaginable to any classical social scientist. Regrettably, this marvelous tool is sometimes thought to spare original thought—in particular, theorizing. But, obviously, sheer volume of data is no substitute for data relevant to hypotheses capable of explaining the facts referred to by the data. True, data can suggest hypotheses, but there is no guarantee that these will be interesting, for some of the most powerful concepts—for example, those of scarcity, ideology, law, and nation—have no perceptual counterparts. On the other hand, interesting hypotheses can suggest the kind of data one should seek. For example, only rates of change in criminality and in the number of bankruptcies, rather than absolute numbers, are indicators of recession or prosperity.

A related view, and the most popular of all, is *inductivism,* a component of empiricism. On this view, data are valuable in themselves, as well as means for generating and evaluating hypotheses and theories. But this is mistaken on several counts. First, direct observation is only skin-deep, because most things and processes are either too small, too large, or too hidden to be detected by the senses. This feature of the world forces us to invent ideas referring to unobservables, such as individual propensities and intentions and social structures and trends. Unlike empirical generalizations, theoretical hypotheses contain predicates denoting unobservable things or properties (see chap. 1 sec. 7). Hence data are not enough to suggest high-level (or deep) hypotheses. For example, decades of econometric analysis have failed to deliver a single economic law.

Second, as noted earlier, observation does not start from scratch but is triggered by some problem and guided by some hypotheses. The latter are often of the programmatic type; that is, they are guesses as to which variables may be relevant and hence worth watching, and some such variables are bound to be inaccessible to direct observation. In short, induction is necessary, particularly in exploring new territory or confronting hypotheses and evidence. But it is never sufficient, for it merely summarizes experience: it is shallow and provides no understanding, much less forecasting power. Thus ancient man knew that water flows downhill and that the sun "rises" every morning, but he did not know why; nor could he have any assurances that one day water might not flow upstream or the sun fail to "rise." Only seventeenth-century physics gave the correct answers, by turning those pieces of inductive knowledge into conclusions derived from Newton's laws of motion and gravity. By the same token, it transformed the uncertain knowledge garnered by observation into the far more certain knowledge included in a formally exact theory supported by an uncounted number of measurements and capable of explaining and predicting. From then on, inductivism became suspect even to scholars who, like Whewell (1847) and Peirce (1958 [ca. 1902]), paid lip service to it.

The sensational success of modern theoretical physics inspired *deductivism*. This is the view that power lies in deduction, not induction: that there is no science except in hypothetico-deductive systems (i.e., theories). An extreme version of deductivism is *refutationism*, according to which the only function of data is to refute hypotheses and theories (e.g., Popper 1959 [1935]). On this view, data play no role in experimental design or in the control of further data. This is mistaken on several counts. First, scientists are interested in positive evidence, or confirmation, as well as in refutation: they wish to know what, if any, empirical support their ideas have, because they are searching for maximally true propositions. Second, the design of any ingenious empirical operation is done in the light of hypotheses or even theories. These auxiliary ideas are taken to be true—not just refutable in principle—in the given context (e.g., the design of any reliable opinion poll requires a statistical theory of random sampling). Third, a well-tried theory may suggest rejecting certain data as implausible.

I submit that actual scientific practice conforms neither to inductivism nor to deductivism: instead, it takes a middle way, using induction to build low-level generalization and evaluate the matching of hypotheses to facts and deduction to derive particulars from generalities and further particulars (Bunge 1960, 1967*b*). Moreover, scientific research adopts scientific realism, according to which data–theory relations are multiple and reciprocal. In fact, (1) data may suggest (never generate by themselves) low-level generalizations—that is, generalizations containing only predicates occurring in the data base; (2) data "activate" theories by supplying them with the information required to carry out the deductive operations involved in the explanation or prediction of facts according to the schema Generalization(s) & Circumstance(s) ⇒ Proposition(s) representing the fact(s) to be accounted for; (3) data may confirm or infirm hypotheses and theories, provided these are testable to begin with, as well as enriched with additional data; (4) theories help evaluate data—in particular, they suggest throwing away outlying figures; and (5) theories help in the design of empirical operations, as well as artifacts and plans of action.

Sometimes data are scarce; at other times they are plentiful. In the former case, the researcher endeavors to produce additional data; in the latter, he must select data. In both cases he needs the guidance of hypotheses suggesting the kind of data to be sought or discarded. Some of these hypotheses may be so general as to deserve being classed as philosophical. For example, a materialist anthropologist will never get enough data concerning reproduction and production, whereas his idealist colleague will never have enough information concerning myth and speech.

Finally, a point of terminology. Just as we distinguished datum from fact, so we must distinguish datum from evidence. An *evidence* is a datum relevant to some proposition: there is no such thing as evidence in itself. Moreover, evidence may be weak or strong. Thus, whereas circumstantial evidence is nearly always weak, experimental evidence can be strong, depending, of course, on the experimental design and execution, as well as the accompanying inferences. If weak, evidence will be inconclusive. If strong, it will be positive (favorable) or negative (unfavorable); only exceptionally will it be conclusive.

4 Hypothesis

In social studies data are plentiful (though often insufficient), but new ideas are scarce, and ideas matching the relevant data are even scarcer. This is partly due to a philosophical bias against hypothesis. Indeed, it is commonly believed that every piece of scientific knowledge is either a datum (given) or a generalization from data—that is, an inductive synthesis. This view, inductivism, is the core of empiricism, which is usually, albeit mistakenly, opposed to rationalism. This opposition is mistaken because collecting, classifying, processing, and interpreting data are conceptual, hence rational, operations, even when computer-assisted.

Inductivism has some empirical support. Indeed, we all learn from examples—that is, from data about particular facts. For example, a normal infant learns language from exposure to snippets of speech. In particular, he learns or makes up grammatical rules from hearing such examples long before he is taught grammar at school. But if Chomsky is right, what the child accomplishes by learning or inventing such rules is the formation of certain hypotheses about linguistic usage. Moreover, he soon learns that there are counter-examples to some of his hypotheses, particularly if the language in question is as unruly as English. And as he grows up, the child learns to make conjectures other than inductive generalizations—for example, that his parents have certain expectations of him.

Data do not "speak for themselves": unless placed in a body of knowledge and suitably "interpreted," they tell us nothing. For example, a smile indicates nothing in itself; but it "means" something to me if I conjecture that the smiling person has a friendly attitude toward me or wishes to win my goodwill or is experiencing a pleasant feeling. In general, the "interpretation" of a set of data is nothing but the adoption of some hypothesis covering them. In other words, data "make sense" only when shown to be instances of a generalization or when explained by being derived from a generalization in conjunction with further data. For example, the news that there have been riots and looting in X "makes sense" (or is explained) if we know that a large fraction of the population of X is very poor and that the government of X has terminated all the food subsidies. The generalization in question is "People revolt when threatened by hunger." Obviously this is a hypothesis and, as such, fallible. In fact, extreme poverty may induce apathy.

Human knowledge is largely, though not totally, conjectural and therefore fallible. Thus, we conjecture other people's feelings, attitudes, and intentions on the basis of their overt behavior. (But, of course, our conjectures are often disproved.) Before crossing the street, we assume that the cars we see coming are not moving fast enough to hit us. (But sometimes we miscalculate.) When studying a demographic trend, we assume that it will persist for some years to come. (But an economic recession, a plague, or a war may break the trend.) When studying a social system, we assume that it is held together by some bonds. (But we may find that these bonds are being weakened by internal conflicts.) And while reviewing the historical documents used by some competent historian, we assume that they are genuine and relevant to our problem. (But they may turn out to be forgeries or to contain falsities or to focus on unimportant details.) In short, human life, particularly the life of a scientist, would hardly be possible without hypothesizing.

The central role of hypotheses is well known in theoretical natural science, and it has been stressed by a number of philosopher-scientists (e.g., Herschel 1830; Whewell 1847; Peirce 1958 [ca. 1902]; Poincaré 1903; Duhem 1914) and popularized by some philosophers (e.g., Popper 1959 [1935]). However, that role is often overlooked in the social sciences. The underrating of hypotheses is largely to be blamed on the empiricist (or positivist) philosophy that still dominates teaching. The empiricist dogma is, of course, that only data matter, experience being the sole source of knowledge. If this were true, then all speculation would be wrong, mathematics would be a kind of shorthand (as Mach thought), and we should try to maximize information rather than under-standing.

The mistrust of hypotheses is such that they often go under the misnomers of 'inference' (in particular, 'conclusion') and 'interpretation.' For example, paleobiologists, prehistorians, and archaeologists are wont to say that they "infer" the behavior and ideas of our remote ancestors from the artifacts and bones found in diggings—as if there were a logic leading from data to conjectures. And anthropologists, sociologists, and politologists (political scientists) influenced by hermeneutic philosophers are likely to say that they "interpret," or "read," human behavior or its traces as if they were texts. The incorrect use of the words *inference* and *conclusion* is often prompted by the empiricist (in particular, positivist) tenet that scientists are only to collect, classify, and summarize data. As for the incorrect use of the word *interpretation*, it is prompted by the idealist tenets that the social is wholly spiritual and the understanding of social facts more intuitive than rational, as well as more subjective than objective, and in any case totally different from the study of nature.

Actually the two cases referred to above are cases of hypothesizing or conjecturing human behavior. Indeed, from a set of data next to nothing can be validly inferred or deduced. (The datum that a given individual is a P implies only that some individuals possess property P. And the datum that all the individuals observed in a sample of a population are P's suggests, but does not prove, that all members of the population are P's.) The archaeologist who ponders the possible origin or use of an ancient artifact does not go from one set of propositions to another in accordance with rules of inference: he guesses—no more, no less. But, far from relying on his intuition, he checks his guess by making a replica of the artifact and putting it to use and in context.

As for the "interpretation" of human behavior, strictly speaking, only artificial signs (i.e., symbols) can be interpreted, and then only provided we know or at least can guess the code or interpretation rule in question. What we actually do when we attribute to someone an intention or some other mental process, on the strength of our experience and our spotty observation of his overt behavior, is to make a guess—that is, a hypothesis. In any case, the hypothesis in question is likely to be challenged. And if found testable and worth checking, sooner or later it will be put to the test by means of further observations and, if possible, in the light of some theory as well. Moreover, if valuable, it deserves to be embedded in a theory, as either a postulate or a theorem. (More on this in chap. 4.)

Another fashionable mistake propagated by the hermeneutic school is that in social studies we should favor analogy or metaphor over hypothesis. This view attracts those who do not care for objective truth, and it spares them the toil of inventing theories and checking them for truth. This view is wrong, because although metaphors can be fruitful, as well as misleading, they can never be true or false. This is why only art and pop philosophy speak in metaphors: the search for truth involves literal discourse. Nor is that view novel. Thus, from time immemorial, society has been regarded as an organism. This metaphor can discharge an ideological function, as it did in La Fontaine's fable about the king being the head of the organism and the commoners its limbs. A more recent instance is the natural selection–social selection analogy, used to justify the elimination of the economically weaker.

Organismic metaphors constitute a root of functionalism in anthropology and sociology. One of its recent offshoots is Luhmann's (1984) view of social systems as "autopoietic" (self-organizing), "self-referential" (endowed with feedback loops), and autonomous, or impervious to external stimuli. (The expression 'self-referential' is borrowed from semantics, where it designates propositions such as "This proposition is false.") Everything specifically socio-logical is lost in this metaphorical text. So is the whole point of designing (or redesigning) and organizing (or reorganizing) defective formal social systems. And conservative ideologies are reinforced, because there is no point in plan-ning, or interfering with, what is allegedly autonomous and runs best by itself.

Still another analogy that has become rather fashionable in social studies is that between society and a closed system obeying the first two laws of thermo-dynamics. This analogy is incorrect, and therefore barren or misleading, for the following reasons. First, the only thermodynamic variable utilizable in social science is energy: the remaining variables, particularly pressure, temperature, and entropy, have no sociological analogs. (One might think that the degree of social order or equilibrium is parallel to entropy; but this analogy does not work, for whereas a thermodynamic system reaches equilibrium when it attains maximum entropy, social disorder is a kind of disequilibrium.) Second, soci-eties are open systems: they interact with nature and among themselves. (Inci-dentally, Comte, Walras, and Pareto favored mechanical analogies and were immoderately partial to static equilibrium. This obsession, and the concomi-tant disregard for change, is still evident in current mainstream economic theory and is one of the reasons why it does not account for reality, which is changeable: see Bunge forthcoming.)

However, the most popular analogies in recent social studies are those be-tween social systems or processes and the market. Thus, one hears about the marriage, crime, educational, political, and even spirituality markets (see, e.g., Becker 1976 and the journal *Rationality and Society*). At first blush this sounds plausible, given that commodification is characteristic of capitalist society. But the analogy is misleading, and so is the research strategy it suggests. Indeed, it shifts the student's attention from society to the market, which is only a subsystem of society. Consequently it impoverishes social science. Second, it reinforces one of the negative aspects of methodological individualism: namely, its view of man as driven only by material interests. Therefore the market approach to noneconomic activities is incapable of accounting for their nonutilitarian features. Third, it invites all social scientists to imitate economists, as if the latter had succeeded in constructing true models of markets proper. (More on "economic imperialism" in Swedberg 1990 and Bunge forthcoming.)

The main function of analogy in science is to form natural classes, or kinds, of things or events (see chap. 2, sec. 5). Occasionally analogies suggest hypotheses, but they cannot replace them, because they are neither true nor false. Moreover, analogies can harm by diverting attention from theory building (as in regarding brains and societies as mere information-processors and viewing the economy, the polity, and the culture as so many intertwining branches of a tree). Hence the postmodern infatuation with metaphor, though justified with reference to literature, is inexcusable with reference to science.

5 Truth

In the postmodern subculture truth is out, and metaphor, myth, convention, consensus, power, and negotiation are in. No matter. We all look for truth in everyday life, because we are curious and wish to survive. And, of course, those who engage in serious research, whether scientific, technological, or humanistic, search for truth or, rather, truths, however partial, and challenge the consensus every time they come up with original truths. (See Rescher 1993 on the consensus cult.) This is what research is all about. That not all truths are full and exact, therefore final, is beside the point, for much research attempts at improving on known partial truths.

If truth were unattainable, communication would be pointless, for every message conveys, presupposes, or elicits some truth (or falsity). This holds not only for any piece of information but for noninformative communication too. For instance, a cry for help presupposes that someone is in distress. A question presupposes that the interlocutor may supply or help find a true answer to it. A proposal presupposes the possible truth of the proposition that the proposed action is feasible and desirable. A promise (or threat) to do *A* elicits in the intended recipient the hope (or fear) that the proposition "*A* will be done" will come true. And whoever states in good faith that truth is a mirage believes this proposition to be true, whence he contradicts himself. In short, the notion of truth is indispensable in all walks of life, even in some subhuman life. Hence both the denial of the possibility of truth—that is, radical skepticism—and the assertion that all truth is mere convention are at best academic games, at worst invitations to live by myth.

Truth in general is studied in semantics and epistemology. The very first truth we should learn about the word *truth* is that it designates at least two very distinct concepts: those of artistic and scientific truth. An example of the former is "Othello was wrong in suspecting Desdemona." However, this is not the place to examine art; we shall be concerned only with scientific truth. There are two radically different kinds of scientific truth: formal and factual, concerning pure ideas and concerning facts, respectively. The abode of the former is mathematics, whereas that of the latter is factual knowledge—ordinary, scientific, technological, or humanistic knowledge. This distinction, first drawn explicitly and forcefully by Leibniz (1981 [1703]), is often denied. Let us see why we should keep it.

Formal truth-values are assigned to propositions lacking any real reference, such as "If $a = b$, then $b = a$" and "$1 > 0$." This is why formal truth-values are assigned and checked by purely conceptual means: deduction (in particular, computation) and finding an exception. By contrast, *factual* truth-values are assigned to propositions referring to possible or actual concrete things. This is why factual truth-values are checked by means of empirical operations. Hence, whereas mathematics is self-sufficient, factual science and technology depend on the world, as well as on reason. Thus, no mathematical theorem is threatened by political upheavals, whereas some of the true statements made about the USSR prior to its dissolution in 1991 are no longer true or even relevant. Only mathematical formulas interpreted in factual terms are sensitive to empirical data.

Since we are centrally interested in social science, which is factual, we shall focus on the concept of factual truth. I adopt the so-called correspondence (or realist) theory of factual truth. According to this theory, a proposition is factually true if it "fits," or "matches," the facts it refers to—that is, if it "corresponds" to its referent(s). Admittedly, this is a vague idea. A more precise definition is the following: *A proposition asserting that fact f is the case is true if and only if f is really (actually, in fact) the case.* For example, a proposition asserting that there are stateless societies is true if and only if, in fact (really, actually), there are stateless societies. An example of a truth about a falsity: The proposition asserting that every society has a collective memory is false if and only if, in fact there is at least one society without a collective memory. Note that the above definition involves three distinct items: a fact f, a proposition p about f, and a (meta)proposition Tp asserting that p is true. (More on truth in Bunge 1974d, 1983b.)

The previous definition of factual truth serves only in cases of ordinary knowledge and simple scientific data. High-level hypotheses—that is, conjectures containing concepts lacking perceptual counterparts—can be contrasted with facts only in an indirect manner, via the relevant data. For example, we do not check the "law" of decreasing returns against business firms but against data concerning the inputs and outputs of such firms. That is, we compare ideas with one another, just as in mathematics. The differences are that, in the case of factual science, both the data and the hypotheses refer to facts, and that the data are obtained by studying facts. However, in the case of factual hypotheses, as well as in that of data, truth, a semantic property of propositions, is made to depend ultimately upon reality, and falsity upon unreality. What there is determines what is true or false. The scientist or technologist proposes: reality disposes.

Ordinary knowledge is replete with full but trivial truths (and falsities). By contrast, complete truths are not easy to come by in factual science or technology. In these fields, more often than not, we must settle for *partial* or *approximate* truths. For example, we cannot know exactly the GDP of any nation, but we can get a fairly good estimate of it. Sometimes we can estimate the probable error, or deviation from the truth, inherent in a run of observations. (This holds particularly for accidental errors.) But most of the time the error is just as unknown as the complete truth we are after. This is the bad news.

The good news is that it is usually possible to detect errors of observation and decrease them by improving on the design or execution of our observations. What holds for data holds, mutatis mutandis, for hypotheses and theories: if found to be in error, we can form and try out alternatives. Moreover, if a scientific theory contains a mathematical formalism involving numerical functions, we can use approximation theory to calculate ever better solutions. A realistic methodology is thus a blend of fallibilism and meliorism.

In science, whether mathematical or factual, the concept of *convergence to the truth* is used. (In mathematics there are even methods of successive approximation to the correct solution, such as Archimedes' "method of exhaustion" for computing the area of a circle.) Moreover, it is an article of scientific faith that some research findings converge, on the whole, to total or nearly total truths. Since there may be temporary setbacks, the convergence in question is not uniform. Furthermore, a process of successive approximation may be discontinued for lack of interest: one may turn to entirely different problems—for example, because the original referents have disappeared.

The sciences and technologies teem with approximate truths and keep finding truer data, hypotheses, and theories. Yet, among philosophers there are radical skeptics, relativists, constructivists, conventionalists, fictionists, pragmatists, and others who deny the possibility of finding any truths of fact. Let us take a quick look at these no-truth epistemologies, which are akin to cultural (in particular, moral) relativism, according to which there are no cross-cultural values or norms.

Radical skepticism, or epistemological nihilism, is the dual of fundamentalism: it denies the possibility of finding any factual truths. This variety of skepticism is to be distinguished from *methodological skepticism*, which is simply the idea that we ought to check ideas before adopting them. Radical skepticism, perhaps justified in antiquity, when so little was known, can now be seen to be false, as shown by the substantial body of knowledge about nature and society. To be sure, this knowledge is only approximately true and seldom definitive. But it is far from being a pile of opinions. (See Bunge 1991*d* for the differences between the two kinds of skepticism: moderate, or methodological, and radical, or systematic.)

Epistemological constructivism-relativism holds that there are no objective truths, hence no objective truth criteria or standards. For any set of facts, there are multiple truths, every one of which is a construction, rather than a representation, of a piece of the world. Moreover, none is superior to any other: "Anything goes" (Feyerabend 1975). In particular, science, on this view, is not superior to myth, ideology, or pseudoscience. In fact, there is no distinction between science and nonscience, hence no point in trying to establish demarcation criteria between them. This quaint opinion cannot explain why some people undergo long scientific apprenticeships or why they invest so much ingenuity, time, and money in doing research or why those who discover new important truths are usually rewarded by their peers.

Constructivism-relativism comes in two varieties: individualist and collectivist. *Individualist constructivism-relativism*, or subjectivism for short, rejects the subject–object distinction, hence the realist hypothesis that every knowing subject is surrounded by an autonomous world that preexists him and which he may attempt to describe and understand. In particular, the feminist theorist Fox Keller (1985) claims—without offering any evidence—that the subject–object distinction is just a male, sexist bias. Subjectivists hold also that truth, like beauty, is in the eye of the beholder: There is your truth, and here is mine, and never the two shall twine. An obvious objection to subjectivism is that it enthrones mere opinion, whereas scientists distrust opinion and reach for propositions whose truth-value they determine by means of empirical and conceptual operations that can be evaluated (hence either corroborated or challenged) by their peers.

The second variant is *collectivist constructivism-relativism*. This is the currently fashionable view that truth is a social construction or convention, so that every social group has its own set of truths. Truth is then coextensive with consensus: agreement makes truth, rather than truth inviting agreement. Thus, on any subject there are feminine versus masculine truths, worker versus capitalist, black versus white, Aryan versus Jewish, Eastern versus Western truths, and so on. All such truths have the same rank, so there is no point in attempting to identify the truest of all, because there are no universal standards of reason or empirical evidence.

Constructivism-relativism is at variance with the ideal of universality, which scientists and technologists adopt throughout the world. It is also at variance with the common experience that competent scientists are often able to either independently replicate or challenge observations or calculations originally made by colleagues of a different sex, ethnic group, social class, or country. Moreover, when they fail to obtain similar results, they usually compare them in the light of the same basic ideas and evaluate them with the help of the same standards. What *is* true is that science is more advanced in some regions or groups than others. It is also true that sometimes ideology colors scientific research. But this coloring can be detected with the help of the most general, therefore least committed, of all tools: logic.

Fictionism holds that truth is unattainable, but that this does not matter as long as we can act on the assumption that things look *as if* they were such and such. In other words, the entire body of human knowledge, or at least all knowledge about human affairs, is a set of fictions. A major root of fictionism is phenomenalism, the view that we have access only to phenomena or appearances, never to real things or things in themselves (recall chap. 1, sec. 7). In other words, everything has the appearance of a sealed unit, or black box, the innards of which will escape us forever. I submit that phenomenalism and, with it, fictionism were first refuted by modern astronomy, when it rejected the geocentric view of the planetary system in favor of the heliocentric one. Further nails were later hammered into the coffin of phenomenalism and fictionism by mechanics, chemistry, electrodynamics, atomic and nuclear physics, genetics, physiological psychology, and the social sciences, all of which posit trans-phenomenal things and sometimes even manipulate them via indicators (see chap. 6, sec. 2).

Finally, *pragmatism,* the philosophy centered on action, asserts that only efficiency matters: that we call 'true' whatever helps survival and success. This opinion, shared by Nietzsche and James, is untenable in everyday life, where one is forced to distinguish between profitable lies and useless truisms. Pragmatism is even less suited to scientific research, the ultimate goal of which is to find or perfect truths. And it is equally inadequate for technology, which consumes scientific truths galore in designing useful artifacts.

The main varieties of anti-realism will be analyzed more thoroughly in chapter 13. For the moment, let us note only that those who uphold them (*a*) contradict themselves when claiming that their no-truth views are true; (*b*) overlook the successes of scientists in piercing the veil of appearance and those of technologists in using scientific truths; and (*c*) do not contribute to the exploration of the world in the interests of establishing ever truer representations of it, for, if truth is unattainable, there is no point in pursuing it. Thus radical skepticism, no less than dogmatism, paralyzes research. Only meth-odological skepticism aids the search for truth. This is part of scientific realism, of which more in chapter 13, section 8. Let us now turn to a constructive task.

What is to be done if an exception (counterexample) to an accepted hypothesis appears? When encountering such an anomaly, our reaction to it will depend critically upon the track record of the hypothesis in question, as well as on the company it keeps. If the track record is not outstanding and the hypothesis is not supported by further generalizations, we should have no qualms about jettisoning it—though, if it is interesting, we might want to keep it in the back of our minds. If, on the other hand, the track record of the hypothesis under suspicion is outstanding and, moreover, it fits with other well-corroborated conjectures, we should attempt to explain the anomaly away by framing an ad hoc hypothesis accounting for the discrepancy, and we should be prepared to have the rescuer checked independently.

A protecting ad hoc hypothesis is scientifically respectable only if it is independently testable—as when we conjecture that the observed anomaly is an "artifact" stemming from a faulty observation or calculation, an unreliable source, or an exogenous shock that can be ascertained objectively and which in fact explains the discrepancy. In this case, when the protecting hypothesis is testable independently, we will say that it is a *bona fide* ad hoc hypothesis. On the other hand, a hypothesis that is not testable independently and is introduced with the sole purpose of saving the generalization in question from refutation is called a *mala fide* ad hoc hypothesis.

Two well-known cases of bona fide ad hoc hypotheses were those of the existence of capillaries (Harvey, 1628) and of the planet Neptune (Leverrier, 1846), both of which entities, though invisible to the naked eye, were discovered eventually. A clear example of a mala fide ad hoc hypothesis is the claim that altruism is really selfish, since it gives pleasure. This is sophism; its only function is to protect the principle of utility, according to which we all act so as to maximize our expected utilities. Another instance of a mala fide ad hoc hypothesis is Freud's repression hypothesis, whose only function is to protect the Oedipus complex hypothesis and similar hypotheses concerning hidden sexuality. (If you are male and happen to love your father, this only proves that you have strongly repressed your hatred for him. If your last dream did not have a sexual content, or if you have no recollection of your father having abused you sexually during childhood, this only proves the efficiency of your superego in repressing your shameful memories.) But the coffee break is over.

6 Criticism

It is only natural to try to confirm our beliefs. Only masochists would wish otherwise. However, intellectual honesty, which includes concern for truth, dictates that this natural impulse be checked by criticism. Whereas dogma is of the essence of ideology, in science and technology almost anything can be the subject of criticism: data, hypotheses, inferences, theories, techniques, tools, valuations, the choice of problems, and entire approaches. (Not everything is doubtful: there are robust findings, such as that all atoms contain protons, that metabolism is necessary for life, and that societies are in a state of flux.) This is so because error can creep in anywhere, and we want our propositions to be maximally true and our techniques and tools maximally suited to the quest for truth or efficiency. We also want comprehensiveness and depth.

Nor are ideas the only possible objects of criticism. All concrete artifacts, especially organizations and social processes, are bound to be or become defective, in need of repair or replacement in the interests of efficiency or fairness or both. This is why freedom to criticize is just as essential in social matters as in science, technology, and the humanities. Indeed, criticism is part of every deliberate correction mechanism, for only if we detect a flaw can we make an effort to understand and repair it.

However, responsible criticism, whether social, technological, or scientific, is rational and rests on the best available knowledge. In particular, responsible social criticism rests on social science. But one cannot criticize everything at once. Indeed, to subject any idea to critical examination is, by definition, to try to find fault by taking temporarily for granted some body of knowledge. This is why we can criticize only one item at a time. Consequently, even the most profound innovations in science, technology, and the humanities are bound to be only partial. Much the same holds for social reforms and even revolutions: none of them can be total, for the simple reason that they must use existing resources, and, by definition, ingrained habits do not change overnight.

A construct may be criticized for having any or all of the following flaws: it is *irrelevant* to the matter at hand; it has some *intrinsic* fault, such as vagueness or failure to be well formed in the case of formulas, circularity in that of definitions, and inconsistency in that of theories; or some *intrasystemic* defect, as when an alleged consequence of some premises does not actually follow from them; or *extra-systemic* fault, such as incompatibility with either the bulk of background knowledge or the available empirical data.

The last-mentioned kind of flaw deserves comment. A theory that contradicts the bulk of well-confirmed knowledge hardly deserves attention, because one of the indicators of truth is precisely compatibility with the background knowledge. As for data, those that do not fit the relevant standard theory are said to be anomalous. According to empiricism, data are more reliable than theories, so that any anomaly indicts the relevant theory. This strategy is certainly reasonable in the case of new theories on probation with respect to "hard" data. But it is not reasonable in the case of new data challenging theories that have rendered distinguished service. There it pays to check the anomaly, for it may be that it originated in flawed observation or calculation.

If a scientific observation, hypothesis, or technique is criticized, the criticism is likely to be met with either argument or new data. By contrast, criticisms of ideologies, as well as of parapsychology, psychoanalysis, and other pseudo-sciences, are most frequently ignored or countered with personal attacks. Consequently they do not make many converts: they merely alert people who have not yet been captured by such belief systems. Criticism can alter belief only when explicitly recognized as a tool for finding the truth. When regarded as a manifestation of hostility, ideological betrayal, rebellion against the "father figure," or a hang-up left over from pre-postmodern thought, criticism may reinforce belief, just as the failure of prophecy reinforces the faith of the religious zealot (see Festinger et al. 1956).

Criticism is essential, but insufficient, for any rational endeavor. Creativity is even more important, for, without it, the critic would have nothing to bite on. One form of creativity is constructive criticism: that is, proposing ways to repair or replace an item that has been found defective. Constructive criticism is less frequent than destructive criticism, however, not only because it is harder, but also because it calls for fairness and friendliness, qualities that get lost when the race for power replaces the quest for truth.

Destructive criticism can be either rational or irrational. The rational kind consists in exhibiting inconsistency, irrelevance, or incompatibility with either empirical findings or sound theory. It offers no alternative, but it clears the pathway. As for irrational destructive criticism, it comes in several sorts. One of them is plain rejection, without offering any reasons. A second is name calling, as in "crass materialist." A third is rejection on the grounds of slanderous imputation of servility to the powers that be. This variety of irrational destructive criticism, sometimes called 'debunking,' is typical of Foucault, the originator of the phrase "another power, another knowledge." It also occurs in the works of some of the constructivist-relativist sociologists of science and some so-called feminist and environmentalist philosophers, who see dark powers beneath such subjects as logic and mechanics, which everyone else regards as politically neutral. But, being irrationalists, they do not bother with evidence. Finally, there is what Derrida and other self-styled postmodern literary critics have called 'deconstruction.' I will not comment on this operation, because in my view it defies intelligible description.

In short, irrational criticism is, by definition, groundless and therefore unjustified. By contrast, rational criticism is a necessary complement of the process of invention and discovery: it helps select and hone new ideas. This is why it is part of the scientific method.

7 Method

I have distinguished research problems from routine ones and suggested that research problems are to routine problems what voyages of discovery are to car trips, however hazardous. There are no known rules for discovering or inventing anything radically new: method and hard work are no substitutes for originality. Therefore the so-called logic of discovery, technique of theory construction, and creative computer program are so many mirages. The creativity involved in spotting interesting problems, hitting on novel solutions, or inventing new theories or procedures, can be trained or stunted, but it cannot be programmed, because the corresponding mental processes are not algorithmic. If they were, all problems would be routine problems, and no original research or new ideas would be needed. There can be no manual for the eccentric.

However, there are research strategies and tactics: this is what methodology is all about. This is what Bernard (1865 [1852]) and Durkheim (1988 [1895]) wrote about in their classics. (Caution: Methodology is the study of methods; substantive research uses methods, not methodologies.) Methods differ in generality. Thus, in principle, the experimental method can be used in all disciplines dealing with facts within our reach. Other methods, such as those of random sampling and successive approximation, are more special. Still others, such as those employed on archaeological sites or when designing social surveys and evaluating social programs, are even more specific.

The most general strategy for working on research problems in science, technology, or the humanities is the *scientific method*. This may be summarized as the following sequence of steps:

choice of a research field—survey of the background knowledge in that field—identification of a knowledge problem—precise formulation or reformulation of the problem—examination of the background knowledge in search of items that might help solve the problem—choice or invention of a tentative hypothesis that looks promising—conceptual test of the hypothesis, to see if it is compatible with the bulk of the existing knowledge on the matter (for it might be a wild conjecture not worth pursuing)—drawing some testable conclusions of the hypothesis (usually with the help of both subsidiary assumptions and data)—design of an empirical (observational or experimental) test of the hypothesis or some consequence of it—actual empirical test of the hypothesis: search for both favorable and unfavorable evidence (examples and counterexamples)—critical examination and, when necessary, statistical processing of the data (e.g., elimination of outlying data and calculation of average error)—evaluation of the hypothesis in the light of its compatibility with both the background knowledge and the fresh empirical evidence—then, if the test results are inconclusive, design and performance of new tests, possibly using different special methods—if the test results are conclusive, acceptance, modification, or rejection of the hypothesis—if the hypothesis is strongly confirmed, check as to whether its acceptance forces some change (enrichment or correction) in the background knowledge—identification and tackling of new problems raised by the confirmed hypothesis—repetition of the test and reexamination of its possible impact on existing knowledge (nil, gain, or loss in precision, qualitatively new results, etc.).

The case of the introduction and checking of new procedures is parallel, except that, here, reliability and accuracy, not truth, are at stake. So is the case of the introduction and tryout of new artifacts such as machines or organizations, except that, here, the checking is for efficiency or fairness.

In addition to methods, both general and special, there are some heuristic guidelines, such as: Start by reviewing the relevant literature, but do not allow yourself to be swamped by it; Place the item under consideration in its context or system; Distinguish the various aspects of the problem but do not separate them; Identify the premises and the unknowns; Look for similar solved problems; Analyze the key concepts and premises; Begin with simple ideas and methods and complicate them only as needed; Always reckon with the unforeseeable; and Revise the research plan as often as necessary (see Pólya 1957). Heuristic maxims, along with general and special methods, facilitate research but are no substitute for originality, audacity, industry, and honesty.

The main function of rules of method and heuristic maxims is to help search for truth. We distinguish three kinds of rules of method in the factual sciences: rules for finding facts, rules for assessing the truth-value of propositions (data and hypotheses) concerning facts, and meta-rules for evaluating the efficiency of such rules. Thus, the operating manual for the use of a measuring instrument contains rules of the first kind. Such rules are specific: they are tied to the particular design of the measuring instrument and the measured object concerned. Hence methodology has little to say about them.

Methodology deals with rules of the other two types. These involve the key concepts of truth and efficiency, which must be distinguished from the corresponding criteria. Indeed, a truth criterion is a rule for assessing the truth-value of propositions of some kind; so it presupposes the concept of truth-value. Likewise, an efficiency criterion is a rule for assessing the efficiency of a rule, procedure, or artifact; hence it presupposes the concept of efficiency. I will now list and sketch some of the most commonly used truth criteria for evaluating factual hypotheses and theories.

Well-formedness. The sentence(s) designating the proposition(s) in question should obey the rules of (linguistic or mathematical) syntax. If they contain magnitudes (numerical predicates), the equations and inequations should be dimensionally homogeneous.

Precision. Predicates should be as precise as necessary; that is, bad vagueness should be minimized, innocent vagueness tolerated.

Meaningfulness. The referent(s) and the sense of the proposition(s) should be explicitly identified with the help of further propositions, especially semantic assumptions (e.g., "K represents the carrying capacity of the territory").

Internal consistency. A theory should contain no obvious contradictions, and if such are discovered, they should be removed by recasting or dropping the assumptions generating them.

External consistency. The proposition(s) should be compatible with the bulk of the background knowledge.

Testability. The proposition(s) should be confirmable (by favorable cases) and, in most cases, refutable (by counterexamples) as well. (Exceptions to the refutability condition are any hypotheses protected by bona fide ad hoc hypotheses and the highest-level axioms of certain sophisticated physical theories, particularly the variational principles: see Bunge 1973*b*.)

Goodness of fit. A hypothesis directly checkable against empirical data should fit them reasonably well.

According to positivism, the last item is the only truth criterion. But I submit that it should be regarded as only one of seven, if only because a good fit can always be attained by assuming that the function is a polynomial of high enough degree and adjusting the coefficients suitably. (For the insufficiency of goodness of fit in econometrics, see Hendry and Richard 1982.)

To sum up, there is one optimal strategy for tackling problems of knowledge—the scientific method—and as many tactics as research fields.

8 The Problem of Knowledge

What is traditionally called the 'problem of knowledge' is actually an entire system of problems. Some of the components of this system are: What is knowledge? What can know: minds, brains, computers, or social groups? Can we know everything, something, or nothing? How does one get to know: from experience, reason, action, a combination of two or all three, or none of them? What kind of knowledge is best—that is, truest, most comprehensive, deepest, and most reliable and fertile? These five problems constitute the core problematics of epistemology, or the "theory" of knowledge—which is still to become a theory proper.

How are these problems best approached? Traditional epistemology handled them in an a priori fashion: it made no use of the sciences of knowledge—that is, cognitive psychology, the sociology of knowledge, and the history of science and technology. I take the view that epistemological problematics lies at the intersection of philosophy, science, and technology, so it should be approached against the background knowledge provided by all three fields of inquiry.

As a matter of fact, this is how we have proceeded in the foregoing. Take, for example, the first problem: What is knowledge? We have regarded every bit of knowledge as the end state of a cognitive process, which, in turn, is a brain process. We have thus distinguished knowledge from cognition, though without separating them. Moreover, we have said what factual knowledge is: namely, a representation of reality, the truer the better.

This leads us to the second problem: What can know? Since cognitive processes occur only in minds (or brains), the collectivist thesis—that what knows is a social group or a communication network—is false. But so is the traditional view of the solitary knowing subject and, even worse, the idealist view—held by Plato, Bolzano, Popper, and others—that there can be knowledge without a knowing subject. Inquiry is not conducted in a social vacuum: like trade and politics, it is a social endeavor involving a tradition (a body of background knowledge) as well as interactions that modify the agents.

The third question—What can we know?—has three conceivable answers: everything, something, and nothing. The first answer is the view of the fundamentalists—religious and philosophical, political and economic—that certain texts, provided they are interpreted correctly, contain all that mankind can or need know. This thesis is false. We know, for instance, that we shall never attain an exhaustive knowledge of the past or even of the present, because most facts are never recorded, some documents are destroyed or lost, and others are forged, as well as because of the more or less myopic and sectoral vision of contemporary chroniclers. The dual of the omniscience dogma—namely, epistemological nihilism or anarchism (or radical skepticism)—is false too, for, as a matter of fact, we do possess a considerable, expanding body of mathematical, scientific, technological, and humanistic knowledge. The mere mention of logic, physics, chemistry, biology, history, engineering, and even medicine should suffice as evidence.

We are then left with the moderate skeptic answer that we can know something. Not everything, because our sources are limited (e.g., our archives are not complete), our resources (especially the human ones) often meager, our curiosity not always intense enough, our brains not always up to the task, and sometimes also because certain philosophical myths stand in the way. One such myth is the idea—held by Vico, Dilthey, Weber, Habermas, and some pragmatists—that man can understand only what he himself makes, in particular, tools, ideas, and social institutions; nature, being alien to ideas and purposes, is opaque to human understanding. This is false because, as a matter of fact, (*a*) we know much more about nature than about society, and (*b*) natural science is necessary (though insufficient) for knowing how social agents and artifacts (whether physical or social) work.

The dual philosophical myth is that we may never get to know how other people feel or perceive, because subjective experience is private. This is part of the empiricist dogma that knowledge is experience. This principle is false, because there is such a thing as knowledge by description, in addition to knowledge by acquaintance. In particular, we can acquire conceptual knowledge about subjective experience: this is what psychology is all about. To be sure, I cannot feel, perceive, or think in exactly the same way as you do. But I can get a rough idea of how you feel, perceive, and think, because all normal human brains and all basic human experiences are similar. In any event, the point of scientific inquiry is not to relive other people's experiences but to understand some of them, as well as facts inaccessible to experience.

The fourth basic question of knowledge—How does one get to know?— has been written off as unimportant by some philosophers, such as Popper. Yet the point of the question How do you know X? is to make sure that the fact or proposition X has been properly checked, rather than imagined. It is a methodological question that cannot be shunned by any serious methodologist. In fact, the question has been taken seriously and answered by intuitionism, rationalism, empiricism, and pragmatism.

Intuitionism claims that there is a special faculty (navel contemplation, inner illumination, insight, Verstehen, or Husserl's vision of essences) that tells us infallibly whether a proposition is true or false. Radical rationalism holds that reason is necessary and sufficient to know anything; radical empiricism, that only raw experience—that is, experience not processed by reason—supplies certain knowledge; and pragmatism, that action is the source and criterion of all knowledge. Let us glance at these doctrines, which will be examined more thoroughly in chapter 12.

While intuitions of various kinds are for real, intuitionism is an obstacle to the advancement of knowledge. Indeed, it is an irrationalist, infallibilist philosophy which pays no attention to argument or test and is thus at variance with the scientific attitude. Rationalism, by contrast, works at least for pure mathematics—not surprisingly, because this is *the* a priori science. But rationalism fails everywhere else, for, unlike ideas, natural facts cannot be invented. Radical empiricism works nowhere, for, in order to learn from experience, we need to reflect upon it, and reflection involves ideas not derived from pure experience, such as those of test, truth, and consistency. This is why there are no radical empiricists left: all the logical empiricists (or neo-positivists) have admitted the need for nonempirical—in particular, logical—ideas. As for pragmatism, it is obviously relevant to ordinary and artisanal knowledge. But it is irrelevant to mathematics and basic science, neither of which is concerned with practical problems. It even fails to do justice to modern technology, which makes intensive use of mathematics and basic science.

The upshot is that while rationalism, empiricism, and pragmatism each hold a grain of truth, none of them gives a true account of all the fields of inquiry into the real world. We need a synthesis encompassing the true components of these traditional epistemologies while going beyond them. This synthesis is scientific realism, which will be expounded and defended in chapter 13, section 8.

The fifth and last basic problem of knowledge was: What kind of knowledge is best—that is, truest, most comprehensive, deepest, and most reliable and fertile? This is not a well-posed question, for the answer to it depends on the field of knowledge and on our goals. Thus, if we seek linguistic knowledge, we will not engage in astronomical research; and if we face a management problem, we will not engage in chemical research. A more reasonable problem is this: What type of inquiry is most likely to yield pertinent, true, comprehensive, deep, and often perfectible solutions to the problems in such and such a field? I submit that if the field in question studies either nature or society, the answer is that scientific inquiry is most likely to yield true, more general, deep (though seldom definitive) answers. This may be called the *scientistic* thesis. There can be hardly any doubt that scientism has triumphed in the study of nature. The question is whether it can work in the study of society. I shall address it at various points in the remainder of this book.

All the higher animals explore their environment. Such inquiry takes it for granted that there is a world out there, that it can be explored, and that it is worth exploring. However, only humans are capable of conducting the special kind of inquiry called "scientific research," and this only from about the fifth century B.C. onward. This is inquiry aimed at forming, checking, and refining clear, testable, and sometimes approximately true ideas about reality. Scientists accomplish this task by combining reason with experience and intuition: by making educated guesses and producing data, as well as by checking both hypotheses and data. The one epistemology that accounts for this procedure and its partial success is scientific realism, according to which there are independently existing things, which can come to be known at least partially and gradually, and known best through scientific research. In short, the scientific community is the ultimate truth squad.

4 :: Systematization

When presented with an interesting new array of facts, we usually attempt to account for them by forming a jumble of rather fuzzy, and perhaps even mutually inconsistent, ideas—a muddle, in short. Critical reflection upon such a muddle may succeed in transforming it into a model, or system of reasonably precise, well-articulated ideas. This may in turn help us to take a second, deeper look at the facts that prompted our modeling effort. This second look is likely to suggest refinements to our model—or perhaps a totally different one. Such zigzagging between ideas and facts may go on until one hits on a sufficiently true model—or else gives up in temporary despair or boredom.

Systems of ideas—in particular, models—are needed not only to represent bits of reality but also to understand ideas. In fact, in order to understand any given idea, we must relate it to other ideas: a stray idea would be unintelligible, hence it would not be an idea at all. (Analogs: An isolated word belongs to no language, and an isolated note has no musical standing.) This is why all ideas come in clusters. But not all such clusters are well organized. For example, a list of geographical or historical data is shapeless and untidy, hence hard to understand, remember, and expand. The ideal cluster of ideas is a conceptual system—that is, a collection of constructs with a clear logical structure. In this chapter we shall examine a few types of conceptual system that occur in science and technology.

Deep hypotheses, exact definitions, accurate data, and precise rules are all very well, but, if taken individually, they do not help us understand, predict, or control anything. In order to understand, predict, or control any facts, we must systematize our data and conjectures about them. Thus, we understand the role of an executive in a firm if we learn the place he occupies in an organization chart. We understand that apes are similar to humans if we recall the hypothesis that we have common ancestors, a hypothesis expressed in our phylogenetic tree, which in turn is represented in the ordering of the species in question. And we explain and predict that nation A will have depleted its natural resource R by a certain time if we know both its present stock of R and the rate at which R is being exploited, as well as the (foolish) policy of the government of A in keeping up or even increasing that rate. In the first case we resort to a classification, in the second to a mini-theory. Both are based on hypotheses and data. Let us analyze the concepts of sketch, classification, model, and theory. Such analysis is of particular importance to social science, which, except for economics, is not characterized by conceptual clarity and systematization. (Lasswell and Kaplan's *Power and Society* [1952], Merton's *Social Theory and Social Structure* [1957], and Coleman's *Foundations of Social Theory* [1990] are exceptions.)

1 Sketch

Most of our knowledge of factual matters is spotty: it consists of a handful of data and guesses united only by their common reference to things of a certain kind. Shorter: Factual knowledge is usually sketchy. We stipulate that a *sketch,* or *schema,* is a set of propositions (or diagrams) outlining the salient known or conjectured features of things of a certain kind. (Exceptionally the set is a singleton.) If these propositions are jointly asserted, the set becomes a conjunction of propositions. Sketches, or schemata, come in various degrees of complexity. The simplest is a list of outstanding properties of the thing in question; for example, "Banania is a small underdeveloped tropical country that produces cash crops and is ruled by a military junta supported by the U.S. government."

More complete sketches are more complex and include, in addition, the structure and environment of the thing. Thus, the simplest sketch, or schema, of a concrete system s at a given time is the ordered triple $m(s) = <C(s), E(s), S(s)>$, whose components stand for the composition, environment, and structure of s, respectively. We shall make frequent use of this qualitative sketch, or CES, when discussing individualism, holism, systemism, and related matters.

Sketches can be verbal, graphic, mathematical, or mixed. For example, the characterization of a university as a social system devoted to research and teaching is of the first kind. Graphs, block diagrams, and flow diagrams illustrate the second kind. Input–output matrices are instances of mathematical sketches.

A diagram is a graphic representation of what are regarded as the outstanding features of a system: its components, the relations among these, and the relations of the system (or its representatives) with its environment. A diagram is actually a graphic display of a system of propositions. But it is not a theory (a hypothetico-deductive system), because the relations among the components are causal, rather than logical. For example, in an organigram the nodes represent units (e.g., individuals), and the edges, or lines joining the nodes, may represent the relations of reporting or supplying. In many cases diagrams are advantageously replaced by matrices. An example is the input–output matrix of an economy, where the cell Mij represents the input of industry i into industry j.

One problem that affects all kinds of representation of real things, from simple sketches to sophisticated theories, concerns detail. Given that we can only get to know so much, or that we only have so much time and talent to spend, how detailed should our representation be? Should it involve only the obviously important features of the referents? Should it represent only the external features, or the composition and structure as well? This is the problem of black box versus alternative representations.

A conceptual *black box* contains only exogenous variables, such as stimuli and responses. A conceptual *translucent box* involves, in addition, endogenous variables representing internal states and their relation to exogenous variables; thus it describes the inner mechanism that is conjectured as explaining the overt behavior of the thing represented. And a *gray box* involves both exogenous variables and what have been called "intervening variables"—that is, variables that do not represent any real properties but discharge a computational function (e.g., the next state function in automata theory).

The choice among the three kinds of conceptual box is dictated by the amount of available information and by the theorist's philosophical stand. If our knowledge is scant, we have no choice but to construct a black or gray box model. This type of representation has been favored by positivists, conventionalists, and other anti-realists. Exclusive attachment to the black box paragon hinders the advancement of knowledge and limits severely its practical use. Indeed, if we ignore what makes a thing tick—that is, what its internal mechanism is—we will not succeed in altering, never mind improving, its behavior. In short, although black boxes are unavoidable at the beginning of a research project, the positivist black-boxist philosophy is negativist.

The construction of schemata raises a number of further interesting methodological and philosophical problems. Here is a short list of them. First, given some information about a real (or putatively real) thing, a choice must be made as to which of its (real or conjectured) traits to include in the model and which to overlook. The decision will depend on the theorist's imagination and philosophical stance, no less than on the information available and the goal. There is no unique solution to the problem, because there is no method or recipe for crafting models.

Second, given two or more representations of a certain thing, it is necessary to find out whether they are equivalent. It is therefore necessary to check whether, for example, two diagrams, or a diagram and a matrix, represent the same system in different ways. Similarly, given two manifestly inequivalent models, it is necessary to investigate whether they represent the same thing to different degrees of accuracy.

The preceding two problems are rather technical. Others are of a more philosophical kind. Here are some examples. First, must every conceptual representation resemble its referents—that is, does it have to be an analog? No. Only some black boxes are iconic, or visualizable. The most sophisticated representations are roundabout or symbolic, for they involve unobservable yet supposedly real entities or properties. (Think of psychology, economics, and history.) Second, can a conceptual model of a real thing be perfect? No. Modeling involves simplification, the initial discarding of details and idiosyncracies. In particular, different items are treated as equivalent in some respect, and these equivalents are treated as if they were identical (recall chap. 2, sec. 5). Further problems raised by the construction of conceptual representations will be tackled in the following sections.

2 Classification

Once we have sketched the things of interest, we may need to group them. To classify a given collection of individuals is to partition it into classes—that is, to group the items in such a way that every individual is attended to and assigned to a single class. For example, with regard to employment, members of a society may be grouped into rentiers, employers, employees, the self-employed, the underemployed, and the unemployed. By contrast, the exploiter–exploited dichotomy does not induce an exhaustive partition, because it makes no room for the jobless or for people who exploit themselves, such as independent professionals, craftsmen, merchants, and farmers who work overtime and do not employ anybody.

Classification starts by forming classes—that is, groups of individuals sharing one or more properties. Consider a collection C of items and call A an attribute (predicate) representing a property P of some members of C. (Remember that any given property may be conceptualized in alternative ways: chap. 1, sec. 1.) The set of all individuals in the collection C that are attributed predicate A (and therefore assumed to possess property P) is $\mathcal{A} = \{x \in C | Ax\}$. A single attribute A and its dual, not-A, allow us to draw a dichotomy—that is, make black-or-white statements of the forms "b is an A" and "c is a non-A." In other words, we get two classes: A and its complement, not-A—for example, the classes of private goods and public goods, democratic and authoritarian political regimes, and progressive and nonprogressive historical periods. (That such dichotomies are often too coarse, since many properties come in degrees, is true, but beside the point.)

If we pick two properties P and Q, represented respectively by predicates A and B, the collection of individuals that are attributed both properties at the same time will be $C = \{x \in C \mid Ax \,\&\, Bx\}$, which in turn can be shown to equal the intersection of the two classes concerned. Including the duals not-A and not-B of the given predicates, we can now form statements of four kinds: "c is an A and a B," "c is an A and a non-B," "c is a non-A and a B," and "c is a non-A and a non-B." In other words, two predicates induce the partition of a collection into four mutually disjoint classes. In general, the conjunction of n predicates induces a partition into 2^n classes.

Different predicates induce different classifications. This would seem to confirm the nominalist thesis that all classes are arbitrary. But not all classifications are equally natural, hence insightful or interesting. Only the classifications induced by important properties give rise to important classifications— that is, groupings that match naturally occurring kinds. This is not to say that such (natural) kinds are real things. Only their individual members can be real. Kinds, whether natural or conventional, are concepts. Thus, the working class is a natural kind, not an arbitrary group, for there are such things as workers, and work is an important socioeconomic category. However, "working class" is a concept, not a concrete thing like an individual worker or a labor union. Consequently it is mistaken to attribute to it, or to any other social group, psychological properties such as a consciousness or a purpose; this is reification.

Whether natural or arbitrary, a classification proper meets certain formal requirements. It is worthwhile listing them explicitly because they are often violated in the social sciences, where many an incomplete enumeration of types (a typology) passes for a classification. The formal conditions for a classification of a collection of individuals are as follows: (1) each member of the original collection is assigned to a single basic class or species (or lowest-rank taxon); (2) each basic class (species) is composed of some of the members of the original collection, and no class is composed of subclasses; (3) membership of each class is determined by a predicate or a conjunction of predicates; (4) each class is clearly demarcated—that is, there are no borderline cases; this is ensured by employing only definite or exact predicates, avoiding vague ones such as "young" and "nice"; (5) any two classes are either mutually disjoint, in which case they are said to belong to the same rank (or taxon), or one of them is included in the other, in which case they belong to different ranks (or taxa); (6) only two relations are involved: the membership relation ($\in$), which holds between the individuals of the original collection and the first-rank classes, and the inclusion relation ($\subseteq$), which relates classes of different ranks (e.g., species to genera); (7) every class of a rank higher than the first (species) equals the union of some or all classes of the immediately preceding rank (e.g., every genus equals the union of its species); (8) all the classes of a given rank are pairwise disjoint, so that no item in the original collection belongs to more than one class of the same rank; (9) every partition of a given rank is exhaustive: the union of all the classes in a given rank equals the original collection; (10) any classification violating any of the previous conditions must be remedied or given up.

3 Theory and Model

Few concepts have fared worse in the social sciences than that of theory. The worst and most popular mistakes in this regard are the following: Theory is any discourse on generalities, however obscure or incoherent; theory is the opposite of hard fact (a vulgar belief); theories are useless: only data and actions are valuable; theories are general orientations or approaches; theories are the same as hypotheses (e.g., Popper); theories are collections of definitions (e.g., conventionalists and Parsons); all theories are generalizations from observed facts (inductivism); there are a priori theories of human behavior (e.g., von Mises 1949); the axioms of a theory are indisputably true (commonsense view); and every axiom system is abstract—that is, uninterpreted (e.g., Debreu 1959, x). Let us examine these odd opinions.

We start with the idea that a theory is any old general discourse, as in "psychoanalytic theory," "critical theory," and "feminist theory." This is not how the word is used in logic, mathematics, theoretical physics, or any other advanced discipline: in these fields the word *theory* designates a hypothetico-deductive system—that is, a system of propositions some of which are hypothesized and the remainder of which are deduced from the former. Next comes the theory–fact antithesis. It is false that theories are opposed to facts and that we therefore have to choose between them. What is true is that some theories do not fit the facts they purport to represent—hence they are false or irrelevant. Nor are all theories less useful than data: what is true is that most of the "grand theories" in traditional social studies have been speculative—hence untested or even partially untestable. Further, theories are not approaches: an approach is neither more nor less than a way of viewing and handling things, problems, or data (chap. 3, sec. 1); hence it may at most suggest a type of theory. Theories are not hypotheses, but systems of such. They may contain definitions, but, far from boiling down to sets of conventions, theories make definite assertions about their subject matter. Like hypotheses proper, and unlike empirical generalizations, theories contain (higher-level) concepts that may not occur in the data relevant to them: they are not data packages (e.g., a theory explaining social cohesiveness, an unobservable, in terms of participation, an observable). However, this does not entail that scientific theorizing can be a priori—that is, dispense with data; data are what theories are supposed to account for or guide the search for. Nor are axioms beyond criticism: they must earn their rank by entailing true, or at least plausible, consequences. Finally, it is false that every axiomatized theory is abstract: this holds only in logic and in abstract branches of mathematics such as set theory and algebra. In short, all ten concepts of theory listed above are wrong.

What, then, *is* a theory? As recalled a moment ago, in all leading fields of scientific research the word *theory* designates a hypothetico-deductive system—that is, a system of hypotheses within which valid arguments (i.e., deductive chains) can be constructed; for example, predicate logic and graph theory, classical mechanics and quantum mechanics, chemical kinetics and the theory of chemical bonding. Obviously dialectics (whether Hegelian or Marxian), phenomenology, psychoanalysis, ethnomethodology, and the like do not qualify as theories proper: they are merely bunches of statements, and not very clear ones at that—on top of which, they are at variance with the facts.

All theories are formally alike: they are all hypothetico-deductive systems. But, whereas theories in pure mathematics are a priori, any theory that purports to describe facts must make room for factual information, so as to be checkable against facts. Every axiom of a factual theory is a hypothesis and therefore subject to possible refutation by empirical data (usually via some theorems, i.e., logical consequences). And only the axioms of an abstract theory, such as logic, set theory, Boolean algebra, group theory, and general topology, are uninterpreted. All other mathematical theories are interpreted in mathematical (e.g., numerical) terms, and all theories in factual science are interpreted in factual terms. Thus, the functions occurring in the infinitesimal calculus relate specific sets, such as subsets of the real line, rather than nondescript ones like those occurring in set theory. And the central functions occurring in a theory in mathematical economics are interpreted in such economic terms as quantity and price. Therefore the claim (e.g., by Debreu 1991) that all axiomatized theories, even in economics, are pieces of pure mathematics is mistaken. Axiomatization bears on the logical ordering of the components (postulates, definitions, and theorems) of a theory, not on their content. Hence all scientific theories are axiomatizable (Hilbert 1918). But whereas some axiomatizations are formal (i.e., they abstract from content), others are not (Hilbert and Bernays 1968 [1934], 1:2).

Obviously, theories are not born fully developed. They start as rather disordered sets of somewhat loosely connected propositions containing more or less fuzzy concepts. Such embryos develop, if at all, through addition and culling, exemplification and generalization, concept refinement (in particular, exactification), and testing against empirical data. But most theory embryos never attain adulthood, either because they are killed by empirical data, or because the people handling them do not know how to cultivate them, or because the problems they address have ceased to be of interest.

The main advantages of theorizing are as follows. (1) A theory unifies a number of previously scattered hypotheses. (2) Such colligation makes it possible to prove (deduce) certain hypotheses on the strength of others. (3) Some of these consequences may be new—that is, unknown before the theory was proposed. (4) The mutual support of the components of a theory makes it easier to examine each of them critically in the light of the others. (5) Every confirmation of one of the components of the theory reinforces indirectly all the others. (6) Every counterexample of one of the components of the theory casts doubt on the others. Obviously well organized—that is, axiomatized—theories have all these virtues to the highest degree. (See Bunge 1967a, 1973c, 1983b.)

A further advantage of theorizing is this: a lone hypothesis may be saved from refutation by conjoining it with an ad hoc hypothesis; but such a maneuver is hardly possible if the hypothesis is a member of a hypothetico-deductive system. In this case the ad hoc hypothesis must be incorporated as a new postulate, which results in a whole new theory with new consequences, some of which may turn out to be untestable or false. A good theory will check the proliferation of "interpretations" of empirical data. As we saw in chapter 3, section 4, any such interpretation is actually a hypothesis that colligates the available data. But, as long as the hypothesis concerned is not a member of some theory, there is no limit to the number of alternative hypotheses that can account for the same data. Such proliferation can turn into what Freese and Rokeach (1979) have called "the alternative interpretation industry," whose workers exploit the data obtained by others to formulate their own alternative hypotheses.

The only effective way of containing such proliferation is to adopt the following rules: (1) Check whether the given hypothesis matches the background knowledge; (2) Try to embed the given hypothesis in an existing theory; (3) If this fails, try to expand the hypothesis into a theory covering not just the original data but also data concerning facts of other kinds; (4) Use the theory (alongside other theories) to redesign the original observation as well as to design new observations; and (5) Reevaluate the original set of data in the light of both the theory and the new data.

Our next subject will be the nature of theoretical models. (I append the qualifier "theoretical" because the word *model* is notoriously ambiguous: almost any representation of a concrete thing is called a model nowadays.) A *theoretical model* of things of a given kind is a specific theory: that is, a narrow-range hypothetico-deductive system. Such a model expands on a sketch of the referent (sec. 2). For example, it states in a precise fashion the manner in which the components of a concrete system are held together. Yet, even the best theoretical model is bound to miss some features of its referent, whence it is likely to be at best only partially true. Theoretical models are smooth, but reality is jagged. Only theories in pure mathematics can be unblemished.

We distinguish two kinds of theoretical model as regards mode of construction: free and bound. A *free model* is one built from scratch, whereas a *bound model* is a specification, or "application," of a general theory to a domain included in the reference class of the general theory. The great majority of theoretical models in biology, psychology, and social science are free, for the simple reason that in these sciences there is a dearth of true general theories. By contrast, most models in physics and chemistry are bound: they result from enriching the set A of basic assumptions (axioms) of a general theory G with a set S of subsidiary assumptions specifying the nature of the things of interest. (In other words, a bound model M equals the infinite set of logical consequences of the union of A and S.) For example, the simplest model of a planetary system results from enriching classical mechanics with a sketch of the system and Newton's law of gravity. An ambitious research project in any science is to build a general theory and check it by crafting a number of bound models. Another is to tackle the inverse problem of imagining a general theory by finding out the common core of a few free models.

Many students of society, particularly rational choice theorists, believe that a single general theory may account for everything social. But this is a methodological fallacy: no general theory G suffices to describe its putatively real referents R without further ado. Indeed, in order to make G account for R, we must enrich G with a set S of subsidiary assumptions that sketch those things. (E.g., to a first, crude approximation, society may be sketched as a system composed of the state riding on top of the civil society; to a second approximation, it may be sketched as a system composed of three interacting subsystems: the economy, the culture, and the polity.) By joining G and S, one obtains a specific theory, or theoretical model, M of the thing(s) to be accounted for. An alternative sketch S' will, when conjoined with G, produce a different theoretical model, M', of either the same things or different entities of the same genus. In the absence of G—that is, when a thing is modeled from scratch—M is a free model coinciding with S. Since the ingredient S of M is an idealization of the things of interest, M may be said to describe directly a model object and only mediately its real referent(s) R. Moreover, since any sketch S is an idealized picture of R, while M describes S accurately, it only describes the real referent(s) R approximately (see fig. 4.1, in which $\Re$ stands for the reference relation).

If the specific theory M turns out not to match its real referent satisfactorily, then G, S, or both must be repaired. If G has a good track record, S will be what is suspect, and a different sketch S' should be tried out. Otherwise G as well as S

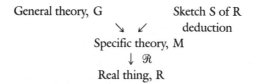

Fig. 4.1. A general theory and a sketch of the thing of interest jointly entail a specific theory of the latter.

may have to be changed. If a theoretical model M proves to be sufficiently true for present purposes, it is often said to "mirror" its real referent, or that model and referent are "isomorphic." However, these expressions are metaphorical, not literal, for the isomorphism relation holds only between sets and, while M is a set (of statements), its referent R is not a set, but a concrete thing. Therefore the "reflection theory of knowledge" held by dialectical materialists, the young Wittgenstein, and some contemporary philosophers, such as van Fraassen (1980), is false. Only mirrors can mirror; sets can only map sets. Metaphor can easily turn realism into fictionism or "as if" talk (recall chap. 3, sec. 5).

The construction of theories and theoretical models raises a number of interesting philosophical problems. Some of them are common to the construction of sketches and were touched on in section 1. Another problem of interest is this: Are "theoretical entities," such as free markets, real or fictitious? Answer: Neither; this is an ill-conceived question. Indeed, by definition, all entities are real or at least putatively real things. The "theoretical entities" in question are actually some of the constructs occurring in scientific theories. The correct question is whether such constructs *refer* to real entities or properties and, if so, whether they *represent* them adequately. And these are hardly questions that can be answered with purely philosophical resources: they also require empirical tests.

A second interesting problem concerns the truth of theories. Assuming that we agree on what it means for a proposition to be factually true, can we extrapolate this notion to a theory, which contains infinitely many propositions? Clearly not, because we could not possibly test all these propositions. However, if the theory is testable, and if we have succeeded in devising suitable indicators and in carrying out good observations or experiments, we should be able to check whether the theory (*a*) is compatible with the bulk of our background knowledge, (*b*) makes no obviously false assertions, (*c*) contains some well-confirmed generalizations in the same field of knowledge, and (*d*) makes some novel and (sufficiently) true predictions.

Hence the expression 'true theory' should be understood to mean "theory containing a substantial set of (sufficiently) true statements and no (blatantly) false ones." Note the vagueness of the terms 'substantial' and 'sufficiently' in the preceding sentence. Vagueness of the former is unavoidable for, in the case of infinite sets of propositions, all examined propositions, regardless of their number, constitute a tiny subset. But the vagueness of the second can be avoided by specifying the acceptable error. Even so, we must be prepared to put up with theories containing a few inaccurate statements. But in science, errors, when detected and when they bear on interesting matters, may spur further research.

A third classical problem concerns the role of simplicity. It is usually held that we should prefer the simplest of all the theories consistent with a given body of data. Moreover, conventionalists (e.g., Goodman 1958) claim that simplicity is decisive in theory evaluation. But they tell us neither what 'simplicity' means nor why we should prefer it to truth, explanatory power, or depth. As a matter of fact, the word *simple* designates many different concepts. For example, a theory may be mathematically simple, but hard to interpret and therefore difficult to test. Or it may be semantically transparent, as well as formally simple, but shallow, of the box-and-arrow type. The moral is clear: While simplicities of all kinds are desirable, they should not be required. The history of knowledge is a sequence of successive complications, not simplifications. One starts with simple problems, hypotheses, or experimental designs, because one knows but little at the beginning. Reality, which is complex, usually forces us to complicate our initial ideas and procedures. Hence simplicity may be an indicator of falsity, shallowness, or both (Bunge 1963).

Our fourth and last problem concerns the "incommensurability" thesis proposed by Kuhn (1962, 1991), seconded by Feyerabend (1975), and popular with postmodernists. According to this thesis, rival scientific theories are mutually "incommensurable" (incomparable), whence the choice among them is either a matter of convention or an act of faith. This thesis is analytically and historically false: analytically, because, by definition, two theories are mutually rival if and only if (*a*) they are different accounts of roughly the same domain of facts, and (*b*) they are comparable in one or more respects—for example, as to coverage, accuracy, predictive power, or depth. Only theories about disjoint domains, such as price theory and evolutionary theory, are mutually incommensurable. And the incommensurability thesis is historically false because rival theories have always been evaluated and compared in at least one respect. In particular, theoretical physicists, starting with Einstein and Bohr, make explicit use of the correspondence principle, which states that a new theory about facts of some kind should be more comprehensive than the older theory and should reduce to the latter at some limit or other—for example, for velocities much smaller than that of light. In sum, the incommensurability thesis is utterly false. Consequently it does not support irrationalism; nor does it help explain theory change or, *a fortiori*, the history of science. (More in Bunge 1973*c*, 1974*c*).

4 Theoretical Law

The concept of a theory allows one to elucidate that of a law statement. Just as in chapter 1, section 1, we distinguished properties from attributes or predicates, so we will now distinguish patterns from the propositions describing them. This holds for laws, quasi-laws, trends, and tacit (internalized) norms. This ambiguity does not affect the explicit norms of human behavior, such as those passed by legislative bodies.

One reason for the pattern–statement distinction is that it allows us to explain a typical endeavor of scientists: that of attempting to uncover concealed regularities. Objective patterns are discovered, not made, but they are discovered with the help of inventions such as mathematical ideas and measuring instruments. The same distinction helps to explain a good portion of the history of science as a sequence of approximations to the true representation of objective patterns. In fact, one and the same objective pattern may be known with different degrees of accuracy and depth.

A second reason for distinguishing between an objective pattern and its conceptualizations is that it helps settle the controversy over realism (Ampère 1843, 28). Subjectivists, conventionalists, and pragmatists claim that what are usually called "laws of nature" are constructions, or even conventions. This claim originates partly in the ambiguity of the word *law* and the corresponding conflation of an objective pattern or regularity with the formula(s) representing it. Once these notions are unfused, it becomes clear that while patterns inhere in the things themselves, the statements representing them are indeed constructions. However, they are not arbitrary constructions: these hypotheses are called 'laws' only if they belong to some theory and are well confirmed. *This* is a (linguistic) convention. (More on this shortly.)

Law statements, trend statements, and norm statements can be collectively called 'pattern statements.' Pattern statements can take a number of forms, depending not only on the things they refer to, but also on the state of scientific knowledge and even on the mathematical ability and goal of the scientists who propose them. Some are verbal statements, others are mathematical formulas. Among the latter we find equations and inequalities of many kinds: algebraic, functional, differential, integral, and so forth.

The most common law statements are functional relations between two or more variables, such as "If all the remaining relevant variables are held constant, then $y = f(x)$." The antecedent of this conditional proposition is called a *ceteribus paribus clause,* a proviso found in all sciences. (See chap. 6, sec. 1, for the widespread erroneous belief that this is characteristic of social science only.) The explicit occurrence of the warning points to the fact that the knowledge in question is limited. An improved knowledge of the pattern concerned would be expressed by a far more complex functional relation. Faith in the possibility of attaining such improvement is called 'meliorism,' just as awareness of the possibility of error in any of the successive approximations is called 'fallibilism.'

So far, most pattern statements in the social sciences are mathematically rather modest by comparison with those in physics and chemistry. Worse, our knowledge of social facts is so primitive that the use of heavy mathematical artillery is often suspect, as being nothing short of window dressing, particularly since the available data are far from precise. Witness the formal refinement of mainstream mathematical economics, conspicuous for its inability to account for the bulk of economic facts (Bunge forthcoming).

(A pattern statement can be defined in terms of the concept of a state function, introduced in chap. 1, sec. 3. A *pattern statement* is a constraint on a state function for things of a certain kind. More precisely, it is either a restriction on the possible values of the components of a state function or a relation between two or more such components. The lawful states lie within a box in the state space.)

From a methodological viewpoint, pattern statements can be divided into two classes: empirical and theoretical. An *empirical* pattern statement, or *quasilaw*, is an empirical generalization: that is, the expression of a regularity that has been obtained with the help of observations, measurements, or experiments but has not yet been embedded in a theory. A *theoretical* pattern statement is, of course, a well-confirmed theoretical condition for some state function. This condition is natural in the case of law statements and trends, and an artifact in the case of norms.

I shall stipulate that a theoretical pattern statement deserves to be called a 'law statement' if and only if it satisfies the following conditions: (*a*) it belongs to a factual theory; (*b*) it or some of its logical relatives (premises or consequences) have been confirmed empirically; and (*c*) the theory is compatible with the bulk of relevant knowledge. Condition (*a*) distinguishes theoretical laws from empirical generalizations, or quasi-laws. Condition (*b*) allows for the situation that the statement in question has not yet been corroborated empirically, but enjoys the indirect support of other well-confirmed formulas in the theory. And the condition (*c*) of external consistency is a tool for identifying and uprooting groundless speculation—in particular, bogus science. So far, the social sciences have come up with very few generalizations fulfilling all three conditions. Most of their generalizations are quasi-laws such as "The older an institution, the wider its distribution."

What should we do if we find facts that do not seem to fall into some pattern? We can try either of two moves: smooth out the irregularities, assuming that they result from errors of measurement or external disturbances; or, its dual, look for a "fine structure" resulting from a hidden mechanism. But either hypothesis must be of the bona fide kind; that is, it must be testable independently.

What if all attempts to account for the observed anomalies fail? Should we give up and declare the unknown to be unknowable, or even miraculous? To do so would be to give up the scientific world view, for this view includes (*a*) the *lawfulness* principle (Every fact satisfies some law(s)), (*b*) the *intelligibility* principle (Reality is knowable, at least partially and gradually), and (*c*) the *explainability* principle (All facts can be explained with the help of laws). (More in chap. 7, sec. 1.) Hence, if one fails to find any patterns in a mass of facts of a certain kind, one should go on hoping that further efforts will uncover such. This is an article of faith, but one which motivates research.

5 Kinds of Theory

Theories—that is, hypothetico-deductive systems—can be classed in respect of subject matter, range, depth, or organization. The *subject matter* (or reference class, or universe of discourse) can be formal, as in the case of pure mathematics, or factual, as in the case of a social science. Whether it is the one or the other depends upon the interpretation (or semantic) assumptions, if any, that accompany the formalism (if any) either explicitly or tacitly. For example, a theory of social networks includes fragments of the mathematical theory of graphs enriched with two semantic assumptions: that the nodes of a graph represent individuals (or else social systems), and that the edges linking the nodes of a graph represent a social relation such as that of subordination (if the graph is directed—that is, the edges are arrows) or exchange (if the graph is not directed).

The domains, or universes of discourse, of factual theories can be classed into three broad kinds: natural (e.g., biological), social (e.g., economic), and socio-natural (e.g., bioeconomic). Given that people are largely artifactual (made and, in particular, self-made), it must be expected that theories in the social and socio-natural fields will differ from those in the natural sciences in at least one respect: that of artificiality. Now, contrary to natural objects, artifacts—such as symbols, tools, and formal organizations—are designed for some purpose or other. Consequently, teleology, or final causation, which has no place in physics, chemistry, or biology, does have one in the social and socio-natural sciences. If only for this reason, it is hard to come up with true models of human behavior. But where descriptive and predictive theories fail, normative or prescriptive ones may succeed. That is, we may be more successful in stipulating how we ought to behave in order to attain certain goals than in describing or forecasting what people actually do.

The *range* of a theory is, of course, its degree of generality. We shall distinguish four kinds of theory with respect to range: narrow, middle, broad, and immense—or models and general, hypergeneral, and scaffolding theories, respectively. More precisely, we have the following variety.

Type 1: special theory or *theoretical model,* such as a model of the simple pendulum, the kinship structure of a given society, business firms of a certain kind, or a particular social process, such as the brain drain. Its semantic features are as follows: (*a*) all the specific concepts of the theory have a factual content— that is, they refer to factual items; (*b*) the reference class is a clear-cut, rather narrow species, whose members are supposed to be represented or modeled by the theory in at least some respects. Its methodological features are that it is (*a*) testable conceptually—that is, it can be checked for consistency with the bulk of the antecedent or background knowledge; (*b*) testable empirically (confirmable or refutable) provided it is enriched with data (i.e., what is subjected to tests is not T itself but $T \cup D$, where T designates theory and D a set of data relevant to T).

Type 2: general theory, such as particle mechanics, the Keynesian model of the economy, and reference group theory in sociology. (These are what Merton [1957, 9] called *middle-range* theories, as opposed to the "grand"—vague, therefore hardly testable—conceptual schemata that had prevailed in sociology up until and including Parsons's time.) Its semantic features are as in (*a*) under type 1 theory, and (*b*) the reference class is a genus (rather than a species), every species of which is representable by a type 1 theory. Its methodological features are that it is (*a*) testable conceptually; (*b*) testable empirically provided it is enriched with subsidiary assumptions (e.g., regarding the number of components and kind of bonds among them), as well as indicator hypotheses, so that it becomes a theoretical model or type 1 theory (i.e., what is subjected to tests is $T \cup S \cup I \cup D$. Here, as before, T and D designate the theory and the relevant data, respectively, whereas S and I designate the subsidiary hypotheses and the indicator hypotheses, respectively).

Type 3: hypergeneral theory, such as continuum mechanics, the synthetic theory of evolution, and neoclassical microeconomics. It has the same semantic features as types 1 and 2, but its reference class is a family or order (rather than a genus), every genus of which is representable by a type 2 theory. Its methodological features are that it is (*a*) testable conceptually—that is, it can be checked for consistency with the bulk of background knowledge, in particular with the corresponding type 2 theory or theories; and (*b*) testable empirically if enriched with subsidiary and indicator hypotheses that transform it into a type 2 theory.

Type 4: scaffolding theory, such as general (classical or quantum) field theory, game theory, statistical information theory, general systems theory, network theory, general machine theory, automata theory, historical materialism, cultural materialism, and the assumptions common to all rational choice models. Its semantic features are (*a*) that some of the symbols may be assigned no definitive factual interpretation—that is, the theory may only be semi-interpreted; (*b*) the reference class is an entire kingdom, every family of which is representable by a type 3 theory. Its methodological features are that it is (*a*) testable conceptually; (*b*) untestable by itself empirically, although it may become testable vicariously upon specification, whereby it may turn into a type 3 theory—thus it is (indirectly) confirmable but not refutable; (*c*) it serves as a scaffolding for the construction of narrower-range theories.

So much for theory range. (See further aspects in Stinchcombe 1968.) Let us now examine the concept of theory *depth*. But first some examples. The quantum theory of solids is deeper than the mechanics of rigid bodies, in that it explains the macro-properties of solids in terms of atomic composition and interatomic forces. Molecular genetics is deeper than classical genetics, in that it explains genotypic changes in terms of gene mutations and recombinations. A biopsychological learning theory is deeper than a behaviorist learning theory, for it explains learning as the formation and reinforcement of neural connections. And a dynamical sociological, economic, or politological theory is deeper than the corresponding static theory, because it accounts for social change.

A shallow theory treats its referents as black boxes with invisible innards. It is often called "phenomenological," for it is thought to represent only phenomena (appearances). But this is a misnomer, because even phenomenological theories in science and technology contain concepts denoting imperceptible properties, such as energy, entropy, and temperature in the case of thermodynamics, the paragon of phenomenological theories. For this reason, 'black box,' 'empty box,' or 'holistic theory' are better names. On the other hand, a *translucent box theory* is one that accounts for the composition, structure, and dynamics of its referents. Finally, a *gray box theory* is one that represents in a schematic way the innards of its referents (their "works"). Network models of social systems are of this kind. They represent the composition and structure of social systems and relate the micro (individual) to the macro (or social) levels. But, because they are static, do not describe any inner mechanism, and omit the system's environment, such models cannot account for growth or decline, let alone for any assembly or breakdown process.

The translucent box–black box distinction appears under different names in different research fields. For example, macroeconomic and econometric models are classed into *structural* and *reduced*. The former contain formulas that exhibit the relation of every dependent variable to independent variables of various levels, whereas the corresponding reduced model exhibits the overall relation between the dependent and the ultimate independent variables. For instance, a structural economic model may boil down to a formula of the type

$$z = f(x,y), \tag{1a}$$

where, in turn,

$$x = g(u), \text{ and } y = h(v). \tag{1b}$$

Substituting (1b) into (1a), one obtains the corresponding reduced model:

$$z = \varphi(u,v). \tag{2}$$

Note the following methodological differences between (1) and (2). First, whereas (1b) "explains" the intermediary variables x and y, which presumably represent important real features of the system under consideration, (2) does not even contain them. In other words, (2) is shallower and therefore simpler than (1) for skipping a level. Second, (1) implies (2), but not the reverse. That is, the task of going from the structural to the reduced model is merely computational (hence deductive), whereas the task of going the other way, from the reduced or descriptive model (2) to the structural or explanatory model (1), is an inverse problem, hence one that has an indefinite number of solutions. Solving this problem is likely to require more ingenuity than inventing the richer model. Moral: Apply your talent to building structural models and leave the reduced ones to computer-aided curve fitting.

A *deep* theory is one that postulates some mechanism at a lower level of organization: it is a mechanismic, multilevel theory, in contrast to a phenomenological, one-level theory. The mechanism need not be mechanical: it may be electromagnetic, chemical, biological, economic, political, or what have you. In most cases the "works" are imperceptible, so they must be guessed before they can be discovered. But, of course, if the theory is scientific, then the mechanism must be experimentally accessible, however indirectly. A deep theory tells us not just (part of) what happens, but also what makes it happen: it involves some causal, stochastic, or mixed mechanism. Hence it has explanatory power. (More in chap. 5, sec. 2.) Moreover, it may prove to be of practical interest, for if we know what makes something tick, we may alter its mechanism to our convenience.

Finally comes the matter of *theory organization*. Most theories are formulated in an untidy fashion, so that one is left wondering what the premises (axioms and definitions) and their consequences are. Moreover, the formal ingredients are usually mixed with semantic assumptions. Such untidiness is only natural at the beginning. It reflects the way the theory was born, nurtured, applied, or taught. But of course untidiness has its price. First, it may prevent us from distinguishing the important from the secondary, definitions from hypotheses, and the latter from their consequences. Second, should the theory fail, it makes it hard to spot the components that are at fault. By contrast, if a theory is well organized, it is easier to spot the parts of it which have been refuted and consequently need to be revised or dropped. Third, untidiness taxes memory with details that could easily be reconstructed with the help of logic or mathematics.

A well-organized theory is one that exhibits explicitly its hypothetico-deductive structure. Such a theory is an *axiomatic* theory. We adopt Hilbert's rule:

Any untidy, but reasonably precise, theory on any subject whatsoever can be axiomatized—that is, reformulated in the axiom–definition–theorem format. In axiomatizing a theory, one starts by identifying its primitive (undefined) concepts and basic assumptions (axioms, postulates) and goes on to lay down definitions. Such identification is performed by collecting the premises that occur in the deductions of typical theorems. Performance of this task is likely to exhibit some previously hidden premises. And the explicit exhibition of all (or nearly all) the premises facilitates the extraction of their logical consequences, to the point of yielding some previously unknown theorems. (See Bunge 1967a, 1973c for the nature and advantages of axiomatics.)

To clarify the foregoing, let us examine a qualitative model of the socio-economics of the arms race, a process that is still going on at the time of writing, despite the official end of the cold war in 1990. Here it is in a nutshell: The arms race ruins the economy and debases the quality of life. It does both by diverting human and financial resources from the renewal of civilian manufacturing industry, the maintenance of public health care and education services, and consumption. (If in need of empirical corroboration, look around.) A possible axiomatization of this intuitive idea follows.

Axiom 1. For any fiscal year the sum of civilian and military investments is constant.

Axiom 2. The rate of technological innovation is an increasing function of investment in R&D.

Axiom 3. Commercial competitiveness is an increasing function of technological innovation.

Axiom 4. The standard of living is an increasing function of civilian investment.

Here are some of the logical consequences of these premises:

Corollary 1. The greater the military expenditures, the smaller the civilian ones. (From axiom 1.)

Theorem 1. As civilian investment decreases relative to military investment, the rate of technological innovation declines. (From corollary 1 and axiom 2.)

Theorem 2. Commercial competitiveness declines with increasing military expenditures. (From theorem 1 and axiom 3.)

Theorem 3. The standard of living declines with increasing military expenditures. (From axioms 1 and 4.)

I will wind up this section with some remarks on the concept of a *metatheory*, a word that is used somewhat loosely in the social sciences. Strictly speaking, a metatheory is a theory about theories, not about the real world: it contains metastatements. (Literary parallel: the narrative–metanarrative distinction.) A metastatement is a proposition about another proposition or a set of such—for

example, "Historical statements are about past events." The distinction between metatheory and theory is sharp. A theory about a certain domain of facts
is not supposed to specify anything about itself: it is about facts. Consequently,
whereas scientific and technological theories are checked by confronting them
with facts (or rather data), metatheories are tested by confronting them with
theories. If a theory matches the relevant data, it stands a chance of being true.
If a metatheoretical statement or a metatheory fits the theory it refers to, it is
true, even if the latter is utterly false. If it does not, it is false, even if it refers to a
true theory.

A metatheory can be descriptive or prescriptive. That is, it says what the
theories in a certain domain, such as sociology, are or ought to be: what their
logical structure, content, and aim are or ought to be and what kind of support,
conceptual or empirical, they do or should enjoy. So far, metatheories proper
exist only in mathematics and formal semantics. What is usually called a metatheory in the social sciences is not a hypothetico-deductive system about theories but a bunch of loosely knit metatheoretical propositions—that is, statements about the nature or goal of theorizing in general or about some
statements of a particular theory.

6 Reduction

In the philosophy of science, reduction is construed as a kind of analysis
bearing either on constructs (such as concepts and theories) or on their referents (things or their changes). The outcome of the exercise is that the reduced
object (construct or thing) is conjectured or proved to depend on some other
object, logically or ontologically prior to it. Examples of conceptual reduction:
all definitions, the deduction of statics from dynamics, and "economic imperialism." Examples of material reduction: heat is random molecular motion;
mental processes are brain processes; and social facts result from individual
actions—or conversely. Let us take a closer look at the reduction operation.

If *A* and *B* are both either constructs or concrete entities, to *reduce A* to *B* is to
identify *A* with *B*, or to include *A* in *B*, or to assert that every *A* is either an
aggregate, a combination, or an average of *B*'s or else a manifestation or an
image of *B*. It is to assert that although *A* and *B* may appear to be quite different
from one another, they are actually the same, or that *A* is a species of the genus
B, or that every *A* results somehow from *B*'s—or, more vaguely, that *A* "boils
down" to *B* or that, "in the last analysis," all *A*'s are *B*'s.

Three kinds of construct may be reduced: concept, proposition, and theory.
To reduce a *concept A* to a concept *B* is to define *A* in terms of *B*, where *B* refers
to a thing, property, or process on either the same or a lower (or higher) level
than that of the referent(s) of *A*. Such a definition may be called a "reductive
definition." (In the philosophical literature, reductive definitions are usually

called "bridge hypotheses," presumably because they are often originally proposed as hypotheses. History without analysis can be misleading.)

We may distinguish three kinds of reductive definition of a concept: (*a*) *same level*, or $L \to L$; (*b*) *top-down*, or *micro-reductive*, $L \to L - 1$; and (*c*) *bottom-up*, or *macro-reductive*, $L \to L + 1$. Example of the first ($L \to L$): "Historical event = $_{df}$ social change." Example of the second ($L \to L - 1$): "Government revenue = $_{df}$ sum of individual taxes." Example of the third ($L \to L + 1$): "Conformism = $_{df}$ bowing to the prevailing values, norms, or habits." So much for concept reduction.

The reduction of a *proposition* results from replacing at least one of the predicates occurring in it by the definiens of a reductive definition. For example, the psychological proposition "Mary was talking" is reducible to the neurophysiological proposition "Mary's Wernicke and Broca areas were active" by virtue of the reductive definition "speech = $_{df}$ specific activity of the Wernicke and Broca areas." The given proposition is said to have been reduced. (More in chap. 5, sec. 2.)

The analysis of *theory* reduction is somewhat more complex. Call T_1 and T_2 two theories (hypothetico-deductive systems). Assume that they share some referents; call R a set of reductive definitions, and S a set of subsidiary hypotheses not contained in either T_1 or T_2. (However, these auxiliary assumptions must be couched in the language that results from the union of the languages of the two theories if they are to blend with the latter.) We stipulate that (*a*) T_2 is *fully* (or *strongly*) *reducible* to $T_1 = _{df} T_2$ follows logically from the union of T_1 and R; and (*b*) T_2 is *partially* (or *weakly*) *reducible* to $T_1 = _{df} T_2$ follows logically from the union of T_1, R, and S.

Ray optics is strongly reducible to wave optics by way of the reductive definition "Light ray = $_{df}$ normal to light wave front." By contrast, the kinetic theory of gases is only weakly reducible to particle mechanics, because, in addition to the reductive definitions of the concepts of pressure and temperature, the former includes the subsidiary hypothesis of molecular chaos (or random initial distributions of positions and velocities). Likewise, quantum chemistry, cell biology, psychology, and social science are only weakly (partially) reducible to the corresponding lower-level disciplines. Even quantum mechanics contains some classical concepts (e.g., those of mass and time), as well as hypotheses about macrophysical boundaries (boundary conditions), so it does not effect a complete micro-reduction. If this holds for atoms, it should hold, with all the more reason, for people. In fact, individual human behavior cannot be described, let alone explained, in a social vacuum. Thus every one of us is born and raised in a particular society with its distinctive economic, political, and cultural features, which contribute to shaping us. If only for this reason, social science is irreducible to psychology. Consequently the collective name 'behavioral science' for psychology and the social sciences is inadequate.

To explain something is to show how it works. And to describe how a system of any kind works, we need to combine micro-reduction with macro-reduction. The reason is that a system is characterized not only by its composition, but also by its environment and structure (sec. 1). Whereas micro-reductionism focuses on composition, macro-reductionism focuses on structure. In other words, the micro-reductionist thesis is that we know a thing if we find out what it is "made" of, whereas the macro-reductionist thesis is that we know something if we can figure out its place in "the scheme of things" (i.e., the larger system). But of course we need both bits of knowledge. Thus, the systems A → B → C and C ← B → A are different because, although they have the same composition, they differ structurally. By contrast, the systems A → B → C and D → E → F have the same structure but differ in their composition. (More on this in chap. 5, sec. 4.)

7 Reductionism

Reduction must not be confused with reductionism, or the thesis that reduction, either micro or macro, is the only legitimate research strategy. Popular examples of reductionism are the claims that genetics (or else the environment) explains every trait of human behavior and that everything social, including marriage, chatter, and musical composition, is preceded and guided by a calculation of expected utilities.

Reductionism is attractive at first sight for being simple and unifying, hence economical. It may be convenient to pretend that people are utility-maximizers in whatever they do or abstain from doing. This reduces all social variables to one: namely, utility (with the eventual addition of probability), and all the principles to that of maximizing expected utility. In this way, all the social sciences seem to be reducible to the utilitarian psychology sketched two centuries ago. But the confrontation of radical reductionism with reality shows that the world is not that simple. This could have been foreseen by noting that the natural sciences employ myriads of variables.

That reductionism is mistaken becomes obvious upon realizing that every thing and every idea is either a system or a component of one and that systems are characterized by their composition, environment, and structure: they fit the CES sketch (sec. 1). Consequently it is doubly mistaken to focus on composition and overlook structure and environment, the way micro-reductionism does.

Micro-reductionism originated with ancient atomism and was revived and considerably reinforced in the nineteenth century. It contrasts with the macro-reductionism characteristic of holism, a prescientific cosmology. The most popular varieties of modern reductionism are physicalism, biologism, psychologism, and sociologism. According to *physicalism*, all things—even social systems—are physical, whence all sciences ought to be reducible to physics ultimately. With regard to social studies, *biologism* holds that social behavior is genetically determined, so biology is the key to social science. (Primitive and archaic biologism asserted that all things are alive, even the universe as a whole.) Modern *psychologism* asserts that all social facts must be explained in psychological terms, particularly in terms of the principle of economic "rationality," or maximizing utility. Finally, modern *sociologism* is the dual, or complement, of psychologism: it is an example of macro-reductionism, in holding that individual behavior is to be explained exclusively by reference to society. Two examples of macro-reductionism are computationalist psychology and textualism. The former claims that all behavior, even that of primitive organisms, is a result of computations according to definite algorithms; whereas the latter (radical philosophical hermeneutics) holds that everything is a text or discourse, the world then constituting a library. Let us examine these views.

Physicalism is false, because organisms happen to be alive, and physics accounts only for the physical components of living things and the physical aspects of living processes. For example, physics tells us what doubly ionized calcium is, but not that it is a neurotransmitter. Likewise, chemistry discloses the composition and structure of genes, but, because these discharge biological functions only within living cells, genetics is not fully reducible to chemistry. Similarly, no social science is reducible to biology, or even to psychology, because only the components of a social system are alive and have a mental life; social systems are not even dead or dumb, except metaphorically. Moreover, a social system is held together not only by biological (e.g., sexual) bonds, but also by economic, political, and cultural ones; and it has specific functions (e.g., manufacture, trade, public transportation, education, or coercion) that no natural science can account for. Finally, social science has concepts, hypotheses, and methods alien to biology and psychology. For example, these sciences have no use for the concept of balance of trade, for the hypothesis that technological innovations bring about economic changes, or for accounting techniques. So much for the most popular micro-reductionist opinions.

Let us now take a quick look at the three macro-reductionist views mentioned above: sociologism, computationalism, and textualism. Sociologism is wrong because the social environment stimulates and inhibits behavior but does not replace visceral and mental processes. Moreover, some of our ideas and actions go against the current, and a few succeed in modifying the social structure: we are never completely passive. As for computationalism, it is wrong even in mathematics, for only numerical functions are computable, and they do not exhaust mathematics. It is also wrong psychologically, because we do not compute our emotions, movements, perceptions, or recalls, any more than planets compute their orbits (Bunge and Ardila 1987). Finally, textualism, a variety of idealism, is wrong because it confuses linguistic expressions with their referents, thereby inviting scientists, technologists, and even laymen to turn from thing and work to word.

We conclude that radical reductionism is not valid, because reduction is seldom complete. In other words, every science has an irreducible core of its own—that is, a set of peculiar ideas and methods. The correct strategy is *moderate reductionism,* whose watchword is: Reduce as far as possible without forcing the issue—that is, do not ignore the formation and breakdown of systems, with the concomitant emergence and submergence of new properties. We shall come back to this point when discussing holism and individualism in social studies (chap. 9).

The failure of the various radical reductionist projects does not entail that every science is separate from the rest of human knowledge. On the contrary, every authentic science overlaps partially with some other sciences, and all the sciences share logic and mathematics. (This partial overlap is so characteristic of science that one of the peculiarities of pseudoscience is isolation.) This could not be otherwise, since the division of scientific work is largely artificial. There are purely physical facts, such as the emission of light; but, above the physical level, all facts have nonphysical as well as physical aspects. In particular, there are no purely social facts: since every social fact involves living persons, it has biological features, which in turn have chemical and physical features. This is one of the reasons why we need interdisciplines, such as neurolinguistics, social psychology, bioeconomics, and historical sociology.

Because every high-level system is constituted by lower-level components, any science studying the former is bound to use some of the findings of the sciences that study the latter. For example, the social sciences make use of some psychology, which in turn utilizes some biology (and much neuroscience), which would be incomprehensible without some chemistry, which in turn requires some physics.

There are thus two conceptual relations between a scientific discipline and its neighbors: the horizontal of partial overlap and the vertical of dependence. The former can be visualized as a rosette, the latter as a pyramid. As we saw a moment ago, this dual epistemological order is rooted in the nature of things. If the world were either a solid block (holism) or an aggregate of separate atoms (atomism), or if science did not attempt to model the world, a single science would suffice.

8 Merger

The limitations of reduction suggest trying the dual strategy: that is, the merger of two or more theories or even entire disciplines. This strategy is needed everywhere sooner or later, because everything is a system or a component of some system, and a system is not just the collection of its components (recall chap. 1, sec. 2). This kind of integrative strategy has paid off handsomely, as can be seen from the achievements of a large number of mergers of initially independent theories or research fields, such as analytic geometry, celestial mechanics, statistical thermodynamics, electromagnetic theory, the synthetic theory of evolution, biogeography, neuropsychology, bioengineering, and socioeconomics.

Let us analyze the concept of merger or amalgamation of two or more theories. The simplest case is the mere union of two or more theories (or, rather, the corresponding set of formulas). But of course not every union of theories results in a theory. For instance, no theory results from joining mechanics with a theory of social networks. A necessary condition for a union to constitute a theory is that the founding theories share referents and therefore specific concepts (variables, functions). Celestial mechanics and the synthetic theory of evolution are two obvious examples of successful theory union.

In most cases the founding theories have to be glued together with additional statements relating some of the concepts of the two theories. For example, the construction of analytic geometry required not only its two precursors, algebra and Euclidean geometry, but also the postulate of a one-to-one correspondence between points in Euclidean n-space and n-tuples of real numbers. We call any extra postulate of this kind a "glue formula."

Different choices of glue formula(s) give rise to alternative mergers (e.g., if in Descartes's glue formula complex numbers are substituted for real numbers, a nonstandard analytic geometry results). In pure mathematics a glue formula need only be justified by the power of the resulting merger. By contrast, glue formulas in factual science relate properties possessed by real things, so they must be tested empirically. For example, if we wish to close the gap between economics and political science, we must conceive, and eventually test, hypotheses gluing economic concepts to political ones—for example, the once-true Marxist hypothesis that every political party represents the economic interests of a distinctive social class.

In general we shall say that a factual theory T is a *merger* of the factual theories T_1 and T_2 if and only if (a) T_1 and T_2 share some referents and some concepts; (b) there is a (possibly empty) set G of (glue) formulas relating some concepts of T_1 to some concepts of T_2; and (c) the (glue) formulas in G are testable empirically. What holds for the merger of theories holds, mutatis mutandis, for the coalescence of research fields.

Integration and reduction are equally important factors in the unity of science. They accompany specialization and compensate for the latter's narrowness and its separatist tendencies. Integration is particularly important and conspicuous in the study of macro-systems, such as multicellular organisms and human societies, because of their multiple aspects and the several levels of organization they cross. This makes the current fragmentation of social science all the more deplorable.

Every concept and every proposition makes sense only in some context—that is, in relation to other bits of knowledge. In particular, concepts and propositions are best understood as components of such conceptual systems as classifications, sketches, and theories. Conceptual systemicity parallels the systemic nature of reality, where there are no monads, no stray properties, and no isolated events—in particular, no stray social facts.

The preceding assertions must not be mistaken for a profession of holistic faith, since holism is hostile to analysis, in particular to reduction. Mine are systemist theses. The point of systemism is not just that there are wholes, conceptual as well as concrete, with (emergent) properties of their own; it is rather that a whole, far from being a block or sealed unit, is a system analyzable in terms of its composition, environment, and structure (CES). This holds in particular for societies, as will be argued in chapter 10.

Not surprisingly, a conspicuous feature of the advancement of science is the progress of systematization, particularly the proliferation of theories and interdisciplines. Theoretical advances occur in a number of ways: through inventing radically new theories or correcting existing ones; through deriving new results in existing theories or refining (in particular, axiomatizing) them; through specifying and generalizing; through reducing and merging; and last, but not least, through metatheoretical analysis, criticism, cleansing, or reorganization in the light of mathematics, empirical data, or philosophical principles.

Such conceptual advances are variously motivated. In some cases the student is moved by the wish to find pattern in a mass of empirical data, in others by the compulsion to interrelate or generalize existing ideas, in still others by the need to derive new predictions that will test a theory or else by the wish to try out a new mathematical tool. His motivation may be practical, as in the case of building or specifying theories that will help to design artifacts (e.g., organizations) or processes (e.g., economic growth); or it may be conceptual or even aesthetic, as when removing inconsistencies or refining and systematizing a disorderly heap of intuitive ideas.

Given the variety of motivations for doing innovative theoretical work and the variety of ways whereby the latter may be accomplished, it would be narrow-minded and short-sighted to favor only one kind. Conceptual diversity is just as important as bio-diversity—but with an important difference: that while we should protect wildlife, we should discourage wild conjectures just as strongly as obviously false factual information. This is best done by examining critically the fruits of theory: namely, explanation, prediction, and the suggestion of new observations or experiments. We will now proceed to examine all three.

PART B :: *From Explanation to Justification*

5 :: *Explanation and Prediction*

Social facts can be produced or prevented; and some of them can be discovered, described, classed, explained, forecast, or evaluated. In this chapter we shall study only the main ways of accounting for facts: namely, description, explanation, and forecast. This study needs to precede that of the practical problems of producing or preventing social facts in a rational way. In particular, objective description should precede everything else, for only a (sufficiently) true description of a social situation qualifies us in advancing explanatory hypotheses, identifying social issues, and designing efficient policies or plans for tackling the latter.

1 Description

The least we should expect from a scientific study is a description of facts of some kind—that is, an answer to some of the what-questions which they elicit, such as What is that? and What happened, and where and when? But before describing a fact, we must make reasonably sure that it has happened or at least could happen. That is, we must start by uncovering or conjecturing the fact in question. This task is comparatively easy when the fact is perceptible, as in the case of riots or troop movements, but hard when it is imperceptible, like a decision, a business takeover, or a demographic or cultural trend. In the latter cases we need special techniques and hypotheses that go well beyond ordinary knowledge. In particular, we need statistical analysis and indicators (i.e., observable–unobservable hypotheses). But in neither case are there rules for discovering facts. If there were, we would seldom if ever engage in arguing over whether certain alleged facts have actually occurred—a favorite pastime of social scientists and politicians.

Once a fact has been discovered or conjectured, we do not normally rush headlong to account for it. Instead, we weigh it to decide whether it is worth describing in any detail. Such evaluation is particularly important nowadays, when we all suffer from information overload and budget cuts. Obviously, the importance or "significance" we attribute to any fact depends on the approach we adopt: on our background knowledge and philosophy, on the problems we are interested in, our aims, and the methods we have mastered or are willing to learn (recall chap. 3, sec. 1).

For example, some historians pay almost exclusive attention to political and military events; others focus on cultural facts; still others, on economic processes. Only a few adopt a systemic viewpoint and study all the pertinent facts: environmental, demographic, biological, economic, political, and cultural. But even the narrowest of specialists must choose among a welter of facts. The choice depends upon evaluation, and the latter depends, in turn, on the researcher's philosophy. If he is an idealist, he will concentrate on culture and politics; if a materialist and nonsystemist, on reproduction and the economy; and so on.

Descriptions can be cast in ordinary language or in a scientific language—not to mention pseudoscientific jargon. Ordinary language descriptions suffice for everyday purposes but are insufficient for scientific or technological purposes. Science and technology add their own words and symbols to designate their specific or technical concepts, some of which refer to entities, properties, and events inaccessible to ordinary inspection or unaccountable in ordinary knowledge terms. Regrettably, in the social sciences it is not uncommon to find trivialities expressed in high-sounding pseudotechnical jargon and sometimes even in poor English (or German or French). For example, this is how Harold Garfinkel (1967, 11) characterizes his brainchild, ethnomethodology: it is "the investigation of the rational [?] properties of indexical [context-dependent] expressions and other practical actions as contingent [?] ongoing accomplishments of organized artful [?] practices of everyday life."

The most precise (though not necessarily the truest) descriptions are *theoretical:* that is, descriptions using the exact languages of a genuine science. For example, change can be accurately described by input–output matrices, differential equations, or other mathematical forms, together with the semantic assumptions that endow some of the predicates occurring in the formulas with factual meaning.

Still, no matter how precise, no description can quench our thirst for understanding. For example, a social mobility table or matrix may be an accurate description: it tells us what happens. But it does not tell us why it happens. If we wish to understand what makes it happen, we must try to explain it—for instance, in terms of opportunity (e.g., job vacancy), connections, individual effort, or any combination of these. Shorter: We want to know what makes things—in particular, people—tick. Bookkeeping is necessary, but it does not satisfy curiosity: only explanation does that.

2 Explanation

Description is necessary but insufficient: we want to know why, not just what, where, when, whence, or whither. For example, social statistics reveal that rises in criminality are associated (strongly correlated) with increases in unemployment. Is this because some people prefer crime to work (as conservatives claim) or because people prevented from earning a livelihood are forced to steal in order to avoid starving (as liberals hold)? Both are explanations of the given data, and only research can decide between them.

Not everything natural calls for explanation. In particular, on a scientific world view the existence of the universe does not: only its evolution calls for explanation. But everything social, starting with society, calls for explanation. Social stasis demands it, given the turnover of people and their conflicting interests; and social change demands explanation, given the slowness to learn and the inertia of institutions. Now, to explain a fact is to exhibit its underlying mechanism(s). For example, the diffusion of cultural things, habits, and traits can be explained by various mechanisms, among them realization of benefit, conditioning, imitation, teaching, and coercion.

To explain a thing, then, is to show how it works, and to explain a fact is to show how it came to be. Thus, we explain pregnancy by ova fertilization and cell division, divorce by unresolved marital conflict, and altruism by empathy and social responsibility. We explain famine by food scarcity, and the latter, in turn, by drought, desertification, overpopulation, undercultivation, hoarding, armed conflict, or whatever. We explain social conflict by divergence of interests, and colonial war by greed for new land or new markets. We explain wholes by their parts, and conversely; the present by the past; actions (or inactions) by interests, choices, and constraints—and so on and so forth.

Explanations may be correct or incorrect, scientific or nonscientific (in particular, magical), deep or shallow, and so on. In all cases we explain facts by invoking some *mechanism* or other, perceptible or hidden, known or suspected. The behavior of simple things does not call for explanation, for they have no "works"—that is, mechanisms that make them tick. But then only physics knows of things with no parts: namely, elementary particles, photons, and the like. As soon as we study systems, from atoms to nations, we experience the need to know how they work. We seldom remain satisfied with descriptions such as black boxes or block diagrams, no matter how accurate they may be. We want explanation, either because we want rational understanding—not some vague intuition or a metaphor, let alone a story—or because we wish to tamper with the thing in question.

Descartes and his followers required that all mechanisms be strictly mechanical. Two centuries later, field physics, evolutionary biology, psychology, historical sociology, and many other scientific disciplines relaxed this condition. We now understand that mechanisms need not be mechanical: they may be physical, chemical, biological (in particular, psychological), social, or mixed. They may be natural or artificial; causal or stochastic or a combination of the two; pervasive or idiosyncratic, and so on. The only condition for a mechanism hypothesis to be taken seriously in modern science or technology is that it be concrete (rather than immaterial), lawful (rather than miraculous), and scrutable (rather than occult).

Here are some examples of social mechanism. The abnormal percentage of unmarried women in postwar periods is a result of male war casualties. The abnormal sex ratio in some Asian countries is caused by girl infanticide, which in turn is caused by poverty and the economic undervaluing of females in male-dominated societies. The rapid growth of shanty towns around Third World cities is caused by (*a*) the decline in traditional agriculture, in turn caused by the growth of market-oriented agriculture (cash crops) or the expansion of cattle ranches; (*b*) industrialization; and sometimes also (*c*) civil war in the countryside. In the industrialized countries, unemployment is caused by industrial obsolescence, increasing productivity, or political change. Everywhere the belief that the standard of living, the quality of life, and particularly survival are at risk moves people to organize themselves, hence the proliferation of mutual societies, unions, lobbies, and the like, as well as the mobilization of organizations, notably churches, originally created for different purposes.

Reductive explanation constitutes an important, particular case of mechanismic explanation. An explanation is said to be *reductive* if and only if at least one of the premises occurring in it is a reductive proposition (recall chap. 4, sec. 6). For example, explanation of the formation of a concrete system in terms of the self-assembly of its components is of the micro-reductive (or top-down) kind. By contrast, explanation of the behavior of a component of a system in terms of the place it occupies or the role it performs in the system is of the macro-reductive (or bottom-up) type. Research on the origin of life or the assembly line induce top-down explanations, whereas the car mechanic and the social psychologist typically resort to bottom-up explanations. However, the fullest reductive explanations are combinations of the two basic types, as when a political event is explained as the outcome of the concerted actions of a number of individuals in reaction to a social issue.

If an explanation is found to be incorrect or shallow, it is the scientist's tacit faith that it can be improved on by conjecturing a different mechanism. Moreover, if no plausible mechanism is found to account for controversial data, such as those concerning miracles, telepathy, or faith healing, the scientist may question the very data: he may suspend his judgment or even deny that the data describe any facts. A scientifically plausible mechanism is one that, no matter how counter-intuitive, satisfies laws. (More on this in sec. 3.)

Some of the earliest explanations of things were mythical, magical, or religious. The earliest scientific explanations were *causal* explanations: that is, explanations in terms of causal mechanisms. Primitive man did not believe in coincidences and did not know about probability. A causal mechanism is of course one activated by events (causes) of a certain kind (recall chap. 1, sec. 5). The causes can be external or internal—that is, environmental stimuli or internal processes. The environmental causes can be natural, social, or a combination of both, such as a sound wave transmitting a command. Among the internal causes are mental events such as decisions, which, in turn, are motivated by intentions. In the latter case, the causes are usually called 'reasons.'

The distinction between cause and reason is real, but it should not be exaggerated the way idealist philosophers have done. Indeed, except in mathematical discourse, reasons are causes which are presumably understood and, moreover, under the agent's immediate control—such as the reasons for doing something. Hence they are quite different from nonrational external causes beyond human control, such as earthquakes, or nonrational internal causes, such as hunger. However, from the point of view of physiological psychology, reasons are brain processes and may thus cause overt behavior. From this standpoint, then, the difference between explanations by (efficient) causes and explanations by (sufficient) reasons boils down to the difference between external and internal causes.

Nor does purposive, or goal-directed, action escape ordinary or efficient causation. If an individual does A in order to achieve goal G, he is being driven to do A by his current mental representation, C, of G, not by G itself. Indeed, nonexistents, such as goals, are devoid of causal efficacy. Thus the causal link is $C \to A$, not $G \to A$. In other words, what is traditionally called 'final causation' is nothing but efficient causation with an effect (goal) in view. 'Rational causation' might be a better name were it not for the fact that we often choose foolish goals or wrong means.

The preceding considerations refute the contentions of Dilthey, Weber, Popper, Davidson, rational choice theorists, hermeneuticists, and ordinary language philosophers that (*a*) causes and reasons are separated by a chasm, and (*b*) human actions, unlike natural events, can be explained only by intentions and reasons, never by causes.

In particular, our conclusion that reasons can be causes refutes the claim that human behavior can be explained only by the so-called logic of the situation. The latter boils down to the following explanatory schema, or practical syllogism:

> An agent in a given situation has goal or intention G.
> The agent reasons that he can best attain G by performing action A.
> Hence he does A.

If the agent is rational, as assumed, he will have some grounds for expecting that his doing A will *cause* (perhaps only with some likelihood) outcome G. And if he is well informed, he will also know that the situation he finds himself in is at least in part the outcome of natural or social *causes*. In short, the rational agent will combine reasons for acting (internal causes) with external causes, instead of detaching them.

However, causality is not enough. Modern social science admits the existence of objective chance—hence the need for stochastic explanations. These, of course, are explanations in terms of probabilities or probability distributions. But they do not allow one to dispense with causal analysis. We need this analysis to distinguish between correlation and causation, as well as between source and symptom. Take, for example, the case of homelessness. It has been known for some time that most of the homeless in the United States have problems that make them incapable of living in normal homes, such as drug addiction, alcoholism, mental illness, a criminal record, or lack of friends. The correlation is strong; but is it a symptom of a causal relation, and, if so, what is the cause, and what the effect? Conservatives hold that only personal disabilities cause homelessness, whereas liberals blame such "structural" circumstances as poverty, unemployment, and the lack of affordable housing. Could it not be that a correct explanation requires combining personal and structural circumstances? Is it not likely that homelessness involves two causal arrows, one bottom-up, or micro–macro, the other top-down, or macro–micro? (More on micro–macro relations in sec. 4.)

Here is another correlation that calls for a causal explanation. It is well known that health and socioeconomic status are directly correlated. On average, the rich live longer and enjoy much better health than the poor. This association has been sustained despite sensational medical advances. Why is this so? I would hazard the following explanatory sketch. Socioeconomic status, jointly with biological (in particular, genetic and psychological) factors, determines an individual's environment and education, which in turn determine his life-style, which in turn determines his state of health. Direct medical intervention in the disease process, when affordable, often comes too late, and in any case it can only do so much (see Evans et al. 1994).

We also need causal analysis to explain how different processes can have roughly the same outcome—the case of *alternative multiple causation*. Think of the different possible sources of wealth accumulation: land ownership, territorial conquest, war, theft (in particular, colonial plundering), industry, trade, banking, and so on. Or think of the different barriers to national development: scarcity of natural resources, overpopulation, dependency, landowner power, militarism, ecclesiastical power, shortage of skilled manpower, bureaucratism, and the rest.

Important social events usually have *joint multiple causes*. Inflation is a case in point, this being why it is hard to control with single measures, such as credit restriction. For instance, the inflation suffered by the industrialized countries between the mid-1970s and the late 1980s has been attributed to the operation of the following mutually independent mechanisms: demand inflation (boosted by advertising), cost inflation, tax cuts, the arms race, and the issuing of government bonds to finance the increasing fiscal debt. This is, of course, only a sketch of an explanation and, like any other, is open to criticism. But the point is that, given the complexity of modern society, *unicausal* explanations of large-scale social facts are implausible. By the same token, sectoral social reforms are bound to fail, particularly if they treat only the symptoms of social ills, instead of their causes.

Causal analysis of the variance (standard deviation) of a distribution is another case of explanation. For example, what accounts for the large variance (spread) in incomes nearly everywhere? It is usually admitted that sex, race, and age (or, rather, sexual, racial, and age discrimination) explain part of the variance, and that education and seniority explain another part. Yet another part may be attributed to opportunity or luck—that is, to the person being available at the right place and the right time. In any event, analysis of variance is the standard statistical method for finding out how much of the variance in a set of data can be attributed to different causes—for example, to nature or nurture in the case of human abilities.

On the other hand, so-called *explanation of variables* is not such. Consider two variables, x and y, the first of which takes values in a set X and the second in a set Y. (In other words, x is an arbitrary member of X, and y of Y. The sets X and Y need not be different.) One usually says that variable x explains variable y if and only if there is a single function, f, that maps X into Y; that is, such that $y = f(x)$ is true for all x in X—perhaps to within a certain margin of error, though. However, this is a case of *analysis*, not explanation proper, since no mechanism, let alone a causal one, is involved.

Our account of explanation is at variance with both descriptivism and historicism. According to the former, which is inherent in empiricism, from Ptolemy to Hume and from Comte to Mach, we should shun explanation, aiming instead to give the most accurate and complete description. The rationale of descriptivism is that only phenomena (appearances) and their mutual relations are accessible to observation: the rest is conjecture and therefore something to be avoided. If this bias against unobservables is jettisoned, it may be admitted that description (though not descriptivism) encompasses explanation insofar as it includes description of mechanisms.

As for historicism, whether idealist, as with Hegel and Dilthey, or materialist, as with Marx and the German historical school, it holds that to explain anything is to place it in a developmental or historical line. Its rationale is that all things are changeable, so the present state of a thing cannot be understood without reference to its past—and its future as well, if a teleological view is thrown in for good measure. This is true but only part of the story, for two reasons: first, before attempting to describe the history of X, we must have some idea about X; second, if we are inquisitive, we will want to find out the change mechanisms—that is, we will want to explain change. So history (though not historicism) can be broadened to encompass both description and explanation.

Our analysis of explanation differs from the standard account. According to the latter, to explain a fact is to subsume it under a generalization. Thus, one explains John's mortality by invoking the generalization "All men are mortal" and the datum that John is human. Actually, this is just a *subsumption* of the particular under the general: it is a logical operation that fails to answer the questions "What (mechanism) makes John mortal?" and "Why must John die eventually?" More on the logic of explanation next.

3 Logical Form

Consider a social fact, such as the crumbling of Soviet and East European communism (actually state socialism together with party dictatorship) around 1990. This fact can be explained as a result of popular dissatisfaction. But such an explanation presupposes the generalization that popular dissatisfaction, everywhere and at all times, causes popular rebellion. We shall see below that this generalization is too simple to be true. For the moment, the point is that we have made tacit use of a lawlike statement. Moreover, by unpacking the compact explanation "Communism fell because of popular dissatisfaction," we obtain the following argument:

Generalization: Every time people are dissatisfied with a political regime, they rebel against it.

Datum: The East European and Soviet peoples were dissatisfied with the Communist regime.

Conclusion: The East European and Soviet peoples rebelled against the Communist regime.

Regardless of the truth of the premises, this is a logically (formally) valid argument. (In fact, it is an instance of the fundamental rule of inference, or modus ponens.) The premises are called the *explanans,* and the conclusion the *explanandum.* The latter is, of course, the proposition describing the fact to be explained. Thus, from a purely *logical* point of view, to explain a fact is to deduce the corresponding explanandum from some explanans premises, at least one of which must be general and another particular. The latter may be called an 'auxiliary datum.' In symbols, the logical structure of the simplest possible explanatory argument is this: For all x: if x is an F, then x is a G. Now, a is an F. Hence, a is a G. In symbols: $(\forall x)(Fx \Rightarrow Gx)$, $Fa \therefore Ga$. So much for the standard or "covering law model" of explanation, expounded by Popper (1959 [1935]) and elaborated by Hempel (1965).

Logical validity is necessary, but insufficient, for correct, or adequate, explanation. The latter requires that the explanans premises be true at least to a first approximation. In short, we stipulate that an explanation qualifies as *correct* if and only if it is a logically valid argument from (sufficiently) true premises, at least one of which is general. Now, not all explanations of animal (in particular, human) behavior fulfill the conditions of validity and truth. In fact, we often offer explanations whose premises are at least dubious. This is particularly so when we impute intentions and rationality to other people or to subhuman animals when habit or conditioning might suffice. Such attributions are conjectural, and they need testing before we can claim that they explain correctly the observed behavior.

This point is obvious in natural science but contentious in social science. Indeed, many students of society claim that their theories need not be true: it would suffice that they allow them to "understand" the facts of interest. But this retreat from the commitment to truth amounts to admitting that the study of society need not be scientific. Indeed, if one is going to settle for "understanding" everything without explaining anything, one may as well condone any myths—for example, that everything that happens is an effect of supernatural, immaterial, or extraterrestrial agencies. Scientific understanding is attained through explanation with the help of true generalizations.

In science, an explanans generalization is either a law statement (or at least an empirical generalization) or a social norm. And the auxiliary datum is an outcome of a run of observations, measurements, or experiments. In other words, a *scientific* explanation is an argument from law (or norm) and circumstance to explanadum. This methodological condition, jointly with logical validity, is necessary for an explanation to qualify as scientific. On the standard, or positivist, view, it is also sufficient. In my view it is not, for it does not include the condition that the explanans must describe the mechanism whereby the fact in question came to be (recall the previous section).

When showing that an explanandum follows validly from certain explanans premises, all we do is to *subsume* the former under a generalization. This amounts to embedding the given particular in a pattern. In other words, we show that the fact in question is an instance of a law, or at least an empirical generalization. For example, we account for the fact that a certain woman earns less than her male colleague by saying that all women are treated like that in the given organization or society. But of course this does not explain anything. Moreover, in a way it justifies the practice in question. By contrast, we do get an explanation proper when told that, in the organization or society in question, women are the object of negative discrimination and that this kind of discrimination is a form of exploitation profitable to the males in charge.

In other words, an explanation proper, unlike a mere subsumption, looks like this:

General explanans premise: a generalization involving reference to a mechanism.

Particular explanans premise: an auxiliary datum concerning the fact to be explained.

Explanandum: a datum concerning the fact to be explained.

We call this the logical form of a *mechanismic explanation*, or explanation proper. The classical paradigm in physics is: Equations of motion & initial or boundary conditions ⇒ body trajectory or field propagation. In biology: Genic variation & environmental conditions ⇒ phenotype. In economics: Price rise & budget constraint ⇒ demand drop.

In sum, an explanation must satisfy three conditions to qualify as scientific: (*a*) *logical*: it must be a formally valid (nonfallacious) argument; (*b*) *semantical*: at least one of its premises must refer to some mechanism or other; (*c*) *methodological*: its premises and conclusion(s) must be testable and preferably reasonably true.

A further desideratum is that the explanans generalizations not be omni-explanatory; that is, they should not purport to explain just about any facts. In other words, there is no universal explanans, a single mechanism that fits everything. For better or for worse, reality is extraordinarily variegated. This is why understanding it calls for a huge collection of hypotheses (in particular, of the mechanismic kind). Classical examples of omni-explanatory, hence suspect, hypotheses concerning human behavior are those resorting to fate, race, utility maximization, and class struggle.

Having stressed the logical form of an explanation, we should not lose sight of its factual content, which is often overlooked in the philosophical literature. That is, we should keep in mind that we explain facts in terms of facts, not propositions. For example, we may explain mass unemployment as an effect of overpopulation combined with increased productivity in some sectors of the economy and decreased profitability in others.

4 Upward and Downward

What is typical of explanation in social science is, of course, that it attempts to explain social facts. To be able to do this, the explanandum, as well as the explanatory premises, must contain some social predicates—that is, predicates representing properties of social systems. In some cases the premises contain predicates of this kind only; that is, a macro–macro link is invoked. Take, for example, the following generalization concerning the Third World: "Servicing the soaring external debt causes a decline in education (E) and health care (H)." This is a true causal statement of the macro–macro, or M–M type. It can be explained in terms of another two M–M generalizations, namely: Increasing debt $\Rightarrow$ decreasing expenditures on E and H and Decreasing expenditures on E and H $\Rightarrow$ decline in E and H, $\therefore$ Increasing debt $\Rightarrow$ decline in E and H.

This explanation is correct but unilluminating, for it does not unveil the causes of the macro-facts referred to by the premises. These causes are of the micro, as well as the macro, kind. A more complete explanatory schema would involve individual needs, desires, and decisions in addition to macro-facts. Consider, for example, the following causal chain for the derivation of the same explanandum: National underdevelopment → individuals wish for national development → people elect government intent on promoting development → adoption of development policy and plan → decision to borrow in order to finance plan → spending decisions → unproductive investments, waste, and theft → deficit → decision to borrow more → soaring debt → decision to ask for loan from the International Monetary Fund → decision to cut social expenditures → cutbacks in social expenditures → negative impact on teachers, health care workers, and the poor → decline in education and health care. Note the combination of macro–micro (M–m), micro–micro (m–m), micro–macro (m–M), and macro–macro (M–M) links.

In general, since social systems are composed of individuals, we must often ask how individual actions combine to produce global effects and how these, in turn, affect individual lives. That is, in social studies we ask m–M and M–m questions as well as M–M ones and leave most m–m problems to psychology. (Durkheim condoned only m–m and M–M accounts. Marx also admitted M–m accounts but underrated m–M ones.)

Consider another example: our previous, admittedly simplistic explanation of the downfall of the Soviet-style dictatorships in recent times (sec. 3). Our explanation was that, ultimately, these events were caused by popular dissatisfaction with the regime. But the predicate "popular dissatisfaction" should be analyzed in individualist terms, as dissatisfaction of most of the adult members of the society. Yet the predicate "regime" (or "social order") cannot be so analyzed, for it represents a systemic or emergent property of the society. I warned earlier that this explanation is simple-minded. Indeed, it invites the question as to why the rebellion did not happen much earlier. A clue to the explanation of why the rebellion occurred when it did appears when two apparently disjoined items, the glasnost and perestroika reforms and Tocqueville's view of the conditions for revolution, are conjoined. Let us take a closer look.

Glasnost and perestroika were initiated from above in 1985 under the leadership of Mikhail Gorbachev. They gave the Soviet people a chance to realize what was wrong with the regime—unchallenged until then—and thus to become dissatisfied with it and discuss its shortcomings openly. Taking advantage of their newly received civil liberties, they eventually vented their anger in the workplace and the street. Read now what Tocqueville wrote in 1853, prompted by his study of the French revolutions between 1789 and 1848: "It is almost never when a state of things is the most detestable that it is smashed, but when, beginning to improve, it permits men to breathe, to reflect, to communicate their thoughts with each other, and to gauge by what they already have the extent of their rights and their grievances. The weight, although less heavy, seems then all the more unbearable" (Tocqueville 1985, 396).

Methodological individualists would claim that Tocqueville's explanation satisfies their requirement of reducing collective events to the "sum" of individual decisions and actions. But this is not what Tocqueville did. His point of departure was macrosocial: namely, the "state of affairs" (or social state) and its improvement. This new state of the social system as a whole is what enabled its members to think and act more freely, and even to judge "the weight" (of the social institutions) in a new light. Far from being individualist, this mode of explanation appears at first glance to be typically holist: it is of the top-down, or structure–agency, type.

But on closer examination, this reading of Tocqueville proves to be just as mistaken as the individualist reading. Indeed, once the oppressed people get a chance to think and act on their own, they get organized, take to the streets, and start to alter the very social order that had begun to improve without their political participation. In other words, a grassroots movement now begins, which ends up by changing the social structure. The corresponding account is of the bottom-up, or agency–structure, type. And this part of the account does satisfy, though only partially, the rule of methodological individualism. But it does so only up to a point, because the radical or consistent individualist rejects the very idea that there is anything above individuals.

In short, then, we have accounted for the most recent and radical social revolution by combining two different modes of explanation: top-down and bottom-up. The former amounts to downward, the latter to upward reduction.

But neither suffices by itself in social matters, because every individual action takes place in a social context and, if effective, the action will in turn alter this context. Hence the two modes of explanation (or reduction) are mutually complementary, rather than exclusive. Consequently neither holism nor individualism matches the practice of scientific explanation. But systemism does (see chap. 10).

Before examining further examples, let me elucidate the expressions "bottom-up" (or "upward") and "top-down" (or "downward"). I will begin by clarifying the notions of micro-fact and macro-fact, for they are involved in the elucidation of upward and downward explanation. Consider a system and its components at some level—for example, a university and the individuals who work or study at it. A *macro-fact* is a fact occurring in the system as a whole. A *micro-fact* is a fact occurring in or to some or all of the members of the system at the given level. For instance, a reorganization of the university is a macro-fact, whereas its members doing their research or homework are micro-facts.

A *top-down (or micro) explanation* of a macro-fact is the deduction of the proposition(s) describing it from propositions describing (micro-)facts in components of the system where the macro-fact occurs. A *bottom-up (or macro) explanation* of a micro-fact is the deduction of the proposition(s) describing it from propositions describing (macro-)facts occurring in the system as a whole. Now, social science studies both micro-facts (insofar as they have macro-effects) and macro-facts (both in themselves and for the impact they have on micro-facts). Hence, in social science we need both top-down and bottom-up explanations, depending on whether we want to explain macro-facts or micro-facts, respectively.

However, top-down (or micro-reductive) explanations are incomplete, because one and the same environmental or social pressure may affect different individuals in different ways. Thus Marxists, who are holists, cannot explain why only some workers rebel against exploitation—let alone why others aid and abet the exploiters. And bottom-up (or macro-reductive) explanations are incomplete, because every individual action occurs in a preexisting social context. Thus Weber, who preached methodological individualism, tried to explain the proliferation of Protestant sects in the United States toward the end of the nineteenth century as a result of the need felt by rootless people, who had recently emigrated from other countries or other regions of the nation, to acquire respectability in order to do business. But since he took the capitalist framework for granted, Weber could not escape the very "collective" concepts that he professed to abhor.

The reason for the incompleteness of both bottom-up and top-down explanations is this. In both cases we start by assuming, explicitly or tacitly, that we are dealing with a *system* and its parts. The only difference lies in the *problem* in question: in the case of micro-explanation the problem is to explain the whole by its parts, whereas in the case of macro-explanation we grapple with the inverse problem. A few examples drawn from the natural and social sciences will help to clarify this important point.

Let us start with what are usually regarded as sensational triumphs of micro-explanation. Ferromagnetism is explained in terms of the alignment of atomic spins and their associated magnetic momenta; however, one starts by assuming that one is dealing with a macro-object such as a chunk of steel. Genetics explains heredity in terms of DNA molecules; but these are assumed to be cell components and, moreover, components of the regulatory subsystem of the cell. Physiological psychology explains learning in terms of the reinforcement of interneuronal connections via neurotransmitters; yet it starts by considering large aggregates of neurons. All feedback systems are explained by analyzing them into their components, each of which "makes sense" only as a system component. Medical models of antisocial behavior, such as drunken driving, take it for granted that the individuals in question exist in society. Neoclassical economics takes the market, a macrosocial entity, for granted; hence it does not exemplify strict methodological individualism. Likewise, social contract theory concerns individuals subject to social constraints: after all, some of the clauses of any contract refer, necessarily, to the institutional framework. None of these is a case of pure micro-reduction, hence none of them supports strict individualism.

Let us now review a few cases of macro-reduction, or bottom-up explanation. The behavior of a molecule in a liquid depends on whether or not it lies on the surface. The peculiarities of deep-sea creatures are explained in part by their isolation and the high pressures they have to withstand. The specific functions of every member of a family or organization depend on his or her place in it. Thus a mother has duties that a childless wife does not have. A professor's teaching duties depend not only on his abilities but also on "the needs of the department." Likewise, his salary depends not only on his competence but also on his connections and on the university budget. None of these is a case of pure macro-reduction.

Since both macro- and micro-reduction are necessary, but neither is completely satisfactory, we must try to combine them. Boudon (1981 [1979]) and Coleman (1984, 1990) have suggested how to combine M–m with m–M analyses, and these in turn with M–M and m–m descriptions. (Incidentally, this shows that Boudon and Coleman practice the systemic approach even while preaching an individualist one.) Consider the collective decisions brought about by voting in a political democracy, where in principle the individual decisions are mutually independent. The electorate is offered a set of alternatives. Each citizen has his own order of preferences, makes his decision, and casts his ballot. The votes are counted, and the election outcome is an-

Macrolevel	$M_1 \rightarrow M_2$	Description
Micro-explanation	$\downarrow$ $\uparrow$	Macro-explanation
Microlevel	$m_1 \rightarrow m_2$	Description

Fig. 5.1. Combination of micro-explanation (top-down) with macro-explanation (bottom-up).

nounced. The macro-facts are the alternatives offered the electorate (M_1) and the election outcome (M_2). M_1 induces the citizen's choice and decision (m_1), which in turn guides his action—that is, his voting (m_2). The aggregation of the outcomes of these individual actions results in the election outcome, M_2. In this particular case the aggregation is merely additive. In most cases macro-facts are the outcome of nonadditive combinations of individual actions, such as two or more individuals joining to constitute, maintain, or alter a social system. But in either case the explanation fits what we shall call a *Boudon–Coleman diagram* (see fig. 5.1).

What holds for facts also holds, mutatis mutandis, for the propositions describing them. That is, when translated into ideas, the Boudon–Coleman diagram becomes a system of at least eight propositions: two macrosociological propositions (concerning M_1 and M_2), two psychological propositions (concerning m_1 and m_2), one further macrosociological proposition (concerning the M_1–M_2 link), one psychological proposition (concerning the m_1–m_2 link), one sociopsychological proposition (concerning the M_1–m_1 link), and one psychosociological proposition (concerning the m_2–M_2 link).

When numerical variables are available, the diagram becomes as shown in figure 5.2. That is, the M–M functional relation $Y = F(X)$ is decomposed into three successive links: $Y = h(y)$, $y = f(x)$, and $x = g(X)$; in short: $F = h \circ f \circ g$. (Malinvaud 1991, 157 uses this diagram to elucidate the microeconomic–macroeconomic relations.)

Some cases call for chains of Boudon–Coleman diagrams. In others the diagram will be more complicated. Consider, for example, the account of social mobility proposed by Lorrain and White (1971). It begins by distinguishing two kinds of mobility: of people and of vacancies. People move when they enter or leave the labor force; they also move when promoted, demoted, or transferred from one department or branch to another. And vacancies "move" when they are filled or left, as well as when new ones are created or old ones eliminated. Both processes occur simultaneously at the micro and the macro levels.

	F		
	$X \rightarrow Y$	Macro-variables
$g \downarrow$	f $\uparrow h$	
	$x \rightarrow y$	Micro-variables

Fig. 5.2. Analysis of a macro–macro functional relation into macro–micro, micro–micro, and micro–macro functional relations.

However, mass mobility results from the aggregation of individual mobilities, whereas the micro mobility of vacancies often results from macro changes such as business expansion or shrinkage. The net social changes are reflected in such variables as employment rate, savings and interest rates, and social expenditures. And an individual's quality of life is determined by these macro-variables as well as by his being in or out of the labor force, climbing up or down the social ladder, or changing his life-style.

In short, from a systemic viewpoint, a satisfactory explanation of any social fact will involve two or more levels—at a minimum, that of the whole and that of its parts. In addition to the components, the explanation will take into account the environment and the structure of the system: that is, it will invoke at least a CES sketch of the system. An explanation involving all this we will call 'systemic.' Systemic explanation combines and subsumes both bottom-up and top-down explanation. In top-down explanation the explanandum concerns a system, and the explanans premises refer to the composition and structure of the system; whereas in bottom-up explanation the expanandum refers to system components, while the explanans premises refer to the structure or the environment of the system.

5 Verstehen

Let us now examine a typically micro-reductionist, or top-down, strategy in social studies: that according to which the student of society should focus on individuals and employ a special mode of cognition, called Verstehen (understanding, insight, comprehension, or "interpretation"), in order to figure out the "meaning" (purpose) of their actions. This strategy is championed by the idealist schools in social metatheory: neo-Kantian, hermeneutic, phenomenological, symbolic interactionist, ethnomethodological, and Wittgensteinian. (See, e.g., Dilthey 1959 [1883]; Weber 1988 [1913], 1922; Schütz 1967 [1932]; Gadamer 1975; Winch 1958; Dallmayr and McCarthy 1977; Mueller-Vollmer 1989.)

The Verstehen school claims that the social sciences differ radically from the natural sciences. The difference concerns not just subject matters and particular methods, as anyone but the most extreme physicalist or sociobiologist will admit. It also concerns the very mode of understanding. Whereas the natural scientist understands through explanation in terms of laws (in particular, lawful mechanisms), the social scientist understands only by means of Verstehen (comprehension or insight), nowadays also called "interpretation" or "hermeneutical understanding."

There are two different construals of the word *Verstehen* and, accordingly, two views on its role in social studies. One is Dilthey's, which is subjectivist and intuitionist; the other is Weber's, which is objectivist and rationalist. For

Dilthey, to "understand" the action of an individual amounts to putting oneself in his place; whereas for Weber, it is to guess its "meaning" in the sense of its purpose. Let us take a closer look at these two construals.

Dilthey, a historical idealist, held that the prime mover in society is the individual mind or spirit (*Geist*), rather than anything material such as the environment, the economy, or biological drives. This is why he called the social sciences *Geisteswissenschaften,* sciences of the spirit, and opposed them to the natural sciences. Now, since mental states are not open to public inspection and since Dilthey could not possibly have anticipated—let alone hoped for—the discovery of physiological indicators of mental processes, he held that the only way one could guess someone else's mental states was by trying to put oneself in his circumstances. In other words, I can understand why so-and-so behaved as he did only if I can imagine myself in his shoes. In short, Verstehen = sympathetic understanding.

Dilthey did not realize how difficult it is to put oneself in someone else's place, particularly if the person belongs to a distant social group or an alien society. Nor did he anticipate two obvious objections that any serious student of society is bound to raise: first, that it is foolish to overlook the existence of biological drives as well as of environmental, economic, and political constraints; and second, that no matter how plausible an explanation in terms of beliefs and intentions may sound, it is hypothetical and, moreover, seldom testable. After all, most human actions can be accounted for by alternative hypotheses. The reasons for this uncertainty are that (*a*) almost any human action may have alternative motivations (needs, wants, beliefs, etc.), and (*b*) motivations are not observable. If we knew the latter, we could predict behavior: this would be a direct problem. But the problem that the "comprehensive" sociologist tackles is the dual, or inverse, of the former, and inverse problems have multiple solutions (recall chap. 3, sec. 2). In light of these objections, it is no wonder that Dilthey's philosophical hermeneutics has not inspired a single important finding or even insight in the field of social studies.

In Dilthey's own view and that of his followers, the appeal to Verstehen is a retreat from objectivity and rationality, hence from science proper. (Even the phenomenologist Schütz [1967 (1932), 240] condemned Dilthey's irrationalism.) Moreover, since most of these scholars were bookish types—in particular, literary critics, historians of ideas, theologians, or philosophers—they focused on texts and their interpretation instead of studying human behavior at first hand. The transition from Dilthey to Husserl, and from the latter's phenomenology to Heidegger and his hermeneutic successors, such as Gadamer and Derrida, was natural. For Dilthey, social facts had to be read off (nonscientific) texts; for his successors all social facts *are*, literally, texts (or "like texts") to be interpreted.

Let us now turn from philosophical hermeneutics to social science and first to Max Weber. Weber, one of the founding fathers of modern sociology, is generally regarded as one of the first to put into practice Dilthey's ideas about Verstehen as well as his idealist version of methodological individualism. I submit that this reading of Weber is only partially true. To be sure, Weber's methodological writings on the sense (*Sinn, Deutung, Bedeutung*) of social actions and their understanding (*Verstehen*) are so muddled that at first sight they do appear to underwrite the intuitionist and subjectivist position. However, reading Weber in the original, rather than in the distorted English translations, and without paying attention to the philosophical authorities he claims to draw on (Dilthey, Windelband, Rickert) and his philosophical interpreters, one is led to a different conclusion. In any event, one should heed the advice of his only student, Alexander von Schelting (1934, 370): to read not just Weber's methodological works but also his substantive ones, for in these he does not follow the former at all closely.

Weber the sociologist and historian does not turn inward and does not indulge in Vico's or Dilthey's psychohistorical fantasies. Instead, he investigates objectively his agents and their circumstances, which have economic, political, and cultural features. Had he not proceeded in this standard scientific way, Weber would have been unable to write about economic history or the objective characteristics of bureaucracy; he would not have conducted his empirical study on agricultural workers east of the Elbe; and he would not have commissioned sociological surveys. In this regard, Weber was no different from his rivals Marx and Durkheim. He did not try to "relive" the experiences (*Erlebnisse*) of others, although on occasion he tried to guess the "meaning" of their actions—which is nothing but their purpose. Besides, Weber warned that, even if self-evident, an account of human behavior in terms of its "meaning" (purpose) is only a hypothesis to be tested like any other (Weber 1988 [1913], 437). Moreover, unlike Dilthey, who rejected the search for causal relations in the social world, Weber looked for them. In particular, he emphasized that people's interests *cause* them to behave in certain ways, and he sought, among others, the social causes of the decline of ancient Rome. By so doing, Weber kept his social studies within the fold of science. (See von Schelting 1934; Albert 1994; Stack 1989.)

Weber the scientist could not help but be a realist, despite paying lip service to anti-realism. But he also recognized the limitation of the naturalist (or behaviorist) approach, which overlooks subjective experience—in particular, emotion, interest, intention, and decision. Had he not been writing in the heavy, muddy, long-winded German academic lingo of his time, Weber might have said simply that an objective study of people must include their subjective experiences. Had he been free of that cultural constraint, he might simply have stated the pseudo-tautology: *Um die Leute zu verstehen, muss man sie verstehen.* (I am playing here on the ambiguity of the term *verstehen*. So did Weber, for whom this term signified both a method and an outcome.) But this would not have sounded academic enough. To write on the "inner actuality" of human processes and on the need to grasp it in a "comprehensive" (*verstehende*) fashion was the thing to do in Weber's stuffy academic environment, dominated as it was by idealism and neo-Romanticism.

Weber's stand in the debate over Verstehen may be summarized as follows. First, to "understand" or "interpret" (*verstehen*) a human action, it is not enough to observe it, and it is not necessary to invoke an empathic projection or identification with the agent. Instead, we must try to conjecture the agent's motivation or purpose. Second, the student achieves understanding when he succeeds in accounting for observable behavior in terms of instrumental rationality—that is, by assuming that the agent will avail himself of the most suitable means to achieve his goal. Third, and consequently, much as he extols the superiority of *Verstehen* over *Erklärung* (explanation), in his substantive works Weber combines the two into what Albert (1990) calls *verstehende Erklärung* (comprehensive explanation). Fourth, Weber is no subjectivist. On the contrary, he often emphasizes the need for an objective, impartial social science, to the point that he is obsessed with value neutrality, for supposing (wrongly) that all value judgments are subjective. Fifth, far from being a consistent methodological individualist, Weber sometimes emphasizes the constraints of social structure upon individual agency. An example is the well-known passage in *Die protestantische Ethik und der Geist des Kapitalismus* (1920–21 [1904–5], 203) where he compares industrial capitalism to a steely cage (*stahlhartes Gehäuse*). The latter, he writes, determines with "overpowering necessity" (*überwältigendem Zwange*) the life-style of every single individual. So much for the myths that Weber took over, unchanged, Dilthey's concept of Verstehen and was a consistent idealist (specifically a hermeneuticist) and methodological individualist.

In short, Weber's point in promoting a "comprehensive" (*verstehende*) social science was that we should take seriously the inner sources of action, but that, far from embracing subjectivism, we should study them in an objective manner. True, at times he exaggerated the importance of belief and intention and, by the same token, underrated the weight of external (material) circumstances. But he was a scientist, not a hermeneuticist. And he was not the only social scientist to oscillate between internalist and externalist modes of explanation. Thus Marx, the holist, dwelt on the greed of Victorian industrialists, on the motives for workers to revolt against them, and on Louis Napoléon's combination of mediocrity and cunning. Consistency is hard to attain.

6 The Role of Verstehen

I hope to have demystified Verstehen and distinguished its two variants: Dilthey's irrational and Weber's rational one, or DV and WV, respectively. Our next task is to find out what role, if any, these play in social science. We begin by admitting that, though fallible, DV—that is, sympathetic understanding—is indispensable for reconstructing the biography of an individual. Obviously, in this case the student must empathize with his subject. But even when written with the help of scientific techniques and reliable data, biography is the one part of history that is not a *social* science: this is what Dilthey and his followers failed to see. Biography supplies, at most, raw material to social science—and not very important material to boot, because it usually concerns only atypical individuals, not "ideal-typical" ones. As for the social sciences proper, they owe nothing to Dilthey, because they are both rational and empirical. (See Harris 1968 for anthropology; Bochenski 1987 for Egyptology; and Albert 1988, 1994 for economics.)

By contrast, WV—that is, the imputation of motives—has a much broader scope than DV, for we do not need to know any biographical details of the individuals in question in order to attribute to them certain intentions if we know roughly their circumstances. For instance, if we know that X is a trader, we can safely assume that he favors free trade; and knowing that Y is a worker is reason enough to suppose that he favors full employment. However, this trick is likely to fail in some cases. For example, knowing that so-and-so is a capitalist does not authorize us to hypothesize that he will vote conservative; likewise, knowing that someone is a worker is not enough reason to suppose that he will vote for the Left. In other words, the general hypotheses underlying the use of WV are just that—conjectures crying out for tests.

Not surprisingly, judging from Weber's major and most mature work, *Wirtschaft und Gesellschaft* (1922), the real accomplishments of verstehende (comprehensive) social science are exceedingly modest. That large work (xxxiii + 1247 pages) is tremendously erudite, but entirely bookish: it does not rely on firsthand empirical research, and it contains almost no statistical data. It contains plenty of definitions, most of them formally flawed, a few hypotheses, but hardly any explanations: it is descriptive and historical, rather than analytical. It does contain a handful of nuggets—for example, some deep insights into the modern state, bureaucracy, and planning—but they are buried in longwinded, foggy paragraphs. In sum, one derives very little *understanding* from it, and what understanding one does derive owes nothing to Verstehen. In fact, Weber pays lip service to Verstehen in the first few pages and then forgets all about it. One is reminded of Marx's praise of dialectics at the beginning of *Das Kapital* and his subsequent neglect of it.

Like Dilthey, Weber does not seem to have realized the magnitude of the task of the "comprehensive" social scientist, particularly since he explicitly declined any help that psychology might offer (Weber 1988 [1913], 432). Indeed, most of the time social scientists have no access to the beliefs and intentions of their subjects: the most they can get to know is some of the outcomes of their subjects' actions. Even declared intentions are not much help, because the real intentions of people are often masked by fear, hypocrisy, ideology, or plain self-deception. Hence any social study (e.g., a history) in terms of individual beliefs and intentions is necessarily speculative. As Durkheim (1988 [1895], 188) put it, matters of intention are too subjective to be studied scientifically—unless, we may add a century later, they are tackled by physiological psychologists armed with such mind-imaging tools as PT scanners and microelectrodes.

As noted in the previous section, if we were told an agent's goals and means, as well as his mental frame, we might be able to figure out what his actions were likely to be. However, the inverse problem of conjecturing goals from observed behavior, or traces of it, has no unique solution. Actually, not even the direct problem is always soluble, and this for two reasons. One is that, as noted above, we seldom, if ever, have reliable information about an agent's intentions. To be sure, Weber and his followers circumvent this problem by assuming simplistically that everyone's overriding goal in whatever he undertakes is to maximize his utilities. But, as we will see in chapter 14, empirical research has abundantly refuted this assumption.

Another obstacle is that every individual is part of several social systems, so his actions combine with those of other people, often unwittingly and in unexpected ways. Only the outcomes of concerted actions are predictable—though not always. When actions are not concerted, or when they are concerted but meet with a strong opposition from other groups, we must expect unintended consequences—in particular, perverse ones. In short, a knowledge (or conjecture) of purposes is not enough to explain human behavior, particularly in social contexts, where people often act at cross-purposes.

Moreover, as Durkheim warned long ago, social science research must not be restricted to the search for purposes, goals, or functions, because some social items are useless, even if, originally, they served a useful purpose. "In fact, there are even more survivals in society than in the organism. There are even cases where a social practice or institution acquires a new function without changing in nature" (Durkheim 1988 [1895], 184). This is why Durkheim recommended that efficient causes be sought independently of final causes or functions.

An examination of any reasonably well-known episode of contemporary political history should show clearly the limitations, and even dangers, of relying on the imputation of motives. Thus, even as the German army was crossing the Soviet western border in 1941, Stalin could not believe his ears, because he held dogmatically to the hypothesis that the only war aim of Germany was to wrest colonies from Great Britain and France. Had Stalin and his sycophants adopted a critical approach to world politics, they would have realized that one cannot guess the real intentions and feelings of one's adversaries or even one's allies. A scientifically minded politician, political analyst, or spy does not presume to read minds, but goes by objective indicators, such as strategic plans, types and quantities of weapons, and troop movements. Nowadays he can also rely on surveillance, particularly electronic intercepts and satellite tracking.

Still, there is no gainsaying that social facts become more intelligible when the data, jointly with more or less tacit general hypotheses concerning human behavior, warrant the guessing of individual motivations, particularly interests and beliefs. However, such motivations are not always rational and predictable: people act not only from calculation but also from habit, emotion, prejudice, and even superstition, as well as impulsively or under compulsion. For example, Moses' flight from Egypt may be explained by the wish of a number of slaves to cultivate their own land at a time when the Nile delta had become overcrowded. But the hazardous exodus into the desert might not have succeeded had Moses and his followers not had faith in his alleged covenant with Yahweh—which reads like a land-lease contract whereby Moses and his followers were allowed to cultivate the promised land in exchange for Yahweh's exclusive worship rights. Another example: Muhammad's military campaigns and the Crusades seem to have been motivated primarily by lust for war spoils, land, and political power. However, steadfast belief in heavenly reward on the part of the foot soldier helps explain his endurance and foolhardiness in battle. In short, the imputation of individual intentions is occasionally enlightening. But it is conjectural, not a matter of infallible intuition. Unless this caution is kept in mind, one may uncritically accept the psychohistorian's fanciful reconstructions of history, such as Freud's.

The conjectural nature of Weber's Verstehen is best seen in the light of the logic of explanation (sec. 3). Consider the general hypothesis schema that all individuals with motive M, when in a situation of type S, engage in actions of kind A. If the motive and the situation are given, the actions follow: this is a valid argument. But it is hardly a useful one, for, normally, only the situation and the action are known, and even then only in part. What the Verstehen enthusiast claims is that he can get at the motive from the situation and the action. But this is logically fallacious: remember that indirect problems do not have unique solutions. Hence he claims to employ a special mode of understanding that does not fit the valid explanation schema, yet yields certainty. By contrast, the scientifically minded student of society acknowledges that imputations of motive are hypothetical and hence need to be tested.

Furthermore, in most cases social scientists deal with social systems on the strength of little if any knowledge about the personalities of their components. For example, a model of the steel industry will not contain psychological variables. Yet such a model may be explanatory. Thus, one may explain the decline in the number of steel mills in the industrialized countries in recent decades as an effect of the decrease in the use of steel in transportation and armaments, jointly with the export of some such mills to Third World countries. This explanation is of the macro–micro type: it does not involve any knowledge of the individuals working in the steel industry. It assumes only that the typical steel mill manager decides to slow down production as demand declines—a question of survival, rather than profit maximization.

In conclusion, WV, or imputation of motives, is useful. But it is limited and dicey because (*a*) we seldom have access to an agent's real motives, (*b*) an agent's circumstances and means are no less important than his goals, and (*c*) social science is about social systems, not individuals, who are the subject of study of psychology. Further, WV is fallible for being conjectural and, moreover, rarely testable. It can be of some use, but only as a soft part of an objective research project, not in place of it. Subjectivity can be accommodated in science, but subjectivism cannot be. (More in chap. 13, sec. 7.)

7 Forecast and Hindcast

To forecast or predict is, of course, to conjecture what will, or at least is likely to, happen. Likewise, to hindcast or retrodict is to conjecture what has, or may have, happened. In ordinary life we perform both operations all the time. For example, we plan as part of our preparation for engaging in rational action, and we attempt to reconstruct the past in order to understand what went right or wrong and thus learn from success or failure.

In basic science, forecast and hindcast have two functions: to help us know the future and the past, respectively, for their own sake and to test hypotheses. For example, economic forecasts picture the future—or, rather, some of the possible futures—and put economic theories and policies to the test. Archaeological and paleontological hindcasts are part of the reconstruction of the past; and, by telling the diggers where and what to look for, hindcasts check certain hypotheses.

Besides having cognitive functions, backward and forward projections have a practical value. The main function of prediction in everyday life, business, politics, and technology is to help design plans of action: to prepare us for the future or to change the present so that it may lead to a more desirable future. (This is why there is nothing, next to competition, that businessmen and politicians hate more than uncertainty deriving from unpredictability.) In the realm of action, hindcast plays a far more modest role than prediction. But, when performed, its aim is not just to discover the past, but to learn from it in order to help shape the future.

A prediction of human behavior can have a practical effect that no other kind of prediction can have. Indeed, if such a prediction becomes known to the relevant actors, it may alter the very behavior that is being forecast. These are the cases of self-fulfilling and self-defeating prophecies (Merton 1957; Jones 1977), now also classified under the somewhat misleading rubric of self-reference (Geyer and van der Zouwen 1990). Examples: (*a*) If someone predicts that action *A* is likely to have effect *B,* those who take cognizance of the prediction and like *B* will do *A,* whereas those who dislike *B* will refrain from doing *A;* (*b*) treating a person as a potential leader (or criminal or what have you) will predispose him to become one; (*c*) in anticipation of unemployment, many African-Americans drop out of school, so decreasing even further their chances of ever getting a job.

So far, we have taken it for granted that human actions are individually and collectively predictable, at least to some extent. What if they are not, as the irrationalists assure us? In this case we would not undertake anything beyond what it takes to meet our most pressing current needs. If the future were totally unpredictable, nobody would study or raise a family, plant trees or manufacture artifacts, take a job or hire employees, save or invest, join an organization or start a business. The carrot drives us no less strongly than the stick—so much so that constructive initiative, particularly investment, drops in times of extreme uncertainty. In short, predictability, even if bounded, is a lure to deliberate action.

Having said this, I hasten to admit that human life is rather uncertain, since it is full of unpredictables. We constantly meet unexpected obstacles and opportunities, new people and new social developments, new problems and new information. By definition of the word *unpredictable,* we cannot foresee such events, either for lack of knowledge or because they are accidental. However, a wise planner allows for unpredictables—for example, by allocating part of his resources to addressing them. That is, he makes the admittedly imprecise, yet useful, forecast that the unexpected will happen.

Scientific prediction must be distinguished from both intuitive forecast and prophecy. Intuitive forecasts are made on the strength of ordinary knowledge and are often colored by groundless optimism, as suggested by the finding that two-thirds of new businesses last fewer than five years. Prophecies are groundless and categorical: they are not based on reliable knowledge and are unconditional, rather than hypothetical. By contrast, scientific forecasts are based on knowledge of present conditions as well as on the laws, norms, or trends peculiar to the thing in question. Consequently they are of the form "If the present state of *X* is such and such, and *X* fits such and such a pattern, then the future state of *X* will be so-and-so." If the future turns out as forecast, the generalization(s) involved in it will be confirmed, so they may continue to be used till further notice. (No conclusion follows validly from $A \Rightarrow B$ jointly with B.) And if future events do not bear out the forecast, we learn that at least one of the conditions occurring in the antecedent of the conditional is false. (In fact, $A \Rightarrow B$ and $\neg B$ jointly entail $\neg A$.) Thus, failures of scientific forecasts are just as useful cognitively as their successes. By contrast, nothing can be learned from the confirmation or refutation of prophecies, for they are not cast in conditional form: they do not test any hypotheses.

Successful forecast or hindcast is of course an important truth indicator, but it is not the only one. Thus, the myth that the cock's crow causes the sun to rise allows us to foresee dawn, and the false geocentric hypothesis allowed Ptolemy to compute fairly exact predictions in planetary astronomy. Still, though insufficient, predictive (or retrodictive) power is a necessary condition for any hypothesis or theory to be regarded as true at least to a first approximation. Explanatory power, though highly desirable, is no substitute for predictive (or retrodictive) impotence. After all, the hypothesis of divine providence can be used to explain anything, but it predicts nothing that can be checked.

There is no logical difference between scientific forecast and explanation. Both are arguments of the form: $A \Rightarrow B$ and A, ergo B. The difference between them concerns content, not form. In fact, unlike explanations, forecasts need not invoke any mechanism. For example, the regularity occurring among the premises of a scientific forecast can be of the black box kind (such as an input–output relation or a rate equation) or even a trend or a statistical correlation. Thus, we need not know any astronomy to forecast that day will follow night, or any economics to forecast that mass unemployment will erode savings.

There are several kinds of scientific forecast and hindcast. The most accurate rely on theoretical laws. That is, they are of the form: Law and circumstance, hence forecast (or hindcast) fact. Actually, theoretical laws concern properties or features of facts rather than whole facts. Hence, the schema is: Law for property P and present value of P, hence final (or previous) value of P. More realistically: laws for property cluster P and initial values of the members of P, hence later (or earlier) values of P.

The generalization(s) involved in a scientific prediction or hindcast may, but need not, involve the concept of time. Example of the former: a population trend. Example of a law statement that does not involve the time concept: If birthrates are inversely proportional to the standard of living, then a doubling of the latter will (eventually) result in the halving of the former. Regularities involving the time concept allow us to predict *when* some facts will occur, whereas time-free regularities allow us to predict only *that* they will happen.

The foregoing holds for stable dynamical systems such as the planetary system. It does not hold for unstable systems, such as radioactive atoms, unregulated economies, coalition governments, and nations bonded by conflict. In these cases there will be different possible futures. Hence, not even a complete, accurate knowledge of the present state could guarantee correct predictions. On the other hand, if a process is stochastic and we know its probabilistic law(s), we will be able to assign a definite probability to each possible future. (In addition, we will be able to predict averages and variances.) Not so if the process is chaotic in the sense of nonlinear dynamics: in this case, branching may occur; and since the underlying laws are not stochastic, there is no way of ascertaining which of the possible branches is more likely to be actualized.

What holds for prediction need not hold for retrodiction. Indeed, in the case of an irreversible process approaching a state of equilibrium, one and the same final state may be reached from different initial states. (Think of life histories or of events with more than one possible cause.) In this case, retrodiction will be impossible, whereas prediction will be possible, for all or nearly all trajectories will converge to a single final state.

Interestingly, if we know the lawful mechanism of a process, we can explain it even while being unable to predict it. For example, geology and evolutionary biology explain but seldom predict. Likewise, with hindsight we can usually explain business crashes and government crises that nobody was able to foresee—which confirms what we already knew about the asymmetry between prediction and explanation despite their common logical form.

Furthermore, although we can uphold the optimistic thesis that all facts can be explained, if not right now, then later on, we cannot sustain a faith in the predictability of everything. Indeed, unlike explanation, predictability is not only a matter of knowledge: some processes are inherently unpredictable. As we saw earlier, this is the case with processes occurring in inherently unstable systems as well as in systems undergoing chaotic processes. In both cases the source of the branching is internal: it inheres in the mechanism itself. Even an omniscient being could not predict the future of such a system. Whether such a being could exist and, if so, what difference its cognitive limitation would make to the lot of humans is an academic or, rather, theological question.

Whether unpredictability stems from lack of knowledge or is in the nature of things, we must face it, particularly when studying human beings or social systems. Consider one case of each kind, and a third where the two types of unpredictability combine. It is well known that some human actions have unintended consequences, some of which are "perverse"—that is, the opposite of what was intended (see, e.g., Merton 1936). This can often be explained in terms of ignorance, such as the failure to adopt a systemic approach, hence the isolation of the thing of interest from its context; disregard for the interests and actions of others; wrong planning, particularly wrong choice of means; incompetence in implementing a good plan; and so on. Failures of this kind are bound to occur when individuals act on insufficient information or in a selfish manner, in which case it must be expected that other people will interfere.

Invention is a classical example of inherent unpredictability. True, Verne, Wells, and a few others prophesied that certain machines would be invented. But they described only their global functions; they did not design them. The reason why a radically original invention cannot be predicted is that to predict an original idea is to have it. In any event, if there are laws of the evolution of knowledge, nobody knows them, so they cannot be used to forecast. However, we can make a few global forecasts in the field of knowledge. For example, we can predict that nearly all routine problems (chap. 3, sec. 2) will be solved eventually, provided they are interesting and suitable means are made available. We can also foresee that if certain problems widely seen as important are not investigated scientifically, they will be taken up by charlatans. That is, culture abhors a vacuum, so it is promptly filled with junk.

Individual human behavior is never fully predictable, because people are fickle, inventive, and, at least in some societies, mobile: they change friends, jobs, tastes, habits, goals, or allegiances; they discover or invent new problems; and they often meet unexpected challenges by coming up with novel ideas. Some such events are likely to fit patterns, and eventually we may be able to discover these patterns. But at present we do not know them, so we cannot successfully predict individual behavior. On the other hand, we can sometimes forecast mass behavior, which is what demographers and actuaries do. For example, although we may not be able to predict how many children, if any, a newlywed couple will have, we can forecast roughly what the total population of a nation will be in the near future, by using the birth, death, and migration rates obtained from recent census figures and plugging them into demographic equations.

Wars and revolutions exemplify the combination of inherently unpredictable processes with unpredictability from insufficient knowledge. Both war and revolution put out of action, sometimes randomly, irreplaceable individuals. Both mobilize individuals who were previously passive and may now unexpectedly undergo a change in attitude and start to play an active role. Both in war and in revolution the leadership, initially unified, is bound to split as a result of rivalries or as the conflict enters a new phase—for example, because of stunning defeats or victories or because of the formation or dissolution of alliances. In both cases the leaders are faced with unexpected problems, which they are forced to tackle in an improvised, hence inefficient, way. If the conflict is protracted, inherently unpredictable new weapons, strategies, or organizational techniques are likely to be introduced and tried with surprising results. Whether in war or in revolution, the leadership is bound to be slowed down by the passive resistance or even sabotage of some groups, such as the bureaucracy. In both cases, the previously prevailing system of values and norms is bound to be eroded without necessarily being replaced by a new system, as a consequence of which, unforeseen changes in behavior may occur. Finally, the victors, if there are any, may not know what to do next, so may not reap any benefits. Or they may end up exhausted or with goals very different from those that drove them initially.

The rate of success of social forecasting is notoriously low. (Examples: Nobody predicted the Great Depression, the massive entry of women into the labor force in the 1970s, the oil crisis, the crumbling of the Soviet Union, the civil war in former Yugoslavia, the decline of the labor unions, or the change in eating, drinking, and smoking habits of Americans starting in about 1970.) In light of the foregoing discussion, there are several possible reasons for such poor forecasting performance. One is that some processes are inherently unpredictable because they occur in unstable social systems. Another is that behavior is partially determined by learning and expectations. A third reason is the dearth of well-corroborated social theories and the fragmentation of social studies. A fourth is the wrong approach often adopted by social forecasters. Let us look at these factors.

The first reason is far from obvious, but it would be unproductive to harp on it at the present time, particularly in view of the third reason. Indeed, we cannot be sure that a system is in fact unstable unless we have a testable theory to explain why it is unstable. The second reason for the frequent failure of social forecasts is that human action is guided not only by the current state of the person and his environment, but also by his expectations, particularly those concerning the possible consequences of his actions, such as the effect of smoking on lung cancer. This is one of the regards in which psychology and social science differ from natural science. (Caution: Our imagining the future, not the future itself, influences our current actions. All the sciences admit the principle of antecedence, or retardation, according to which every event is determined by the states of the thing in question and its environment at all times preceding the event of interest.) The third reason given above will be rejected by those who believe that we can predict human behavior by means of rational choice theories. However, these have proved to lack predictive power, whence they are claimed to enjoy only a normative status (see chap. 14).

Now, in the absence of well-corroborated dynamical theories, social forecasters usually resort to extrapolating current trends. Such extrapolations may be successful in the short term but are likely to fail in the long term. In fact, they can lead to absurdity, such as forecasting that eventually drug consumption will exceed food consumption, that there will not even be standing room left on the planet—or, on the contrary, that the AIDS epidemic will bring about the extinction of the human species. Yet, combining several trends— for example, demographic, economic, and cultural—may suggest correct forecasts. For example, the rise of mass unemployment in the West since about 1970, though unforeseen, could have been predicted from the passing of the baby boom wave, the increased participation of women in the labor market, and the introduction of labor-saving devices (Malinvaud 1984, 72–73). Moral: Do not equate the unforeseen with the unpredictable.

As for the approach adopted by social forecasters, it is often speculative, sectoral, and biased. Wild speculation is particularly rampant among futurologists and stockbrokers. Theirs are not scientific predictions but prophecies: they belong to science fiction. By contrast, demographic projections, which come in sheaves, are serious extrapolations from current trends. One of their functions is to alert people to the catastrophic consequences of unbridled reproduction. This is all predictive futurology can do: sound the alarm. However, this is a subject for the next section.

Another flaw of most forecasts of social trends is their sectoral, or nonsystemic, nature. Characteristically, economic forecasts seldom take demographic or political factors into account, and, in turn, political forecasts usually overlook nonpolitical factors. A third common flaw is bias: most futurologists are committed to a rosy vision of the future. In other words, they often engage in wishful thinking. (However, as will be seen in the next section, there is not necessarily anything wrong with a dose of wishful thinking when envisaging the future, because, up to a point, we shape it ourselves.) In any event, whatever the shortcomings of social forecasting, it may be safely predicted that social forecasting services will continue to multiply and prosper for a long time. (See, e.g., the *International Journal of Forecasting*.)

Some of the people concerned with preserving freedom think that we should not try to improve our ability to predict human behavior. The underlying idea is that freedom amounts to unpredictability. But this opinion is mistaken. Indeed, by definition, a free action is one that an agent performs by choice rather than as a result of external compulsion; moreover, such a decision is sometimes made with full awareness of the consequences and even against the current. Hence, far from being indeterminate, free actions are inwardly determined and thus predictable by the agents themselves. (The predictability of the outcome or effect of an action is another matter.) On the other hand, impulsive actions—that is, actions performed by people overcome by strong emotions—are unpredictable, as are their outcomes. Rational action is action guided by reliable knowledge, particularly knowledge of laws, norms, and circumstances. In a lawless universe, freedom would be impossible, because deliberation and action according to plan would be impossible.

So far we have dealt with what may be called *passive* forecasting, in which the forecaster does not intervene to change the course of events. (Example: "You'll age.") In ordinary life, politics, and technology, we also issue *active* forecasts, which express an agent's intention to do something about a course of events, as in "I'll help you." Such forecasts are involved in designing and shaping the future—on which more anon.

8 Designer Future

There are two ways of getting things done: by talking or by doing. The former is to broadcast a datum, a lie, or a prophecy, expecting that someone will believe it and act on it. The second is harder: it calls for resources, careful planning, hard work, help from others, and luck. Let us examine briefly the two methods for shaping the future.

The rumor-spreading method is this: An individual holds, states, or propagates a datum, a falsity, or a prophecy that modifies his own or other people's behavior in such a manner that it brings about the final state of affairs envisaged. For example, the fatalistic driver or skier is likely to crash more often than the optimist. The expectation of inflation sustains inflation, and that of war facilitates the start of hostilities, and so on. All these are *self-fulfilling prophecies*. (See the previous section.) *Self-defeating prophecies* are similar. They consist in issuing forecasts that induce people to act in such a manner as to prevent the prophesied events from coming to pass. For example, if an opinion pollster forecasts the defeat of a certain political party, many of its supporters will change allegiances, so that its defeat will be even worse than anticipated.

Presumably, the number of self-fulfilling and self-defeating prophecies has increased dramatically in recent years in part as a result of the huge increase in communications. The mechanism at work in both cases is the same. Belief in a prophecy leads people to act so as to bear it out. Only a minority respond by trying to prevent the prophesied event from coming to pass: they are the nonconformists.

Both kinds of prophecy highlight one of the differences between the social and the natural sciences. Whereas the mere prediction of a natural event does not alter the latter, that of a social event may strengthen or weaken the possibility that the event will actually happen. In addition, weather forecasts and (in the future) the prediction of natural disasters, such as cyclones, floods, and earthquakes, if broadcast, will affect human behavior. In short, in social science we must reckon with belief (true or false), because it steers human action—for better or for worse.

The second, far more effective method for affecting the future is doing: in particular, acting on the strength of well-conceived plans. I discuss planning elsewhere (Bunge forthcoming). The following remarks will suffice here. Futurology can be passive or active, oracular or scientific. That is, it can either foresee or design the future on the basis of forecasting and in light of some desiderata. For instance, if we want to stop the growth of something, such as population or pollution, we must devise efficient means to check the relevant process. This requires unveiling not just the current growth rate but also the growth mechanism, for it is only by tampering with the latter that we may be able to alter the course of events. In other words, designing the future is a matter not just of refining forecasting techniques, but also of explaining what is going on. Shorter: Planning involves explanation as well as prediction.

(More precisely, if x_t is the value of a variable x at time t, and x^*_{t+1} the desired, possible value of x at a later time $t + 1$, the technologist's task is to devise at least one function f such that $x^*_{t+1} = f(x_t, y, t)$, where y is a strategic variable—that is, one that may be manipulated in order to get the desired result. Clearly, the design of such a function leading from an *is* to an *ought* involves solving a prediction problem. The action that accomplishes such a leap across the is–ought gap is up to men and women of action—workers, managers, or politicians—or their artificial proxies, not to technologists.)

Paradoxically, successful planning reckons with unpredictables, such as unexpected changes in the environment and sudden shifts in human behavior patterns. Not, of course, that we can predict such changes; but we must make room for them, hence for corresponding changes in our plans. (In particular, any reasonable budget will contain a slot for unforeseen expenses.) Shorter: Successful plans are adaptable.

Finally, at this time of severe global issues that threaten the survival of humankind, the most important question concerning the future is not what it will be like, but whether our species can earn one. Consequently, active futurology, concerned with designing a livable future, is needed to supplement passive social forecasting. We cannot know the future, but we can shape it at least in part: this is what intelligent management and politics are all about.

The logic, epistemology, and methodology of description, explanation, and forecast are the same in all the sciences, natural, social, and hybrid. In all of them one attempts to account objectively for real facts, or, at least, putatively real ones, in terms of data and hypotheses consistent with the data. The only difference between the social and the natural sciences with regard to description, explanation, and forecast is that the former must take beliefs, interests, and purposes ("meanings") into account, for these guide human action. All such assumptions are hypotheses, not "interpretations." Hence the scientific study of social facts goes far beyond text interpretation, which, incidentally, is only possible when intelligible texts are available.

However, since hypotheses about other people's subjective experiences are hard to test, any accounts in social science which include them are likely to be somewhat unreliable. This feature renders these sciences even more conjectural than astrophysics. Still, it does not make them subjective, because (*a*) those mental states (or rather the brains in such states) are hypothesized to be real, and (*b*) the corresponding hypotheses, far from being arbitrary fantasies, are designed to be testable and, moreover, compatible with the data as well as with psychology. However, the matter of tests deserves a separate chapter.

6 :: *Empirical Operations*

Whoever cares for truth should care for truth tests, because truth-values can be assigned responsibly only on the strength of truth tests. Of course, so-called revealed truths are exempt from such tests, some for being untestable, others for being asserted as dogmas: they are handed down, or imposed, rather than proposed. By contrast, the conjectures proposed by mathematicians, scientists, technologists, humanist scholars, and ordinary folk are supposed to be testable. Moreover, if interesting, it is expected that they will eventually be put to the test.

Since mathematical conjectures refer to mathematical ideas, not concrete things, they are tested in a purely conceptual manner. (But, since all tests are carried out by human beings or their artificial proxies, they may make use of a computer as well as the traditional pencil and paper.) By contrast, scientific and technological conjectures refer to real—or, at least, putatively real—things, so they must be checked against the latter in order to find out whether they fit. However, this is easier said than done.

What does it mean that a test for the truth of a factual proposition consists in "confronting" it with the facts it refers to, in order to check whether it "fits" them? This question looks easy but is not, because the notions of confrontation and fit are taken from ordinary knowledge. One may check literally the fit of a glove, for in this case fitting consists in comparing two concrete things; and one may "confront" two ideas, such as an equation and its solution(s). But it is not clear how one could bring an idea face to face with the fact it describes.

Besides, why was it stated above that empirical checking is *a* truth test rather than *the* one and only such test?

These and a few other philosophical problems will be investigated in the present chapter. The critical role of indicators in testing will be emphasized, particularly because they are systematically ignored by philosophers of science. However, we shall skip most of the technical methodological problems, in particular, statistical ones, such as goodness of fit tests and analysis of concomitant variations, for there are plenty of adequate books about them (see, e.g., Blalock and Blalock 1968; Blalock 1974; Boudon 1967).

1 Testability

When do we say that proposition *p*, referring to fact(s) *f*, is true? When *f* is the case as described by *p*. (For more on this, the correspondence "theory" of factual truth, see chap. 3, sec. 5.) But how do we check whether *p* describes *f* adequately—that is, truly? We resort to empirical operations: observations, measurements, or experiments. But how can these help when the facts in question are not directly accessible to observation or experiment, as is the case with most social facts? We resort to indicators. Let me explain.

We have no direct access to the outside world. We grasp it only through experience and reason. To indulge in metaphor, experience—perception and action—occurs at the interface between ourselves and our external world. (Your external world includes me, and mine includes you.) Perception and action mediate between the world and our ideas about it, providing us with raw material for imagination and reasoning. The resulting elaboration is a set of ideas: images, concepts, propositions, diagrams, sketches, classifications, models, and theories. We check these ideas about reality by comparing them with empirical data, not with the world itself. In particular, we do not confront a proposition *p* about fact(s) *f* with *f* itself, but with some datum (or data) *e* relevant to *f*, some evidence for or against *p*. We can do this because both *p* and *e* are propositions, which *f* is not.

Moreover, whenever the facts being studied are not directly observable, we resort to further intermediaries: namely, indicators, or diagnostic signs. Thus, the state of the economy of a country is as imperceptible as the economy itself. Therefore economists estimate it through such indicators as GDP, rate of inflation, balance of payments, and unemployment rate. Physical analog: the height of a column of liquid is a temperature indicator; chemical: *aqua regia* is an indicator of gold; biological: any of the "vital signs," such as heartbeat; psychological: reaction speed. We "see" hidden facts through indicators. Any factual item (thing, state, event) observable through one or more indicators is said to be *indirectly observable*. (More on this in secs. 2 and 3.)

However, before rushing to design indicators or make observations, we should ascertain whether the hypothesis that we want to check is testable in principle. A first, necessary condition for a proposition to be testable empirically is that it refer to facts of some kind. On this count, the formulas of pure mathematics are not testable empirically. A second necessary condition is that the proposition not be a tautology—that is, a logical truth—for such a statement holds no matter what may be the case. For example, the statement "If two persons interact, then the action of each either rewards or does not reward the action of the other" is tautological, hence impregnable to fact.

A third necessary condition of testability is that the predicates occurring in the proposition represent directly or indirectly observable properties. Thus Freud's claim that everyone is abnormal is untestable, because it rules out the possibility of finding "square" persons with whom to compare the others in order to impute abnormality. A fourth testability condition is that the proposition at stake does not contain a proviso rendering it untestable in real time. One such proviso is "ultimately," or "in the last analysis," occurring in the propositions "All social facts depend ultimately upon subjective values" and "In the last analysis all cultural processes depend on economic factors." These propositions are untestable, because it is not specified when "ultimately" might be or what "the last analysis" is, let alone who is to perform it or when. Hence there is always the hope that if current analysis yields an inconclusive or even a negative result, further analysis will bring confirmation.

The *ceteris paribus* (other things being equal) condition would seem to discharge a similar function. Indeed, it allows one to explain away negative evidence as an effect of changes that the model does not contemplate. However, the ceteris paribus condition is quite legitimate with reference to any open concrete system. It merely points to a limitation of the model; it does not make it invulnerable when, in fact, the other factors do not vary. Moreover, notwithstanding a widespread belief, ceteris paribus conditions are not peculiar to social studies, but occur in all research fields. For example, when stating a thermodynamic formula, it may be necessary to warn that it holds only at constant pressure or temperature. (Moreover, the concept of a partial derivative includes that of ceteris paribus.)

Finally, a fifth testability condition is that the given proposition not be shielded from refutation by a second proposition which is not independently testable and whose only function is to protect the first (see chap. 3, sec. 4, on mala fide ad hoc hypotheses).

Let us now put our testability criteria to the test. Einhorn and Hogarth (1978) studied the way in which hits and misses affect our personal belief system and trust in our own judgment. They proposed a model of learning from experience that boils down to this. Suppose the subject makes judgments or decisions of a certain kind, and that only two categories are distinguished: right and wrong. Suppose, further, that the outcomes of his judgments or decisions can be only hits (H) or misses (M). Call h and m the reinforcing values of the positive and negative feedbacks, respectively. The model postulates that the total feedback, F, of outcome on self-confidence is

$$F = hH - mM, \text{ with } h + m = 1.$$

Using this formula we can divide people into at least the following three classes:

(a) the *gullible*: $h = 1$, $m = 0$, whence $F = H$ (success builds overconfidence);

(b) the *hypercritical*: $h = 0$, $m = 1$, whence $F = -M$ (failure destroys confidence);

(c) the *balanced*: $h = m = \frac{1}{2}$, whence $F = \frac{1}{2}(H - M)$ (success and failure contribute equally strongly to F).

This model is interesting, clear, and exact. Unfortunately, it is untestable, because neither F nor the parameters h and m are measurable. Being untestable, we do not know whether it is true. But, of course, the model is perfectly meaningful, which is a counterexample to both operationalism and the so-called verifiability theory of meaning.

2 Indicator

The most interesting scientific constructs (concepts, hypotheses, and theories) refer to imperceptible facts such as dispositions, mental processes, social trends, and past events—hence the need for objective, reliable indicators of such unobservables (which Pareto called "residues"). Typical indicators in the social sciences are footprints, human bones, artifacts, written documents, income inequality indices, GDPs, unemployment rates, discount rates, polling results, and frequency of political riots. For example, longevity is a quality-of-life indicator. (For a large sample, see, e.g., the *World Handbook of Political and Social Indicators*.)

Any relation between an indicator and the corresponding unobservable feature is neither a convention nor a rule, but a hypothesis. As such, it must be justified both analytically and empirically, rather than adopted uncritically. If reasonably reliable, we shall call it an 'indicator hypothesis,' although its traditional name is 'operational definition.' I reject the latter because definitions proper are conventions and, as such, arbitrary except for practical considerations; whereas an indicator hypothesis can be true or false to some degree. However, I shall retain the term 'operationalization,' for lack of a better name, to denote the preparation of a hypothesis or theory for empirical tests.

What is usually called the 'operationalization' of a construct consists in relating it to data via one or more indicator hypotheses. Examples: (*a*) the color that litmus paper takes is an acidity indicator; (*b*) phenotype is a genotype indicator; (*c*) in the more advanced sciences a theoretical concept U is operationalized by an indicator hypothesis of the form $U = f(O)$, where O is a directly observable or measurable property and the function f is specified and, moreover, has been shown to be adequate.

A hypothesis or theory that has not yet been operationalized cannot be tested, though it may be a promising speculation. On the other hand, a hypothesis or theory that cannot in principle be operationalized does not qualify as scientific. For example, the notions of an invisible hand, rational expectation, and shadow price, widely used in mainstream economics, are not operationalizable. (Even the far more useful concepts of uncertainty, social cost, and opportunity cost are exceedingly vague and so far unmeasured.)

Indicators can be qualitative or quantitative. Examples of the former: utterances that indicate beliefs, actual preferences among choices, and intentions underlying actions. Examples of quantitative indicators: the volume of trade among firms in a region, which indicates the latter's economic integration; frequency of political meetings, which indicates the intensity of democratic life; and the average number of books sold per capita, which indicates cultural level. If quantitative, indicators can be single numbers (scalars) or n-tuples of numbers (vectors). For example, productivity is a scalar, whereas any reasonable indicator of quality of life or of development is a vector whose components are figures for life expectancy, protein consumption per capita, family size, median disposable income, and average school years (see Bunge 1975, 1981*b*).

Many, if not most, of the indicators used in everyday life and in the social sciences are inaccurate or ambiguous and consequently unreliable. This holds, in particular, for the behavioral indicators of mental states and for the economic, social, and political indicators. Think of the ambiguity of facial expressions, gestures, or even words; of the poverty of any economic indicator taken by itself (e.g., GDP, which indicates total wealth, not social welfare, in that it says nothing about income distribution); of the limited value of knowing the number of schooling years regardless of school quality, and so on.

Some indicators are unreliable for being ambiguous. Thus a small number of hospital beds may indicate either a high level of public health or a high morbidity rate; a large number of public rallies may indicate a high level of civic concern or well-disciplined party troops; and so on. Ambiguity can be reduced by using entire batteries of indicators. For example, if a manufacturer wishes to find out the degree of customer satisfaction with his product, he will be ill-advised to restrict his inquiries to his habitual buyers, for these are, by definition, the satisfied ones. He should also look at the market share of his product.

Another example: Income cannot be taken as the sole, or even the best, indicator of quality of life, for it may be insufficient to meet needs and wants that the market does not supply or that the consumer does not want.

Let us now analyze both ambiguous and unambiguous indicator hypotheses. The former are of the form "If U then O," where O stands for an indicator of the unobservable U. It says that U is sufficient for O, and O necessary for U. If U is assumed, then O follows by the modus ponens rule. This inference is valid but unhelpful, because we want to get access to U through O, not the other way round. Moreover, since U is sufficient but not necessary for O, the latter might be imputed to a different unobservable. That is, given O, U is merely possible, not necessary. For example, a large number of industrial firms per million people may suggest a high level of industrialization, a low concentration of wealth, or low productivity.

By contrast, an unambiguous indicator hypothesis is of the form "If O, then U." If, in fact, O is observed, then we are allowed to conclude that U is the case, even though we have not perceived U. But for this logically valid inference to be methodologically correct, the hypothesis "If O, then U" must not only have been invented to begin with, but must also have been empirically confirmed and justified by an independently corroborated theory. And neither invention nor empirical confirmation is an easy task. For example, only electrodynamics can tell us that the tangent of the angle through which the pointer of an ammeter turns under the action of an electric current is proportional to the intensity of the current. So far, social scientists have not come up with indicator hypotheses of similar accuracy.

In order to obtain unambiguous, accurate indicators, one must craft theories involving high-level hypotheses: that is, conjectures about unobservable (but not occult) things or features of things. For example, physiological psychologists conjecture neural mechanisms and experiment with them, in order to explain overt behavior. Engineers proceed in like manner when designing materials, mechanisms, or processes with the desired global properties. And rational choice theorists attempt to explain social facts in terms of conjectures concerning certain mental processes of agents. (Whether these conjectures are true is beside the point.) All these students know what phenomenalist philosophers have yet to learn: namely, that composition and internal structure determine output and that systems with different composition and structure may have roughly the same output. (There is even a theorem to this effect in general systems theory.) Think of mechanical and electronic watches or of economies with similar outputs.

Once adequate indicator hypotheses are available, we can conjoin them with some of the propositions of the theory, so as to "read" the latter in empirical terms and thus be able to confront them with data. In short, indicator hypotheses provide bridges between theories and data. (For details, see Appendix 2.)

This view is at variance with the story told by classical (positivist) philosophy of science. According to the latter, a theory is a three-layered pyramid of hypotheses. The highest level contains only theoretical constructs, the middle level both theoretical and empirical ones, and the lowest level only observational concepts and hypotheses. Moreover, the relation between these layers is strictly deductive: the higher-level hypotheses imply the lower-level ones. Thus, the empirical content of theories emerges automatically at the bottom of the deductive chain: the lower in the logical chain, the closer to the ground. How this happens without the help of indicator hypotheses and data is never explained. This view, attractive for its simplicity, is widely accepted on authority, not for having passed any tests.

The positivist view is false for the following reasons. First, all the concepts occurring in a theory are theoretical. In other words, a theory has no empirical content by itself: it merely has some blanks that can be filled in with empirical data. Empirical concepts occur in observational or experimental protocols, but even here they are often combined with nonempirical concepts, such as nationality, marginal propensity to save, and political attitude. Second, logic cannot perform the miracle of producing empirical propositions out of nonempirical ones. If we wish to confront a theory with experience, we must build theory–observation bridges. This is done by operationalizing the theory—which would be unnecessary if its low-level statements could be confronted directly with data.

3 Social Indicator

A social indicator is an observable feature of a social fact pointing to an unobservable feature of the same social fact. Until about 1970, almost all the indicators used in social science were economic. Since then, the so-called social indicators movement has emerged, and sociologists and politologists have designed and used hundreds of new indicators (see, e.g., the journal *Social Indicators Research*). An examination of a few behavioral, social, and economic indicators will exhibit some of the problems they raise: in particular, some of the preconceptions that must be overcome in designing them (see, e.g., Bunge 1975, 1981*b*; Sheldon and Moore 1968; van Dusen 1974).

Actual choice is usually regarded as a reliable indicator of preference. And so it is, as long as all the options are known to the subject and are available at roughly the same cost. If some cost much more than others, actual choice will be a function not only of preference, but also of affordability. And if the options emerge and disappear in the course of time or are widely spread in space, then the opportunity factor enters in: We should reach for the good without waiting for the better, let alone the perfect (March and Simon 1958).

Income is usually taken to be the major, or even the only, indicator of social well-being (or quality of life). Yet this indicator is misleading, particularly in the case of societies with low birthrates and infant mortality, high life expectation, relatively high age of women at marriage, strong social networks, adequate public health, education, transportation, and leisure facilities; it is even more so where house rental is low and the climate benign. The Indian state of Kerala is a well-known example: it enjoys the highest quality of life in the subcontinent, despite having an average annual income of only just over $100 per capita.

Income is an insufficient measure of well-being because (*a*) biological well-being depends on the quality of the environment as well as on the quality of housing and the value of household assets, and (*b*) psychological well-being depends on job security, savings and pension plans, absence of social stress, access to cultural facilities, and status recognition. In sum, income is not a reliable indicator of either personal well-being or social welfare. On the other hand, large income differentials are reliable indicators of social inequality—in particular, of sexual or racial discrimination. Moreover, a large change in the income structure of a society is a good indicator of profound social transformation.

A faithful poverty index should rest on a clear concept of poverty. (The same holds, of course, for the dual concept of wealth.) Let us agree that poverty is the inability to meet basic needs without resorting to over-exertion, begging, crime, or public welfare. To quantify this concept, assume that it is possible to measure the degree, s_i, to which a person can satisfy the *i*th basic need with what he earns by honest toil. A person's degree of poverty in the *i*th respect, p_i, can then be defined as the complement of s_i to unity: that is, $p_i = 1 - s_i$. The total poverty index for a person is then definable as the average over all the *n* basic needs of the individual:

$$P = (1/n) \Sigma_i p_i = (1/n) \Sigma_i (1 - s_i).$$

This is an objective indicator. (It can be refined by assigning a weight to each need.) In addition to objective indicators, social scientists, particularly sociologists, use some subjective indicators. For example, to find out about the quality of life in a given community, they ask people in a random sample not only what their income is and how they spend it, but also how they feel about a number of features of their lives (see Michalos 1980–82). Such data are undoubtedly important, but they may not represent faithfully real-life conditions. For example, it has been reported that in the United States subjective well-being remained roughly constant during the 1980s (Andrews 1991). Yet income inequality has been increasing since 1969, and most people became poorer through inflation, unemployment, corporate downsizing ("leaner and meaner"), a shift from industrial jobs to ill-paid service ones, erosion of Social Security, deterioration of public services, and so on (Harrison and Bluestone 1988). Such a discrepancy between real and perceived quality of life serves as a warning against undue reliance on subjective measures and on the questionnaire method generally. It also poses an interesting problem for social psychologists: Have the responses in question been truthful, and if so, are they the effect of self-delusion? If the latter, what has caused that self-delusion?

Regrettably, the vast majority of social indicators are empirical; that is, they are not backed up by any social theory. Therefore they are ambiguous, sometimes even conventional, and often inadequate. For example, energy consumption per capita is usually taken as an indicator of economic development. But it can also be an indicator of energy waste, as suggested by a comparison of the United States with Sweden. Another example: Okun's misery index is the sum of the inflation and unemployment rates. This index may work satisfactorily for prosperous countries, but it fails for others—for example, those with full employment and little or no inflation, but where most people live below the poverty line. Besides, since the index does not include real income (after inflation), it does not represent faithfully the rise in poverty that has occurred in the United States and elsewhere between 1969 and 1996.

In sum, we need plenty of social indicators to link social theory to social reality. And we need not just *more* indicators, but *better* ones: clearly defined, related to social theories, and checked for adequacy.

4 Reality Check

Empirical tests designed to check the matching of ideas with facts are essential in all factual sciences. This is not always understood in the field of social studies, however, where many received beliefs about humans and social systems look self-evident and therefore in no need of tests. For example, some paleoanthropologists still believe that hominids were hunters rather than gatherers, scavengers, and only lastly hunters; and mainstream economists assume that everyone's preferences are constant and transitive. The stubborn rejection of adverse empirical evidence is a mark of nonscience, especially pseudoscience. And denying the possibility of attaining objective truth is a mark of antiscience.

For better or worse, intuition and nonscientific data are poor guides to social research, if only because (*a*) unsupported intuitions and hearsay may be rejected out of hand; (*b*) only very small social groups are visible; (*c*) overt individual behavior is an unreliable clue to an agent's intentions; and (*d*) the social scientist nearly always deals with the past, whether remote or recent. For these reasons, the social scientist is forced to make conjectures about unobservables, just like the nuclear physicist or the molecular biologist. But unless he puts those conjectures to the test, he will be creating or supporting myths.

In addition to the difficulty of access to his objects of study, the social scientist often works under the pressure of ideology. For example, it is widely accepted that the major source of social inequality is educational inequality, whence popular education is bound to have an equalizing effect. Sorokin challenged this optimistic hypothesis in 1927, and Boudon (1974) subjected it to empirical investigation. He found that, at least in contemporary France, a rise in educational level is accompanied by a decline in social status. Boudon himself explained this finding as follows. Where everyone gets an education, the waiting line for high positions gets longer. In other words, a rise in educational level is compensated for by a rise in the height of the barrier to entry into a higher social level. Where everybody is somebody, nobody is anybody. On the other hand, where nearly everybody is nobody, as in the Third World, anybody with an education is somebody: there, education is an effective social mobilizer.

Another interesting case of theory testing is Blaug's (1976) examination of the empirical status of Becker's well-known theory of human capital. Blaug concluded that, while the theory has inspired much research, it has not been well corroborated. For example, it is not true that, when faced with career choice, most students behave as well-informed and "rational" (i.e., maximizing) economic agents—so much so that in several fields the return on graduate education is low or even negative, and in the United States almost half of undergraduates in the natural sciences and engineering shift to the social sciences and humanities. Worse, the testable parts of the theory do not fare better than rival theories.

A still more instructive case is the empirical test of Milton Friedman's 1957 theory on the relation between planned consumption and income. Whereas some of the data used by Friedman confirm his theory, others do not. "If they fit, Friedman reports the fit as confirmation. . . . If they do not fit, Friedman either rejects the data as bad . . . or offers ad hoc explanations for the poor fit" (Diesing 1982, 137–38). Consequently the theory is never tested: only the reader's gullibility is.

Factual hypotheses can be tested by observation, measurement, or experiment. Observation may be direct or indirect. In social science the former bears on individuals or small groups. In particular, one may choose to observe face-to-face encounters in daily life. This kind of observation is of course necessary to test, or even generate, hypotheses concerning interactions. But it is insufficient, particularly in modern society, where people in positions of power may treat their subordinates as equals in order to manipulate them better. That is, the observable social structure may mask the real structure, much as a coat of paint may obliterate the difference between pine and oak. (See Bourdieu 1989, 16.) This is why the atheoretical recording of observable encounters, conducted by symbolic interactionists and ethnomethodologists, is of little use in unveiling social structure—or any other important feature of a social system, for that matter. A social scientist embracing scientific realism goes beyond appearances: he searches for the unobservable yet real things, processes, or patterns that manifest themselves in the phenomena (recall chap. 1).

Indirect observation in social science employs such means as questionnaires, interviews, statistics, surveys, ledgers, archival documents, and discarded tools or food remains. (The interview qualifies as indirect observation in that it activates a subject's memories.) Interviews and questionnaires are useful but limited and somewhat unreliable tools. First, the person questioned may lie, deceive himself, or be the victim of a trick of memory. Second, questionnaires and interviews elicit responses to the questions that the researcher is interested in; they seldom ask what bothers or intrigues the subject. For example, the question "Do you know how to do X?" may reveal that the subject does or does not have skill X, but it fails to elicit whether he has any alternative skills, which may be more important than X (R. Collins 1987).

Next comes measurement. One can measure either the numerosity of a collection or the intensity of a property (i.e., the value of a magnitude). In the first case one counts, as in making inventories or taking censuses. In the second case one avails oneself of a measuring instrument, such as a ruler, scale, chronometer, or more complex device like an electric meter. Whichever, the measurement technique depends on the property of the object of interest, and every technique and measuring instrument calls for its own special theory. There is no such thing as a universal meter capable of measuring crops, migration fluxes, industrial absenteeism, or what have you. Consequently, contrary to what many philosophers believe, there can be no general theory of measurement except for the theory of random measurement errors.

(What is often called "measurement theory" in the methodology of psychology and social science [e.g., Suppes and Zinnes 1963] is nothing of the sort. It deals exclusively with the formation of additive measures—extensive magnitudes such as length—detached from the theories in which they occur. It has nothing to do with measurement proper, which is an empirical operation. Ironically, the theory seems to have originated in a mistranslation of the German word *Mass* (measure), a mathematical concept, as "measurement" [Bunge 1974*b*]. Since measurements are empirical operations, they cannot be accounted for by a single theory, much less an a priori one. The design and execution of a measurement depend as much on the *mensurandum* as on the available empirical means—so much so that the measurement of any given magnitude, when performed with different measuring instruments, calls for different theories. Moreover, many measurements are indirect; that is, they involve indicators, and these depend on both the mensurandum and our body of theoretical and empirical knowledge about the mensurandum. No amount of mathematical sophistication can make up for empirical research.)

An important feature of measurement results is that they are subject to error, both systematic (due to flawed design or execution) and random. Whereas the former is human, random error inheres in both the thing measured and the measurement instrument. It originates in small random changes, such as Brownian motion and the "noise" in a telephone cable. In the natural sciences and psychology, it is standard practice to note the probable error of every measurement result. But this practice is still rare in the social sciences. Such slackness has two negative consequences. One is excessive confidence in data. The other is inconclusiveness with regard to the confrontation of theory with data: if the latter are affected by a wide margin of error, then they may be taken to confirm any number of theories.

Do social scientists make measurements? Most social scientists hardly ever measure anything, at least personally. When they do use numbers, they rely almost exclusively on figures supplied by nonscientists such as clerks, census-takers, government inspectors, and accountants. Moreover, many such figures, such as costs, prices, and profits, are read or calculated, rather than measured; and some of them are of little value in times of inflation. (Other features, such as transaction and opportunity costs, are at best guessed.) This is in vivid contrast to measurements in the natural sciences, which are designed and carried out by scientists in the light of well-confirmed theories. (See Morgenstern 1963; Bunge 1967*b*.)

One reason why social scientists hardly ever measure anything is that most of them rarely, if ever, meet the objects they study. (Management experts sometimes perform measurements proper, but they are at best technologists, not scientists.) None of them designs or operates measuring instruments, and most of their information is secondhand. Moreover, much of the empirical information they handle is qualitative, or "soft"—which is not to imply that it is unimportant. In short, measurement plays a much more modest role in social science than in natural science—which is one more reason not to confuse measurement with quantitation (for the latter, see chap. 2, sec. 4). So much for measurement. Let us now look at experiment.

An experiment is a deliberate alteration of the value of one or more properties (or variables) to see which other properties are affected and, if possible, to what extent. Like scientific observation and measurement, only more so, experiment is preceded by careful design and planning and followed by data processing. We all know the advantages of experiment over observation: only the former allows us to discover the relevant variables and to ascertain what depends on what. (See, e.g., Bernard's 1952 [1865] classic.)

Regrettably, there is an old philosophical prejudice against the very possibility of performing experiments in social science, which would make of it a branch of the humanities, in the same league as literary criticism and art history. This idealistic bias was punctured more than a century ago by the birth of experimental archæology, followed later by experimental social psychology, sociology, economics, and marketing. Yet, the old prejudice dies hard.

Three levels of experiment can be distinguished in contemporary social science: micro, meso, and macro, bearing on individuals, small groups, and communities, respectively. For example, a micro-experiment may investigate the economic (e.g., consumer) behavior of individuals (see, e.g., Davis and Holt 1993); another may check political attitudes (see, e.g., Laponce and Smoker 1972); a third may probe a subject's ideology (see, e.g., Cacioppo and Petty 1983). A meso-experiment studies how members of a small group behave to one another (see any textbook on social psychology). And a macro-experiment (or field experiment) may study, say, the impact of a certain public health program on some communities, using those which do not have it as controls (see, e.g., Greenwood 1945; Hausman and Wise 1985). So, once again, it is not true that social science is necessarily nonexperimental. What is true is that too many students of society believe that speculation, particularly if clad in mathematical garb, can stand on its own.

Most experiments in psychology and social science employ Fisher's theory of experimental design. This theory revolves around the notion of a *null hypothesis*. This is the hypothesis that the variables in question are mutually unrelated, so that the data are "due to chance." (I.e., H_0 is the hypothesis that the variable in question does *not* depend on the suspected variable. E.g., if $H = (y = ax + b)$, then $H_0 = (a = 0)$.) If the null hypothesis is refuted, it is time to try one or more of the alternative or substantive hypotheses.

Fisher's theory is indispensable in the preliminary stages of experimental research, when all one has to go on is a hunch that two given variables may be correlated. Refutation of the null hypothesis clears the way for crafting a substantive hypothesis or theory. Once this is in hand, it should help one design a more sophisticated experiment aimed at answering a more precise question, of the form: Are the variables in question related in such and such a manner?

Social science experiments have a property that no experiment in natural science can have: they can either be or fail to be realistic. That is, the experimental group may or may not exhibit the key features of the population from which it was taken. For example, an experiment in social psychology may force the subjects to remain silent and passive; one in economics may involve play money; or—and this is nearly universal—the subjects may not constitute a social system, so they will be unlikely to become involved or exhibit reciprocity and solidarity.

Not all experiments are real: some are thought-experiments, others of the *ex post facto* type. A thought-experiment consists in imagining what would happen if certain facts were to occur or had (or had not) occurred. Computer simulations are the most precise of all thought-experiments. They are particularly valuable as techniques for forecasting the behavior of complex systems.

Indeed, if we know or suspect the mechanism that makes a system tick, we can program a computer to simulate the system and show us how the system will evolve. And by varying the values of certain parameters in the model, we can assess their weight in such a process. Such exercises are particularly important in technology, for showing whether certain systems are likely to be stable under particular perturbations and whether certain courses of action are likely to be successful.

Thought-experiments may also spark off interesting hypotheses. In fact, the very design of a real experiment is a thought-experiment. And every student of the past is constantly making thought-experiments. For example, the economic historian Robert Fogel imagined what the history of the United States would have been without railways. (Whether such an exercise proves that railways made little difference to American development is another matter.) However, being chains of thoughts, or their computer surrogates, thought-experiments have no empirical force. This must be stressed at a time when many social scientists and animal rights activists believe that computer simulation can replace real experiments.

As for ex post facto experiments, they are not really experiments at all, but unplanned events analyzed with hindsight. For example, reports on people's behavior during and after a natural disaster, such as an earthquake, reveal the degree of social cohesion and level of solidarity of the people affected. Thus, sociologists have noted the contrast between the selfish behavior of Nicaraguans in the aftermath of the earthquake that destroyed Managua and the solidary behavior of the Chinese and Mexicans in similar (later) circumstances.

The process of checking the adequacy of our factual ideas to their referents may be summarized as follows:

1. Choose the proposition or theory, p, to be tested or to be used as a baseline for testing a new method.

2. Uncover the fact(s), f, referred to by p.

3. Find out whether p is testable with the means at hand.

4. Devise an indicator, I, of fact f referred to by proposition p.

5. Design an empirical test, t, of p with the help of I and possibly with the help of some theory other than p as well.

6. Set up the checking device.

7. Check the checking device for eventual systematic errors.

8. Perform a run, t, of empirical tests.

9. Collect the raw data, E, that test t yields.

10. Screen data E for possible errors.

11. Compute average value and experimental error.

12. Discard suspect data (those in excessive error).

13. Translate E into the language of p by means of indicator I, thus getting E^*.

14. Select translated datum e^* in E^* relevant to p.

15. Contrast e^* with p.

16. Assuming e^* to be true, calculate the error ϵ_1 in p, and conclude that p is true (or false) to within ϵ_1 relative to evidence e^*—until further notice.

17. Assuming p to be true, calculate the error ϵ_2 in e^*, and conclude that e^* is true (or false) to within ϵ_2 relative to hypothesis p—until next notice.

This procedure is at variance with the standard view proposed by logical empiricists as well as by some of their critics, notably Popper, according to which the propositions to be tested are confronted directly with raw empirical data. Actually, as we have just seen, the confrontation is indirect, for there are at least two additional components: the indicator hypotheses and the (auxiliary) hypotheses or theories used to design the observation or experiment. Neither the indicators nor the auxiliary hypotheses (or theories) are included in the construct that is being put to the test. (If what is being tested is a hypothetico-deductive system, a third component must be added: viz., the subsidiary hypotheses and the data that specify the particular object under observation.) Yet these additional components may well contain serious errors masking the truth of the tested construct (Bunge 1973*c*, 1983*b*).

The conclusion is obvious: neither the logical empiricists nor their opponents have proposed a realistic account of hypothesis or theory testing. The reason seems obvious: none of them has bothered to analyze (much less perform) a single laboratory test.

5 The Weight of Evidence

It is only natural to wish to see one's pet hypotheses confirmed. Only a masochist would wish otherwise. The prospect of confirmation is thus a powerful lure to research. Moreover, strong confirmation is the only truth indicator we have. However, like all indicators, it is unreliable, since further research may reveal counterexamples. For example, it is widely believed that keeping one's fingers crossed during takeoff and landing averts air crashes. But the available favorable evidence, though overwhelming, may be inconclusive, for, after all, passengers' fingers do not seem to be relevant to flight dynamics. It is therefore advisable to seek not only positive evidence but also possible negative evidence.

Which weighs more in assessing the truth-value of scientific hypotheses, confirmation or refutation? Or should they be assigned equal weight? Opinion is divided among philosophers, though not among scientists. In fact, the former are split between confirmationists (or inductivists), like Carnap and Reichenbach, and refutationists (or deductivists), like Peirce and Popper. Confirmationists claim that a few exceptions hardly matter, whereas refutationists hold that they are damning. The former think of the degree of confirmation of a hypothesis as the ratio of the number of favorable cases to the total number of cases. (And because of the analogy between this ratio and Laplace's definition of probability, they tend to identify the two and equate probability with degree of truth.) By contrast, refutationists care only for negative evidence. They argue that while no number of confirmations of the consequent *B* of a conditional hypothesis of the form "If *A*, then *B*" suffices to confirm its antecedent *A*, a single negative case suffices to refute it, according to the *modus tollens* inference rule "If *A*, then *B*, and not-*B*, then not-*A*."

Actual scientific practice fits neither the confirmationist nor the refutationist schema. For one thing, the two share the empiricist belief that empirical data are firm, whereas scientists know that data are just as fallible as hypotheses. That is why they test data of a new kind against well-tried hypotheses (recall the preceding section). This is also why they protect well-tried hypotheses with (bona fide) ad hoc hypotheses when negative data seem to refute them. Shorter: There is no rock-bottom empirical base, and not all hypotheses are equally flimsy. In fact, some are supported by other hypotheses which, in turn, have been confirmed satisfactorily. Thus, support for a hypothesis comes partly from empirical data and partly from the extant body of relevant knowledge— so much so that hypotheses are checked against the latter before being subjected to empirical tests (Bunge 1967*b*).

Popper's (1959 [1935]) refutationism is a useful warning against naive confirmationism, but it is not a viable alternative to it. First, it exaggerates the importance of criticism. After all, theories must be created before they can be criticized. Second, refutationism ignores the fallibility of empirical data. Third, it denies the importance of confirmation, which, after all, is a truth indicator. Fourth, refutationism restricts the function of observation and experiment to the checking of theories, whereas these are also necessary to design experiments, to produce the data required to make forecasts or hindcasts, to "discover" problems, and even to suggest (modest) hypotheses, in the form of empirical generalizations.

If refutationism were correct, we would be justified in upholding all testable hypotheses that have not yet been refuted empirically—for example, we would be justified in believing in the sunken continents Atlantis and Mu. The methodological skeptic rejects these myths not because they have been refuted by observation or experiment, but because they are not supported by any positive evidence. And he refuses to believe in telepathy, not only because it lacks empirical support, but also because it is inconsistent with physiological psychology.

In sum, real-life scientists are equally interested in positive and negative empirical evidence, either of which may be inconclusive. In addition, they also check the compatibility or otherwise of the hypothesis or theory on trial with the bulk of background knowledge—its external consistency, for short. (Recall that the background knowledge includes a handful of philosophical principles:

in the first place, those of the existence, lawfulness, and knowability of the external world.) Their verdict is favorable only when the conditions of compatibility and overwhelming confirmation are jointly met—and even then only until further notice.

Thus there are two indicators of factual truth: empirical confirmation and external consistency. But they do not have the same weight in all circumstances. In fact, empirical confirmation is decisive only if external consistency has been satisfied, while external consistency is decisive only in the case of empirical confirmation. And even such decisions hold only till further notice.

The above can be compressed into the following methodological principles:

M1. If a factual hypothesis or theory is compatible with the bulk of scientific background knowledge, then the former's truth-value will depend exclusively upon the outcome of rigorous empirical tests. Shorter: If h is externally consistent, then h is true if and only if h has been confirmed empirically.

M2. If a factual hypothesis or theory has been strongly confirmed by rigorous empirical tests, its truth-value will be determined exclusively by its compatibility (or otherwise) with the bulk of scientific background knowledge. Shorter: If h has been confirmed empirically, then h is true if and only if h is consistent externally.

Both rules are subject to two qualifications: (a) the truth in question may be only partial (e.g., to within the error of observation or computation), and (b) the valuation in question is subject to revision in the light of new theoretical or empirical information.

There is no genuine factual science without empirical data garnered by observation, measurement, or experiment. Yet, however relevant and accurate, data have only an instrumental or derivative value. In fact, they serve four functions: (1) to form preliminary (pretheoretical) descriptions; (2) to motivate or even suggest conjectures; (3) in conjunction with hypotheses or theories, to explain or predict facts; and (4) to subject hypotheses and theories to empirical tests. Such tests are anything but straightforward: indeed, they call for indicators, experimental designs, and subsidiary assumptions. The latter are used in the course of research even though they may be the subject of criticism in alternative research projects.

The intertwining of data and theory in actual scientific research refutes the simplistic accounts of data collection and theory testing offered by the classical philosophies of science. In particular, it refutes both inductivism (data $\Rightarrow$ theory) and deductivism (according to which the only function of empirical operations is to test theoretical predictions). Inductivism is best refuted by pointing out that no concepts denoting unobservables, such as those of a decision, an economy, or a nation, can occur in any observational or experimental protocols. And deductivism is best refuted by recalling that scientific advances occur not only through criticizing and testing theories but also through several other means, mainly by crafting new ideas.

Indeed, scientific progress involves not only theoretical advances, but also the invention of new measuring instruments and techniques, new observations or measurements (of known as well as of novel facts), new indicators, critical revisions of other workers' empirical results, the reorganization (in particular, axiomatization) of existing theories, and last, but not least, the philosophical examination of such theories with a view to either refining or weeding out fuzzy notions and unjustified assumptions. Such philosophical examination is particularly pertinent in the case of theories in the social sciences, for some of these are contaminated by obsolete philosophies and ideologies. However, this is a subject for the next chapter and my companion volume.

7 :: Science et al.

Science, technology, and ideology are the main fountainheads of modern culture. Yet all three have been widely misunderstood, confused with one another, and often jointly blamed for all the evils of our time, from environmental degradation to nuclear weapons, from unemployment to consumerism. Moreover, some people, such as Marcuse (1964) and Habermas (1971), have accused the couple science–technology of being the ideology of late capitalism. Others, such as Feyerabend (1975), have claimed that this couple is no better than pseudoscience, or even anti-science. In this chapter we shall attempt to dispel these confusions. This will help us later on when we come to tackle such questions as the scientific status of social studies, the value freedom and moral neutrality of science, and the role of ideology in sociotechnology—the branch of technology that tackles social issues. It will also help us to evaluate the claims of the postmodern constructivist-relativist philosophy and sociology of science and technology.

Whereas philosophers are interested in knowledge in itself, social scientists study, among other things, knowledge communities: how they produce, utilize, spread, and distort knowledge, true, half-true, or false. They study such communities in themselves, as well as in relation to one another and to other sectors of culture and to the economy and the polity. The main sectors of intellectual culture in relation to the economy and the polity in an industrialized society may be pictured as in figure 7.1.

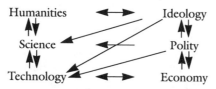

Fig. 7.1. Sketch of modern culture. The arrows represent influences.

This system is made up of two interconnected three-tiered towers. The humanities supply science with world views, problems, and goals, in exchange for which they get both findings and new problems. Science feeds knowledge to technology, which in turn provides the former with problems and tools. In the second tower, the economy provides the polity (in particular, government) with resources, in exchange for which it gets a skilled labor force, contracts, and regulations designed to save it from itself. Ideology, which caps this tower, guides or misguides government, which in exchange supplies it with power. The two towers are linked. In particular, the polity influences technology, which feeds industry and the state in exchange for support. And ideology, jointly with the polity, can stimulate or inhibit the humanities, science, and technology by encouraging or discouraging research and the development of new products. For example, whereas an enlightened ideology favors the scientific approach to social problems, an obscurantist ideology inhibits or misguides it. And whereas an altruistic moral philosophy will condemn social injustice and militarism, an egoistic one is likely to justify them.

The anthropological, sociological, economic, politological, and historical studies of science, technology, and ideology are interesting in themselves, and they can be useful in helping design cultural policies and programs, as long as they employ correct ideas about the nature of science, technology, and ideology. But it behooves philosophers to study this nature. Hence, far from being able to replace philosophy, social-scientific studies of science, technology, and ideology presuppose clear philosophical ideas about them. This does not mean that any philosophy will do. A philosophy of X should be checked for relevance and truth against X itself. For example, an irrationalist philosophy is incapable of accounting for the rational component of inquiry and evaluation; an idealist philosophy is bound to underrate empirical tests; an empiricist philosophy is bound to underrate theories; an anti-realist philosophy, such as conventionalism, phenomenalism, subjectivism, and pragmatism, makes no room for the concepts of test, truth, and error; and a linguistic philosophy is not interested in ontological, epistemological, ethical, or historical considerations (recall Introduction, sec. 3). In the following I shall sketch a realist philosophical view of science, technology, pseudoscience, and ideology.

1 Basic Science

There are several kinds of knowledge: genuine and bogus, ordinary and specialized, artisanal and humanistic, formal and factual, disinterested and mission-oriented, and so on. In the present section we shall deal with a very special kind of knowledge: namely, basic factual science, as exemplified by biology and sociology, but not management science and social medicine, which will be treated as science-based technologies.

Science starts where ordinary knowledge stops or fails as being either false or shallow. This does not entail that familiarity with the environment (e.g., one's social universe) is the main obstacle to the progress of science, as Bourdieu, Chamboredon, and Passeron (1991, 13) claim. Indeed, such familiarity is double-edged. On the one hand, it keeps the naive from seeing through the veils of appearance and tradition (in particular, superstition). On the other, it helps the sophisticate to keep his feet on the ground, thereby reducing irrelevant or wild speculation. Such closeness to reality is particularly important in social studies, with their tradition of grand speculation and minimal testing.

There is no consensus about the proper definition of the word *science*, either among scientists or among philosophers of science. Every metascientific school seizes on a single trait. Thus, according to some, science is uniquely characterized by the scientific method. (If this were true, then an experimental study of ghosts would rank as scientific.) Positivists hold that the distinctive trait of science is empirical manipulation. (But then alchemy might pass as a science, whereas history might not qualify.) Popper maintains that the mark of science is refutability. (But if this were so, astrology would be a science, whereas some extremely general physical hypotheses, which are confirmable but not refutable, would have to be regarded as nonscientific.) Still other scholars claim that anything mathematizable is scientific. (But then any bunch of equations, no matter how far removed from reality, would qualify as scientific.) Pragmatists look only for the "cash value" of ideas and "what is better for us to believe," as William James put it. (Accordingly, in a theocratic society, theology would qualify as a science.) Still others claim that what is characteristic of science is the consensus of expert opinion. (But surely every active field of research teems with controversy, and rational consensus is a social by-product of truth.) Finally, there are those who say that science is what scientists do. (But this does not allow us to distinguish genuine science from the quackery in which some scientists occasionally indulge.)

Since none of these popular views is adequate, I shall propose one of my own (Bunge 1983*b*). It covers all the major features of basic science conceived of as an activity, a changeable body of knowledge, and involving a community. In this way I hope to account for the epistemological, methodological, social, and historical aspects of science. The principal idea is that any given basic factual science is a member of a scientific system and is characterized by the conceptual and empirical study of some section or aspect of reality, with a view to representing the latter in the truest, deepest way possible. This idea can be spelled out as follows.

The *system of factual scientific research fields* is a variable collection, every member $\mathfrak{R}$ of which is representable by a 10-tuple

$$\mathfrak{R} = <C, S, D, G, F, B, P, K, A, M>,$$

where, at any given time,

1. *C*, the *research community* of $\mathfrak{R}$, is a social system composed of persons who have received a specialized training, hold strong communication links among themselves, share their knowledge with anyone who wishes to learn, and initiate or continue a tradition of inquiry (not just of belief) aimed at finding true representations of facts;

2. *S* is the *society* (complete with its culture, economy, and polity) that hosts *C* and encourages, or at least tolerates, the specific activities of the components of *C*;

3. the *domain*, or *universe of discourse*, *D*, of $\mathfrak{R}$ is composed exclusively of (actual or possible) real entities (rather than, say, free-floating ideas) past, present, or future;

4. the *general outlook* or *philosophical background*, *G*, of $\mathfrak{R}$ consists of (*a*) the ontological principle, that the world is composed of concrete things that change lawfully and exist independently of the researcher (rather than, say, ghostly or unchanging or invented or miraculous entities); (*b*) the epistemological principle, that the world can be known objectively, at least partially and gradually; and (*c*) the ethos of the free search for truth, depth, understanding, and system (rather than, say, the ethos of religious faith or that of the quest for sheer information, utility, profit, power, consensus, or good);

5. the *formal background*, *F*, of $\mathfrak{R}$ is the collection of up-to-date logical and mathematical theories (rather than being empty or made up of obsolete formal theories);

6. the *specific background*, *B*, of $\mathfrak{R}$ is a collection of up-to-date and reasonably well-confirmed (yet corrigible) data, hypotheses, and theories and of reasonably effective research methods, obtained in other fields relevant to $\mathfrak{R}$;

7. the *problematics*, *P*, of $\mathfrak{R}$ consists exclusively of cognitive problems concerning the nature (in particular, the regularities) of the members of *D*, as well as problems concerning other components of $\mathfrak{R}$;

8. the *fund of knowledge*, *K*, of $\mathfrak{R}$ is a collection of up-to-date and testable (though rarely final) theories, hypotheses, and data compatible with those in *B*, obtained by members of *C* at previous times;

9. the *aims, A,* of the members of *C* include discovering or using the regularities (in particular, laws) and circumstances of the *D*'s, systematizing (into theories) general hypotheses about *D*'s, and refining methods in *M*;

10. the *methodics, M,* of ℜ consists exclusively of scrutable (checkable, analyzable, criticizable) and justifiable (explainable) procedures, in the first place the general scientific method (background knowledge → problem → solution candidate → check → candidate evaluation → eventual revision of either solution candidate, checking procedure, background knowledge, or even problem).

In addition, there is at least one other *contiguous* scientific research field, in the same system of factual research fields, such that (*a*) the two fields share some items in their general outlooks, formal backgrounds, specific backgrounds, funds of knowledge, aims, and methodics, and (*b*) either the domain of one of the two fields is included in that of the other, or each member of the domain of one of the fields is a component of a concrete system in the domain of the other.

Further, the membership of every one of the last eight components of ℜ *changes,* however slowly at times, *as a result of inquiry* in the same field (rather than as a result of ideological or political pressures or "negotiations" among researchers), as well as in related (formal or factual) fields of scientific inquiry.

Any field of knowledge that fails to satisfy even approximately all the above conditions will be said to be 'nonscientific' (e.g., theology, philosophy, and literary criticism). A research field that satisfies them approximately may be called a 'semi-science' or 'proto-science' (e.g., economics and political science). If, in addition, the field is evolving toward full compliance with them all, it may be called an 'emerging' or 'developing science' (e.g., psychology and sociology). On the other hand, any field of knowledge that, being nonscientific, is advertised as scientific will be said to be 'pseudoscientific' or a 'fake' or 'bogus' science (e.g., parapsychology, psychoanalysis, and psychohistory). Whereas the difference between a science and a proto-science is one of degree, that between a proto-science and a pseudoscience is one of kind. (More in sec. 5.)

I submit that the above definition captures the essential conceptual, empirical, social, and historical features of any basic factual science, from physics to history. It also includes Merton's (1973, chap. 13) ethos, or "institutional imperatives," of basic science: universalism (as opposed to nationalism or racism), epistemic communism (i.e., publiic property of knowledge), disinterestedness (as opposed to the utilitarian orientation of technology), and organized skepticism (as opposed to dogmatism). By the same token, this characterization disagrees with the fashionable constructivist-relativist philosophy and sociology of science, which has not proposed a clear definition of science and refuses to demarcate it from nonscience anyway. (More in sec. 6.)

Note the following points. First, every scientist belongs to a scientific community, which is a social system (or network), not a mere aggregate of mutually independent scholars. Characteristically, quackery is marginal. Second, not every society constitutes a suitable matrix for a scientific community: only minimally affluent and tolerant societies do. Third, condition (3) excludes the ghostly as a possible subject for scientific inquiry but does not preclude speculation on still undiscovered entities, such as superluminal fields or fully democratic societies.

Fourth, the philosophical background, G, of factual science is usually ignored or underrated. Moreover, according to all the popular philosophies, science is disjoint from philosophy. Yet, there is no scientific research without an ontological, epistemological, and moral basis, even if this is usually hidden. For instance, if we do not believe in the independent existence, lawfulness, and knowability of the external world, we will not explore it. And whoever violates the norms of intellectual honesty and common property of scientific knowledge risks being ostracized.

Fifth, the formal background, F, of a factual science varies from one sector to the next, between a bare minimum of elementary logic to highly sophisticated mathematical theories. In principle, all of mathematics is utilizable in science. Which mathematical theories find application depends not so much on the subject matter as on the mathematical proficiency and imagination of the scientist. Caution: The degree of mathematical sophistication of a science is an ambiguous indicator of the level of development of the latter. For example, mainstream economics is far more mathematical, but also far less realistic, than history.

Sixth, the specific background, B, of a science is an indicator of its place on the ladder of the sciences. Thus, psychology and anthropology presuppose (utilize) biology; sociology, economics, and politology presuppose psychology and anthropology, but there is no order of precedence between the three disciplines mentioned first; on the other hand, history depends upon sociology, economics, and politology. Only logic has no presuppositions. A discipline other than logic that borrows nothing from any other discipline is either extremely backward or bogus.

Seventh, the problematics, P, of a science depends exclusively on the problems that its researchers choose to work on. As we saw in chapter 3, section 2, in every discipline one can pose problems of many different kinds: routine or research, substantive or methodological, theoretical or empirical, and so on.

Eighth, the fund of knowledge, K, of a science may be poor or rich, depending on its age and level of development. But it is never empty, for problems are not posed in a cognitive vacuum but against some background knowledge. Even the newest branch of social science possesses some fund of knowledge borrowed from preexisting branches.

Ninth, the aims, A, of a science are description, explanation, and possibly prediction, with the help of laws or norms. Only the proto-sciences and pseudosciences are totally bereft of laws. Even history, though not a fertile source of laws, makes use of law statements borrowed from other sciences.

Tenth, the methodics, M, of any science is constituted by the general scientific method (chap. 3, sec. 7) plus techniques (special methods) of its own. Obviously, methods are only tools for solving problems: even the most sophisticated techniques are worthless unless applied to sizable problems.

So much for the ten components of any scientific research field. As for the conditions of systemicity and changeability, suffice it to say at this point that isolation and stagnation are typical of pseudoscience, scholastic philosophy, and ideology. (More in secs. 5–8.) Every genuine scientific discipline interacts with its neighbors and changes as a result of research, which can include controversy over anything other than the desiderata of precision and consistency.

Readers of Kuhn (1962) may wonder why the word *paradigm* does not occur in my characterization of science, although I did elucidate it earlier (chap. 3, sec. 1). There are two reasons for this omission. First, it is simplistic to claim that a science can be identified by a single feature, such as a paradigm: I have found it necessary to list ten different features. Second, Kuhn's thesis that every "normal" science has a single paradigm is close to the truth for the seventeenth and eighteenth centuries, when mechanics was the paragon science, but does not hold for the next two centuries. For example, in physics since the middle of the nineteenth century, the field-theoretic thought style has coexisted with the corpuscular one, and probabilistic reasonings have intertwined with deterministic ones; chemists use classical or macro-descriptions (in chemical kinetics) and semi-classical ones (e.g., in the ball-and-spoke models of molecules) along with atomic explanations; biologists go on describing and classifying organisms while at the same time studying their molecular components and investigating whole populations and ecosystems, both synchronically and diachronically; physiological psychology coexists with mentalism; some social scientists are individualists, whereas others are holists and still others systemists; and so on. In sum, it is not true that every "normal" science is monoparadigmatic. Moreover, to demand that a single paradigm (or thought style or approach) be adopted in every field is to invite narrow-mindedness and dogmatism. Thus Himmelstrand (1986, 2:7): "sociology, in order to be scientific . . . , necessarily must be multi-paradigmatic."

My characterization of a science is designed to fit all the factual sciences: natural (like biology), social (like economics), and socio-natural (like social psychology). It is also designed to fit the auxiliary, or service, sciences, such as archaeology and descriptive statistics, as well as the substantive ones, such as sociology and history. But it does not describe the formal or mathematical sciences, for these do not deal with independently existing things, hence they do not contain propositions vulnerable to empirical data.

Finally, how scientific are the social studies? I have investigated this question elsewhere (Bunge forthcoming). The result is this. Some fields, such as demography and history, are scientific to a high degree, in that they comply fairly well with the above conditions. They are short only on theory, hence on laws. Others, such as sociology, economics, and politology, have plenty of theories, but few of these happen to be true, whence they qualify only as semi-sciences. Still others, such as the humanistic (in particular, hermeneutic) social studies, are utterly nonscientific. So there is plenty of room for improvement—unless, of course, one believes, against all evidence, that social studies can never become scientific.

2 The Unity of Science

Mathematicians need not pay any attention to fields of learning other than their own. By contrast, physicists make ample use of mathematics, chemists of mathematics and physics, biologists of physics and chemistry, psychologists of neuroscience, sociologists of psychology, and so on. Why this difference? Because mathematicians deal in pure ideas—that is, ideas without real counterparts—whereas factual scientists not only borrow some tools from mathematics, they also borrow some findings from other factual sciences when dealing with systems whose components are studied by those sciences. For example, the sociological study of social networks makes use of graph theory, a chapter of pure mathematics, as well as of some results of psychology concerning interpersonal relations.

There is a clear, simple criterion for finding out whether a research field is autonomous or, on the contrary, depends upon other disciplines. It is this: A science S_1 will be said to be *independent* of another science S_2 if and only if all the problems in S_1 can be solved without using any findings in S_2. Otherwise S_1 *depends* upon S_2. And if S_1 depends upon S_2, and conversely, then these sciences are *interdependent*. Thus, mathematics is independent of economics, but not conversely. By contrast, all the social sciences are mutually interdependent, for in every one of them there are problems that require findings from one or more of the sister sciences. For example, a deep study of any economy goes beyond economics: it examines natural and human resources, social relations, cultural constraints, the political system, and the recent past of the society. The fact that few economic studies follow this line merely suggests that disciplinary independence in social studies can be had only at the cost of depth and truth.

There is a bewildering variety and number of scientific disciplines—at least a thousand and still growing. Yet the preceding considerations presuppose that all sciences are one in some respects. Otherwise it would be impossible to propose a general definition of science. What, if any, are the bonds that hold all the sciences together? How can geology, neurobiology, history, and other disciplines be components of a single system? Several answers to this question have been proposed.

One answer is reductionism, which we first met in chapter 4, section 7. The three most popular radical reductionist strategies have been psychologism, physicalism, and economicism (or same-level reductionism). *Psychologism* was proposed by Berkeley, Avenarius, and Mach and adopted at one time by Russell and Carnap. Its master idea is that we should stick to sense-data: these are the ultimate bricks, or "atoms," of which the world is made. This project has failed, even in psychology. Thus perception goes beyond sensation, and the distinction between correct and incorrect perception presupposes the hypothesis of the autonomous existence of physical objects. Besides, physiological psychology rests on the assumption that mental processes are neurophysiological processes. So radical psychologism, or sensationism, is out. On the other hand, a moderate version of it won strong support in the 1960s and 1970s, when all the social sciences were called "behavioral sciences," on the tacit assumption that they were "ultimately" reducible to (behaviorist) psychology. (See, e.g., Berelson and Steiner 1964; Homans 1974.)

Physicalism is the dual of psychologism. According to this, every science is "ultimately" about physical entities, so all the sciences are to be unified through the method and language of physics. This update of seventeenth-century mechanism was the original program of the *Encyclopedia of Unified Science* (1938–62) devised by the sociologist Neurath and the philosopher Carnap. This project miscarried for several reasons, the most important of which is that micro-reduction is at best partial (recall chap. 4, secs. 6 and 7). In particular, no social science is reducible to biology, or even to psychology, because only the components of a social system are alive and can have a mental life. Social systems are held together by social (economic, political, or cultural) links as well as by biological (e.g., sexual) and psychological (e.g., empathy) ties. Moreover, they discharge suprabiological functions, such as education, security, production, and exchange.

Finally, *economicism* is a much more modest reductionist program, confined to the social studies. Indeed, it is the attempt to reduce all social sciences, and sometimes psychology as well, to economics. The first version of economicism was historical materialism, which exerted a strong (though often unacknowledged) influence on all social studies. It did so by shifting the focus from disembodied ideas to the economic or "material basis" of society. But it failed ultimately because it underrated the power of culture and politics, either of which may occasionally gain the upper hand. The latest version of economicism, called 'economic imperialism,' was proposed by Becker (1976) and adopted by Coleman (1990) and several others (see Swedberg 1990). This reductionist program attempts to account for everything social in terms of neoclassical microeconomics—stable preferences, maximizing behavior, and market equilibrium. But this nineteenth-century theory does not explain even the modern economy, on top of which it hangs two fuzzy notions, those of subjective value (or utility) and subjective probability, which will be examined in the next chapter. (See Bunge 1995*b*, Bunge forthcoming, for more.)

All three reductionist prescriptions for achieving the unity of the sciences have failed. Still, the unity of science, and indeed of all genuine knowledge, is desirable for mutual enrichment and checking. Moreover, it is being achieved through different means: the building of interdisciplines, the use of mathematics, the ubiquity of philosophy, and the systemic approach. Let us take a look at these four unifying factors.

An *interdiscipline* is, of course, a discipline bridging two or more disciplines. More precisely, an interdiscipline (*a*) overlaps partially with two or more disciplines, sharing some referents, concepts, hypotheses, and methods with them, and (*b*) contains hypotheses bridging the original disciplines—the glue formulas we met in chapter 4, section 8. Social psychology, neurolinguistics, bioeconomics, and political sociology are clear cases of interdisciplines. By contrast, sociology and geology are not, because they do not connect two or more disciplines: they satisfy condition (*a*), but not (*b*).

There are hundreds of interdisciplines, and more are being born as specialists dare to trespass the borders of their own fields. (Psychoneuroendocrinoimmunology is only one of the recent arrivals.) Every serious interdiscipline contributes to cementing the unity of science. The mushrooming and success of most existing interdisciplines suggests the following methodological postulate:

Any two scientific research fields can be bridged by one or more research fields.

This assumption, jointly with the definition of a system, entails that the collection of scientific research fields constitutes a system. In turn, this theorem entails the corollary that any discipline that fails to be related to at least one scientific research field is not a science. This condition is included in our definition of a scientific discipline. The failure to comply with it is a mark of pseudoscience (see sec. 5).

Another powerful interdisciplinary glue is mathematics, which is a vast generalization of logic. Indeed, anyone knowing some mathematics can cross disciplinary boundaries with little discomfort, though of course not without some effort. This is because mathematics has no ontological commitment; that is, it makes no assumptions concerning the nature of reality. The same holds for logic, the lowest basement of the mathematics skyscraper (recall chap. 2, sec. 2). The ontological neutrality of mathematics explains why so many scientific research fields share some mathematical ideas. What changes from one field to another is the interpretation assigned to mathematical ideas. Thus, whereas in population ecology the sigmoid, or S-shaped, function may represent the growth of a population, in psychology it may represent a learning process; a vector may represent a force in mechanics and a bundle of goods or their corresponding prices in economics; and so on. By itself, no mathematical idea represents anything real. Only a mathematical idea together with its interpretation in factual terms can represent something real. In other words, theories in pure mathematics are devoid of factual (in particular, empirical) content. Therefore every mathematical theory in science, technology, or the humanities contains interpretation (or semantic) assumptions that endow some of its mathematical concepts with an extra-mathematical content, as we saw in chapter 2, section 4.

The sensational success of mathematics in all fields of scientific research suggests our next methodological postulate:

Every clear and powerful idea, in any research field, can be made even clearer and more powerful by being mathematized (i.e., by being assigned a precise construct belonging to a definite mathematical theory).

This postulate entails that all the sciences can be constructed on a single formal basis: namely, mathematics (inclusive of logic). An immediate consequence of this is that any discipline refractory to mathematics is either nonscientific, prescientific, or proto-scientific.

Another discipline that underlies every factual science, thus contributing to the unity of the sciences, is philosophy. Indeed, all the factual sciences share a number of concepts and hypotheses which, in being extremely general and pervasive, belong to philosophy. I have argued this point before. Suffice it now to recall the concepts of thing, time, and truth and the principles of lawfulness and of the intelligibility of reality. Scientists are seldom conscious of these presuppositions, and some, when on a philosophical foray, argue against them. What matters, however, is whether a philosophical principle does some work, if only tacitly. And this can be discovered only by analyzing cases of actual research, not by quoting *obiter dicta* of famous scientists or philosophers. For instance, take the principle that, far from being constructed by scientists, the world exists by itself. If scientists did not hold this principle, they would not explore reality but would construct mathematical theories or just myths: they would invent, but not discover. Or take the principle that, though fallible, our knowledge of facts is perfectible. If scientists did not hold it, they would make no effort to estimate errors, check data, or improve their theories. The fact that they do make such efforts and that some of these pay off handsomely shows that scientists care for truth and trust in the possibility of attaining ever greater accuracy and depth, which in turn shows that the subjectivist (in particular, constructivist), conventionalist, and pragmatist philosophies of science are false and pernicious, if only because none has any use for the concept(s) of truth.

It may also be objected that not all philosophies promote the search for scientific truth. *Touché*: for example, Hegelianism is inimical to science in being aprioristic, phenomenology in being subjectivist, existentialism in being irrationalist, and all three in being obscure. But this does not disprove our thesis that philosophy is one of the ingredients of the glue holding the sciences together. It only goes to show that there is good philosophy, bad philosophy, and pseudo-philosophy. If we believe that scientific research is the best way to get to know the world, ourselves included, we shall favor a philosophy that stimulates scientific research rather than hinders it. It would be silly for a scientist to attempt to conduct his research in accordance with an unscientific philosophy. And it is wasteful, or even destructive, for a philosopher living in the age of science and technology to prop up an unscientific or technophobic philosophy.

Let us finally mention a fourth way of overcoming the fragmentation of knowledge: namely, the systemic, or analytico-synthetic, approach. This is an alternative to both the individualist (or analytic or micro-reductionist) and the holist (or synthetic or macro-reductionist) approaches. *Systemism* boils down to the following postulate:

Every object (whether concrete, conceptual, or symbolic) is either a system or a component of one or more systems.

Because it stresses the interconnections among things, as well as among ideas, systemism favors the integration of the sciences and, indeed, of the totality of human knowledge. In particular, it discourages the sectoral approach and encourages interdisciplinary and multidisciplinary work, all of which is particularly important for the social sciences. (More on systemism and its rivals in chaps. 9 and 10.)

However, even granting that the systemic approach contributes to the unity of science, the specialist might ask why he should care for such unity, given that depth calls for specialization. There are at least three reasons for cherishing and promoting the unity of the sciences. One is that most hybrid scientific disciplines have proved fertile. (Most, not all, because psychohistory, human sociobiology, and biopolitology are below par.) A second reason is that awareness of the unity of the sciences beneath their diversity facilitates the mobility of investigators from one field to another. A third reason is that some interdisciplinary borders have no counterparts in reality, but derive from myopic views, philosophical bias, turf protection, or historical accident. In particular, the fragmentation of social studies is artificial and pernicious, because society is a single system, though, of course, one with several subsystems with strong couplings.

To be sure, the various components and properties of a system must be analyzed and distinguished, not confused. But analysis should help synthesis rather than hinder it, much less replace it, and distinction should not entail separation. In other words, specialism, though necessary, should not be overdone: it should be tempered by generalism. The reason is that, though complex, the world is a single system, whence the collection of fields of knowledge, however complex, should also be a system if it is to constitute an increasingly true representation of the world and thereby an increasingly efficient tool for transforming it.

To conclude: The unity of scientific knowledge is fact, not unrealistic aspiration. This system is never cohesive enough, and thus its unity may not be obvious to the narrow specialist, but it does not escape the generalist, particularly if he happens to have a philosophical frame of mind. Indeed, all scientists study reality, employ the scientific method, can help themselves freely to a common mathematical toolbox, and they all share, albeit usually tacitly, certain comprehensive philosophical assumptions concerning the world and our knowledge of it. Besides, no scientific field is isolated: each one overlaps with others, some of which are interdisciplines. Furthermore, a number of theories can be totally or partially reduced to other, more comprehensive or deeper ones. Finally, the systemic approach, which calls for multidisciplinary work, can be adopted with great profit in all research fields. So even though unification through reduction to a single science has proved to be just a dream, science is one, after all.

3 Applied Science

There is no consensus on the signification of the expression 'applied science.' In the field of social studies, 'applied' often means concern with particular problems, such as stagflation, as opposed to investigating highly idealized theories such as general equilibrium economics. We shall adopt its prevalent usage in natural science and engineering, where it denotes the link between basic science and technology. Examples: pharmacology, biomedical research, and epidemiology.

Applied science is the research field in which scientific problems of possible practical import are investigated on the basis of findings in basic (pure) science. It is targeted, or "mandated," rather than free research: from some of it one expects eventually some findings of practical interest, such as the effects of chemical pollution or social inequality upon health. However, applied research is expected to yield knowledge, not designs for artifacts or plans of action, which are the products of technology. Typically, the applied scientist uses generalizations and theories instead of either inventing or testing them. And, in turn, the technologist makes use of some of the outputs of applied science.

Clinical psychologists, psychiatrists, and education experts are applied scientists to the extent that they engage in original scientific research, but not in their professional practice, where they rank as highly skilled craftsmen or servicemen. So are the social scientists who investigate particular social issues, such as marginality, drug addiction, corruption, criminality, illiteracy, fanaticism, cultural deprivation, inflation, and development. Only those who design social policies or programs qualify as sociotechnologists. And those who implement them may be called sociotechnicians.

Applied science uses basic science but does not flow automatically from the latter: it involves original research. If it did not involve research and did not yield new knowledge, it might qualify as expertise, but not as science. Still, the main task of the applied scientist is to exploit part of the fund of knowledge produced by basic research. He is expected to make discoveries but not to discover any deep properties or general laws. Also the scope of applied science is narrower than that of the corresponding basic science. For example, instead of studying social conflict in general, the applied sociologist may study industrial conflict in a given region, industry, or firm, with a view to finding (though not implementing) practical (though not necessarily fair) solutions to it. Implementation is left to civil servants, managers, or union leaders.

Applied science, like technology, has a practical goal: both are targeted. For instance, during the colonial period some anthropologists were hired by governments to study the natives in order to figure out how best to maintain colonial domination. Developmental sociologists and economists study the problems of underdevelopment not just out of scientific curiosity, but in order to pinpoint the hurdles that a suitable development plan must address. They are asked to supply knowledge to policymakers for use in designing specific plans aimed at solving specific social issues.

Applied science connects basic science with technology, but there are no precise borders between the three—so much so that what begins as pure research may end up as applied, and the latter as technological. (Pharmacology, biotechnology, and bioeconomics are exemplary.) However, the channels between the three are often clogged, and each of the three activities has its peculiarities and calls for its own specific intellectual background, interest, and ability. Whereas the original scientist, whether basic or applied, is essentially an explorer, the creative technologist is basically an inventor: he designs systems or processes. In particular, the sociotechnologist designs or redesigns social systems or methods for managing them. However, we are bordering on the subject of the next section.

4 Technology

Most people confuse technology with either science or industry, and some scientists exploit this vulgar confusion to obtain research grants by promising vague practical results. The confusion is understandable, because modern technology and industry make intensive use of scientific findings, and also because of the pervasiveness of pragmatism, which has no time for disinterested inquiry. Yet there are sharp differences between the three fields despite their commonalities. The main difference between science and technology is that the former, whether basic or applied, produces new knowledge, whereas R&D laboratories, workshops, and offices use knowledge only as a means to design artifacts (e.g., machines, towns, or formal organizations), norms (e.g., emission standards), or plans of action (e.g., literacy or immunization campaigns). These and other peculiarities of technology are studied by a growing number of philosophers of technology (see, e.g., Mitcham and Mackey 1972; Agassi 1985; Bunge 1985*b*; Mitcham 1994).

Some of the differences between science and technology can be detected in the vocabulary of technical reports, where such typically technological words as *use, repair, reliability, efficiency, safety, user-friendly, quality control, productivity, rule, norm, policy, plan,* and *cost-effective* are bound to occur. This difference in vocabulary is an indicator of differences in referents, means, and goals. The central objects of technology are artifacts, whether things or processes, inanimate, living, or social; its main cognitive means is applied science; and its goal is to control natural or social systems or processes for the benefit of some social group. The scientist comes up with new propositions thought to be true, the technologist with proposals, original or well tried, aimed at efficiency.

We start by distinguishing between technics and technology: the former is prescientific craftsmanship, the latter, science-based research and development (R&D). (There is no such thing as Stone Age or even Iron Age technology.) The technologist refines technics with the help of science and exploits findings of pure and applied science. He may engage in original research, but only temporarily and as a means. His specific task is not to explore the world but to craft tools (material or intellectual) to change it—for better or worse. He does this by making designs, plans, or norms with the help of some of the best available pure knowledge.

The technologist employs well-confirmed generalizations—in particular, laws—as bases for technological rules, which in turn are the grounds for his designs or plans. For instance, knowing that C is or could be valuable to industry, the biotechnologist, upon learning from genetics that genic change A in organism of kind B brings about the latter's production of C, sets up, tests, and eventually implements the rule: Induce change A in large numbers of B's in order to produce C's in industrial quantities. If, on the other hand, C proved to be noxious, the very same piece of scientific knowledge would be the ground for the dual rule: Prevent change A in all B's in order to prevent them from producing C's. As we saw earlier (chap. 2, sec. 8), this ambivalence of technological knowledge is the root of its moral ambivalence. That is, technology can be used or misused. Hence we should frisk the technologists, not the scientists. (More in chap. 8, sec. 5.)

A technological design, norm, or plan may bear on inanimate things, organisms, mental processes, social systems, or information. Hence technology, in this broad sense, includes the following fields: hardware technology, which includes physiotechnology (e.g., civil, electrical, and nuclear engineering) and chemotechnology (industrial chemistry and chemical engineering); biotechnology (e.g., agronomy, therapy, and genetic engineering); psychotechnology (e.g., clinical and marketing psychology); sociotechnology (e.g., management science and military strategy); and software technology or knowledge engineering (e.g., information science and robotics).

The R&D process can be analyzed into the following main stages: choice of field → formulation of a practical problem → acquisition of the requisite background knowledge → invention of technical rules → invention of artifact in outline → detailed blueprint or plan → test (at the workbench or in the field or on the computer) → test evaluation → eventual correction of design or plan. We call this sequence the 'technological method.'

The final product of an R&D process is a prototype for an artifact, a preliminary plan, or a set of norms to be proposed to the employer or client. In the case of sociotechnology, the artifact is a formal organization, such as a business firm or a government department; and the norm or plan is one of rational (and hopefully efficient) action. For example, a management consultant may be called in to diagnose the sources of trouble of a business firm and to propose a plan to solve its problems.

The adoption and execution of the final technological design, norm, or plan is usually in hands other than the technologist's. The latter gives advice but does not make the final decisions or implement them. In particular, in social matters the sociotechnologist makes proposals, which may well be ignored, adopted, corrected, or rejected by his employer or client (political or business body). If the boss approves the final project, he instructs the bureaucrats (civil servants or business executives) to have it implemented by yet other people or their artificial proxies (robots).

With regard to originality, there are two kinds of technological invention: primary and secondary, or innovation and improvement. A problem requiring a primary invention looks like this: It is desirable to attain goal G; so inquire whether some means M (machine, organization, process, product, or plan) could be designed and eventually brought into existence to attain G. Should you find a plausible M, try to develop it into a technically feasible and economically (or politically or culturally) profitable item. Example: A reduction in the birthrate is desirable. Design a medically, culturally, politically, and economically feasible program to institute massive voluntary family planning.

By contrast, an improvement problem looks like this: Existing artifact M for achieving goal G is defective (cumbersome, unsafe, inefficient, slow, expensive, wasteful, or associated with undesirable side effects). Conduct research aimed at designing a variant M' of M to the same end G, but lacking some of the flaws of M. Example: Social program S is effective but wasteful. Streamline S so as to increase its efficiency.

Both primary invention and improvement problems call for the design of artifacts (inanimate, living, or social) or processes for doing or making something useful to somebody in the most efficient manner. But there are obvious ontological and epistemological differences between the two. Primary invention may lead to radical novelty, whereas secondary invention leads only to a minor alteration of the former. There is also a psychological difference. Unlike superficial improvements, primary inventions spring from curiosity, are fueled by creative imagination, and are stimulated by the successes and failures of the creative process itself. By contrast, improvements are mostly guided by the carrot of practical success. Finally, there is an interesting social difference as well: whereas most improvements are generated within a given sector, radical inventions are often the work of outsiders or interdisciplinary teams. This feature of technological invention seems to be related both to the routine inherent in most permanent jobs and to the inertia of large organizations, but is otherwise poorly understood.

Whether primary or secondary, once adopted and implemented, an invention becomes an innovation. Innovations are not ideas but social events, such as the Industrial Revolution, the diffusion of domestic appliances, social legislation, and the ongoing information-processing revolution. Resistance to technological innovation is ambiguous: it may be either an indicator of backwardness, reluctance to learn and adapt, or fear that the innovation in question may have undesirable social consequences, such as mass unemployment, pollution, or cultural degradation.

We are now ready to propose a general definition of the concept of a technology, which will supplement and refine the foregoing as well as exhibit the commonalities and differences of technology vis-à-vis basic science (sec. 1). A family of technologies is a system every component $\mathcal{T}$ of which is representable by an 11-tuple:

$$\mathcal{T} = \; < C, S, D, G, F, B, P, K, A, M, V >,$$

where, at any given moment,

1. the *professional community*, C, of $\mathcal{T}$ is a social system composed of individuals who have received a specialized training, hold information links among themselves, share certain values, and initiate or continue a tradition of design and evaluation of artifacts or processes of some kind;

2. S, the *society* that hosts C, supports, or at least tolerates, the professional activities of the members of C;

3. the *domain,* or universe of discourse, D, of $\mathcal{T}$ is composed exclusively of (certified or putatively) real entities, past, present, or future, some natural and others artificial;

4. the *general outlook* or *philosophical background,* G, of $\mathcal{T}$ consists of (*a*) an ontology of lawfully changing things—in particular, natural resources and

things under possible human control; (*b*) a realist epistemology with a touch of pragmatism; and (*c*) the professional ethics of the utilization of natural and human (in particular, cognitive) resources;

5. the *formal background*, F, is a collection of up-to-date logical and mathematical theories;

6. the *specific background*, B, of $\mathcal{T}$ is a collection of up-to-date, reasonably well-confirmed (yet corrigible) data, hypotheses, and theories, of reasonably effective research methods, and of useful designs, norms, and plans found in other fields of knowledge, particularly in the sciences and technologies related to $\mathcal{T}$;

7. the *problematics*, P, of $\mathcal{T}$ consists exclusively of cognitive and practical problems concerning the members of the domain, D, as well as problems concerning other components of the 11-tuple;

8. the *fund of knowledge*, K, of $\mathcal{T}$ is a collection of up-to-date, testable (though not definitive) data, hypotheses, theories, and methods, as well as designs, norms, and plans, compatible with the specific background, B, and obtained by members of C at previous times;

9. the *aims*, A, of the members of C include inventing new artifacts or processes, new ways of using known ones, or norms and plans for realizing or evaluating them;

10. the *methodics*, M, of $\mathcal{T}$ consists exclusively of scrutable (checkable, analyzable, criticizable) and justifiable (explainable) procedures, in particular, the scientific method and the technological method;

11. the *values*, V, of $\mathcal{T}$ consist in a collection of value judgments about natural or artificial things and processes—in particular, raw materials and finished products, human resources, work processes, social organizations, and norms.

In addition, there is at least one other *contiguous and partially overlapping* technology with the same general characteristics as $\mathcal{T}$. Further, the membership of every one of the last nine components of $\mathcal{T}$ *changes* over time, however slowly, as a result of R&D in $\mathcal{T}$ or related technologies, sciences, and mathematics or in response to social demands.

Any field of knowledge that fails to satisfy, even approximately, all the preceding conditions will be said to be *nontechnological*. A field of knowledge that shares the utilitarian aims, A, of technology but satisfies only partially some of the other conditions can be said to be a 'proto-technology.' Most sociotechnologies, particularly normative macroeconomics and law, are of this kind. By contrast, a technology with a bulky, specific, scientific background, such as electrical engineering or biotechnology, is called a 'high' (or 'advanced') technology. A technology that comes up with artifacts or plans which employ few scarce resources, are benign in their effect on the environment, and can be handled by individuals or small groups—thereby promoting a labor-intensive economy—is called a 'soft' (or 'intermediate,' or 'appropriate') technology. Examples: the technologies involved in the design of rural dwellings with modern conveniences, built with local manpower and materials. Finally, a field of knowledge that is nontechnological in lacking a scientific basis or in failing to employ scientific and technological methods, yet is advertised or sold as technological (or scientific), may be said to be a 'pseudo-technology' (or fake or bogus technology). Examples: most psychotherapies, monetarism, "scientific socialism," and economic "shock therapies."

Note the following points. First, a family of technologies is not an aggregate but a system, for every development (or delay) in any of its components is likely to have an impact on other components: that is, they all hang together. Second, the professional community of a technology is a social system, not an isolated individual or an aggregate of loners. This systemicity is ensured by professional societies, publications, and meetings. However, technological communities are far less cohesive and open than scientific ones, because their products are the private property of their clients rather than the common property of society. Such property rights are secured by patents, as well as by industrial and military secrecy. Still, patents can be circumvented by small innovations, and secrecy can be violated by espionage. Moreover, in recent years, technological cooperation among firms and between these and governments, prompted by escalating costs of R&D, and by the high costs of unbridled competition, has begun to mesh with competition.

Third, not every society can sustain a community devoted to R&D. Thus, theocratic and underdeveloped societies may buy some new industrial products, but the former inhibit original thinking in all fields, and the latter claim that they cannot afford to fund it—while in fact they cannot afford not to support it, for they are underdeveloped largely because they are deficient in original thinking. Fourth, the domain, or universe of discourse, *D,* of any technology, unlike that of a natural science, contains not only natural things but also artifacts such as machines and formal organizations.

Fifth, the philosophical background, *G,* of technology is usually overlooked, although every R&D project presupposes it. To begin with, technology shares with science plenty of philosophical concepts, such as those of thing and property, event and process, causation and randomness, law and rule, organism and society, the natural and the artificial. In addition, when engaging in R&D, the technologist makes tacit use of a number of ontological and epistemological principles, such as those of the reality, changeability, lawfulness, and knowability of the external world. (Moreover, certain comprehensive technological theories, such as the general theories of machines, automata, and control, qualify as ontological as well as technological: see Bunge 1971.)

However, the technologist's philosophical perspective is somewhat different from that of the scientist. First, the technologist is primarily interested in things for us and under our possible control, rather than things in and for themselves. For example, he is more interested in formal schooling than in learning in general, in socioeconomic programs than disinterested social or economic analyses, and so on. Second, he tends to prefer the simpler theories, which are easy to work with, even if shallow—although he has no objection to learning complex theories when the simple ones lead to inefficient designs or programs. Although he tacitly acknowledges the existence and value of objective truth, he is usually content with rough approximations: he cannot afford perfectionism. Thus he laces scientific realism with a dash of pragmatism.

As for the ethical component of the philosophical background of technology, it differs somewhat from the ethos of basic science. The technologist's job is mission-oriented, and his mission is utilitarian: far from being an autonomous agent, he is expected to adopt his employer's interests. Consequently he is likely to appropriate knowledge acquired by others, without, however, sharing the knowledge produced at his employer's expense. He may have no moral qualms about designing mass murder weapons or useless or shoddy products. If he blows the whistle on anti-social projects, he is likely to be fired. Still, technologists, like scientists, cherish objective truth, if only as a means to efficient design or planning. If they did not, they would be inefficient.

Sixth, the formal background, F, of any technology is one of the indicators of its level of advancement. For example, until World War II, management and military logistics were empirical technics. Nowadays they sometimes make use of sophisticated operations research models and quality control methods involving higher mathematics.

Seventh, the volume of the specific background, B, of a technology is yet another indicator of its degree of development. The more a technology owes to basic science, the more credit it deserves. For instance, operations research and marketing are more efficient (for better or worse), the more they make intensive use of psychology, sociology, and economics.

Eighth, the problematics, P, of a technology is unlimited, yet constrained by socioeconomic circumstances. In every technology we may distinguish the following kinds of problem: (*a*) *domain*, or reference class, problems, such as, What is criminology about: criminals, societies, or criminals-in-society? (*b*) *philosophical* problems, such as, Is the sociotechnologist morally justified in designing organizations with the goal of maximizing profit regardless of social costs? (*c*) problems of *formal background,* such as, Is there a special mathematics for sociology (or economics or politology)? (*d*) problems of *specific background,* such as, Which sciences underly environmental management? (*e*) problems of *problematics,* such as, Is problem p soluble with means m? (*f*) *fund-of-knowledge* problems, such as, How good (exact, true, or serviceable) is decision theory? (*g*) problems about *aims,* such as, How can military industries and technologies be converted into civilian ones when peace breaks out?

(*h*) *methodological* problems, such as, How can the performance of a social organization or a social program be measured?

Ninth, the fund of knowledge, K, of a technology may be modest or impressive, but it cannot be empty, or it would not be a technology. The very formulation of a technological problem presupposes some fund of knowledge.

Tenth, the aims, A, of technology include the design or redesign of artifacts, norms, or processes and the drawing or redrawing of plans for their utilization, each with the help of some mathematics and science. For this reason, professionals using the fruits of R&D without engaging in the latter may be experts, but they are not technologists proper.

Eleventh, the methodics, M, of a technology includes its particular techniques, such as those of accounting and social surveying. It also includes the scientific method and what I am calling the technological method.

Twelfth, the value judgments in V bear on natural or artificial entities or processes in the light of the aims, A. The V's are supposed to be a result of analyses and tests, rather than impulsive. V must be distinguished from internal value judgments about any of the components of the R&D process—for example, technical problems of design or planning. V has no counterpart in basic science. Thus, a political scientist may describe a given political movement, whereas a political analyst may prescribe how best to steer or weaken it.

Thirteenth, there are no stray, self-sufficient, let alone self-propelling technologies. They all hang together, and they all depend on socioeconomic circumstances.

Fourteenth, all technologies teem with novelty. A technology that ceases to evolve becomes an obsolete technic.

Fifteenth, like science, art, law, and philosophy, technology is an abstraction. Actually there are only individual technologists, communities of such, and sociotechnological systems such as modern farms, factories, transportation, communication, or sanitation networks, banks, hospitals, schools, and armies. (A sociotechnological system is a social system in which technology plays a decisive role. In such a system, technologists or experts using technologies and sophisticated equipment are crucial, perhaps even decisive, but never dominant. Ultimately, control is always exerted by management or government. Technocracy is politically unrealistic and is undesirable in not being democratic.)

Sixteenth, since technology is a means to an end, any account of an artifact must involve some teleological explanation (explanation in terms of goals) in addition to whatever causal, stochastic, or mixed mechanisms explain the way it works or fails. (By contrast, physics, chemistry, biology, and much of psychology must refrain from using the concept of finality. A screwdriver is made to turn screws, but a hand is not made.) Thus, in order to account for the achievements and shortcomings of management science, we must keep in mind that the goal of managers is to optimize (not necessarily maximize) the technical and economic performance of the sociotechnological systems in their charge.

So much for a general characterization of technology. As for sociotechnology, its practitioners are expected to recommend the most efficient ways of setting up, maintaining, reforming, or dismantling social systems, as well as of triggering, quickening, regulating, or slowing down social processes. In particular, they are expected to cure social ills. But it is generally admitted that social therapy is today just as empirical and backward as medical therapy was at the beginning of the twentieth century, when drugs were mostly prescribed just because they seemed to do good in some cases, rather than on the strength of clinical research based on physiology and pharmacology. However, I tackle sociotechnology in the companion volume (Bunge forthcoming).

Let us now turn to two nonscientific components of every culture that are sometimes mistaken for either science or technology: pseudoscience and ideology.

5 Pseudoscience

A pseudoscience is a body of belief or practice advertised or sold as scientific without really being such (recall sec. 2). Pseudoscientists either do not conduct any research at all (like the psychoanalysts) or they conduct flawed research (like parapsychologists). In either case, when sincere, they are gullible and on the whole impervious to criticism. They fail to comply with the moral and institutional imperative that Merton called "organized skepticism."

There are pseudosciences galore: alchemy and astrology, dowsing and UFO-logy, "scientific" creationism and Lysenko's plant "science," parapsychology and psychoanalysis, homeopathy and holistic medicine, graphology and all projective techniques, starting with Rorshach's ink-blot test. (See the bimonthly the *Skeptical Inquirer*.) Most scientists diagnose these bodies of popular belief correctly for what they are, and believers or practitioners thereof are correspondingly outside the scientific community.

Though easily detected and refuted, popular pseudoscience is dangerous because (*a*) it is accessible to the public, whereas genuine science is difficult and therefore elitist; (*b*) it can be expensive in terms of health, money, and time; (*c*) it reinforces uncritical (in particular, magical) thinking; (*d*) it misrepresents the scientific approach by passing off wild speculation or uncontrolled data as scientific findings; (*e*) it enjoys the support of powerful pressure groups, such as religious groups, political parties, and professional lobbies; and (*f*) it contaminates some immature fields. This last point deserves a paragraph or two.

It is well known that social studies and sociotechnics have been contaminated by psychoanalytic fantasies, although the latter are at variance with experimental psychology—abhorred by Freud himself (1929) and his disciples. For example, some sociologists, teachers, and criminologists have adopted the psychoanalytic hypothesis that watching violent actions provides a cathartic discharge of hostility. They either ignore the fact that laboratory and field studies have refuted this fantasy long ago or do not care for such scientific findings. In either case, their readers, pupils, or wards are ill served.

The popularity of psychoanalysis has several causes. One, of course, is gullibility. A second cause is that there are no prerequisites for reading psychoanalytic writings. A third is that Freud hit the jackpot when he decided to deal with emotions, which had been overlooked by academic psychology and were later ignored by behaviorism as well. Whenever scientists overlook an important subject, some nonscientists are bound to exploit it. A fourth cause of the popularity of psychoanalysis is that it has facile explanations for everything in terms of a handful of ingenious, funny hypotheses, without any worry over testing them empirically. Thus, it explains conformism as submission to the "father figure," and rebellion as revolt against it; civilization as due to the repression of instinct, and hostility to civilization as the victory of instinct; religion and morality as by-products of the Oedipus complex; and so on. In short, psychoanalysis claims to explain everything personal and social. (Incidentally, it is a case of ontological and methodological individualism, for it purports to explain everything social in terms of individual life histories.) But it is at loggerheads with scientific psychology. Moreover, it does not account for sociality, much less for the emergence and breakdown of social systems; it does not account for history; and it makes no predictions about either individuals or social groups. Worse, psychoanalytic explanations are unsound because their premises are either untestable or, if testable and actually tested (by nonanalysts), they have been soundly trounced.

The latest casualty is "repressed memory" therapy, based on Freud's false hypothesis that there is no such thing as forgetting: the superego represses every painful memory, such as that of having been a victim of sexual abuse during childhood. The "repressed memory" therapist claims that he can reawaken memories of such long-forgotten episodes, thereby helping his patients sue the putative offenders for substantial sums and wrecking lives and families in the process. Until recently, many American courts admitted uncritically the testimonies of such therapists, imposing heavy fines and prison terms on thousands of probably innocent people. Thanks to the intervention of qualified psychologists and to the campaign launched by the False Memory Syndrome Foundation, in 1993 judges started to learn that most "reactivated repressed memories" are false memories implanted by the therapist, sometimes with the assistance of drugs. What began as a lucrative swindle aided by the vulgar confusion of psychoanalysis with psychology is ending with the discredit of the most popular pseudoscience of the century.

Sadly, some pseudoscientific doctrines are not mere popular superstitions but products of the academic industry. As argued elsewhere (Bunge 1985*a*, 1985*b*, 1991*b*, 1991*d*, forthcoming), the following belong in academic pseudoscience: (1) so-called measurement theory, which confuses measurement, an empirical procedure, with quantification, a conceptual one (recall chap. 6, sec. 4); (2) human sociobiology, which minimizes the effects of social stimuli on human development and ignores the vast array of different cultures; (3) much of information-processing psychology, particularly of the computational variety, which conflates various meanings of the term 'information,' takes the mind–computer analogy to be an identity, denies the relevance of neuroscience to psychology, and ignores emotion as well as creativity; (4) talk of information theory in social studies, which is metaphorical, does not identify the various components of the putative information system, fails to tell us how to measure probabilities or entropies, and consequently is untestable; (5) talk of catastrophe and chaos theories in social studies, which in most cases does not involve any equations, so is just hand waving, and when it does involve equations, is speculative in being unsupported by hard empirical evidence (recall chap. 1, sec. 6); (6) all applications of decision theory and game theory involving subjective utilities, probabilities, or both; (7) economic theories that use undefined utility functions and subjective probabilities and describe nonexisting free markets; (8) Austrian school of economics, which is aprioristic and refuses to make use of mathematics; (9) hermeneutic sociology, which equates social facts with discourses or texts and dispenses with empirical tests; (10) constructivist-relativist sociology of science, which denies reality and objective truth, as will be seen in the next section. (More examples of social pseudoscience in Sorokin 1956; Andreski 1972; Boudon 1990*a*.)

Academic pseudoscience is harder to spot and fight than popular superstition, because it is produced within the scientific community and is protected by the principle of academic freedom. It is also more dangerous for science, because it lowers research standards and brings discredit upon the scientific community. Regrettably, most philosophers and sociologists of science have failed to identify this Trojan horse and consequently to attack it, for lack of an adequate characterization of genuine science. Detection of forgery involves an adequate understanding of the genuine article.

If one adopts the definition of a scientific research field proposed in section 1, then diagnosis of a body of belief as pseudoscientific becomes a classroom exercise. (The same holds, mutatis mutandis, for spotting pseudo-technologies.) Recall the conditions for a field of knowledge $\Re = \; < C, S, D, G, F, B, P, K, A, M >$ to qualify as a science, then compare them with the corresponding pseudoscience. A pseudoscientific community, C, is a bunch of believers, rather than an association of creative, critical researchers. The host society, S, either supports C for practical (e.g., commercial) reasons or tolerates it while marginalizing it. The domain, D, of a pseudoscience contains unreal—or, at least, not certifiably real—entities, properties, or events, such as archetypes, national wills, collective minds, and free markets. The general outlook, *G,* of a pseudoscience includes either (*a*) an ontology countenancing immaterial entities or processes, such as disembodied spirits (or else unreal entities such as labor markets that clear instantly); or (*b*) an epistemology that makes room for paranormal cognitive abilities, arguments from authority, or "data" drawn from a hat; or (*c*) an ethos that, in defense of dogma, blocks the free search for truth. The formal background, *F,* of a pseudoscience is very poor, fraudulent (e.g., it involves pseudoquantities), or purely ornamental (e.g., it dresses up untestable or obviously false assumptions). For example, most rational choice models contain undefined utility functions. (See Appendix 4.)

Further, the specific background, *B,* of a pseudoscience is nil or minute: bogus scientists learn little or nothing from science. (The only pseudoscience that does make use of a science—viz., astronomy—is astrology.) Nor does pseudoscience contribute anything to science or technology. The problematics, *P,* of a pseudoscience is largely either imaginary or practical: it does not include any important, topical basic research problems. The fund of knowledge, *K,* of a pseudoscience contains numerous untestable or false conjectures in conflict with well-confirmed scientific hypotheses. And it contains no universal, well-confirmed hypotheses belonging to hypothetico-deductive systems. The aims, *A,* of a pseudoscience do not include the finding of laws or their use to explain or predict any real facts. The methodics, *M,* of a pseudoscience contains procedures that cannot be checked by alternative means or are not justifiable by well-confirmed scientific theories. In particular, criticism and empirical tests are not welcome. Finally, (*a*) there is no contiguous field of knowledge, except possibly another pseudoscience; and (*b*) a pseudoscience is typically stagnant or, if it changes, it does so as a result of squabbles or external pressures, rather than research. In other words, the pseudosciences are isolated and tradition-bound.

I will wind up this section by noting that pseudoscience must not be mistaken for either scientific error or heterodoxy. Errors will occur in all human endeavors, and truths abound in fields other than science. What is peculiar to science (as well as to mathematics and technology) is not so much absence of error as self-correction through research. Nor is consensus a peculiarity of science—notwithstanding a fashionable opinion. Scientific heterodoxy is just unconventional science, and, as Poincaré said, scientific controversy is the salt of science. A new idea or procedure will be regarded as scientific if, regardless of its popularity or lack of it, it fits an adequate definition of science. Deviations within science should be welcome, deviations from science not.

6 An Example: The New Sociology of Science

The modern sociology of science was born in the 1930s around Robert K. Merton, and it has become an established branch of sociology (see, e.g., Merton 1973). It attempts to investigate in a scientific way scientific communities and the interactions between scientific research and social structure and holds the former to be realist, disinterested, critical, and subject to a moral code. In the mid-1960s an irrationalist, idealist reaction against the Merton school was born. The new sociology of science (henceforth NSS), usually described as constructivist and relativist, claims to paint a far more realistic image of scientific research by jettisoning the ideals of disinterested research and objective truth. (See, e.g., the journal *Social Studies of Science;* Barnes 1977; Bloor 1976; H. M. Collins 1981; Knorr-Cetina and Mulkay 1983*b*; Latour and Woolgar 1979.) I will proceed to show that this image is neither true nor new and, moreover, that the NSS is a clear example of a pseudoscience. (For details see Bunge 1991*b*, 1992*a*.)

To begin with, most new style sociologists of science mistrust science. They regard it as an ideology, a power tool, an inscription-making device with no legitimate claim to universal truth, and just one more social construction on a par with myth. They regard scientists as skilled craftsmen but somewhat unscrupulous wheeler-dealers and unprincipled politicians. In short, they laugh at Merton's (1957, 1973) classical characterization of the scientific ethos.

Subscribers to the NSS regard all facts, or, at least, what they call 'scientific facts,' as social constructions. But actually, in matters of knowledge, the only genuine social constructions are the exceedingly uncommon scientific forgeries committed by a team. A famous forgery of this kind was the Piltdown fossil man "discovered" by two people in 1912, certified as authentic by a number of experts (among them Teilhard de Chardin), and unmasked as a fake only in 1950. According to the existence criterion of constructivism-relativism, we should admit that the Piltdown man did exist—at least between 1912 and 1950—because the scientific community believed in it. Are we prepared to believe this? Or should we rather suspect that the NSS is incapable (or even unwilling) of telling hot air from cold fact?

Because constructivist-relativists deny that there is any conceptual difference between science and other human endeavors, some of their evaluations of science overlap with those of the counterculture, to the point that the NSS is in some important respects a component of it. Let us look at a few examples. Michael Mulkay (1969), a pioneer of the NSS, waxes indignant over the way in which the scientific community treated Immanuel Velikovsky's allegedly revolutionary *Worlds in Collision* of 1950. He scolds scientists for their "abusive and uncritical rejection" of Velikovsky's speculations and for clinging to their "theoretical and methodological paradigms"—among them the equations of celestial mechanics. He claims that astronomers had a duty to put Velikovsky's fantasies to the test.

Mulkay's complaint ignores the facts that (*a*) the burden of proof rests on the would-be innovator; (*b*) empirical tests are unnecessary when a new theory violates well-confirmed theories or successful methods, on top of which it does not solve any outstanding problems; (c) nearly all Velikovsky's claims have been proved wrong (the exception being his conjecture that there had been collisions between galaxies, a lucky guess for which he offered no evidence); and (d) scientists have more important tasks than testing the fantasies of an outsider without scientific credentials. However, a number of scientists, headed by Carl Sagan, did take time to criticize in detail Velikovsky's fantasies, and the AAAS devoted an entire symposium to them (Goldsmith 1977).

Second example: Yaron Ezrahi (1971) claims that Arthur Jensen's alleged findings on the innate intellectual inferiority of African-Americans were rejected by the American scientific establishment for ideological reasons. And he holds that geneticists were particularly vehement in their criticisms of Jensen's work out of concern, at least in part, with their own "public image and support." Ezrahi does not bother to analyze the very IQ tests from which Jensen's conclusions were derived. Had he done so, he might have learned that (a) at that time such tests were indeed culture-bound and thus likely to favor whites over blacks, and (b) no IQ test is fully reliable unless backed up by a well-confirmed theory of intelligence—which is overdue (Bunge and Ardila 1987).

Other vocal constructivist-relativists have mounted a spirited defense of astrology and parapsychology. (See, e.g., Pinch and Collins 1979, 1984; Pinch 1979; Collins and Pinch 1982.) They attack the critics of these pseudosciences for espousing what they call "the standard model of science," which they dub "ideology." Regrettably, they do not propose an alternative "model" of science. They call only for a "re-appraisal of scientific method" to make room for astrology, parapsychology, psychoanalysis, and other "extraordinary sciences." It would go against the grain of their school to propose clear-cut criteria of scientificity, since it holds science to be an ordinary "social construction." But how is it possible to discuss rationally the scientific status of an idea or practice except in the light of *some* definition of scientificity? As for the truth-values of the alleged findings of astrologers, parapsychologists, and the like, how can we discuss them in the constructivist-relativist framework, where truth is said to be a social convention on a par with table manners?

Our last case will be Lynch's ethnomethodological study "Sacrifice and the transformation of the animal body into a scientific object: Laboratory culture and ritual practice in the neurosciences" (1988). Taking his cue from Durkheim's studies in the sociology of religion, Lynch claims that the killing of laboratory animals at the end of a run of experiments is part of a ritual practice whereby the body of the animal is transformed into "a bearer of transcendental significances." Regrettably, he omits to present any evidence for this extraordinary claim. It was bad enough when Latour and Woolgar (1979) compared the scientific laboratory to a political committee. Now that the laboratory bench has been presented as an altar for the enactment of sacrifice, it would not be surprising if laboratory scientists were to put a ban on visitors from the enemy camp. The popular misperception of science is bad enough without help from the NSS.

To conclude this section, the failure to distinguish science from pseudo-science is an indicator of philosophical shallowness and is practically, as well as theoretically, disastrous. This is particularly so in the fields of social studies and politics, because pseudoscientific views of man and society can become the conceptual basis of, and justification for, pernicious governmental (or anti-governmental) policies. Think of the myth of the superiority of the "white race" as a tool of slavery, colonialism, and racial segregation; of the free market myth as a weapon against social justice; or of the myths of the dictatorship of the proletariat and of "democratic centralism" as tools of Stalinism.

7 Ideology

An ideology may be defined as a system of ideals. More precisely, it may be characterized as a system of sweeping beliefs, particularly value judgments and moral norms, aimed at organizing and mobilizing people of a certain kind to work or fight in order to attain certain individual or social goals. So defined, the term 'ideology' is neutral: it lacks the derogatory signification that Marx gave it. This is useful for understanding why nobody can, or even should try to, escape all ideology and why some people are willing to fight and even die for theirs. It is also required to explore the question of whether a scientific ideology is possible.

Many an ideology, like many a philosophy, originates in the uncontrolled inflation of a single idea. Thus liberalism emerged from a love of liberty, socialism from a love of equality, and anarchism from an aversion to state oppression. Thus most ideologies are sectoral: only a few are world views. Thomism was the most outstanding, comprehensive, and coherent of all pre-modern ideologies. Its earliest modern successor and rival is the ideological component of the eighteenth-century Enlightenment. It is worth recalling, if only because it is the target of the "counterculture," "New Age," and post-modernist movements.

The Enlightenment ideology can be compressed into the following modern-ist decalogue: (1) trust in reason and learning; (2) rejection of myth, supersti-tion, and generally groundless belief (dogma); (3) free inquiry; (4) secularism; (5) naturalism (as opposed to supernaturalism) and scientism; (6) utilitari-anism (as against duties-only morals); (7) respect for craftsmanship, enthusi-asm for industry, and reverence for the machine; (8) progressivism and opti-mism: criticism of present social ills and trust in the future; (9) individualism together with libertarianism, egalitarianism (to some degree or other), and political democracy—at least for white males; and (10) universalism—for example, human rights and education for all. Some of these principles are part of a world view, others are value judgments, and still others part of a political program to change society.

Diffusion of Enlightenment ideology caused three successive backlashes. The first was constituted by the philosophical and political strands of Romanticism (e.g., Hegel and Adam Müller). The second was the anti-science movement spearheaded by Nietzsche, Dilthey, and Bergson. The third began with Husserl's phenomenology, was followed by Heidegger's existentialism, and culminated in the counterculture and postmodernism born in the mid-1960s. Each of these reactions against the Enlightenment was narrower and shallower than the preceding one. (More in Bunge 1994a.)

There are many differences between ideology, on the one hand, and science and technology, on the other. The most obvious difference is that, in contrast to science and technology, ideologies, like pseudosciences, are belief systems rather than research fields. Consequently they are isolated from the system of the sciences and technologies, and they seldom evolve—or, if they do, it is not in response to either scientific research or social practice. Being detached from science and technology, extant ideologies do not presuppose a body of scientific or technological knowledge. Worse, they are at variance with the fund of scientific and technological knowledge—though not necessarily so, as will be seen below when discussing the possibility of scientific ideology.

We distinguish *global* ideologies (or world views) from *sociopolitical* ones. Thomism, the Enlightenment, and Marxism are unique in being comprehensive, detailed world views, each including philosophical and sociopolitical components, whence part of their power of persuasion. Marxism is the most complex of the three, in being a global, modern, secular ideology (world view) combined with what has become largely outdated social science. (By the way, an analysis of Marxism in terms of philosophy, sociopolitical ideology, and social studies is overdue and a prerequisite for evaluating it correctly and seeing what deserves to be salvaged from its shipwreck.)

Let us now tackle sociopolitical ideologies, such as anarchism, liberalism, fascism, and socialism. A sociopolitical ideology deals only with the social order and usually favors special interests, although a philanthropic ideology is possible in principle. Contrary to what a cynic might contend, every sociopolitical ideology contains or presupposes a rich fund of ideas, however sketchy and false some of them may be. This is why an ideology can become the glue and propellant, rallying cry and flag, of a social movement.

Sociopolitical ideologies are certainly important, for some of them mobilize large masses or permeate institutions, rendering some of them dysfunctional. But ideologies are not more important than a number of nonideological social items such as the firm and the family. (Yet the structuralist Marxist Althusser included the family in the "ideological apparatus of the state"; moreover, he claimed that it is the most oppressive of all. But this was just an ideological claim unsupported by empirical research.)

The beliefs composing a sociopolitical ideology are of the following kinds: (*a*) ontological theses concerning the nature of persons, groups, and societies in general; (*b*) a collection of hypotheses about the particular society that the party or movement intends to control; (*c*) theses concerning the environmental, economic, political, or cultural issues (real or imaginary) faced by societies of a given type at a given time; (*d*) value judgments about persons, races, classes, institutions, and the like; and (*e*) action (or inaction) programs for the solution (or masking) of social issues and the attainment (or thwarting) of individual or group goals. The first three sets of theses constitute knowledge, true or otherwise, whereas the values and plans in the remaining two sets are noncognitive. Could all five sets be filtered by science and technology? In other words, is a scientifico-technical ideology possible, or just an oxymoron? Let us examine this question, because it is both theoretically interesting and practically important.

My answer is that a *scientifico-technological ideology* is in principle possible. We characterize it as the 10-tuple

$$\mathcal{I} = <C, D, G, F, B, I, P, V, A, M>,$$

where

C = a lay political party and its sympathizers;

D = a society and its subsystems;

G = the world view of science and technology and, in particular, the general conception of society inherent in the most advanced social sciences of the time;

F = the full panoply of logical and mathematical tools that may be needed to build social theories, policies, and plans;

B = the whole of social science and sociotechnology;

I = the issues faced by S, as well as the problems concerning the struggle for power and the administration of natural resources and the economic, political, and cultural systems;

P = a collection of policies and programs for social action, aimed at solving the problems in $\mathcal{I}$, and consistent with both G and B;

V = a value system concerning the good society, as well as right social behavior, consistent with both G and B;

A = a set of feasible goals—short-, middle-, and long-term ones—to be attained by C;

M = a set of means deemed (in the light of B) adequate to attain the aims, A.

In sum, a scientifico-technological ideology is one inspired by genuine contemporary social science and sociotechnology rather than by either myth or pseudoscience. It contains the utopian element occurring in V—namely, the idea of the good society—but this ideal should be feasible and should jibe with social science and sociotechnology.

Still, there is nothing intrinsically good, except conceptually, about an ideology being scientifico-technological. Such an ideology will be good or bad according as it includes or fails to include noble values and moral principles to regulate the means as well as the goals. In other words, being scientifico-technological should be only necessary for an ideology to be admissible: we must also look into the accompanying moral and political philosophy. Consequently, instead of looking at ideologies separately from other components of our culture, we should evaluate them in light of both social science and technology and moral and political philosophy. Otherwise we may end up either in chaos or in concentration camps run by operations research experts.

This treatment of ideology has been sketchy: the subject deserves detailed social studies. The point of bringing up ideology was (*a*) to note its philosophical (in particular, ethical) content; (*b*) to use our analysis, later in this volume and elsewhere (Bunge forthcoming), to identify the ideological components of certain social views and policies; and (*c*) to stress the differences between ideology, on the one hand, and science and technology, on the other—particularly since such differences are denied by both the constructivist-relativist sociology of science and so-called critical theory. More on this below.

8 Confusing Science with Ideology

Marcuse (1964), Habermas (1971), and other members of the Frankfurt school, which engendered critical theory, claimed that science (including mathematics) and technology have an ideological content. More precisely, they held that science and technology (which they conflated) have become the ideology of late capitalism, so discharge the function of legitimating the powers that be. A fair number of practitioners of the constructivist-relativist sociology of science examined in the previous section have adopted this bold thesis. But what is the *evidence* for it? Its defenders see no need to say, because they reject the scientific approach.

Now, it is well known that modern science and technology have evolved hand in hand with capitalism—but then so have the humanities. It is also true that ideology is occasionally passed off as science, as was the case with the myth that blood (or the genome) tells. Lewontin (1991) makes this point in his *Biology as Ideology*, which he should have entitled *Ideology as Biology*, since it debunks reactionary ideology masquerading as science.

Nor is there any doubt that ideology contaminates the *social* sciences, especially economics and politology (see, e.g., Robinson and Eatwell 1974; Galbraith 1987; Lang 1981, 1990; Pasinetti 1981). But all the above are examples of *pseudo*scientific Trojan horses which have infiltrated the citadel of science, not evidence for the claim that science is the ideology of capitalism. In particular, economic theories and methods, unlike economic policies, must be ideology-free if they are to count as scientific, by definition of *science* and *ideology*. For example, since input–output models and econometric methods are portable

across societies, there is no reason to suspect that they are ideologically contaminated. In any event, no *evidence* has been produced to show that they are.
The charge that pure mathematics and natural science are ideological, and
political weapons of capitalism to boot, is even more preposterous. What, pray,
is the economic or political content of the Pythagorean theorem or the infinitesimal calculus? What is the social content of the assertions that the hydrogen
atom has a single proton, that carbon has four valences, that ribosomes synthe-
size proteins, that lead is toxic, that the brain is composed of many subsystems,
or that children resemble their ancestors? To be sure, mathematics and science
can be *utilized* for economic or political purposes. But the fact that they can be
utilized for pro-social as well as antisocial goals is an argument in favor of the
thesis that they are just as neutral as language.

If every mathematical or scientific statement is imputed some (undefined)
social content, it follows that all scientific controversies (*a*) have an ideological
component and (*b*) are terminated by means other than experiment, calculation, or logical argument. These theses are, indeed, favorites with the new
generation of sociologists of science, whom we met in the preceding section.
Again, I ask: What is the *evidence* for them? The only supposed evidence is that
some scientific controversies have indeed had ideological overtones because one
of the views in conflict was a component of the ideology of the powers that be.
This was, of course, the case with Galileo's trial, the evolutionism–creationism
controversy, racism, the genetics–Lysenkoism scandal, and a few others. However, the final verdict was scientific, not political: it was a triumph of truth, not
power.

Only a very primitive inductivist will leap from *some* to *all* without paying
attention to counterexamples. Now, it so happens that ideology-free scientific
controversies by far outnumber ideology-laden ones. Here is a random sample
of heated controversies of the first kind: that over cold fusion in 1989; the
ongoing controversy about the existence of black holes; the polemics between
gradualists and saltationists in evolutionary biology; the dispute in the 1930s
and 1940s over the (electrical or chemical) nature of interneuronal contacts;
the controversies over the interpretation of quantum theory since its inception
in 1926; the spirited debate over special relativity during the two decades that
followed its advent in 1905; controversies about the very existence of atoms
and discussions of logic and set theory around 1900; the Darwin–Lamarck
confrontation and the polemics between field theorists and partisans of action
at a distance in the mid-nineteenth century; and the conflict between Newtonians and Cartesians in the seventeenth and eighteenth centuries.

This is not to deny that some of these controversies had some *philosophical*
load. The last-cited one did have such a component. But the two rival views,
Newtonianism and Cartesianism, were ideologically progressive at the time,
in that both were mechanistic. However, the point is that all these scientific

controversies were ideology-free and were terminated eventually by strictly scientific means. (In particular, the Newtonians won by showing that they could calculate—indeed predict—the real trajectories of bodies in a number of cases, whereas the Cartesians could not.) The above counterexamples, which could easily be multiplied, refute the thesis that in *all* cases consensus in science depends on who elbows the hardest, shouts the loudest, or wields the most power.

The above-mentioned cases also refute the thesis that crucial experiments test only theorists, never theories (Pinch 1985). Experiments, when conclusive (which they are not always), test the truth claims of theories as well as the competence of scientists. Why would experimentalists bother to design and perform experiments if these had no cognitive content and their only function were to put their own reputation at risk? If science were only about prestige and power, scientists would turn to less demanding tasks, such as the nonscientific sociology of science.

At the beginning of this section I mentioned one of the roots of the belief that all science is tainted by ideology: namely, the critical theory school. There is a second root: namely, the transposition of the Feuerbach–Durkheim hypothesis that primitive cosmogonies and religions are modeled on the corresponding societies. The drafter of the "strong programme" in the constructivist-relativist sociology of science (Bloor 1976, chap. 2) believes that what holds for primitive cosmogonies and religions holds for modern science too. But why should it, given that science, far from being a belief system, is a research field, hence one where belief must be justified by test rather than by authority?

A third root of the claim that scientific controversies can be resolved only by extra-scientific means is the thesis of the "underdetermination" of theory by data, introduced by Ptolemy, revived by Duhem and the neo-positivists, and popularized by Quine. According to this thesis, any set of empirical data may be accounted for by two or more theories, which are then said to be "empirically equivalent." Conventionalists such as Duhem and empiricists such as Frank and Reichenbach have used this alleged fact against scientific realism and in favor of the view that scientific controversies are settled by recourse to some nonscientific (but still conceptual) criterion, such as simplicity (see, e.g., Bunge 1963). And the constructivist-relativists use it to support their claim that all scientific controversies can be terminated only by noncognitive means, such as political maneuvers.

Actually the problem of empirical underdetermination, though real, is not as bad as it looks, and there is no evidence that scientists resolve their differences in noncognitive ways. For one thing, the usual underdetermination situation concerns hypotheses (single propositions), not comprehensive theories (vast systems of hypotheses). Unlike the former, the latter hang together and are supposed to account for a number of apparently disparate collections of data.

SCIENCE ET AL. 217

What amounts to the same thing, general scientific theories are supposed to predict facts which, *prima facie*, look unrelated. Hence a classical test to which rival theories are subjected is designed to ascertain which of them predicts more accurately the greater variety of facts. This is how Maxwell's field theory came to be preferred to action-at-a-distance electrodynamics, relativistic mechanics to classical mechanics, quantum physics to classical physics, the synthetic theory of evolution to Darwin's, and so on. (No parallels in social science come easily to mind.)

Still, it is true that neither explanatory nor predictive power is enough: scientific theories are subjected to a whole battery of additional tests. But all these are conceptual rather than either empirical or political (Bunge 1963, 1967*b*, 1983*b*). One of them is the test of external consistency: that is, compatibility with the bulk of the background knowledge (see chap. 6, sec. 5). Another is compatibility with the world view prevailing in the scientific community—which may be at variance with the ruling ideology. This is not surprising, for the scientific world view grew hand in hand with science itself. For example, if two contemporary learning theories are compatible with the same experimental data, but one of them involves some neurophysiological mechanism while the other does not, it is reasonable to prefer the former, and this for the following reasons: first, because the former theory will help to explore neurophysiological learning mechanisms and may thus come to enjoy additional empirical support; second, because the hypothesis that mental functions are brain functions, rather than functions of an immaterial mind, is consistent with the world view prevalent in the contemporary scientific community. In short, philosophy does play a role in (some) scientific controversies. But politics does not, or when it does, it interferes with the search for truth.

There must be something seriously wrong with a study of science incapable of telling science from ideology and, worse, that conflates the two. One source of this confusion is likely to be sheer ignorance, particularly willful ignorance. Another is the vulgar opinion that knowledge "is whatever men take to be knowledge. It consists of those beliefs which men confidently hold to and live by" (Bloor 1976, 2)—with the proviso that the word *knowledge* be reserved "for what is collectively endorsed, leaving the individual and idiosyncratic to count as mere belief" (ibid., 3). Shorter: Knowledge is whatever belief enjoys social sanction. (For criticisms of the view that knowledge is a kind of belief, see Popper 1972 and Bunge 1983*a*.) Accordingly, abstruse scientific theories, such as quantum electrodynamics, do not qualify as knowledge. On the other hand, all popular superstitions qualify.

Let us not quibble over the correct definition of the tricky concept of knowledge (for which see Bunge 1983*a*). What is crucial here is whether or not the student of science should distinguish between truth and falsity. According to the proponents of the "strong programme," the sociologist is not interested in the true–false and objective–subjective dichotomies. He must give "equal time" to all theories, and his own theories "will have to apply to both true and false beliefs" and "regardless of how the investigator evaluates them" (Bloor 1976, 3). Consequently the new-style sociologist of science, who follows Feyerabend (1975), is both unable and unwilling to distinguish science from nonscience, in particular pseudoscience (recall sec. 6). He thus disqualifies himself from the task of characterizing science vis-à-vis other branches of culture, authentic or junk.

Science, technology, and ideology are the three most potent cultural engines of the modern world. Science is powerful because it is capable of delivering general and profound, if mostly partial and temporary, truths. Technology is potent because it taps science to design novel and efficient, if not always beneficial, artifacts and plans that feed industry and government and are constantly changing everyday life in the advanced countries. And ideology is potent because it shapes or deforms minds and guides or misguides social behavior.

Of the three forces, science and technology are the most rational and innovative and are the trademarks of modern culture. Any ideas or practices incompatible with them are obsolete or inefficient or both; or, if preferred, they are either premodern or postmodern. This holds for the study and control of both nature and society. The same should hold for philosophy too. But alas, this is not the case. Most philosophies, particularly when dealing with science and technology, are far removed from the latter. This state of affairs is not just an indicator of the backwardness of philosophy. It may also affect scientists and technologists in either of two adverse ways: by turning them away from philosophy or by suggesting to them philosophical ideas that may hinder their work. For this reason it behooves scientists and technologists to cooperate with philosophers in constructing a philosophy in harmony with science and technology.

8 :: *Values and Morals*

Social science students are usually warned to heed Weber's injunction: Keep your work value-free and morally neutral. But they are seldom told what values and morals are, much less why these should be shunned in social research. Moreover, they are not told why they should refrain from making any commitment to social causes, even though they were probably drawn to social studies out of concern over social issues. I will therefore attempt to answer these questions.

Social actions and their outcomes are valuable or disvaluable to someone or other in some respects, and they either follow or break some of the prevailing moral norms. Therefore we must study the key concepts of valuation and morality before examining the precepts of value freedom and moral neutrality. (For details, see Bunge 1989.)

1 Nature and Roots of Values

Value judgments are statements of the form "*A* is good (or bad)" or "*A* is better (or worse) than *B*." When analyzed, they turn out to be somewhat more complex. For example, "*A* is good (or bad)" is analyzable as "*A* is good (or bad) for person (or social system) *B*, in respect *C*, in circumstance *D*, and in view of goal *E*." In other words, the predicate "is good" is not unary but, at least, of the fifth degree (Bunge 1962*a*). Moreover, as regards commodities, goodness and badness can be quantitated: in this case we have to do with a variable depending on five independent variables. Shorter: Goodness and its dual are relational properties, not intrinsic ones (recall chap. 1, sec. 1).

The preceding analysis, though sketchy, should suffice to dispel the idea that values are objects on a par with things and ideas or intrinsic properties such as fertility and population. Instead, values are properties of things or processes and, moreover, relational ones. Hence "X is a value" is short for "X is valuable for someone or something, in some respect and in certain circumstances, and to some end." Since whatever is valuable is so to someone, there are no values in themselves. In particular, values are not autonomous, otherworldly Platonic ideas that may or may not be "embodied" or "instantiated."

The preceding does not imply that all values are subjective, culture-bound, or both. It shows only that, far from being absolute or self-existing, values are *relative* to people or other organisms. Thus, air and water, well-being and security, as well as love and friendship, are objectively valuable to all people: these value judgments can be confirmed empirically. By contrast, it does not seem possible to prove that smoking or poker are objectively valuable. So far, so good: all values are relational properties, and some of them are objective, whereas others are subjective. However, this analysis stops short of telling us what values are.

Axiology, or value theory, is the branch of philosophy that deals with the general concept of value and with the status of value judgments. Here we shall tackle briefly only three problems in axiology: the nature and source of values, the objectivity or otherwise of value judgments, and the value–fact gap. We submit that all human values have two roots: objective needs and subjective wants. In other words, we judge something as valuable to the extent that it meets or helps meet some need or wish. However, we do not set great store by the necessities we have easy access to and thus take for granted, like clean air and water in bygone days. For something to be valuable, it must be not only useful or pleasant, but also scarce or vulnerable, like love, trust, goodwill, justice, peace, and a satisfactory job. If nothing were scarce, nothing would be valuable—and we would never compete for anything.

Now, a need or want can be either personal or social. Accordingly, values are either personal or social. That is, some things or processes are directly valuable to individuals, whereas others are valuable to social systems and thus only indirectly to individuals. For example, persons feel the need to love and be loved and thus value love. By contrast, an organization, lacking a brain, cannot impute value to anything. But since it requires manpower, management, and energy, these can be said to be valuable to the organization. This being so, its stakeholders—that is, the individuals who have a stake in the organization's existence—are advised to evaluate those key items.

(Warning: The personal–social distinction for values does not coincide with the private–public dichotomy for goods. Thus, certain private goods, such as gardens, are socially valuable as city lungs; and some public goods, like state-owned hospitals, are directly valuable to everyone. The personal and the private coincide only in the cases of toothbrushes and privacy, which are not shared. Likewise, the social and the public coincide only in cases such as those of cooperatives and the mail service.)

Personal values are biological, like health and longevity, or psychological, like feelings of well-being and of being wanted. Social, or impersonal, values are those we attribute to things other than ourselves, although they relate to ourselves. We may group social values into four genera: environmental (e.g., climate and clean air), economic (e.g., productivity and low cost), political (e.g., justice and self-government), and cultural (e.g., truth and beauty).

Not all needs are equivalent: some are more basic than others. A *basic need* is one that must be met for someone to stay alive. A *secondary need* is one that must be met for a person to be able to be in good physical and mental health. As with needs, so with wants or desires. On an egoistic morality, all wants or desires are legitimate. If I want X, then I have the right to try to get X. On an unselfish (i.e., either altruistic or egoistic) morality, some wants are legitimate, others not. A *legitimate want* is one whose satisfaction does not prevent anyone else from meeting his basic needs, though it may interfere with someone else's pursuit of a want.

We need some things or processes in themselves and others as means to certain ends. We impute intrinsic values to the former, and instrumental values to the latter. In other words, we value some items as goals in themselves and others as means to attain some goals. However, the means–ends distinction is not absolute, for what is a goal at one stage of the deliberation or action process may become a means at the next stage. Hence the intrinsic–instrumental distinction is not absolute either: it is situational—that is, it depends on circumstances. For example, in a monetary economy one needs money (M) in order to live (L). But in order to earn (not just get) money, one must work (W), so W is a means to attain the subgoal M. In turn, to get a satisfactory job, one needs to acquire certain skills by undergoing some course of study or training (S). W is now the subgoal, and S the submeans. The upshot is that we need to study in order to live. (In obvious symbols, $L \Rightarrow M$, & $M \Rightarrow W$, & $W \Rightarrow S$, $\therefore L \Rightarrow S$.)

The preceding distinctions allow one to tackle the problem of the status of value judgments. Are all of these subjective, or are some objective? I submit that some value judgments concerning basic needs or wants are objective, whereas others are not. For example, "Education is good" is an objectively true value judgment, because it can be shown that having an education is nowadays necessary (though not sufficient) to earn one's living in an honest way. On the other hand, "Smoking is good" is objectively false, because smoking is known to impair health and is economically wasteful. But "Smoking makes *x* feel good for a while" is true for some instances of *x*. That is, smoking is subjectively (psychologically) valuable for some people, even though it is objectively disvaluable for everyone except the tobacco industry and its political lackeys.

Let us finally tackle the fact–value gap. Hume pointed out that there is a chasm between what there is and what there ought to be. This gap is conceptual as well as factual, in that value judgments and prescriptions cannot follow logically from descriptions, whence morals cannot follow from science. For example, "Unemployment is high now" does not entail the value judgment "Unemployment is *too* high now," let alone the imperative "Unemployment *ought* to be reduced."

Thus the fact–value, or is–ought, gap is real. However, we cross it every day, just as we put ideas into practice. For instance, if the economy goes into a recession, most macroeconomists recommend lowering the interest rates, arguing, rightly or wrongly, that this will promote borrowing, which promotes investment, which creates jobs, which stimulates consumption, all of which helps us to pull out of a recession. In sum, in social life, values and facts, though distinct, are not separate. We evaluate most of the things we handle and most of the actions that affect us. In particular, we evaluate means and goals, and try to make happen what we value most. The pervasiveness of evaluation is one of the things that distinguishes the social from the natural world, as well as their corresponding sciences.

The above distinction between objective and subjective value judgments and the corresponding distinction between real needs and mere desires are not usually drawn in social studies. Worse, focus on subjective value, or utility, has become standard not only in mainstream economic theory, but in all social studies. This is largely due to the influence of utilitarianism, which in turn presupposes an individualist world view, a semi-subjectivist epistemology centered on belief rather than truth, and an emotivist ethics which focuses on passion and overlooks cognition. Be this as it may, the truth is that a number of theories in all branches of social science employ the notion of subjective utility—which, as will be shown in due course, is fuzzy.

2 Utility

The concept of utility, or subjective value, is central to neoclassical economics and all other rational choice theories. But, alas, it is not an exact concept. Indeed, although a popular dictionary of economics asserts confidently that "[t]he concept of utility is not contentious," experts in utility theory have often expressed qualms about it, as can be seen by perusing the journal *Theory and Decision* and the volumes of the Theory and Decision Library.

I submit that the general quantitative concept of utility has two fatal flaws. The first is that the utility function is seldom defined—unlike, say, the logarithmic function, which exactifies Bernoulli's special concept of utility. Whereas great generality is desirable in abstract mathematics, it is a severe shortcoming in any branch of applied mathematics, where computation using precise figures is necessary for empirical tests. The second flaw is that, being subjective, utility is hardly measurable or even subject to interpersonal comparison. In other words, ordinarily, the values of the utility functions are not assigned either rationally (by calculation) or empirically (by measurement). This is why in the vast majority of rational choice models utilities are assigned either arbitrarily or intuitively—hardly a triumph of rationality.

In fact, the standard von Neumann–Morgenstern (1947) axioms state only the conditions for the *existence* of a utility function characterizing a given decision-maker. They do not *define* any particular utility function. (For a clear presentation of a somewhat different postulate system, see Luce and Raiffa 1957.) No wonder that in the vast majority of cases utility functions are subject to just two qualitative constraints: that they be monotonically increasing and decelerated with respect to quantities (see, e.g., Marshall 1920 [1890], Mathematical Appendix). Obviously, these conditions define any of a nondenumerable infinity of functions, hence none in particular.

Thus the alleged law of decreasing marginal utility, du/dx, with increasing quantity x, is assumed more or less tacitly. Those unwilling to commit themselves to this "law" do not require even the above mild restrictions. For example, in his memorable analysis of the market for "lemons" (shoddy goods) Akerlof (1984, 9–10) postulated a linear utility function—which, of course, fails to satisfy one of the two standard conditions. To misquote Humpty-Dumpty, "When *you* use the word 'utility' it means just what you choose it to mean—neither more nor less."

Like beauty, subjective utility and changes therein are largely in the eye of the beholder. This makes it impossible to state, let alone prove, that a given person or group is *objectively* better or worse off than another or that one business or political deal is *objectively* preferable to another. One consequence of this is that there is no such thing as objective inequality or social injustice—a convenient result for conservatives. Do not attempt to reform society; wear rose-tinted glasses instead.

A second consequence is that since subjective utility statements are not rigorously testable, the theories in which they play a key role, such as neoclassical economics, are in the same boat as philosophical aesthetics (as distinct from psychological aesthetics). That is, they are nonscientific. No wonder that some of the more methodologically sophisticated social scientists, from Pareto to Samuelson, have treated cardinal utility in a cavalier fashion or dispensed with it altogether. (Further criticisms in Appendix 4; Blatt 1983; Hammond 1967; Kahneman and Tversky 1979; and MacCrimmon and Larsson 1979.)

Still, suppose that someone did come up with a utility theory involving definite, objective utility functions whose values could be measured. This is possible, and, as a matter of fact, one such objective measure is suggested in Appendix 5. However, its usefulness would be restricted by the fact that every instance of complex social behavior has several mutually incommensurable effects—for example, pecuniary loss accompanied by moral satisfaction. But being incommensurable, their partial values cannot be added up to find the total value of an action. For example, a politician may ponder the costs and benefits of an important political reform, such as his region becoming a sovereign nation, to take a fashionable example. He expects, say, an economic loss (or gain) along with a cultural or political gain (or loss). Supposing he succeeded in quantitating the former, how would he go about pinning numbers on the latter, and what units would he use? Even assuming that he solved this problem, he would be unable to add or subtract the two or three numbers—the x dollars and y units of culture or z units of politics. In short, he would be unable to estimate the total utility of the proposed political reform.

What holds for subjective utility holds, a fortiori, for the concept of expected subjective utility, which occurs in the formulation of the so-called rationality principle: Always act so as to maximize your expected utility. Expected utility is weighted utility, where the weights are probabilities. Consider the simplest case involving uncertainty: that of an action with only two possible outcomes, 1 and 2, with utilities u_1 and u_2, respectively. In this case the expected utility of the action is, by definition, $Eu = pu_1 + (1 - p)u_2$, where p is the probability of the first outcome, and $1 - p$ that of the second. There is nothing wrong with this definition if the utilities (and probabilities) are well defined, as in games of chance. But, as was pointed out above, this is not usually the case in social studies.

Furthermore, the probabilities involved in expected utilities are usually not well defined either—except, again, in the case of games of chance. In fact, in most rational choice models probabilities are assigned in the same arbitrary manner as utilities. Or, to be more precise, they are usually taken to be *subjective*, or *personal*, probabilities. The adoption of subjective, or personal, probabilities betrays a nonscientific approach, for objectivity is of the essence of science and technology, just as subjectivity is peculiar to art (recall chap. 1, sec. 6). Moreover, the subjectivist approach encourages wild guessing and guarantees inaccurate results, for intuitive probability estimates are notoriously inaccurate (see, e.g., Kahneman and Tversky 1973).

(Von Neumann and Morgenstern [1947, 19] constitute an exception. They rightly rejected subjective probability, embracing instead what they called "the perfectly well-founded interpretation of probability as frequency in long runs."

Obviously, they were unaware that the frequency school had been shot down by Jean Ville in 1939 and even earlier, though with only a modest technical apparatus, by Herbert Feigl in his unpublished doctoral dissertation at the University of Vienna.)

To return to value. My objection to the fuzzy notion of utility does not entail that it is impossible to define and measure value in a correct manner. One way of doing so is to recall that utility was originally conceived of as the amount of satisfaction of either a need (an objective deficit) or a want (a subjective wish or desire) procured by an action. This suggests equating value with deficit or deprivation (see Appendix 6). Granted, we do not always know the quantity of a good necessary to meet a given need or want, or even the quantity of it accessible to us. In the absence of such information, the (epistemologically) rational agent will refrain from pretending that he can handle (objective) values in an exact way. By proceeding in this fashion, he will abide by the ancient skeptic rule: In the absence of sufficient reasons or data, suspend belief, and refrain from acting.

A major drawback with most utility theorists is that they tend to overlook adverse empirical evidence. One of the earliest such pieces of evidence was published in 1953 by Nobel laureate Maurice Allais and was replicated decades later by several other workers—to no avail. The result, known as "Allais' paradox," is that real people violate the linearity of the probabilities involved in the very definition of expected utility (Allais and Hagen 1979; Anand 1987; Machina and Munier 1994). Besides, Shoemaker (1992) showed that, contrary to the standard theory, subjects do not estimate probabilities and utilities independently of each other. In particular, they underrate probabilities under certain conditions, and payoffs under others. Several other behavioral economists, by exploring the variety of human motivations, have refuted the myth that man is above all a utility-maximizer. (For a review addressed to economists, see Earl 1990.) By refusing to face such mounting adverse empirical evidence and sticking instead to nineteenth-century armchair psychology, rational choice theorists behave like true believers, not rational agents.

Finally, empirical studies have exhibited a moral dimension absent from rational choice theory. For example, Kahneman and colleagues (1987) found that people tend to behave fairly even at some cost to themselves. And Frank and his coworkers (1993) found that studying neoclassical microeconomics renders people selfish. However, the moral dimension calls for a new section.

3 Morals

A code of conduct is a system of norms steering social behavior in a given social group or in society at large. In other words, such a code specifies what is to count as right conduct of individuals and organizations, particularly their rights and duties. There are at least three kinds of code of conduct: professional, legal, and moral. Here we shall focus on moral codes, which are sometimes at odds with professional or legal codes.

A *moral code* is a system of moral norms, or rules. These specify the basic (or human) rights and duties of people in a given society, regardless of what any professional or legal codes may prescribe. We are particularly interested in the moral norms that enjoin us to observe rights and duties deriving from basic needs and legitimate desires, for these are the sources of objective values according to section 1.

Any such moral rules may be deemed *realistic* if they correspond to objective needs and wants of real people; *fair* if they enjoin us to act so that such needs and wants are met; and *ratio-empiricist,* as opposed to dogmatic, if they are subject to both argument and evaluation in light of the consequences of actions guided by them. I submit that a realistic, fair, ratio-empiricist morality is far more fundamental, universal, and legitimate than any legal or professional code, bound as these are to special interests and historical accidents. Thus, I submit that a realistic, fair, ratio-empiricist morality ought to take precedence over both the law of the land and the code of conduct of any profession.

Moral norms are learned and internalized early on in life, and they may surface and be discussed in the face of moral issues—that is, whenever there is a conflict between norms or whenever self-interest (or rights) conflicts with other interests (or duties). This does not entail that social life is the only source of morality, however. Like values, morals have biological and psychological roots too, because the point of morality is to help realize (or inhibit) human values, which have sources of all three kinds. This suggests that morals should be studied in the light of biology, psychology, and social science. But, lest we confuse description with prescription (or *is* with *ought*), we should retain our freedom to question any prevailing moral norms in the light of rational argument and empirical testing (by evaluating the consequences of the actions ruled by the norm).

I submit that a *moral right* is the right to meet a basic need (such as to breathe, eat, work, learn, or make friends) or a legitimate want (such as to obtain a higher education or earn promotions). Likewise, a moral duty is a duty to help someone else exercise his moral rights. Furthermore, I submit that, in any realistic, fair, ratio-empiricist moral code, every right implies a duty, and conversely. (For a proof, see Bunge 1989.) For example, my right to ask for help implies my duty to help others, and my civil duties imply my right to vote and run for office. Such a trade-off, or balance, between rights and duties is summarized in the principle: *Enjoy life and help live.* This is the maximal norm of the moral doctrine that I have expounded elsewhere (Bunge 1989) and that will be discussed in section 5.

Moral codes are neither natural nor God-given: they are social inventions with biological, psychological, and social roots. They "reflect" society, change along with it (though seldom at the same time), and react upon it by regulating social behavior. This thesis differs from the sociologistic view that conflates morals with mores, so that ethics becomes nothing but *la physique des moeurs* (Durkheim). The latter view overlooks the differences between right and wrong customs and underrates the political power of moral criticism. Morality is a social leaven as well as a device for social control; this is why it is not the same as law and why it now supports, now undermines, the law of the land.

This view of the nature of moral norms differs from emotivism, which is the ethics of both intuitionism and empiricism, particularly positivism. According to emotivism, morality is purely a matter of feeling and taste, whence it cannot be subjected to critical analysis, much less empirical test. Contrariwise, I would emphasize the biological and social roots of morals and submit that although norms are not testable for truth, they are testable for both consistency (with other norms in a given normative system) and practical efficiency.

This view of the function of norms, moral or otherwise, is at variance with two alternative, extreme views. One is irrationalism, according to which norms play no role at all: we always act blindly, either in response to current stimuli (behaviorism) or pulled by drives and emotions (psychoanalysis), or "gratuitously"—that is, arbitrarily (existentialism). The dual of this view is hyperrationalism, according to which doing anything, even perceiving and speaking, involves following rules.

Ethical irrationalism is false, because we keep creating, observing, enforcing, reforming, or breaking rules of conduct. Ethical hyperrationalism is also false, because we often act spontaneously or impulsively and think of rules only when some new issue arises (Cicourel 1974). Moreover, these views are morally wrong, on top of being false, in that they relieve us of the duty to examine our conduct in the light of moral principles, and the latter in the light of the consequences of our actions. After all, we all enjoy some measure of freedom not only to do what we want, but also to resist some selfish temptations. The truth, then, lies somewhere between ethical irrationalism and ethical hyperrationalism.

4 Freedom

We have just recalled the platitude that morals are about duties as well as rights. Now, if we were totally free, we would have rights but not duties, hence we would have no use for morals. But sociality involves duties, hence artificial (made) restrictions upon freedom. And even without such moral and legal constraints, we would be unable to do everything we fancied, for we are all limited by our environmental, biological, economic, cultural, and political circumstances.

In other words, as Marx and Weber taught, we live in cages. Each cage is in part natural, in part made. Insofar as it is natural, no human being can break away from it. But, insofar as it is social, certain human actions can expand, and others shrink or deform, the cages we live in. The point of every social movement of moral, legal, or political reform is precisely to bring about changes in the boundaries to human freedom.

(A cage in this context is no mere metaphor. Indeed, we may represent the state of any individual, at any given time, as a point in an abstract space—a state space—with as many axes as properties [recall chap. 1, sec. 3, and see Appendix 1]. As we live, the representative point moves in that space. But it does not move arbitrarily. The laws of nature and prevailing conditions confine everyone of us within a box, and moral and legal norms confine us within an even smaller box contained in the former. However, neither the natural box nor the social sub-box is rigid. New axes sprout, and others are pruned, as we learn or unlearn skills or habits, and as we engage in new activities or give up old ones. In sum, as we age and move around in society, our cages change in number of dimensions and size.)

If we find it necessary to limit freedom, it is because we admit that free will, however bounded, is for real. Were it not, we would be robots without initiative, plans, compassion, or rebellious impulses. We need some measure of freedom to meet our needs and wants, as well as to perform our duties. We also need freedom to work or, if necessary, fight for our rights or those of others. In short, humans enjoy bounded freedom, which they must largely conquer.

We are not born free: we are born dependent. But most of us in the West gain in freedom as we grow up and learn and interact with one another and become interdependent. We are sometimes free to choose between certain options. But these options are usually given to us: we seldom set them up. Worse, most of our contemporaries do not enjoy the freedom to choose even what they need, much less what they want: so far, freedom of choice has been a rare privilege. In short, some people are freer than others. Yet, this is not to say that what is now a privilege may never become a right, or conversely. Although we do live in cages, we can shrink or expand them.

The preceding has obvious consequences for social science and political philosophy. One of them is that individualism, which assumes that full freedom is possible and desirable, is just as false as holism, which denies freedom altogether. (More in chap. 9.) The consequences for ethical theory are equally obvious: since we are neither fully free agents nor robots, we cannot accept radical libertarianism any more than radical necessitarianism.

5 Ethics

Ethics is defined here as the study of morals. Ethics is to morals as meteorology is to the weather. Just as there can be bad meteorology of good weather, so there can be bad ethics of good morals. And just as "selfish morality" is a contradiction in terms, so there can be good ethical studies of selfishness.

Ethics can be divided into scientific and philosophical. Scientific, or empirical, ethics studies the moral codes prevailing in different social groups: it lies at the intersection of social psychology, anthropology, sociology, politology, and history. For instance, it studies the way industrialization enforces the "work ethic" and the way the latter is eroded by endemic mass unemployment. By contrast, philosophical ethics, or moral philosophy, analyzes, codifies, evaluates, or even builds systems of moral principles. We shall not deal here with empirical or descriptive ethics. Instead, we shall glance at a few classical ethical theories of interest to social science: deontologism, egoism, neo-libertarianism, contractualism, and utilitarianism. My own theory will be sketched at the end.

Deontologism is a duties-only moral philosophy. It enjoins us to do what is regarded as right, regardless of the consequences. Traditional deontologism was either tribal and part of some religion (the case in the Old Testament) or nationwide and part of politics (the case of Confucianism). Deontologism comes in two varieties: holistic and individualistic. Holistic deontologism, whether religious or secular, enjoins the individual to subordinate his interests to some social whole or other, such as the fatherland, the church, or the party. On this view, the whole is everything, whereas the individual is expendable. Individualistic deontologism, first clearly expounded by Kant, is universalist and secular, hence humanistic rather than theistic. It postulates that people are free to act, but that they should subject themselves voluntarily to a cross-cultural moral law that is stated only vaguely, however. Indeed, the famous moral imperative is not a moral principle at all, but a metaethical one: it prescribes that all moral maxims should be universalizable—that is, applicable to all human beings. This humanistic metaethical rule entails rejecting privileges of all kinds (biological, economic, cultural, or political). It is also incompatible with moral duplicity, such as the military morality according to which a soldier must be a good Samaritan to his comrade and a devil to the "enemy."

Whether holistic or individualistic, deontologism has two fatal flaws. One is that, in being nonconsequentialist, it condones irresponsibility, which makes it useless or worse. The other is that it pays no attention to personal needs and aspirations and consequently makes no room for rights. No wonder that Kant's moral philosophy has far more admirers and commentators than adepts. Rational, fair, responsible people are expected to weigh the possible consequences of their actions (and inactions) for themselves and others: they are consequentialists, not deontologists. Moreover, a duties-only ethics, though adequate for keeping subordinates in line, is inconsistent with democracy.

All other moral philosophies are consequentialist. Most of them revolve around the idea of free rational choice—the very same idea that inspires neoclassical economics and other theories in social studies. This holds in particular for rational egoism (e.g., Rand 1964), neo-libertarianism (e.g., Nozick 1974), contractualism (e.g., Gauthier 1986), and utilitarianism (e.g., Smart 1973). The first two hold that everyone ought to enjoy total freedom to choose, do, and become what he wants, with little or no regard for others. Hence these doctrines are variants of straight egoism, so do not qualify as moral philosophies at all. Indeed, the utterly selfish individual is one who flouts all morality. When faced with any choice, he asks only, "What's in it for me?" If he can avoid it, he will never ask, "What can I do for you?"—unless it is a potential customer whom he is addressing. No wonder that rational egoism and neo-libertarianism are part of the intellectual baggage of the New Right, obsessed as it is with protecting privilege, as well as of the self-indulgent, permissive member of the baby boom generation (born during the 1946–64 period) whose slogan is "Anything goes" in matters of conduct as well as knowledge.

As for contractualism and utilitarianism, they implement the norm of enlightened self-interest. This norm presupposes, correctly, that every one of us depends upon others, so that it is in our own interest to do something for others. Let us have a quick look at these influential doctrines. The gist of contemporary contractualism (or contractarianism), by contrast to the classical contractualism of Hobbes and Rousseau, is that (*a*) it is inegalitarian, (*b*) it asserts that an action is good or right if and only if it conforms to an agreed-on deal, and (*c*) it holds that morals are a by-product of contracts. Modern-day contractualism "has no place for duties that are strictly redistributive in their effects, transferring but not increasing benefits, or duties that do not assume reciprocity from other persons" (Gauthier 1986, 16). It follows that we have no obligations to children, the weak, the poor, or future generations, and that there can be no moral objections to pimping or indented labor, for they are subject to contract. Contractualism is a code of behavior for the powerful and the hard—those who write contracts, not those who have no choice but to sign (mostly metaphorically) on the dotted line. It makes no room for the noncontractual ties such as those of love, friendship, respect, solidarity, or compassion that help individuals live or hold social networks together. (Rawls [1971], usually regarded as the model contemporary contractualist, is hardly such, for he is centrally concerned with fairness and welfare and tolerates inequities only as rewards for services rendered to the community.)

Some contractualists (notably Gauthier 1986) worship the market, which is not concerned with distributive justice, the core issue of public morality. In particular, market-oriented contractualists have nothing to say to the vast masses of the Third World who participate only marginally, if at all, in market economies—or, when they do participate, do so by underselling their labor or the cash crops that they grow in place of the foodstuffs needed to nourish their families and by buying goods such as cigarettes, beer, and guns that no one really needs.

However, as anyone who has been in business knows, contractualism does not work for interfirm relations any more than it does for intrafirm ones. Indeed, no contract can foresee every problem, and most business issues are tackled by thinking, consulting, negotiating, bargaining, threatening, or cajoling with a modicum of trust, not by invoking contracts. Thus, although contractualism looks at first blush like the businessman's code of conduct, the latter would be ill-advised to adopt it. Indeed, a contract that fails to conform to the norms of common decency and fairness is likely to be broken sooner or later. It may even be contested in a court of law. The wise businessman is not out for the blood of his employees, clients, and suppliers: he wishes to keep them; he is not eager to fight with his competitors, if only because he knows that he may lose the fight; and he does not knowingly strike deals with crooks, for he knows that they can outsmart him. Dishonest practices not only have high individual costs: by driving honest dealers out of the market, they may destroy the market itself (Akerlof 1984). Therefore, contractualism notwithstanding, there *is* such a thing as business morality (see, e.g., Etzioni 1988; Sen 1987; Iannone 1989). In short, morality precedes contract (as well as law), not the other way round. Putting the agora before morality is like putting the trailer before the car. Remember the wise ancient maxim: *Leges sine moribus vanae.* So much for contractualism.

The paragon of rational choice ethical theory is of course utilitarianism, whether egoistic or altruistic. The egoistic utilitarian strives to maximize his own expected utility regardless of other people's needs and wants, whereas the altruistic utilitarian endeavors to maximize the aggregate, or social, expected utility. Now, whether egoistic or altruistic, utilitarianism can be of either of two kinds: act or rule. The act utilitarian estimates the expected utility of every action, whereas the rule utilitarian abides by general norms subsumed under the rationality principle (sec. 2).

Egoistic utilitarianism coincides with rational egoism, so we need not dwell on it. By contrast, classical utilitarianism, from Bentham and Mill to Harsanyi and Smart, proposes that the aggregate, or social, utility, or collective welfare, be maximized. Regrettably, this principle, at first sight as clear as it is noble, is incurably fuzzy. The reason is that it involves the notion of subjective utility, which, as we saw in section 2, is mathematically and empirically suspect. Consequently the payoff matrices invoked by some utilitarians to defend warfare, and by others to bolster cooperation, are phony. They assign arbitrary values to undefined (hence nonexistent) key functions. This procedure is anything but rational.

Worse, utilitarianism has no moral code: it contains no precise moral norms capable of guiding people's actions. In particular, act utilitarianism shares the tenet of rational choice theory that every action should be weighed on its own merit regardless of the norms of social behavior entrenched in tradition. By contrast, rule utilitarians are committed to proposing general norms of conduct. But, as a matter of fact, they have done nothing of the sort: frequently they just borrow the rules of conventional morality (see e.g., Harsanyi 1985). In practice, then, utilitarianism is as much an empty hulk as contractualism and Kantianism. Yet it has undeniable merits: it is secular, consequentialist, and concerned with both individual and social welfare. So, despite its shortcomings, it is the least bad of the rational choice ethical theories.

Finally, I want to raise two objections to all rational choice ethical theories. One is that they overlook moral feelings, such as compassion, fairness (equity), solidarity, and the wish to help others without necessarily expecting reciprocity. Yet social life is hard to imagine without such feelings. (Even Pareto, no bleeding-heart liberal or even a Christian, said as much.) And those moral feelings are more relevant to social justice than rationality—which, when understood as economic rationality, is incompatible with social justice.

A second objection concerns the uncritical assumption that all agents are free to choose. This postulate is highly controversial, if only because of the fog surrounding the very notion of freedom. Some thinkers have denied free will altogether—which of course contradicts the common experience of choice under no external compulsion. Others have admitted it with what the Jesuits call "mental reservations." Thus, according to Spinoza, Hegel, and Engels, freedom is nothing but the knowledge of necessity—a sophism if ever there was one, as anyone who has done time in jail can attest. Still other philosophers equate freedom with predictability—an obvious category mistake, for it confuses an ontological category with an epistemological one.

At least two different concepts of freedom have been distinguished: passive, or freedom *from*, and active, or freedom *to*. If this much be admitted, a look at ordinary life, psychology, and social science suggests that nobody is fully free from internal and external constraints. But we also know that every able-bodied adult of sound mind (*a*) can work or fight to free himself from some external constraints, and (*b*) is capable of devising options not given him at the start. For example, we can overcome certain hurdles by learning, changing jobs, fighting some people, or cooperating with others.

However, nobody is entirely free to choose anything except in trivial matters. Indeed, everyone has to submit to the general limitations of the human condition and to the particular conditions of his station in life (recall sec. 4). We are only partially free: semi-autonomous, semi-heteronomous. Ironically, rational choice theorists themselves admit severe limitations upon active freedom when presupposing that our options are given and our preferences constant—an unnecessary restriction on the rationality principle.

The most interesting cases are those in which neither of the available choices can or ought to be made. In such cases we must try to work out compromises between the given options or create new ones. As for preferences, it is unreasonable to keep them if they prove unrealistic or harmful. The rational individual learns, among other things, to change his preferences as needed: he is living disproof of the dogma of preference constancy upheld by most neoclassical economists (e.g., Stigler and Becker 1977). And the moral individual adjusts his preferences to his moral code.

In sum, rational choice models are not good moral guides to social behavior because (a) they revolve around self-interest, whereas ethics is mainly about duties, fairness, and mutual help; and (b) they are inconsistent with the psychology and sociology of pro-social behavior.

Deontologists may do the wrong thing for high-minded reasons; contractarians and utilitarians may do the right thing for the wrong reasons; and moral nihilists and libertarians will do the wrong thing for the wrong reasons. But who is likely to do the right thing for the right reasons? Only those who value whatever helps people (including themselves) meet their basic needs or legitimate wants, and who hold that there ought not to be rights without duties, or conversely. We call them *agathonists* (from the Greek word *agathon*, meaning good), for they strive for the good of self and other.

Agathonism rests on the value theory sketched in section 1. Thus, it assumes that values can be objective or subjective, and that anything that helps meet a basic need or a legitimate desire of some human being is valuable to him. The central ideas of agathonism are the following (Bunge 1989). First, everyone has moral rights and duties, as defined in section 3. Second, there are five main types of rights and duties: environmental, biopsychological, cultural, economic, and political; hence any moral code that excludes rights and duties of any of these kinds is incomplete. Third, rights and duties come in pairs and imply one another, so there is a trade-off between rewards and burdens. In other words, egoism is to be tempered with altruism, and competition in some regards should be combined with cooperation in others. In this way morality becomes compatible with prudence. These principles lead to, and are encapsulated in, the maxim *Enjoy life and help live.*

6 Science, Technology, and Morals

If it be admitted that knowledge—or, at any rate, some of it—is intrinsically valuable, then basic scientific research needs no justification, for it is nothing but the pursuit of knowledge. Not so technology, which uses knowledge as a means to attain practical results. Since these may be valuable, indifferent, or of no value, technologies can be good, worthless, or evil. (Just think of the technologies of mass murder, public deception, and mass production of junk.) Basic science and technology thus have different value systems. Correspondingly, they have different moral codes. That of science can be compressed into the commandment (or norm)

N1. Thou shalt search for the truth, pursue it wherever it may lead, and communicate it to whoever may be interested in it.

Technological research and development also abide by this norm. If they did not, they would be ineffectual. But the goal of technology is utilitarian, and it so happens that what is useful to some may be indifferent or harmful to others (e.g., overconsumption in the First World, achieved at the expense of underconsumption in the Third). Hence norm N1, while necessary, is not sufficient to ensure that technology is beneficent. If we wish the technologist to care for the good and the right, we must have him observe an additional norm of conduct:

N2. Thy design, norm, or plan shalt help people meet their basic needs or legitimate desires.

This is not the place to discuss how to bell the cat—a matter for social philosophy, political theory, and, above all, politics. Suffice it to point out the need to subject technological development to social control, by contrast with the need for freedom in basic research (see Agassi 1985; Iannone 1987; Mathews 1989).

Scientific research has, then, an internal moral code, or endo-morality, without which it would degenerate into charlatanism. The implementation of norm N1 calls for:

1. *intellectual honesty,* or the "cult" of truth: concern for rationality, objectivity, and testability and contempt for wishful thinking and black lies. Fulfillment of the demands of intellectual honesty requires in turn

2. *independence of judgment:* the habit of searching for evidence or proof without appealing to ultimate authority. Intellectual honesty and independence of judgment demand, in order to be practiced, a dose of

3. *intellectual courage:* the disposition to tackle hard and even embarrassing problems, defend truth, criticize error, and expose hoaxes regardless of their source. Criticism and self-criticism (not to be mistaken for self-flagellation), if practiced with courage, inspire one with

4. *love of intellectual freedom:* the freedom to investigate, criticize, and take

sides, as well as love of the individual rights and civil liberties that protect the freedom of research. The practice of science induces contempt and hatred for illegitimate authority, whether cultural or political, as well as for unjust power. Intellectual honesty and love of freedom lead, then, to reinforcing a

5. *sense of justice*, or fairness, which is not so much servitude to positive law (sometimes unjust) as the disposition to reckon with other people's rights, opinions, and feelings, always giving credit where credit is due.

Science is a school of morality, but, as is well known, not all its pupils graduate with honors. Occasionally a researcher skirts a touchy problem, refrains from criticizing error, plagiarizes, or even fakes data or contorts arguments. No matter: others are likely to tackle the dangerous problem or attack the widespread error; and fakes and thefts will eventually be uncovered—though their victims may never be compensated. The point is that in basic science truth and depth, not practical usefulness, power, or consensus, have the last word. Ideally, truth commands consensus, not conversely, constructivism-relativism notwithstanding.

Because scientific research is a search for truth, distortion and cover-up of truth are the most serious of all forms of scientific misconduct, even more so than plagiarism. Stealing some findings hurts the victim, and it may make him suspicious and even secretive. But faking data or computations hurts everybody: it is analogous to counterfeiting money. This is, of course, unacceptable to the constructivist-relativist school of the sociology of science. This school denies the possibility of finding objective truths, and it claims that science can be neither value-free nor morally neutral on account of being supported or tapped, watched or censored, hence misguided or distorted, by business or government. On this view, science is an ideology, and the thesis of its neutrality a myth. The alleged evidence for this view is the engagement of science with military, industrial, agricultural, and political research. But, of course, this view merely betrays ignorance of the difference between science and technology—in particular, ignorance that the goal of scientists is to find truths, whereas that of contemporary technologists is to find out how to get things done with the help of scientific truths.

What holds for science in general holds for social science. Here, too, truth is the highest value. In other words, norm N1 ought to be upheld in social science. This is what Leopold von Ranke demanded in 1824 from historians: that they tell *wie es eigentlich gewesen* (what really happened). It also harmonizes with Max Weber's *Wertfreiheit* (value neutrality) principle for social science in general—which, as we shall see, does not carry over to sociotechnology.

It has been suggested that Weber's espousal of the value neutrality principle was nothing but a gimmick to maintain the balance between the requirements of scientific inquiry and those of the absolutist state that supported it (Gouldner 1973). This is not true. Weber wanted to promote the objective study of social facts. Moreover, he was quite outspoken politically: he studied and condemned the power of the *Junkers*, the tyranny of the bureaucrats, and the continuation of World War I. (On the other hand, he was blind to sex and race discrimination, economic inequality, and colonialism.) In proclaiming the value neutrality of science, Weber wished only to defend the search for truth against the distortions of both conservatives and Marxists.

Now, truth about society can endanger deeply held, yet groundless, beliefs and can jeopardize vested interests and the associated ideologies. Not surprisingly, ideology and politics sometimes get in the way of social scientists. Worse, the enemy is often within and unrecognized as such. In fact, much pseudoscience and political opinion are passed off as social science (see, e.g., Andreski 1972; Lang 1981). Because of the danger of ideological contraband under the guise of social science, the demarcation between science and nonscience is even more important in the case of social studies than in that of the study of nature—all the more so because a number of scholars deny the very possibility of drawing the line in question (recall chap. 7, secs. 5–8).

The basic social scientist makes intrascientific value judgments: he evaluates problems, hypotheses, techniques, and findings. And because he is supposed to pursue the truth, he must not mistake value judgments about social facts for true statements about the latter. Yet, he cannot avoid letting his value system and ideology orient his choice of research problems, much less his policy recommendations. For example, he may prefer to study real economic disequilibria rather than fictitious static equilibria, dictatorships rather than the paradoxes of voting rules, and the causes and consequences of war rather than the exploits of successful mass murderers. There is no harm in weighing problems in the light of some value system or ideology, as long as one's research abides by the moral code of science. What matters in scientific research is strong motivation (of any kind) and scrupulous respect for the truth. (That not all students of society actually respect the truth is another matter, to be taken up in Part C.)

The case of applied scientists and technologists—in particular, sociotechnologists—is altogether different. They are committed not only to truth (as a means) but also to the interests (values and goals) of their employers or clients, who are usually business firms or political organizations. These interests may be broad or narrow, pro-social or antisocial. Hence the resulting technical recommendation, design, norm, or plan cannot be unbiased: it is likely to benefit some people at the expense of others. Suffice it to think of the design of new mass murder weapons or useless gadgets, of heavily polluting factories or oppressive organizations. And recall that, between about 1940 and 1990, nearly half the engineers in the industrialized world were employed in military technology.

What holds for technology in general applies, of course, to sociotechnology. The expert who examines social issues is morally obliged to "declare his values," as Gunnar Myrdal (1969) demanded. He must take a stand with regard to such social issues as inequality, unemployment, inflation, unfair taxation, external debt, sexual or racial discrimination, political oppression, militarism, war, and bureaucratism. This is because he is expected to make proposals to tackle such issues, and the public—at least in a democracy—has the right to know which side he is on, so as to be able to take a rational stand. Regrettably, many proposals of this kind, particularly those concerning the macroeconomy, are presented as unbiased technical blueprints and are seldom offered for public debate (see details in Bunge 1996).

But even if he tries to pass off a political program as an unbiased technical proposal, the scientific policymaker will seek to make *objective* value judgments so that his recommendations or plans will benefit his employer. As Durkheim (1988 [1895], 142) wrote, we must find "an objective criterion, one inherent in the facts themselves, that will allow us to distinguish in a scientific fashion health from sickness in the various orders of social phenomena. . . . [In this way] science will be in a position to shed light on practice while keeping faithful to its own method." For example, the value judgments "Poverty is bad" and "War is bad" are not subjective, for it is true that poverty and war cause hardship, stunt personal development, and incite people to antisocial behavior. In sum, in practical matters partiality is compatible with objectivity.

To sum up, whereas scientists come up with propositions, technologists come up with proposals. A proposition may be false but not harmful. By contrast, proposals are neither false nor true: they can only be effective or ineffective, beneficial or harmful to someone. Scientists are accountable to society for the fruitfulness of their search for truth, cogency, depth, and transparency. But this is all we should expect of them. We should not ask them to deliver practically useful items too, because most of them do not have a technological mind-set. On the other hand, technologists are socially responsible and therefore accountable for the results of the implementation of their proposals. Whereas it is impertinent to ask a basic scientist "Whose side are you on?" this question should be posed to technologists. In short, unlike basic science, technology is morally and socially committed. Hence, citizens of a democracy should have a different attitude toward basic research than toward technology. They should defend the freedom of basic research, because it can enrich culture—for example, by helping to explain social facts. But the citizenry should get involved in the control of the development and implementation of any technologies likely to jeopardize the well-being of any human beings, born or yet to be born.

Every social system adopts some moral code. In a democratic society, there are a number of alternative moral codes which nevertheless share some principles. In addition, there is a family of professional codes, as well as a legal code. But the law is never enough, for, even if it enshrines some basic rights and duties, it will be broken unless sustained by a matching moral code entrenched in custom.

When a social order breaks down suddenly, then, until a new order has been built, people tend to feel free to act as they like—a chaotic state of affairs, which hinders the construction of the new order. This is one of the reasons why politics should go hand in hand with morals. It is also one of the reasons why gradual (yet global) reform is preferable to revolution (see Bunge forthcoming).

Not all societies are equally fair and viable. (Absolute moral relativism, inherent in anthropological functionalism and legal positivism, is morally wrong in that it ignores fairness.) Where unemployment is massive and chronic, the work ethic sounds hollow. Where unrestricted liberty to promote self-interest prevails, the social order is morally illegitimate and politically unstable. Injustice is greatest where individual rights are suppressed for the greater glory of some supra-individual entity, real or imaginary. Only a social order that entrenches the agathonist maxim "Enjoy life and help live" can be expected to be both fair and stable—though not static. The problem of designing such a social order is tackled elsewhere (Bunge 1989 and forthcoming).

Our next task will be to examine the family of philosophical *isms* involved in controversies over social studies.

PART C :: *General
Philosophical
Problems in
Social Science*

9 :: *Individualism and Holism*

The question of the nature of society lies at the very foundation of social science and social policy. I submit that there are only three general, coherent views on this matter: individualism, holism, and systemism. They can be compressed into the following formulas: "The individual is the alpha and the omega," the Nazi slogan *Du bist nichts, dein Volk ist alles* ("You are nothing, your people is everything"), and "We shape society, and it shapes us," respectively. Ironically, both individualism and holism write off social ills and discourage social protest in identical terms: "Blame yourself (or your genes), not the system." Hence neither bodes well for social engineering.

According to individualism—also called atomism, voluntarism, and intentionalism—a society is just a collection of individuals; consequently all social studies are ultimately studies of individuals. By contrast, holists (or collectivists or structuralists) hold that a society is a whole that transcends its membership and that it can only be understood on its own level. Finally, systemism maintains that a society is a system of interrelated, interacting individuals, and that it possesses emergent, or supra-individual, properties, so that it ought to be studied at both micro and macro levels. Individualists proceed from the bottom up, holists from the top down, and systemists start from individuals embedded in a society that preexists them and watch how their actions affect society and alter it.

Here are some examples of the general views in question. On the whole, Protestantism, liberalism, and the New Right are individualist, whereas Roman Catholicism, Islam, fascism, communism, and nationalism are collectivist. Hobbes, Locke, Smith, Hume, Bentham, Tocqueville, Mill, Dilthey, the neoclassical economists, Simmel, and Weber were individualists, whereas Plato, Ibn Khaldûn, the Romantics (particularly Hegel), Comte, Marx, Durkheim, Parsons, and members of the Frankfurt school and the social constructivists were holists. However, none of these thinkers has been a consistent individualist or holist. In particular, Tocqueville, Mill, and Weber admitted that every individual is subject to rigid institutional constraints; whereas Marx, Durkheim, and Parsons knew that these constraints are ultimately the doing of individuals. Whoever places individual action in a social context, or explains social change in terms of individual actions, acts like a systemist, even as he recites an individualist or holistic credo. In particular, Aristotle was a systemist in focusing his attention on the community held together by individual goodwill and reciprocity. Likewise, democratic socialists and liberals who advocate the welfare state behave as systemists even while reciting their respective original credos.

Paradoxically, anyone of the three approaches can promote the unity of the social sciences: individualism, because its unit of analysis in all fields of social research is the person, usually the "rational," or maximizing, agent; holism, because it views society as a whole whose parts can be singled out only in an arbitrary fashion; and systemism, because it regards society as a system composed of strongly linked subsystems ultimately composed of individuals. Hence the isolationism practiced in most social sciences, particularly mainstream economics, cannot be due to the general approach. Perhaps it originates in historical accident, tunnel vision, myopia, and the wish to protect turf. However, this is another story (see Bunge forthcoming).

Every conceptual view of any natural object has two components: an ontological and a methodological one. The former concerns the nature of the object, the latter the proper way to study it. But if the object is social, such as a school or a business firm, a third feature must be added: namely, values and morals, for these are what guide or misguide human behavior. That is, in metatheoretical matters concerning social science,

X-ism = <Ontological X-ism, Methodological X-ism, Axiologico-moral X-ism>.

The *isms* to be analyzed in this chapter and the next are, of course, individualism, holism, and systemism. The inclusion of an ontological component in any X-ism is bound to raise positivist eyebrows, particularly for assigning it pride of place in the ordered triple. Such priority may be justified as follows. First, being precedes knowing: cognition is only one of the functions of the human being (as well as of other higher vertebrates). Second, whoever investigates a real object assumes, at least tentatively, that the latter exists or may exist. Moreover, the investigator starts by having at least a rough idea of the nature of the object of interest, since he must know what to investigate and why. Third, the explorer or investigator chooses his research method according to what (little or much) he knows or suspects about the nature of his object. Thus ontology precedes (or ought to precede) epistemology and, in particular, methodology.

The inclusion of the third coordinate, axiologico-moral (hence behavioral) X-ism, may raise even more eyebrows, at least among those who, following Weber, believe that all value judgments are subjective, all moral norms nothing but social conventions, and that the social scientist should steer clear of them anyway. This is not my own view (see chap. 8). But even if it were, the inclusion of the values and morals held by (most of) the members of a social system is apposite because, for better or worse, they contribute to shaping the social behavior of all members of the system.

This chapter focuses on individualism and holism. It examines their ontological, epistemological, and axiologico-moral aspects. The merits and flaws of each will be shown. (See also Watkins 1952; Mandelbaum 1955; Brodbeck 1968; Krimerman 1969; Gellner 1973; O'Neill 1973; Bunge 1979*a*, 1985*b*; Smelser 1986; Lloyd 1991.) This analysis will help us to grasp systemism in the next chapter.

1 Individualism

Individualists focus on individuals and either deny the existence of social bonds and social systems or assert that these are fully reducible to individuals and their actions. Margaret Thatcher summarized this view in her famous dictum: "There is no such thing as society: there are only individuals." It is a view that goes back to Hobbes, and it was shared by all the utilitarians. Thus Bentham (1982 [1789], 12): "[T]he community is a fictitious *body*, composed of the individual persons who are considered as constituting as it were its *members*. The interest of the community then is, what?—the sum of the interests of the several members who compose it." Much later, Mill (1962 [1875], 573) stated confidently that "The laws of the phenomena of society are, and can be, nothing but the laws of the actions and passions of human beings united together in the social state. . . . Human beings in society have no properties but those which are derived from, and may be resolved into, the laws of the natural or individual man. In social phenomena the Composition of Causes is the universal law." In short, there are neither social facts nor social regularities characterized by emergent properties.

Individualism is still going strong in social science and its philosophy. Witness neoclassical microeconomics and the numerous rational choice theories in sociology and politology that ape the former and thus exemplify what has been called 'economic imperialism' (see, e.g., Becker 1976; Swedberg 1990).

Homans (1974) is a clear contemporary case of radical individualism. He denies that there are supra-individual (i.e., social) entities and asserts that all humans act "rationally"—that is, from self-interest. At the same time he is a behaviorist, in holding that any two individuals placed in the same circumstances will act in the same way, so as to maximize their expected utilities. This view is attractive in promising to explain all human behavior with the help of a single law, thus unifying all the social sciences under the collective name 'behavioral science.' However, this is only a dream. In fact, psychologists have known for many years that, because they have different pasts and expectations, as well as different internal states, different members of the same animal species often react differently to the same external stimuli. (This is sometimes called the zeroth, or Harvard, law of psychology.) Not even rats are identical black boxes (input–output devices).

Individualism is even stronger in social, political, and moral philosophy. For example, Popper (1957, 1974) claimed that there are no social wholes, so social scientists can study only individuals—for example, soldiers rather than armies. And Winch (1958), following Wittgenstein, held that social scientists study only intentional and, moreover, rule-directed behavior, not social groups. If Popper and Winch were consistent, they would deny the very possibility of social science. In fact, Winch does deny it, asserting that social studies belong in epistemology—a view that Gellner (1973, 53) has called "profoundly and significantly wrong" in being alien to the practice of social research.

The current popularity of individualism can be explained by the following factors: (*a*) it is clear and simple; (*b*) it is rationalist; (*c*) it boasts a large scope and a strong unifying power—indeed, it claims to cover all the sciences of man, from psychology to history; (*d*) it matches the nonfascist pro-capitalist ideologies, whether liberal or conservative; (*e*) it promotes utilitarianism, whether egoistic or altruistic. Alas, as we shall argue shortly, along with these real or virtual virtues, individualism has fatal flaws, not least of which is that it fails to match social reality, if only because it denies the existence of social wholes with characteristics of their own, such as the specific functions and assets or the prosperity or decline of schools, business firms, and states.

As noted at the beginning of this chapter, we distinguish the ontological from the methodological and moral aspects of individualism. We start with the first coordinate of the ordered triple. *Ontological individualism* may be compressed into the following theses:

OI1. A society is an aggregate of persons. Supra-individual totalities are fictitious. In particular, institutions are nothing but conventions ruling individual behavior.

OI2. Since social wholes are abstractions, they cannot behave as units or have emergent, or global, properties: every social property is the resultant or aggregation of properties of the individual members of society.

OI3. Being fictions, social wholes cannot interact, they cannot act on any of their members, and they cannot evolve. The interaction between two societies consists in the totality of the interactions among their individual members. Group pressure is the resultant of the pressures exerted by each group member on other members. And social change is the totality of changes in the individual components of society.

The matching theses of *methodological* (or *epistemological*) *individualism* are as follows:

EI1. The proper topic for social study is the individual.

EI2. To explain a social fact amounts to explaining the actions of the individuals involved in it.

EI3. Hypotheses and theories in social science can be tested only by observing the behavior of individuals.

Finally, *moral (or behavioral) individualism* boils down to the following principles:

MI1. Individuals, or, at any rate, some of them, are maximally valuable.

MI2. The *summum bonum* is self-interest together with the liberty to pursue it.

MI3. The only legitimate function of institutions is to safeguard or advance individual liberties and interests.

Let us examine the above theses. Ontological individualism is untenable because, when consistent and radical, it involves the denial of social relations or their exile to the world of ideas. Thus Popper (1974, 14): "[S]ocial relations belong, in many ways, to what I have more recently called 'the third world,' or 'world 3,' the world of theories, of books, of ideas, of problems." This is a consequence of the thesis that a society is nothing but its membership, since a relation between individuals x and y is neither in x nor in y. But it so happens that social bonds constitute the glue that holds social groups together and endows them with (emergent) properties of their own. Moreover, the collection of social relations in a society constitutes the latter's social structure. So, consistent individualism is bound to discourage research on the central problem of sociology: namely, the unveiling and analysis of social structure. A fortiori, it will discourage any movements aimed at changing the social structure; that is, ontological individualism supports social conservatism.

(The individualist may wish to use the nominalist thesis that a binary relation, such as that of employment, is nothing but a set of ordered pairs of individuals, such as ⟨Boss, Secretary⟩; and that an n-ary relation is a set of ordered n-tuples. But this will not do, because the very notion of an ordered n-tuple involves that of relation—otherwise one has an unordered n-tuple, that is, a homogeneous set of n elements. What is true is only that the extension or graph of an n-ary relation is a set of n-tuples of individuals: namely, those among whom this relation holds. A relation is not identical with its extension, just as a unary property is not the same as the set of individuals who happen to possess that property at a given moment. In sum, relations, particularly social relations, are not reducible to sets of individuals. If only for this reason, the nominalist project of eliminating properties and relations in favor of individuals has failed.)

Individualism not only fails to explain the existence of social wholes: it does not even account for simple, private individual actions such as writing and posting a letter. Indeed, when writing letters, we make use of such socially produced goods as pens, sheets of paper, and envelopes, as well as of public goods, such as common knowledge and language. And in posting a letter, we make use of further public goods: sidewalks, streets, stamps, and the mail. Individual actions, then, cannot be an absolute beginning of social studies, any more than institutions. We start either with an individual in society or with a social system sustained (or undermined) by its individual components.

(To take a somewhat more sophisticated example, consider the social relation of belonging, as exemplified by "Person b belongs to social group G_i," or $b \in G_i$ for short. It so happens that the concept of belonging, $\in$, is not definable as a set of ordered pairs. In fact, $\in$ is a basic (undefined) concept in set theory. Moreover, before stating $b \in G_i$, we must have formed the idea of the social group G_i. And this requires splitting the membership S of the given society into social groups, one of which is G_i. This partition of S must have been induced by some equivalence relation, such as that of having roughly the same occupation, income, or political attitude. That is, the statement in question, $b \in G_i$, presupposes that the given society, far from being an unstructured collection of individuals, can be analyzed as a family of social groups. Mathematically, G_i is a member of the quotient of S by an equivalence relation $\sim$, or $G_i \in S/\sim$. The same holds for any of the more complex statements in social science involving some social relation.)

In sum, every statement made in social science asserts or presupposes that a society—nay, any social system—is a structured collection of individuals rather than either a mere aggregate (individualism) or a whole within which the individual is lost (holism). The *social structure* of S consists of a certain set R of (social) relations in the collection S of individuals composing the society. Surely the set S is an abstraction in being a set; and so is R, since there are no relations in themselves, detached from their relata. (Sets and relations do not consume or produce, cooperate or fight: they are no more and no less than concepts.) But what is a structured collection if not a system, and a concrete one at that if composed of concrete interacting individuals?

The individualist may concede this point, but, if consistent, he will insist that the structure of a system must somehow be contained in, or be deducible from, the properties of the individual members of the system. In short, he will contend, as Homans (1958, 1974) does, that every predicate in social science is reducible to a bunch of predicates concerning individuals. However, this claim is logically untenable, as shown by the following counterexample. The property of being salaried consists in bearing the relation "is in the pay of" somebody. (In general, call R the binary relation in question and P the unary property of being R-related. Then $Px =_{df}$ for some y: Rxy.) In short, it is not true that a study of the individual members of a social system suffices to reveal the global features of the system. Only a study of socially related individuals, couples, triads, and so on can yield the desired result. In other words, if we want to know something about society, we must study not only its components, but also the society as a whole, as well as its subsystems. In short, we must adopt the systemic approach (see next chapter).

The ontological individualist views society as analogous to a low-density gas, the individual agents being the analogs of the molecules, and their utility functions being counterparts of the laws of motion. As in the elementary kinetic theory of gases, the individuals are assumed to act independently of one another, being constrained only by the container (or its analog, the institutional framework or the market). Incidentally, neither the gas container nor its social analog is ever analyzed into individuals: both are handled as wholes, a strategy that violates methodological individualism.

But social systems, from the family and the firm to the transnational corporation and the state, are more like lumps of condensed matter than gases. And theories of condensed matter bear little resemblance to the theory of gases—which is as it should be, since condensation is accompanied by qualitative changes. In these theories interaction is of the essence: it is what makes a body fluid or solid, just as face-to-face interaction turns an amorphous social group into a social system. This is why few, if any, social scientists (unlike social philosophers) practice ontological individualism even when they preach it.

In sum, ontological individualism is false. This renders methodological individualism barren and moral individualism suspect. The first is obvious. If there are social systems with (emergent) properties of their own, they must be studied, and their components ought not to be studied in isolation from one another, because the behavior of each individual depends in part on that of fellow members of the system, as well as on the structure of the latter. (Physical parallel: the properties of an atom are not deducible from separate studies of its nucleus and its electrons.) In short, the individualist approach to society cannot account for the emergence, maintenance, or breakdown of social systems.

Finally, moral individualism is suspect, if only because it denies the value of social systems. By rejecting cooperation, solidarity, and social responsibility, moral individualism undermines all social systems, even business firms. In particular, the current plight of American society has been attributed in part to the pathological individualism of the baby boom generation (see Russell 1993).

2 The Case of Rational Choice Theory

There are few, if any, *consistent* upholders of ontological individualism or social atomism. Even such eloquent preachers of radical ontological individualism as Weber, Simmel, Hayek, Homans, and Popper have resorted to such unanalyzed wholes as "social order," "the market," "the state," or "the situation" (or "state of affairs") and have occasionally criticized the fallacy of composition—without realizing the inconsistency. Likewise Dilthey, the champion of philosophical hermeneutics, is usually regarded as an individualist. Yet he insisted that the social conditions of a period, the climate of opinion, the legal system, and other "social totalities" have to be treated as such and, moreover, that they constitute the "objective spirit," an unanalyzed given with which the individual spirit or mind is confronted.

Weber is a clear example of inconsistent individualism. In a brilliant posthumous, little-known essay (1924), he proposed a systemist, and even materialist, explanation of the decline of imperial Rome. In fact, contrary to the traditional individualist and moralist explanations in terms of effeteness and corruption, Weber holds that the ancient Italian economy could not advance as long as it relied on slave work. In fact, the slave market dried up when the expansion of the empire (caused by wars of conquest) ceased, which happened at the time of Tiberius, long before the barbarian invasions. In turn, the decline in the slave work force caused the drop in state revenues—hence the shrinking of the army—as well as in the incomes of landowners. As the *latifundia* were replaced by the "natural" (small farm) economy, production fell, and the cities declined.

In short, Weber does not explain the decline of the Roman empire in terms of individual decisions resulting from free choices, the way a rational choice theorist should. The owner of a large Sicilian wheat plantation did not have the choice of buying or not buying slaves to replace the old and the dead, for few, if any, slaves were for sale. The senators did not have the choice of mounting or not mounting a new expansionary war, for the treasury was half empty, and the barbarians at the borders would not let them, anyway. On the other hand, it is likely that in most cases the decision-makers did act in their own (short-term) interests—but such actions often had "perverse" effects.

Homans (1987, 72), one of the most radical of all contemporary individualists, does not manage to be completely consistent either. Thus, after insisting (against Weber and Popper) that social science is reducible to individual psychology and, like them, denying the existence of "true emergents" in social science, he writes about social structures as "any features of groups that persist for any period of time." Coleman (1990, 300), another champion of methodological individualism, indicts ontological individualism or atomism as a fiction. And Boudon, also a self-styled methodological individualist, emphasizes the emergence of systemic properties and admits that one and the same individual is likely to behave differently in different macro-circumstances (see, e.g., Boudon and Bourricaud 1986).

While there are few, if any, consistent ontological individualists, there are plenty of *methodological* individualists: that is, students of society who claim that the understanding of social facts requires only the investigation of the beliefs, intentions, and actions of the individuals concerned. But methodological individualism, hence rational choice theorizing, comes in at least two strengths: strong, or radical, and weak, or moderate. According to *radical* methodological individualism, a single theory, containing concepts referring exclusively to individuals, suffices to explain all kinds of social behavior and social system. Homans (1974) and the self-styled "economic imperialists," such as Becker (1976) and lately Coleman (1990), who claim that neoclassical microeconomics suffices to explain everything social, from marriage to war, belong to this party.

By contrast, *moderate* methodological individualism holds that certain universal premises concerning individuals, though necessary, are insufficient to account for social life. It asserts that different kinds of social fact call for different models sharing those universal premises, but that each model contains hypotheses concerning both the specific kind of interaction and the particular institutional framework. Moderate individualism comes close to systemism. Thus Coleman (1986, 1312) is behaving like a closet systemist when he writes: "The central theoretical problems: how the purposive actions of the actors combine to bring about system-level behavior, and how these purposive actions are in turn shaped by constraints that result from the behavior of the system."

Let us take a closer look at the two varieties of methodological individualism, starting with the radical one, according to which all social groups must be accounted for by a single, overarching theory. This assumption presupposes uniformity and constancy of human nature. Indeed, if all individuals act only when impelled by self-interest and behave in disregard of what other people do, then all social groups are basically similar, and consequently a single theory should fit them all. Moreover, since self-interest is the key concept of the paragon discipline, neoclassical microeconomics, all rational choice models must be variations of the latter; thus all social science is ultimately reducible to microeconomics. This may still be a minority view, but it has been gaining ground steadily since the 1970s.

There are at least three objections to this radical view. The first is summarized in the classical formula *Dictum de omni, dictum de nullo*—what is said about everything says nothing. (In semi-technical semantic jargon: Sense or content is inversely related to extension or truth domain.) Put another way, an extremely general theory can cover only features common to all members of its reference class, hence it will miss all particularities and most mechanisms. For example, such a theory will fail to distinguish honest work from crime, families from stores, nonprofit organizations from business firms, schools from armies, and so on. And being unable to account for differences among individuals, as well as for the diversity of social interactions, systems, processes, and institutions, the theory is bound to be unrealistic, hence false.

A second objection to the individualism involved in rational choice theorizing is that by postulating that all individuals are well-informed, shrewd utility-maximizers, it makes no room for the uniqueness of every individual. In particular, it makes no room for the outstanding individual—the entrepreneur, the political or cultural leader, or even the role model. Now, if all individuals are roughly the same, they should behave similarly in the same circumstances—which, of course, is contrary to fact. So, paradoxically, rational choice theory leads to the same result as holism: namely, that nobody is indispensable—or even that everybody is expendable. In short, the theory is self-defeating.

A third objection to radical individualism is that social facts, and even individual behavior, cannot be accounted for without the help of certain "macro-concepts" that do not seem definable in terms of "micro-concepts." (We call 'macro-concept' a concept referring to a macro-entity, such as a business firm, whereas a 'micro-concept' is one concerning a micro-entity, such as an individual person.) For one thing, behavior does not happen in a social vacuum, but in a social matrix. For another, as Karl Polanyi (1944) first stressed, and as recent empirical research has confirmed, "most behavior is closely embedded in networks of interpersonal relations" (Granovetter 1985, 504). Far from being perfectly designed and controlled, such networks are nonhierarchical, informal, and plagued by delays and congestion. But they can also make up for the rigidity of the chains of command, thus beating the neat charts designed by managers (White 1973).

A consequence of the embeddedness of the individual in social systems of various kinds is that an authentically rational decision-maker will take his social environment into account. For example, a businessman cannot make rational choices unless he takes account of the global entities or processes referred to by such concepts as occur in the following laundry list: "policy of the firm," "state of the market," "organization," "technology," "product quality," "scarcity," "bottleneck," "economic situation," "development," "business opportunity," "social order," "government," "value-added tax," "inflation rate," "discount rate," "labor movement," "code of commerce," and "political stability."

None of these concepts is about individual persons or is definable in terms of individual dispositions or activities: they are "irreducibly social," as Arrow (1994) would say. All of them transcend biology and psychology. They are peculiar to social science, because they concern social systems embedded in even larger systems, and every system possesses (emergent) properties that its components lack. For instance, a country may be at war without every one of its inhabitants taking up arms. Another example: Capitalism, socialism, and their various combinations are features of entire economies, not of individuals. A third example: Parliamentary democracy and one-party dictatorship can be properties only of a political system. (For precise definitions of the concepts of social system and emergence, at variance with the holistic views of Parsons and Luhmann, see Bunge 1979*b*.)

The emergence and breakdown of systems endowed with radically new properties sets objective limits to micro-reduction, or the construal of a whole as the collection of its components (recall chap. 4, sec. 7). It cannot be otherwise if our ideas are to match the real world, which is composed of changeable systems. Interestingly enough, this is the case with atomic physics as well as with social science. Indeed, every well-posed problem in quantum theory involves a formulation of the boundary conditions, which represent the environment of the thing in question in a global manner, rather than in terms of concepts representing micro-entities. Irreversibility is another case of emergence, one that holds not only for physical systems but also for biological and social ones. In particular, life histories and historical processes cannot be run backward.

The following examples from social science highlight the limits that the emergence of novelty sets on micro-reduction. Consider, first, social inertia, in particular the slowness of any large organization, such as a corporation or a state bureaucracy, to react to new situations. Every individual in the organization may be quick to grasp that something new is afoot and that such novelty calls for restructuring the organization. Still, everyone may have his own ideas as to what ought to be done, and everyone will tend to defend his own turf, occasionally to the point of sabotaging the instructions coming from above. The result is that systemic inertia can be far greater than individual inertia.

Our second example is social forecasting. According to radical individualism, every aggregate outcome is merely the "sum" of individual decisions. Consequently, in order to make, say, macroeconomic forecasts, we would have to know the decisions made by every single economic agent. But of course this is impossible: only an omniscient being could have access to such a huge amount of information. (Besides, individual decisions are constrained by the state of society.) Hence the consistent individualist must either abstain from making economic forecasts, or he must make them on the unrealistic assumptions that every single agent has "rational" expectations and behaves in a perfectly "rational" way. The former option leads to inaction, the latter to wrong forecasts and thereby to inefficient action. (See Blinder 1989 for the failure of the rational expectations school in macroeconomics.) Either way, radical individualism leads us astray.

Another objection to radical individualism is this. If physical entities, such as atoms and molecules, behave differently when coupled in different manners, as in the case of isomers, why should people be any different, particularly given the variety of social relations? Think of the differences between a cloud, the water in a jug, a snowflake, an ice cube, and a glacier—despite the fact that all these systems are composed of identical H_2O molecules. Is there any reason for social systems to differ less among themselves than physical systems composed of molecules of the same species? Why should we make do with a single theory in social science, when physics needs different theories for different states of aggregation? Granted, this objection is analogical, but it should have some heuristic power in theory construction. In particular, it should help discourage physico-social analogies.

Besides, even assuming that the link (e.g., force) between two things is known, in physics only two-body and very-many-body problems are soluble exactly. Intermediate-body-number problems, starting with the three-body problem, are not generally soluble in an exact or closed manner. (Our planetary system is an exception, because the solar mass is many times greater than any planetary mass, so that the calculus of perturbations can be applied.) In the case of physics, very-many-body problems are solved by adding statistical assumptions; but, even so, the system must have a large number of components to be manageable. This is one of the reasons why large physical (and chemical and biological) systems are studied on their own level in addition to being analyzed into their components. There is no reason to think that social systems are more amenable to the radical micro-reduction strategy. So much for radical micro-reductionism.

The weak, or *moderate*, version of rational choice theorizing admits the need for subsidiary hypotheses concerning both the specific type of social group and (though often in an underhand fashion) the institutional framework or social environment as well. (Every rational choice model M_i of this kind may then be regarded as the set of logical consequences of the union of two sets, G and S_i. G is a set of general premises common to all such models: maximizing behavior, ontological individualism, and methodological individualism. And S_i is a set of subsidiary, or special, assumptions describing the specific features of the system or process in question. In short, $M_i = Cn(G \cup S_i)$, where i is a numeral. The role of G is thus similar to that of the general principles of evolutionary biology, which are insufficient to account for the differences between, say, moss and elephants.)

This weak version of rational choice theorizing is not open to the two objections raised against the strong version. However, even this moderate version is unrealistic, because G itself is unrealistic. Indeed, people act from custom, obligation, or passion, as well as on the strength of cold calculation. Moreover, not even calculated behavior can be perfect, and this for at least two reasons: first, the information required for any realistic calculation is never complete, on either the theoretical or the empirical side; second, the goal aimed at may not be realistic, or it may be morally objectionable.

Another unrealistic assumption of both the weak and the strong versions of rational choice theory is that of total freedom of choice. Even a quick reflection on any of the major events in anyone's life suffices to refute this view. For example, we cannot choose whether or when to be born or to come of age, whether to grow up in an advanced or a backward country, in good times or bad. In hard times we cannot be choosy about jobs or life-styles; we can seldom choose whether to live in a hovel or a mansion; the education we get and the occupation we engage in depend crucially on our family's socioeconomic status and connections; the citizens of most nations, however democratic, have little if any say in choosing between peace and war; even world leaders have a limited "menu" of choice (Russett and Starr 1981); and so on and so forth. No doubt we ought to promote the cause of rights—albeit checked and balanced by the concomitant duties. But total freedom is at best a mirage, at worst an ideological bait (recall chap. 8, sec. 6). And if our choices cannot be totally free, then they cannot be fully rational either, except conceptually. We shall take a closer look at rational choice theory in chapter 14. Let us now examine two approaches that, though usually presented as individualist, violate key principles of individualism.

3 Individholism and Crypto-Systemism

As we have just seen, by definition of the word *moderate,* every moderate rational choice theorist takes for granted certain macro-entities (such as markets and governments) or macro-variables (such as scarcity and fiscal debt). Now, the corresponding macro-concepts are not definable in terms of individual features or actions. Hence the moderate rational choice theorist cannot be strictly faithful to the postulates of methodological individualism—the very approach he intends to implement.

We saw that this is the case with Weber (chap. 5, sec. 5). It is also the case with Boudon (1987, 46), an admirer of Weber's, who, while stating that any macrosocial fact M is to be explained as the outcome of a set of individual actions m, admits that, in turn, "the actions of individuals are made understandable, in the Weberian sense, by relating them to the social environment, the situation S, of the actors: $m = m(S)$. Finally, the situation itself has to be explained as the outcome of some macrosociological variables, or at least of some variables located at a higher level than S. Let us call these higher-level variables P, so that $S = S(P)$. On the whole, $M = M\{m[S(P)]\}$." (For a similar formulation, see Bunge 1985b, 116.) I submit that this is not individualism, but closet systemism like Mill's (1952 [1875], 586, 595–96). A consistent individualist would write equations only of the form $M = f(m)$.

Upholders of the so-called structural interdependence hypothesis, rampant in contemporary social studies, are guilty unwittingly of a similar inconsistency (see, e.g., J. W. Friedman 1977 and Coleman 1990). Let us glance at it. *Structural interdependence* means mutual dependence of agents through an impersonal third party, such as the market or the state. According to this hypothesis, each agent makes decisions in the light of the state of some social whole, but without any concern for the values, goals, intentions, or actions of his fellow agents. That is, everyone assumes that other people's actions are independent of his own and takes into consideration only the constraints imposed by the social matrix, which he takes as given and fixed. Thus, each individual is assumed to exert full control over the variables that interest him. In particular, each person's utility function is assumed to be independent of other people's utilities.

One flaw of this hypothesis is that it is at variance with reality. In fact, every one of us, with the possible exception of autistic patients and megalomaniacs, regulates his behavior by taking into account what other individuals may feel, think, or do. (Examples: conversation, face-to-face competition and cooperation, keeping up with the Joneses, and the bandwagon effect.)

A second defect of structural interdependence is this. The assumption that agents are connected only via a supra-individual agency, such as the market, and never come in touch with one another is actually a holistic hypothesis, just as the assumption of the mutual independence of agents is a typically individualistic one. In fact, the market, the institutional framework, and the "situation" are holistic skeletons in the individualist's closet. Thus the structural interdependence hypothesis combines the worst of individualism with the worst of holism. This unholy (and unwitting) alliance may be called 'individholism.' The differences between it and its rivals are shown schematically in figure 9.1.

What Bourricaud (1975) and Boudon (1979) call 'neo-individualism' is a more consistent stand and one close to systemism. Both admit that people are seldom fully rational, well informed, and free to act; but they insist (rightly) that individuals have "a strategic capacity with regard to the roles that are proposed to them." Further, they attribute to social constraints and the interference of others the "perverse effects" of individual and collective action pointed out by Marx and Keynes and more recently by G. Hardin. This self-styled "well-tempered Hobbesianism" comes close to systemism, for, unlike radical individualism, it does not deny the existence of social systems.

Likewise, contractualism, or social conventionalism, also called "institutional individualism," lies midway between individualism and systemism. Indeed, from Rousseau onward, contractualists have recognized the existence of distinct social "entities" such as societies, customs, and institutions. But, lacking a clear, comprehensive, consistent ontological framework, they fail to analyze the very notion of a social "entity," to the point of collecting in the same

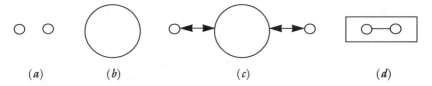

Fig. 9.1. (a) *Radical individualism: everyone for himself.* (b) *Holism or collectivism: the social whole is everything, the individual nothing.* (c) *Individholism: agents interact through an unanalyzed whole.* (d) *Systemism: interpersonal interactions build, maintain, or break up systems and are constrained by the overall structure.*

bag social systems, their functions, social norms, and traditions. Thus Agassi (1987, 147) defines society as "the *conventional means of co-ordination* between individual actions" (emphasis in original). This is confusing a thing (society) with one of its functions (coordination). And it involves exaggerating the role of contracts and conventions, which perform only a (modest) explanatory role and even then only during periods of stasis: they do not explain the emergence and breakdown of social systems. By contrast, social ties and conflicts, as well as shared (or conflicting) needs and beliefs—in sum, cooperation and competition—do explain social change. Contracts and conventions are made or unmade as features of the processes of the emergence or disintegration of social wholes. They are part of the glue, not the things glued. In sum, institutional individualism is muddled.

The failure of radical individualism has led many social scientists to move toward individholism, an inconsistent stand halfway between individualism and systemism. Thus Randall Collins (1987, 195) states that "macroconcepts are only words we apply to . . . aggregations of microencounters." But he immediately adds that "microevents, the behavior of individuals in situations, are themselves determined by where they are located in the larger network of microencounters around them in time and space" (1987, 196). Why not adopt a clear-cut consistent systemist viewpoint from the start?

4 Shortcomings of Individualism

By asserting the absolute primacy of the individual, as well as the legitimacy of the relentless pursuit of individual interests, individualism leads to a uniformitarian, ahistorical view of human nature. An epistemological partner of this ontological thesis is that there is no need for any specific sociological, economic, or politological categories and regularities. The result is utter failure to account for the peculiarities of different social systems, societies, social movements, and historical periods. This failure has disastrous practical consequences, as when the International Monetary Fund admonishes the Third

World to copy the First World, rather than tackle its own issues with its own resources.

Moreover, individualism is incapable of accounting for the emergence, decline, or even existence of social systems of any kind. In particular, it does not help elucidate any of the central notions of social science, such as those of social structure and social change mechanism. Nor does it help us to model social systems in a realistic fashion, for any minimally adequate model of a system will include the system's emergent properties, not all of which result from aggregation. For example, we all agree that a society is politically democratic if and only if every one of its citizens has the right to vote for its public officers and run for public office. At first blush this is a definition of an emergent property in terms of individual rights. But the definiens includes the concept of public office, which is irreducible to individualistic terms, for it makes sense only in relation to a political system.

Being incapable—nay, unwilling—to tackle social systems as emergents, individualism does not account even for individual behavior, which is always socially embedded and thus socially conditioned. Hence it ignores the problems of the micro-to-macro and macro-to-micro relations. (In particular, one will search in vain for any details on these problems in Weber's work.) Thus, it does not explain why one individual, who is competent but lacks the right connections, is not promoted, while another, who is incompetent but belongs to the right network, gets ahead.

It is naive or worse to pretend that all individuals are fully self-propelled and free to choose unless the government rides on their backs. Take, for example, the daily life of a worker. He wakes up an hour or two before his shift starts, a time set not just by his employer, but by the entire sector in which he works. He goes to work using a public transportation vehicle or a car pool—in either case a component of a sociotechnical system. He carries out a task assigned by his supervisor, who in turn acts on instructions of engineers and managers. The product of his work contributes to the social product of his firm, which delivers it to the market. Moreover, our worker interacts, both directly and indirectly, with fellow workers as well as with some officer in his union local—still another social system. At the end of the week, he receives a wad of bank notes issued by his government—the supreme political system of his country. This money will allow him to purchase a number of goods and services offered by other firms—and so on.

Our worker is, of course, free to quit his job and try elsewhere—provided there are openings and that he has skills on demand and belongs to some effective network. But what good does the freedom to change jobs, as well as to choose his breakfast cereal, do him if he lacks tenure and has no say in the running of his workplace, which is the very source of his subsistence? And are his bosses any freer from social constraints? Even the most powerful world leader is the prisoner of special interests and is constrained by circumstances. Of course, we are all free to some extent, but at some risk. Kant's fully autonomous individual is a philosopher's stone. We are all semi-autonomous and semi-heteronomous.

At one point Coleman (1964, 242) admitted that there is a practical obstacle to the implementation of the individualist project: namely, that it would require writing down and solving a system of n simultaneous equations, where n is the number of persons in the group of interest. (This would be the sociological analog of the n-body problem in physics.) But even if these equations were known, which they are not, an even greater difficulty would remain, namely this: No proposition regarding an isolated individual could possibly be both true and relevant to social science, for every individual lives and acts in a number of social systems, in which he interacts with other persons. In other words, the above-mentioned n equations would have to be supplemented by at least as many equations representing interpersonal exchanges, as well as the environmental constraints on individual actions and interactions. The analog of the latter in continuum mechanics, field theory, and quantum theory is constituted by constraints and boundary conditions. (Not even physical atomism abides by philosophical atomism: see Bunge 1991c.)

In short, ontological individualism yields an "undersocialized" view of man and society (Granovetter 1985), just as holism proposes an "oversocialized" picture (Wrong 1961). We should therefore steer clear of both extremes, as well as of the crypto-holism involved in what we have called individholism. So much for ontological individualism, whether straight or diluted.

Unsurprisingly, methodological individualism inherits all the shortcomings of ontological individualism. Familiar examples of irreducibly systemic (or emergent) categories in social science are those of public good, state, social order, institution, legal system, state, wealth distribution, capitalism, history, and progress. Even key notions of microeconomics, such as those of scarcity, market demand, price, and equilibrium, are irreducible to (undefinable in terms of) individual actions.

If consistent, the methodological individualist will attempt to reconstruct the feelings, ideas, valuations, and intentions of all his agents—who, in the case of history, are no longer available for questioning. To accomplish his task, he can count on few, if any, reliable data concerning a few heroes or knaves. (Who but an omniscient deity could get to know what goes on in the brains of myriads of individuals at any given instant?) In view of the scarcity of personal data, the methodological individualist has only two options: either he makes up the required information, or he assumes that it is irrelevant, because all human beings are alike and satisfy the same laws (e.g., they are all rational maximizers). If he chooses the first procedure, he may claim to be a storyteller but certainly not a scientist. If the second, he must show that he uses well-confirmed, universal psychological generalizations. This is exactly what all the neoclassical economists, particularly the founding fathers—Walras, Jevons, Menger, Pareto, and Marshall—claimed to do. But in fact none of them used any findings of experimental psychology—particularly the recent discovery that real people are not habitual maximizers. (Moreover, Dilthey, Weber, Hayek, Popper, and other individualists have explicitly stated, though not argued, that social science is in no need of psychology.)

Hence, to carry out his program, the methodological individualist is forced to make up psychological laws. But few have admitted that this is what they actually do, and, consequently, that they write fiction rather than science. Only Simmel (1923 [1892]), a radical individualist and idealist, was candid enough to admit that the individualist must frame a "formal" or "abstract" psychology—that is, one that does not bother to test its hypotheses. In short, the methodological individualist faces a dilemma. And whether he solves it by making up data or psychological laws, he does not behave like a scientist.

As for the political and moral (or behavioral) individualist, his maxims are at best innocuous, at worst obnoxious: innocuous for ignoring the social constraints on individual action, obnoxious for underrating, or even ignoring altogether, our duties to others, in particular our civic duties. In fact, individualism is socially dissolving and incompatible with political democracy (Tocqueville 1952–70 [1835]; Bunge 1989; Camps 1993). Indeed, freedom can be enjoyed only among peers: if some individuals are more powerful (economically, politically, or culturally) than others, they will be able to clip the wings of the weaker. Equality and freedom are mutually complementary, not exclusive.

In short, individualism is scientifically, morally, and politically untenable. Its sole virtue is its opposition to holism, but this it shares with systemism.

5 Holism

Holism (or organicism, or collectivism) is the exact opposite of individualism: it negates every one of the latter's theses. In particular, it holds that nature and society are "organic wholes" which cannot be understood by breaking them down into their components. Holism is attractive at first sight because of its insistence on the need to study everything as a part of some whole and for its thesis that "the whole is greater than the sum of its parts"—a clumsy way of saying that wholes possess (emergent) properties that their parts lack. However, we shall argue that holism is even more inadequate than individualism.

Ontological holism is inherent in aggressive nationalism and in traditionalist communitarianism (or communalism), which opposes the cohesive *Gemeinschaft* (community) to the atomized *Gesellschaft* (society) (see Tönnies 1979 [1887]). It is also inherent in the German historical school headed by G. Schmoller and in the institutionalist economics founded by T. Veblen.

Likewise, Ibn Khaldûn, the only medieval social scientist; the conservatives Edmund Burke, Adam Müller, and Hegel; Comte, the mature Marx, Tolstoy, Durkheim, Tönnies, Malinowski, Gini, and Parsons, unlikely bedfellows though they may seem, were holists. In fact, they all held that society precedes the individual and shapes his every feeling, thought, and action. The immediate methodological consequence of this ontological thesis is that social studies have to be of the top-down (or macro-to-micro) kind. The moral, political, and legal consequences are just as obvious: the individual must bow to the superior interests of the group; duties dominate rights.

Thus, in a famous passage, Marx stated: "Upon the different forms of property, upon the social conditions of existence, rises an entire superstructure of distinct and peculiarly formed sentiments, illusions, modes of thought and views of life. The entire class creates and forms them out of its material foundations and out of the corresponding social relations. The single individual derives them through tradition and upbringing" (Marx 1986 [1852], 118–19). Likewise, Durkheim (1970, 250) writes: "[S]ocial life must be explained, not by the conceptions of those who participate in it, but by the deep causes which lie outside consciousness." In both cases the individual is treated not as an agent, but as a patient at the mercy of social forces, economic in the case of Marx, spiritual in that of Durkheim. Moreover, both men claimed that ideas are held by social groups and constitute social facts—determined for Marx, determiners for Durkheim.

Ontological holism is inherent in anthropological and sociological functionalism: remember, for example, Radcliffe-Brown and Parsons. Functionalism holds that every social item, however destructive or morally repugnant it may seem, discharges a useful function, one that contributes to the preservation of society. It emphasizes cohesion through solidarity and consensus, overlooks conflict, and minimizes the role of power and coercion. Likewise, Bourdieu (1989) is a holist, since he regards the individual as a product of a "field" or social whole existing above individuals. Thus an artist exists only because there is an artistic field; in turn, a field is "a system of objective relations" prior to and above their relata—an obvious logical howler. Holism is also evident in the collectivist subjectivism of the constructivist-relativist sociology of science, which claims that all "scientific facts" are social constructions or conventions (see chap. 7, sec. 6). It underlies the anti-psychiatry movement, according to which mental disorders are not brain malfunctions but nonadaptive reactions to social pathologies. Holism is tacit among management experts who write about a firm's goals, intentions, and strategies, as if it had a brain of its own. Last, but not least, the best, most beautiful exposition of holism is Tolstoy's monumental *War and Peace*.

As for methodological holism, it is upheld by all those who, like the anthropologists and sociologists influenced by intuitionism, phenomenology, and related philosophies, reject analysis or underrate mathematical modeling and even statistics. Moreover, a holistic morality is obvious in every totalitarian ideology, since for such an ideology individuals are only tools in the service of some higher whole such as the People, the Nation, the Church, or the Cause.

Let us now ferret out and collect the general ontological, methodological, and axiologico-moral principles of holism as they relate to social studies. *Ontological holism* can be compressed into the following theses:

OH1. A society is a whole transcending its members.

OH2. A society has gestalt, or global, properties. These properties are emergent: that is, irreducible to any properties of the parts.

OH3. Societies behave as units. The interaction between two societies is a whole–whole affair. Society acts on its members far more strongly than these react upon society. Further, social change is supra-individual, though it affects the individual members of society.

The *epistemological*, or *methodological*, theses matching the preceding social ontological theses are these:

EH1. Any proper social study is a study of social wholes.

EH2. Social facts are explainable only in terms of supra-individual units such as the state or supra-individual forces such as collective memory, the will of the people, national destiny, and historical fate. Individual behavior is understandable (though perhaps not rationally explainable) in terms of the action of the entire society upon the person.

EH3. Hypotheses and theories in social science are either beyond empirical testing (unscientific holism) or are testable only against macro-data (science-oriented holism).

Finally, *moral holism* boils down to the following principles:

MH1. Social wholes are maximally valuable.

MH2. The summum bonum is the whole, together with the duty to preserve it.

MH3. Individuals are valuable only to the extent that they pursue the good of the totality.

Let us now evaluate all the above theses, beginning with ontological holism. It is true that social systems are wholes with emergent properties such as viability and stability. Consequently they behave as wholes; in particular, they interact and change as wholes in certain regards. For example, a school (or a factory or an entire nation) may advance or decline as a whole, even if the competence and industry of its individual components remains roughly constant. (Sometimes progress or decline may be attributed to the type of organization, i.e., to the way the components of the system interact among themselves and with members of other social systems.)

But it is false that social systems hover above their components and lead, as it were, a life of their own: there is no system without components. Social systems are nothing but systems of interconnected persons together with their artifacts. Nor is it true that all global or systemic properties are emergent: some of them, such as demographic variables (e.g., total population and birth and death rates), are resultant—so much so that they are obtained by mere aggregation. Nor can society act upon its members. What is true is that individual agency is constrained by social structure: that is, the behavior of each individual is determined not only by his genetic makeup and his development, but also by his place in society. (E.g., morbidity and longevity depend on socioeconomic status: see McKeown 1979.) Finally, social change is indeed global, by definition, but it is effected by individual action. (E.g., Tolstoy tells us that, upon occupying Moscow in 1812, Napoleon's experienced, disciplined soldiers scattered throughout the city and became marauders. From then on "the army *qua* army ceased to exist.") In sum, ontological holism does not tell the whole truth.

How about methodological holism? I submit that EH1 is true by the very definition of social science. But the other two principles have at best a grain of truth each, and they inhibit research rather than stimulate it. Thus, the functionalist principle EH2 rightly suggests looking for the function(s) of the part in the whole; but, since it takes the latter for granted, it fails to explain its emergence, subsistence, or decline. And EH3 is unduly restrictive: social psychologists, anthropologists, sociologists, microeconomists, and historians often collect information about individuals in an effort to understand the behavior of systems. For example, how are we to uncover the mechanisms of the current decline of such traditional institutions as the family, the labor union, and the church unless we get information about the behavior of their members as well as about society at large?

In general, wholes, social or others, must be studied not only at their own level but also as complex entities. Social circumstances constrain and stimulate individual behavior but do not determine it fully: spontaneity and creativity, hence bounded freedom, are for real, after all (recall chap. 8, sec. 4). If they were not, deviance and rebellion would be unexplainable. Finally, to explain social facts, we need and in fact often use data about individuals as well as about social systems. For example, recovery from an economic recession may be explained as an effect of the return of consumer confidence, hence increased spending, in view of the hope generated by a new government.

Methodological holism is nothing but intuitionism, which conflicts with both rationalism and empiricism. According to intuitionism, we grasp wholes in a direct, immediate way. Analysis, when necessary at all, comes only after perceiving or intuiting the whole, because the part can be understood only by the role it performs in the whole. Intuitionism is obscurantist, because of the subordinate roles it assigns to both reason and experience and because of its dogmatic claim that intuition supplies instant, complete, deep, and final truths. (A detailed examination of intuitionism will be made in chap. 12, sec. 1.)

As for moral holism, it clearly enjoins moral heteronomy. It comes in two versions: moderate and radical. Moderate moral holism enjoins us all to work and make sacrifices for the common good. This includes helping the poor through private charity and social legislation. It is the moral philosophy underlying "Tory socialism" from Disraeli onward, the Roman Catholic social policy proclaimed by Pope Leo XIII, and present-day communitarianism. By contrast, radical moral holism advocates abject submission to the powers that be. It is the morality which totalitarian leaders would like their subjects to adopt and practice. Remember the fascist slogan: *Believe, obey, fight.* Though quite different from each other, neither variety of moral holism encourages individual responsibility and the enjoyment of life.

To conclude: Holism contains a couple of ontological nuggets: the theses that there are wholes, which differ from mere aggregates, and that they have emergent properties. But methodological holism is obscurantist, and moral holism degrading. No wonder, then, that no serious student of society has been a consistent ontological, epistemological, and moral holist.

Individualism and holism are not arbitrary inventions. Tocqueville (1952–70 [1835], pt. II, chaps. 1–4) conjectured that the former represents the fragmentation of capitalist societies, whereas holism fits roughly the cohesiveness of medieval societies. However, neither of these views accounts faithfully for any society. Ontological individualism fails because of its radical reductionism—a reductionism that does not work even in physics. Its methodological partner fails because it overlooks data and hypotheses concerning systemic behavior. And moral individualism does not work, either because it undermines viable moral and social norms, or because it encourages antisocial behavior. We must look for an alternative to individualism, then. However, this alternative should retain the valid individualist theses that social facts are "ultimately" the result of individual actions and that the study of society requires reason and experience in addition to intuition.

The opposite of individualism—namely, holism—fares even worse. Due to its anti-analytic stand, holism has attracted not only scholars who have realized the real shortcomings of individualism, but also many irrationalists. It is subscribed to by practitioners of holistic "medicine," proponents of the Gaia hypothesis, and the anti-scientific wings of the feminist and environmentalist movements, particularly New Age feminism and "deep ecology." Holism also attracts all those who think that individuals exist for the sake of State, Church, or party, rather than the other way round. No wonder holism is common to all authoritarian ideologies. Because science involves analysis along with synthesis, holism is not the correct alternative to individualism. It is not enough to point out that a triangle, a body of water, and a government have features that their components lack: we also want to know how these components combine to constitute systems. We need such knowledge both to understand systems and to manage them.

With regard to society, holism is the no-person view, just as individualism is the no-society view. Consequently, neither of them can guide effectively the study of social facts, in particular, micro–macro relations. No wonder that the best contemporary social researchers overcome the holism–individualism opposition (see, e.g., Boudon and Bourricaud 1986, 210–12). They adopt, albeit tacitly in most cases, the systemist view, to be expounded in the next chapter.

10 :: *Systemism*

The alternative to both individualism and holism is systemism, since it accounts for both individual and system and, in particular, for individual agency and social structure. Indeed, systemism postulates that everything is a system or a component of one. And it models every system as a triple ⟨composition, environment, structure⟩, or CES for short, so it encompasses the valid features of its rivals. Furthermore, systemism offers some globalizing principles that prevent the specialist from getting bogged down in details and thus losing perspective. (For details see Bunge 1979*a*, 1979*b*. For earlier essays on systemism, see Buckley 1968 and Optner 1973.) These claims will be justified below.

I submit that most social scientists adopt systemism in their everyday work, even if they pay lip service to either individualism or holism. Sometimes, however, they adopt different approaches in different fields. (Thus Marx, a systemist in economics, adopted holism in sociology and individualism in politology. And Pareto, an individualist in economics, was a pioneer of systemic sociology.) Systemists explain social systems in terms of individual actions and the latter in terms of social context. For example, they characterize the roles that individuals enact by reference to the social systems (e.g., business firms or government departments) in which they are active. (Recall the proverbial case of the bewildered tribesman who visits a bank without ever having heard about legal tender or interest rate: Mandelbaum 1955.) They characterize such systems in global terms—for example, by the kinds of goods or services they supply or by their relations to other systems.

And they study systemic features such as cohesiveness, equilibrium, progress, and their duals.

Yet systemism has often been misunderstood or attacked. One such misunderstanding consists in the fuzzy characterization of a system as an "organic whole," which invites biological metaphors. Of course, all organisms are systems, but the converse is false. For example, atoms and rigid bodies, as well as clubs and business firms, are systems, but there is nothing literally "organic" about them: they are not alive. Another such misunderstanding consists in a woolly notion of a system. Thus the most famous historical sociologist of the day writes: "[A] basic tenet of my work is that societies are not systems" (Mann 1993, 736). What are they, then? "Societies are constituted of multiple overlapping and intersecting sociospatial networks of power" (Mann 1986, 1). But all networks are systems, hence all social networks are social systems, so the preceding sentence boils down to: Societies are (supersystems) composed of social systems held together by power relations. Shorter: Society is a system of systems. (Do not ask what "sociospatial network" means in the sentence quoted above, or the difference between overlap and intersection. Mann does not elucidate.)

A third common misunderstanding is the belief that systemism overlooks social conflict and change. This is indeed how some functionalists and followers of Parsons have conceived of social systems. But this is a narrow, mistaken construal: any adequate theory of social systems will make ample room for conflict (as well as cooperation) and change.

Still, we must admit that, in addition to these misunderstandings, there are two *legitimate* grievances against the "systems theory" of some social scientists. One is that it is so vague as to be trivial and indistinguishable from holism. The other is that some "systems theorists" believe that a single theory can explain social facts of all kinds, which renders empirical research unnecessary. This, of course, is a serious mistake, for systemism is only an approach, and every general systems theory is just a skeleton to be fleshed out with specific hypotheses and data concerning the particular kind of system of interest. However, neither reproach can be leveled against systemism per se.

1 The Systemic Approach

Recall that an approach, or way of looking at things or handling them, is made up of a body of background knowledge together with a set of problems (problematics), a set of aims, and a set of methods (methodics) for wrestling with such problems: $\mathcal{A} = \langle B, P, A, M \rangle$ (chap. 3, sec. 1). Since the systemic approach is hypergeneral, the only items that can occur in its background knowledge are certain philosophical hypotheses. These consist essentially in an ontological principle and its epistemological counterpart. The former is the principle that every concrete thing is either a system or a component of such. Its epistemological partner is the norm that every system must be studied on its own level, as well as analyzed into its interacting components. So much for the first component of $\mathcal{A}$.

The problematics of the systemic approach is the totality of problems, cognitive or practical, that may be posed concerning systems of any kind. Its aims, like those of science and technology, are to describe, understand, predict, and control. And its methodics includes analysis as well as synthesis, generalization as well as systematization, mathematical modeling, and empirical testing in the laboratory or in the field. Thus the systemic approach is applicable in every discipline and retains the positive aspects of atomism (attention to individual components) as well as holism (attention to the whole).

Failure to adopt the systemic approach to the study or design of systems of any kind is bound to result in failure to address some of the issues concerned or, worse, to create pointless problems. By contrast, adoption of the systemic approach will avoid the pitfalls of tunnel vision which the narrow specialist invariably falls into, incapable as he is of taking into account any features that are not studied in his field. In other words, systemism favors interdisciplinarity and multidisciplinarity. By the same token, it helps to avoid the costly mistakes made by the specialist—scientist or technologist, policymaker or manager—who overlooks most of the features of the real system he studies, designs, or steers. A few examples will illustrate this point.

A sociologist may miss the most important features of the system of interest if he ignores either the needs and beliefs of its members or the macro-systems in which the system of interest is embedded. An economist will not build realistic models of any economic system if he pays attention only to its individual components, overlooking the relations among them, the environmental constraints, or the effects of political and cultural circumstances. The statesman will not introduce effective new legislation aimed at addressing social issues unless he realizes that these are multidimensional: environmental, bio-psychological, cultural, economic, and political. Moral: A necessary—but, alas, insufficient—condition for efficient policymaking is the adoption of a systemic view of society. The preceding may be compressed into the following postulate:

Every real thing is either a system or a component of a system; every construct is a component of at least one conceptual system; every symbol is a component of at least one symbolic system; and every research field is a component of the system of human knowledge.

This assumption entails, among others, the following consequences. First, studying or designing a concrete thing as if it were simple and isolated, and working in a discipline as if it had no neighbors worth cultivating, can get one only so far. Second, anything other than the universe which is not a component of some system is unreal. Third, any discipline that borrows nothing from, and gives nothing in return to, other disciplines is worthless.

Now two words of caution against confusing the systemic approach with what is loosely called "systems theory": first, whereas the former is an approach that can be used as a scaffolding for the construction of theories, "systems theory" is actually a collection of theories used mostly in advanced technology, such as linear systems theory, general control theory, automata theory, and statistical information theory; second, the so-called systems theories found in social studies and popular in the 1960s and 1970s have fallen into some disrepute, the verbal ones having been discredited for being just rehashed, flabby holistic doctrines, and the more precise ones for boiling down to either box-and-arrow or flow diagrams that exaggerate the weight of environmental variables and overlook internal variables, such as interest and intention, as well as mechanisms and processes. But to reject the systemic approach just because in some cases it has been wrongly implemented is a case of throwing out the baby along with the bathwater.

Finally, the systemic approach is not the same as systems analysis, although the former underlies the latter. Systems analysis studies concrete systems by building mathematical models, then running these on computers, so as to observe and forecast their performance. This procedure is perfectly legitimate as long as (*a*) the models are checked independently against data, and (*b*) computer simulation is not regarded as a substitute for empirical testing (see Dawson 1962). The method is particularly useful when the equations in the model are not tractable in exact form—for example, because they are nonlinear. A philosophical offshoot of systems analysis is that analysis is the enemy not of wholeness but of obscurity. The fact that in some cases systems analysis has been shallow and that in others it has been used for evil political purposes is beside the point, for all tools, from knives to words, can be misused.

2 Systemism in Social Science

Let us now look at society and social science from a systemic viewpoint. To begin with, the *social ontology of systemism* is reducible to the following principles:

OS1. Society is a system of changing subsystems.

OS2. Being a system, society has systemic, or global, properties. While some of these are resultant (or reducible), others are emergent, though rooted in the individual components and their interplay.

OS3. Interaction between two social systems is an individual–individual affair, where each individual acts on behalf of the system he represents. The members of a social system can act severally upon a single individual, and the behavior of each individual is determined by the place he holds in society, as well as by his genetic endowment, experience, and expectations. And every social change is a change in the structure of a society, hence a change at both the social and the individual levels.

The matching theses of *systemic epistemology or methodology*, as regards social science, are as follows:

ES1. Social science is the study of social systems: their changing composition, environment, and structure.

ES2. Social facts are to be accounted for (described, explained, or forecast) in terms of social systems and their individual components—with their needs, wants, beliefs, intentions, actions, and interactions—in their natural and social environment. In turn, individual behavior is to be accounted for in terms of all the relevant features, biological, psychological, and social, of the individual-in-society.

ES3. Hypotheses and theories in social science are to be tested against environmental and social (in particular, demographic, sociological, economic, political, and cultural) data. However, some social data are built out of data concerning individuals, for these alone are directly observable.

Finally, *moral systemism* can be compressed into the following principles:

MS1. Whereas all individuals can be valuable, the more valuable ones are those who render useful services to others.

MS2. Enjoying (biopsychosocial) well-being and helping others to live constitute the summum bonum.

MS3. The only legitimate function of a social system is to promote the (biopsychosocial) well-being of its members or those of other social systems, without preventing anyone from meeting his basic needs.

I submit that the systemic ontology of society retains the grains of truth found in both social individualism and social holism. In particular, it shares with the former the idea that individuals, not impersonal social forces, are ultimately the prime movers of society; it refrains from reifying social groups unless their members happen to constitute a system; and it requires that certain holistic sentences be translated into sentences referring to individuals-in-their-environment. Thus, instead of saying that society punishes deviant behavior, we had better say that some members of any society punish any members of it who behave in a deviant manner. However, this statement does not involve a reduction to individuals, for it contains the irreducible (though analyzable) concepts of society and of deviance. That the former is irreducible follows from the assumption SO1 that, far from being an aggregate, society is a system. That "deviance" is not reducible either follows from the observation that this concept only makes sense relative to what is taken to be normal behavior in a given society. Let us take a closer look at these complementary concepts. We shall see that analysis, frowned upon by holists, need not be reductionistic.

The dual concepts of normal and deviant behavior are not purely individualistic, because they involve the concept of a society: they represent a mutual property of an individual and a social system. (This holds for every feature studied by social psychologists.) Yet this mutual property (or variable) can be analyzed (explained) in terms of properties of individuals and their social positions or roles. Thus, consider an individual property P, such as performance, work satisfaction, income, or number of books read per year. Assume, for the sake of simplicity, that P has been correctly quantified and that the data show that, in society S, the distribution of P around the mean $E(P)$ is roughly bell-shaped, with standard deviation σ. Then we can make the following definitions:

For any member x of S:

x conforms in S with respect to $P =_{df} |P(x) - E(P)| < \sigma$;

x is deviant in S with respect to $P =_{df} x$ does not conform in S with respect to P.

In these formulas $E(P)$ and σ are collective properties of the society, S, whereas P is a property of an arbitrary member, x, of it. However, both are statistical artifacts rather than emergent properties of S, since they characterize mere aggregates as well as systems. But the point is that both collective properties are computable from individual data.

This example shows that while the individualist refuses to countenance wholeness and the holist extols it but refuses to analyze it, the systemist recognizes wholes and encourages their analysis. He takes the best of the two worlds of ideas and is thus in the best position to distinguish what belongs to society from what belongs to its individual members. No wonder, then, that most social scientists from Aristotle on, regardless of their declared philosophies, adopt a systemic viewpoint insofar as they study groups of interrelated individuals (in particular, their structure and evolution) and recognize the specificity of social systems such as formal organizations. (For the typical position of the practicing sociologist, see Blau 1974.) Nowadays only some philosophers and ideologists are either radical individualists or radical holists (see Brodbeck 1968; Krimerman 1969; O'Neill 1973). As for the epistemology of systemism, it coincides with that of scientific realism. It is thus opposed to the intuitionism inherent in holism and avoids the risk of subjectivism inherent in individualism. Finally, a systemist morality promotes both self-interest and solidarity and is thus equidistant from moral individualism, or selfishness, and moral collectivism, the morality of the tyrant for use of his subjects. It coincides with agathonism (see chap. 8, sec. 5).

Since I view the problematics and the metatheory of social science from a systemic perspective, it would be good to illustrate the latter. I shall do so by examining four key ideas in social science: those of social system, social structure, social change, and micro–macro links. (For details see Bunge 1974*b*, 1979*b*, 1981*c*.)

3 Social System

I begin by defining the general concept of a system, whether concrete, conceptual, or symbolic. A *system* is a complex object, every part or component of which is related to some other component(s) of the same object (e.g., families, schools, firms, and informal networks). An object is a *subsystem* if it is both a system and part of another system (e.g., universities and governments). And an object is a *supersystem* if it is composed of systems (e.g., a chain of supermarkets or an entire society).

(I do not adopt the standard definition of a system as a *set* of interrelated elements, because sets are concepts, whereas some systems, such as social ones, are concrete. Second, a set has a fixed membership: once a member, always a member; whereas the composition of a concrete system may change over time.)

We distinguish three main kinds of system: conceptual, concrete, and symbolic. A *conceptual* (or formal) system is a system all the components of which are conceptual (e.g., propositions, classifications, and hypothetico-deductive systems—i.e., theories). A *concrete* (or material) system is a system all the components of which are concrete, or changing (e.g., atoms, organisms, and societies). And a *symbolic* (or *semiotic*) system is a concrete system some components of which stand for or represent other objects (e.g., languages, computer diskettes, and diagrams). (By contrast, a collection of commercial posters is not a system.)

The simplest representation of a concrete system at any given time is the list of its composition, environment, and structure (see chap. 4, sec. 1). We call this kind of sketch the CES model and write it thus: $m(s) = \langle C(s), E(s), S(s) \rangle$. The first component of this ordered triple, the *composition*, $C(s)$, of s, is the collection of the parts of s at the time concerned (e.g., the members of a tribe). The *environment*, $E(s)$, of s is the collection of things not in s that are connected to parts of s (e.g., the physical surroundings of a tribe plus the human outsiders with whom members of the tribe have relationships). And the *structure*, $S(s)$, of s is the collection of relations among the members of s plus the relations among these and those of $E(s)$. The former will be called the 'endostructure,' the latter the 'exostructure' of the system (e.g., the endotribal kinship relations and the trade relations between the tribe and outsiders, respectively). The part of the system whose components are linked directly to environmental items may be called the system *boundary* (e.g., the representatives, salesmen, and PR officers of a business firm constitute the latter's boundary). On this definition, a system boundary need not have a definite geometric shape (Bunge 1992*b*). In particular, social systems, unlike organisms, are shapeless. And, unlike Parsons's definition (1951, 481ff.), our definition of a system does not include the condition of boundary constancy.

A *social system* is a concrete system composed of gregarious animals that (*a*) share an environment and (*b*) act upon other members of the system, directly or indirectly, in ways that are cooperative in at least one respect. A *human social system* is a social system composed of human beings and their artifacts. (Durkheim 1897 noted the need to include artifacts, such as tools and roads.) Caution: Cohorts, occupational groups, and social classes are not systems. Social classes, like biological species, are variable collections. By contrast, labor unions, like biopopulations, are concrete systems.

Another concept worth noting is that of a network (Polanyi 1944; Lorrain and White 1971; Granovetter 1974). A network is a system representable as a graph: that is, a collection of nodes connected (fully or partially) by edges (not arrows). A *social network* is a network composed of gregarious animals (e.g., people) and artifacts (e.g., collections of close and distant relatives, circles of friends, clubs, scientific communities, Internet). A social network is held together by pro-social feelings (e.g., of friendship and solidarity) and acts of reciprocity, rather than relations of dominance: it is informal and nonhierarchical. All networks are systems, but the converse is false. For example, a formal organization is a system, but not a network. Ditto a market. But every participant in a market is a member of at least one network and often deals through it (Granovetter 1985).

Two kinds of social system are often distinguished: natural or spontaneous, on the one hand, and artificial or formal (organizations), on the other. Whereas the former are self-organized, the latter are designed, set up, maintained, transformed, or dismantled in accordance with explicit goals, plans, and rules. Thus families, street-corner gangs, and information networks are spontaneous social systems, though not all of them natural, whereas schools, firms, and government departments are organizations.

We assume that, in contrast to animal societies, a *human society* is a social system composed of four subsystems: (*a*) the *biological* or *kinship* system, whose members are held together by relations of descent, sex, reproduction, child rearing, or friendship; (*b*) the *economic* system, held together by relations of production and exchange; (*c*) the *political* system, whose specific function is to manage the social activities in the society; and (*d*) the *cultural* system, whose members are busy discovering or inventing, teaching or learning, designing or planning, singing or dancing, advising or healing, or engaging in similar activities which are not primarily biological, economic, or political. This is the *quadripartite*, or BEPC, model of society (Bunge 1979*b*).

Clans, bands, factories, schools, hospitals, sports teams, clubs, car pools, churches, armies, and political parties are social systems, whereas hamlets, towns, provinces, and nations are that and more: they are societies. There are also human *supersocieties*, or systems composed of two or more societies, such as the European Community and the former USSR. Finally, there is the *world* (social) system: that is, the human supersociety born in 1492, and composed of all human societies.

A social *process* (or activity) is a process occurring in a social system, like getting married or rearing children, working together or fighting, trading commodities or information, organizing or disorganizing. Obviously, there are social processes of all sizes, from those occurring in families to worldwide ones. Finally, a *social movement* is a mass social process occurring in at least one artificial system (or organization) and dragging along a number of people not belonging to the latter (e.g., social reform movements and the popular diffusion of new artifacts or customs).

So much for definitions. Let us now put them to work with reference to social systems. Here are some generalizations, every one of which contains at least one of the concepts defined above.

1. Every human being is a member of at least one social system; hence there are no totally marginal persons: even marginal people in a shantytown build their own systems in order to survive (Lomnitz 1977).

2. Social systems are held together by links of various kinds: biological, psychological, economic, political, or cultural; hence it is mistaken to privilege any one type of link.

3. A person's beliefs, preferences, expectations, choices, and actions are socially conditioned by his membership in social systems; but it does not follow that mental states are social processes or that all ideas have a social content.

4. Every social system has a specific function, one that no system of another kind can perform; but it does not follow that every social system is beneficial to all its members.

5. Every social system is engaged, at any time, in some process or other, an assumption that should allay the fear of those who believe that talk of systems presupposes immobility, or at least stability.

6. A system's changes result from either endogenous changes in its components or interactions among its components or among some of these and environmental items.

7. Every social process or activity modifies the state of the social system(s) in or between which it occurs.

8. All members of a social system cooperate in some respects but compete in others; this thesis combines Marx's emphasis on conflict with Durkheim's on solidarity.

9. As long as it is not violent, hence destructive, competition stimulates initiative and innovation, whereas cooperation favors cohesion and security.

10. A social system emerges (spontaneously or by design) if and only if it is perceived as promising to meet some of the needs or wants of some of its members.

11. A social system breaks down (peacefully or otherwise) if and only if it ceases to benefit most of its members, or if the losses caused by internal conflicts are perceived to outweigh the benefits of cooperation.

12. The performance of a social system improves through competition as long as the latter does not destroy the bonds that hold the system together.

Let us now turn from social systems to the systemic approach in social studies. In a preliminary study we need only the following two postulates.

S1. Every social system can be analyzed into its composition (persons and artifacts), environment (natural or social), and structure (the collection of biological, economic, political, and cultural relations): $m(s) = \langle C, E, S \rangle$.

S2. The social sciences study social systems and their subsystems and super-systems.

These two assumptions, together with some of the preceding definitions, imply the following consequences among others. First, an adequate under-standing of any social system involves the (empirical and theoretical) investiga-tion of its composition, environment, and structure. Second, an adequate understanding of any society involves the (empirical and theoretical) investiga-tion of its biological (or kinship), economic, political, and cultural subsystems. Third, no particular social science is self-sufficient. Fourth, because all concrete things are changeable, the social sciences ought to study social dynamics. Fifth, the efficient management of a social system involves a consideration of its changeable composition, environment, and structure.

If the preceding is admitted, if only for the sake of argument, then the strengths and weaknesses of the alternatives to the systemic view of society become apparent. The strength of holism lies in its emphasis on the qualitative difference between a society and its components; its weakness in its rejection of analysis in general, in particular our CES analysis into composition, environ-ment, and structure. As for individualism, its strength lies in its attention to the members of social systems, in particular their mental lives; its weakness in its minimization of material constraints and stimuli. The *forte* of environmen-talism (in particular, behaviorism and ecologism) lies in its study of environ-mental constraints and stimuli; its weakness in its minimization of individual initiative and social structure. Finally, the strength of structuralism lies in its attention to the bonds among people; its weakness in its minimization of the role of individuals and their environment. Besides, Lévi-Strauss and Bourdieu, like Marx, are guilty of the logical fallacy of trying to define individuals and groups as sets of relations—as if there could be relations without relata (see, e.g., Bourdieu 1968).

I submit that systemism has all the virtues and none of the shortcomings of the alternatives. I will now proceed to show its value in exactifying two key notions that usually occur in a fuzzy state (see Bunge 1974*b* and 1979*b* for details).

4 Social Structure and Social Change

We have defined the structure of a system as the collection of relations among members of the system plus those between them and environmental items. We now distinguish two kinds of relation: *binding* and *nonbinding*. A bond, or tie, is a relation that makes a difference to the entities it connects. Only binding relations contribute to holding the components of a system together and thus qualify as members of the structure of the system. For example, relations of trade and employment, as well as those of cooperation and competition, are among the binding social relations and thus belong to the structure of a social system. By contrast, relations of being older or more educated than, or residing north of, are not binding. (Spatiotemporal relations, which are of the non-binding kind, only render the emergence of some ties possible; e.g., in most traditional societies being older than implies wielding more power than.)

Social bonds or connections are relations among different people: they do not hold between an individual and himself. In other words, they are not reflexive. A fortiori, they are not equivalence relations such as, for example, that of equal occupation, for these are reflexive, symmetric, and transitive. (R is an equivalence relation in a set S if and only if for any members x, y, z of S, (a) Rxx; (b) if Rxy, then Ryx; and (c) if Rxy and Ryz, then Rxz.) The methodological interest of equivalence relations lies in the fact that they allow one to partition the population of a social system into pairwise disjoint homogeneous groups, or equivalence classes, such as the classes of married and unmarried people, traders and nontraders, and so on. Every occupational group and every social class is an equivalence class, but neither is a system.

Since most social ties are not equivalence relations, they do not lend themselves to splitting a population into homogeneous groups, such as social classes. Think of the relations of working, employing, buying, voting, or teaching: none of them is reflexive, symmetric, or transitive. However, any such relation can be associated with one or more equivalence relations. Consider, for example, the relation of teaching: it generates the classes of teachers, the taught, and those who are neither. Every one of these is an equivalence class, for any two members of it stand in an equivalence relation. Indeed, all teachers, however different, are equivalent in that they teach; likewise students and those who neither teach nor study. We have thus partitioned the initial population into three pairwise disjoint classes of individuals who are equivalent in one respect.

What holds for binary relations, such as that of teaching, holds for higher-order relations, such as that of buying. This is a ternary relation: x buys y from z. By seizing on the first variable, we form the class of buyers; on the second, that of commodities; on the third, that of sellers; finally, the complement of the union of all three classes is the group of items in the given collection that are neither buyers nor goods nor sellers. The original collection has thus been partitioned into four pairwise disjoint equivalence classes.

In general, an equivalence relation $\sim_k$ in a collection S induces the splitting of S into n_k disjoint equivalence classes. The family of all such groups is designated $S/\sim_k$ and is called the quotient set of S by $\sim_k$. Call S_{ik} the ith member of this family. If the equivalence class $\sim_k$ is rooted in a social relation, we call S_{ik} a 'social cell.' In other words, every equivalence relation $\sim_k$ based on a social relation induces a partition P_k of the original collection S into n_k pairwise, disjoint social cells S_{ik}; that is, $P_k = S/\sim_k = \{S_{ik} | 1 \le i \le n_k\}$.

Suppose, now, that an empirical synchronic study of a social system s with composition (membership) S has led us to identify a certain number of social cells in it, such as those whose members have (roughly) the same occupation and the same income, adopt (roughly) the same political attitude, or have (roughly) the same number of school years. Every such social group S_{ik} may be construed as being generated by some equivalence relation $\sim_k$, where k ranges between 1 and m, the total number of relations being considered. We stipulate that the social structure $S(s)$ of the given social system s equals the family of all such homogeneous (equivalence) classes. That is, we set

$$S(s) = \{P_k | 1 \le k \le m\}, \text{ where } P_k = S/\sim_k.$$

The partition of the population S by the equivalence relation $\sim_k$ may be pictured as the division of a pie into a certain number of slices, n_k. Then $S(s)$ can be pictured as the stack of all m such divided pies. It is up to the social scientist, of course, to identify the relevant relations and thus the interesting partitions. This does not imply that Lévi-Strauss and the hermeneuticists (or interpretationists) are right in holding that social structures are only in the mind of the student. What is true is that different students may come up with different representations (or conceptualizations) of an objective property of the social system in question, such as its structure. Moreover, these representations need not be equally fictitious and thus equivalent: some may be finer or deeper than others.

A convenient way of displaying the structure of a social system is to form the matrix $\|S_{ik}\|$ of all the social cells. (Some of the entries of this matrix are likely to be empty or, rather, occupied by the empty set.) This representation has the advantage that it suggests how to bring in numbers. Indeed, by counting the number N_{ik} of people in each cell S_{ik} at a given time and dividing by the total population N at that time, we obtain the density matrix $D = (1/N)\|N_{ik}\|$ of the given social system. A comparison of the populations of the various social cells gives an idea of their relative numerical importance at any given time, as well as of their growth or decline over time. (More on this model in Bunge 1974a.)

Note that structures, particularly social structures, are imperceptible. Hence they must be conjectured. (Once conjectured, some of them may be diagrammed and thus rendered visualizable.) Moreover, the social scientist must not only uncover (by way of guess and test) objective social structures. He must also discover the way they are "perceived" by the members of the systems he studies. The reason is that beliefs, whether true or false, influence actions. For example, a person will act in one way if he believes that a structure is unchangeable and in a different way if he believes that it can be altered. For every triad society–actor–sociologist we must thus reckon with four different structures: (*a*) the objective structure and (*b*) the subjective representation of it imagined by the agent, and the theoretical models of the former and the latter, which the social scientist constructs. This fourfold division embraces both the objective and the subjective aspects, without mixing them up the way structuralists, ethnomethodologists, hermeneuticists, and other subjectivists do. These complex relations are sketched in figure 10.1.

The density matrix, D, defined above allows us to refine the notion of social change as structural change; that is, the change over time of the densities of the social cells S_{ik} (e.g., relative increase or decrease in the memberships of occupations, social classes, and nongovernmental organizations). More precisely, the *net structural change* of society s between times 1 and 2 may be defined as $D_{12} = D_2 - D_1$. A socially stagnant society is one in which the densities of the social cells hardly change over time—that is, $D_{12} = 0$. On the other hand, gradual (or revolutionary) social changes are described by gradual (or abrupt) changes in the density matrix.

Any matrix E_{12} such that $E_{12}D_1 = D_2$ may be called a 'social evolution operator.' Hence the net structural change between times 1 and 2 can be rewritten as $D_{12} = [E_{12} - I]D_1$, where I is a unit matrix of suitable rank. By exhibiting counterexamples, it can be shown that the operator E is not unique. (On the other hand, given D_1 and E_{12}, D_2 remains uniquely determined. This is a direct problem, the former an inverse one.) The interpretation of this mathematical result in social science terms is obvious: any given structural change in a society can be brought about in alternative ways (each represented

Theory	Model of society	←	Model of agent's model of society
↑	↑		↑
Reality	Society	→	Agent's model of society

Fig. 10.1. *A realistic model of a society includes an account of the way its members perceive society.*

by a different E). Shorter: There is more than one means to effect any given social structural change. (In state space terms: Any given point in the state space of a society can be reached along more than one trajectory from any other given point.) The moral of this for social policy is clear: if a given net structural social change is agreed upon, the various possible means for bringing it about must be evaluated (as to morals as well as cost–benefit ratios) before any of them is chosen. Shorter: Think before doing.

The preceding analysis of social change is precise and general, but only descriptive: it involves no change mechanisms ("social forces"), hence it lacks explanatory power. To discover such mechanisms, we must analyze society. The first step in this direction is to distinguish internal from external sources of possible social change, such as social conflicts from international relations. The second is to analyze a society into its major subsystems, biological, economic, political, and cultural, in accordance with the BEPC model outlined in section 3. Each of the two steps suggests three families of theories concerning the engines of social change. The external–internal (or exogenous–endogenous) distinction suggests externalism (e.g., geographical and meteorological determinism), internalism (e.g., technological innovation and social conflict), and systemism. The latter holds that social change is sometimes caused by external factors and at other times by internal ones. And the quadripartite, or BEPC, division is associated with such views as cultural materialism (all change originates ultimately in biological and economic factors), idealism (which assigns primacy to ideas), and systemism. According to the latter, social change may originate in any of the four subsystems, but, once it gets going, it is likely to drag other subsystems along, because all subsystems intersect and interact. (See Mann 1993 for a different, though cognate, view couched in somewhat fuzzy terms of "entwinings of sources of social power.")

5 Micro–Macro Relations

The problem of micro–macro relations is central to both contemporary social science and its metatheory (see, e.g., Alexander et al. 1987). I will address it by combining my concept of a social system with my semantic theory of reference (see chap. 2, sec. 2). The first decision that an investigator must make is what to study. That is, he must start by identifying his referents or units of analysis: individuals, groups, or systems of some kind. Now, every scientist is interested in one or more kinds of referent or unit with regard to complexity, from the individual component of some system on up. One thus speaks of levels of analysis, each corresponding to a different real level of organization—for example, that of the person, the firm, and the nation.

Since there are different levels of organization, there is no such thing as the one, absolutely appropriate level of analysis regardless of one's aims. In some cases one may be interested in individuals, in others in the world system. However, every unit of analysis (or referent), except for the universe as a whole, is embedded in a higher-level system. Hence, when describing the former, we must not overlook the latter. That is, our discourse ought to refer to both the *central* (or target) referent and the *peripheral* (or environmental) referent. Thus, in the proposition "The manager's main duty is to ensure the viability of his firm" the manager and his firm are the central referents, and the social environment the tacit peripheral referent (since viability is relative to the environment).

The simplest distinction of levels is between a micro-level, composed of individuals of some kind, and a macro-level, composed of the systems to which those individuals belong. A system may be treated as a unit in a given context if, in fact, it behaves like one in certain respects. For example, although persons are complex systems, social scientists treat them as if they were units. Likewise, a business firm is a system, and whereas an organization sociologist is interested in its composition and structure, an economist or a historian may treat it as a black box.

Such a distinction of levels evokes Eddington's familiar two-desk problem. Which is the real desk: the whole piece of furniture or the system of its component atoms—that is, the one of ordinary experience or the one that is a result of scientific analysis? From a systemic and realistic viewpoint there is a single desk, albeit described in two different, but mutually complementary, ways. (Actually we may interpolate a third level of both existence and analysis: the meso-level composed of the wood fibers.) Every adequate analysis focuses on one real level of organization, or system level. For example, every modern nation has a single economy that can be described at the micro-, meso-, and macro-levels—that is, in micro-, meso-, and macroeconomic (and even mega-economic) terms. The individual firm (like the atom), the business conglomerate (like the fiber), and the entire economy (like the whole desk) are equally real, though each has its peculiar properties.

Systems come in many sizes and degrees of complexity, so it may be convenient to distinguish several sublevels within a macro-level. In particular, in a social study it may be necessary to distinguish the following levels:

Nano-level. Central referent: the individual. Sample of problems: the effects of sex, age, social origin, educational background, and family connections on career choice, salary, or status in an organization.

Micro-level. Central referent: the small or primary social system—for example, the family, soccer team, clique, or cottage industry. Sample of problems: the dependence of family size upon income and level of education, the viability of a cottage industry, the mechanisms of clique formation and dissolution.

Meso-level. Central referent: the medium-size system, such as a clan, medium-size business, school, church, or village. Sample of problems: the social structure, competition or cooperation with similar systems, relations with natural or social environment.

Macro-level. Central referent: the large system—for example, the community, corporation, town, or local government. Sample of problems: the cohesiveness and stability of the system, splittings and mergers, effects of technological innovation, upkeep of social services, garbage recycling.

Mega-level. Central referent: the superlarge system—for example, the transnational corporation, nation, region, or world system. Sample of issues: conservation or reform of the social order, globalization of the economy, stabilization of international relations, global environmental protection, scope of the United Nations.

Corresponding to these distinctions in reality, we have several levels of discourse or analysis. In social science the following distinctions among levels are common. Social psychology studies individuals in relation to social systems. It addresses such problems as consumer and voting behavior, choice of mate or career, expectations and education, *anomie* and alienation, suicide and crime. Micro-sociology, microeconomics, micro-politology, and micro-history study small social groups, such as families, cliques, work teams, committees, small farms, retail shops, gangs, and neighborhood organizations: in short, groups characterized by face-to-face interactions. These raise such problems as the emergence, maintenance, and breakdown of hierarchies in systems of that kind and the impact of larger systems such as oligopolies and governments. By contrast, macro-sociology, macroeconomics, macro-politology, and macro-history deal with macro (as well as meso and mega) social systems, such as megacorporations, transportation or communications networks, and national, regional, or international economies or governments, all of which raise qualitatively different scientific and policy problems from those raised by micro-systems.

Obviously, it is not enough to distinguish real levels and the corresponding levels of analysis. Once such distinctions have been made, one must tackle the interesting, challenging problem of micro–macro relations and, in particular, the ways in which the components of a system (or subsystem) contribute to the efficient (or inefficient) performance of the system (or supersystem). This is the problem of m–M and M–m relations, which we first met in connection with reduction (see chap. 5, sec. 4). Let us take a further look at it.

There are two kinds of relations between a concrete entity and the system of which it is a part: part–whole and causal relations. We stipulate that thing *a* is *part* of thing *b* just in case the concatenation, juxtaposition, or physical addition of *a* and *b* equals *b* (Bunge 1977*b*, chap. 1). (The part–whole relation differs from the set membership relation, because systems are not sets, and because, unlike the part–whole relation, the membership relation is not transitive. But the latter does hold between a system component and the composition of a system.)

As for causal relations between part and whole, we cannot view them in a holistic fashion, because the whole contains its parts. In line with section 4, we stipulate the following conventions:

1. *m–M link* (or *agency–structure relation*) is short for the proposition that one or more units on level m act, independently or in combination, in a way that alters the state of one or more systems on level M. Examples: (*a*) a citizen's complaint about police brutality brings about an inquiry which results in a reorganization of the police force; (*b*) the income distribution of a society, hence its overall social structure, is altered by people joining together in production and consumer cooperatives or in political parties working for a restructuring of society.

2. *M–m link* (or *structure–agency relation*) is short for the proposition that the behavior of a unit on level m is constrained or stimulated by the place (function, role) it holds in a system on level M. Examples: (*a*) the collusion or merger of several major firms in a given industrial sector effects a sudden rise in the price of the commodities they produce or market, thus lowering the standard of living of their consumers; (*b*) the introduction of health insurance in a region improves the well-being of every inhabitant of the region.

In addition to m–M and M–m links, there are m–M–m and M–m–M loops. Example of an m–M–m loop: A popular political leader pushes for new social legislation which increases social expenditures, which in turn improve the quality of life of many people. Example of an M–m–M loop: As the standard of living and the level of education rise, couples have fewer children, which decreases the number of new home-buyers, which depresses the construction industry, which in turn contributes to a decline in overall economic growth.

This last example can be represented by what was previously (chap. 5, sec. 4) called a Boudon–Coleman diagram (see fig. 10.2). Whereas holists focus on the upper tier and individualists on the lower one, systemists take in both of them and can thus supply a far richer account. Consequently they can also suggest more effective social policies than either of their rivals. For example, they will argue that, since health depends on both personal and social factors, an effective health policy will combine care with cure—that is, prevention of, and intervention in, the disease process—together with radical social measures to decrease social inequality and improve sanitation, housing, and nutrition. (See Evans et al. 1994.)

What holds for the objective part–whole and causal relations among entities on different levels has its counterpart in their study. That is, in some cases a top-

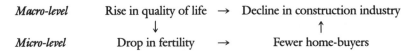

Macro-level   Rise in quality of life → Decline in construction industry
                              ↓   ↑
Micro-level   Drop in fertility   →   Fewer home-buyers

Fig. 10.2. Analysis of a macro–macro causal arrow into macro–micro, micro–micro, and micro–macro causal relations.

down strategy is indicated, at other times a bottom-up one, and in still other cases a mixed strategy. For example, a company that creates a new job category writes specifications for it and advertises for it, screening candidates one by one: it proceeds from the top down, whereas the candidates adopt the converse perspective. On the other hand, if we want to discover the function or role that a particular individual performs in a social system, we must observe him at work in the place he occupies in the system; so in this case a mixed strategy is called for.

In the light of the occurrence of m–M, M–m, m–M–m, and M–m–M links,the agency–structure dichotomy appears contrived. Indeed, all agency is agency within some social system, and all social systems exist (or break down) through the actions of their components. Hence the dichotomy is just as fictitious as the body–motion, air–wind, face–smile, and brain–mind dichotomies. We must distinguish things from features and processes, but we must not detach them, much less oppose them, because features are possessed by things, processes are changes in things, and all things are in flux (see chap. 1).

I have argued that the systemic approach is superior to its alternatives, if only because it contains the grains of truth found in the latter. It handles wholes without being holistic and studies their individual components without being individualistic. It is analytic without being radically reductionist. It tells us that the correct way to ascertain whether something is indeed a system, rather than either indivisible or an aggregate, is to analyze it into its constituents and study the links among these. Last, but not least, it recognizes a multiplicity of legitimate levels of analysis: as many levels as levels of reality.

Unlike its rivals, the systemic approach is universal in its scope. Indeed, it is either tacitly or explicitly employed in the scientific study of systems of all kinds: conceptual, concrete and symbolic, natural and social—from atoms to societies. But its explicit adoption is particularly useful in social science, where holism and individualism are still paid lip service, not because they are fertile but because of philosophical inertia and ideological bias.

11 :: *Idealism and Materialism*

Idealism and materialism are ontological doctrines: they concern the furniture of the world. Crudely put, idealism (or spiritualism) is the doctrine that ideas exist separately from and above (or instead of) matter, while materialism holds that everything in the world is material or concrete, ideas being bodily (brain) processes. (Caution: The admission that we ideate and that we can understand reality only in terms of our own ideas is not a mark of idealism but of common sense.) But there are several varieties of idealism and materialism: crass and sophisticated, clear and confused, total and partial, consistent and inconsistent, and so on.

Idealism, expelled from natural science in the seventeenth century, has survived to this day in theology, philosophy, mathematics, psychology, and social studies. In the last, it asserts that all social facts are either ideas or embodiments of ideas, by contrast with materialism, which holds that all social facts are states or changes of state of concrete entities, from persons to social systems. Sample of idealist views: (*a*) the thesis that the state is a "spiritual reality"; (*b*) the structuralist thesis that societies are languages, or "like" languages, and the hermeneutic claim that they are texts, or "like" texts; (*c*) the fashionable constructivist-relativist doctrine that there is no theory-free reality. By contrast, any social study that assumes that people are concrete entities with biological needs and that no social system could subsist without material resources is clearly materialist.

It should be obvious why the idealism versus materialism question is important to social science. The idealist focuses on ideas and thus underrates or even ignores the physical environment, animal needs and drives, and factors of production—in particular, work. He is likely to be more interested in the lives of heroes and villains than in those of the populace. And his approach will tend to be bookish and nonquantitative. The materialist, on the other hand, will focus on environmental, biological, demographic, and economic aspects, as well as on the ways ordinary people live and, in particular, reproduce and earn their livelihood. He will be just as interested in artifacts, statistics, and surveys as in norms, doctrines, and written documents and will foster quantification.

For example, idealists tend to attribute the current social crisis in the United States to the "breakdown of family values" and immorality. Consequently they limit themselves to recriminating, preaching, and punishing. By contrast, materialists are likely to blame the crisis on chronic poverty and ethnic segregation, which erode traditional values and cause despair, anomie, and criminality. Consequently they support social programs aimed at reducing poverty and segregation through job creation, education, and community organization. The epistemic consequences are clear: whereas the idealist has a ready answer to all social issues, the materialist is likely to press for more social studies of poverty and antisocial behavior in order to design better social policies.

I will argue that, although idealism is at best irrefutable, the so-called spiritual (i.e., cognitive and emotional) aspects of life are for real and should be studied scientifically—that is, in a materialist fashion. However, let us first glance at the history of this millennial philosophical saga. Animism, shamanism, and beliefs in magic, telepathy, ghosts, supernatural beings, and an afterlife are idealist. So are the philosophies of Pythagoras, Plato, Plotinus, Leibniz, Berkeley, Hegel, Bolzano, Dilthey, Frege, Husserl, and most contemporary philosophers. On the other hand, the ancient atomists, Hobbes, Spinoza, Diderot, Holbach, and Marx did not believe in separate souls or in gods: they were materialists. Others—in particular, Aristotle, Averroës, Descartes, and Newton—stood halfway between materialism and spiritualism. For example, Descartes regarded the cosmos as a self-rewinding clock, though one originally built by the supreme Clockmaker. Moreover, he reinforced the dualism of mind and body, still popular among philosophers despite the achievements of physiological psychology. Still others, such as Hume, Kant, Comte, Mill, Mach, and the members of the Vienna Circle—in sum, positivists of all hues—believed that they stood above the fray. But in fact they were close to idealism in denying the existence of things in themselves—that is, independently of our perceiving them. (Yet, the mistaken conflation of positivism with materialism is quite common.)

Idealism is still going strong in psychology and social science after having been soundly beaten in the natural sciences. Indeed, in their scientific work, physicists, chemists, and biologists seldom, if ever, condone self-existing immaterial entities. (Caution: Electromagnetic and other fields count as material, even though they carry no mass; and energy, unlike radiation, is a property of material things, not an entity.) True, here and there one encounters vestiges of idealism among natural scientists, but the main thrust of natural science is naturalistic. For instance, some cosmologists claim that the Big Bang was an act of creation out of nothing, in violation of all the conservation laws. Some theoretical physicists believe that measurement is the only cause of microphysical processes. Molecular biologists use metaphors of genetic "information," "instruction," "translation," and "transcription," and some even talk about nucleic acid molecules as sequences of "symbols." But these are merely avoidable *façons de parler*. Some biologists still invoke teleology (under the fancy new name "teleonomy") to "explain" function, although evolution and development do the job nowadays. A handful invoke no less mysterious and immaterial "morphogenetic fields" to account for morphogenesis. But these fantasies are nonfunctional vestiges, even though, like the human appendix, they cause trouble once in a while. And, like the appendix, they can be removed without danger to the bulk of natural science—which, unsurprisingly, is definitely naturalistic.

Things are very different in psychology, the social sciences, and the socio-natural sciences like linguistics. Here idealism is still widespread, though often in subtle forms and sometimes unknown to the very people who subscribe to it. The most popular example is folk psychology—in particular, psychoanalysis, according to which the mind or soul is immaterial and the only source of action. Another is the view that mind and society are information-processing devices. A third is that, with regard to social behavior, all that matter are the mental processes of choice and decision making.

There are several reasons for the survival of idealism in the sciences of man. First, these disciplines were born in the humanities, which were dominated first by theology and later by idealist philosophy. Second, social studies deal with people, and people have mental experiences, which in earlier times were accounted for in terms of immaterial entities. Of course, since the mid-nineteenth century, mental processes have increasingly come to be explained in neurophysiological terms and thus in a materialist fashion. (See, e.g., Hebb 1949, 1980; Bindra 1976; Bunge and Ardila 1987.) But physiological psychology is still young and not widely known. Besides, it is at variance with folk psychology, in particular psychoanalysis, as well as with religion and the bulk of academic philosophy. Third, idealism has been reinforced by the failure of such crude versions of materialism as biologism, inherent in social Darwinism and human sociobiology. In short, tradition, ideology, and vulgar materialism have hindered the progress of scientific materialism in social studies. And this, in turn, has retarded the maturation of the social sciences, by underrating or even overlooking work and environmental and demographic factors.

To be sure, some idealists, like Durkheim and Weber, have made important contributions to social science by studying the role of ideas in social life. But these contributions can be interpreted in materialist terms by assuming (*a*) that all ideas are brain processes, and (*b*) that all social systems, even cultural ones, such as schools, are concrete, or material, in being composed of flesh-and-bone people. Such materiality does not entail that social systems and practices are natural and can therefore be studied by physics, chemistry, or even biology. Though material, such systems are irreducibly social. Hence naturalism is inadequate to study them. The study of society calls for a more sophisticated materialism, one accounting for artificial systems and practices, such as firms and schools, manufacture and trade, language and ceremony, management and politics: that is emergent materialism (see Bunge 1981*c*).

We proceed to examine idealism and materialism as they relate to contemporary social studies, rather than in general.

1 Idealism

Philosophical idealism (or spiritualism) is the family of doctrines that hold the autonomous existence and primacy of ideas. Although in modern times idealism is often rationalist and secular, it started off as the philosophical offshoot of magic, shamanism, sorcery, and religion. The spiritualist nature of magic, shamanism, and sorcery is clear. They attribute to the magician, sorcerer, or shaman spiritual powers over things or people—for example, to cause rainfall without seeding clouds, to cure the sick without medication or surgery, or to harm the enemy without wielding weapons. This mode of thinking involves magical causation and makes no allowance for coincidence and chance; above all, it is uncritical. For example, the rainmaker is allowed to perform his rituals at the beginning of the rainy season, and his failures are explained away as the result of interference by rivals.

To be sure, the believer in magic, sorcery, or shamanism may give "reasons" of sorts, rather than invoking dark irrational forces, in which case he can be said to be "subjectively rational." But his reasons are fanciful: in actual fact, there are no psychic powers, mind does not move matter—there is no telekinesis. (There is, of course, voluntary motion, but it is the muscular result of a neurophysiological process that in primates starts in the frontal lobes.) In short, magical beliefs are not mere errors: they are wrong-headed and are held on the strength of lucky coincidences and despite exceptions.

As for the spiritualist component of religion, it is too obvious to need elaboration. Suffice it to recall that every religion proper postulates the existence of supernatural, immaterial, hence unobservable, beings. Correspondingly, every theology contains an idealist ontology—which, however, may be combined with a realist epistemology, as in the case of Thomism. The main task of medieval philosophers was to elaborate that idealist ontology as the handmaiden of theology.

Let us now jump from magic, sorcery, shamanism, and religion to modern social studies. Rather than conduct a methodical search, I shall take a random sample of idealist opinions, starting with the so-called marginalist revolution of 1870, which was actually an idealist counterrevolution. Classical economists, from Smith and Ricardo to Mill and Marx, emphasized natural resources, capital, and labor, to which Marx added class warfare. By contrast, neoclassical economists, starting with Walras, Jevons, and Menger, overlooked nature and underrated work. They focused instead on subjective values (utilities) and subjective probabilities and postulated that every agent is wholly free and acts on the sole strength of his rational choice—a clear case of replacement of materialism by idealism. Eventually this body of theory became mainstream economics, but until the 1960s it exerted no appreciable influence outside economics. Since then it has invaded much of the territory of the other social sciences. Whether this movement has been successful is another matter (for which, see Bunge 1995a, 1995b). The point is that this is an idealist movement, since it overrates the social impact of certain ideas at the expense of natural resources, work and social structure. It is the rationalist wing of idealism in the field of social studies. Its irrationalist complement comes next.

The most influential idealist rival of rational choice theorizing in social studies over the past century has been philosophical hermeneutics. This school, founded by Dilthey (1959 [1883], 1959 [1900]), has attracted mostly theologians, classical philologists, literary critics, historians of nonscientific ideas, and irrationalist philosophers. It blends Kant's subjectivism with Hegel's objective idealism and holds that the object of what others call social studies is not the social world but the human spirit. Consequently these studies should be called Geisteswissenschaften (sciences of the spirit). Their task is to understand the "inner reality" of the lucky few who left behind written documents.

On this view, these disciplines are disjoint from the natural sciences not only in subject matter and special techniques but also in method: this is the "comprehensive understanding," or Verstehen, which we met in chapter 5, sections 5 and 6. The proper task of the heremeneuticist is to attempt to grasp the Sinn (sense) or Deutung (meaning) of the individual actions in question—in plain English, to figure out the agent's purpose. This leaves out the problems of the genesis, structure, and change of social systems, from family to nation—a particularly remarkable omission at the time of the birth of large corporations, strong governments, and powerful labor unions and political parties.

Simmel (1923 [1892]) followed Dilthey's lead in regarding the social sciences as Geisteswissenschaften. According to him, their subject matter is *geistig* (spiritual), not material. (Other influential writers, particularly Spengler and Collingwood, held the same view.) Simmel criticized not only the materialist Marx (whom he admired on several counts) but also the objectivist idealist historian Ranke, who stated that the historian's task is to tell what really happened. Simmel was certainly right to reject naturalism in social science, but he was right for the wrong reason: namely, that to him everything social is an outcome of mental processes, which are immaterial. He was also right to deny the possibility of giving a full description of social reality and to insist that we must "stylize," simplify, or idealize facts. But he did not realize that this is common to all the sciences and that every scientific model of a given real object is supposed to capture some of its real features (recall chap. 2, sec. 5 on ideal types).

Finally, Simmel's extravagant subjectivist claim that the student "makes nature and history" is clearly at variance with scientific practice and even everyday practice. Fortunately, he himself did not abide by that thesis when writing his celebrated monograph on the history of money. Moreover, in this study Simmel found that life in a monetary economy depersonalizes individual and social relations—a blow to the very individualism he preached. In sum, Simmel the scientist contradicted Simmel the philosopher. As we saw earlier (chap. 5, sec. 5), the same was true of Weber.

Weber, Simmel's contemporary and a fellow neo-Kantian, launched an explicit attack on historical materialism and was seen by many as the anti-Marx. In particular, whereas Marx, following Feuerbach, regarded religion as an ideological translation and legitimation of the social order, Weber rightly saw Christianity as an important social force. But he went too far in holding that Protestantism and its work ethic were the driving force of early capitalism. As the Catholic theologian J. B. Kraus (in Neurath 1981 [1931], 401–5) put it, this was a case of belief in the magic power of the spirit. (Besides, the cases of northern Italy and France refute Weber's thesis.) Ironically, where Hinduism was concerned, Weber (1920–21, 2: chap. 1) proposed a materialist view. Indeed, he described the Hindu caste system before the Hindu religion and noted how well the latter—in particular, the doctrine of karma—fitted the former. (On the other hand, our contemporary, Dumont [1966, 52], states that "caste is a state of mind" and explains caste by religion. This is a clear case of sociological idealism. Worse, it trivializes the unfairness and tragedy of the Hindu caste system.)

I suggest that the idealist philosophy borrowed from Dilthey, Windelband, and Rickert played only a minor role in Weber's substantive work. To begin with, as noted earlier (chap. 5, sec. 5), notwithstanding his defense of Verstehen in his methodological writings, Weber hardly used it in his scientific work, where he proceeded in a realist, if bookish, way. Second, far from neglecting the economy, he devoted his major work, *Wirtschaft und Gesellschaft* (1922), to it. In fact, Weber's "later sociology of modern society is not much different from that of Marx" (Alexander and Giesen 1987, 18). Third, Weber (1920 [1904–5], 205–6) concluded his famous book on Protestant ethics and the spirit of capitalism by stating that "there can be no question of replacing a one-sided 'materialist' conception of the meaning of culture and history with an equally one-sided spiritualist one." In sum, Weber was not a consistent spiritualist. But he rightly stressed the role of ideas in social life. Materialists cannot object to this as long as ideas are not regarded as self-existing.

Let us now turn from the German to the French branch of spiritualism, which was strongly indebted to the former. Weber's rival, Emile Durkheim, was no less of an idealist, albeit an equally inconsistent one. Durkheim's ideas of collective consciousness, representation, and memory are not just instances of the fallacy of composition; nor are they secular successors to the Romantic *Weltgeist* (world spirit) and *Zeitgeist* (spirit of the times). They are key concepts in Durkheim's idealistic and holistic view of the social. Indeed, for him and his followers, particularly the young Mauss, (*a*) a social fact, though objective, is an event in the consciousness of a society, and (*b*) "a society consists . . . above all, in the idea that it forms of itself." All social facts occur in the sphere of public opinion, which is "the system of collective representations. Social facts are then causes because they are representations or act upon representations. At bottom social life is a set of representations" (Fauconnet and Mauss 1968 [1901], 26). After his teacher's death, Mauss turned his attention to the so-called material aspects of society—but he never rid himself of the idea of collective mentality.

Idealism may have motivated some of Durkheim's scientific research, in particular that on the religion–suicide connection, but it certainly did not stand in the way of his research. In fact, he stressed that social facts should be studied just as objectively as physical facts. He also embraced the distinctly materialist hypothesis that certain belief systems, notably religion and folk biological systematics, are ideal translations of social organizations. This is why French scholars credit him with having founded the modern sociology of knowledge.

Four decades after Durkheim's death, the idealist component of his view of social life crossed the channel under Wittgenstein's flag. Thus Winch (1958, 23) held that "social relations are expressions of ideas about reality." The social relations among men "exist in and through their ideas," so that "social relations must be a species of internal [conceptual] relations" (1958, 123–24). But "to understand the nature of social phenomena in general . . . [is] precisely the aim of epistemology" (1958, 42). His fellow Wittgensteinians Louch (1969) and Malcolm (1968) concurred. Moreover, Malcolm stated explicitly that the hypotheses of social science are a priori, ergo empirically untestable. Hence the social scientist has no need to get up from his armchair. This disastrous methodological consequence follows from the idealist view of the nature of social life, as well as from confusing two uses of the word *meaning:* namely, as the sense of a linguistic expression and the purpose of an action. (See Gellner 1973 for more.)

A closely related school is that of *symbolic interactionism* (Mead 1934; Blumer 1969). Its central theses are that humans are above all symbolic animals (Cassirer 1944) and that people react not to each other's actions, but to the way they themselves "interpret" these actions. No doubt, both theses have important true components: people do invent or use symbols of various kinds, and they act in accordance with the way they "read" (conjecture) the intentions of others. However, there are no symbols in themselves: a symbol is a means that cannot be understood when detached from what it stands for—or, rather, from what it is (rightly or wrongly) assumed to represent. Hence social facts are not bunches of symbols. Second, our "interpretation" of the actions of others is not the only determinant of our own actions: we are motivated or inhibited by a number of material (natural and social) constraints as well as by the way we "interpret" the actions of others. In sum, symbolic interactionism rightly emphasizes the importance of symbols, in particular words, but errs in detaching the symbolic from the material and in overrating the former at the expense of the latter.

A related idea is that information can be detached from its material carrier or substratum, because statistical information theory is so general that it makes no assumptions concerning the nature of the information transmitter, channel, and receiver. This idea is sometimes expanded into the thesis that all things, from molecules to societies, are nothing but information bundles. This not only dematerializes things but erases their differences in kind, as well as the corresponding laws, and thus effects a radical impoverishment (oversimplification) of the world.

Our final example of idealism is anthropological and sociological structuralism, as represented by Lévi-Strauss (1963) and Bourdieu (1968, 1989). According to this school, (*a*) all the sciences study structures in themselves rather than structured objects (i.e., systems); (*b*) structures are only in the heads of the students; and (*c*) all social structures are basically linguistic and, more particularly, syntactic. Thesis (*a*) is logically false, for, by definition, a structure is a set of relations, and there are no relations without relata. Far from being self-existing entities, structures are properties of objects. For example, every chemical structure is the structure of some molecule, and every social structure is the structure of some social system. Thesis (*b*) renders the findings of structuralists suspicious, for why should we believe people who confess to making up social structures instead of uncovering them? Thesis (*c*) is blatantly false, if only because the basic classical syntactic categories—subject (S), verb (V), and object (O)—have no social correlates. For example, the SVO ordering that prevails in modern English, as in "John wrote the paper," tells us nothing about the British social order, let alone the radical changes it has undergone since the birth of the English language. On the other hand, social and military history do have something to say about linguistic change: remember, for example, the sea changes brought about in Old English by the Norman conquest.

Because of its thesis that language is the key to social structure, structuralism overlaps partially with philosophical hermeneutics, to which we now turn.

2 Contemporary Hermeneutics

Hermeneutics is criticism and interpretation of texts. It is not so much a discipline as an activity that all scholars engage in. Dilthey's hermeneutic approach to the study of social facts, which we met briefly in the preceding section, is a different matter altogether. It is the view that (a) the goal of the student of society is to attain a Verstehen ("comprehensive understanding") of written documents and, through them, of their authors, and that (b) interpretation is a subjective, intuitive, incorrigible procedure. We noted earlier (chap. 5, sec. 5) the limitations of Verstehen, regarding objectivity as one of the marks of science in contrast to art (chap. 7, sec. 1). Let us now examine a new version of hermeneutics: what has been hailed as the "textual revolution" or "linguistic turn" in humanistic and social studies.

Contemporary hermeneutics, or textualism, is a radical extension of Dilthey's hermeneutics. It adds to the latter the ontological thesis inherent in magical thinking that word and object are equivalent, or in any case inseparable from one another. It holds that social facts are symbols, texts, or text analogs to be "interpreted." Thus Ricoeur (1971) claims that actions are similar to texts, whence they must be handled by hermeneuticists. (Obvious objection: Mary may be *like* a rose, but she certainly *is* not a rose, hence not something to be put in a vase.) Charles Taylor (1971) holds the same thesis and adds his famous formula: "Man is a self-interpreting animal." And Geertz (1973, 14), the founder of "interpretive anthropology," asserts that culture (in the broad anthropological sense) is an "assemblage of texts," and, more particularly, an "interworked system of construable signs." The epistemological and methodological consequence of this view is that the study of society is a task for semioticians, linguists, and literary critics—not for scientists.

Some of the best-known members of this school are Derrida (1967), Foucault (1969), Geertz (1973), Gadamer (1975), Lachmann (1973), Ricoeur (1971, 1975), and Taylor (1971). (See also Bloom et al. 1990; R. H. Brown 1987; Burke 1989; Dallmayr 1987; Kearney 1986; Mueller-Vollmer 1989; Wagner 1986.) Because of their glossolatry and subjectivism, Heidegger (1986 [1927]), Wittgenstein (1953), and Lévi-Strauss (1963) are often counted among the founding fathers of contemporary hermeneutics. (Besides, Heidegger regarded himself as a follower of Dilthey, and he exerted a strong influence on Gadamer, Derrida, and others.) And, because of their belief that communication is the hub of social life, Habermas (1981) and Luhmann (1984) may also be counted as hermeneuticists. The motto common to all of them could be said to be *Totus in verba*. And their common ancestor is Dilthey's (and Weber's) equivocation over the words *Deutung* (interpretation) and *Sinn* (meaning, function, goal), which in colloquial German can bear on actions as well as linguistic expressions.

The key concepts of hermeneutics are, of course, those of text and interpretation. The first is left undefined, and the second is taken in the broadest possible sense. Indeed, according to the hermeneutical school, not only signs, but also human behavior, and perhaps natural events as well, can and must be "interpreted." And in both cases 'interpretation' means the disclosure of 'meaning,' which in turn seems to mean nothing but intention, purpose, or goal. Note the double equivocation whereby two traditional semiotic terms, 'sign' and 'interpretation,' are assigned nonstandard significations. In fact, in mainstream philosophy, at least since Frege, only a construct or its symbol is assigned a meaning, and this is taken to be its sense, its reference, or both together (see, e.g., Bunge 1974*c*).

That double equivocation leads readily to the radical hermeneutic thesis that "the word is the dwelling of Being" (Heidegger 1959, 267). Consequently, "there is no outside-the-text" (Derrida 1967). Or, as the sociologist of science Woolgar (1986, 312) puts it, "there is no reality independent of the words (texts, signs, documents, and so on) used to apprehend it. In other words, reality is constituted in and through discourse." In short, the world is the library of libraries—a comforting thought for a bookworm but a nightmare for the rest of us. Let us see how these views on interpretation stand up to methodological analysis.

First of all, normal people distinguish between signs, such as words, and their referents. Moreover, they do not attribute syntactic, semantic, or phonetic properties to such things as stars, people, and societies, for the simple reason that we cannot read, write, or interpret them. This is why we study them empirically and build conceptual models of them, rather than consulting dictionaries and grammars. To be sure, in the process we use or produce texts, but only as records of the conceptual and empirical operations concerning our objects of study—stars, people, or what have you. Even in literate societies, social facts, such as those involving kinship, work, trade, and political power, are not texts, or even "like" texts. Consequently linguists, hermeneuticists, and literary critics are not equipped to study social life.

Second, it is not true that there is a single concept of interpretation, one that applies equally to artificial signs such as words, social signals (not signs) such as gestures, and natural "signs" such as dark clouds. Artificial signs, such as words and road signs, are interpreted with the help of explicit conventions; social signals are "interpreted" with the help of more or less explicit generalizations; and natural "signs" are "interpreted" in the light of natural laws. Far from distinguishing and analyzing the various concepts designated by the word *interpretation,* hermeneuticists confuse them. This confusion leads them to believe that social science is a branch of semiotics, the science of signs.

(In technical terms, we have to do here with at least four different functions, or maps, each with its own domain and co-domain. The domain and co-domain of the "interpretation" of natural signs are natural facts; the domain and co-domain of the "interpretation" of social signals are social facts; the domain of musical interpretation is a set of musical notes, and its co-domain a set of sounds; the domain of the interpretation of a mathematical, scientific, or technological text is a set of mathematical symbols, and its co-domain a set of constructs, some of which refer to extralinguistic objects.)

Third, what hermeneuticists call an "interpretation" of a human action is actually a *hypothesis.* Indeed, when one "interprets" an action as pro-social or antisocial, harmless or dangerous, and so on, one makes a guess about the feelings, ideas, or intentions of a fellow human being. One "reads" worry in the wrinkles of his forehead, mirth in his laughter, determination in the angle of his mouth, aggressiveness in his body posture, and so on. In other words, one treats a piece of overt behavior as an (uncertain) *indicator* of a hidden mental state or process. (For social indicators, see chap. 6, sec. 3.)

One frames such hypotheses on the strength of one's fund of knowledge of self and others. But empirical knowledge is notoriously unreliable; in particular, ordinary behavioral indicators are ambiguous and culture-bound. (For instance, among Westerners a smile is usually associated with pleasure, understanding, or approval, whereas among Orientals it may signal displeasure, incomprehension, disapproval, or even a threat.) In daily life one seldom bothers to check such hypotheses; one just suffers the consequences of mistaken "interpretations." But in science one is expected to check one's hypotheses, because one realizes that they are fallible, and one is interested in truth. This is the crux of the matter. By rechristening 'hypothesis' as 'interpretation,' the hermeneuticist skirts the problems of the empirical test for truth. He relies on his intuition—in particular, his empathic understanding, which he seems to regard as infallible—rather than on objective tests. He can then claim that social science is not an empirical science but a branch of the humanities, a Geisteswissenschaft to be cultivated exclusively in the library.

But social studies would be extraordinarily impoverished and debased if they relied exclusively on unchecked "interpretations," for, even when some of these hypotheses happen to be true, they explain nothing—nor are they intended to explain, because the hermeneuticist claims that social science should not attempt to explain anything but only to "understand" in an immediate (intuitive, preanalytic) manner. Scientists are far more rigorous and ambitious: to them, the understanding of any piece of human behavior amounts to an explanation with the help of a theory linking beliefs, intentions, expectations, and evaluations to corresponding actions in the given social milieu.

To conclude: Since humans are, among other things, symbol-making animals who think and interact with the help of symbols, it would be foolish for a social scientist to disregard symbols altogether. But to regard individuals and societies as texts is an idealist extravagance (more in Gellner 1985; Albert 1988, 1994; Spiegel 1990). This extravagance is indulged in by a number of fashionable schools in social studies: structuralism and poststructuralism, symbolic interactionism and symbolic anthropology, critical theory and feminist "philosophy," ethnomethodology and phenomenology. Let us take a look at the last of these.

3 Phenomenology

Husserl, the founder of phenomenology as well as the mentor of Heidegger, was never seriously interested in social matters, and few, if any, social scientists have read his abstruse prose. Their knowledge of phenomenology is mostly secondhand, through the writings of Alfred Schutz (Schütz, Schuetz). Yet the latter once admitted that "The task of reproducing faithfully Husserl's language, which in the original German offers serious difficulties even to German readers, is, I believe, really creative work" (Schütz 1940, 164). Clearer: Husserl is so obscure that he can be interpreted in almost any way his students and translators like.

Husserl was a radical, consistent spiritualist, a dogmatist—he never argued for his *obiter dicta*—and a declared enemy of science proper, as well as a conservative to boot. He started out as a subjective spiritualist interested only in the study of self ("egology"). Toward the end of his life, he claimed to be interested in the *Lebenswelt* (life-world or everyday life), though only as a community of individual spirits. This later phase is the one that has influenced some anthropological and sociological schools, particularly ethnomethodology.

Here is a random sample of quotes from Husserl's second phase, which I have translated as far as possible: "The spirit [Geist], and only the spirit, is in itself and for itself [*ist in sich selbst und für sich selbst seiend*]" (1954 [1935], 345); "Only the spirit is immortal" (ibid., 348). "The spirit knows itself, and the scientific spirit knows itself scientifically" (ibid., 345). However, "this knowledge is subjective, not objective" (ibid.). Therefore, "there never was and there never will be" an objective science of the spirit or soul (ibid.). Shorter: Scientific psychology is impossible because only I can know my own soul.

Moreover, according to Husserl (1954 [1936], 70), subjectivity is ontologically prior to objectivity. Or, as Schütz (1940, 168) put it, "transcendental subjectivity . . . alone has the ontic sense of absolute being." The "transcendental ego" is "correlative" to the world, and the latter is "constituted by the intersubjective community of individuals" (Husserl 1954 [1936], 138). In other words, "I as primaeval I [*Ur-Ich*] constitute my horizon of transcendental others as cosubjects of the transcendental intersubjectivity that constructs the world" (ibid., 187). "Accordingly phenomenology cannot ignore the world any longer [as it used to], but must perform the *épaché* [bracketing out] with regard to all the objective sciences" (ibid., 138). And, because it turns scientific objectivism into transcendental subjectivism, phenomenology is "the greatest revolution" in history (ibid., 69). No comment.

Husserl is rightly regarded, along with his star pupil, Heidegger, as a precursor of postmodernism for having blamed the exact sciences, naturalism, and objectivism for what he saw as "the crisis of the European sciences"—which, incidentally, at the time were flourishing everywhere in Europe except in Nazi Germany. He went so far as to claim that science is to be blamed for skepticism and nihilism and even for irrationalism (Husserl 1954 [1935], [1936]). Yet Husserl also attacked rationalism and, in a typically Romantic mood, prescribed a return to the *Lebenswelt* as a cure. His villains were not Nietzsche, the archnihilist, or Heidegger, the arch-irrationalist, but Descartes and Galileo, the founding fathers of modern thought.

Social scientists might not have noticed phenomenology, had it not been for Schütz (1967 [1932]), who endeavored to merge it with the Austrian school of economics. Both schools were aprioristic, individualistic, subjectivistic, and politically conservative; but whereas phenomenology was intuitionist, the Austrian school of economics was definitely rationalist. Schütz attempted to fuse them by purging the Austrian school of its rationalism and its naive view of concept formation. He thus hoped to salvage the Austrian school, which was bankrupt on account of its apriorism and ahistoricity, as well as its laisser-fairism at the time of the Great Depression, which called for and elicited strong state intervention.

Schütz reassured his teacher Ludwig von Mises that economic principles such as the law of diminishing marginal utility are statements "of what necessarily must happen," rather than empirically testable hypotheses. He misused Menger's (1969 [1883]) and Weber's (1922) concept of an ideal type to bolster von Mises's claim that economics, like geometry, deals with ideal objects, not with the real world. More precisely, he stipulated that we call 'economic' any action that conforms to the allegedly a priori principles of (neoclassical) economics. And, in Husserlian jargon, he postulated that "the very objectivity of economic knowledge consists in the ordering of subjective meaning-contexts (such as subjective valuations) into the objective meaning-context of scientific knowledge" (1967 [1932], 246). But he did not elucidate the meanings of "subjective" and "objective"; nor did he explain how subjectivity can be embedded in objectivity. For all his denunciations of irrationalism, Schütz was an irrationalist.

The originality, depth, and fertility of Schütz's work can be judged by the following fragment: "My social world with the *alter egos* in it is arranged, around me as the center, into associates (*Umwelt*), contemporaries (*Mitwelt*), predecessors (*Vorwelt*), and successors (*Folgwelt*), whereby I and my different attitudes to others institute these manifold relationships. All this is done in various degrees of *intimacy* and *anonymity*" (Schütz 1940, 181). How this platitude can help us understand, let alone stem, such social processes as overpopulation or environmental degradation, industrialization or militarization, colonization or democratization, mass unemployment or massive diffusion of cultural goods and evils, is left as an exercise for the reader.

In sum, phenomenology has contributed the following to social studies: impenetrable, pretentious jargon, lack of rigor, subjectivism, contempt for empirical research, and exclusive interest in the minutiae of everyday life at the expense of their social and historical context. This is particularly obvious in the case of ethnomethodology.

Finally, existentialism, the major offspring of phenomenology, is hardly analyzable, for it is the pit of irrationalist verbiage. Let the reader judge for himself from the following sample of Heidegger's celebrated *Sein und Zeit* (1986 [1927]), dedicated to his teacher, Husserl. On human existence, or being-there (*Dasein*): "Das Sein des Daseins besagt: Sich-vorweg-schon-sein-in-(der Welt-) als Sein-bei (innerweltlich begegnendem Seienden)" (ibid., 192). On time: "Zeit ist ursprünglich als Zeitigung der Zeitlichkeit, als welche sie die Konstitution der Sorgestruktur ermöglicht" (ibid., 331). I challenge anyone to make sense of these wordplays, or even to translate them into comprehensible German. That is no ordinary rubbish: it is unrecyclable academic garbage.

4 Ontological Constructivism

Philosophical constructivism is the view that all is constructed: nothing is given. There are two different kinds of constructivism: epistemological and ontological. The former, from Aristotle to Kant, Engels, Einstein, Piaget, and Popper, holds that all concepts and theories are human constructions. It opposes empiricism, which claims that all ideas are percepts or derive directly from them. The empirical, analytical, and historical study of concept formation supports epistemological constructivism (recall chap. 2).

Ontological constructivism is a totally different thing: it is the idealist view that all facts are human constructions. It can originate in either of two errors:

the belief that, because all we know about any object X is constructed rather than found ready-made, then X itself must have been constructed; the opinion that, because some existential hypotheses, such as those about witches and of the ether, turned out to be false, there can be no self-existing things, let alone objective truths about them.

Ontological constructivism, now fashionable, is anything but novel: it goes back at least to Berkeley's famous formula "To be is to perceive or to be perceived" (1713) and Schopenhauer's "The world is my idea" (1836). Mill (1843) defined matter as "a permanent possibility of sensation," and Mach (1886) held that the world is composed of sensations. Carnap analyzed and systematized this view in the book that launched him: *The Logical Construction of the World* (1928). Fleck (1979 [1935]) gave constructivism a new twist: not individuals, but communities—in particular, scientific communities—construct the world.

The latter view became fashionable in academic circles, thanks to Kuhn (1962), Foucault (1969), and Feyerabend (1975). Thus, in an influential book, Latour and Woolgar (1986, 182) claim that "'out-there-ness' [i.e., the external world] is the *consequence* of scientific work rather than its *cause*." One might think that these writers were just philosophical unsophisticates who confuse facts with statements. Indeed, Latour and Woolgar assert that "A fact is nothing but a statement with no modality [i.e., no indication that it is entertained as a hypothesis, or that it has been confirmed] and no trace of authorship" (1986, 82). But, since they subsequently (ibid., 174ff.) launch an attack on realism, one is forced to take their subjectivism seriously. They leave no doubt as to their subjectivism when they state that "reality is the consequence rather than the cause of this construction" (ibid., 237). Other members of the school concur. Thus H. M. Collins (1981, 3) writes that "the natural world has a small or nonexistent role in the construction of scientific knowledge." And, because laboratories are full of artifacts, Knorr-Cetina (1983, 119) claims that "nowhere in the laboratory do we find 'nature' or 'reality' which is so crucial to the descriptivist interpretation of inquiry."

In short, according to ontological constructivism, reality is not independent of the knower but his product. Scientific research is "the process of secreting an unending stream of entities and relations that make up 'the world'" (Knorr-Cetina 1983, 135). For example, the celestial bodies are "cultural objects" (Garfinkel et al. 1981). Indeed, every object is "an icon of laboratory temporality" (whatever that may mean) (Lynch et al. 1983). A major philosophical mentor of the new sociology of science wrote: "*Scientific entities* (and, for that matter, all entities) *are projections and are thus tied to the theory, the ideology, the culture that projects them*" (Feyerabend 1990, 147, emphasis in original). Schopenhauer's formula "The world is *my* representation" now reads "The world is *our* construction."

That ontological constructivism inheres in age-old subjective idealism is recognized by only a few constructivists. Thus H. M. Collins (1981) admits that the new sociology of science has been influenced by such idealist philosophies as phenomenology, structuralism, poststructuralism, deconstructionism, and the word worship of the later Wittgenstein and the French school of general semiotics. And Woolgar (1986, 312) explains that the discourse analysis that he, Latour, Knorr-Cetina, and others practice is indebted to poststructuralism (in particular, Foucault and Derrida), which "is consistent with the position of the idealist wing of ethnomethodology that there is no reality independent of the words (texts, signs, documents, and so on) used to apprehend it. In other words, reality is constituted in and through discourse." The world is a library, and even "*praxis* cannot exist outside discourse" (ibid.).

If facts and theories were indeed the same, no fact could be used to test a theory, and no theory could guide the search for new facts—the way Merton (1957) and other scientists believe. Since theory testing and theory-steered exploration are facts of daily scientific life, it follows that the denial of the distinction between them is contrary to fact. Moreover, if fact and theory were identical, facts would have theoretical properties (e.g., consistency and explanatory power), and theories would have physical, chemical, biological, or social properties (e.g., viscosity and toxicity). Since this is not the case, the postulated identity is a mere confusion. Yet this muddle and the epistemological relativism that comes with it are characteristic of the "strong programme" in the sociology of science (see Bloor 1976). Its advocates claim that all of reality is a human construct, that all is invention and nothing discovery, and that all constructs have a social content.

Whereas constructivists write about "the social construction of scientific facts," most scientists and all realist philosophers would refer to the process of interaction among scientists (either face-to-face or via the literature). This process starts with a decision to explore a field and pose a question, proceeds to make an observation, a conjecture, or a critical remark, and ends up in one or more statements that are generally accepted (as sufficiently true), at least for the time being, for having passed the required tests. Thus, whereas a realist would say that the molecular composition and biological function of the TRF compound were *discovered* by scientists working in two rival (yet often cooperating) research teams, according to Latour and Woolgar (1986, 152) that finding was "a thoroughly social construction." This version of the story is a travesty of history; moreover, it is blatantly inconsistent with evolutionary biology, as well as with the scientific method.

In conclusion, ontological constructivism is neither true nor new. Worse, it discourages exploration of the world and thus the search for objective truth. Worse still, when put into practice, it is akin to shamanism and may thus have a negative social impact. For example, a professional who reads in *Social Work* an editorial entitled "Words create worlds" (Hartman 1991) is likely to advise a battered child or a homeless person: "Just talk yourself out of your dire circumstances."

5 Materialisms

No philosophy has been more misunderstood or vilified than materialism, largely because it is usually accompanied by irreligiosity. In ordinary language, materialism is often conflated with cupidity. In the metatheory of social science, it is often confused with naturalism, economicism, or even positivism. Naturalism is the version of vulgar materialism that denies the specificity of the social and consequently attempts to reduce social studies to natural science. Behaviorism, human sociobiology, and genetic determinism are three of the failed naturalistic versions of materialism. Another is economicism, the view that all human behavior is driven only by material or economic interests. In any event, philosophical materialism is not a single doctrine, but a whole family of world views.

Philosophical materialism is the family of ontologies which assert that all existents are material (concrete), though not necessarily tangible. Aside from this common thesis, materialisms differ widely. It is only by adding further requirements that a definite materialist ontology can be built or identified. This is how we can distinguish, among others, the following species: mechanism, naturalism (in particular, geographical and biological determinism), historical materialism, cultural materialism, and emergent materialism. We proceed to characterize them briefly with special reference to society.

Mechanism is the earliest kind of materialism: it was inherent in ancient atomism. It holds that everything in the world boils down to bodies or corpuscles in motion; so every science should be reducible, at least in principle, to mechanics. Examples: Hobbes's *De corpore* (1655), Descartes's posthumous *Traité du monde* (1664), and La Mettrie's *L'homme machine* (1747). Mechanism remained the nucleus of the modern world view until the middle of the nineteenth century, when field physics, thermodynamics, and evolutionary biology emerged.

Naturalism is an extension of mechanism. It holds that persons and societies are parts of nature and must therefore be studied in the same way as natural things. This is how social physics, social chemistry, social Darwinism, behaviorism, and human sociobiology came into being. Naturalists pay little or no attention to the beliefs, values, expectations, decisions, or strategies of individuals. (Some of them, the nominalists, radical behaviorists, and so-called eliminative materialists, deny even the existence of mind.) Nor do they admit the peculiar properties and patterns of social systems. In short, they exclude much and are radical, downward reductionists.

What holds for naturalism in general holds a fortiori for its main varieties: namely, environmental and biological determinism. The former, as represented by behaviorism, asserts that people are products of their natural environment alone, whereas the latter claims that we are the products of our genes, and that social differentiation is the outcome of natural selection. Each of these views contains a grain of truth: no serious social scientist can ignore environmental constraints and stimuli, heredity, or our animal condition. But neither view makes room for creativity, initiative, disinterested inquiry, or convention; neither explains the diversity or changeability of individuals and social systems; and neither has anything reasonable to say about any social systems above the family, such as the economy, the polity, and the culture. They purport to explain much with little and ignore the rest: they are simplistic.

The idealists, in particular such neo-Kantians as Simmel and Weber, as well as their successors, the rational choice theorists, rightly rejected naturalism in social science. But they were right for the wrong reason, in that they believed that social processes (to the extent that these are admissible to an individualist) are the outcome of mental processes alone. For example, Morgenstern (1972, 702) wrote: "An 'ethereal network' of decisions, expectations, plans, valuations, moves these physical objects [the tangible ones] around."

To a materialist, every mental process, whether affective or cognitive, is a brain process. He denies that ideas in themselves can move things, not because ideation, as a brain process, is causally ineffective, but because there are no ideas in themselves. Instead of speaking of the action of the mind on the body, he speaks of the action of certain parts of the brain on the rest of the body. If he is consistent, he will also hold that persons and social systems are material and satisfy some natural laws. However, materialists need not be radical reductionists or, in particular, naturalists. They may be emergentists: that is, admit that persons and social systems are largely made (are artifactual), whence they possess properties unknown to natural science. Shorter: Naturalism is right in holding that people and societies are material, wrong in denying their emergent features. This is the gist of *emergentist materialism*, of which more shortly.

Historical materialism, the social philosophy of Marxism, adds a much-needed social dimension to naturalism (see Marx and Engels 1986). Its central theses are that (*a*) every society has a material infrastructure, the economy, capped by an ideal superstructure (*ideelles Überbau*), composed by the polity and the culture; (*b*) the economy is the prime mover of every society: the superstructure merely reflects and consolidates the relations of economic production; and (*c*) all stratified societies are conflictive, and all social change derives ultimately from the clash of economic interests. When first proposed in the mid-nineteenth century, these ideas were original, shocking, and powerful, both intellectually and politically. They redirected much social research and formed the nucleus of an ideology that eventually affected one-third of humankind, leading to a radical redrawing of the political map of the planet. This is not the place to inquire into the causes of the ultimate failure of this vast social movement in recent years (for which, see Bunge forthcoming). Here we will ask only what, if anything, is wrong with the above three tenets of historical materialism.

The infrastructure–superstructure thesis is a version of the old matter–soul dualism, whence it is inconsistent with materialism. Nor is this the only vestige of idealism in historical materialism. Another is the well-known view that the characters who appear on the economic stage are but the personifications of the economic relations that exist among them (Marx 1967 [1867]). In short, every individual is "an ensemble of social relations" (Marx 1973 [1857–58]). This structuralism *avant la lettre* is a piece of Platonism, for it amounts to positing the existence of relations prior to and above the terms related. (If *Rab* is the case, a Platonist holds that the individuals *a* and *b* merely exemplify the preexisting *R*, whereas a nominalist holds that only *a* and *b* exist.)

A further vestige of idealism is found in Lenin (1947 [1908], 251), who scolded Dietzgen for rejecting the dualistic opposition between matter and ideas, without which Lenin thought there could be no opposition between materialism and idealism. In the same work (ibid., 121) he equated objective truth with absolute truth, and defined it as "truth not dependent upon man and mankind." He thus unwittingly adopted Plato's, Leibniz's, and Bolzano's idealist thesis about propositions in themselves—which was to be resurrected by Popper (1972). Even more remarkable is Lenin's anticipation of Popper's "three worlds" typology. Indeed, in his *Philosophical Notebooks* (Lenin 1972 [1914], 182) he wrote with reference to our knowledge of the external world: "Here there are *actually,* objectively, *three* members: (1) nature; (2) human cognition = the human *brain* (as the highest product of this same nature); and (3) the form of reflection of nature in human cognition, and this form consists precisely of concepts, laws, categories, etc." It is not easy to be a consistent materialist.

A consistent materialist will not turn the mind-over-matter dogma upside down and adopt the matter-over-mind tenet instead. He will refuse to detach the ideal from the material, just as he will abstain from detaching a smile from a face. He will talk about ideating brains, along with beating hearts, and will regard the polity and the culture as material (though not physical) systems in being composed of concrete entities, namely people. This will lead him to reject the second Marxist tenet, the thesis that society is "ultimately" driven by the economy—a special case of the alleged primacy of the material over the spiritual. He may hold instead that either the environment or any of the four main subsystems of society—the biological, economic, political, or cultural—may initiate changes likely to drag along the rest in their wake (e.g., a technological invention or a new piece of legislation may trigger economic changes).

This is indeed what our BEPC model of society boils down to (see chap. 10, sec. 3).

The failure of the second thesis of historical materialism will induce the consistent materialist to reject the third tenet. While agreeing on the centrality of conflict, he will point out that there are plenty of social conflicts in addition to those that oppose the poor to the rich—for example, sexual, ethnic, religious, and international conflicts. Some conflicts are of the top-down or bottom-up types, but others are of the in–out kind; they all occur in parallel, and some of them intertwine (see, e.g., Mann 1986, 1993). Moreover, cooperation is just as pervasive as conflict: think of families, schools, firms, and NGOs.

In short, historical materialism is wrong not for being materialist but for being one-sided and inconsistent. A consistent materialist will favor a five-dimensional—environmental, biological, economic, political, and cultural—approach to society and history. He will also admit cooperation along with conflict. And, if he happens to have a scientific mind-set, he will update his philosophy in the light of scientific advances.

Historical materialism lies midway between idealism and emergent materialism. From the former it has inherited not only the opposition between matter and spirit, but also conceptual fuzziness and dogmatism. In fact, historical materialism has never been formulated in a precise way; in particular, its central notion of dialectical "contradiction" is as fuzzy as Hegel's (see Bunge 1981c). Further, although historical materialism has left a deep imprint on social science—particularly on anthropology, economics, and history—it has not learned much from it and has failed to keep up with the momentous transformations in both the industrialized societies and the Third World. This reluctance of most Marxists to change along with social science and society is surely in part responsible for the failure of the ruling Marxist parties to respond adaptively to the deep economic and political crises in the so-called socialist countries around 1990—a cruel irony in the case of a dynamicist philosophy. So much for Marxist materialism.

Cultural materialism, championed by Marvin Harris (1979) and deservedly popular among anthropologists, starts where historical materialism left off. It differs from the latter in that it rejects the obscurities of dialectics and includes environmental challenges, as well as sex and biological reproduction, as powerful motivations of human behavior. Consequently, cultural materialism—which perhaps ought to be called "ecobioeconomic materialism"—pays close attention to environmental and demographic variables, in particular to the economic causes and effects of population growth. Thus, one of its most fruitful central theses is this: Reproduction pressure → overproduction (in particular, overhunting, overfishing, and overcultivation) → depletion of natural resources → misery → social decline. This is the by now familiar tragedy of the Sumerians, the Mayas, and other peoples.

While cultural materialism has much to its credit (see Ross 1980), it is open to three major objections. One is that it takes over from Marxism the idealist thesis of the "superstructure" as a disembodied entity, instead of regarding it as a subsystem of society. The second is that it espouses the empiricist (inductivist) view of concept formation as deriving always from data and the naive view of theory construction as being rule-directed. (However, empiricism is a professional hazard for anthropologists and in any event is far less crippling than subjectivism.) The third objectionable feature of cultural materialism is that it is a rational choice version of functionalism. Indeed, Harris assumes that all social inventions, from agriculture to the state, from dietary taboos to fertility cults, are introduced on the basis of cost–benefit considerations, albeit mostly unconsciously. For example, according to Harris, the Aztecs practiced human sacrifice because they were short on animal proteins—even though, as a matter of fact, they got only a few grams of human flesh each year. There are at least three problems with this thesis. One is that it underrates human stupidity, cruelty, and mythmaking. Another is that it underrates the need and ability of the ruling class to stage impressive public spectacles (see León-Portilla 1980). A third is that it fails to explain why people tend to retain certain habits even after they have become dysfunctional—as is nowadays the case with the right to reproduce.

The flaws in both historical and cultural materialism suggest how to proceed in order to overhaul materialism and render it formally precise and up-to-date in light of contemporary science. As a matter of fact, I employed this strategy in Part A to elucidate the concepts of thing (in particular, system), property (in particular, emergent), process, pattern, and several others. In particular, I defined a material entity as one capable of changing and a concrete system as one composed exclusively of material things connected to one another (chap. 1). The key postulates common to all materialisms can be stated as follows:

M1. An object is real (or exists really) if and only if it is material.

M2. The real world is the system composed of all material things.

In particular, a system is real (material) if and only if it is composed exclusively of real (i.e., material) parts. Accordingly, social systems are material systems. (On the other hand, institutions, such as the family and the mail, if conceived as kinds or families of social systems, are just as immaterial as sets.) If we now define the word *matter* as the collection of all material objects and *reality* as the collection of all real objects, we come up with the identity: reality = matter. Note that this is an assumption, not a definition. Indeed, by definition, a real object is one that exists independently of the knower. But objective idealists, like Plato, Hegel, and Bolzano, postulate that ideas exist by themselves; they are ontological realists but not materialists. Yet many scholars, in particular Marxists, equate materialism with realism, thus confusing an ontological doctrine (materialism) with an epistemological one (realism).

Using some elementary formal tools and keeping close to contemporary science and technology, it is possible to build a materialist ontology which is (*a*) *precise:* every key concept is exact or exactifiable; (*b*) *systematic:* every statement is a member of a hypothetico-deductive system; (*c*) *scientific:* every hypothesis is consistent with contemporary science; (*d*) *dynamicist:* every entity is changeable; (*e*) *systemic:* every entity is a system or a component of such; (*f*) *emergentist:* every system has properties that its components lack; (*g*) *evolutionist:* every emergence is a stage in some evolutionary process. We call this ontology *emergentist* (or *scientific*) materialism (Bunge 1977*b*, 1979*b*, 1981*c*).

The upshot of this discussion for social science is that, unlike its predecessors, emergent (or scientific) materialism focuses on social systems and assigns ideas an important function in social life, yet without falling into idealist extravagance. It takes human beings in their entirety, with their needs and desires, ideas and social behavior, without attempting to reduce everything social to either biological or economic factors. In particular, scientific materialism does not limit human life to procreation, production, consumption, or fighting: it also encompasses friendship and cooperation, contemplation and rationality, morality and the law. This broad view is materialist, because it refuses to detach ideas and their symbols from living brains and behavior, and also, far from regarding culture as an autonomous sphere, views it as one of the three major artificial subsystems of society—neither passive mirror nor prime mover. This view suggests that all the social sciences are equally important components of a single cultural system.

Social systems, particularly formal organizations such as firms and schools, could not exist without some thinking. But this does not entail that they exist only insofar as they are thought of, as spiritualists claim (e.g., Burdeau 1967, 2: 252: *"L'Etat n'existe que parce qu'il est pensé"*). Admitting and even stressing the role of invention, reasoning, choice, evaluation, decision, and the like does not commit one to embracing idealism, all the more so since the latter is inconsistent with science. Indeed, factual scientists study and handle only material things, from electrons and fields to people and societies. And far from working under the delusion that such things come into being as a result of their thinking, natural and social scientists presuppose that their objects of study exist or may exist on their own, whether in the present, the past, or the future.

In short, materialism has triumphed, whereas spiritualism has failed in scientific social studies as well as in natural science. Hence any philosophy compatible with factual science will be materialist. To be sure, social relations pass through the heads of people, but it is such heads, not immaterial minds, that do the feeling, perceiving, thinking, and the like. It is also true that scientists map the world with ideas, but these are processes in their brains and are thus objects of scientific study rather than the property of idealist philosophers. The materialist view of ideas helps to explain why some knowledge of the world is adequate: being part of the world, some animals can get inside knowledge of it. However, knowledge is the subject of the next two chapters, devoted to the major epistemological doctrines that have surfaced so far in the metatheory of social studies.

12 :: Intuitionism, Empiricism, Pragmatism, and Rationalism

This chapter deals with four influential families of doctrines about knowledge—intuitionism, empiricism, pragmatism, and rationalism—as well as with some of their combinations. We first met intuitionism in chapter 9, section 5, where we identified it with the epistemology of holism. Intuitionism claims that human beings, or at least some of them, have the ability to grasp things or ideas in an immediate fashion, without analysis. Bergson is perhaps the best and clearest representative of modern radical intuitionism. By comparison, Kant and Dilthey were moderate intuitionists, for they acknowledged the need for intellect, which Bergson held in contempt.

In the field of social studies, only Dilthey and his few followers—in particular, the hermeneuticists (e.g., Geertz), phenomenological sociologists (e.g., Schütz), symbolic interactionists (e.g., Blumer), and ethnomethodologists (e.g., Garfinkel)—are intuitionists. In particular, Dilthey conceived of Verstehen (insight, perceptiveness, comprehension, or interpretation) as irrational and synthetic (or global), unlike Erklärung (explanation), which was admittedly rational and analytic but allegedly limited to mathematics and natural science.

Empiricism is inimical to intuitionism, and it comes in two basic varieties: epistemological and ontological. According to epistemological empiricism, all knowledge originates in experience, particularly in perception, whether spontaneous, as in daily life, or tutored, as in scientific research. We shall not be concerned here with ontological empiricism, according to which to be is to perceive or to be perceived. This view, held by Berkeley, Avenarius, Mach, the later William James, and the young Carnap, has remained a curiosity.

By contrast, epistemological empiricism is the most influential epistemology in all the factual sciences except for neoclassical microeconomics. Even some sophisticated textbooks of theoretical physics start off with a declaration of empiricist faith, only to plunge immediately into conceptual constructions, such as field theories and quantum mechanics, which are devoid of any constructs distilled from sense experience. I will criticize the narrowness of empiricism without, however, joining the positivism bashers who reject all concern for fact finding and empirical testing.

Pragmatism is action-centered: according to this doctrine, doing is the source, content, test, and worth of all knowledge. Pragmatism comes in two versions: moderate, or refined, and radical, or crass. Peirce, Dewey, and C. I. Lewis were moderate pragmatists. The proverbial red-neck who despises and hates intellectuals is a radical pragmatist; so was Nietzsche. But both versions of pragmatism discourage disinterested research and thus unwittingly destroy the source of the very technology they extol.

Finally, rationalism is at variance with both intuitionism and empiricism. Crudely put, rationalism is trust in reason. It, too, comes in two strengths: moderate and radical. Whoever regards reason as necessary though insufficient to understand anything embraces a moderate version of rationalism, one that can be combined with either moderate intuitionism, as in the case of Weber, or moderate empiricism, as in the case of nearly every scientist.

Radical rationalism, fathered by Plato, is the thesis that reason is both necessary and sufficient not only in mathematics but also in science and technology. Many rational choice theorists, particularly the neo-Austrian economists and the self-styled "economic imperialists," have embraced radical rationalism. They are apriorists; that is they do not care for empirical data. Apriorism is the one feature that radical rationalists share with intuitionists and that unites them against positivists and scientific realists.

We will examine these various positions, find them unsatisfactory, and end up by proposing a particular synthesis of rationalism and empiricism.

1 Intuitionism

Intuition is, of course, immediate cognition: knowledge attained with little or no reflection. It can be perceptual or conceptual (intellectual). Thus we normally recognize effortlessly familiar faces—though sometimes we make mistakes. We can also "see" without cogitation that two propositions, such as "It is raining" and "The TV set is set on," are not equivalent to one another, whereas the logical equivalence of two mathematical formulas may require laborious proof.

Intuition, then, is for real, but it is at least as fallible as perception and reasoning. However, like these, intuition can be trained. Such training comes with experience and reflection. Thus, through doing mathematics, one may acquire intuition with regard to abstract matters. In this case, far from being pre-analytic, intuition is a bonus of reason. And in all cases intuition must be checked against either reasoning or experiment. This is particularly true of objects, such as those studied in mathematics, nuclear physics, and social science, that are inaccessible to ordinary experience.

In short, intuition is only one phase of cognition. Therefore the claim that a given problem, whether cognitive, practical, or moral, can be handled only intuitively is a tacit admission of ignorance or sloth. Hence intuitionism, the view according to which intuition is infallible and, moreover, the highest cognitive faculty, is false. (More in Bunge 1962*b*.) Moreover, intuitionism opens the gates to wild fantasy and induces gullibility. Witness radical "feminist theory." For example, Shepherd (1993) endorses Jungian psychology, parapsychology, holistic metaphysics, and holistic medicine along with intuitionism.

Although there is no logical relation between intuitionism and spiritualism, they are correlated in fact. Bergson (e.g., 1903) and Dilthey (e.g., 1959 [1883], [1900]) are cases in point. We will disregard the former, since he never influenced social studies except indirectly, through his anti-intellectualism. (For an early criticism, see Benda 1912.) On the other hand, Dilthey is familiar to some social scientists for his spiritualist and intuitionist claims that (*a*) the social sciences are Geisteswissenschaften (sciences of the spirit) and therefore disjoint from the natural sciences; (*b*) unlike the natural scientist, the social scientist makes ample use of empathy (*Mitempfindung*) and aims at comprehension (*Verstehen*) rather than explanation (*Erklärung*); (*c*) the *Geisteswissenschaftler* is interested only in the particular and the whole, never in the general or the part, and they can be grasped at one stroke, not through rational or analytic effort; (*d*) in research we must rely on "the power of personal life" rather than "the mere force of intelligence"; and (*e*) complying with the preceding rules will result in infallible knowledge.

Dilthey did not offer any evidence for these claims, other than that biographers try to put themselves in the shoes of their subjects and historians do not discover any laws. But then intuitionists claim to have instant, certain knowledge of things: they have no use for either tests or the (positive or negative) evidence that these may yield. The reader is invited to apply these intuitionist theses to the description, understanding, steering, or redesign of a business corporation or a government department. He is, moreover, invited to preface his report to his supervisor or client with the caution: "Not to be checked, questioned or revised, for it is the product of my infallible intuition."

Husserl (1950 [1931] 1952 [1913]), the father of phenomenology and the grandfather of existentialism, pushed intuitionism a step further. He held that we can grasp the immutable *eidos,* or essence, of all things—ideal or concrete, natural or social—through a special intellectual yet nonrational intuition called "vision of essences" (*Wesensschau*). Such intuition would proceed independently of ordinary experience; moreover, it could be exercised only by "bracketing out" real things—that is, pretending that they do not exist. In short, we grasp essence by ignoring existence. Husserl called this operation which characterizes methodological solipsism 'époché' (see chap. 11, sec. 3).

Characteristically, Husserl did not bother to elucidate his notion of essence. His disciple Heidegger used the same word even more indiscriminately. For example, in his essay on truth, Heidegger (1976 [1943]) claimed that (*a*) the essence of truth is freedom, and (*b*) the essence of freedom is truth. Now, the combination of these sentences yields "The essence of the essence of truth is truth" and "The essence of the essence of freedom is freedom." Neither of these word strings is meaningful, even assuming that "essence of essence" equals "quintessence." But, of course, Heidegger was not concerned with sense.

According to phenomenology, the vision of essences would yield truths that, though not formal, are impregnable to criticism on the strength of either rational argument or empirical data. Of course, no evidence for the existence of either autonomous essences or that extraordinary faculty is offered. On the other hand, any number of cases can be cited of scientific discoveries of essential or basic properties and laws—for example, those of nuclear physics and genetics—through imagining and testing counterintuitive theories. Interestingly, phenomenology does not bar doubt and criticism in general; it merely confines them to empirical data and factual science. The latter would then be fraught with uncertainty: it would be a second-class field relative to the "eidetic sciences," or sciences of essences, which are said to yield absolute, definitive truths. Husserl himself (1950 [1931], 30) emphasized that phenomenology "forms the *extremest contrast to sciences in the hitherto accepted sense,* positive, *'objective'* sciences." Moreover, as we saw above, he (1954 [1936]) blamed naturalism and the exact sciences for what he saw as "the crisis of European science." Given the anti-scientific stand of phenomenology, it is hard to understand why it has lately become respectable among some students of society (see chap. 11, sec. 3).

In sum, intuitionism is not a true and fruitful philosophy of knowledge. And phenomenology is the worst of all varieties of intuitionism, for postulating the existence of a Wesensschau, or ability to "see" essences in a direct, immediate fashion. It is the worst in exempting the student from the tasks of collecting data and building theories—in particular, mathematical models—as well as from the scientific and moral responsibility of putting them to the test. In short, phenomenology is dogmatic.

This is not to deny the role of intuitions of various kinds. We often do start with some intuitive ideas. But, after checking and refining or rejecting them, we end up with different ideas, most of which are counterintuitive. However, with reference to facts or ideas that lie beyond everyday life, initial intuitions are rare or, when they do occur, are usually mistaken. This holds in particular for large social systems and vast social processes, no less than for elementary particles and galaxies. In all such cases reliance upon intuition is bound to lead either nowhere or to disaster. This is why intuitionism is at best barren and at worst disastrous, in social studies and policymaking as well as in physics.

2 Contemporary Obscurantism

Obscurantists dispense with reason, experience, or both. Consequently they reject rationalism, empiricism, and any combination of the two. Moreover, many of their writings are unintelligible and sometimes even ungrammatical. Regrettably, irrationalism is becoming increasingly fashionable once again— which is both an indicator and a cause of cultural decadence. Though particularly strong in literature and communications departments (see Livingston 1988, 1991), it is spreading through arts faculties too. Consider the following course description from the New School for Social Research in New York: "Kierkegaard was the first to deconstruct metaphysics; he was also the first to realize that the task cannot be accomplished. This makes him the first postclassical philosopher." Shorter: Kierkegaard realized that it is impossible to "deconstruct" (unmask?) metaphysics; yet, at the same time, he accomplished this task. Parallel: Levitation is of course impossible, but I do it all the time. These are instances of self-contradictory, hence irrational, statements.

Rational animals try to avoid contradicting themselves for several reasons. A first, logical reason is that contradictions are (formally) false. A second, is that a contradiction implies anything, whether true or false, relevant or irrelevant, whence it cannot be judged by its consequences. (For any proposition $A: A$ & $\neg A \Rightarrow B$, with B arbitrary. Proof: By definition, $A \Rightarrow B =_{df} \neg A \vee B$, which is true if A is false, regardless of the truth-value of B.) The methodological reason for avoiding contradiction is that every empirical confirmation of A disconfirms $\neg A$ and thus invalidates the conjunction A & $\neg A$. (The effect of refutation is, of course, the same.) The practical reason is that we cannot carry out two mutually incompatible actions at the same time. And the moral reason is that good and evil are mutually exclusive.

It might be contended—as Hegel, Kierkegaard, and Sartre did—that reality itself is absurd (or contradictory). But this is absurd, because reality is not a proposition, hence it has no logical properties such as consistency or its dual. True, some concrete systems and some processes contain mutually opposing components, aspects, or forces. But these are cases of ontic opposition, not logical contradiction. It is also true that the conflation between real opposition and logical contradiction, as well as the corresponding confusion of ontology with logic, is unavoidable in idealist philosophy, particularly Hegel's. However, this only goes to show that idealist philosophy is not a reliable guide to either scientific research or rational action.

A number of students of society, swayed by intuitionism, pragmatism, existentialism, or psychoanalysis, hold that humans are basically irrational. They overlook the fact that many people, at several periods of history, have engaged in rational discourse, overcome superstition, adopted rational beliefs, and engaged in rational action, even without having had the benefits of a college education. A good example of this is the rather quick manner in which Amerindians lost their faith in animism, shamanism, and magic when confronted by their European conquerors. At the beginning they believed the Spaniards to be supernatural, invincible, and immortal. But, as they saw them being taken sick and dying, and as they got used to European artifacts, the Amerindians realized that their new masters were human beings like themselves (Trigger 1991, 1211).

A more recent, sudden, massive, and tragic example of loss of faith in a belief system, in the face of its inability to explain and stem the course of events, is the downfall of "scientific communism" in the former Soviet bloc. This does not entail that the superstitions that are replacing it are any better. But it does go to show that one must not exaggerate the power of traditional belief systems compared with that of experience and reason. Recall Lincoln's law about nobody being able to fool all the people all the time.

Finally, brief mention must be made of a more subtle assault on reason: namely, the linguistic philosophy introduced by the later Wittgenstein (1953). This philosophy lies on the fringe of irrationalism in being about words, not ideas or facts, and in discouraging formalization, theorizing, and curiosity about science and technology. Consequently it turns students away from logic, science, and technology and unwittingly makes them sympathetic to philosophical hermeneutics, according to which everything is a sign or a symbol to be interpreted (recall chap. 11, sec. 2). A product of this "linguistic turn" is the recent revival of rhetoric and the birth of so-called rhetorics of the social sciences. Its effect on social studies can be gauged from the popularity of Rorty's *Philosophy and the Mirror of Nature* (1979) and McCloskey's *The Rhetoric of Economics* (1985). A key thesis of both books is that doing science is just engaging in conversation. McCloskey adds that the end results of scientific research are persuasive metaphors rather than maximally true data or theories.

To be sure, communication is essential to all research. But it is no less true that fruitful conversation is possible only when there are interesting ideas to be discussed: the weather and sports are unlikely to be subjects of fruitful scientific chats. It is also true that argumentation, even in the sciences, is sometimes rhetorical and spirited, rather than rigorous and dispassionate, and that some of what passes for theory is just metaphor. But the rhetoricians do not limit themselves to noting these platitudes: they claim that the whole point of social science is rhetoric aimed at persuasion rather than argumentation aimed at truth. Thus McCloskey (1985, xvii) claims that all economic constructs, including mathematical models and statistical tests, "may be seen as figures of speech—metaphors, analogies, and appeals to authority." We are told that "Good science is good conversation" and that "Methodology is bourgeois." The implications are clear: Do not take economics and methodology seriously and, in general, reject "scientism" and "modernism." Shorter: Switch off the light.

Given the strong influence of obscurantism on social life and even in academic circles, it should be studied and criticized scientifically, for its diffusion interferes destructively with that of the scientific approach to research and policymaking.

3 Vulgar Empiricism and Crypto-Empiricism

Empirical research, a component of every serious exploration of reality, is sometimes confused with empiricism, a philosophy. Empiricism is the family of philosophies according to which only experiences exist (ontological empiricism), and these are the sole source and test of ideas (epistemological empiricism). We distinguish two main empiricist schools: vulgar (or naive) empiricism and logical empiricism (or neo-positivism). The former holds that all knowledge is experiential, so scientific knowledge is not qualitatively different from ordinary knowledge. This was the view of Bacon, Locke, and Hume, as well as of the later Wittgenstein, his followers, and a number of sociologists of science. Logical empiricists, by contrast, draw a sharp boundary between science and nonscience, and within the former they distinguish logic from what they call the empirical sciences (what I call the factual sciences). We shall examine logical empiricism in the next section. But first we will examine vulgar empiricism and its unwitting adoption by some sociologists of science.

Naive empiricism is common sense, or untutored philosophy. Although it may be suited to the lower animals, it does not suit the higher ones. Thus, it has been known for many years that even rats have expectations, and that these guide their search for sensory stimulation and influence their perception. We also know, particularly since the birth of modern physics, that high-level scientific concepts have neither perceptual counterparts nor (*pace* Kant) intuitive contents (see Einstein 1936). Think, for example, of the concepts of relation, variance, structure, mass, energy, entropy, stress (mechanical, physiological, or social), probability, metabolism, evolution, society, culture, history, the state, or justice. All these are nonempirical concepts, in not being related directly to perception or action; yet they are indispensable in accounting for factual items.

What holds for high-powered scientific concepts holds, a fortiori, for the hypotheses containing them. All such constructs are intellectual constructions invented by highly evolved individual brains. Think, for example, of the trivial theorem: "In a social system divided into n groups there are $\frac{1}{2} n (n - 1)$ logically possible symmetric intergroup relations." This simple counterexample suffices to refute all kinds of empiricism. Another argument against empiricism is the failure of ontological and methodological individualism (see chap. 9). Indeed, because individuals are observable but societies are not, empiricism implies individualism. Therefore, if the latter falls, it drags empiricism down with it. ($E \Rightarrow I$ & $\neg I \therefore \neg E$.)

However, empiricism is far from being totally groundless. Indeed, some low-level nontechnical concepts are suggested by experience (e.g., the non-technical [prescientific] concepts of thing, place, duration, person, behavior, and exchange). Still, for science, these are only precursors of the corresponding scientific concepts. It is also true, as well as more important, that in science all hypotheses are supposed to be empirically testable, at least in principle, if only indirectly, through the direct test of logically related hypotheses. *This* is the important, valid, durable contribution of empiricism. It is incorporated in what will be called "ratio-empiricism" (sec. 6).

The failure of naive or vulgar empiricism may best be seen by examining a contemporary example. A major tenet of the constructivist-relativist sociology of science championed by Barnes, Bloor, H. M. Collins, Garfinkel, Knorr-Cetina, Latour, Mulkay, Pinch, Woolgar, and others is that there is nothing peculiar about science: it is just one more "social construction," one more "way of world-making" (Goodman's phrase), one more "political arena." But what can one expect from research conducted with this presupposition, which may be called 'ordinarism'? Can we expect it to teach us what *distinguishes* authentic science from ordinary knowledge, bogus science, or other fields of human endeavor, such as technology and ideology, or industry and government, and how it *interacts* with them? Obviously not, since it denies such differences and therefore the very possibility of such interactions. Can we expect it to discover the social factors that stimulate the advancement of science and those that inhibit it? Clearly not, since it regards all social factors as themselves constructions, specifically, scientific constructions. Nor can we expect it to *discover* anything else, since it denies the very possibility of discovering anything existing out there, for the simple reason that it holds that there is nothing "out there" (recall chap. 11, sec. 4, on ontological constructivism). If we take constructivism at its word, we can expect it to deliver only what it makes up itself. And if we take the associated relativism at its word, we can expect its deliveries to be no better than fables. So why believe anything this school tells us?

The classical empiricist Francis Bacon—not a hero of the constructivist-relativist school—believed that he had hit on a handful of rules, whereby just a few ordinary people could make scientific findings. The advocates of constructivism-relativism (in particular, Knorr-Cetina 1981 and Latour 1983) concur with the grandfather of positivism, though without giving him credit. They go even further, asserting that there is nothing special about science, "nothing of any cognitive quality." Thus Latour (1983, 162): "Scientific fact is the product of average, ordinary people and settings, linked to one another by no special norms or communication forms, but who work with inscription devices." Never mind what the inscriptions mean and how their content is checked for consistency and truth: only the "technology of inscribing (writing, schooling, printing, recording devices)" is said to matter. "To take up Feyerabend's saying: 'in the laboratory anything goes, except the inscription devices and the papers'" (Latour 1983, 161).

The constructivist-relativist view of scientific research is an oversocialized version of Bacon's naive empiricism. According to this view, scientists occupy themselves by collecting (or rather constructing) data, making "inscriptions," or texts, "negotiating" with one another, and changing their "rules" (even their "rules for seeing") in mysterious ways. (See, e.g., H. M. Collins 1983.) Spotting problems, conceiving hypotheses, designing and carrying out experiments, and checking for either truth or consistency do not occur in what Collins calls the "Wittgensteinian/phenomenological/Kuhnian model of scientific activity." In other words, this is not a model of real scientific research: it is a philosophical fantasy.

Because constructivism-relativism covertly espouses vulgar empiricism, it pays no attention to conceptual problems and scientific theories. Or, when it does, it mistakes them for sets of symbols that can be subjected to ordinary language (or "semiotic") analysis. Thus Latour (1988) subjected Einstein's special relativity theory to such analysis and concluded that it was about "communication among long-distance travelers" rather than bodies embedded in electromagnetic fields—which, of course, fails to square with the assumption that the theory holds everywhere, even in outer space. Nor does it tell us how the famous formula $E = mc^2$ could be of any use to long-distance travelers.

Because this school overlooks or misinterprets scientific theories, it fails to give an adequate (true) account of modern laboratory operations, all of which presuppose some theories, and some of which are designed to test theories. Thus Latour and Woolgar (1979), as well as Knorr-Cetina (1981), believe that the essence of laboratory work is the manipulation of artifacts. In the process, scientists do not discover or invent anything—not even the instruments themselves. They merely acquire and accumulate "new skills in manipulating things," especially laboratory equipment (Knorr-Cetina 1981; Latour 1983). Actually, the handling of laboratory equipment is often left to lab technicians or even to automated devices, for instruments are only means—means to produce items of objective knowledge about the world. When means are systematically mistaken for goals, something is seriously amiss, not only in morality, but everywhere.

Presumably, on this operationist view of scientific research, Newton did not investigate moving bodies (the referents of mechanics) but was busy handling measuring instruments, which, alas, he did not particularly care for. Moreover, withdrawn though he was, Newton must have engaged in "negotiating" with his rivals, in particular the Cartesians and Leibniz, whom he in fact criticized mercilessly. His ultimate victory over them was presumably a result of his superior ability in outmaneuvering rivals: he was the better politician. Likewise, Crick and Watson should presumably be presented as spending their time in Cambridge making measurements (which they never actually did) and "negotiating" with Rosalind Franklin and other crystallographers, as well as with Linus Pauling via his son, under the delusion that they were intent on figuring out the composition and structure of hereditary material. If they had only known about the constructivist-relativist program, they would have realized what they were actually doing: nothing like consulting your constructivist-relativist therapist to rid yourself of your delusions.

Advocates of the new sociology of science claim over and over again that, far from neglecting the "technical content" of the scientific projects they study, they provide "detailed accounts of the 'nuts and bolts' of scientific activity" (Pinch 1985, 3). This they accomplish not by undergoing a normal, rigorous, lengthy scientific apprenticeship but by visiting scientific laboratories. Thus Pinch (1985, 5) tells us that he became "familiar" with the tricky problem of solar neutrinos from "having visited the site of the experiment [Raymond Davis's] and having spent several days talking with and 'observing' the experimental group." No solid background in theoretical or experimental physics seems to be required to accomplish this task. All one needs is enough pluck to ask for permission to visit a laboratory and sufficient command of a natural language to understand the simplified version that the host is prepared to hand out to the intruder. Although this passes for participant observation, it is only pre-Malinowski verandah observation.

Every serious student knows that in order to participate effectively in a scientific project, in any capacity other than that of either journalist or lab technician, it is necessary to understand the problem that is being investigated. For example, to understand the so-called problem of solar neutrinos, one must be able to make sense of the complex mathematical equations for the neutrino flux. And to grasp the experimental design, one must understand, among other things, the principle of neutrino detection that is being employed, which calls for some theoretical atomic physics. Otherwise the problem, which is that of explaining the discrepancy between the measurement data and the theoretical calculation, cannot be understood, let alone expounded, in any depth. Only the specialist can account for the "nuts and bolts" of any particular piece of scientific research. Science is not that ordinary, after all.

The constructivist-relativist does not bother to learn the language of the tribe he claims to study. Once or twice in a lifetime he visits a physics or biology laboratory, without knowing any physics or biology. Yet he claims to possess a quick, foolproof method for acquiring "native competence" in any science— that is, for mastering the tacit, as well as the explicit, rules of any scientific "game." The recipe is this: "Tacit knowledge is best acquired through face-to-face contact" with scientists—never mind their subject matter (H. M. Collins 1983, 92). Yet the same author admits that "The method of full participation can rarely be attained in practice . . . but a series of depth interviews can be an acceptable substitute" (ibid., 93). Shorter: To master a research field, one need not undergo any training in it, let alone conduct original research; a stint at journalism suffices.

No wonder the findings of sociologists of science who believe that scientific research is an ordinary endeavor are themselves ordinary. In fact, their findings are of two kinds: correct, but unoriginal, or outrageously false. The former are few and obvious: that scientific research is performed not in isolation but in the midst of a social network; that every member of a research team exchanges information, questions, evaluations, proposals, and so forth with other members; that scientists make statements of different kinds (e.g., tentative or assertive); and that there is an ongoing transformation of items of one kind into items of another.

Side by side with such platitudes, we find such obvious blunders as assertions that every statement has a social content; that "a statement becomes a fact" when "freed from the circumstances of its production" (Latour and Woolgar 1979); that reality is constructed and "deconstructed" in the same way as a literary text; that "the whole process of fact construction has been shown to be accountable inside a sociological framework" (Latour 1980, 53); that even the notion of a contradiction, as well as the operations of instrument calibration and statistical analysis, can, and must, be construed in sociological terms (H. M. Collins 1983, 111); that "inferences from the general to the particular actually have an inductive character" (Barnes 1982, 101); and so on and so forth.

In short, as the old chestnut goes, what is true in the new sociology of science is not new, and what is original is false. Its dismal performance suggests the following morals: (*a*) If you wish to learn about science, start by studying some; (*b*) if you ignore philosophy, you will end up reinventing bad philosophy; (*c*) where anything goes, nothing goes well.

So much for vulgar empiricism and its unlikely bedfellow, constructivism-relativism. Neither of them tells us what makes scientific practice different from any other. Let us turn next to the most refined, interesting version of empiricism.

4 Logical Empiricism

Logical empiricism (or neo-positivism), born and nurtured in the short-lived but intense Vienna Circle (1926–36) and its Prague and Berlin satellites, is the most sophisticated kind of empiricism. In contrast to classical empiricism, it favors exactness and stresses the importance and autonomy of logic and mathematics. Like its ancestor, it is centrally concerned with empirical testability and induction, is scientistic, and fights nonsense and anti-science. It regards sense-data as the solid foundation of all knowledge, attempts to minimize the role of theoretical terms or even to eliminate them altogether, and professes to despise metaphysics—while engaging in phenomenalist metaphysics.

This school culminated and exhausted itself in the *International Encyclopedia of Unified Science* (1938–62). The project, conceived by the sociologist Otto Neurath and seconded by the philosopher Rudolf Carnap and the semiotician Charles W. Morris, aimed to unify the sciences through the adoption of a common language and a common method: those of physics. However, theirs was only a halfway physicalist project. It fell short of physicalism, or vulgar materialism, in demanding the linguistic and methodological, but not the conceptual (hence ontological), reduction of all the sciences to physics. This was perhaps a result of a compromise among the founders: Neurath was a radical physicalist, Carnap a follower of Mach's sensationalism, according to which physical objects are just bundles of sense-data, and Morris was interested in signs.

The original project was never carried through. For one thing, most of the fascicles of the *Encyclopedia* were specialized monographs: there was little inter-disciplinarity and even less physicalism. In particular, no attempt was made to reduce biology and psychology, let alone social science, to physics. Worse, by the time the *Encyclopedia* had become well known, logical positivism was dying out—so much so that the last monograph to be published under the umbrella of the *Encyclopedia* was Kuhn's best-seller, the *Structure of Scientific Revolutions* (1962), a decisively anti-positivist work and, to some extent, irrationalist to boot. Indeed, among other things, Kuhn exalted intuition and metaphor, overlooked the function of mathematics in theory construction, and mini-mized the role of adverse empirical evidence and criticism in the rejection of theories. Furthermore, like Bachelard before him, Kuhn exaggerated the dis-continuities in the history of science, claiming that rival approaches ("para-digms") and theories are actually mutually incomparable ("incommensur-able"). Besides, he did not believe in the unity of science—the very rallying cry of the *Encyclopedia*.

Since then, positivism bashing has become fashionable, and "post-Kuhnian," or postmodern, philosophers and sociologists indulge in this sport. Now, there are two kinds of anti-positivism: enlightened and obscurantist. The former shares the precision and (unrequited) love of science of the logical positivists but attacks their limitations and seeks to overcome them, in particular their attachment to empiricism, their phenomenalist metaphysics, and their mistrust of theory, inherent in their failed attempt to reduce all theoretical concepts to empirical ones. By contrast, obscurantist anti-positivism takes issue with all that is best in logical positivism, particularly its love of science, conceptual clarity, use of formal methods, demand for tests, and criticism of obscurantism. Logical positivism is also attacked for its alleged realism and materialism, whereas in fact it is semi-subjectivistic and claims to stay above the materialism—idealism dispute.

To conclude, logical positivism was progressive compared with the classical positivism of Ptolemy, Hume, d'Alembert, Comte, Mill, and Mach. It was even more so by comparison with its contemporary rivals—neo-Thomism, neo-Kantianism, intuitionism, dialectical materialism, phenomenology, and existentialism. However, neo-positivism failed dismally to give a faithful account of science, whether natural or social. It failed because it remained anchored to sense-data and to a phenomenalist metaphysics, overrated the power of induction and underrated that of hypothesis, and denounced realism and materialism as metaphysical nonsense. Although it has never been practiced consistently in the advanced natural sciences and has been criticized by many philosophers, notably Popper (1959 [1935], 1963), logical positivism remains the tacit philosophy of many scientists. Regrettably, the anti-positivism fashionable in the metatheory of social science is often nothing but an excuse for sloppiness and wild speculation.

5 Pragmatism

The word *pragmatism* is ambiguous: depending on the context, it can mean horse sense, opportunism, or a kind of philosophy. Philosophical pragmatism is the doctrine according to which action, not just any kind of experience, is the source, test, and *raison d'être* of all knowledge worth acquiring. According to pragmatism, all thought is only a means to action. And "the true is the name of whatever proves itself to be good in the way of belief" (James 1975 [1907], 42). For example, if belief in God "works" for you, then this belief is true. A consequence of this equation of truth with efficiency is the underrating of theory, or at least of any theory that cannot be used as a tool for action. Another result is the widespread cynical view that theoretical models are to be used but not believed.

(Earlier on, Engels had claimed that the only test of ideas of any kind is praxis: the proof of the pudding is in the eating. Even earlier, Marx had berated philosophers for "interpreting" the world, the point being to change it. Paradoxically, while some Marxists, following Antonio Labriola, call their philosophy "the philosophy of praxis," they fail to see its kinship with the pragmatism of Peirce, James, Dewey, and C. I. Lewis.)

Pragmatism has not had many followers among social scientists. Nowadays its influence seems confined to the constructivist-relativist sociology of knowledge. Thus Barnes (1977, 2) states that knowledge is "developed actively and modified in response to practical contingencies." Theoretical problems and developments are not within the purview of pragmatism. There is no room in it for the works of Darwin or Maxwell, Cajal or Einstein, even less for those of historians, mathematicians, or philosophers—unless, of course, they are conveniently distorted beyond recognition. This is precisely what the fashionable "post-Mertonian" sociology of science does.

Latour and Woolgar (1979, 171) write: "A useful maxim is Heidegger's observation that *Gedanke ist Handwerk*": thinking is craftwork. At other places they pooh-pooh ideas in general and "stories about minds having ideas." In their view, there is nothing special about laboratory research and no essential difference between their activity and that of their informants. "The only difference is that they have a laboratory" (ibid., 257). And Knorr-Cetina (1981, 7) claims that "If there is a principle which seems to govern laboratory action, it is the scientists' concern with making things 'work,' which points to a principle of success rather than of truth." Good constructivist that she is, Knorr-Cetina (1983) combines pragmatism with subjectivism and, borrowing a phrase from Goodman (1978), claims that scientific research is a "way of world-making."

Like Monsieur Jourdain, who did not know that he had been talking prose all his life, the proponents of the new sociology of knowledge have reinvented Nietzsche's and James's pragmatist concept of truth as efficiency (or cash value). Thus Bloor (1976, 35) reveals that the realist notion of (factual) truth as the matching of ideas to reality can be dispensed with: "It is difficult to see that much would be lost by its absence." What matters in a theory, he asserts, is that it should "work"—but he does not say what it is for a theory to "work." The fact of the matter is that every conceptual or empirical test of a hypothesis is a test for its *truth,* regardless of its credibility or potential usefulness. If the hypothesis passes the tests, we declare it (sufficiently) true—*pro tempore.* Once this happens, the hypothesis is available for further arguments, tests, or applications. In short, truth precedes consensus or "social convention," not the other way round.

Pragmatism (or instrumentalism) does not "work" with regard to science, because scientific theories and experiments aim at constructing maximally consistent, true, deep accounts of the real world. If they did not, there would be no point in checking or perfecting such accounts. Only technological theories, designs, and plans are tested for efficiency—that is, effectiveness together with low cost, low risk, and significant benefit. To be sure, technology is pragmatic in the sense that it pursues practical rather than purely cognitive aims. But, ironically, pragmatism fails to deliver a faithful picture of modern technology, for the latter feeds freely on disinterested inquiry. Technology can "work" only if there is some truth to its underlying science. True, an artifact or a process is occasionally designed on scant scientific knowledge, as were the steam engine, the airplane, and the light bulb. But, if efficient and important, an invention is bound to elicit scientific research that will ultimately vindicate its design and help improve it.

The instrumentalist does not bother to ask questions of the form "Why does theory T succeed (or fail)?" Worse, he takes *success* to be a self-explanatory word—which it may be in ordinary life, but not in science or technology. (How successful is a technology whose implementation causes unemployment or pollution?) By contrast, the realist holds that the concept of (partial and factual) truth is methodologically prior to that of (partial and practical) success. Consequently he is in a position to offer a rational answer to the question concerned. In fact, he can say that theory T "works" in practice because T is (sufficiently) true: T "fits" the facts that the practical user of T is intent on controlling. If, on the other hand, T is not adequate (does not represent more or less faithfully a chunk of reality), it will not be useful in controlling or transforming any real thing. By failing to explain the practical success or failure of modern technology in terms of the truth of the underlying scientific ideas, the pragmatist fails to account for (rational) action, which alone interests him. In short, pragmatism does not work either epistemically or practically.

Operationism (Bridgman 1927) is the application of pragmatism to scientific concept formation. It consists of just two theses, one ontological, the other semantical. The ontological tenet is *Esse est metiri:* to be is to be measured. That is, whatever cannot be measured does not exist, at any rate insofar as science is concerned. And the semantic thesis of operationism is that scientific concepts are "defined" by laboratory operations. Thus, the concept of population is defined by the operation of census taking.

Both theses are mistaken: the first because there are plenty of things and processes, some real, others possibly so, whose properties we have not yet managed to measure. (Think of most social systems and processes.) All we can say about the relation between observability and existence is this: first, that if something exists, then we may hope to discover it; second, that if an observation is novel and interesting, we should scrutinize it further to find out whether it points to an independently existing thing or process or is just appearance or fantasy.

The semantic thesis of operationism is mistaken for the following reasons:

first, one cannot measure anything without a prior notion of what one wants to measure; second, definition is a conceptual operation, not an empirical one, and consists in equating two concepts (chap. 2, sec. 6); third, almost any quantitative property can be quantitated in more than one way. (Moreover, it is desirable that there be different techniques for measuring any given property, as checks on one another.) Hence, if operationism were true, there would be as many concepts of time, say, as kinds of time-keeping pieces.

The only virtue of operationism is its rejection of woolly ideas—except for its own idea of a definition. In this regard, it has exerted a healthy influence on psychology and the social sciences, by demanding the operationalization of such fuzzy notions as those of frustration and satisfaction of a nation. However, its influence on natural science, particularly physics, has been negative, through discouraging the invention of constructs without an empirical counterpart, such as the idea of light propagating in a vacuum.

Constructivist-relativist sociologists of science have unwittingly reinvented Bridgman's operationist concept of meaning as a set of laboratory operations. Thus Latour (1988, 26): "[W]e refuse meaning to any description that does not portray the *work* of setting up laboratories, inscription devices, networks; we always relate the word 'reality' to the specific trials inside specific laboratories and specific networks that measure up the resistance of some actants." Accordingly, all of mathematics, history, philosophy, and theoretical science (especially theoretical physics, chemistry, biology, psychology, and sociology) is meaningless. But, by the same token, so is constructivist-relativist sociology, since its practitioners do not work in laboratories, but only visit them occasionally.

In short, pragmatism—in particular, operationism—does not yield a true picture of science and technology.

6 Rationalism

As stated earlier, we must distinguish two kinds of rationalism: moderate and radical. The former is just faith in reason. In this respect, many philosophical schools, from Aristotelianism and Thomism to historical materialism and logical empiricism, have been rationalist to some extent; so too was the Enlightenment, of course. Moderate rationalism holds that reason is necessary but insufficient to understand the world and, a fortiori, to change it. On the other hand, radical rationalism, such as that of Descartes, Spinoza, Leibniz, Menger, and von Mises, is identical with faith in the ability of reason, unaided by perception, experiment, or action, to unveil reality or even to construct it: it is aprioristic. (Oddly, Mill [1952 (1875)] was an apriorist with regard to social science and an empiricist with regard to natural science.)

In either version, rationalism is the foe of irrationalism, which refuses to engage in rational discussion and trusts only gut feeling, intuition, and blind ("gratuitous") action. Examples: mysticism, intuitionism, existentialism, the Nazi "blood and soil" ideology, and postmodernism. Plotinus, Meister Eckhart, Fichte, Schelling, Herder, Kierkegaard, Unamuno, Heidegger, Jaspers, Marcel, Sartre, and Derrida are paragons of irrationalism. "If you think, you stink," the motto of Skid Row, a heavy metal rock group, is the intersection of all irrationalisms.

Rationalism *lato sensu* is inherent in all scientific, technological, and humanistic work, for it is not possible without some coherent reasoning. In this sense, moderate rationalism is an essential component of modernity, not only in cultural matters, but also in business and government. It is inherent in valid argumentation and critical discussion, and it is the force behind rational action, as well as a weapon against superstition, dogma, and authoritarianism. By contrast, radical rationalism is impracticable in factual science and technology, because real things are not creations of the mind. It does not even work in philosophy for, as Peirce (1935 [1898]) noted, all philosophy makes use of observation.

To be sure, general conjectures and forecasts are conceived prior to experience. But such prior expectations must be checked before being pronounced true or false (to some extent). Hence they are not synthetic a priori propositions à la Kant. Such need for empirical tests is precisely one of the differences between factual science and technology, on the one hand, and mathematics, theology, and art, on the other. In other words, apriorism, whether rationalist or intuitionist, amounts to denying Leibniz's (1981 [1703]) correct distinction between truths of fact and truths of reason.

Rationalist apriorism flourished and failed in scholastic physics, which was definitively overthrown by Galileo and his followers. However, this failure has not deterred those who, like Ludwig von Mises (1949), believe that action theory and economics are a priori sciences about the social world. Not surprisingly, this aprioristic approach has been just as barren as scholastic physics: it has not advanced social science. The moral is obvious: To *understand* the world, we must explore *the world*. (That we do so with the help of constructs, that we discover by means of inventions, is obvious and beside the point.)

Science and technology retain the Enlightenment's trust in reason—that is, rationalism in the broad sense. In particular, social scientists are expected to work rationally—that is, to abide by logic and scrutinize critically every idea even, nay particularly, when studying irrational behavior. However, the investigator's commitment to rationality has nothing to do with the hypothesis that all the agents he studies are themselves rational, in any of the many senses of 'rational' (conceptual, instrumental, etc.). This hypothesis flies in the face of experience. In science and technology we must be realists as well as rationalists.

While emphasizing the increasing importance of rationality in economic and political life, as well as in the intellectual sphere, Weber and Schumpeter admitted that we are often actuated by affect, passion, or error. In particular, Weber regarded the hypothesis of rational behavior as an ideal type, allowing us to explain certain actions as outcomes of rational decisions and others as deviations from rationality—much as the hypothesizing of a force explains the departure of a body from rectilinear uniform motion. Moreover, he warned explicitly that the rationality hypothesis has a methodological status only: it must not be understood as the thesis that human life is fully ruled by reason (Weber 1922, 3).

In short, the scientific researcher espouses rationalism *lato sensu* and has no use for radical rationalism because the latter is aprioristic, hence dogmatic.

7 Ratio-Empiricism

Reason and experience are each necessary but insufficient to understand the world. We understand facts in explaining them with the help of theories and data. Theories are products of reason, but they must be checked by empirical operations, and these in turn must be designed in the light of theories. To put it negatively, unchecked speculation and blind empirical trial are equally barren. The philosophical moral is that an adequate philosophy of factual science and technology, one that is both true and fruitful, combines the true features of rationalism and empiricism. We call this synthesis "ratio-empiricism" (Bunge 1983*b*).

Kant recognized the need to combine rationalism with empiricism, but he combined the bad halves of both: in fact, he took the apriorism of radical rationalism and the phenomenalism inherent in empiricism. Logical empiricism was another brave attempt to join empiricism with rationalism. It rejected Kant's apriorism concerning the basic categories, such as those of space, time, and causation, but retained phenomenalism and inductivism. Popper's (1959 [1935]) criticism of logical empiricism helped discredit inductivism. But his medicine was worse than the sickness, for he claimed that there can be reasons or experiences only against, never for, any ideas. This view, which may be called "negative ratio-empiricism," ignores the fact that every investigator looks for both positive and negative evidence, conceptual or empirical. He does so because he wants to attain truths, not just eliminate errors. In science, just as in a court of law, truth emerges from the interaction of defense with prosecution; or, as Bernard (1952 [1865], 97) put it, truth emerges from supplementing the *preuve* with the *contre-épreuve*. Odysseus, rather than Sisyphus, is the hero of the truth-seekers.

We should combine the good halves of the two great epistemological traditions. These are the practices of conceptual analysis, hypothesizing, theorizing, proving, and discussing, together with observation, measurement, experiment, and praxis—as Bacon preached on occasion and Galileo practiced. Three glues keep these two halves together: (*a*) moderate or *methodological skepticism*, which urges us to inquire and doubt and consequently discourages complacency and dogma; (*b*) *critical realism*, which asserts that we can build approximately true theories of reality and thus combines fallibilism with meliorism; and (*c*) *scientism*, the thesis that scientific research is the best way to explore reality. The resulting synthesis may be called "scientific ratio-empiricism," or "scientific realism."

Scientific realism accounts for the conceptual components of scientific research without being rationalist and for its empirical components without being empiricist. It encourages doubt without falling into systematic (or destructive) skepticism; it admits intuition but rejects intuitionism, as well as convention, but not conventionalism. It is justificationist in that it requires that every proposition, whether hypothesis or datum, as well as every norm, be justified theoretically or empirically. But it adds that any particular justification is fallible and perfectible: it is fallibilist and meliorist. And it is scientistic, while neither admitting blindly every result of scientific research nor being radically reductionist. (More in chap. 13, sec. 8.)

Figure 12.1 exhibits the relations between the main contemporary epistemological trends. (Intuitionism and irrationalism have been left out, because they do not include any theories of knowledge.) Rationalism and empiricism, as well as intuitionism and pragmatism, are *foundationalist:* that is, they assume that there is a rock bottom upon which the rest can be securely built (see, e.g., Haack 1995). Being fallibilist, our epistemology is not foundationalist. But it is not radically skeptic either, for every science has foundations, albeit transient ones. It is the task of axiomatics to dig them up. Analytical advances may require a reorganization or overhauling of a body of theory, and empirical findings may call for the alteration or even rejection of some or all of the postulates of a theory. Knowledge has no ultimate epistemic foundation, either rational or empirical. It has only an ultimate factual or material foundation: namely, the real world. This is where scientific realism joins scientific materialism (chap. 11, sec. 5).

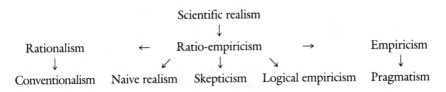

Fig. 12.1. Relations among the major epistemological schools. The more comprehensive views embrace the less comprehensive ones. The arrow represents a sort of projection operation, whereby a system is reduced to one of its components or versions.

Materialism makes a crucial contribution to epistemology, by treating both the inquirer and his community as concrete entities to be investigated by factual science (in particular, psychology and sociology) as well as by philosophy. By the same token, it eliminates the traditional subject–object opposition, for the knowing (or rather inquiring) subject is seen as part of the world—in particular, as a social animal.

In this chapter and the foregoing we have examined a number of academically respected views about factual knowledge. Regrettably, most of their champions do not bother to put them to the only tests that should count. These are: (*a*) Does any of them account for the way real people explore the world and try to understand or control it in a non-magical fashion? and (*b*) Does any of them promote the advancement of knowledge?

Consider, for instance, the theory–data relation, one with which every factual scientist must come to grips sooner or later. Irrationalists, particularly intuitionists, care for neither theories proper (hypothetico-deductive systems) nor empirical data, so the problem of their relation does not bother them. Constructivist-relativists, especially the proponents of the "strong programme" in the sociology of science, maintain that there is no data–theory distinction: both are collections of conventional inscriptions, and both are ultimately dictated by ideology or even political power. Hence the problem of checking theory against data and conversely does not arise for them either. In short, neither irrationalism nor its next-door neighbor, constructivism-relativism, has anything helpful to say about the theory–data relation. The reason is that neither is interested in truth, the ultimate goal of all genuine scientific research.

Radical rationalists, such as Eddington and Thom, have claimed that a good mathematical theory is capable of delivering all the empirical data we need (see Bunge 1994*b* for a criticism of Thom's apriorism). It follows that we may close down all laboratories and statistical bureaus—a proposal that few would dare to implement. On the other hand, radical empiricists, such as Mach, hold that theories are just summaries of economic data, so in principle are dispensable—a view that only the most hardened behaviorists hold nowadays. And conventionalists claim that theories are merely computation devices (algorithms)—something that only computer programmers might be prepared to admit.

We are left, then, with ratio-empiricism, which blends the positive features of both rationalism and empiricism, adds the thesis that science contains some philosophy, which in turn interacts with ideology, and through the latter with society at large. For instance, Darwin admitted that he drew inspiration from the writings of Smith on economic competition and of Malthus on overpopulation. However, evolutionary biology has severed its ideological connection: it was never about human society, and it was eventually accepted by the scientific community, despite its disagreement with the dominant ideology. It was

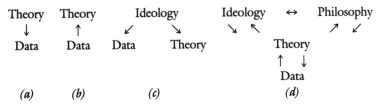

Fig. 12.2. Theory–data relation according to (a) apriorism, (b) empiricism, (c) constructivism-relativism, and (d) ratio-empiricism.

accepted for jibing with a secular, dynamicist world view and for having passed numerous tests, among them the successful prediction that fossil remains of our apelike ancestors would eventually be dug up. Once it had passed truth tests, it earned acceptance and started influencing other sciences, as well as philosophies and ideologies, both reactionary and progressive. Eventually it was corrected and enriched, first by genetics and more recently by ecology as well.

In conclusion, the relations between empirical data, theories, philosophy, and ideology are far more complex than imagined by most philosophers (see fig. 12.2).

13 :: *Subjectivism and Realism*

Objectivity is of the essence of science, just as subjectivity is of the essence of art. Natural scientists are natural objectivists—except when on the occasional philosophical foray. But it is harder to be scientific, hence objective, about human affairs than about nature. This is so because it is always difficult and often impossible to guess correctly other people's attitudes and intentions; we are influenced by social conventions and personal experience, with its attendant interests, expectations, emotions, and prejudices; and ideology, often fueled by political or economic interests, is likely to distort our perceptions of social facts or even keep us from approaching them in a disinterested way. This is why social science is so much more backward than natural science. It is also why we often mistake opinions for data, value judgments for descriptive statements, and prophecies for forecasts. Further, this is why it is so important, for the advancement of social studies, to identify and expose the subjectivist philosophies that compound the natural obstacles to the objectivist or realist approach to social facts.

Realism is "the view that material objects exist externally to us and independently of our sense experience" (Hirst 1967). It is the epistemology that all of us adopt tacitly when not under the influence of narcotics or anti-scientific philosophies. It may be compressed into the following rules which we learn in elementary school, in the street, or at work:

R1. Distinguish fact from both opinion and fiction.

R2. Get your facts right; that is, gather or produce reliable data.

R3. Check your opinions and hypotheses against facts: search for objective truth.

All natural scientists have been, or at least have behaved as, realists. Until recently, nearly all social scientists were realists too: they took the reality of the social world for granted and assumed tacitly that their task was to describe and perhaps also explain it as objectively and accurately as possible. They were innocent of subjectivism, conventionalism, constructivism, and epistemological relativism: these old, barren philosophical games were ignored or regarded as inconsequential extravaganzas. This did not prevent some of them from taking sides over social issues. Far from it, they understood that the success of policies, plans, and actions aimed at either conserving or changing social reality depends in part upon objective accounts of it. In other words, the pre-postmoderns were realists, and they distinguished objectivity from impartiality.

For example, even though Marx and Engels took sides in politics and even denied the possibility of impartial social science, they stressed the need to study the social world in an objective and, moreover, a scientific manner. (On the other hand, some of their followers, such as Gouldner [1970, 496], reject "the myth that social worlds are merely 'mirrored' in the sociologist's work.") Further, Marx and Engels made use of plenty of economic and social data in their (alas, unsuccessful) attempt to discover the objective "laws of motion" of society. Likewise, Simmel and Weber conducted their sociological and historical research as realists, even while adopting neo-Kantianism and taking issue with realism in their methodological writings. (This was the respectable thing to do in the German academic establishment of the time, which was dominated by idealism, particularly neo-Kantianism.) What is true is that Simmel and Weber were not naturalists or, as one may now say with hindsight, behaviorists. Indeed, they rightly held that one must take the inner life of people into account, particularly their beliefs, motivations, and intentions (recall chap. 5, secs. 5 and 6 on Verstehen). True, they stated that this approach committed them to subjectivism. But this was a slip on their part, since one can be objective about other people's subjective experiences, provided one employs reliable indicators and as long as every imputation of belief, motivation, or intention is treated as a conjecture subject to empirical tests.

It is also true that neoclassical economists and their imitators in other disciplines ("economic imperialists") postulate subjective utilities and subjective probabilities and that they seldom bother to test their models. But they do not claim that social facts are their own constructions, or even that they are social conventions. Far from it, they claim truth for their theories. Even the arch-apriorist Ludwig von Mises made this claim. Whether it is correct is beside the point right now. The point is that even the most farfetched neoclassical models are offered as faithful representations of economic reality.

This situation started to change in the 1960s, when anti-realism went on the rampage in the social science community, to the point that some students asserted that there must be witches, since some people act on a belief in witchcraft (see, e.g., Fiske and Schweder 1986). This movement seems to have had two sources: one philosophical, the other political. The former was a reaction against positivism, which was wrongly supposed to be objectivist. (This assumption is mistaken, because positivism, from Comte and Mill to Mach and the Vienna Circle, is a variety of empiricism. And the latter equates reality with the totality of human experience, so that it is basically subjectivist: recall chap. 12, sec. 4.)

This particular "anti-positivist" reaction is regressive. Indeed, instead of pointing out the negative features of positivism, such as its exaltation of data at the expense of theory, it denounces rationality and the concern with empirical testing. And it proposes replacing positivism with all manner of anti-scientific philosophies, such as conventionalism, constructivism, intuitionism, Hegelianism, phenomenology, hermeneutics (in particular, desconstruction), and even existentialism. But it does not do so consistently. For example, much of the field research conducted by ethnomethodologists, who are given to quoting Husserl and even Heidegger, falls squarely within the pedestrian tradition of empiricism and, in particular, behaviorism. In fact, all they offer are data about minutiae of everyday life: they practice the very philosophy they condemn (recall chap. 12, sec. 3).

The political source of contemporary anti-realism was the rebellion stirred up by the Vietnam War and the May 1968 generation of radical student activists, feminist advocates, and environmentalists against the establishment, which was (wrongly) identified with the all-powerful, diabolical power behind science and pro-scientific philosophy. So fighting science and pro-scientific philosophy was regarded as part of the fight against the establishment—a typically primitive reaction. Something similar happened in Mexico after 1910, when Porfirio Díaz's dictatorship, which had espoused Comte's philosophy and called itself "scientific," was toppled. In both cases many political progressives embraced the anti-scientism that had characterized the traditional Right.

Some of the philosophical gurus of the 1960s student revolt declared that the real world was mythical, and science only a weapon of political power. Consequently truth was pronounced nonexistent, and science a tool of capitalism. Thus, according to Foucault (1969), there is no objective truth: there are only "regimes of truth and power," whence "another power, another truth." But social critics and activists who take this stand shoot themselves in the head, for any successful political criticism or action, whether from below or from above, must assume that the adversary is real and can be known and that such knowledge is instrumental in the struggle against it. (Thus Foucault's [1975] essay on the modern prison system is valuable for containing some true descriptions.) In any event, those who do not believe at least tacitly in truth will not search for it and consequently will not find it: they are epistemically barren. No wonder that we owe to the postmoderns no important new findings about the social world.

In this chapter (which follows closely Bunge 1993) I will examine the main kinds of realism (or objectivism) and subjectivism currently being discussed in social metascience. I will be using the following definitions. An account of a fact (or group of facts) is *objective* (or *impersonal*) if and only if it is about one or more facts occurring in the external world—which, of course, includes the brains of others. (Whether the account is true as well as objective is another matter. Factual truth implies objectivity, but the converse is false.) On the other hand, a statement is *subjective* (or *personal*) if and only if it is about one's own feelings or beliefs, regardless of its truth-value. For example, the proposition "The USSR broke up in 1991" is an objective (moreover, true) statement, whereas "The breakup of the USSR makes me happy (or sad)" is a subjective one. Finally, an account is *intersubjective* in a given community if and only if (nearly) all the members of the community agree on it (regardless of its truth-value).

The concepts of objectivity and intersubjectivity are logically independent of one another. While the concept of objectivity is epistemological and semantical, that of intersubjectivity is psychosociological. However, within a scientific community intersubjectivity is an indicator of objectivity. Yet, like most, if not all, indicators, it is unreliable. For example, all the members of a given group of people may perceive or conceptualize a given fact in the same, wrong manner. Thus, during two decades, almost all Soviet citizens believed Stalin to be genius, hero, and saint all rolled into one. Consensus is not a truth criterion: it is primarily a psychosocial fact.

Social scientists deal with both objective facts and their "perceptions," so they have to reckon with subjective and intersubjective statements, as well as objective ones. But to the extent that they abide by the canons of science, even their assertions about other people's subjective statements will be objective—though not always true. For example, a social psychologist may conclude a study by asserting that most members of group X believe Y, but he may not write: "I believe that most members of X believe Y," for a statement of this sort has only autobiographical value. Scientists are supposed to find at least approximate truths and to believe only such. Of course, sometimes they err, but when they discover error, they are expected to report it and attempt to correct it. (The latter is, of course, a moral norm.)

Objectivism (or *realism*) is the view that, except in the arts, we should strive to eliminate all subjective elements from our views about reality. Objectivism does not entail the rejection of subjectivity: it merely enjoins us to study it objectively, the way experimental psychology does. In particular, a scientific theory may refer to subjective experiences, such as illusions, but it must do so in an objective manner. Let us next examine the opposite of objectivism.

1 Subjectivism

Subjectivism is the philosophical view that the world, far from existing independently, is a creation of the knower. Subjectivism provides a cheap explanation of differences of opinion and spares one the trouble of confronting one's beliefs with the relevant facts. Thus Breit (1984, 20) asks why J. K. Galbraith and M. Friedman, two of the most distinguished social scientists of our time, held mutually conflicting views of economic reality. He answers: "There *is* no world out there which we can unambiguously compare with Friedman's and Galbraith's versions. Galbraith and Friedman did not discover the worlds they analyze; they decreed them." Breit then compares economists to painters: "Each offers a new way of seeing, of organizing experience," of "imposing order on sensory data" (as Kant would have said). From this perspective the problems of objective truth and of the difference between science and non-science do not arise. But then, why hire economists, rather than painters, to address economic issues?

(Caution: Hayek [1955] and others have confused subjectivism with the recognition of the existence and importance of feelings, beliefs, and interests. A realist, or objectivist, should be willing, nay eager, to admit the relevance of feeling, belief, and interest, hence bias, to social action; but he will insist that they be studied objectively. This attitude is to be contrasted with both subjectivism and the positivist—or behaviorist, or black box—approach to human behavior.)

Subjectivism is a component of infantile and magical thinking, with their irrepressible tendency to reify ideas, to impute reality to whatever is imagined. Thus, belief in the superiority of a given ethnic or social group leads its members to behave as if they were actually superior, and belief in witchcraft leads people to treat those accused of practicing witchcraft as witches. Of course, scientists are not supposed to indulge in magical thinking. But critical thinking, a central feature of the Enlightenment, is nowadays on the wane. Thus, radical feminist "theorists" extol intuition over reason, which they regard as a tool of male domination, and regard subjectivism as feminine (see, e.g., Harding 1986, 1991; Shepherd 1993; and Patai and Koertge 1994 for criticisms). And an influential anthropologist claims that "ghosts, spirits, demons, witches, souls, and other so-called religious or supernatural concepts are, in some important sense, real and objective" (Shweder 1986, 172). By the time Weber wrote about the *Entzauberung* (decharming or demystification) of the world that accompanied modernization, anthropologists and sociologists had started to practice the maxim: Scratch a myth and find a fact. Today's subjectivists have turned this principle upside down, to read: Scratch a fact and find a myth. They regard facts as symbols or metaphors for something else and tend to equate facts with our descriptions of them.

A popular argument against objectivism is that everyone, not least scientists, has passions, is socially embedded, has group loyalties, and has inherited a tradition. This is obvious, but in scientific research the point is to keep one's idiosyncratic likes and dislikes under control and disregard one's tribal ties, in order to search for the truest possible account of facts—doing it passionately. Biological and social categories, such as sex, ethnicity, nationality, social class, and political sympathy, apply to individual scientists, not to their findings. In particular, there is no feminine, homosexual, Aryan, American, proletarian, or conservative science: authentic science is universal, and so is philosophy. Certainly, being a woman or a member of a minority group may help one note certain problems disregarded by researchers belonging to the socially dominant group. But such problems will not be solved adequately unless approached objectively with the help of such universal tools as theorizing, experiment, and criticism.

Idealist philosophers (e.g., Goodman 1978), ethnomethodologists (e.g., Goffman 1963; Garfinkel 1967), constructivist-relativist sociologists (e.g., Latour and Woolgar 1979; Knorr-Cetina 1981), and a number of feminist theorists (e.g., Shepherd 1993) hold that the world is subject-dependent: that all facts, natural or social, are "constructions," either individual or social. They confuse the map(s) with the territory. And neither of them offers any empirical *evidence* for the claim that for any concrete entity X, X comes into being only at the moment we think of X—much as, according to the book of Genesis, God created any X he fancied simply by uttering "Let X be." Let us glance at one of the philosophical schools that has most strongly influenced the recent retreat from realism in social studies: phenomenology.

Phenomenology is a modern paragon of subjectivism. In fact, according to its founder, the gist of phenomenology is that it is a "pure egology," a "science of the concrete transcendental subjectivity" (Husserl 1950 [1931], 68). Not surprisingly, the very first move of the phenomenologist is the "phenomenological reduction," or "bracketing out" (*époché*), of the external world. "One must lose the world through *époché* in order to regain it through universal self-examination" (ibid., 183). He must do this because his "universal task" is the discovery of himself as transcendental (nonempirical) ego (ibid., 76). Once he has pretended that real things such as chairs and colleagues do not exist, the phenomenologist proceeds to uncover their essences, making use of a special intuition (*Wesensschau*), the nature of which is not explained, and for which no evidence is offered. The result is an a priori, intuitive science (ibid., sec. 34). And this science proves to be nothing but transcendental idealism (ibid. 118).

This subjectivism is not only epistemological but also ontological: "[T]he world itself is an infinite idea" (ibid., 97). How could anyone think that this wild fantasy could shed any light on anything except the decadence of German philosophy?

This extravagance can have at least one of two negative effects on social studies. One is to focus on individual behavior and deny the real existence of social systems and macrosocial facts: these would be the products of such intellectual procedures as interpretation and aggregation. The other is to alienate students from empirical research, thus turning the clock back to the era of armchair ("humanistic") social studies. The effect of the former move is that *social* science becomes impossible; that of the second that social *science* is rendered impossible. Either or both of these effects are apparent in the work of phenomenological sociologists (e.g., Schütz 1967 [1932]), ethnomethodologists (e.g., Garfinkel 1967), and hermeneuticists (e.g.,Geertz 1973).

Traditional subjectivism was individualist: it regarded the knower as an individual (e.g., Berkeley, Schopenhauer, Mach and Husserl). Consequently it could not face the objection that there should be as many worlds as people and thus no intersubjective agreement would be possible unless it added the theological assumption that God takes care of the uniqueness of the world. This objection would not worry the sociologist Luhmann (1990), according to whom there are as many realities as observers, for every one of these is "a construction of an observer for other observers." Consequently there is no objective truth. Worse, the individual relates only to his own constructs. He cannot communicate with others, because "only communication can communicate"—an echo of Heidegger's "Language speaks," "The world worlds," and "Nothingness nothings."

Subjectivism is incompatible with the factual sciences, whether natural, social, or mixed, since they attempt to account for reality in as objective a manner as possible. Yet subjectivism is often found in social studies, not only in those influenced by idealist philosophies but also wherever the notions of subjective probability and utility are employed, as will be seen in section 6.

2 Conventionalism

The view that scientific hypotheses and theories are useful conventions rather than more or less true (or false) representations of facts is called "conventionalism." Conventionalism rings true in pure mathematics, which is a free mental creation constrained only by the requirements of exactness and noncontradiction. Yet even here one distinguishes notational conventions and definitions, on the one hand, from axioms and their logical consequences (theorems), on the other. Since a theory contains infinitely many theorems and only a finite number of definitions and notational conventions, the conventional component of any theory is tiny. Hence conventionalism is false even for mathematics.

Radical conventionalism is obviously impracticable with regard to factual science, because here we are engaged in finding and explaining empirical data, which are anything but conventional. But one might try a moderate version of conventionalism, according to which the choice among theories which account equally well for the data is ultimately a matter of convention. Let us look into this possibility. Any given body of empirical data can be "covered" by an unlimited number of different hypotheses: this is the problem of empirical *underdetermination*. A common case is this: the dots on a plane (or a higher-dimensional space) representing experimental results can be joined by any number of continuous curves (or surfaces). It would seem that the choice among such competing hypotheses is arbitrary—for example, we may choose the simplest of them. This leads to equating truth with simplicity, or at least to regarding simplicity as a test for truth—as proposed by Goodman (1958) and others. (See Bunge 1963 for a criticism.)

This is not how scientists actually proceed in all cases. A scientist is likely to prefer the simplest of all the hypotheses compatible with a certain body of data as long as he knows nothing else about the matter in hand. But if he pursues his research, he will want to explain the data in question. To this end, he will cast about for and, if need be, invent more comprehensive or deeper hypotheses, or even hypothetico-deductive systems—that is, theories. He will then check not only whether any of them matches the old data, but also whether they predict correctly any new data. He will end up preferring the hypothesis or theory with the largest coverage and the greatest explanatory power, even if it does not fit the original data exactly. And he will expect that further research (his own or other people's) will result in an even more potent hypothesis or theory, which is likely to be more complex for referring to deeper mechanisms. His goals are truth and depth, not simplicity: he is a realist, not a conventionalist. For this reason, he regards (approximate) empirical fit as only an indicator of factual truth: he also requires compatibility with a comprehensive and, if possible, deep theory (recall chap. 6, sec. 5).

Conventionalism, then, is false with respect to factual science, for failing to account for the relentless search for ever deeper explanations, hence for scientific progress. It fails because it rejects the concept of objective truth. This rejection is, of course, peculiar to all versions of subjectivism. Thus Kant held that there can be no objective truth, because it is impossible to know things in themselves. To him, what we call "knowledge" is always construction, never representation. His follower Lange elaborated on this point and emphasized the illusory character of human knowledge and the relativity of the distinction between truth and falsity. Nietzsche adopted Lange's view and, under Spencer's influence, gave it a biological twist: true is whatever promotes life, false whatever puts it at risk. (Hence the need for "noble lies"—in particular, socially expedient myths.) James's version of pragmatism, though not Peirce's, included this ignoble idea. Rorty's (1979) attack on realism and defense of pragmatism (and existentialism) take a similar line.

Fictionism combines conventionalism with pragmatism. According to fictionism, all hypotheses and theories are at best useful fictions. It is not that things *are* so-and-so: we can assert only that they look *as if* they were so-and-so and that some of our ideas work *as if* they were true (Vaihinger 1920). This doctrine has a small grain of truth. In fact, every factual theory includes some fictions in the form of idealizations, simplifications, or approximations (recall chap. 2, sec. 5 on ideal types). Still, these are not fictions on a par with those of fantastic literature or surrealist art—they are accepted only when found to be approximately true. When not, they are rejected.

Fictionism has survived in at least three doctrines. One is the view that scientific theories, and even historical narratives, are metaphors rather than literal representations of real things or processes (Hesse 1966; Ricoeur 1975; Hayden White 1978; McCloskey 1985). If this view were true, there would be no point in subjecting theories and historical accounts to "reality checks." But since scientists and historians do care for empirical evidence and often debate matters of truth and error, fictionism is utterly false.

Another survival of fictionism is the methodology of economics proposed by Milton Friedman (1953). According to this, the assumptions of a theory need not be true: all that matters is that their consequences be realistic. But of course one may validly and trivially infer true propositions from the wildest assumptions, particularly from contradictions, which are picturesquely said to be "vacuously true." Since scientists do not seek triviality, Friedman's view is false. A third vestige of fictionism is the version of contractualism according to which all human intercourse is ruled by contract, whether explicit or tacit. Thus, even if two interacting individuals, or an individual and a formal organization, are not bound by any explicit contract, they can still be seen "as if" they had signed a contract. This gimmick renders contractualism empirically irrefutable.

Should any doubt remain that fictionism is at variance with modern science, the following examples should dispel it. Electrons behave in certain circumstances as if they were particles—but they are not. Chaotic (in the technical sense) systems look as if they were random—but they are not. DNA molecules work as if they contained instructions for the synthesis of proteins—but they do not. Spider webs look as if they were the work of intelligent beings—but they are not. Social systems look as if they were alive and had a mind of their own—but they do not. In all these cases, a shallow analogy was first proposed, then checked and refuted. Appearances were found to be misleading and fictionism false.

Traditionally conventionalists and fictionists were methodological individualists: they held that conventions and fictions are proposed by the individual scientist and then adopted by their fellow scientists if found expedient. In recent times a kind of *collectivist conventionalism*, combined with subjectivism (or constructivism) and anthropological relativism, has spread throughout science studies. The reasoning behind this view is this. If all cultures are equivalent, if none is superior to any other, and if there are not even different kinds of knowledge (e.g., scientific and ideological), then the adoption of any one idea is a social convention and merely a matter of usefulness to a given community.

Collectivist conventionalism holds, in particular, that (*a*) "proper usage [of, e.g., classificatory terms] is agreed usage," and (*b*) *"different* [conceptual] *nets stand equivalently as far as the possibility of 'rational justification' is concerned. All systems of verbal culture are equally rationally-held"* (Barnes 1983, 33; emphasis original). Barnes reaches these conclusions from an examination of the ways in which different *preliterate* peoples classify animals and from his readings of Wittgenstein's *Philosophical Investigations* (1953), which, of course, was concerned only with *ordinary* language seen from an *ordinary* knowledge perspective, not a linguistic one.

Barnes has generalized to *all* knowledge, even mathematical, scientific, and technological knowledge, what he believes to have found in the literature on primitive ordinary knowledge. (Durkheim and Mauss [1968 (1903)], who were among the first to conjecture that primitive classifications mirror a tribe's social structure, particularly in the case of totemism, did not commit Barnes's error.) Barnes does not study the way in which *contemporary* chemists or biological systematists classify things or the way physicists build theories and check them. Presumably, he would not be budged by the objection that statements such as "Whales are fish" and "There are witches" are false, period. After all, relativist anthropologists are epistemological relativists, conventionalists, and often subjectivists as well.

In conclusion, conventionalism is not true of science, or even of mathematics.

3 Social Constructivism

Social constructivism is a blend of subjectivism and collectivism. In fact, it claims that all social facts, and possibly all natural facts as well, are constructions of "thought collectives" such as scientific communities. Different "thought collectives" hold different and, moreover, mutually incommensurable views of the world. Thus, whether collectivist or individualist, constructivism denies objective universal truths: it is relativist.

Collectivist or holistic subjectivism was first expounded by Ludwik Fleck in his *Genesis and Development of a Scientific Fact* (1979 [1935]), which exerted a decisive influence on the young Thomas Kuhn (see Kuhn's preface to the English translation). This was a study of the history of syphilis, which Fleck called a "scientific fact"—just because it was (sometimes) studied and treated in a scientific way. Fleck denied that science studies independently existing things. He held that every "scientific fact" is the product of a "thought collective," or community of people united by a "thought style." He denied that a person can think by himself. Hence every scientific fact (in particular, every discovery or invention) is a social fact.

Moreover, the converse is said to hold as well. Indeed, according to Fleck, there is no such thing as the external world: "[O]bjective reality can be resolved into historical sequences of ideas belonging to the collective" (Fleck 1979 [1935], 41). This holistic form of subjectivism, adumbrated by the later Husserl (1954 [1936]), has been adopted by a number of sociologists (e.g., Berger and Luckmann 1966) and sociologists of science (e.g., Latour and Woolgar 1979; Knorr-Cetina and Mulkay 1983). In fact, it has become rather fashionable to write about the "social construction of reality." For example, the feminist theorists Belenky, Clinchy, Goldberger, and Tarule (1986) hold that truth is context-dependent and that "the knower is an intimate part of the known"—just because some of the women they interviewed felt so. Harding (1986) and MacKinnon (1989) claim that not only science, but also human sexuality, is a social construction. Are pregnancy, birth pangs, and birth included? If so, why not adopt more convenient conventions?

Constructivists confuse reality with our representations of it: the explored with the explorer, the known with the knower, the territory with its maps, America with Vespucci, facts with data, objective patterns with law statements. Moreover, they do not usually distinguish epistemological constructivism from ontological constructivism. Let us address this latter confusion. Epistemological constructivism holds, in opposition to empiricism, that concepts and hypotheses are not just distillations of perceptions, but intellectual creations or constructions. In particular, the scientific observation of objective (theory-free) facts involves (some) theoretical concepts. Such concepts occur not only in the design and interpretation of empirical operations, but also in some experimental protocols. All this is important and true, but it does not entail "the abolition of the fact/theory distinction" (Barnes 1983, 21). In other words, epistemological constructivism does not imply ontological constructivism: only the converse implication holds.

When not on a philosophical foray, an anthropologist is likely to claim that the *concepts* of a human being found in the various anthropological views are theoretical, while at the same time admitting that there are people out there, whether or not we theorize about them, and, moreover, that there were people long before anthropology emerged. Likewise, any sober sociologist will admit that the various *concepts* of social stratification are theoretical, while at the same time holding that all modern societies are objectively stratified and that every scientific study of social stratification attempts to represent such an objective feature. In short, all but vulgar empiricists agree that concepts, hypotheses, and theories are constructed; only subjectivists claim that all facts are constructed as well. Thus, whereas *epistemological* constructivism is in order up to a point, *ontological* constructivism is not, for it flies in the face of evidence. Love and hate, birth and death, are not constructions, social or otherwise. Nor are work, trade, war, or any other social facts. Facts are facts are facts, even when discovered or produced in the light of ideas (see chap. 11, sec. 4).

There is more than careless use of key terms such as 'fact' and 'construction' in the writings of constructivists. There is also deliberate neglect of the "technical" aspect of the research process—that is, the problems, hypotheses, arguments, experimental designs, and measurements that accompany the exchanges of views, plans, and findings among members of research team(s), and without which such exchanges would be pointless. There is even explicit refusal to employ such methodological terms as 'hypothesis' and 'proof,' perhaps for being stigmata of internalism (Latour and Woolgar 1986, 153).

Such neglect of the technical meanings and truth-values of the "inscriptions" produced in the laboratory is not accidental, but the product of a deliberate choice: that of choosing to study the tribe of scientists as if it were a primitive society such as a tribe of hunters and gatherers. In the case of a social system, such as a fishing village, even a traveler or an investigative journalist can learn something from untutored observation, through being familiar with basic, cross-cultural human activities. He learns the alien language and undertakes an in-depth study only if he wishes to understand the political organization, the mythology, or the ceremonies of the group.

A scientific research team is radically different from a primitive tribe—not in its operations being mysterious, but in their having an extremely specialized function, that of producing *scientific* knowledge through processes that, unlike gathering, hunting, or fishing, are not in full view. The layman visiting a laboratory observes only behavioral manifestations of the mental processes locked in the brains of the researchers and their assistants. To the layman, the problems that trigger a research activity are even less intelligible than its results. Hence he is bound to take only a superficial look, much as the behaviorist psychologist limits his task to describing overt behavior.

Despite the layman's obvious limitations, Latour and Woolgar (1986, 153) claim that "observation of actual laboratory practice" yields material that "is particularly suited to an analysis of the intimate details of scientific activity." They do not explain how a total stranger, who does not even understand the language of the "tribe" whose daily life he "shares" (by moving around in the same rooms), can have access to such intimate details, which take place inside the skulls of the subjects of study. Nor do they explain how mere verbal exchanges and "negotiations" can "create or destroy facts," rather than alter constructs such as problems, data, hypotheses, or methods.

Not only do these amateurs not apologize for butting into a team engaged in a serious research project which they cannot understand, which is like illiterates taking part in a literary workshop, they do not believe such ignorance to be a serious handicap: "We take the *apparent* superiority of the members of our [*sic*] laboratory in technical matters to be insignificant, in the sense that we do *not* regard prior cognition . . . as a necessary prerequisite for understanding scientists' work" (Latour and Woolgar 1986, 29, emphasis added). Unsurprisingly, these ill-equipped observers conclude that scientists do not engage in any distinctive thought processes, that scientific activity is "just one social arena," and that a laboratory is just "a system of literary inscriptions." How would they know if they do not understand any scientific "inscriptions"? And, given their deliberate confusion of facts with statements about facts, how would they know when "a statement splits into an entity and statement about an entity" or when the converse process occurs, during which reality is "deconstructed"—in ordinary parlance, when a hypothesis is falsified? On the strength of such elementary confusions and borrowings from anti-scientific philosophies, they conclude that the world does not exist independently of the knowing subject. Paradoxically, constructivists claim that only their own "empirical studies" supply an adequate (i.e., realistic, true) account of scientific research. Woolgar (1986) notes this paradox, but it does not bother him. Postmodernity is beyond truth and cogency.

4 Relativism

If reality is a social construction, and if facts are statements of a certain kind, then there are no objective universal truths. In other words, if there is nothing "out there" that was not previously "in here," then the very expression "correspondence of ideas with facts" makes no sense. And if there is no objective truth, then scientific research is not a quest for truth. Or, to put it in a somewhat milder way, "[W]hat counts as truth can vary from place to place and from time to time" (H. M. Collins 1983, 88). This is the kernel of epistemological relativism, originally invented by German Romantic irrationalists. (Cultural— in particular, moral—relativism seems to have emerged in the eighteenth century along with the noble savage doctrine. Epistemological relativism implies cultural relativism, but not conversely.)

The most extreme kind of epistemological relativism is radical or *systematic skepticism* of the kind held in antiquity by Sextus Empiricus, in the late Renaissance by Francisco Sánchez, and in our own day by Feyerabend under the heading of "epistemological anarchism." The radical skeptic denies the possibility of objective, universal knowledge and is thus purely destructive. He rejects all canons and standards: "[H]e recognizes no rules, not even the rules of logic" (Feyerabend 1975, 182). He takes pleasure in defending "the most trite, or the most outrageous statement. . . . His favorite pastime is to confuse rationalists by inventing compelling reasons for unreasonable doctrines" (ibid., 189). Being a sophist and a jester, the epistemological anarchist is not committed to the ideals of rationality and truth and thus feels free to treat lightly the best scientific theories we have, while demanding tolerance for all manner of superstition and pseudoscience. In this way he discourages serious research, and his view has the same result as dogmatism: namely, stagnation or regression. (For more on Feyerabend's views, see Bunge 1991*b*.)

Radical or systematic skepticism must be distinguished from the moderate or *methodological skepticism* advocated by Descartes. This consists in practicing methodical doubt, believing only what is supported by either formal proof or strong empirical evidence—and even then, only until further notice. Whereas systematic skepticism is barren for its denial of all truth, methodological skepticism is fruitful for keeping us on our toes and promoting constructive criticism as well as scientific cooperation alongside competition. Merton (1938), who called it "organized skepticism," rightly regarded it as a central epistemic and social feature of science.

A variety of radical skepticism is *epistemological relativism.* This is the view that truth is at best local: bound to tribe and time. This, of course, is nothing new: it was stated long ago in the concise formula *Veritas filia temporis.* It is a naive reaction to the variety of cultures and the multiplicity of conflicting views about the same facts. Such multiplicity inspires systematic skepticism, particularly in light of the externalist view that social circumstances and interests determine, or even constitute, all scientific statements.

All epistemological relativists reject the universality inherent in mathematics and sought by basic scientists. If relativism were true, there should be, at least potentially, as many "alternative" mathematics as social (or ethnic or other) groups: masculine and feminine mathematics, white and black, Gentile and Jewish, Western and Eastern, and so on. As Bloor (1976) and Restivo (1983) remind us, this was indeed a thesis of the once-popular obscurantist philosopher of history Spengler, whom Wittgenstein admired. It was also a favorite Nazi thesis: thus, whereas Aryan mathematics and physics are concrete and intuitive, their Jewish counterparts are abstract and counterintuitive.

This thesis about alternative mathematics can be refuted by showing that mathematical statements do not refer to anything real (in particular, social) and are not justified (in particular, proved) by recourse to empirical operations (in particular, social actions). (See, e.g., Bunge 1985*a*, chap. 1.) What is true is that mathematics cannot flourish in a backward society, whose members have neither the education nor the motivation, means or leisure, to devote themselves to the purest of all the pure sciences. It is also true, though perhaps of no interest to our relativist sociologist, that modern mathematics contains a large number of "alternative" mathematical theories *alongside* the "canonical" ones (e.g., intuitionist logic, nonstandard set theories, modulo arithmetics, non-Euclidean geometries, and nonstandard analysis). Hence mathematical truth *is* relative, as has been known for more than a century. (E.g., the equality "12 + 1 = 1," false in number theory, holds in clock arithmetic. Another old example: Inside a circle there are infinitely many "parallels"—i.e., noninter-secting lines—to any given straight line. A third example: The elements of a Lie algebra are not associative.)

However, every mathematical truth is relative to some *theory,* not to society. And any departures from canonical, standard, or classical mathematical theo-ries are prompted by purely intellectual reasons, mainly the wish to prove or to generalize—that is, to overcome the restrictions of earlier theories. Any such changes are brought about by pure intellectual curiosity: they are not re-sponses to social pressures, industrial needs, or ideological demands. They are answers to conceptual problems, not social issues. If mathematical problems were social problems, most of the latter would be soluble, and, moreover, they would get solved along with the advancement of mathematics—which, alas, is impossible, if only because mathematics has no social content.

"Deviant" mathematical theories have nothing to do with social deviance. Not only do they all fail to refer to anything social, but they are cultivated *along with* their standard counterparts in the same mathematical community, regard-less of economic or political factors—except, of course, that poor societies cannot afford to support much mathematical research, and dictators may dis-like certain branches of mathematics. (Incidentally, under the 1976–83 Argen-tine military dictatorship, two provincial governors banned modern mathe-matics, including the vector calculus, regarding it as Marxist. Little did they know that in so doing they were subscribing to the relativist thesis, popular with some neo-Marxists.)

The falsity of epistemological relativism is even more obvious with reference to factual science. Indeed, the multiplicity of simultaneous or successive mutu-ally incompatible theories about one and the same domain of facts only goes to prove that scientific research does not guarantee *instant, complete, and final truth.* But, as observational and experimental tests show, we often hit on *par-tially true* hypotheses. (Incidentally, partial truth has nothing to do with rela-tive or contextual truth.) And, as the history of science shows, if a hypothesis is interesting and sufficiently true, it will stimulate further research that may result in truer or deeper hypotheses. What holds for hypotheses and theories holds also, mutatis mutandis, for experimental designs. There *is* scientific pro-gress after all, because there *is* such a thing as objective (though usually only partial) truth.

As for the suspicion that if a scientific project has been motivated or distorted by material or ideological interests, it cannot yield objectively true results, this is an instance of what philosophers call the 'genetic fallacy,' which consists in judging a piece of knowledge by its birth (or baptismal) certificate. (The *argumentum ad hominem* is a special case of the genetic fallacy.) A hypothesis, datum, or method may be correct (true in the case of a proposition) regardless of the motivation of the research that produced it. Or it may prove to be false even if prompted by the purest of intentions. In short, the correctness of an idea is independent of its origin and utilization, and it must be established by strictly objective means. The same holds for the content of an idea. For instance, Durkheim held that all logical ideas, among them that of set inclusion, have a social (in particular, a religious) *origin,* but he did not claim that they also have a social (in particular, a religious) *content.*

Another popular source of contemporary epistemological relativism, one used by Kuhn (1962), is the perception of ambiguous figures first studied by Gestalt psychologists. If I see now a human face, now a vase, what is there *really* to be seen, and how can I claim that either perception is the correct one? The constructivist replies: "The nicest feature of this example is that we can see how foolish it is to ask which of these it *really* is" (H. M. Collins 1983, 90). But of course an ambiguous figure is, *by definition,* one that can be perceived (successively) in two different ways, neither of which is truer than the other. The ambiguity resides in the figure–subject system, not in the real face or the real vase separately. Collins suggests that such ambiguity affects *all* scientific problems, data, hypotheses, and methods. But neither he nor anyone else has advanced any *evidence* showing that this is indeed the case. Moreover, as anyone knows, ambiguity and vagueness will happen but can be corrected.

Although constructivist-relativists say that they have no use for the concept of truth, they do not ignore the fact that everyone makes mistakes. It is just that they cannot *define* the concept of a mistake or error in terms of departure from truth, as is done in the theory of errors of observation and in epistemology. They conveniently leave it undefined. Moreover, some of them seem to prefer error to truth. For example, Latour (1983, 164–65), ever eager to *épater le bourgeois,* assures us that scientists "can make as many mistakes as they wish. . . . Each mistake is in turn archived, saved, recorded and made easily readable again. . . . When you sum up a series of mistakes, you are stronger than anyone who has been allowed fewer mistakes than you." Thus the laboratory "is a technological device to gain strength by multiplying mistakes" (ibid., 165). Anyone who suspects that Latour is mistaking science for politics is right. In fact, Latour and Woolgar wrote earlier that "there is little to be gained by maintaining the distinction between the 'politics' of science and its 'truth'" (1979, 237). Shorter: As Hegel and the legal positivists said, might makes right.

Scientific controversy is alleged to be in the same boat. According to the relativist, all scientific controversies are conceptually unending, because there is no objective truth. Hence *"even in the purest of sciences,* if debate is to end, it must be brought to a close by some means not usually thought of as strictly *scientific"* (H. M. Collins 1983, 99). In other words, there are no crucial observations or experiments, no new predictions, no logical or mathematical proofs, no decisive counterexamples, no tests of (internal or external) consistency, and so on. There is only either the arbitrary decision of the "core set," or clique, in power or a negotiation and final compromise between the rival factions. "Politicking" would be the name of the scientific game.

Philosophers have taken care of epistemological relativism or skepticism either with the help of purely logical arguments or by listing some of the lasting findings of science, such as the heliocentric model of the planetary system, the circulation of the blood, the existence of electromagnetic fields, atoms, and genes, and the evolution of biospecies. These and most of the truths of logic and mathematics are surely some of the many full (not just partial) and eternal truths established from the beginning of the modern era—pace such skeptics as Hume, Engels, and Popper.

As noted earlier, epistemological relativism must not be mistaken for methodological skepticism, or fallibilism. According to the latter, all *propositions de fait* are *in principle* fallible—but also corrigible. The scientific researcher adopts tacitly what we have called methodological (or moderate) skepticism by contrast with systematic (or radical) skepticism. He doubts only where there is some (logical or empirical) *reason* to doubt: "If it ain't broke, don't fix it." Moreover, he cannot doubt *everything at once,* but only what is dubious in light of some body of knowledge. Nor does he doubt some of the very philosophical principles which drive scientific research, but which the new sociology of science rejects, among them those of the independent existence and objective intelligibility of the external world. Shorter: Most of the truths about the world are likely to be only *partial,* but they are *truths* nonetheless, not just equally uncertain conjectures, let alone fables.

Furthermore, scientific truths, whether total or partial, are supposed to be *universal* or cross-cultural, rather than the property of this or that social group. There are no such things as proletarian science or Aryan science, black mathematics or feminine philosophy: these are just political or academic rackets. To be sure, learning prospers more in some groups or societies than others, but so does superstition. If a view is acceptable only to the members of some social group, then it is ideological, not scientific. Even when an idea originates within a special group, it must be *universalizable* to count as scientific. Unless this criterion of scientificity is accepted, it becomes impossible to distinguish science from ideology, pseudoscience, or anti-science—which is, of course, one of the claims of the new sociology of science. (See further criticisms of relativism in Jarvie 1984; Gellner 1985; Trigg 1985; Archer 1987; Siegel 1987;

Livingston 1988; Boudon 1990*a*, 1990*b*; Bunge 1992*a*; Sebreli 1992; Boudon and Clavelin 1994; Albert 1994; Rescher 1994.)

5 Epistemological Hermeneutics

As we saw in chapter 11, section 2, the ontological thesis of philosophical hermeneutics, or textualism, is that the world, and in particular society, is a text or discourse. To take off on Berkeley, *to be is to be an inscriber or an inscription.* Let us now examine the epistemological concomitant of this extravagant view, which I shall call "epistemological hermeneutics," though it is often called "general semiotics."

If the world is indeed the longest speech ever or the largest library, it follows that if one wishes to understand it, all one has to do is to listen, read, and interpret. In particular, one must "interpret" human action (i.e., guess its purpose) and treat it as a discourse, subjecting it to hermeneutic or semiotic analysis. Dilthey (1959 [1883], [1990]), the founder of philosophical hermeneutics, restricted the range of the latter to the human sciences; but Gadamer (1975) and Feyerabend (1981) claimed that hermeneutics is valid even for natural science. But they did not explain how Verstehen works in, say, weighing a body.

We showed earlier (chap. 11, sec. 2) how hermeneuticists conflate several concepts of interpretation and how what they call "interpretation of human behavior" is actually hypothesizing intention from behavior. (Such hypotheses are often wrongly called "inferences.") Now we add that because any given behavior is consistent with more than one purpose, we must regard such hypotheses ("interpretations") as tentative and therefore in need of empirical test. A trivial example should suffice to make the point. Datum: Individual *X* puts up his home for sale. Possible hypotheses in the absence of further data: (*a*) *X* is desperately in need of cash; (*b*) *X*'s house is now too big for him because his children have left home; (*c*) *X* believes this is a seller's market; (*d*) *X* fears a real estate crash and wishes to cut his losses; (*e*) *X* knows that his house has a structural fault and wishes to sell before it becomes apparent; (*f*) *X* intends to move out of town; (*g*) *X* is about to divorce, retire, die, or what have you. Thus we have (at least) seven different interpretations of the "House for sale" sign. Only some inquiry can pick the true one.

What holds for behavioral signals holds, mutatis mutandis, for texts, particularly if they convey technical knowledge unfamiliar to the reader. However, mere ignorance does not stop the hermeneuticist (or general semiotician), according to whom (*a*) even science is just a heap of inscriptions to be deciphered with the sole help of hermeneutics, and (*b*) since doing science or metascience—or anything else, for that matter—is only a matter of wordmanship or language-games, any literate person should be able to play (Latour and Woolgar 1979).

Thus, in the hermeneutic perspective, the distinction between expert and layman evaporates. So does the annoying requirement that interpretations be put to the test. Indeed, objectivity is merely "conformity to orthodox practices of writing and reading" (R. H. Brown 1990, 188). The consequence for the fact–fiction and truth–falsity distinctions is obvious: "[T]he distinctions between fact and fiction are thereby softened because both are seen as the products of, and sources for, communicative action" (ibid., 189). Why, then, should anyone worry about the concept of truth (other than consensus), let alone with truth tests?

The textualist approach conveniently allows one to tackle even the most abstruse scientific ideas solely with the tools of semiotic analysis. Thus Latour (1988) performed such an analysis of the special theory of relativity (SR), as expounded by Einstein in his 1920 popular book *Relativity: The Special and the General Theory.* (The reasoning is clear: if a layman can read popular science, then science must be accessible to all.) Since this popular exposition uses the prop of a bunch of travelers who take trains, measure times, and send signals, Latour concludes that SR is not about the electrodynamics of moving bodies (the title of Einstein's 1905 seminal paper), or even about space and time.

Latour (1988, 11) reveals to us that what counts in SR are certain human activities. He goes so far as to suggest that Einstein chose the wrong title: "His book could well be titled: 'New Instructions for Bringing Back Long-Distance Scientific Travellers'" (ibid., 23). Moreover, Einstein's work would be similar to the Smithsonian Institution's initial plan for setting up a nationwide network of weather observers in order "to build up meteorological phenomena [*sic*]." The deep changes introduced by SR in our concepts of space and time, mass and energy and their relations, as well as in the relation between mechanics and electrodynamics, are invisible from the hermeneutic-constructivist-relativist viewpoint.

This travesty of SR leads Latour to vindicate the old, discredited philosophical misinterpretation of SR (and of quantum mechanics) as a confirmation of *epistemological* relativism, a form of subjectivism according to which all scientific facts are created by "independent and active observers." (One source of this elementary mistake is the erroneous identification of "reference frame" with "knowing subject.") Hence the title of his paper: "A relativistic account of Einstein's relativity." It did not occur to Latour that in order to evaluate any claims concerning the role of the observer in a scientific theory, it is necessary (*a*) to axiomatize the theory, so as to separate the scientific grain from the didactic and philosophical chaff, and (*b*) to analyze the theory with the help of some theory of reference, so as to ferret out its genuine referents.

If these tasks are carried out, it can be *proved*, not just *claimed*, that SR and quantum mechanics are about independently existing physical things (Bunge 1967*a*, 1973*c*), *not* "about the ways of describing any possible experience" (Latour 1988, 25). In particular, by proving that the referents of relativistic mechanics are bodies interacting via an electromagnetic field (as suggested by the title of Einstein's founding paper), one disproves the quaint claim that the speed of light and the Lorentz transformations are "part of the normal business of building a society" (ibid.). As everyone knows, societies have been in existence since long before the birth of science; and, for better or worse, their emergence, maintenance, and breakdown is utterly foreign to theories of relativity.

Like Pythagoreanism, Cabalism, and psychoanalysis, philosophical hermeneutics views all things as symbols of other things. (A character in Umberto Eco's novel *Foucault's Pendulum* maintains that the penis is a phallic symbol.) It is a regression to magical thinking. By contrast, the distinction between a symbol and its *denotatum* is a basic feature of rational or critical thinking. The sentence "The cat lies on the mat" bears no resemblance to the fact it describes or even to the sounds one makes when uttering it. Hence a linguistic (e.g., syntactic, phonological, or stylistic) analysis of the sentence will not reveal what it stands for. The conflation of fact and symbol is not just mistaken, but insane.

Neither people nor social systems, any more than atoms or plants, have linguistic properties. Not even our ideas about things can be identified with their linguistic wrappings, if only because these differ from one language to the next. In particular, theories have logical, mathematical, and semantic properties, not linguistic or literary ones. This is why scientific theories are created by scientists and analyzed by logicians and scientific philosophers, not by hermeneuticists or linguistic philosophers, let alone by literary critics. Therefore hermeneutic philosophy has nothing to teach social scientists.

Yet a few competent social scientists, from Weber (1988 [1913]) to Hodder (1992), have claimed that their work fits the hermeneutic model rather than the scientific one. This view rests on two misunderstandings: one on the nature of method, the other on the nature of the hermeneutic procedure. The former consists in the wrong positivist belief that the scientific method can be applied only to observable facts, not to unobservable ones such as the feelings, thoughts, and intentions of our remote ancestors. Actually the scientific method can be applied to all knowledge problems and is the only method that can turn coarse intuitions into testable and in some cases true (yet seldom totally certain) hypotheses, and raw data into (more or less solid) evidence for or against hypotheses. As for the hermeneutic procedure, when legitimate, it can be translated into the standard method with the help of the following glossary:

Meaning (of an action or an artifact) → function or purpose.
Interpretation, or Verstehen (of an action or an artifact) → hypothesis or theory.
Hermeneutic circle → data–hypotheses–data zigzag.

To conclude: Scientists are supposed to keep one eye on ideas, the other on facts. However, some students of society (typically, anthropologists and historians) are blind to theory, whereas others (typically, mathematical economists) are blind to fact. Only a few, particularly the hermeneuticists, are blind in both eyes. In short, philosophical hermeneutics has no redeeming qualities. (More in Albert 1994.)

6 Probability: Objective and Subjective

Philosophical controversies over the concept of probability are part of the age-old controversy between realism and anti-realism. The modern theory of probability is neutral with regard to these controversies, because it assigns probabilities to abstract sets—that is, sets of nondescript elements. But controversy is likely to arise as soon as these elements are assumed to represent factual items such as physical events or states of mind; that is, when the probability concept is used to reason about facts.

The main controversy concerns the question of whether probability is a measure of objective chance or a measure of our degree of belief or uncertainty. For example, if we flip a fair coin, it has equal probabilities, namely $\frac{1}{2}$, of landing heads or tails. To an objectivist, these probabilities are objective, but once the coin has landed, they vanish—whether or not we look at the coin. Or, if preferred, once the coin has landed, one of the probabilities has expanded to 1, while the other has shrunk to 0. (*Alea jacta est*, as Roman gamblers said once they had thrown the sheep knuckles.) Hence, to the objectivist, it makes no sense to ask of a blindfolded person, after the coin has landed, what is the probability that he will see the coin showing its head. Beliefs cannot be assigned probabilities—not until some psychologist comes up with a well-confirmed probabilistic theory of belief acquisition and change.

By contrast, the subjectivist (or personalist, or Bayesian) believes that probabilities are states of mind. Hence he will assign a probability not only to a random event but also to his belief in anything, particularly a nonrandom event that he cannot predict for want of knowledge. For example, he will say that the probability that the blindfolded spectator will find that the coin has landed head up is $\frac{1}{2}$. Or, to take another example, suppose a woman is known to have two children, one of them a boy. Obviously, the other child is either a boy or a girl. The subjectivist, who ignores the sex of the second child, will say that the probability of the child being a boy is $\frac{1}{2}$. But the realist will refuse to assign a probability to the belief in question. He will argue that such an assignment makes sense only during the very short period of egg fertilization, for this is indeed a process of random gene shuffling, where the sexes have almost the same chance of prevailing. Moreover, he will scold the subjectivist for confusing the probability of an event with the degree of certainty of his belief in the occurrence of that event—a case of mistaking physics for psychology.

What practical difference can it make which of the two interpretations of probability is chosen? A great deal. First, realism promotes the scientific investigation of random processes, whereas subjectivism denies their existence or even fosters idle speculation. Indeed, subjective estimates, even by experienced observers, are no serious substitute for measurement or theoretical calculation, however approximate these may be. For one thing, it is practically impossible to give a reasonable subjective estimate of a probability smaller than, say, 0.1, whereas a physicist will think nothing of calculating or measuring probabilities even less than 10^{-10}. For another, people have a well-known tendency to underrate the probabilities of highly likely events while overrating the probabilities of very unlikely events.

Third, the subjectivist interpretation is rife with paradox. Consider again the example of the woman who admits to having two children, one of them a boy, but asks the subjectivist to guess the sex of the second child. At first sight, the probability of this child being a boy too is $\frac{1}{2}$. But, if he is inquisitive, the subjectivist will go further. He may reason that, if there are two boys, and they are not twins, one of them is older than the other: call him B1, and B2 his kid brother. Now there are not two, but three equally likely beliefs: B1 and a girl, B2 and a girl, and the boys B1 and B2. Only one of these beliefs can be true, and the "probability" of each of them being true is $\frac{1}{3}$, not $\frac{1}{2}$ (Gardner 1992, 131). The moral is that whatever credences (belief strengths) may be, they do not behave like probabilities.

Let us next examine, in light of the foregoing, the way probabilities are interpreted in an important school of social studies: namely, rational choice theory. The central concept of this theory (or, rather, family of theories) is the notion of expected utility. This is the sum of the products of the utilities (payoffs) of the possible outcomes of an action by their respective probabilities. In the vast majority of cases, the utilities and probabilities are taken to be subjective, for what is at stake is the manner in which the agent "perceives" his options and chooses a course of action. Consequently different persons are likely to assign different expected utilities to any given action. And none of them can be said to be objectively more correct than the others: it is all a matter of opinion or taste, not science. Only the use of mathematical symbols gives it a scientific appearance. Furthermore, subjective probabilities (or, rather, degrees of belief) cannot be inferred from an observation of the subject's actual choices, because these may not reveal his real preferences, especially if he has a stake in the events or is just risk-averse (see Karni and Safra 1995).

The adoption of subjective, or personal, probability values is of course central to the Bayesian (or personalist) school of mathematical statistics defended in recent years by de Finetti, Jeffreys, Carnap, Savage, Good, Lindley, and others. It is also part of Bayesian decision theory. (For detailed criticisms, see du Pasquier 1926; Fréchet 1946; Bartlett 1975; Bunge 1988*a*.) But the subjectivist stand is inconsistent with the way in which probabilities are assigned in mature disciplines such as statistical mechanics, quantum theory, genetics, engineering, and even some branches of social science, such as demography, epidemiology, and social mobility theory. In these disciplines probabilities (or probability distributions) are treated as objective properties on a par with lengths and populations, neither of which is supposed to be estimated subjectively (except provisionally and subject to experimental checking). In particular, no prior (a priori) probabilities occur in the "hard" sciences, except as hypotheses to be checked against relative frequencies.

Moreover, in the hard sciences probabilities are introduced only when there is reason to believe that a chance process, such as random shuffling or random sampling, is at work: No probability without objective randomness. Yet Milton Friedman (1976, 84) assures us confidently that "individuals act *as if* they assigned personal probabilities to all possible events." The fictionist *as if* trick renders the statement untestable and thus frees the theorist from the burden of empirical testing—very convenient for the lover of free speculation. But it leaves the statistician baffled and helpless, for the Bayesian cannot exactify the concepts of randomness, randomization, and random sample.

The adoption of subjective probabilities can have disastrous consequences—for example, in the case of risk evaluation. For instance, people tend to underestimate high risk, such as the likelihood of critically ill people dying or becoming "vegetables"—an error that can have serious moral and pecuniary consequences (see, e.g., Knaus et al. 1991). A memorable dramatic case was the explosion of the *Challenger* space shuttle in 1986. When asked to investigate the causes of the disaster, Feynman (1989, 179–80) discussed the matter with some of the engineers and managers involved in it. A competent, forthright expert told him that 5 out of 127 rockets inspected by him had failed—a rate of about 4 percent. Assuming that a manned flight would be safer than an unmanned one, he estimated that there was about a 1 percent chance of failure. But the NASA managers did not believe in estimating probabilities on the strength of relative frequencies. They had insisted that the probability of failure was only one in 100,000—that is, 10,000 times smaller than the figure estimated by the engineer. How had the managers come by that fantastic figure? They did not and could not say: theirs was a subjective, or personal, probability guess of the kind that occurs in most rational choice models.

A less dramatic case is that of the risks faced by insurance companies. An ordinary insurance company will calculate its insurance premiums on the basis of actuarial tables for life expectancies, fires, or automobile accidents. It will not insure against any risk unless it can avail itself of such tables, which give objective probabilities estimated on the strength of the corresponding relative frequencies. But the famous Lloyd's of London was willing to issue insurance policies against such comparatively rare events as the theft of a van Gogh painting, the shipwreck of a jumbo tanker, or an earthquake, acting on the expectation that no string of rare calamities of this sort could happen in a single year. But 1990 happened to be such a year, and, as a consequence, Lloyd's came to the brink of bankruptcy. Moral: Acting on subjective probabilities amounts to gambling—a bad, mad, sad business.

In short, in any rigorous scientific discourse, probabilities (*a*) are part of a model concerning some random (or stochastic) thing or process, (*b*) represent objective properties of the things in question, and (*c*) are supposed to be objectively measurable, though not necessarily in a direct manner (Bunge 1988*a*). Not so in most rational choice models. The expected utilities occurring in most rational choice models are neither mathematically well defined nor objectively measurable. Subjective probabilities are, of course, in the same boat with subjective values or utilities.

Note that I am not suggesting that the outcomes of our actions are fully determinate, rather than more or less probable. To be sure, chance is for real, not just a synonym of ignorance. Thus in many cases, and in all choice situations, we are confronted with real (not just conceptual) possibilities, and it is often in our power to actualize some of them and block others. But the point is that (*a*) some possibilities (e.g., those of car collisions) are nonrandom, whence they cannot be assigned probabilities; and (*b*) we rarely have a clue as to the precise values of the probabilities of random social events, if only because there are few reliable (probabilistic or other) mathematical models of human action. By contrast, in the hard sciences probabilities (or probability densities) occur in exact theories, where they are related to other magnitudes, some of which are measurable either directly or via indicators. (Thus, in quantum physics one may measure probabilities indirectly through such variables as energy, temperature, or light intensity.)

Decision theory has been constructed on the analogy of games of chance. (This is ironic, because in games of chance, utilities and probabilities are objective and knowable, hence they do not have to be guessed, much less made up.) Now, life is not a gamble, even though it is chock full of accidents and chance events. It is not just that we can make some events happen at will. Nor is it only that usually we do not know the odds and utilities of the possible outcomes of our actions. The point is that in most cases we do not even know the full set of such possible outcomes—this being why we encounter surprises at every turn. (Hence, even if every foreseeable branch in a decision tree could be assigned a probability on some reasonable grounds, the sum of the probabilities for the various known branches originating in a node could not add up to unity, as it should, because we do not know all the branches.)

To put it another way, no decision tree can include all the possible outcomes of a real action. But in compensation, when disaster threatens, we can often prevent it—something we are not allowed to do once the dice have been rolled. Because in principle we can alter in mid-course almost any course of deliberate action, and because we ignore so many factors, decision theory and its kin, modeled as they are on games of chance, are not reliable guides to rational action. Rational people are not gamblers: they attempt to master chance or even avoid it, instead of throwing themselves on its mercy. (More in Bunge forthcoming.)

Nor am I suggesting that social scientists should ignore subjective phenomena, such as beliefs, uncertainties, expectations, and intentions. We must try to find out about them and examine them critically. But subjectivity must be studied scientifically—for example, by means of reliable objective (physiological or behavioral) indicators. The arbitrary assignment of probabilities to states of mind or to the possible outcomes of intended actions is not a scientific procedure, precisely in being arbitrary.

The same holds, a fortiori, for the assignment of probabilities to propositions and, in particular, to hypotheses. No precise rules for making such assignments are known. Moreover there *can* be none, because hypotheses are neither generated nor adopted at random. (Yet there is a whole academic industry, viz., inductive "logic," which presupposes that every proposition can be attributed a probability.) The whole point is that such "probabilities" are subjective, hence rather arbitrary. 'Subjective probability' is just a fancy name for strength of belief, credence, or plausibility.

There can be no reasonable objection to studying subjective "probabilities," credences, or plausibilities in an objective manner. As a matter of fact, they have been so studied, and two major findings have been obtained. First, a subjective probability is not a linear function of the corresponding objective probability. (There is some experimental evidence for the psychophysical power law $S = \alpha p^\beta$, with $\alpha > 1$ and $0 < \beta < 1$.) Second, and consequently, subjective probabilities do not satisfy the laws of the calculus of probability. (Thus, if the power law holds, then the subjective estimate of the objective probability $p = p_1 + p_2$ of an alternative is $S = \alpha(p_1 + p_2)^\beta \neq S_1 + S_2$. The same qualitative consequence follows from any other nonlinear relation between S and p.) In short, probability can be neither defined nor interpreted in terms of belief. Only the realist (propensity) interpretation of probability is utilizable in science and technology.

7 Objective Study of Subjectivity

The power of belief is such that if a person believes X to be real, he will behave as if X is real, even if, in fact, X is nothing but a figment of his imagination (see Merton 1957, 421ff.). Since subjectivity is an important feature of human life, the realist should favor its objective study. In fact, psychologists and social psychologists do study the way in which subjective factors, such as perceptions, beliefs, valuations, and attitudes, influence objective items, such as actions, and, in turn, how the actions of other people influence our subjective experiences. In other words, social scientists are interested not only in objective situations, but also in the ways these are "perceived." But they are supposed to study objectively such perceptions as well as external circumstances, and in fact this is what they try to do (see, e.g., Nagel 1961, chap. 13). To see how subjective and objective factors can combine, let us examine the problem of objective versus subjective ("perceived") fairness.

Whenever benefits and burdens can be quantified, we may define the *degree of justice* (or fairness) done an individual over a given time span as the ratio of his benefits, b, to his duties or burdens, d, during that period; that is, $J = b/d$. Perfect justice or equity is represented by a straight line at 45° on the d–b plane. Injustice or inequity is represented by the region below this line (underprivilege) and that above (privilege). So much for objective justice.

Now social scientists, from Aristotle to Tocqueville and Marx, have known that conformity and nonconformity with regard to the distribution of benefits and burdens depend on "perceived" rather than objective justice. (In particular, both the underdog and the top dog tend to justify inequity in terms of desert, real or alleged.) Therefore, in addition to the concept of objective justice, we need a subjective measure of justice. In a pioneering paper, Jasso (1980) proposed the following formula for "perceived" or *subjective justice:*

$$J_p = k \log(b/b_f),$$

where b and b_f denote the objective and the "perceived" fair shares of benefits, respectively, and k is a constant characteristic of the particular person. If a person is easily satisfied, he has a large k; if picky, his k is small. Perceived justice is positive (privilege), null (equity), or negative (underprivilege), according as the actual benefit b is respectively greater than, equal to, or smaller than the "perceived" fair share b_f of benefits. Jasso's formula should ring a bell familiar to psychophysicists and utility theorists.

The preceding formula captures the "rights" side of justice but overlooks its "duties" side, which is unacceptable to anyone who believes that justice consists in a balance between the two (Bunge 1989). This omission is easily remedied by dividing the argument of the logarithm by the ratio d/d_f of actual to fair (but still "perceived") burden. The result is

$$J_p = k \log[(b/b_f)/(d/d_f)] = k \log (b.d_f/b_f.d).$$

According to this formula, a person will feel (justifiably or not) that justice has been done him if and only if $b/b_f = d/d_f$; that is, if the ratios of actual to "fair" benefits and burdens are the same. Obviously (mathematically) and interestingly (psychologically), the above condition can be satisfied in infinitely many ways. One (sufficient) condition is of course $b = b_f$ and $d = d_f$, which may be referred to as ideal subjective justice. However, $b = cb_f$ and $d = cd_f$, where c is an arbitrary real number other than 0, will do just as well. In particular, the following combinations are possible:

$b = 2b_f$, and $d = 2d_f$,
$b = (\frac{1}{2})b_f$, and $d = (\frac{1}{2})d_f$.

That is, doubling the "fair" share of duties can be compensated by doubling the "fair" share of benefits. And halving d_f can be balanced by halving b_f.

So far, we have tacitly interpreted b_f and d_f as outcomes of self-appraisals or subjective evaluations. However, they can also be interpreted as figures arrived at by persons other than the individual in question. For example, the manager of a firm or the chairman of an academic department may determine what constitute "fair" benefits and burdens for an individual who carries out a given task. And he may do so using objective performance indicators. Still, the individual in question may have a different "perception."

Social scientists, then, are expected to study objectively not only how things really are, but also how they are "perceived." Nor is this enough. People do not just "perceive" society: they sustain or alter it by acting on others. This points to an important difference between knowing subjects in the theory of knowledge about nature and those in the theory of social knowledge. Whereas in the former the knowing subject studies natural things, in the latter he studies people who not only know but also act on the strength of their knowledge, or rather belief. In particular, unlike theories in natural science, some of the theories in social science cannot help but refer to people who are led (or misled) by social theories. For example, social movements differ from the movements of bodies or fields, in that their members have social goals and are inspired by ideologies.

This difference has led some scholars to challenge the belief in the possibility of social science and others to suggest that although social science is possible, the corresponding epistemology must be changed. The former claim is disposed of by recalling that social science does exist, even though, admittedly, not always on a high level. The second claim is more interesting and, at first blush, correct. Indeed, it would seem that, since social facts are the deeds of people, they are not out there: everything social is constructed or invented, and nothing discovered. Consequently realism, which might work for natural science, is inadequate for social science: here we need a radical constructivist epistemology that shuns objectivity. This view is often called "constructivism," less often "second-order cybernetics." But of course it is as old as philosophy itself; it has traditionally been called "subjective idealism," as we saw in chapter 11.

In sum, the fact that people create social facts and are influenced by their own beliefs does not render objective social studies impossible; nor does it call for a change in epistemology. All it does is force us to impute to people (conjecturally, hence subject to tests) interests, beliefs, intentions, doubts, and other mental processes. In other words, all we have to do is to widen and deepen the scope of social studies, taking it far beyond the mere recording of overt behavior (see Searle 1995). Shorter: Since society and nature, though different, are equally real, they ought to be studied in the same realist way. Even shorter: Naturalism implies realism, but realism does not imply naturalism.

8 Scientific Realism

Realism is the philosophical view that the external world exists independently of our sense experience and ideation and that it can be known, if only in part. The first conjunct is an ontological thesis, whereas the second is an epistemological one. Hence it is possible to assert the former while denying the latter. That is, one can hold that material objects exist of themselves but cannot be known except, perhaps, by their appearances. Or one can claim that the world is intelligible because we construct it ourselves, much as we construct stories and mathematical theories. Full-blooded realism asserts jointly the theses of the autonomy and knowability of the external world.

Science and technology do more than try to prove full-blooded realism: they *presuppose* it. Indeed, if the external world did not exist independently of the subject, how could he explore it? And if the external world did exist independently but was unknowable, how could we account for the success of scientific exploration? To be sure, scientists have emotions and foibles; they make mistakes, and some of their actions have impure motives. In short, they are human, not angelic. But spotting error—particularly someone else's—and trying to correct it are part of the scientific job description. Scoundrels will make a scientific career only if they produce (or plagiarize) some genuine science: if they find out some objective truths about the world. In short, science is "objectivity without illusions" (Kitcher 1995).

Realism is opposed to subjectivism in all its forms. In particular, it clashes with conventionalism, constructivism, and phenomenalism. On the other hand, realism is consistent with some forms of immaterialism, such as Aquinas's, though not, of course, with Berkeley's or Mach's. In particular, it is possible to be a realist while believing that there are disembodied souls and angels. By the same token, realism must not be confused with materialism, which is an ontological view, not an epistemological one (see chap. 11, sec. 5). Nor must realism be confused with empiricism or positivism, both of which restrict the knowable to what can be experienced (see chap. 12, secs. 3 and 4); and even less with pragmatism, which rejects the very idea of mapping reality and is interested only in action (see chap. 12, sec. 5). Such confusions result from superficiality and cause time to be wasted. Witness Putnam's (1994) reluctant admission of realism after attacking it for decades.

The ontological thesis of realism can be restated thus: There are things in themselves—that is, independent of the knowing and acting subject. Its epistemological companion can then be reformulated as follows: We can know things in themselves, not just as they appear to us. These two theses are presupposed in any scientific research (see chap. 7, sec. 1) and are confirmed by all scientific successes. For example, some popularizations of quantum physics notwithstanding, physicists treat electrons, photons, and other imperceptible things as things in themselves, independent of any observers. This is no dogma: it is easily proved by inspecting the basic equations (i.e., axioms) describing such entities. In fact, those equations do not contain any variables referring to the knowing subject (Bunge 1967*a*, 1973*c*).

One of the recurrent objections to mainstream mathematical economics is that it is not realistic enough—for example, that it assumes equilibrium and perfect competition when, actually, neither pertains. Still, even the most orthodox economist will admit only so much fiction. For example, it may happen that the price (or the quantity) equations for an economy have two mathematically exact solutions, one for positive, the other for negative prices (or quantities). Since real prices and quantities are positive, the economist will declare the negative solutions economically meaningless, because unrealistic. That is, he will tacitly endorse realism even while building models that are far from the truth.

Another example of tacit realism is this. When a new hypothesis or theory fails empirical tests, it is rejected for not fitting the facts—that is, for not being realistic. But this may not be the end of the story. One may try modifying the original hypotheses or theories in the hope of coming up with truer—that is, more realistic—ones. Should this move fail, one may attempt to construct entirely different ideas, or even adopt a different approach. In either case, one admits tacitly that one's ideas ought to pass reality checks.

We must distinguish three varieties of realism: naive, critical, and scientific. *Naive* or *commonsensical realism* asserts that things are such as we perceive them. This view does not distinguish between a thing in itself and that thing for us (i.e., as it appears to us), or it demands that every real item have a counterpart in the corresponding theory. In other words, naive realism holds that true knowledge (or language in the case of the early Wittgenstein) "mirrors" reality, or is "isomorphic" to it. The naive realist is uncritical and consequently prey to sensory delusion and self-deception, as well as a sitting duck for skeptics and idealists. And since he believes in the possibility of attaining complete, definitive truths about matters of fact, he can explain neither errors nor efforts to correct them by constructing ever more complex theories containing concepts increasingly removed from perception and intuition. Naive realism is particularly unsuited to the study of things, such as electrons and social systems, and processes, such as atomic collisions and stagflation, that are not directly perceptible and have counterintuitive properties.

There are two ways of responding to the inadequacies of naive realism: to reject it altogether or to try to refine it. The former is the anti-realist response. The anti-realist reasons that since scientists keep discovering errors in their own work, as well as changing their ideas and even their data, truth is unattainable. Shorter: Reality, if it exists at all, is unknowable. This is a naive, defeatist response to naive realism. It overlooks the fact that scientific error is corrigible: that we can usually go from error to partial truth to higher-order approximations. Worse, anti-realism is blatantly unrealistic—that is, false—because the whole point of scientific research is to explore the real world in order to get to know it. In particular, what would be the point of checking scientific hypotheses against facts if they did not purport to represent facts? And what would be the point of technological proposals if they did not intend to alter certain features of real things, to assemble new ones, or to dismantle existing ones? Scientists and technologists are not paid to play games, but to explore reality or devise means to alter it.

The *critical realist* acknowledges that perception is limited and can be deceptive, and that complete, exact truth is hard to come by. He admits that the way we perceive things depends in part upon our beliefs and expectations. This inclines him to adopt a critical or skeptical attitude: he is a fallibilist. He also realizes that perception must be corrected and supplemented by conception— that is, the construction of concepts, hypotheses, and theories referring to imperceptible things such as social networks and nations. Moreover, he realizes that scientific theories cannot be isomorphic to their real referents because they contain (*a*) constructs without real counterparts (such as those of logical consequence and identity), (*b*) simplifications and idealizations, and (*c*) conventional elements, such as definitions, units, scales, and coordinate systems. (Besides, isomorphism can hold only between sets, and reality happens not to be a set.) In short, the critical realist holds that we explore reality and account for it by using our own ideas. This is no concession to idealism, any more than the use of conventions commits one to conventionalism.

Scientific realism is a refined version of critical realism and the culmination of ratio-empiricism (see chap. 12, sec. 7). In addition to the ontological and epistemological postulates of realism, it asserts (*a*) the methodological principle that scientific research is the most advanced mode of inquiry into any matters of fact, even though it is not infallible, and (b) the article of (justified) meliorist faith that, though fallible, scientific research can yield increasingly true representations of the world. These two additional principles are jointly called "scientism." (The signification of the word *scientism* here is the traditional one: see, e.g., Lalande 1938. By contrast, Hayek [1955] proposed the Pickwickian, malicious definition of *scientism* as a "slavish imitation of the method and language of science." To be scientistic, in the traditionally accepted sense of the word, is to practice the scientific approach, not just ape it. The imitation of science is called "pseudoscience.")

Scientific realism is not just a recent philosophical fad. It was explicitly defended by Galileo and was the focus of his infamous trial. As is well known, Galileo held that heliocentric planetary astronomy was true and, in particular, that our planet revolves around the sun, not the other way round. This statement contradicted naive realism, phenomenalism, conventionalism—and the book of Genesis. His inquisitor, Cardinal Bellarmino, took the phenomenalist and conventionalist view, defended earlier by Ptolemy, that the astronomer's task is to account for appearances, not to find out how things really are. The Inquisition did not press Galileo to adopt the old geocentric view: it just wanted him to declare that the two rival views were equivalent in both being compatible with the data, so that the new astronomy would make no dent in Scripture.

In short, the Inquisition fought the newly born scientific realism and defended phenomenalism and conventionalism. The Church terminated the controversy by force, but scientific realism was vindicated a few years later. In fact, Newtonian celestial mechanics justified the heliocentric hypothesis by showing that, because the solar mass is at least a thousand times larger than the masses of the planets, the latter really revolve around the former. This news does not seem to have reached contemporary philosophers like van Fraassen (1980) who reject realism and require only the empirical adequacy of models of the phenomenal world.

(Ironically, by defending phenomenalism against scientific realism, the Inquisition betrayed the realism inherent in Thomism, which was the official Roman Catholic philosophy at the time. Even more ironically, one century later, Kant, who in some ways belonged to the Enlightenment, attempted to revive phenomenalism, freshly killed by Newton's science. Worse was to come: two centuries later the logical positivists—in particular, Philipp Frank—repeated the Cardinal's contention that the two "systems of the world"—that is, planetary astronomies—are equivalent. Will philosophers ever learn not to lag too far behind science? And can theologians afford to keep up with science?)

Scientific realism is tacitly embraced by all who search for or utilize objective (factual) truth, particularly practicing scientists and technologists when not on philosophical holidays. Remember the gist of the realist conception of truth: A proposition asserting that a fact f is the case is true if and only if f is really (actually, in fact) the case (chap. 3, sec. 5). The very notion of factual, or objective, truth presupposes realism, and, in turn, realism involves the realistic (or adequacy) conception of truth. However, scientific realism does not require total, final truth: it will settle for partial (approximate) and provisional truth when nothing better is available or required. The path to truth is winding, long, and sometimes unending.

How do we know that scientific research presupposes (and confirms) scientific realism? Certainly not by circulating questionnaires among researchers or philosophers, but by analyzing the role of real existence hypotheses in some typical research projects. For instance, an anthropologist interested in investigating the life-style of the tribe X, of which he has only hearsay, starts by traveling to the land of X. On arrival, he looks for people who display characteristics similar to those portrayed in the preliminary report he has. That is, he tries to make sure that X exists. If he succeeds in making contact with some X's, he attempts to study them from as close a range as they will allow.

Our anthropologist will not believe right away everything he is told by his informers, particularly since these may believe in nonexistents. In other words, he will check their reports. Moreover, he will try to unveil some features, such as the social structure of the tribe X, which may not be apparent to the X's themselves. In short, he will proceed like a good scientific realist. And when submitting his study of the X for publication, his referees will take pleasure in pointing out flaws which prove that he did not discover or grasp correctly all the facts: his critics, too, try to be good scientific realists, even if they profess subjectivism or relativism.

An additional argument for realism is provided by the following thought-experiment. If a researcher were not at least a closet realist, he would remain content with recording his own mental states, particularly appearances, and would construct only egocentric (or at most lococentric) views. He would make no effort to explain appearances in terms of hidden, though presumably real, entities and processes. He would not entertain hypotheses about unobserved, but presumably real, entities or properties and, a fortiori, he would not put them to the test. Worse, he might turn to nonscience or even anti-science instead of doggedly pursuing objective truth. (He may hold unscientific beliefs while not engaging in scientific research; but this shows only that weekend philosophy may be inconsistent with workday philosophy.) And if he had no faith in the possibility of correcting error and converging to the truth, the scientist would not attempt to perfect either observations or theories. Incidentally, only realism can account for error, because error is, by definition, deviation from truth, and, in turn, (factual) truth is fitting the facts. Thus the normal state of alert to the ever-present possibility of errors of various kinds, together with faith in the ability to detect and correct them, is just as strong an argument for realism as is the strong, steady output of partial truths about the real world.

By denying the autonomous existence of the external world, or at least the possibility of knowing it objectively, anti-realism discourages its scientific exploration and its rational control. Shorter: Anti-realism is anti-scientific and impractical. By contrast, realism is not just one more philosophical extravagance: it is the epistemology tacitly inherent in factual science and technology. It inheres in the former, because the declared aim of scientific research is to explore and understand reality. And realism inheres in technology, because the latter's job is to design or redesign feasible artifacts or plans aimed at altering reality.

Moreover, the philosophy of knowledge that we adopt tacitly in everyday life is realist—albeit, of the commonsensical variety. There is a powerful biological motivation for this: Know your environment or perish. No complex animal can survive unless it is capable of modeling adequately (truthfully) its immediate environment, at least in some respects. It will starve to death unless it can identify what it can eat and what can eat it, and it will get lost unless it is able to chart its surroundings. Realism is thus necessary for animal survival, as well as for understanding and altering the world in a rational manner. If there ever were subjectivist animals, they either died very young from exposure to the world they denied, or they were appointed professors of philosophy. Indeed, philosophers are the only animals that, because they are protected by academic freedom, can afford to ignore or even deny reality—as long as they are tenured.

14 :: Between Reason and
Fact: Rational Choice
Theory

The concepts of rational choice, decision, and action are at the center of a large and growing number of theories, broad or narrow, in all the social sciences: the theories of utility, decision, and games, as well as neoclassical microeconomics. These rational choice theories are as controversial as they are popular and interesting. An examination of the assumptions common to all of them will clarify and help us to evaluate them. It will also be an occasion to apply, and thus consolidate, what we have learned in the foregoing.

Let us start by recalling that the family of schools of thought which hold that the world is intelligible and extol the virtues of conceptual rigor and rational discussion is called "rationalism." As we saw earlier (chap. 12, sec. 6), rationalism comes in two strengths: radical and moderate. The former claims that reason is necessary and sufficient to understand the world: it is aprioristic. The latter makes room for experience, hence for arguments from empirical evidence. It thus coincides with the synthesis of rationalism and empiricism which we called "ratio-empiricism" and claimed was practiced by scientists and technologists (chap. 12, sec. 6).

All rationalists agree that the study of society should proceed rationally. But only some rationalist students of society impute full rationality to all their subjects and build or apply rational choice models. Before examining these models, we will analyze the word *rationality*, for it is anything but unambiguous. This analysis is indispensable if we are to avoid confusion and dispel the widespread illusion that any one discipline, such as logic or economics, can have a rightful monopoly on rationality. Moreover, unless one realizes the ambiguity of the word *rationality,* any failures of rational choice theory risk being misinterpreted as a vindication of irrationalism—as was actually suggested by Ryan (1991).

The word *rationality* is notoriously polysemic: it designates at least twelve different concepts: (1) *semantical:* clarity or minimal fuzziness; (2) *logical:* internal consistency—that is, noncontradiction; (3) *dialectical:* inferential validity—that is, absence of logical fallacies; (4) *erotetic:* posing only problems that make sense in some context—that is, avoidance of pseudo-problems; (5) *methodological:* questioning and justifying assumptions and methods; (6) *epistemological:* requiring empirical support and compatibility with the bulk of background knowledge; (7) *ontological:* admitting only ontological assumptions compatible with factual science; (8) *valuational:* choosing only goals attainable with the available means; (9) *prohairetic:* observing the transitivity of preference—that is, complying with the principle that if $a > b$, and $b > c$, then $a > c$; (10) *moral:* caring for individual and social welfare; (11) *practical, instrumental,* or *means–ends:* choosing or devising, in light of the best available information, the means most likely to help attain the given goal(s); (12) *economic:* self-interest understood as the maximization of one's expected utility. We shall group the first six rationality concepts under the rubric "conceptual rationality," the last six under "substantive rationality."

One may say of any intellectual process, even if flawed, that it is rational, whereas automatic and emotional mental processes are nonrational. Only intellectual processes that involve the deliberate flouting of the principles of rational discourse—in particular, the imperative of clarity and the principle of noncontradiction—can be said to be irrational. Thus, talk of concrete abstraction, reasons of the heart, the meaning of existence, and democratic centralism is not just mistaken and wrong-headed; it is irrational. Unlike error, the irrational is beyond repair.

What holds for mental processes also holds, mutatis mutandis, for actions controlled by the former. That is, we may class actions as rational and nonrational in a given respect. Some actions can be rational in one respect, irrational in another—which can give rise to paradox. Thus the smoker who anticipates the future consequences of his addiction is said to be rational (Becker and Murphy 1988), even though he is irrational in preferring momentary gratification to good health and longevity.

Whereas irrationalists deny that it is possible or desirable to explain anything, or at any rate anything important, rationalists attempt to understand everything, even the nonrational. This is why scientists and technologists must be regarded as rational beings even when they only collect empirical data. However, it is one thing to explain the nonrational and quite another to attempt to reduce it to rationality—as when a psychologist talks about a fly "computing" its flight and an anthropologist writes about an innumerate tribesman "calculating" the costs and benefits of a rain dance. The scientific rationalist makes use of reason to understand both rational and nonrational processes, but he does not impute rationality to the whole world. In particular, he values rational theories of both rational and nonrational choice, and he may wish to see a rational explanation of the upsurge of irrationalism in social studies since the mid-1960s.

1 Foundations of Rational Choice Theory

Rational choice theory is actually a whole family of rather fashionable theoretical models. They all assume that (*a*) choice and exchange constitute the hub of social life, and (*b*) every choice is motivated by self-interest and, more precisely, is guided by the principle of economic "rationality," or utility maximization. Rational choice models have been mushrooming over the past few decades in all the so-called human sciences, from psychology to history, and even in theology. (See, e.g., Becker 1976; Booth et al. 1993; Boudon 1979; Brams 1980; Coleman 1990; Benn and Mortimore 1976; Luce and Raiffa 1957; Moser 1990; Olson 1971; Rapoport 1989; Stigler and Becker 1977; von Neumann and Morgenstern 1947; and the journals *Theory and Decision* and *Rationality and Society*.)

Rational choice theory may be regarded as the culmination of the rationalist view of man held by such diverse thinkers as Hobbes and Spinoza, the members of the French and Scottish Enlightenments, and the English utilitarians, as well as Comte, Marx, and Weber. All these thinkers stressed the role of interests and rationality, equated the latter with modernity, and rejected the religious and Romantic views of man. However, there are important differences between contemporary rational choice theorists and their precursors. Whereas these older thinkers held a rather broad concept of rationality, rational choice theory uses the narrow instrumental concept of economic rationality, or utility maximization, sketched by eighteenth-century utilitarian philosophers and refined by marginalist economists between 1870 and 1890. Further, rational choice theory disregards the problem of the rationality of goals (Weber's *Wertrationalität*), as well as that of the morality of both goals and means. And whereas Comte, Marx, and Weber thought in terms of a historical process of rationalization and Entzauberung (demystification) in all domains of belief and action, rational choice theory takes it for granted that preferences are constant and that utility-maximizing behavior is inherent in human nature: thus it is an ahistorical view.

Rational choice theory has been criticized either for being rational or for not being rational enough. The former kind of criticism is inherent in the writings of Schütz, Goffman, Geertz, Garfinkel, and Derrida, who in turn drew their inspiration from two of the main irrationalist philosophical schools of this century: phenomenology and existentialism (recall chap. 11, sec. 3 and see, e.g., Denzin 1990). A closely related criticism of rational choice theory is the anti-modernist "rhetoric of the human sciences," which claims that all intellectual activity is nothing but chatting and producing persuasive metaphors, rather than maximally true data or hypotheses (see, e.g., McCloskey 1985).

The irrationalist criticism of rational choice theory is uninteresting except insofar as it occasionally makes a valid point, such as that real humans are seldom fully "rational"—that is, selfish and calculating—and that even mathematical economists sometimes indulge in hand waving and make use of metaphors. My quarrel with rational choice theory is that it involves an unrealistic view of man, ignores empirical findings, and is all too often conceptually fuzzy. I will criticize it not for being scientistic, but for being pseudoscientific.

Believers in the power of reason are expected to build, apply, teach, or at least admire rational views of human behavior—which behavior is itself not always rational in any of the many senses of that ambiguous word. But it stands to (scientific) reason that this expectation is justified only if such views are supported by empirical evidence. In other words, rationalism is not enough: it must be combined with realism—that is, a concern for the matching of theory with facts. Moreover, realism may be regarded as a condition of integral rationality, for it is irrational, both epistemically and instrumentally, to press for untestable or untested theories about any domain of reality.

This caution, unnecessary in the case of a mature science, is mandatory in immature research fields such as sociology, economics, and politology. Indeed, in these fields, theory is often disjoined from data, and empirical research is frequently conducted in a theoretical vacuum. Worse, the philosophy underlying most social studies is either classical rationalism (reason is all-powerful) or classical empiricism (empirical data are the alpha and the omega of research). Rational choice theory illustrates the former research strategy, whereas trial-and-error search for statistical correlations exemplifies the latter. In the following I intend to substantiate the first conjunct of the preceding claim.

Being a rationalist of sorts—more precisely, a ratio-empiricist—my view of rational choice theories is sad rather than jaundiced. Though an enthusiast of conceptual and practical rationality, I believe that rational choice theory has failed abysmally in being simplistic and far removed from reality. And I regret that this failure has brought discredit upon the whole enterprise of serious theorizing in the field of social studies. By the same token, this discredit has brought aid and comfort to such foes of rationality as symbolic interactionists, phenomenologists, ethnomethodologists, rhetoricians, and hermeneuticists. Therefore my criticisms are intended as a contribution toward making way for a more realistic, hence more effective, use of reason in the field of social studies.

There is a large variety of rational choice theories, including utility theory, decision theory, and game theory, as well as their specializations, or models, such as neoclassical microeconomics, Olson's model of collective action, Becker's model of the marriage market, Coleman's linear system of action, and the game-theoretic models of political behavior (see, e.g., Bunge forthcoming). Let us ferret out the assumptions common to all such theories.

A rational choice theory, or model, of individual or social behavior is one that rests on the following axioms:

A1. *Utility and probability:* Every agent has a "stable" (unchanging) utility (subjective value) function, and he can assign a (subjective) probability to any (actual or possible) event that interests him.

A2. *Rationality:* All agents are rational, in the sense that they act exclusively from self-interest and, moreover, so as to maximize their utilities, whether simple or expected.

A3. *Ontological individualism:* Social groups are nothing but collections of individuals.

A4. *Methodological individualism:* The properties and changes of any social group can be understood by studying the behavior of its members.

These assumptions entail the following immediate consequences:

C1. Given the relevant information about the actual and possible facts being envisaged, all agents can calculate the expected utility of any of the courses of action open to them.

C2. Habit, imitation, external compulsion, compassion, impulse, publicity, ideology, and commitment, whether contractual, emotional, moral, or ideological, are irrelevant.

C3. Social groups have no emergent or systemic features: they have only resultant properties—that is, properties deriving from the aggregation (summation) of individual ones.

C4. Social science has no need of irreducibly collective or systemic concepts such as those of social system, social structure, social cohesion, or even social fact.

C5. Social science is reducible to a study of the utility-maximization behavior of individuals.

The first consequence follows from A1 together with the assumption about information (which some authors take to be complete). The three subsequent consequences are just negative restatements of the corresponding axioms A2–A4. The fifth is a corollary of the latter.

To begin with, the occurrence of the word *rational* in the expression "rational choice theory" is unfortunate because, as noted at the beginning of the chapter, the word is ambiguous. However, this criticism affects only the label of the product. Far more serious are the following objections to the product itself.

First, A1 is heroic—a common euphemism for "utterly false." Of course people have preferences, but these are not "stable" but changing, if they ever learn anything. But empirical investigation has yet to establish that people have definite utility functions in the mathematical sense. (Does the reader know his own? I don't know mine. I am not even sure I have got one.) In any event, most rational choice models do not specify such functions: they specify only their qualitative features. (The same holds for indifference "curves": they too are drawn, not plotted.) And those few scholars who do specify such functions choose them for computational convenience rather than on the strength of empirical evidence. Moreover, they often feign that everyone has the same utility function. (The favorites are $u = \log x$, $u = \log (x - a)$, $u = ax^{\frac{1}{2}} + b$, and $u = ax - bx^2$, with a, $b > 0$.) See Appendix 4.

Something similar holds for the assumption about subjective probabilities, the second part of A1. This may be why Milton Friedman (1976) weakened it somewhat to read: We assume that agents act *as if* they assigned a probability to every event. But this will not do, for in factual science and technology, in contrast to pure mathematics and art, we are interested in fact, not fiction. Moreover, in those fields we are interested in objective probabilities of random events, as estimated, for example, by the corresponding observed relative frequencies. (Randomness, as in games of chance, induces uncertainty and may involve risk, but the converse is false.) "Subjective science" is a contradiction in terms. To be sure, a psychologist may investigate subjective probabilities (or, rather, likelihoods); but he is expected to investigate them objectively. Moreover, it behooves him to measure the errors his subjects make when estimating objective probabilities. So much for A1.

Second, utility (or gain or profit) maximization is usually taken for granted, but seldom put to the test. Moreover, we are never told the actual results of efforts to maximize payoffs. We know only that they can be "irrational"—namely, whenever accompanied by shortsightedness, waste of human or natural resources, exploitation, oppression, war, or cutthroat competition—and may end up in self-destruction. This suggests that the use of 'rationality' in that particular sense is persuasive or ideological, rather than either descriptive or normative: it may serve to disguise self-interest. (I am rational; you use people; he exploits them.)

These criticisms do not involve a rejection of the rational *approach* to the study and management of society—in the conceptual senses of 'rational.' Science and technology are eminently rational endeavors. Nor do these criticisms entail a denial that planning and rational decision making do play a role in human behavior, particularly in modern society. I am criticizing only a misappropriation of the ambiguous term 'rationality,' as well as the thesis that self-interested calculation is the only or even the major, let alone the best, guide to human action.

My fourth criticism is that rational choice theory is far too ambitious. It claims to explain everything social in terms of just two variables (utility and probability) and four hypotheses that would hold for all individuals in all social groups in every historical period. But a theory of everything social does not explain any particular social fact. In particular, it cannot explain synchronic or diachronic differences among individuals, groups, or societies. A theory of everything may belong in logic or ontology, but it is out of place in factual (or empirical) science. (Thus, because logic refers to anything, it describes nothing in particular, whence it is insufficient to model any particular factual domain.)

In particular, a theory of everything social cannot account for both the band and the family, the small farm and the agribusiness firm, the corner store and the transnational corporation; for barter and commerce, marriage and divorce, education and politics, health care and law; for competition and cooperation, committee decision and social welfare judgment, war and peace, progress and decline; and so on and so forth. No wonder rational choice models are either far removed from reality, or, when they do capture particular features of real systems or processes, they do so by considerably enriching, in an underhand manner, the postulate system expounded above—for example, by assuming that individual agents interact via the market in macrosocial circumstances that are never analyzed in individualist terms.

My fifth criticism is that, in being radically reductionist (in particular, individualist), rational choice theory fails to account for systemic constraints on individual behavior—in other words, for the effect of structure on agency. Shorter: The assumption that agents are completely free to choose ignores the constraints, compulsions, and traditions of various sorts that shape individual action. The theory overlooks the fact that one and the same individual behaves differently in different social systems, just as a molecule in a liquid body behaves differently at the bottom and at the surface. True, the rational choice theorist is apt to invoke changing "situations" or "circumstances," but, as noted earlier, he treats these as black boxes and thus in a holistic manner inconsistent with methodological individualism. (For individholism, see chap. 9, sec. 3.)

This flaw has the important consequence that the norm "Maximize your utilities" cannot be put into practice for want of knowledge concerning the intentions, preferences, and actions of the people with whom we interact. Von Neumann and Morgenstern (1947, 11) admitted this fatal flaw: "If two or more persons exchange goods with each other, then the result for each one will depend in general not merely upon his own actions but on those of the others as well. Thus each participant attempts to maximize a function . . . of which he does not control all variables." Shorter: Utility-maximization problems are not mathematically well posed; hence the norm "Maximize your utilities" is hollow.

So much for general critical remarks. They will be spelled out in the balance of this chapter. Let us start by taking a closer look at the rationality postulate.

2 Five Versions of the Rationality Postulate

As noted above, the word *rationality* designates at least a dozen different concepts, only one of which has been singled out by most rational choice theorists. Consequently, one should be able to conceive of at least eleven "rationality postulates" in addition to the rationality postulate designated A2 in section 1. For example, in Arrow's social choice theory, rationality boils down to respecting the transitivity of preference relations. And in action theory (or praxiology), an action is called "rational" just in case it is conceived and executed in light of the best available information.

It is instructive to place A2 alongside four alternatives found in the relevant literature. They are:

R1. *Principle of adaptable behavior:* "Agents always act in a manner appropriate to the situation in which they find themselves" (Popper 1967, 361).

R2. *Principle of instrumental (or functional) rationality:* Agents always adopt the means most likely to produce the desired results.

R3 (= A2). *Principle of (economic) rationality:* Agents always act so as to maximize their expected utilities.

R4. *Principle of least effort:* Agents always choose the least expensive means to attain their goals.

R5. *Principle of subjective rationality:* Agents always act on their beliefs about the situation in which they find themselves, as well as on their beliefs about the most suitable means and the possible consequences that their actions may have for themselves and others, and aim for the consequences they judge best.

R1 is so vague that it might be said to hold for an electron in an external field as well as for a human being faced with a practical problem: indeed, both act according to their circumstances. Popper (1967) has admitted that R1 is (*a*) "almost empty," subsequently adding that (*b*) it is false (hence nonempty), yet (*c*) "as a rule sufficiently near the truth" and (*d*) "an integral part of every, or nearly every, testable social theory," in being the key to the explanation of individual behavior (which would in turn explain social facts). Since (*a*) contradicts (*b*), which in turn contradicts (*c*) and (*d*), what is the rational choice theorist to do? In any case, R1 is hardly testable, if only because the very concept of "appropriate behavior," on which it hinges, is fuzzy. Not being rigorously testable, R1 is neither true nor false. Hence, notwithstanding Popper's opinions (*c*) and (*d*) above, R1 should not occur in any scientific theory. So much for Popper's version.

The principle R2 of instrumental rationality is false. (A restatement of it will be proposed in sec. 5.) Few people are smart enough and well informed enough, as well as sufficiently resourceful and strong, to be able to employ the best available means, much less do so always. It has been found experimentally that many people do not even identify correctly the choices before them, let alone evaluate them properly (Kahneman and Tversky 1973; Tversky and Kahneman 1981).

If R2 were true, people would seldom, if ever, resort to violence to settle their differences. The price of shares would be consistently related to both earnings and assets, whence they would not fluctuate wildly. The price of household goods such as dishwasher liquids would not be inversely correlated with their efficiency, as the Consumers Union found in 1984. Furthermore, if R2 were true, there would be no market for "lemons" (shoddy products). Yet there is such a market, because the buyer ignores something that the seller knows and keeps to himself (Akerlof 1984). Hence, at best, R2 could be regarded as a definition, or else a norm or ideal, of instrumental rationality. More on this matter below.

Interestingly enough, R2 is not only false, but also ambiguous—so much so that it may be coupled either to idealism, as in the case of Weber, or to materialism, as in Marx's historical materialism and Harris's (1979) cultural materialism. Thus, the latter explains why orthodox Hindus treat cows as sacred and people of the lowest caste as untouchable; but it fails to explain why fertility rites are still practiced in an overpopulated country or why its inhabitants put up with ubiquitous, annoying, if cute, monkeys. Hindus, like everyone else, would seem to behave rationally except when they behave otherwise. Having disposed of the myth that all human beings abide at all times by the principle R2 of instrumental rationality, let me hasten to admit that the more we learn, the closer we come to abiding by it. For example, as the Amerindians watched the European conquerors, they soon came to prefer knives to stone scrapers and guns to spears. In short, instrumental rationality can be learned. But this does not entail that everyone practices it at all times, so that we can explain all human beliefs and actions in terms of it.

The norm R2 of instrumental (or means–ends) rationality may be called the "principle of act rationality." On the other hand, the rule R3 of economic rationality (our old acquaintance A2) may be regarded as the trademark of rule rationality. (Note the analogy with the act and rule versions of utilitarianism.) Whereas R2 enjoins us to examine each case on its merit alone, R3 purports to be a universal recipe. But, for better or worse, R3 is false in implying the weaker principle R2, which is false, as we saw a moment ago. (Remember the modus tollens rule of inference: If A, then B. Now, not-B. Ergo, not-A.)

However, R3 can also be indicted independently of R2. First, as the historian Marc Bloch (1949, 101) wrote, the *homo oeconomicus* of classical economists is unrealistic, "not only because he was supposed to be exclusively concerned with his own interests: the worse illusion consisted in imagining that he could form such a precise idea of these interests." Second, maximizers risk being ostracized. Third, they are perfectionists, hence procrastinators, rather than efficient agents ready to grab an opportunity when it appears. Indeed, R3 presupposes that there is an *ideal* price at which a commodity is to be purchased or sold: namely, the price that maximizes the agent's profits. Whoever holds this Platonist belief will wait until he can strike the perfect deal—and may thus incur stiff opportunity costs. The realistic businessman would rather do business today, possibly at a modest profit, than wait for the ideal day to come. (More in sec. 3.)

No wonder, then, that the maximizer is an extremely ideal type. In fact, several empirical studies have found that most ordinary people do not attempt to maximize their utilities: they set themselves more modest objectives and are strongly motivated by collectively shared beliefs, particularly values and norms (see, e.g., Reich 1988, chaps. 1–3). For example, according to recent surveys, most Americans, though reluctant to pay taxes, believe that their government spends too little on helping the poor, public health, education, environmental protection, and social security (Coughlin 1991). But, as recent experiments suggest, training in mainstream microeconomics, the paragon of rational choice theory, makes people more selfish and dishonest than the ordinary: they take to heart the principle that self-interest is the prime mover of human behavior (Frank et al. 1993).

It might be argued that R3 is neither true nor false, in that it is a norm or rule of behavior, rather than a descriptive statement—so much so that if people "deviate from the theory, an explanation of the theory and of their deviation will cause them to readjust their behavior" (Morgenstern 1979, 180). An obvious rejoinder is that R3 is a poor guide to action and predictor of same, if only because it does not specify whether one should seek to maximize one's expected utility in the short, medium, or long term. If these three terms are conflated, and particularly if short-term self-interest is allowed to prevail, one may end up by falling into "social traps" (Hardin 1968). These are social situations that "draw their victims into certain patterns of behavior with promises of immediate rewards and then confront them with consequences that the victims would rather avoid" (Cross and Guyer 1980, 4). Examples: overexploitation of people or natural resources (e.g., overgrazing and overcultivation), overindustrialization, overurbanization, overautomobilization, welfare abuse, and "standing tall in the world." In conclusion, the maximizing behavior postulate R3 is not just false in most cases, its observance is a major cause of the global disasters that humankind is facing nowadays.

Having refuted the principle of economic "rationality," it is only fair to admit that it does hold a grain of truth, which is why it has been embraced so readily by so many students of society. We often do act out of self-interest: otherwise we would not survive, much less advance. This explains, for example, why entrepreneurs and self-employed people often work themselves to death; it also explains why slaves, serfs, and salaried people do not do this. But even those of us who are driven mainly by self-interest make no use of utility functions (except when teaching rational choice models) and usually take the interests of others into account, if only to induce them to cooperate with us. When we do not, we pay the price of our shortsightedness or we fall into social traps. In short, the principle of economic "rationality" has to be subjected to so many qualifications that it loses explanatory and normative powers. So much for R3.

R4, the principle of least effort, or cost minimization, is false for the same reason that R2 is. But it can be evaluated independently of R2. Psychologists have known for quite a while that most people do not regard all work as a disutility, the way the book of Genesis and neoclassical economists do. A healthy person is naturally active to the point that, when forced into idleness, he invents tasks to keep himself busy—as anyone who has done time in jail will attest. Hebb (1955) and others have shown experimentally that people, and even rats, prefer activity to idleness, even if the former brings a lower external reward. Lane (1981) reports on a number of recent studies refuting the dogmas that work is a disutility and money the main source of happiness. And the empirical research of Juster (1985) and others has shown that among Americans the intrinsic rewards of work outrank those of leisure.

Activity is often its own reward: think of craftsmen, artists, scientists, and amateur sportsmen. Moreover, external rewards, when unnecessary, as in the cases of playing and learning, may distort the activity itself and even warp personality (e.g., studying for grades, not for the joy of learning, and playing baseball for money, thus distorting the very nature of sports). Cost minimization, doubtless an economic desideratum, can be achieved in a morally acceptable way through work incentives, management rationalization, and R&D. In short, labor-saving devices and procedures are products of hard work, not of laziness or greed. In sum, R4 is not true.

Finally, R5 is my own version of the principle of subjective rationality (Pareto 1935 [1916], 183; Weber 1922, chap. 1; Boudon 1989). It is so weak as to be almost tautological, hence practically irrefutable and thus useless in any scientific theory.

On balance, three of the five so-called rationality principles—R2, R3, and R4—are false, and two, R1 and R5, are hardly testable. Indeed, suppose someone behaved in a manner that an observer, such as a social scientist, would ordinarily regard as irrational—for example, from habit, on impulse, from love of gambling, under coercion, out of commitment to an absurd doctrine, without sufficient information, or in a highly original way. The agent could argue that, under the circumstances, his action was rational after all, particularly since he knows best what is in his own interest. Worse, if blamed for acting on insufficient information, the agent might retort that he had no time to collect the relevant information, or even that collecting it would have been prohibitively expensive. Sure enough, he would find support from some economists, who would confirm that in such circumstances ignorance is preferable to knowledge, and gambling better than inaction. And if any of these gambits were to fail, the agent could still excuse himself by blaming the circumstances—preferably other people. In every case, his own rationality, along with the suitability of any of the above rationality principles, would remain unscathed.

Let us take a closer look at some of the above principles.

3 Maximizers or Survivors?

Let us return for a moment to R3—that is, the principle A2 of economic rationality or expected utility maximization. Even such a methodologically perceptive economist as Samuelson (1976, 436) held that "it is not merely a law of economics, it is a law of logic itself." This is of course mistaken: the laws of logic, or tautologies, are independent of subject matter. (Think, e.g., of "For any proposition p, it is false that p and not-p.") On the other hand, the maximization principle is a factual or empirical statement. Whether it is true to fact is another matter and one that cannot be decided before examining whether it is testable. (Keep in mind the sequence: Meaningful?—testable?—tested?—true?)

The maximization hypothesis is only weakly testable, if at all, whenever the expected utility is "calculated" in terms of subjective utilities and probabilities. Indeed, in this case, no instance of behavior can refute it conclusively, since the utilities and probabilities in question are subjective and therefore can be freely manipulated to save the principle from being refuted by any ugly facts. Things look different from the observer's viewpoint—for example, that of the psychologist or the sociologist. If he has independently assigned his own utilities and probabilities to the events in question, he can judge whether, from *his* point of view, his subjects behave in a "rational" way—which is not to say that the observer's evaluations are always correct. The test can be observational or experimental. Let us start with the former.

Even casual observation shows that people usually overrate large gains (or losses) associated with very small probabilities (for which intuition fails). Otherwise lotteries would not sell, and people would pay more attention to clean life-styles than to taking expensive precautions against extremely rare diseases. Psychologists, anthropologists, and sociologists who have studied the matter, such as B. Malinowski, R. H. Lowie, R. Firth, R. C. Thurnwald, T. Parsons, K. Polanyi, and D. O. Hebb, have found that minimizing effort behavior is far more widespread than maximizing gains behavior. All humans have needs and desires and do something to meet them, but few people work driven exclusively by the profit motive. In short, the profit motive is not a psychological universal: it is not inherent in human nature. This holds particularly, though not exclusively, for subsistence economies. For instance, during the colonial period, Indians of subarctic Canada sought out better terms of trade among competing fur-buyers. But when offered higher prices, they brought in fewer furs in exchange for manufactured goods. "The Indians purchased only enough . . . to meet their basic needs, to satisfy their love of adventure and ceremony, and to gain status amongst their fellows" (Ray and Freeman 1978, 223). In short, as a behavioral economist would say, the Indians were not maximizers, but "satisficers." Even in industrial societies, most people work at intrinsically unrewarding tasks only as much as they need to satisfy their basic needs and legitimate wants, as well as those of their dependents. And most computer hackers are driven more by the challenge of breaking codes than by profit.

A number of observations and experiments have confirmed these findings that people do not behave the way rational choice theory says they do and should. (See Allais and Hagen 1979; Herrnstein 1990; Hogarth and Reder 1987; Kahneman et al. 1982; Tversky 1975. Warning: These authors are not put off by either subjective utilities or subjective probabilities.) Indeed, these and other empirical studies have found that most people are risk-averse. For example, most of us prefer job security to a high but insecure income, and we buy insurance if we can afford it. Maximizers do exist, but they are rare and are perceived as such. True, some experimenters have reached different conclusions. But this is not surprising because, as Davis and Holt (1993, 67) admit candidly, the experimental subjects are "maximizing individuals"—that is, they are instructed to maximize.

Given the mounting empirical evidence against the universal maximizing behavior postulate, it is distressing to find that some psychologists admit it on the neoclassical economist's word. Thus Rachlin and colleagues (1981, 388) state: "We do not ask whether value is maximized; we assume that value is maximized and ask what it is that organisms therefore value." This is like saying: "We do not question the existence of the Devil; we assume that he exists and ask what he makes people do." Interestingly, there is a precedent for this in the history of science. A century ago, Poincaré noted that physicists used the bell-shaped error curve in the belief that mathematicians had proved it, whereas mathematicians accepted it, believing that physicists had confirmed it experimentally.

Even when the possible gains and the corresponding probabilities can be estimated in an objective fashion, it is unlikely that all the variables can be maximized at the same time. If a variable y is an increasing function of a variable x, the two will be maximized at the same time. But if y happens to be inversely proportional to x, then maximizing x will result in minimizing y, and conversely. The latter is usually the case with such pairs as ⟨price, quality⟩, ⟨firm size, technological innovation⟩, and ⟨risk, return⟩. In short, simultaneous maximization problems, even when well posed, are not generally soluble. (See Afriat 1987 for the history and mathematics of the universal maximization myth.)

In short, R3 (i.e., A2), and consequently all theories that include it, are *irrefutable* if the utilities and probabilities are taken to be the subject's and *false* if they are taken to be the observer's. (We are never told what happens when the observer is his own subject—i.e., in the case of self-observation or introspection.) Moreover, empirical research on firms has shown R3 to be false (Allais and Hagen 1979; March and Simon 1958). In particular, it fails for the megacorporations that nowadays dominate the economies of most advanced countries. Indeed, the main goal of the manager of a megacorporation is to maximize the market share, hence the rate of expansion. Unlike a classical firm, a megacorporation can afford not to pay dividends for a few quarters if it embarks on an overhauling, expansion, or takeover project. Whether such behavior is rational is beside the point.

So, in fact, firms do not exhibit consistent maximizing behavior. But could R3 be taken as a norm rather than a statement of fact? This is what many scholars believe. Thus Scherer (1980, 38) claims that the proof that firms maximize profits is that those that fail to turn profits go down. But this reasoning is fallacious: of course a firm must make a profit over the long haul if it is to stay in business, but this is no proof that it must endeavor to *maximize* profit. Given possible perverse effects of profit maximization, the prudent manager, unlike the speculator and the raider, ignores R3. Now, if maximization does not work either in fact or as a norm, what does? Simon (1955) and March and Simon (1958) have proposed a well-known plausible alternative: namely, that reasonable decision-makers attempt to *satisfy* only their needs or aspirations—which, except in the case of tycoons and conquerors, are seldom excessive. If you insist on maximizing, you will have to wait until all options are in sight, thus running the risk of incurring opportunity costs. Instead of waiting until all the alternatives have emerged and have been duly evaluated, the reasonable decision-maker stops his search the moment he believes he has caught a satisfactory opportunity that may not recur. He is a *satisficer*, not a maximizer. Simon calls this alternative "bounded rationality." I prefer to call it "bounded ambition," as opposed to the maximizer's vaulting ambition.

One may argue on general grounds that in human affairs *optimization* is the ticket and that optima lie between minima and maxima. Thus we ought not to minimize costs (or maximize profits), for this can be done only at the price of untold misery to some. Nor should we attempt to maximize quality, for this would render most commodities inaccessible to all but the very wealthy. (In cultural endeavors, quality maximization equals perfectionism, which in turn results in endless procrastination.) Likewise, we should optimize, not maximize, growth rates (which should often be null or even negative), rates of technological innovation, wages, returns, leisure times, number of years of schooling, public services, popular participation in public affairs, and population densities. And whereas in some cases we can settle for mere satisfaction, particularly when waiting for optima to show up may involve unreasonable risks, at other times we must aim for higher goals. In sum, we ought to be optimizers rather than either maximizers or minimizers as regards our *goals*. On the other hand, since we should try to maximize the chances of attaining our goals, we should be maximizers (or minimizers) with regard to the effectiveness of the *means* chosen to implement our goals.

To be sure, the commandment "Thou shalt maximize (or minimize, as the case may be)" is universal and mathematically convenient, whereas "Thou shalt optimize" requires the building of specific realistic models in response to particular problems. But positive economics is supposed to represent reality, not just to afford an excuse for doing mathematics. And normative economics is supposed to be in the public interest, and thus in harmony with a morality higher than the individualist code.

Now, if optima replace maxima (or minima) as regards the goals of economic activity, then equilibria lose their pride of place, for, in general, equilibrium points correspond to maxima or minima. This, together with the fact that the modern economy is constantly evolving, suggests that any general equilibrium theory in economics is bound to be theoretically unrealistic and practically misleading. It may be good for academic promotion and winning a Nobel prize, but not for understanding or running the economy.

Finally, the principle R4 of least effort or cost is testable. Moreover, it is a principle of sound management—at least when tempered by the rule that economies should not deprive anyone of his bowl of rice. Regrettably, R4 is not always observed: witness the universal waste of human and material resources, particularly during wars and economic slumps. In short, R4 is not true, but, when recast in the normative mode and conjoined with suitable principles of social justice, it is a good norm.

4 Subjective and Unconscious Rationality?

The principle of subjective rationality, R5, presupposes that people always know what is best for them. But this is not true. As Marx would say, subjective interests, those that guide deliberate action, do not always coincide with objective, or real, interests. Indeed, the latter may be masked by ignorance or ideology. Think of sacrifices to cruel gods or parties, of acts of bravery carried out in the service of tyrants, or of workers voting conservative.

Pareto, Weber, and Boudon have therefore written about *subjective rationality*, in an attempt to account for the subjective component of decision making and at the same time salvage the hypothesis of rational choice. Thus, a maladaptive action, a dysfunctional social institution, or an absurd belief system may be subjectively rational even while being objectively irrational. Pareto (1935 [1916]) gave the example of the ancient Greek sailor to whom sacrifice to Poseidon was just as "logical" as the act of rowing. In my view, the sacrifice is objectively irrational, while rowing is objectively rational. Giving bad reasons for one's actions is not necessarily behaving in a rational way: one's "reasons" may be quite unreasonable.

Marx's hypothesis of dual interests and the Pareto–Weber–Boudon hypothesis of dual rationality are methodologically flawed. Indeed, they render the rationality postulate just as untestable as Freud's hypothesis that all dreams without an explicit sexual content have a latent one. For this reason I suggest that the expressions 'subjective interest' and 'subjective rationality' be replaced by 'unenlightened self-interest' and 'error,' respectively. The explicit recognition that some human beliefs and actions are irrational (in some of the senses of the word) makes room for both failure and learning.

On the other hand, the concept of objective interest is methodologically sound. Indeed, in principle it is possible to test a proposition of the form "Action A of individual X is in X's best interests (or is likely to safeguard or enhance X's well-being)." What is to be done when someone fails to act in his own best objective interests? Just say so and attempt to explain the action in question in terms of nonrationality, such as habit, impulse, ignorance, or ideological blinkers. Nonrationality is a fact of life, whence any social theory that ignores it is unrealistic. This fact was recognized by Pareto, who distinguished "logical" (instrumentally rational) from "illogical" actions and held that whereas economics studies the former, sociology investigates the latter. (See also Scitovsky 1976; Frank 1988.)

In short, the various rationality postulates we have just examined are not so much blatant falsities as excessively bland, therefore hardly testable, conjectures. As Arrow (in Swedberg 1990, 148) puts it: "The rational choice hypothesis is . . . a very weak hypothesis and the trouble is not so much its correctness or incorrectness, but that it says relatively little." One of the apostles of rational choice theory sees virtue in such poverty and fuzziness: "Since rationality can be pretty flexible and the data are often limited, I don't frequently encounter decisive evidence against rationality" (Becker, in Swedberg 1990, 41). Soothsayers, astrologers, and psychoanalysts are in the same boat— which is hardly flattering news for a genuine rationalist.

Even assuming, for the sake of argument, that some rationality principle were true, it would not suffice to frame specific explanations or predictions of human behavior, and this for the logical reason that extremely general principles must be conjoined with auxiliary hypotheses as well as data if they are to yield explanations or predictions of particular facts—if only because conditions change from one case to the next. Now it may happen that two different rational choice models contain mutually incompatible subsidiary assumptions and that only one of the models is found to fit the facts. In this case, clearly only one of the subsidiary hypotheses deserves credit. Furthermore, it may well happen that the hypothesis in question does all the work, the rationality principle functioning merely as a general foil, a heuristic device, or even mere decoration. This seems indeed to be the case with a number of rational choice models in politology (Simon 1985).

Another kind of rationality that has been postulated is unconscious cost–benefit analysis, a materialist version of rational choice theory. According to Harris (1979) and other cultural materialists, people always come up with solutions that minimize the cost–benefit ratios, though admittedly they seldom do this consciously. They claim, for example, that the first farmers did not start by having the idea of crops: when their folk became too numerous, they just switched from collecting to cultivating, and in due course they saw that they now had enough to eat. I take this view to be a crude naturalistic reaction against cultural idealism. All it does is to replace the idealist mystery of the victory of spirit over matter with the mystery of a blind cost–benefit force without explicit analysis or evaluation. I find it more plausible to think that once in a while people use their brains, proceeding sometimes by blind trial and error and at other times by intelligent (though often equally inefficient or even counterproductive) design. This is no concession to idealism, for it does not involve the view that the spirit exists independently of matter and dominates it.

A related theory is optimal foraging theory, popular in ecology and anthropology. This too is a naturalist version of rational choice theory, but it does not involve the paradox of unconscious cost–benefit analysis. It just states that foragers, such as hunter-gatherers, tend to maximize the net rate of energy gain. The more efficient foragers out-reproduce the less efficient ones (i.e., they have a higher Darwinian fitness). This behavior pattern would be a result of random genic change and blind selection. Possession of a highly evolved brain would confer an added advantage only in the search for the optimal diet. Optimal foraging theory is paradox-free: it involves only objective variables, such as net energy cost and yield and handling time, and it has been mathematized. For these reasons, the theory is empirically testable. Whether it is also true, at least for hunter-gatherers, is another matter (see, e.g., Bettinger 1991).

In short, there is neither subjective nor unconscious rationality. When rationality does operate, it is objective and conscious. Even so, rationality is always combined with—and sometimes smothered by—nonrational factors, such as habit, passion, compulsion, or dogma. Besides, it is always constrained by laws, norms, and circumstances.

5 Instrumental Rationality

I submit that in addition to a rational (as well as empirical) approach to human behavior of all kinds, rational and nonrational, we need (*a*) a sufficiently clear concept of practical or instrumental rationality and (*b*) a normative, or pre-scriptive, rather than descriptive, principle of instrumental rationality. The following are offered for discussion:

Definition of 'instrumental rationality': An action is *instrumentally rational* if and only if it is likely to produce the desired outcome with the least effort.

Norm of instrumental rationality: A rational individual engages deliber-ately in an action M at a certain time if and only if (*a*) M is an effective means to his goal G, as suggested to him by the best available information; (*b*) G has priority over other goals of his at that time; and (*c*) the cost of M, added to that of the undesirable effects accompanying G, is smaller than that of any other means known to him, as well as substantially smaller than the value of G. (The task of constructing the definition of the dual concept of refraining rationally from performing an action is left to the reader.)

This is a prescription, rather than a description, because it is restricted to instrumentally rational individuals. (On the other hand, it is not restricted to humans. It may well apply to some subhumans as well.) It is also restricted to instrumental rationality: the norm does not touch on alternative concepts of rationality, let alone on overall rationality. In particular, no mention is made of maximizing any utilities.

If an individual makes the (practically) wrong choice of means, he should be said to behave in an instrumentally objectively irrational (or unrealistic) fash-ion, not in a subjectively rational way. But the means he chooses, though instrumentally irrational, may happen to be rational in some other ways, such as morally. That is, he may have to trade off rationality in some regard for irrationality in another. Finally, the genuinely rational agent is supposed to weigh his various values and goals at any given moment, as well as to refrain from sacrificing everything to the overriding value or goal of the moment. Total commitment to a single value or goal other than welfare is self-defeating in the long run, because life is many-sided. (Remember never to put all your eggs in the same basket.)

In sum, none of the various rationality principles found in the literature has a descriptive value. Simpler: Real people do not always act rationally, in any of the senses of 'rational.' Moreover, we often act pulled by tradition or swayed by passion. (How many of us observe consistently the rational maxim "Speak not, act not, in anger"?)

However, the principle R2 of instrumental rationality is valuable when reworded in the normative mode: that is, as a guide to action. Moreover, it is useful even in the original declarative mode: namely, as a methodological or heuristic tool. This is in fact how Weber (1922, 3) understood the principle: as an idealization allowing one to explain certain human actions as outcomes of (instrumentally) rational decisions and others as deviations from (instrumental) rationality, originating in nonrationalities of all kinds, such as affects and mistakes, not to mention natural and social factors beyond the agent's control. (Mechanical analog: departures from either static equilibrium or rectilinear uniform motion are accounted for in terms of forces, constraints, or both.)

Moreover, Weber (ibid.) warned that the rationality principle "must not be understood as a rationalist prejudice of sociology, but only as a methodological means, hence it must not be reinterpreted as the belief in the actual predominance of rationality in life." Regrettably, this is not how contemporary rational choice theorists understand A2, even while invoking Weber. Worse, they adopt A3 in preference to A2.

6 Explanation by Reasons versus Explanation by Causes

It is often claimed that because humans are rational beings, their behavior must be explained in terms of reasons rather than causes, let alone accidents. According to this view, nature is the realm of causation and chance, and society that of sufficient reason—in particular, instrumental reason or even utility maximization. This dualistic view goes back to Kant and other idealist philosophers and was elaborated by Dilthey, Weber, and the rational choice theorists. It is open to the following objections.

First, reasons can be causally efficient only because they are brain processes, hence at least in part causal ones. Consequently the cause–reason dichotomy does not hold in a scientific perspective. To be sure, the premises of an argument do not cause its conclusion, and arguments are not validated or invalidated by resorting to causal (e.g., neurophysiological) considerations. But the point is that thinking is a brain process and therefore one that presumably satisfies natural laws, among them causal ones. (See any textbook on physiological psychology.)

Second, because every one of us is part of nature and a member of at least one social system, all our actions are now constrained, now facilitated, by our natural and social environment. Moreover, our very reasons for doing or refraining from doing anything are likewise determined, in part, by external circumstances. When conforming, we bow to causal chains; when rebelling, we intend to use some of them. In either case we reason about causes, and some unexpected external events prompt us to revise our reasons. In short, reasons combine with causes: we use causal relations as tools to put our reasons into practice.

Third, reasons—in particular, the principle of instrumental rationality—are not enough to explain social facts in a bottom-up fashion: we also need to know something about the circumstance or particular situation surrounding the action in question. Some scholars, such as Popper (1957), speak therefore of the "logic of situations," or "situational logic," as peculiar to social science. But actually there is no such special logic. The explanatory schema in question is just a specification of the general schema found in all sciences: Law & circumstances ∴ fact to be explained. In this case the "law" is the principle of instrumental rationality (Nadeau 1993). Besides, the social circumstance or situation is not analyzable in individualist terms. It is nothing but the momentary state of the social system concerned.

This is not to deny the differences between an explanation in terms of reasons and one in terms of laws. One of them is that the principle of instrumental rationality is not a law but a norm—moreover, one that it is not always wise or right to apply. Another difference is that, unlike the case of scientific explanations, explanations according to "situational logic" are rather insensitive to hard fact. Thus a businessman may attribute his firm's successes to his own smart management while blaming his firm's failures on the unfavorable economic situation. And this may not be just a self-serving ruse: the person may actually be right. But the only way to find out the truth is to go beyond methodological individualism and investigate the macroeconomic situation.

7 Evaluation of the Rational Choice Approach

It is time to collect together our thoughts about the rational choice approach. We start by noting what it leaves out. By wishing to encompass everything, rational choice theory leaves out almost everything—in particular, environmental constraints, social structure, and people's passions, especially love and hate. To be sure, no theory in factual science is or can be complete. Indeed, when modeling any chunk of reality, one seizes on some salient traits of it and deliberately overlooks the rest. All the same, one hopes that subsequent efforts will include some of the features that were initially overlooked or left aside as negligible. One thus jumps from an imperfect model to a less imperfect one— or, at least, one holds on to this scientistic article of faith sustained by past successes. This hope motivates the invention of alternative models, more precise and truer than the previous ones. And all the time empirical research furnishes values of the free parameters occurring in the theory, poses new problems, and tames the imagination. So much for mature science.

The rational choice models do not fit this description. They are somewhat fuzzy for revolving around the notions of subjective probability and subjective utility; they cast no light on what they are supposed to account for—namely, social systems; most of them are static; they overlook some major determinants of choice; they leave a gap between choice and action; and they do not care much for empirical validation. Having addressed the first four shortcomings in the previous sections, let us now examine the last three.

The rationality postulate denies implicitly the effect of nonrational factors upon behavior involving choice. Indeed, according to it, all our actions are free and exclusively motivated by self-interest ("rationality"). But, as Marx (1986 [1859], 182) rightly stressed in a famous passage: "In the social production of their life, men enter into definite relations that are indispensable and *independent of their will*, relations of production which correspond to a definite stage of development of their material productive forces" (emphasis added). This is not to endorse Marx's holistic thesis that individuals are nothing but cogs in a machine over which they exert no control, but to remind ourselves that our freedom of choice, though real, is rather limited. We do not have to choose between Marx's holism cum determinism and Weber's individualism cum voluntarism: we can use the true insights of both, and we ought to adopt a systemic approach to the study of society, since the latter happens to be a system of systems.

Not only are many of our choices not autonomous, but some of them are inopportune. Furthermore, most people are willing to devote some of their scarce resources (in particular, time) to helping others. For example, we give much information for free, and, unsolicited, we volunteer well-meaning advice; we run the occasional risk for the sake of others or for causes that we deem worthy; we join organizations from which we expect nothing but their meeting our need to feel useful, to "belong" to a group, or just to do what we feel is right; most of us are not "free riders": we work and pay our dues and taxes, however grudgingly; and, above all, most of us do not attempt to maximize our utilities through crime.

Moreover, most of us realize that utter selfishness is self-destructive, for breeding mistrust and contempt, hence social ostracism, and sometimes for leading us into social traps. Few people are so callous as not to be motivated at least in part by feelings of benevolence toward some of their fellow human beings. Most of us know that we would achieve nothing without the cooperation of others, a cooperation that calls for a modicum of willingness to reciprocate, care, and share. Some management scientists (e.g., Porter 1980) have noted that unbridled competition is dangerous. Japanese industrialists reduce R&D costs by forging technological alliances, which even some American corporations (such as the three major car-makers and Merck and Dupont) have begun to try to do. And anyone minimally familiar with the worlds of business and politics knows that the most successful entrepreneurs and politicians are organizers and fighters who take more pleasure in getting things done than in earning profits or perks. I am not arguing here from moral principles: I am just pointing out that real people are smart enough not to behave the way rational choice theories assume.

In some respects we are smarter than narrow-sighted utilitarians give us credit for. For example, we are often willing to forgo profit for the sake of health or peace of mind. In other cases we are sillier: we hold on to principles and rules that have proved disastrous, or we act on insufficient information; we postpone the important for the urgent, act on impulse, procrastinate, or blame others for our own mistakes; we spend more than we can afford, buy lottery tickets, bet on horses, consult soothsayers or psychoanalysts; we vote for crooks or admire mass murderers; we smoke, drink, pass on unchecked gossip, or watch sitcoms; we contemplate passively the decay of good traditions or the deterioration of the environment; and we are often gullible—sometimes to the point of believing the rationality postulate (see Boudon 1990a for an analysis). And, whether dumb or smart, "fortune [accident] is the ruler of half our actions" (Machiavelli 1940 [1513], 91)—something that rational choice models do not count on.

Rational choice theory has been berated for ignoring emotion. This charge is only partly justified, because emotions steer preferences, which constitute the starting point of the theory (Stinchcombe 1990). What is true is that rational choice theory takes preferences for granted and assumes them to be rational, radical, and constant. Indeed, rational choice theorists do not investigate how preferences emerge and change as a result of circumstances, persuasion, compulsion, learning, and argument. It is not just that those theorists leave the problem of preference change to other specialists: they often assert that preferences are in fact constant—that, as Stigler and Becker (1977) held, de gustibus non est disputandum. Experiment has proved them wrong (see, e.g., Scitovsky 1976). In fact, the most important disputes are about values. As Hirschman (1992, 147) puts it, de valoribus est disputandum. This holds in particular for political values, which are formed and deformed through social interaction and discussion (see, e.g., Sen 1995).

As for passion, or very strong emotion that cannot easily be swayed by argument, it cannot be denied that rational choice models leave it out, in spite of its being a major determinant of our choices. (See Hirschman's [1977] fascinating story of the conflict between interest-centered and passion-centered views in economic and political thinking.) To be sure, Hume's radical view, that reason is the slave of passion, is refuted by anyone who engages in rational discourse for the sake of truth. However, many a calculated piece of behavior is intended to satisfy some nonrational, or even irrational, drive. For example, as the banker Felix Rohatyn said, capital is nervous, as well as greedy.

In any event the reason–passion (or head–heart) dichotomy, taken for granted by rational choice theorists, belongs to archaic psychology. (In general, rational choice theorists ignore contemporary psychology.) We have learned that, though distinct, ratiocination and emotion interact because the cerebral cortex, the organ of cognition, is anatomically linked to the limbic system, the organ of emotion. This connection renders pure reason even more problematic than pure passion (Bunge 1980). Moreover, allometric studies suggest that, in the course of evolution, the limbic system has increased at about the same pace as the neocortex. This balance is required for social life, since without the ability to evaluate social stimuli, especially symbols, culture would be impossible (Armstrong 1991).

The anatomical and physiological connection between the organs of cognition and emotion explains why passion can fuel or distort reason and why reason can excite or steer passion. It explains why we feel motivated to do certain things rather than others, why we sometimes change our preferences, why at other times we refuse to listen to the voice of reason, and so on. In short, reason and passion are mutually complementary, rather than exclusive. This being so, the rationality postulate is just as false as the existentialist dogma that reason plays no role at all in human existence. The truth lies somewhere in between these two dogmas: reason and passion interact (see Frank 1988).

Let us now address the choice–action gap. Rational choice models cover only choice. They do not touch on the inputs—the practical issues posed by needs, wants, beliefs, and so forth—or the outputs—the actions and their outcomes. There is nothing wrong with such deliberate restriction of subject matter, for every theory has a restricted domain or reference class. What is wrong is to claim that a theory of rational choice can be a theory of everything social, when in the best of cases it can account for only one of the steps in the action process. (For action theory, see Bunge forthcoming.)

It is not merely that this process contains many more links than those envisaged by rational choice theories. There is also the matter of the gaps between such links and the changes in such links. (Spanish proverb: *Del dicho al hecho hay un buen trecho* [there is a big jump between word and deed].) In particular, the action taken, if taken at all, is likely to differ in some respects from the one decided upon. This may be so for either or all of the following causes: unforeseen events (hence alteration of the original problem), insufficient resources, incompetence, intra-agency conflict, disobedience, or sabotage. (For the ubiquitous presence of conflict and contravention of orders in formal organizations, see, e.g., Dexter 1990.)

Our last topic is the relation between rational choice theory and social reality. In principle, a factual theory can bear the following relations to its referents. It can handle genuine problems concerning the nature of its referents; it can incorporate empirical data (e.g., as particular values of variables or parameters); it can be confronted with available observational or experimental findings; it can predict facts; or it can help design policies aimed at altering reality. Let us pretend, for the sake of brevity, that rational choice models do address genuine problems and make use of empirical information. We ask next: How do these models fare in matching the evidence, predicting, and policymaking?

Critics of decision theory, game theory, neoclassical microeconomics, and other rational choice theories have noted again and again that such theories do not match individual psychology and are far removed from social reality. In particular, most real people follow custom or rules of thumb, rather than well-thought-out strategies; they are half-selfish and half-altruistic, rather than purely self-seeking; they seldom, if ever, get to take part in perfectly competitive markets in equilibrium; they seldom choose rationally either their careers or their mates; during an economic recession they never choose to lose their jobs (or "decide to invest in leisure")—as would be the case if they were complying with the dogma that everything that happens to an individual is a result of his free rational choice. In short, rational choice theory is too far removed from reality.

This fatal flaw is hardly surprising if one bears in mind that the theory was invented long before psychologists started to study experimentally the way people actually make choices. One finding of such studies is that usually we do not behave according to carefully laid-out plans with clearly indicated goals. The studies suggest instead that "choices are made as we go along, that decisions are made on the basis of relatively insignificant local details, and that we only know the destinations after we have arrived" (Cross and Guyer 1980, 16). So, even if its methodological individualism ingredient were right, which it is not, rational choice theory would be bound to yield wrong results because it presupposes a false, obsolete psychology.

This does not entail that rational action is impossible. It is possible, particularly if planned on the basis of a scientific study of the system in question. The engineering design of industrial plants, operations research, business budgeting, military logistics (unlike strategy), and macroeconomic policymaking are good examples of rational action. But rational choice theories—in particular, decision theory and game theory—are conspicuously absent from these fields.

How about prediction? It is no secret that economic theorists have been incapable of predicting any major economic booms or slumps, much less stagflation (inflation cum unemployment), deindustrialization (as a result of the massive export of industrial plants to developing countries), the economic impact of technological innovation, and the destabilizing effect of the free movement of capital on a global scale. As for politology, nobody on the "scientific" (game-theoretic) side seems to have forecast correctly any major political event. In particular, none of them seems to have predicted the break-up of the Soviet Union in 1991. On the other hand, Hélène C. d'Encausse (1978), a traditional politologist—one who reads newspapers and talks to people on the street—did forecast the latter a decade in advance. And the sociologist Randall Collins (1986) predicted the same events from macrosocial conditions, such as geopolitical overextension, paralysis of the state, and struggle among rival factions of the elite. By contrast, all rational theorists can do is to analyze past events.

In sum, rational choice theory fails to account for the behavior of real people and, a fortiori, that of social systems. The question of why it must fail will be tackled next.

8 The Fatal Flaws of Rational Choice Theory

Rational choice theorists have offered rather simple, hence attractive, explanations of social facts of very many kinds. All these explanations assume individualism, free choice, and maximizing behavior—the core hypotheses of mainstream economic theory and utilitarian ethics theory from Adam Smith and Jeremy Bentham onward. Although rational choice models have become increasingly sophisticated, they all share some or all of the following fatal flaws.

1. The (subjective) utility functions, which play a central role in these models, are either undefined or posited arbitrarily, often only for computational convenience; hence, except for the rare bird, despite their symbolic apparatus, the models are pseudo-mathematical.

2. The vast majority of the models contain the concept of subjective probability—which, being subjective, does not belong in science except as a subject of study.

3. Some of the models involve the concept of subjective rationality, or rationality in the eye of the agent, whose only function seems to be that of protecting the rationality postulate.

4. Nearly all the models are static: in particular, they assume fixity of options and constancy of preferences (or utilities).

5. Although they are supposedly strictly individualistic, all the models smuggle in unanalyzed holistic notions such as those of "the situation" and "the institutional framework"—whence they deserve to be called "individholist" rather than individualist (see chap. 9, sec. 3).

6. All the models overlook the power of elites, governments, bureaucracies, corporations (in particular, oligopolistic and transnational firms), networks of all kinds, lobbies, and other groups and systems, all of which distort preferences, restrict the freedom of choice, and justify La Fontaine's dictum "La raison du plus fort est toujours la meilleure."

7. The models cover only one type of social interaction—namely, exchange—and even then, often via some unanalyzed whole, such as the market.

8. The models omit every motive for human action other than self-interested calculation. In particular, they overlook habit and impulse, fear and suggestion, passion and compassion, commitment to individuals or causes, and moral scruples.

9. By focusing on choices and means, the models take motivations and goals for granted and overlook side effects.

10. The models ignore micro–macro relations and, in particular, do not account for agency–structure relations or for the emergence, decline, and breakdown of social systems as a result of action or negligence.

11. Because of their excessive generality, the models have no predictive power.

12. For the same reason, the models are unrealistic: they are mostly *jeux d'esprit*, even though some of them have been commissioned by big business or by the military establishment.

13. Being unrealistic, at times surrealistic, the models are not suitable policy tools.

In sum, rational choice theories are inadequate—that is, at variance with reality. We have found them wanting in being trapped within the individualist and utilitarian dogmas, in overrating the "rationality" (calculating and maximizing ability) of people, in containing fuzzy basic notions and untestable key assumptions, and in idealizing the free market.

There is more. The overwhelming majority of rational choice models do not contain the time variable, whereas the exact opposite is the case with the vast majority of scientific theories. The reason, of course, is that science deals with reality, which is ever changing, whereas rational choice theory ignores reality. Furthermore, the most general of all rational choice theories, that of games, involves no parameters to be determined empirically: it locks experience out. In this regard too, game theory is utterly different from all genuine scientific hypotheses and theories. For example, sociologists generally admit that criminality, C, is a linear function of unemployment, U; that is, $C = a + bU$, with a, b > 0, where the values of the parameters a and b are supposed to be determined from social statistics. But game theorists do not bother with this sort of thing: they proceed a priori. They perpetrate synthetic a priori judgments and get away with them. (For further criticisms, see Pareto 1974 [1906]; Gini 1952; Scitovsky 1976; Rapoport 1989; Smelser 1992; Green and Shapiro 1994; Bunge forthcoming.)

This is not to say that all rational choice theories are utterly false and useless. In fact, they can perform three services: (*a*) they may help hone the preliminary formulation of some problems, by forcing the student to distinguish the options, draw decision trees, and take costs and benefits into account; (*b*) some of them show that the pursuit of self-interest may lead to "social traps"—that is, collective disasters; (*c*) others may suggest experiments aimed at testing those very models, such as the experiments which have been conducted to check the expected utility axioms and game-theoretic models; and (*d*) by failing to represent reality, they show how much actual behavior departs from "rationality" and may suggest a search for deeper, more complex theories—much as the failure of the flat earth hypothesis stimulated the elaboration and checking of the round earth one.

In sum, rational choice models, if not taken too seriously, may serve heuristic purposes. Anatol Rapoport (personal communication, 1991) thinks that "their most valuable contributions stem from their failures rather than from their successes." Regrettably, too many rational choice models serve only as intellectual acrobatics for academic promotion, justification for aggressive military strategies, or accounts of failures of the latter. (For game-theoretic theology, see Brams 1980; for Newcomb's problem, a parlor game favored by some philosophers, see Campbell and Sowden 1985, and Bunge forthcoming.) None of these models discharges the function intended: namely, to help guide rational action. At best, they shed some uncertain light on the past. (See, e.g., Malitza 1971 for a decision-theoretic model of an episode in Balkanic history and Bunge 1973a for a decision-theoretic analysis of the American defeat in Vietnam showing that the Pentagon was anything but rational.)

Why, then, does rational choice theory enjoy such enormous prestige? For the following reasons: (a) it is basically simple; (b) it presupposes no knowledge of experimental psychology, sociology, politology, or history; (c) it claims to explain all human behavior with the help of a single principle; (d) it makes liberal use of symbols, which, though they often designate ill-defined mathematical concepts, never fail to intimidate the nonmathematical reader; (e) it endows market worship and warmongering with intellectual respectability; (f) it is often criticized for the wrong reasons, mainly for being on the side of reason; and (g) so far it has not been threatened by serious rivals.

To sum up, rational choice theory is not a solid, substantive theory of society. This failure can be traced back to the specific assumptions of the theory; it is not due to the rational approach to social studies. Any serious study of society will be rational, but no realistic account of social facts will assume that people always act rationally—in particular, selfishly. After all, "[a]ssuming too much rationality is silly" (Agassi 1977, 265).

The reader may feel that my criticism is excessive: that I am throwing out the baby along with the bathwater. My response is that there is no baby. In fact, rational choice theory was born in 1789 in the field of moral and political philosophy (Bentham's utilitarianism) and in 1871 in the field of economics (neoclassical microeconomics), so it is anything but young. Moreover, it died long ago from mathematical malnutrition and psychological anemia, from deficiency of the enzymes required to digest the simplest social facts and moral principles and from exposure to the sound and fury of social storms.

Where does this leave us? Must we conclude that rationality is impossible both in social theory and in practice? This is what Elster (1989) and other students of rational choice theory have concluded. One of them, the politologist Alan Ryan (1991), has gone so far as to declare—hopefully, tongue in cheek—that "it is more rational to be irrational than rational." This contradiction would have been spared upon realizing that the word *rationality* designates at least a dozen different concepts, among them those of logical and economic rationality. If this distinction is drawn, the intent of the phrase in question may be reworded thus: It is (often) more rational to be economically irrational (i.e., selfless) than rational (i.e., self-seeking).

The proper conclusion is not that rationality is expendable, but rather that (a) *rationality should be conceived of in a broad fashion,* both conceptually and substantively (sec. 1), rather than narrowly, as self-interested calculation; (b) *conceptual rationality, though necessary, is not enough:* to bear fruit in the study of reality, it must be combined with hard-nosed realism, which in turn calls for rigorous empirical testing as well as for the inclusion of nonrational features of human behavior; (c) *substantive or practical rationality does not suffice either,* not even in combination with conceptual rationality, to design effective policies and plans: it must be supplemented with a commitment to social progress, which involves social justice.

To conclude, allow me to propose seven insolent, though perhaps pertinent, maxims for the guidance of the perplexed student of rational action:

M1. Do not mistake greed for rationality.

M2. Being rational does not involve imputing rationality to everyone else.

M3. Regardless of how much you admire conceptual rationality, never underrate the power of irrationality, especially your own.

M4. Mathematics should be servant, not master, in the task of modeling the world.

M5. Get in touch with social reality once in a while. Meet people, mix with them, and join with them in common enterprises, so as to get a feel for social systems and their changeability and overcome the prejudice that everyone else is a selfish bastard.

M6. Avoid inbreeding. Do not just read other scholars' papers; also read the popular press and statistical reports, and listen to what people have to say.

M7. When all else fails, try the scientific approach: it has been known to work.

To sum up, we must uphold conceptual rationality for being an ingredient of the scientific approach, and the norm of instrumental rationality for being a guide to efficient action. But we cannot accept any of the so-called rationality principles that occur in rational choice theory. Indeed, we reject R1 for being vague and therefore untestable, R2, R3, and R4 for being false, and R5 for being nearly tautological.

These conclusions have important methodological consequences. First, a rational study of society, or anything else, does not involve imputing rationality, in any of the twelve acceptations of this word, to the subjects of our study. To do so would be unrealistic. As Schumpeter (1991, 319) wrote: "So far all there is of rationality in the social sciences emanates from the analyst."

A second methodological consequence is that because the norm of instrumental rationality is a guide to efficient action, we must place it in sociotechnology, not in basic social science. The task of the latter is to describe, explain, and predict, not to prescribe. And description, explanation, and prediction are best performed in terms of objective laws, such as those of the actual (normally nonmaximizing) behavior sought by psychologists and sociologists. By contrast, it is the task of sociotechnologists, as of engineers, to devise rules and plans that will enable people to make things happen according to rule or plan. That is, they are engaged in self-fulfilling prophecy, rather than detached prediction.

This concludes our study of the most general philosophical ideas inherent in the social sciences and in some of the topical debates as to their nature and status. The philosophy of the individual social sciences, as well as of the socionatural or mixed ones and the social technologies, is the object of the companion volume *Social Science under Debate*.

Appendixes ::

APPENDIX 1 :: *State Space Representation*

Consider an arbitrary concrete thing of a given kind. Call n the total number of its known properties, and P_i its ith known property, where $i = 1, 2, \ldots n$. Further, call F_i an attribute representing P_i. (Properties are real features, whereas predicates are their corresponding conceptualizations.) The list of such attributes (or mathematical functions) is called a *state function* of the thing in question or, rather, of any thing of the same kind. Shorter: A state function for things of a given kind is a list $F = \langle F_1, F_2, \ldots, F_n \rangle$, which may be pictured as an arrow in an n-dimensional space. Since n is the total number of known properties, and since our knowledge of matters of fact is always bound to be incomplete, we can never be sure that any given state function is the last word.

The state of a thing at a given time is the list of all its properties at that time. Since these are values of the functions representing the respective properties, the *state* of a thing at a given time can be represented by the list of such values. That is, $s_t = \langle F_1(t), F_2(t), \ldots, F_n(t) \rangle$. That is, a value of a state function, F, for a thing at time t represents the state of the thing at t. Whether such a representation is faithful (true) is another matter, one to be checked by empirical investigation. This is one of the reasons that we talk about a, rather than *the*, state function for things of some kind.

The set of possible states of a thing can be represented in a *state space* for the thing. This is the abstract n-dimensional space spanned by the corresponding state function, $F = \langle F_1, F_2, \ldots, F_n \rangle$. If only two properties of the thing are either known or taken into account, the corresponding state space is a region of the plane determined by the axes F_1 and F_2—for example, the population and total production of a society (see fig. A1). A state space for a thing with n known properties is n-dimensional.

Every state of a thing of a given kind can be represented as a point in a suitable state space. As time goes by, the values of some of the properties of the thing are bound to change, so the representative point will move along some

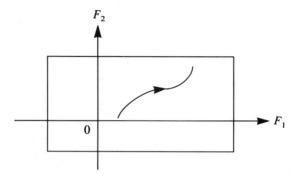

Fig. A1. State space for things characterized by two quantitative properties, F_1 and F_2. The box is the set of lawfully possible states of the things. The curve represents a possible history or sequence of lawful states of a thing.

trajectory. The stretch of such a trajectory over a time period T is called the *history* of the thing concerned during T. However similar to one another, two different things are bound to have different histories, because of differences either in their composition or in their environment. But if they are of the same kind, their histories will be representable in the same state space.

The concept of a state function can be used to elucidate the notion of a concrete system, such as a labor union, in contradistinction to an aggregate, such as the working class. Indeed, a state function for an aggregate for noninteracting things is uniquely determined by the state functions of the components. Typically in this case, the state function of the whole equals either the sum or the product of the state functions of the parts. This is not the case with a system proper. Here the state of every component is determined, at least in part, by the states of the remaining components. Think, for example, of a society composed of a population of peasants and a population of landowners occupying the same territory. The rate of growth of each population depends on the numerosities and the birth and death rates of both populations. Hence, the total state function is no longer separable either additively or multiplicatively. The contributions of the parts become inextricably entangled. Moreover, the system state function may be constrained by one or more global conditions. (The Pauli principle in atomic physics is such a global constraint.) Hence the construction of a state function for systems of some kind must proceed from scratch rather than on the basis of the state functions of the components. (More on state and event spaces in Bunge 1977a, 1977b.)

APPENDIX 2 :: *Law and Rule*

Laws and rules are regularities. In ordinary knowledge, they are often confused, but actually they are quite different. Whereas laws are objective patterns that we cannot change, rules are man-made prescriptions for doing things and, as such, can be altered. The following formal analysis will sharpen the distinction.

Consider a collection of things of kind K with a state space S_K. A law L_K of K's is a mapping of S_K into itself; that is, $L_K: S_K \to S_K$. Thus, if a thing of species K happens to be in state s belonging to S_K, then $L_K(s) = t \in S_K$ represents the passing of the thing to state t.

Now let M denote an animal species, such as humankind, and call A_M the set of all the actions that individuals of kind M are capable of performing. Then a rule for animals of kind M dealing with things of kind K is a mapping from the states of such things to the actions of those animals; that is, $R_{KM}: S_K \to A_M$. Thus, if s is in S_K, then $R_{KM}(s) = a \in A_M$ is the action that rule R_{KM} prescribes for individuals of kind M facing a system of kind K when in state s.

Unlike laws, then, rules are man-made prescriptions. However, (*a*) every enforceable rule is consistent with the underlying laws; and (*b*) if internalized, a rule gives rise to regularities in behavior that look very much like laws—until people change or drop the rule for whatever reason.

APPENDIX 3 :: *The Logic of Theory Operationalization*

Even the simplest scientific theory contains concepts that, though referring to facts, have no experiential counterparts (e.g., the concepts of institution, structure, productivity, price elasticity, state budget, and cultural decline). In science such concepts are related to empirical concepts by means of indicator hypotheses, which are used to operationalize factual theories (see chap. 6, sec. 2). We proceed to sketch the operationalization process. (For details see Bunge 1973*c*).

Given are a general theory, T, and a set, S, of subsidiary assumptions specifying particular features of the referents of T and S, such as their composition, environment, and structure. From T and S we build a (bound) model, or specific theory, M. M is the set of logical consequences of the union of T and S, inclusive of T and S. We now add the set, I, of indicator hypotheses constructed with the help of some antecedent knowledge and perhaps T itself. We hope that the members of I, the indicator hypotheses, are well confirmed and thus reliable. Further, call E the set of available empirical data concerning the referents of M. Again, we hope that the members of E are not only relevant to M but also reasonably accurate (true). These data are absent from and far removed from the theory, which is why we need the indicators I to build a bridge between the model M and the empirical evidence E.

So much for the information in hand. The problem is to use this information to "read" the empirical data in theoretical terms—for example, to "interpret" items of overt behavior in mental terms or economic indicators in terms of some macroeconomic theory. I call this a 'translation' of the available data into the language of the model. The translated data, E^*, follow logically from the raw data, E, jointly with the indicators, I. These translated data are fed into the model, M, to yield the "translated" model, M^*. Finally, using once again the indicator hypotheses, I, that result is translated back into the language of experience. That is, M^* is joined with I to entail M^{**}. The latter is the *operationalization* of the theoretical model, M. What confronts the data, E^*, is M^{**}, not the original model, M.

Note that not the theory T itself, but some consequences of T, together with the subsidiary assumptions, S, the indicator hypotheses, I, and the data, E, face whatever experience may be relevant to T. Consequently, if M^{**} fails the empirical tests, we may blame T, S, I, or E. Surprisingly, the standard discussions of confirmation and refutation ignore these complications: they assume that theories confront data in a direct fashion.

APPENDIX 4 :: *Utility: A Skeleton in the Closet of Rational Choice Theory*

Most rational choice models fail to specify the utility functions that rational agents are supposed to maximize. That is, they pivot around undefined functions. For example, a much quoted paper by Stigler and Becker (1977), both Nobel laureates in economics, is crammed with such "functions," of which only the general shape is specified. (Among such functions, or rather symbols, are the amount of music appreciation produced and consumed by an arbitrary subject and the corresponding shadow price he must pay for it.) In this way the authors are able to "prove" what all ordinary mortals and experimental psychologists know to be *false:* namely, that tastes are constant over time and similar among people (see, e.g., Scitovsky 1976).

Such lack of specificity is peculiar to philosophy and abstract mathematics. For example, in the general theory of metric spaces it is required that the distance function should comply with just three extremely lax conditions. (For all elements, or "points," x, y, z in an arbitrary set S, $d(x,x) = 0$, $d(x,y) = d(y,x)$, and $d(x,y) + d(y,z) \geq d(x,z)$.) These conditions define any of infinitely many distance functions in spaces of arbitrary dimensionality. By the same token, they do not specify any particular space. Hence they do not enable one to compute or measure any distances. In order to compute or measure the distance between two points in a particular metric space, one needs a specific distance function, such as the one defined by the Pythagorean theorem. (Moreover, any such applicable distance function will involve a length unit and, in the case of relativistic physics, a reference frame as well. Hence it will be a more complex concept than the d considered above.) Consequently, a physicist who limited himself to asserting that physical space (or space-time) is a metric space, without committing himself to the precise metric (or distance function, or line element), would be laughed out of his profession. On the other hand, social scientists can get away with similar generalities concerning utility and other functions. (Allais 1986; Shubik 1987; and Coleman 1990 are among the few exceptions.)

Likewise, the Kolmogoroff axioms define the entire, infinite family of probability functions, and are thus necessary but insufficient for handling particular problems in either pure or applied probability theory. While such generality is inherent in abstract mathematics and philosophy, it is intolerable in factual science. Here we are dealing with things, such as atoms and social groups, that belong to special classes and are therefore characterized by specific properties and relations among these—that is, laws. In factual science one may certainly guess the values of the functions of interest, provided such guesses are supported by some evidence and are testable and corrigible at least in principle. But when guessing without any possibility of testing is the only "method" for finding the values of functions—for example, because these are assumed to be purely subjective—we are not talking science.

To put it another way, a function u about which one stipulates only that it increases monotonically with a decreasing slope, is an unknown. Hence, to claim that one understands an action by saying that its actor, a, is attempting to maximize his u amounts to saying that a behaves the way he does because the actor has a certain occult quality. This is a case of explaining the obscure by the more obscure—which may fly in theology, but not in science.

Let me try again. The propositional schema $u(x) = y$, where u stands for an undefined utility function and y for its (arbitrarily assigned) value at x, has nearly the same methodological status as the schema "The blah of x equals y." Neither u nor blah has a precise meaning. Consequently, no statement containing either is testable empirically. (Recall from chap. 2, sec. 2, that meaning precedes testing, not the other way round.) True, we do have some intuitive notion of utility, whereas we have none of "blah." However, although some intuitive constructs are precursors of scientific concepts, the notion of utility holds no such promise, even though it was introduced as far back as 1738 (see Blatt 1983, 170).

That an indeterminate utility function is a fuzzy, artificial construct was recognized by the great mathematician Henri Poincaré as early as 1901. In a letter to Léon Walras, one of the three founding fathers of marginalism, Poincaré pointed out that utility is an arbitrary function, and while he admitted that arbitrary functions may be used in certain mathematical reasonings, he emphasized that one must try to eliminate them in the end results or consequences of such reasoning. He wrote that "if the arbitrary functions still occur in these consequences, the latter won't be false, but they will be devoid of interest, because they will be subordinated to the arbitrary conventions laid down at the beginning" (1901).

It may be rejoined that Newton's laws of motion contain a general concept of force. True, but this concept is precise, for it is defined implicitly by a postulate system; moreover, particular physical forces are usually measurable. By contrast, the general utility concept is fuzzy, and utilities are unmeasurable in an objective, precise manner. (Preferences may only be ordered.) Furthermore, when an author does assume a definite utility function, such as $u_1(x) = \log x$, $u_2(x) = \log (x - a)$, $u_3 = ax^{\frac{1}{2}} + b$, or $u_4(x) = ax - bx^2$, he usually does so mainly for computational convenience: he seldom if ever adduces any empirical evidence for his choice.

Yet the precise shape of a utility curve may make a big difference. Thus, following Blinder (1989), let us compare the first two functions indicated above, interpreting x as the actual consumption and a as the subsistence consumption of a person. Suppose that in a given year $x = \$10,000$ and $a = \$5,000$. Assume further that a recession reduces consumption by $p = 20$ percent to $x^* = x - 0.2x$. The corresponding drops in utility are dramatically different for seemingly similar choices of the utility function, namely:

$$\Delta u_1 = \Delta x/x^* = p/(1 - p) = \tfrac{1}{4};$$
$$\Delta u_2 = \Delta x/(x^* - a) = px/(x - px - a) = \tfrac{2}{3}.$$

This example refutes the standard contention that only the qualitative features of utility functions matter.

It may be rejoined that, unlike grand theories in traditional social studies, some rational choice models are chock full of numbers. True, but most if not all of these figures have been taken out of a hat. It does not help to assign the utility functions definite values (in particular, maxima) if these values are posited rather than either calculated or measured. And this is precisely what most rational choice models do; namely, postulate the basic utilities instead of either computing or measuring them.

Now, when u is not a well-defined function, it makes no sense to speak of its derivative, du/dx, or marginal utility. (Hence the marginalist school should be renamed the "unknown function school.") For the same reason, a rate of change of an undefined utility over time cannot be written explicitly, much less measured accurately—which is just as well, because most rational choice theorists assume that utilities are time-independent or, what amounts to the same thing, that preferences are unchangeable. This weaker (qualitative or ordinal) assumption is testable. But it is patently false: our preferences do alter as we learn (or unlearn) and as our circumstances change. Advertisers, preachers, and political activists count on such plasticity—contemporary teachers much less so.

Likewise, the qualitative version of the so-called law of decreasing marginal utility of money is empirically testable. But it is obviously false for collectors, whether they hoard stamps, money, or power. In particular, the "law" fails for borrowed money in the case of ambitious corporate executives. Indeed, these individuals find that the more money they can lay their hands on, the more numerous their opportunities become, from expansion to mergers to take-overs, so their appetite increases as they eat. Presumably, they think that the utility of money increases exponentially with the quantity of money itself—as Galanter (1962) suggested three decades ago on the strength of an experiment performed on ordinary subjects. The case of the delinquent bankers and speculators of the "greedy 1980s and 1990s" bears this out.

Presumably, if psychologists were to hit on a reliable method for plotting the utility curves of their experimental subjects, they would come up with as many curves as personality types. (The same would hold for indifference curves.) Moreover, they might find that (a) the utility of a commodity depends not only on the satisfaction it procures but also on the pain its purchase costs (in the simplest case, $u = s - p$); and (b) if the upward path for a subject is convex, his downward path is concave—that is, losses are felt more intensely than gains. As a matter of fact, this dependence of valuation upon the subject's past history, especially his initial endowment, has been experimentally confirmed (Knetsch 1992).

APPENDIX 5 :: *Futility Theory*

The theory to be proposed presently is a general theory of rational choice. Its mathematical status is just as vague as that of utility theory, its scope equally wide, and its empirical support equally shaky. It is offered for amusement as well as to show how easy it is to concoct theories of everything social smacking of exactness.

Futility theory is about individual human action. It rests on the following axioms:

A1. Every human action, a, at any given time t has an intensity $a(t)$, which is a positive real number.

A2. There is a function, F, defined for every value $a(t)$ of the intensity of an action, which is twice differentiable and represents the degree of futility of the action.

A3. All agents are futility-minimizers. More precisely, F is negatively slanted and positively accelerated (i.e., $dF/da < 0$ and $d^2F/da^2 > 0$).

A4. Futility is sub-additive; that is, the total futility of a group (or collective) action is less than or equal to the sum of the futilities of its members.

Examples: (1) People work to decrease the futility of their existence. When work does not have the desired effect, they idle. (2) People observe the law when this behavior decreases futility; otherwise they break it. (3) People cooperate in order to decrease futility; when cooperation fails, they compete or even fight. (4) People marry to decrease their combined futility; when this fails, they split up. (5) People join voluntary associations in hopes of decreasing their futility; when this fails, they defect.

Don't ask how futilities are measured or compared or how the above axioms might be refuted, unless you are prepared to answer similarly unsettling questions concerning the axioms of rational choice theories.

A somewhat deeper, and mathematically far more sophisticated, theory is this. We start by defining the effeteness of an agent as a function, E, of the intensity $a(t)$ of his action, its rate of change $v = da(t)/dt$, and time t. The effeteness function is subject to the condition that its integral with respect to time be a minimum, and we identify this integral with the futility function. That is,

$$F(t) = \int_0^t E[a(u), v(u), t]du = \text{min.},\tag{1}$$

which is equivalent to

$$\delta F(t) = 0,\tag{2}$$

where δ stands for the first-order variation in the sense of the calculus of variations. Upon carrying out the indicated operation, we get the Euler differential equation for the agent's effeteness:

$$d(\partial E/\partial v)/dt - \partial E/\partial a = 0.\tag{3}$$

Determination of the form of E suited to every agent is a matter for the rational choice of the futility theorist. (If he is as smart as he is lazy, he will be guided exclusively by considerations of computational convenience.) Once that choice has been made, the solution of the differential equation (3)—that is, the computation of the value of the action of the effete at any instant—is a straightforward technical problem. And, as with utilities, the problem of empirical tests does not even arise.

Let us now get serious. It is well known that, given any differential equation, such as (3), it is possible to fashion a variational principle, such as (1), that entails the former. In other words, it is always possible to find *something* about *any* process that gets minimized or maximized. This task is rather trivial mathematically, although it is an inverse problem, not a direct one, for it consists in guessing an assumption (i.e., eq. 1) entailing the desired consequence (i.e., eq. 3). But all the functions involved are supposed to be mathematically well-defined. And in the case of physics, they are also supposed to have precise physical meanings. In sum, the name of the game is not to hit on *something* that gets maximized or minimized, for that is included in the bargain from the beginning. The real problem is to hypothesize the *true laws* of the process in question. But such laws are missing in rational choice theory.

APPENDIX 6 :: *Objective Value*

The following is an excerpt from a fragment of a previous work (Bunge 1989, 81). We restrict our universe of discourse to goods that meet some basic needs of human beings, such as food and shelter, which can be quantitated in an objective fashion. We assume further that the (basic) value of an item is the degree to which it satisfies a basic need, and the (basic) disvalue of an item the degree to which it generates a basic need. More precisely, we propose the following postulate.

Let x be a kind of item capable of either satisfying or generating a basic need, y, of a given animal in a given state, and call $A(x)$ the amount of x available to the said animal, and $N(x,y)$ the amount of x that the animal needs to fully satisfy y. We posit that the value of x for the given animal in the given state, relative to y, is:

$$V(x,y) = \text{sgn}\,(x,y).\,[1 - A(x)/N(x,y)],$$

where $\text{sgn}(x,y) = \begin{cases} +1 \text{ if and only if } x \text{ satisfies } y, \\ -1 \text{ if and only if } x \text{ generates } y. \end{cases}$

See figure A2.

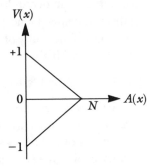

Fig. A2. Value of item x for a fixed need or want y, as a function of the amount A(x) of items capable of meeting need or want y. The value is maximal when the item meets a need, minimal when it generates a need.

APPENDIX 7 :: *Utility as a Set*

We proceed to introduce two set-theoretic notions of utility that, being qualitative, are not open to the objections that have repeatedly been raised against cardinal (numerical) utility over the past century. The first concept elucidates the intuitive idea that something is useful or beneficial if and only if it meets some need or desire of someone. We take these notions of need and desire (or wish) for granted and stipulate that the *utility* of object x for animal (e.g., human being) or social group y is the collection of needs (N) or wants (W) of y that x meets or satisfies. That is, we stipulate that

$$U(x,y) = \{z \in N \cup W | Mxzy\},$$

where $Mxzy$ is short for "x satisfies need or want z of y."

This qualitative concept allows one to introduce a comparative one. In fact, we can say that object a is *preferable* to object b for subject y (i.e., $\geq_y$) if and only if the utility of b for y is included in that of a; that is,

$$a \geq_y b =_{df} U(b,y) \subseteq U(a,y).$$

Clearly, the preference relation thus defined inherits the antisymmetry and transitivity of the inclusion relation, $\subseteq$.

The above definitions make no explicit reference to the disvaluable side effects of every human action, even the most beneficial. This shortcoming will be remedied in the following. Let a be an action with beneficial (or pleasurable) consequences $P_1, P_2, \ldots, P_m$ and negative (or nocent) effects $Q_1, Q_2, \ldots, Q_n$. We define the *utility* of the action a as the set of P's, and its *disutility* as the set of Q's. In self-explanatory symbols, $U(a) = \{P_1, P_2, \ldots, P_m\}$, and $D(a) = \{Q_1, Q_2, \ldots, Q_n\}$. So much for definitions. Let us now put them to work.

If we are consequentialists rather than deontologists, we shall rank actions by the utility of disutility of their outcomes. Hence we may stipulate that action a is *preferable* to action b if and only if the utility of a includes that of b and the disutility of a is included in that of b. That is:

$$a \geq b \text{ if and only if } [U(b) \subseteq U(a)] \ \& \ [D(a) \subseteq D(b)].$$

This preference relation, $\geq$, has the desired formal properties. In fact, it is antisymmetric and transitive because of the antisymmetry and transitivity of the inclusion relation. This concept of utility does not have the flaws of the standard concept used in rational choice theory. True, it is not quantitative; but an honest qualitative concept is certainly preferable to a pseudoquantity.

References ::

Afriat, S. N. 1987. *Logic of Choice and Economic Theory.* Oxford: Clarendon Press.

Agassi, J. 1977. *Towards a Rational Philosophical Anthropology.* The Hague: Martinus Nijhoff.

———. 1985. *Technology. Philosophical and Social Aspects.* Dordrecht: Reidel.

———. 1987. Methodological individualism and institutional individualism. In *Rationality: The Critical View,* ed. Agassi and I. C. Jarvie, pp. 119–50. Dordrecht: Martinus Nijhoff.

Agger, B. 1991. Critical theory, poststructuralism, postmodernism: their sociological relevance. *Annual Review of Sociology* 17:105–31.

Akerlof, G. A. 1984. *An Economic Theorist's Book of Tales.* Cambridge: Cambridge University Press.

Albert, H. 1988. Hermeneutics and economics. A criticism of hermeneutical thinking in the social sciences. *Kyklos* 41:573–602.

———. 1990. Methodologischer Individualismus und historische Analyse. In *Theorie der Geschichte,* Vol. 6: *Teil und Ganzes,* ed. K. Acham and W. Schulze, pp. 219–39. Munich: Deutscher Taschenbuch Verlag.

———. 1994. *Kritik der reinen Hermeneutik. Der Antirealismus und das Problem des Verstehens.* Tübingen: Mohr.

Alexander, J. C., and Giesen, B. 1987. From reduction to linkage: the long view of the micro–macro debate. In Alexander et al., 1–42.

Alexander, J. C.; Giesen, B.; Münch, R.; and Smelser, N.J., eds. 1987. *The Micro– Macro Link.* Berkeley: University of California Press.

Alker, H. R.; Deutsch, K. W.; and Stoetzel, A. H., eds. 1973. *Mathematical Approaches to Politics.* San Francisco: Jossey-Bass.

Allais, M. 1986. Determination of cardinal utility according to an intrinsic invariant model. In *Recent Developments in the Foundations of Utility and Risk Theory,* ed. L. Daboni, A. Montesano, and M. Lines, pp. 83–120. Dordrecht: Reidel.

Allais, M., and Hagen, O., eds. 1979. *Expected Utility Hypotheses and the Allais Paradox.* Dordrecht: Reidel.

Ampère, A.-M. 1843. *Essai sur la philosophie des sciences,* vol. 2. Paris: Bachelier.

Anand, P. 1987. Are the preference axioms really rational? *Theory and Decision* 23:189–214.

Andreski, S. 1972. *Social Sciences as Sorcery.* London: André Deutsch.

Andrews, F. M. 1991. Stability and change in levels and structure of subjective well-being: USA 1972 and 1988. *Social Indicators Research* 25:1–30.

Archer, M. 1987. Resisting the revival of relativism. *International Sociology* 2:235–50.

Armstrong, E. 1991. The limbic system and culture. *Human Nature* 2:117–36.

Arrow, K. J. 1994. Methodological individualism and social knowledge. *American Economic Review* 84, no. 2:1–9.

Barnes, B. 1977. *Interests and the Growth of Knowledge.* London: Routledge and Kegan Paul.

———. 1982. On the implications of a body of knowledge. *Knowledge: Creation, Diffusion, Utilization* 4:95–110.

———. 1983. On the conventional character of knowledge and cognition. In Knorr-Cetina and Mulkay, 19–51.

Barnes, B., ed. 1972. *Sociology of Science: Selected Readings.* London: Penguin.

Bartlett, M. S. 1975. *Probability, Statistics and Time.* London: Chapman and Hall.

Baumol, W. J., and Benhabib, J. 1989. Chaos: significance, mechanism, and economic applications. *Journal of Economic Perspectives* 3:77–105.

Becker, G. S. 1976. *The Economic Approach to Human Behavior.* Chicago: University of Chicago Press.

Becker, G. S., and Murphy, K. M. 1988. A theory of rational addiction. *Journal of Political Economy* 96:675–700.

Belenky, M. F.; Clinchy, B. McV.; Goldberger, N. R.; and Tarule, J. M. 1986. *Women's Ways of Knowing. The Development of Self, Voice, and Mind.* New York: Basic Books.

Benda, J. 1912. *Le Bergsonisme ou une philosophie de la mobilité.* Paris: Mercure de France.

Benn, S. I., and Mortimore, G. W., eds. 1976. *Rationality and the Social Sciences.* London: Routledge and Kegan Paul.

Bentham, J. 1982 [1789]. *An Introduction to the Principles of Morals and Legislation,* ed. J. H. Burns and H. L. A. Hart. London: Methuen.

Berelson, B., and Steiner, G. A. 1964. *Human Behavior: An Inventory of Scientific Findings.* New York: Harcourt, Brace and World.

Berger, P., and Luckmann, T. 1966. *The Social Construction of Reality.* Garden City, N.Y.: Doubleday.

Bergson, H. 1903. Introduction à la métaphysique. *Revue de métaphysique et de morale* 11:1–36.

Bernard, C. 1952 [1865]. *Introduction à l'étude de la médecine expérimentale,* 2d ed. Paris: Charles Delagrave.

Bettinger, R. L. 1991. *Hunter-Gatherers. Archaeological and Evolutionary Theory.* New York: Plenum.

Bindra, D. 1976. *A Theory of Intelligent Behavior.* New York: Wiley.

Blalock, H. M., Jr., ed. 1974. *Measurement in the Social Sciences: Theories and Strategies*. London: Macmillan.

Blalock, H. M., Jr., and Blalock, A., eds. 1968. *Methodology in Social Research*. New York: McGraw-Hill.

Blatt, J. M. 1983. How economists misuse mathematics. In Eichner, 166–86.

Blau, P. M. 1974. Presidential address: parameters of social structure. *American Sociological Review* 39:615–35.

Blaug, M. 1976. Human capital theory: a slightly jaundiced survey. *Journal of Economic Literature* 14:827–55.

Blinder, A. S. 1989. *Macroeconomics under Debate*. New York: Harvester Wheatsheaf.

Blitz, D. 1992. *Emergent Evolution: Qualitative Novelty and the Levels of Reality*. Dordrecht: Kluwer.

Bloch, M. 1949. *Apologie pour l'histoire, ou Métier d'historien*. Paris: Armand Colin.

Bloom, H. 1990. The breaking of form. In H. Bloom et al., 1–38.

Bloom, H.; de Man, P.; Derrida, J.; Hartman, G. H.; and Miller, J. H. 1990. *Deconstruction and Criticism*. New York: Continuum.

Bloor, D. 1976. *Knowledge and Social Imagery*. London: Routledge and Kegan Paul.

Blumer, H. 1969. *Symbolic Interactionism*. Englewood Cliffs, N.J.: Prentice-Hall.

Bochenski, J. M. 1987. Logische Stichproben aus der Aegyptologie. In *Logik, Wissenschaftstheorie und Erkenntnistheorie. Akten des 11. Intern. Wittgenstein Symposium*, ed. P. Weingartner and G. Schurz, pp. 303–14. Vienna: Hölder-Pichler-Tempsky.

Booth, W. J.; James, P.; and Meadwell, H., eds. 1993. *Politics and Rationality*. Cambridge: Cambridge University Press.

Boudon, R. 1967. *L'Analyse mathématique des faits sociaux*. Paris: Plon.

———. 1974. *Education, Opportunity, and Social Inequality*. New York: Wiley.

———. 1977. *Effets pervers et ordre social*. Paris: PUF.

———. 1979. *La Logique du social. Introduction à l'analyse sociologique*. Paris: Hachette. Engl. trans.: *The Logic of Social Action: An Introduction to Sociological Analysis*. London: Routledge and Kegan Paul, 1981.

———. 1987. The individualistic tradition in sociology. In Alexander et al., 45–70.

———. 1989. Subjective rationality and the explanation of social behavior. *Rationality and Society* 1:173–97.

———. 1990a. *L'Art de se persuader des idées fausses, fragiles ou douteuses*. Paris: Fayard.

———. 1990b. On relativism. In *Studies on Mario Bunge's Treatise*, ed. P. Weingartner and G. Dorn, pp. 229–43. Amsterdam: Rodopi.

———. 1991. What middle-range theories are. *Contemporary Sociology* 20:519–52.

Boudon, R., and Bourricaud, F. 1986. *Dictionnaire critique de la sociologie*, 2d ed. Paris: Presses Universitaires de France.

Boudon, R., and Clavelin, M., eds. 1994. *Le Rélativisme est-il résistible?* Paris: Presses Universitaires de France.

Bourdieu, P. 1968. Structuralism and theory of sociological knowledge. *Social Research* 35:681–706.

———. 1989. Social space and symbolic power. *Sociological Theory* 7:14–25.

Bourdieu, P.; Chamboredon, J.-C.; and Passeron, J.-C. 1991. *The Craft of Sociology: Epistemological Preliminaries*. Hawthorne, N.Y.: Walter de Gruyter.

Bourricaud, F. 1975. Contre le sociologisme: une critique et des propositions. *Revue française de sociologie* 16 suppl.:583–603.

Bradburn, N. W.; Rips, L. J.; and Shevell, S. K. 1987. Answering autobiographical questions: the impact of memory and inference on surveys. *Science* 236:157–61.

Brams, S. J. 1980. *Biblical Games: A Strategic Analysis of Stories in the Old Testament.* Cambridge, Mass.: MIT Press.

Breit, W. 1984. Galbraith and Friedman: two versions of economic reality. *Journal of Post-Keynesian Economics* 7:18–28.

Bridgman, P. W. 1927. *The Logic of Modern Physics.* New York: Macmillan.

Brock, W. A. 1990. Chaos and complexity in economic and financial science. In *Acting under Uncertainty: Multidisciplinary Conceptions,* ed. G. M. von Furstenberg, pp. 423–50. Dordrecht: Kluwer.

Brock, W. A., and Dechert, W. D. 1991. Non-linear dynamic systems: instability and chaos in economics. In *Handbook of Mathematical Economics,* vol. 4, ed. W. Hildenbrand and H. Sonnenschein, pp. 2209–35. Amsterdam: North Holland.

Brodbeck, M., ed. 1968. *Readings in the Philosophy of the Social Sciences.* New York: Macmillan.

Brown, C. 1994. Politics and the environment: nonlinear instabilities dominate. *American Political Science Review* 88:292–303.

Brown, R. H. 1987. *Society as Text. Essays on Rhetoric, Reason, and Reality.* Chicago: University of Chicago Press.

———. 1990. Rhetoric, textuality, and the postmodern turn in sociological theory. *Sociological Theory* 8:188–97.

Buckley, W., ed. 1968. *Modern Systems Research for the Behavioral Scientist.* Chicago: Aldine.

Bunge, M. 1951. What is chance? *Science and Society* 15:209–31.

———. 1959. *Causality.* Cambridge, Mass.: Harvard University Press. Rpt. as *Causality in Modern Science.* New York: Dover, 1979.

———. 1960. The place of induction in science. *Philosophy of Science* 27:262–70. Rpt. in *Through Time and Culture,* ed. A. P. Iannone, pp. 239–46. Englewood Cliffs, N.J.: Prentice-Hall, 1994.

———. 1962a. An analysis of value. *Mathematicae Notae* 18:95–108.

———. 1962b. *Intuition and Science.* Englewood Cliffs, N.J.: Prentice-Hall. Rpt. Westport, Conn.: Greenwood Press, 1975.

———. 1963. *The Myth of Simplicity.* Englewood Cliffs, N.J.: Prentice-Hall.

———. 1967a. *Foundations of Physics.* Berlin: Springer-Verlag.

———. 1967b. *Scientific Research,* 2 vols. Berlin: Springer-Verlag.

———. 1971. Is scientific metaphysics possible? *Journal of Philosophy* 68:507–20.

———. 1973a. A decision theoretic model of the American war in Vietnam. *Theory and Decision* 3:328–38.

———. 1973b. *Method, Model and Matter.* Dordrecht: Reidel.

———. 1973c. *Philosophy of Physics.* Dordrecht: Reidel.

———. 1974a. The concept of social structure. In *Developments in the Methodology of Social Science,* ed. W. Leinfellner and W. Köhler, pp. 175–215. Dordrecht: Reidel.

———. 1974b. On confusing 'measurement' with 'measure' in the methodology of the behavioral sciences. In *The Methodological Unity of Science,* ed. M. Bunge, pp. 105–22. Dordrecht: Reidel.

———. 1974c. *Treatise on Basic Philosophy,* Vol. 1: *Sense and Reference.* Dordrecht: Reidel.

———. 1974d. *Treatise on Basic Philosophy,* Vol. 2: *Interpretation and Truth.* Dordrecht: Reidel.

———. 1975. What is a quality of life indicator? *Social Indicators Research* 2:65–79.

———. 1977a. States and events. In *Systems: Approaches, Theories, Applications*, ed. W. E. Hartnett, pp. 71–95. Dordrecht: Reidel.

———. 1977b. *Treatise on Basic Philosophy*, Vol. 3: *The Furniture of the World*. Dordrecht: Reidel.

———. 1979a. A systems concept of society: beyond individualism and holism. *Theory and Decision* 10:13–30.

———. 1979b. *Treatise on Basic Philosophy*, Vol. 4: *A World of Systems*. Dordrecht: Reidel.

———. 1980. *The Mind–Body Problem*. Oxford: Pergamon.

———. 1981a. Analogy between systems. *International Journal of General Systems* 7:221–23.

———. 1981b. Development indicators. *Social Indicators Research* 9:369–85.

———. 1981c. *Scientific Materialism*. Dordrecht: Reidel.

———. 1983a. *Treatise on Basic Philosophy*, Vol. 5: *Exploring the World*. Dordrecht: Reidel.

———. 1983b. *Treatise on Basic Philosophy*, Vol. 6: *Understanding the World*. Dordrecht: Reidel.

———. 1985a. *Treatise on Basic Philosophy*, Vol. 7: *Philosophy of Science and Technology*, Part I: *Formal and Physical Sciences*. Dordrecht: Reidel.

———. 1985b. *Treatise on Basic Philosophy*, Vol. 7: *Philosophy of Science and Technology*, Part II: *Life Science, Social Science, and Technology*. Dordrecht: Reidel.

———. 1988a. Two faces and three masks of probability. In *Probability in the Sciences*, ed. E. Agazzi, pp. 27–50. Dordrecht: Reidel.

———. 1988b. Why parapsychology cannot become a science. *Behavioral and Brain Sciences* 10:576–77.

———. 1989. *Treatise on Basic Philosophy*, Vol. 8: *Ethics*. Dordrecht: Reidel.

———. 1991a. A critical examination of the new sociology of science, part 1. *Philosophy of the Social Sciences* 21:524–60.

———. 1991b. A skeptic's beliefs and disbeliefs. *New Ideas in Psychology* 9:131–49.

———. 1991c. The power and limits of reduction. In *The Problem of Reductionism in Science*, ed. E. Agazzi, pp. 27–49. Dordrecht: Kluwer.

———. 1991d. What is science? Does it matter to distinguish it from pseudoscience? A reply to my commentators. *New Ideas in Psychology* 9:245–83.

———. 1992a. A critical examination of the new sociology of science, part 2. *Philosophy of the Social Sciences* 22:46–76.

———. 1992b. System boundary. *International Journal of General Systems* 20:215–19.

———. 1993. Realism and antirealism in social science. *Theory and Decision* 35:207–35.

———. 1994a. Counter Enlightenment in contemporary social studies. In *Challenges to the Enlightenment*, ed. P. Kurtz and T. J. Madigan, pp. 25–42. Buffalo, N.Y.: Prometheus.

———. 1994b. L'Ecart entre les mathématiques et le réel. In *Passion des formes: à René Thom*, ed. M. Porte, 1:165–73. Fontenay-St Cloud: E.N.S. Editions.

———. 1995a. A critical examination of the foundations of rational choice theory. In *Towards a Theory of Man and Society*, ed. J. Götschl, pp. 211–28. Dordrecht: Kluwer.

———. 1995b. The poverty of rational choice theory. In *Critical Rationalism*,

Metaphysics and Science, ed. I. C. Jarvie and N. Laor, 1:149–68. Dordrecht: Kluwer.

———. 1995*c*. Quality, quantity, and pseudoquantity in social science. *Journal of Quantitative Linguistics* 2:1–10.

———. Forthcoming. *Social Science under Debate*.

Bunge, M., and Ardila, R. 1987. *Philosophy of Psychology*. New York: Springer.

Burdeau, G. 1967. *Traité de science politique*, 2 vols. Paris: Librairie générale de droit et de jurisprudence.

Burke, K. 1989. *On Symbols and Society*. Chicago: University of Chicago Press.

Cacioppo, J. T., and Petty, R. E., eds. 1983. *Social Psychophysiology*. New York: Guilford Press.

Campbell, R., and Sowden, L., eds. 1985. *Paradoxes of Rationality and Cooperation: Prisoner's Dilemma and Newcomb's Problem*. Vancouver: University of British Columbia Press.

Camps, V. 1993. *Virtudes públicas*, 2d ed. Madrid: Espasa-Calpe.

Cassirer, E. 1944. *An Essay on Man*. New Haven: Yale University Press.

Cicourel, A. V. 1974. *Cognitive Sociology*. New York: Free Press.

Coleman, J. S. 1964. *Introduction to Mathematical Sociology*. New York: Free Press.

———. 1984. Microfoundations and macrosocial behavior. *Angewandte Sozialforschung* 12:25–37. Rpt. in Alexander et al. 1987, 153–73.

———. 1986. Social theory, social research, and a theory of action. *American Journal of Sociology* 91:1309–35.

———. 1990. *Foundations of Social Theory*. Cambridge, Mass.: Harvard University Press, Belknap Press.

Collingwood, R. G. 1946. *The Idea of History*. Oxford: Clarendon Press.

Collins, H. M. 1981. Stages in the empirical programme of relativism. *Social Studies of Science* 11:3–10.

———. 1983. An empirical relativist programme in the sociology of scientific knowledge. In Knorr-Cetina and Mulkay, 85–113.

Collins, H. M., and Pinch, T. J. 1982. *Frames of Meaning: The Social Construction of Extraordinary Science*. London: Routledge and Kegan Paul.

Collins, R. 1981. On the microfoundations of macrosociology. *American Journal of Sociology* 87:984–1014.

———. 1986. The future decline of the Russian Empire. In *Weberian Sociological Theory*, pp. 186–209. Cambridge: Cambridge University Press.

———. 1987. Interaction ritual chains, power and property. In Alexander et al., 193–206.

Coughlin, R. M. 1991. The economic person in sociological context: case studies in the mediation of self-interest. In Etzioni and Lawrence, 35–58.

Cross, J. G., and Guyer, M. J. 1980. *Social Traps*. Ann Arbor: University of Michigan Press.

Dahrendorf, R. 1988. *The Modern Social Conflict: An Essay on the Politics of Liberty*. London: Weidenfeld and Nicolson.

Dallmayr, F. R. 1987. *Critical Encounters: Between Philosophy and Politics*. Notre Dame, Ind.: University of Notre Dame Press.

Dallmayr, F. R., and McCarthy, T. A. 1977. *Understanding and Social Inquiry*. Notre Dame, Ind.: University of Notre Dame Press.

Davis, D. D., and Holt, C. A. 1993. *Experimental Economics*. Princeton, N.J.: Princeton University Press.

Dawson, R. E. 1962. Simulation in the social sciences. In *Simulation in Social Science*, ed. H. Guetzkow, pp. 1–15. Englewood Cliffs, N.J.: Prentice-Hall.

Debreu, G. 1959. *The Theory of Value*. New York: Wiley.

———. 1991. The mathematization of economic theory. *American Economic Review* 81:1–7.

d'Encausse, H. C. 1978. *L'Empire éclaté*. Paris: Flammarion.

Denzin, N. K. 1990. Reading rational choice theory. *Rationality and Society* 2:172–89.

Derrida, J. 1967. *De la grammatologie*. Paris: Editions de Minuit.

Dexter, L. A. 1990. Intra-agency politics: conflict and contravention in administrative entities. *Journal of Theoretical Politics* 2:151–72.

Diesing, P. 1982. *Science and Ideology in the Policy Sciences*. New York: Aldine.

Dilthey, W. 1959 [1883]. Einleitung in die Geisteswissenschaften. In *Gesammelte Schriften*, vol. 1. Stuttgart: Teubner; Göttingen: Vanderhoeck and Ruprecht.

———. 1959 [1900]. Die Entstehung der Hermeneutik. In *Gesammelte Schriften*, 4:318–31. Stuttgart: Teubner.

Duhem, P. 1914. *La Théorie physique: son objet et sa structure*, 2d ed. Paris: Rivière.

Dumont, L. 1966. *Homo hierarchicus. Essai sur le système des castes*. Paris: Gallimard.

Du Pasquier, G. 1926. *Le Calcul des probabilités, son évolution mathématique et philosophique*. Paris: Hermann.

Durkheim, E. 1897. *Le Suicide*. Paris: Alcan.

———. 1970. *La Science sociale et l'action*, ed. J.-C. Filloux. Paris: Presses Universitaires de France.

———. 1988 [1895]. *Les Règles de la méthode sociologique*. Introduction by J.-M. Berthelot. Paris: Flammarion.

Durkheim, E., and Mauss, M. 1968 [1903]. De quelques formes primitives de classification. In *Essais de sociologie*, by M. Mauss, pp. 162–230. Paris: Editions de Minuit.

Earl, P. E. 1990. Economics and psychology: a survey. *Economic Journal* 100:718–55.

Eichner, A. S., ed. 1983. *Why Economics Is Not yet a Science*. Armonk, N.Y.: M. E. Sharpe.

Einhorn, H. J., and Hogarth, R. M. 1978. Confidence in judgment: persistence in the illusion of validity. *Psychological Review* 85:395–416.

Einstein, A. 1936. Physics and reality. *Journal of the Franklin Institute* 221:313–47.

Elster, J. 1989. *The Cement of Society. A Study of Social Order*. Cambridge: Cambridge University Press.

Etzioni, A. 1988. *The Moral Dimension: Toward a New Economics*. New York: Free Press.

Etzioni, A., and Lawrence, P. R., eds. 1991. *Socio-Economics. Toward a New Synthesis*. Armonk, N.Y.: Sharpe.

Evans, R. G.; Barer, M. L.; and Marmor, T. R., eds. 1994. *Why Are Some People Healthy and Others Not?* New York: Aldine de Gruyter.

Ezrahi, Y. 1971. The political resources of American science. Rpt. in Barnes 1972, 211–30.

Fauconnet, P., and Mauss, M. 1968 [1901]. Sociologie. In *Essais de sociologie*, by M. Mauss, pp. 6–41. Paris: Editions de Minuit.

Featherstone, M., ed. 1988. Special issue on hermeneutics. *Theory, Culture and Society* 5:195–576.

Festinger, L.; Riecken, H. W.; and Schachter, S. 1956. *When Prophecy Fails.* Minneapolis: University of Minnesota Press.

Feyerabend, P. K. 1975. *Against Method.* London: Verso.

———. 1981. *Philosophical Papers,* 2 vols. Cambridge: Cambridge University Press.

———. 1990. Realism and the historicity of knowledge. In *Creativity in the Arts and Science,* ed. W. R. Shea and A. Spadafora, pp. 142–53. Canton, Mass.: Science History Publications, U.S.A.

Feynman, R. P. 1989. *What Do You Care What Other People Think?* New York: W. W. Norton.

Fiske, D. W., and Shweder, R. A., eds. 1986. *Metatheory in Social Science. Pluralisms and Subjectivities.* Chicago: University of Chicago Press.

Fleck, L. 1979 [1935]. *Genesis and Development of a Scientific Fact.* Foreword by T. S. Kuhn. Chicago: University of Chicago Press.

Foucault, M. 1969. *L'Archéologie du savoir.* Paris: Gallimard.

———. 1975. *Surveiller et punir: naissance de la prison.* Paris: Gallimard.

Franck, R., ed. 1994. *Faut-il chercher aux causes une raison? L'explication causale dans les sciences humaines.* Paris: Vrin.

Frank, R. H. 1988. *Passions within Reason. The Strategic Role of the Emotions.* New York: W. W. Norton.

Frank, R. H.; Gilovich, T.; and Regan, D. T. 1993. Does studying economics inhibit cooperation? *Economic Perspectives* 7:159–71.

Fréchet, M. 1946. Les définitions courantes de la probabilité. In *Les Mathématiques et le concret,* pp. 157–204. Paris: Presses Universitaires de France.

Freese, L., and Rokeach, M. 1979. On the use of alternative interpretations in contemporary social psychology. *Social Psychology Quarterly* 42:195–201.

Freud, S. 1929. *Introductory Lectures on Psychoanalysis,* 2d ed. London: Allen & Unwin.

Friedman, J. W. 1977. *Oligopoly and the Theory of Games.* Amsterdam: North Holland.

Friedman, M. 1953. The methodology of positive economics. In *Essays in Positive Economics,* pp. 3–43. Chicago: University of Chicago Press.

———. 1976. *Price Theory.* New York: Aldine.

Gadamer, H.-G. 1975 [1960]. *Wahrheit und Methode,* 4th ed. Tübingen: Mohr.

Galanter, E. 1962. The direct measurement of utility and subjective probability. *American Journal of Psychology* 75:208–20.

Galbraith, J. K. 1987. *A History of Economics.* London: Hamish Hamilton.

Gardner, M. 1992. Probability paradoxes. *Skeptical Inquirer* 16:129–132.

Garfinkel, H. 1967. *Studies in Ethnomethodology.* Englewood Cliffs, N.J.: Prentice-Hall.

Garfinkel, H.; Lynch, M.; and Livingston, E. 1981. The work of a discovering science construed with materials from the optically discovered pulsar. *Philosophy of the Social Sciences* 11:131–58.

Gauthier, D. 1986. *Morals by Agreement.* Oxford: Clarendon Press.

Geertz, C. 1973. *The Interpretation of Cultures.* New York: Basic Books.

Gellner, E. 1973. *Cause and Meaning in the Social Sciences.* London: Routledge and Kegan Paul.

———. 1985. *Relativism and the Social Sciences.* Cambridge: Cambridge University Press.

Geyer, F., and Zouwen, J. van der, eds. 1990. *Self-Referencing in Social Systems*. Salinas, Calif.: Intersystems Publications.

Gini, C. 1952. *Patologia economica*, 5th ed. Turin: UTET.

Glass, L., and Mackey, M. C. 1988. *From Clocks to Chaos*. Princeton: Princeton University Press.

Goffman, E. 1963. *Behavior in Public Places*. New York: Free Press.

Goldsmith, D., ed. 1977. *Scientists Confront Velikovsky*. Papers from an AAAS Symposium. Ithaca, N.Y.: Cornell University Press.

Goodman, N. 1958. The test of simplicity. *Science* 128:1064–69.

———. 1978. *Ways of World-Making*. Indianapolis, Ind.: Hackett.

Gouldner, A. W. 1970. *The Coming Crisis of Western Sociology*. New York: Basic Books.

———. 1973. *For Sociology. Renewal and Critique in Sociology Today*. New York: Basic Books.

Graaff, J. de. 1967. *Theoretical Welfare Economics*. Cambridge: Cambridge University Press.

Granovetter, M. 1974. *Getting a Job: A Study of Contacts and Careers*. Cambridge, Mass.: Harvard University Press.

———. 1985. Economic action and social structure: the problem of embeddedness. *American Journal of Sociology* 91:481–510.

Green, D. P., and Shapiro, I. 1994. *Pathologies of Rational Choice Theory. A Critique of Applications in Political Science*. New Haven: Yale University Press.

Greenwood, E. 1945. *Experimental Sociology: A Study in Method*. New York: King's Crown Press.

Griliches, Z. 1994. Productivity, R&D, and the data constraint. *American Economic Review* 84:1–23.

Haack, S. 1995. *Evidence and Inquiry*. Oxford: Blackwell.

Habermas, J. 1971. *Toward a Rational Society*. London: Heinemann.

———. 1981. *Theorie des kommunikatives Handelns*, 2 vols. Frankfurt: Suhrkamp.

Hammond, J. S. III. 1967. Better decisions with preference theory. *Harvard Business Review* 45:123–41.

Hardin, G. 1968. The tragedy of the commons. *Science* 162:1243–47.

Harding, S. 1986. *The Science Question in Feminism*. Ithaca, N.Y.: Cornell University Press.

———. 1991. *Whose Science? Whose Knowledge? Thinking from Women's Lives*. Ithaca, N.Y.: Cornell University Press.

Harris, M. 1968. *The Rise of Anthropological Theory*. New York: Crowell.

———. 1979. *Cultural Materialism*. New York: Random House.

Harrison, B., and Bluestone, B. 1988. *The Great U-Turn: Corporate Restructuring and the Polarization of America*. New York: Basic Books.

Harsanyi, J. C. 1985. Does reason tell us what moral code to follow and, indeed, to follow any moral code at all? *Ethics* 96:42–45.

Hartman, A. 1991. Words create worlds. *Social Work* 36:275–76.

Harvey, D. 1989. *The Condition of Postmodernity. An Inquiry into the Origins of Cultural Change*. Oxford: Blackwell.

Hausman, J. A., and Wise, D. A. 1985. *Social Experimentation*. Chicago: University of Chicago Press.

Hayek, F. A. 1955. *The Counter-Revolution of Science*. Glencoe, Ill.: Free Press.

Hebb, D. O. 1949. *The Organization of Behavior: A Neuropsychological Theory.* New York: Wiley.

———. 1955. Drives and the C.N.S. conceptual nervous system. *Psychological Review* 62:243–54.

———. 1980. *Essay on Mind.* Hillsdale, N.J.: Lawrence Erlbaum Associates.

Heidegger, M. 1959. *Unterwegs zur Sprache.* Tübingen: Neske.

———. 1976 [1943]. *Vom Wesen der Wahrheit,* 6th ed. Frankfurt: V. Klosterman.

———. 1986 [1927]. *Sein und Zeit,* 16th ed. Tübingen: Niemeyer.

———. 1987 [1953]. *Einführung in die Metaphysik,* 5th ed. Tübingen: Niemeyer.

Hempel, C. G. 1965. *Aspects of Scientific Explanation.* New York: Free Press.

Hendry, D. F., and Richard, J.-F. 1982. On the formulation of empirical models in dynamic econometrics. *Journal of Econometrics* 20:3–33.

Herrnstein, J. W. 1990. Rational choice theory: necessary but not sufficient. *American Psychologist* 45:356–67.

Herschel, J. F. W. 1830. *Preliminary Discourse on the Study of Natural Philosophy.* London: Longmans.

Hesse, M. 1966. *Models and Analogies in Science.* Notre Dame, Ind.: University of Notre Dame Press.

Hilbert, D. 1918. Axiomatisches Denken. *Mathematische Annalen* 78:405–15.

Hilbert, D., and Bernays, P. 1968 [1934]. *Grundlagen der Mathematik,* 2 vols. Berlin: Springer-Verlag.

Himmelstrand, U., ed. 1986. *Sociology: From Crisis to Science?* 2 vols. London: Sage.

Hirschman, A. O. 1977. *The Passions and the Interests. Political Arguments for Capitalism before Its Triumph.* Princeton, N.J.: Princeton University Press.

———. 1992. *Rival Views of Market Society.* Cambridge, Mass.: Harvard University Press.

Hirst, R. J. 1967. Realism. In *Encyclopedia of Philosophy,* 7:77–83. New York: Macmillan and Free Press.

Hodder, I. 1992. *Theory and Practice in Archaeology.* London: Routledge.

Hogarth, R. M., and Reder, M. W., eds. 1987. *Rational Choice. The Contrast between Economics and Psychology.* Chicago: University of Chicago Press.

Homans, G. C. 1958. Social behavior as exchange. *American Journal of Sociology* 62:597–606.

———. 1974. *Social Behavior. Its Elementary Forms,* rev. ed. New York: Harcourt Brace Jovanovich.

———. 1987. Behaviorism and after. In *Social Theory Today,* ed. A. Giddens and J. Turner, pp. 58–81. Stanford, Calif.: Stanford University Press.

Husserl, E. 1950 [1931]. *Cartesianische Meditationen.* In *Husserliana: Gesammelte Werke,* vol. 1. The Hague: Martinus Nijhoff.

———. 1950, 1952 [1913]. *Ideen zu einer reinen Phänomenologie und phänomenologischen Philosophie.* In *Husserliana: Gesammelte Werke,* vols. 3, 4. The Hague: Martinus Nijhoff.

———. 1954 [1935]. Die Krisis des europäischen Menschentums und die Philosophie. In *Husserliana: Gesammelte Werke,* 6:314–48. The Hague: Martinus Nijhoff.

———. 1954 [1936]. *Die Krisis der Europäischen Wissenschaften und die transzendentale Phänomenologie.* In *Husserliana: Gesammelte Werke,* vol. 6. The Hague: Martinus Nijhoff.

Iannone, A. P., ed. 1987. *Contemporary Moral Controversies in Technology.* New York: Oxford University Press.

————. 1989. *Contemporary Moral Controversies in Business.* New York: Oxford University Press.

James, W. 1975 [1907]. *Pragmatism.* Cambridge, Mass.: Harvard University Press.

Jarvie, I. C. 1984. *Rationality and Relativism.* London: Routledge and Kegan Paul.

Jasso, G. 1980. A new theory of distributive justice. *American Sociological Review* 45:3–32.

Jones, R. 1977. *Self-Fulfilling Prophecies: Social, Psychological and Physiological Effects of Expectancies.* Hillsdale, N.J.: Erlbaum.

Juster, F. T. 1985. *Preferences for Work and Leisure.* Ann Arbor: University of Michigan Press.

Kahneman, D.; Knetsch, J.L.; and Thaler, R. 1986. Fairness as a constraint on profit seeking: entitlements in the market. *American Economic Review* 76:728–41.

————. 1987. Fairness and the assumptions of economics. In Hogarth and Reder, 101–16.

Kahneman, D., and Tversky, A. 1973. On the psychology of prediction. *Psychological Review* 80:237–51.

————. 1979. Prospect theory: an analysis of decision under risk. *Econometrica* 47:263–91.

Kahneman, D.; Slovic, P.; and Tversky, A., eds. 1982. *Judgment under Uncertainty: Heuristics and Biases.* Cambridge: Cambridge University Press.

Karni, E., and Safra, Z. 1995. The impossibility of experimental elicitation of subjective probabilities. *Theory and Decision* 38:313–20.

Kearney, R. 1986. *Modern Movements in European Philosophy.* Manchester: Manchester University Press.

Keller, E. F. 1985. *Reflections on Gender and Science.* New Haven: Yale University Press.

Kitcher, P. 1995. *The Advancement of Knowledge.* New York: Oxford University Press.

Knaus, W. A.; Wagner, D. P.; and Lynn, J. 1991. Short-term mortality predictions for critically ill hospitalized adults: science and ethics. *Science* 254:389–94.

Knetsch, J. L. 1992. Preferences and nonreversibility of indifference curves. *Journal of Economic Behavior and Organization* 17:131–39.

Knorr-Cetina, K. D. 1981. *The Manufacture of Knowledge: An Essay on the Constructivist and Contextual Nature of Science.* Oxford: Pergamon.

————. 1983. The ethnographic study of scientific work: towards a constructivist interpretation of science. In Knorr-Cetina and Mulkay, 115–39.

Knorr-Cetina, K. D., and Cicourel, A. V. 1981. The micro-sociological challenge of macro-sociology: towards a reconstruction of social theory and methodology. In Knorr-Cetina and Cicourel, 1–47.

Knorr-Cetina, K. D., and Cicourel, A. V., eds. 1981. *Advances in Social Theory and Methodology: Towards an Integration of Micro- and Macro-sociology.* London: Routledge and Kegan Paul.

Knorr-Cetina, K. D., and Mulkay, M. 1983a. Emerging principles in social studies of science. In Knorr-Cetina and Mulkay, 1–18.

Knorr-Cetina, K. D., and Mulkay, M., eds. 1983b. *Science Observed. Perspectives on the Social Study of Science.* London: Sage.

Krimerman, L. I., ed. 1969. *The Nature and Scope of Social Science.* New York: Appleton-Century-Crofts.

Kuhn, T. S. 1962. *The Structure of Scientific Revolutions.* Chicago: University of Chicago Press. Rev. ed. 1970.

———. 1991. The road since *Structure.* In *PSA 1990,* 2:3–13. East Lansing, Mich.: Philosophy of Science Association.

Lachmann, L. M. 1973. *Drei Essays über Max Webers geistiges Vermächtnis.* Tübingen: Mohr.

Lalande, A. 1938. *Vocabulaire technique et critique de la philosophie,* 3 vols. Paris: Alcan.

Lane, R. E. 1981. *The Market Experience.* New York: Cambridge University Press.

Lang, S. 1981. *The File.* New York: Springer.

———. 1990. Case study of political opinions passed off as science and mathematics. Videotape. American Mathematical Society and Mathematical Association of America.

Laponce, J. A., and Smoker, P., eds. 1972. *Experimentation and Simulation in Political Science.* Toronto: University of Toronto Press.

Lasswell, H. D., and Kaplan, A. 1952. *Power and Society: A Framework for Political Inquiry.* London: Routledge and Kegan Paul.

Latour, B. 1980. Is it possible to reconstruct the research process? Sociology of a brain peptide. *Sociology of the Sciences Yearbook* 4:53–76.

———. 1983. Give me a laboratory and I will raise the world. In Knorr-Cetina and Mulkay, 140–70.

———. 1987. *Science in Action. How to Follow Scientists and Engineers through Society.* Cambridge, Mass.: Harvard University Press.

———. 1988. A relativistic account of Einstein's relativity. *Social Studies of Science* 18:3–44.

Latour, B., and Woolgar, S. 1979. *Laboratory Life: The Social Construction of Scientific Facts.* Beverly Hills, Calif.: Sage.

———. 1986. *Laboratory Life: The Construction of Scientific Facts.* Princeton, N.J.: Princeton University Press. (Revision of Latour and Woolgar 1979.)

Lazarsfeld, P., and Menzel, H. 1965. On the relations between individual and collective properties. In *Reader on Complex Organizations,* ed. A. Etzioni, pp. 422–40. New York: Holt, Rinehart and Winston.

Leibniz, G. W. 1981 [1703]. *Nouveaux Essais sur l'entendement humain.* Eng. trans.: *New Essays on Human Understanding.* Cambridge: Cambridge University Press.

Lenin, V. I. 1947 [1908]. *Materialism and Empirio-Criticism.* Moscow: Foreign Languages Publishing House.

———. 1972 [1914]. Conspectus of Hegel's Science of Logic. In *Philosophical Notebooks, Collected Works,* vol. 38. Moscow: Progress Publishers.

León-Portilla, M. 1980. *Toltecáyotl: Aspectos de la cultura náhuatl.* Mexico D.F.: Fondo de Cultura Económica.

Leontief, W. 1982. Academic economics. *Science* 217:104–7.

Lévi-Strauss, C. 1963. *Structural Anthropology.* New York: Basic Books.

Lewontin, R. C. 1991. *Biology as Ideology: The Doctrine of DNA.* Concord, Ont.: Anansi.

Livingston, P. 1988. *Literary Knowledge.* Ithaca, N.Y.: Cornell University Press.

———. 1991. *Literature and Rationality: Ideas of Agency in Theory and Fiction.* New York: Cambridge University Press.

Lloyd, C. 1991. The methodologies of social history: a critical survey and defense of structurism. *History and Theory* 30:180–219.

Lomnitz, L. 1977. *Networks and Marginality.* New York: Academic Press.

Lorrain, F., and White, H. C. 1971. Structural equivalence of individuals in social networks. *Journal of Mathematical Sociology* 1:49–80.

Louch, A. R. 1969. *Explanation and Human Action.* Berkeley: University of California Press.

Luce, R. D., and Raiffa, H. 1957. *Games and Decisions. Introduction and Critical Survey.* New York: Wiley. Rpt. New York: Dover, 1989.

Luhmann, N. 1984. *Soziale Systeme. Grundrisse einer allgemeinen Theorie.* Frankfurt: Suhrkamp.

———. 1987. The evolutionary differentiation between society and interaction. In Alexander et al., 112–31.

———. 1990. *Die Wissenschaft der Gesellschaft.* Frankfurt: Suhrkamp.

Lynch, M. E. 1988. Sacrifice and the transformation of the animal body into a scientific object: laboratory culture and ritual practice in the neurosciences. *Social Studies of Science* 18:265–89.

Lynch, M. E.; Livingston, E., and Garfinkel, H. 1983. Temporal order in laboratory work. In Knorr-Cetina and Mulkay, 205–38.

McCloskey, D. N. 1985. *The Rhetoric of Economics.* Madison, Wis.: University of Wisconsin Press.

MacCrimmon, K. R., and Larsson, S. 1979. Utility theory: axioms vs. "paradoxes." In Allais and Hagen, 333–409.

Machina, M. J., and Munier, B., eds. 1994. *Models and Experiments on Risk and Rationality.* Dordrecht: Kluwer.

Machlup, F. 1955. The problem of verification in economic theory. *Southern Economic Journal* 22:1–21.

McKeown, T. 1979. *The Role of Medicine.* Princeton, N.J.: Princeton University Press.

MacKinnon, C. 1989. *Toward a Feminist Theory of the State.* Cambridge, Mass.: Harvard University Press.

Macpherson, C. B. 1962. *The Political Theory of Possessive Individualism: Hobbes to Locke.* Oxford: Clarendon Press.

Macy, M. W. 1990. Learning theory and the logic of critical mass. *American Sociological Review* 55:809–26.

Malcolm, N. 1968. The conceivability of mechanism. *Philosophical Review* 77:45–72.

Malinvaud, E. 1984. *Mass Unemployment.* Oxford: Blackwell.

———. 1991. *Voies de la recherche macroéconomique.* Paris: Odile Jacob.

Malitza, M. 1971. A model of Michael the Brave's decision in 1595. In *Mathematics in the Archaeological and Historical Sciences,* ed. F. R. Hodson, D. G. Kendall, and P. Tautu, pp. 516–23. Edinburgh: Edinburgh University Press.

Mandelbaum, M. 1955. Societal facts. *British Journal of Sociology* 6:305–17.

Mann, M. 1986. *The Sources of Power,* Vol. 1: *A History of Power from the Beginning to A.D. 1760.* Cambridge: Cambridge University Press.

———. 1993. *The Sources of Power,* Vol. 2: *The Rise of Classes and Nation-States, 1760–1914.* Cambridge: Cambridge University Press.

March, J. G., and Simon, H. A. 1958. *Organizations.* New York: John Wiley.

Marcuse, H. 1964. *One-Dimensional Man.* Boston: Beacon Press.

Marshall, A. 1920 [1890]. *Principles of Economics,* 8th ed. London: Macmillan.

Marx, K. 1967 [1867]. *Capital*, vol. I. New York: International Publishers.
———. 1973 [1857–58]. *Grundrisse: Foundations of the Critique of Political Economy.*
New York: Penguin.
———. 1975 [1847]. *The Poverty of Philosophy.* Moscow: Progress Publishers.
———. 1986 [1852]. The eighteenth Brumaire of Louis Bonaparte. In *Selected
Works*, by K. Marx and F. Engels, pp. 95–180. New York: International
Publishers.
———. 1986 [1859]. A contribution to the critique of political economy. In *Selected
Works*, by K. Marx and F. Engels, pp. 181–85. New York: International
Publishers.
Marx, K., and Engels, F. 1986. *Selected Works.* New York: International Publishers.
Mathews, J. 1989. *Age of Democracy. The Politics of Post-Fordism.* Melbourne: Oxford
University Press.
Mauss, M. 1968. *Essais de sociologie.* Paris: Editions de Minuit.
Mead, G. H. 1934. *Mind, Self, and Society,* ed. C. W. Morris. Chicago: University of
Chicago Press.
Menger, C. 1969 [1883]. *Untersuchungen über die Methode der Socialwissenschaften,
und der politischen Oekonomie insbesondere.* Leipzig: Dunker and Humblot. Vol. 2
of *Gesammelte Werke,* 2d ed. Tübingen: Mohr.
Merton, R. K. 1936. The unanticipated consequences of purposive social action.
American Sociological Review 1:894–904.
———. 1938. Science and the social order. *Philosophy of Science* 5:321–37. Rpt. in
Merton 1973, 254–66.
———. 1957. *Social Theory and Social Structure,* rev. ed. New York: Free Press.
———. 1973. *The Sociology of Science. Theoretical and Empirical Investigations.*
Chicago: University of Chicago Press.
———. 1987. Three fragments from a sociologist's notebooks. *Annual Review of
Sociology* 13:1–28.
Michalos, A. 1980–82. *North American Social Report,* 5 vols. Dordrecht: Reidel.
Mill, J. S. 1952 [1875]. *A System of Logic,* 8th ed. Rpt. London: Longmans,
Green.
Miller, D., ed. 1985. *Popper Selections.* Princeton, N.J.: Princeton University Press.
Mitcham, C. 1994. *Thinking through Technology. The Path between Engineering and
Philosophy.* Chicago: University of Chicago Press.
Mitcham, C., and Mackey, R., eds. 1972. *Philosophy and Technology.* Chicago:
University of Chicago Press.
Morgenstern, O. 1963. *On the Accuracy of Economic Observations,* 2d ed. Princeton:
Princeton University Press.
———. 1972. Descriptive, predictive and normative theory. *Kyklos* 25:699–714.
———. 1979. Some reflections on utility. In Allais and Hagen, 175–83.
Moser, P. K., ed. 1990. *Rationality in Action. Contemporary Approaches.* Cambridge:
Cambridge University Press.
Mueller-Vollmer, K., ed. 1989. *The Hermeneutic Reader: Texts of the German
Tradition from the Enlightenment to the Present.* New York: Continuum.
Mulkay, M. 1969. Some aspects of cultural growth in the natural sciences. In Barnes
1972, 126–42.
Myrdal, G. 1969. *Objectivity in Social Research.* New York: Pantheon Books.
Nadeau, R. 1993. Confuting Popper on the rationality principle. *Philosophy of the
Social Sciences* 23:446–67.

Nagel, E. 1961. *The Structure of Science.* New York: Harcourt, Brace and World.
Neurath, O. 1981. *Gesammelte philosophische und methodologische Schriften,* 2 vols., ed. R. Haller and H. Rutte. Vienna: Hölder-Pichler-Tempsky.
Nozick, R. 1974. *Anarchy, State and Utopia.* New York: Basic Books.
Olson, M. 1971. *The Logic of Collective Action,* 2d ed. Cambridge, Mass.: Harvard University Press.
O'Neill, J., ed. 1973. *Modes of Individualism and Collectivism.* London: Heinemann.
Optner, S. L., ed. 1973. *Systems Analysis.* Harmondsworth: Penguin.
Pareto, V. 1935 [1916]. *A Treatise on General Sociology,* 4 vols. New York: Harcourt, Brace and Co. Rpt. New York: Dover, 1963.
————. 1966. *Sociological Writings.* Selected and introduced by S. E. Feiner. Totowa, N.J.: Rowman and Littlefield.
————. 1974 [1906]. *Manuale di economia politica.* Padua: Cedam.
Parsons, T. 1951. *The Social System.* New York: Free Press; London: Collier-Macmillan.
Pasinetti, L. L. 1981. *Structural Change and Economic Growth.* Cambridge: Cambridge University Press.
Patai, D., and Koertge, N. 1994. *Professing Feminism. Cautionary Tales from the Strange World of Women's Studies.* New York: Basic Books.
Peirce, C. S. 1935 [1898]. *Scientific Metaphysics.* In *Collected Works,* vol. 6. Cambridge, Mass.: Harvard University Press, Belknap Press.
————. 1958 [ca. 1902]. Scientific method. In *Collected Papers,* ed. A. W. Burks, 7:37–75. Cambridge, Mass.: Harvard University Press.
Piaget, J. 1965. *Etudes sociologiques.* Geneva: Librairie Droz.
Pinch, T. J. 1979. Normal explanations of the paranormal: the demarcation problem and fraud in parapsychology. *Social Studies of Science* 9:329–48.
————. 1985. Towards an analysis of scientific observation: the externality of evidential significance of observational reports in physics. *Social Studies of Science* 15:3–36.
Pinch, T. J., Collins, H. M. 1979. Is anti-science not-science? *Sociology of the Sciences Yearbook* 3:221–50.
————. 1984. Private science and public knowledge. *Social Studies of Science* 14:521–46.
Poincaré, H. 1903. *Science et hypothèse.* Paris: Flammarion.
————. 1965 [1901]. Letter to L. Walras. In *Correspondence of Léon Walras and Related Papers,* ed. W. Jaffé, 3:164–65. Amsterdam: North Holland.
Polanyi, K. 1944. *The Great Transformation.* New York: Rinehart.
Pólya, G. 1957. *How To Solve It.* New York: Doubleday Anchor Books.
Popper, K. R. 1957[1944–45]. *The Poverty of Historicism.* London: Routledge and Kegan Paul.
————. 1959 [1935]. *The Logic of Scientific Discovery.* London: Hutchinson.
————. 1962 [1945]. *The Open Society and Its Enemies,* 2 vols. London: Routledge and Kegan Paul.
————. 1963. *Conjectures and Refutatons.* New York: Basic Books.
————. 1967. The rationality principle. Rpt. in Miller, 1985, 357–65.
————. 1972. *Objective Knowledge.* Oxford: Clarendon Press.
————. 1974. Intellectual autobiography. In *The Philosophy of Karl Popper,* ed. P. A. Schlipp, pp. 3–181. La Salle, Ill.: Open Court.
Porter, M. E. 1980. *Competitive Strategy.* New York: Free Press.

Portes, A., and Sassen-Koob, S. 1987. Making it underground: comparative material on the informal sector in Western market economies. *American Journal of Sociology* 93:30–61.

Putnam, H. 1994. The Dewey Lectures 1994. *Journal of Philosophy* 91:445–517.

Rachlin, H.; Battalio, R.; Kagel, J.; and Green, L. 1981. Maximization theory in behavioral psychology. *Behavioral and Brain Sciences* 4:371–417.

Rand, A. 1964. *The Virtue of Selfishness: A New Concept of Egoism.* New York: American Library.

Rapoport, A. 1989. *Decision Theory and Decision Behavior.* Dordrecht: Kluwer.

———. 1990. Comments on Tsebelis. *Rationality and Society* 2:508–11.

Rawls, J. 1971. *A Theory of Justice.* Cambridge, Mass.: Harvard University Press.

Ray, A. J., and Freeman, D. B. 1978. *"Give Us Good Measure": An Economic Analysis of Relations between the Indians and the Hudson's Bay Company before 1763.* Toronto: University of Toronto Press.

Reich, R. B., ed. 1988. *The Power of Public Ideas.* Cambridge, Mass.: Harvard University Press.

Rescher, N. 1987. *Scientific Realism.* Dordrecht: Reidel.

———. 1988. *Rationality.* Oxford: Clarendon Press.

———. 1993. *Pluralism.* Oxford: Clarendon Press.

———. 1994. *A System of Pragmatic Realism,* vol. 3. Princeton, N.J.: Princeton University Press.

Restivo, S. 1983. *The Social Relations of Physics, Mysticism and Mathematics.* Dordrecht: Reidel.

Ricoeur, P. 1971. The model of the text: meaningful action considered as a text. *Social Research* 38:529–62.

———. 1975. *La Métaphore vive.* Paris: Seuil.

Robinson, J., and Eatwell, J. 1974. *An Introduction to Modern Economics,* rev. ed. London: McGraw-Hill.

Rorty, R. 1979. *Philosophy and the Mirror of Nature.* Princeton, N.J.: Princeton University Press.

Rosenau, J. N. 1990. *Turbulence in World Politics.* Princeton, N.J.: Princeton University Press.

Ross, E., ed. 1980. *Essays in Cultural Materialism.* New York: Academic Press.

Rossi, P. H. 1988. On sociological data. In Smelser, 131–54.

Russell, C. 1993. *The Master Trend: How the Baby Boom Generation is Remaking America.* New York: Plenum.

Russett, B., and Starr, H. 1981. *World Politics: The Menu for Choice.* San Francisco: W. H. Freeman.

Ryan, A. 1991. When it's rational to be irrational. *New York Review of Books* 38, no. 15:19–22.

Samuelson, P. A. 1966 [1952]. Utility, preference and probability. In *Collected Works of Paul A. Samuelson,* 1:127–36. Cambridge, Mass.: MIT Press.

———. 1976. *Foundations of Economic Analysis.* New York: Atheneum.

Schelting, A. von. 1934. *Max Webers Wissenschaftslehre.* Tübingen: Mohr (Paul Siebeck).

Scherer, F. 1980. *Industrial Market Structure and Economic Performance,* 2d ed. Chicago: Rand-McNally.

Schütz, A. 1940. Phenomenology and the social sciences. In *Philosophical Essays in*

Memory of Edmund Husserl, ed. M. Farber, pp. 164–86. Cambridge, Mass.: Harvard University Press.

———. 1953. Common sense and the scientific interpretation of human action. *Philosophy and Phenomenological Research*, 14:1–38.

———. 1967 [1932]. *The Phenomenology of the Social World*. Evanston, Ill.: Northwestern University Press.

Schumpeter, J. A. 1950 [1942]. *Capitalism, Socialism and Democracy*. Introduction by T. Bottomore. New York: Harper Torchbooks.

———. 1991. *Joseph A. Schumpeter: The Economics and Sociology of Capitalism*, ed. R. Swedberg. Princeton, N.J.: Princeton University Press.

Scitovsky, T. 1976. *The Joyless Economy*. New York: Oxford University Press.

Searle, J. 1995. *The Construction of Social Reality*. New York: Free Press.

Sebreli, J. J. 1992. *El asedio a la modernidad: Crítica del relativismo cultural*. Barcelona: Ariel.

Sen, A. K. 1987. *On Ethics and Economics*. Oxford: Blackwell.

———. 1995. Rational and social choice. *American Economic Review* 85:1–24.

Sheldon, E. B., and Moore, E., eds. 1968. *Indicators of Social Change: Concepts and Measurements*. New York: Russell Sage Foundation.

Shepherd, L. J. 1993. *Lifting the Veil. The Feminine Face of Science*. Boston: Shambala.

Shoemaker, P. J. H. 1992. Subjective expected utility theory revisited: a reductio ad absurdum paradox. *Theory and Decision* 33:1–21.

Short, J. F., ed. 1986. *The Social Fabric*. Beverly Hills, Calif.: Sage.

Shubik, M. 1987. *A Game-Theoretic Approach to Political Economy*. Cambridge, Mass.: MIT Press.

Shweder, R. A. 1986. Divergent rationalities. In Fiske and Shweder, 163–96.

Siegel, H. 1987. *Relativism Refuted: A Criticism of Contemporary Epistemological Relativism*. Dordrecht: Reidel.

Simmel, G. 1923 [1892]. *Die Probleme der Geschichtsphilosophie. Eine erkenntnistheoretische Studie*, 5th ed. Munich: Duncker und Humblot. Eng. trans.: *The Problems of the Philosophy of History*. New York: Free Press, 1977.

Simon, H. A. 1955. A behavioral model of rational choice. *Quarterly Journal of Economics* 69:99–118.

———. 1985. Human nature in politics: the dialogue of psychology with political science. *American Political Science Review* 79:293—304.

Smart, J. J. C. 1973. An outline of a system of utilitarian ethics. In *Utilitarianism For and Against*, by J. J. C. Smart and B. Williams, pp. 1–74. Cambridge: Cambridge University Press.

Smelser, N. J. 1986. From structure to order. In Short, 33–38.

———. 1992. The rational choice perspective: a theoretical assessment. *Rationality and Society* 4:381–411.

Smelser, N. J., ed. 1988. *Handbook of Sociology*. Newbury Park: Sage.

Sorokin, P. A. 1937. *Social and Cultural Dynamics*, vol. 3. London: Allen and Unwin.

———. 1956. *Fads and Foibles in Modern Sociology and Related Sciences*. Chicago: Henry Regnery.

Spaulding, A. C. 1988. Archaeology and anthropology. *American Anthropologist* 90:263–71.

Spiegel, G. M. 1990. History, historicism, and the social logic of the text in the Middle Ages. *Speculum* 65:59–86.

Stacey, R. D. 1992. *Managing the Unknowable*. San Francisco: Jossey-Bass.

Stack, G. 1989. The meaning and value of *Verstehen*. *Dialogos* (Puerto Rico) 24, no. 54:129–64.

Stigler, G. J., and Becker, G. S. 1977. De gustibus non est disputandum. *American Economic Review* 67:76–90.

Stinchcombe, A. L. 1968. *Constructing Social Theories*. Chicago: University of Chicago Press.

———. 1990. Comment. *Rationality and Society* 2:214–23.

Suppes, P. 1970. *A Probabilistic Theory of Causality*. Amsterdam: North Holland.

Suppes, P., and Zinnes, J. L. 1963. Basic measurement theory. In *Handbook of Mathematical Psychology*, ed. R. D. Luce, R. R. Bush, and E. Galanter, 1:1–76. New York: John Wiley.

Swedberg, R. M. 1990. *Economics and Sociology. Redefining Boundaries: Conversations with Economists and Sociologists*. Princeton, N.J.: Princeton University Press.

———. 1991. "The battle of methods": toward a paradigm shift? In Etzioni and Lawrence, 13–34.

Taylor, C. 1971. Interpretation and the science of man. *Review of Metaphysics* 25:3–51.

Tocqueville, A. de. 1952 [1835]. *De la démocratie en Amérique*. In *Oeuvres complètes*, vol. 1. Paris: Gallimard.

———. 1985. *Selected Letters on Politics and Society*, ed. R. Boesche. Berkeley: University of California Press.

Tönnies, F. 1979 [1887]. *Gemeinschaft und Gesellschaft*, 8th ed. Darmstadt: Wissenschaftliche Buchhandlung.

Tolstoy, L. 1982 [1865–69]. *War and Peace*. London: Penguin.

Trigg, R. 1985. *Understanding Social Science*. Oxford: Blackwell.

Trigger, B. G. 1991. Early native North American responses to European contact: romantic versus rationalistic interpretations. *Journal of American History* 77:1195–1215.

Tversky, A. 1975. A critique of expected utility theory: descriptive and normative considerations. *Erkenntnis* 9:163–73.

Tversky, A., and Kahneman, D. 1981. The framing of decisions and the psychology of choice. *Science* 211:453–58.

Vaihinger, H. 1920. *Die Philosophie des Als Ob*, 4th ed. Leipzig: Meiner.

Van Dusen, R. A., ed. 1974. *Social Indicators, 1973: A Review Symposium*. Washington, D.C.: Social Science Research Council.

Van Fraassen, B. 1980. *The Scientific Image*. Oxford: Clarendon Press.

Ville, J. 1939. *Etude critique de la notion de collectif*. Paris: Gauthier-Villars.

Vining, D. R. 1986. Social versus reproductive success: the central theoretical problem of human sociobiology. *Behavioral and Brain Sciences* 9:167–216.

von Mises, L. 1949. *Human Action: A Treatise on Economics*. New Haven: Yale University Press.

von Neumann, J., and Morgenstern, O. 1947. *Theory of Games and Economic Behavior*, 2d ed. Princeton, N.J.: Princeton University Press.

von Schelting, A. 1934. *Max Webers Wissenschaftslehre*. Tübingen: Mohr.

Wagner, R. 1986. *Symbols That Stand for Themselves*. Chicago: University of Chicago Press.

Watkins, J. 1952. Ideal types and historical explanation. *British Journal for the Philosophy of Science* 3:22–43.

Weber, M. 1920–21 [1904–5]. *Die protestantische Ethik und der Geist des Kapitalismus.* In Weber, *Religionssoziologie,* 1:1–206. Tübingnen: Mohr, 1920.

———. 1920–21. *Gesammelte Aufsätze zur Religionssoziologie,* 2 vols. Tübingen: Mohr.

———. 1922. *Wirtschaft und Gesellschaft. Grundriss der Verstehende Soziologie,* 3 vols., 5th ed. Tübingen: Mohr (Paul Siebebck). Eng. trans.: *Economy and Society.* Berkeley: University of California Press.

———. 1924. Die sozialen Gründe des Untergangs der antiken Kultur. In *Gesammelte Aufsätze zur Wirtschafts-und Sozialgeschichte,* pp. 289–311. Tübingen: Mohr.

———. 1988 [1913]. Über einige Kategorien der verstehenden Soziologie. In *Gesammelte Aufsätze zur Wissenschaftslehre,* pp. 427–74. Tübingen: Mohr.

Whewell, W. 1847. *Philosophy of the Inductive Sciences,* rev. ed., 2 vols. London: Parker.

White, H[arrison]. 1973. Everyday life in stochastic networks. In Alker et al., 287–300.

White, H[ayden]. 1978. *Tropics of Discourse.* Baltimore: Johns Hopkins University Press.

Winch, P. 1958. *The Idea of a Social Science.* London: Routledge and Kegan Paul.

Wittgenstein, L. 1953. *Philosophical Investigations.* Oxford: Blackwell.

Woolgar, S. 1986. On the alleged distinction between discourse and praxis. *Social Studies of Science* 16:309–17.

Wrong, D. 1961. The oversocialized conception of man in modern sociology. *American Sociological Review* 26:183–93.

Zak, M. 1994. Postinstability models in dynamics. *International Journal of Theoretical Physics* 33:2215–80.

Index of Names ::

Afriat, S. N., 372
Agassi, J., 198, 234, 253, 385
Agger, B., 75
Akerlof, G. A., 223, 231, 367
Albert, H., 152, 293, 343, 346
Alexander, J. C., 4, 277, 288
Allais, M., 225, 371, 372, 395
Althusser, L. 212
Ampère, A.-M., 119
Anand, P., 225
Andreski, S., 207, 236
Andrews, F. M., 173
Archer, M., 342
Armstrong, E., 381
Arrow, K. J. 250, 274

Bachelard, G., 316
Bacon, F., 58, 313
Barnes, B., 209, 315, 318, 335, 336
Bartlett, M. S., 348
Baumol, W. J., 41
Becker, G. S., 94, 175, 192, 233, 243, 249, 360, 374, 380
Belenky, M. F., 336
Bellarmino, R., 356
Benda, J., 307
Benhabib, J., 41
Benn, S. I., 361
Bentham, J., 231, 243, 383

Berelson, B., 192
Berger, P., 336
Bergson, H., 212, 305
Berkeley, G., 296
Bernard, C., 102, 322
Bernays, P., 114
Bettinger, R. L., 375
Bindra, D., 34, 48, 284
Blalock, A., 35, 167
Blalock, H. M., 35, 167
Blatt, J. M., 224, 395
Blau, P. M., 269
Blaug, M., 175
Blinder, A. S., 251, 396
Blitz, D., 20
Bloch, M., 367
Bloom, H., 56, 290
Bloor, D., 209, 216, 217–18, 296, 318, 339
Bluestone, B., 174
Blumer, H., 289, 305
Bochenski, J. M., 154
Bohr, N., 118
Booth, W. J., 361
Boudon, R., 20, 45, 148–49, 167, 175, 207, 248–49, 253, 254, 263, 343, 361, 369, 380
Bourdieu, P., 175, 186, 259, 273, 289
Bourricaud, F., 45, 249, 254, 263
Bradburn, N. W., 87

Brams, S. J., 385
Breit, W., 330
Bridgman, P. W., 319
Brock, W. A., 41
Brodbeck, M., 243, 269
Brown, C., 40
Brown, R. H., 290, 344
Buckley, W., 264
Burdeau, G., 303
Burke, K., 290

Cacioppo, J. T., 178
Campbell, R., 385
Camps, V., 258
Carnap, R., 4, 180, 192, 295, 315
Cassirer, E., 289
Cicourel, A. V., 227
Clavelin, M., 343
Coleman, J. S., 20, 109, 148–49, 192, 248, 249, 254, 257, 395
Collingwood, R. G., 287
Collins, H. M., 209, 210, 295, 313, 315, 338, 341, 342
Collins, R., 176, 255, 382
Coughlin, R. M., 368
Cross, J. G., 368, 382

Dahrendorf, R., 66
Dallmayr, F. R., 150, 290
Darwin, C., 88, 324
Davis, D. D., 178, 371
Dawson, R. E., 178, 267, 371
Debreu, G., 55, 113, 114
Dechert, W. D. 41
de Graaff, J., 55
d'Encausse, H. C., 382
Denzin, N. K., 362
Derrida, J., 12, 101, 150, 290
Descartes, R., 58, 283, 298
Dexter, L. A., 381
Diesing, P., 175
Dilthey, W., 150–52, 212, 248, 286, 305, 343, 377
Duhem, P., 42, 92, 216
Dumont, L., 287
Du Pasquier, G., 37, 348
Durkheim, E., 20, 25, 84, 102, 145, 152, 210, 216, 227, 237, 259, 271, 285, 288, 335, 341

Earl, P. E., 225
Eatwell, J., 214
Einhorn, H. J., 168–69
Einstein, A., xii, 4, 118, 311, 344

Elster, J., 385
Engels, F., 58, 232, 299, 327
Etzioni, A., 231
Evans, R. G., 280
Ezrahi, Y., 210

Fauconnet, P., 288
Featherstone, M., 75
Feigl, H., 225
Festinger, L., 101
Feuerbach, L., 216
Feyerabend, P. K., 25, 59, 97, 118, 184, 218, 295, 339, 343
Feynman, R. P., 348
Fielding, H., 63
Fisher, R., 178
Fiske, D. W., 328
Fleck, L., 80, 295, 335–36
Fogel, R. W, 179
Foucault, M., 101, 290, 295, 328–29
Fox Keller, E., 97
Franck, R., 35, 225
Frank, P., 216, 356
Frank, R. H., 368, 374, 381
Fréchet, M., 348
Freeman, D. B., 371
Freese, L., 115
Freud, S., 5, 99, 156, 168, 206
Friedman, J. W., 254
Friedman, M., 55, 175, 334, 364

Gadamer, H. G., 150–51, 290, 343
Galanter, E., 397
Galbraith, J. K., 214
Galilei, G., 356
Gardner, M., 347
Garfinkel, H., 136, 305, 332
Gauthier, D., 230–31
Geertz, C., 290, 305, 332
Gellner, E., 243, 244, 289, 293, 342
Geyer, F., 158
Giesen, B., 4, 288
Gini, C., 384
Glass, L., 40
Goffman, E., 331
Goldsmith, D., 210
Goodman, N., 118, 318, 331, 333
Gouldner, A. W., 235, 327
Granovetter, M., 250, 257
Green, D. P., 384
Greenwood, E., 178
Griliches, Z., 85
Guyer, M. J., 368, 382

Haack, S., 323

Habermas, J., 184, 214, 291
Hagen, O., 225, 371, 372
Hammond III, J. S., 224
Hardin, G., 254
Harding,. S., 330, 336
Harris, M., 154, 301–2, 375
Harrison, B., 174
Harsanyi, J. C., 231, 232
Hartman, A., 398
Harvey, D., 75
Harvey, W., 99
Hausman, J. A., 178
Hayek, F. A., 86, 248, 330, 356
Hebb, D. O., 34, 48, 284, 369
Hegel, G. W. F., 4, 54, 58, 64, 88, 232
Heidegger, M., 12, 50, 151, 290–91, 308, 318
Hempel, C. G., 143
Hendry, D. F., 104
Herrnstein, J. W., 371
Herschel, J. F. W., 92
Hesse, M., 334
Hilbert, D., xii, 114
Himmelstrand, U., 190
Hirschman, A. O., 84, 380
Hirst, R. J., 326
Hobbes, T., 230, 243, 298
Hodder, I., 345
Hogarth, R. M., 168–69, 371
Holt, C. A., 178, 371
Homans, G. C., 192, 244, 246, 248, 249
Hume, D., 32, 222, 380
Husserl, E., 10, 12, 106, 151, 293–95, 305–6, 331, 336

Iannone, A. P., 231, 234
Ibn Khaldûn, 242, 259

James, W., 186, 317
Jarvie, I. C., 342
Jasso, G., 352
Jensen, A., 210
Jones, R., 158
Juster, F.T., 369

Kahneman, D., 224, 225, 367, 371
Kant, I., 58, 64, 229, 257, 322, 333, 377
Kaplan, A., 109
Karni, E., 347
Kearney, R., 290
Keynes, J. M., 84, 254
Kitcher, P., 353
Knetsch, J. L., 397
Knorr-Cetina, K. D., 209, 295, 313, 318, 336

Koertge, N., 330
Kraus, J. B., 287
Krimerman, L. I., 243, 269
Kuhn, T. S., 6, 81, 118, 190, 295, 316, 336, 341

Labriola, Antonio, 318
Lachmann, L. M., 290
Lalande, A., 356
La Mettrie, J. de, 298
Lane, R. E., 369
Lang, S., 214, 236
Lange, F. A., 333
Laponce, J. A., 178
Larsson, S., 224
Lasswell, H. D., 109
Latour, B., 16, 209, 210, 295, 296, 313, 315, 318, 320, 336, 337, 341, 344–45
Lazarsfeld, P., 19
Leach, E., 86
Leibniz, G, W., 35, 95, 321
Lenin, V. I., 300
León-Portilla, M., 302
Leverrier, U.-J.-J., 99
Lévi-Strauss, C., 273, 275, 289, 290
Lewontin, R. C., 214
Livingston, P., 309, 393
Lloyd, C., 243
Lomnitz, L., 272
Lorrain, F., 149, 271
Louch, A. R., 288
Luce, R. D., 223, 361
Lucjmann, T., 336
Lucretius, 41
Luhmann, N., 59, 93, 291, 332
Lynch, M. E., 210, 295

McCarthy, T. A., 150
McCloskey, 310–11, 334, 362
Mach, E., 92, 295, 324
Machiavelli, N., 380
Machina, M. J., 225
Machlup, F., 55
McKeown, T., 261
Mackey, M., 40
Mackey, R., 198
MacKinnon, C., 336
Malcolm, N., 288
Malinvaud, E., 149, 163
Malitza, M., 385
Mandelbaum, M., 243, 264
Mann, M., 64, 265, 277, 301
March, J. G., 172, 372
Marcuse, H., 184, 214

Marshall, A., 7, 223
Marx, K., 4, 58, 68, 84, 145, 152–54, 211,
 228, 254, 259, 264, 299–300, 327, 379
Mathews, J., 234
Mauss, M., 288, 335
Mead, G. H., 289
Menger, C., 66, 294
Menzel, H., 19
Merton, R. K., 4, 109, 122, 158, 188, 205,
 208–9, 296, 351
Michalos, A., 173
Mill, J. S., 84, 231, 243, 295, 320
Mitcham, C., 198
Moore, E., 172
Morgenstern, O., 85, 177, 223, 224, 299,
 361, 368
Morris, C. W., 315
Mortimore, G. W., 361
Moser, P. K., 361
Moses, 156
Mueller-Vollmer, K., 150, 290
Muhammad, 156
Mulkay, M., 209, 336
Müller, A., 212
Munier, B., 225
Murphy, K. M., 360
Myrdal, G., 8, 84, 237

Nadeau, R., 378
Nagel, E., 351
Neurath, O., 192, 315
Newton, I., 314
Nietzsche, F., 212, 333
Nozick, R., 230

Olson, M., 361
O'Neill, J., 243, 269
Optner, S. L., 264

Pareto, V., 43, 84, 169, 223, 232, 264, 369,
 374, 384
Parsons, T., 113, 122, 259, 271
Passinetti, L. L., 214
Patai, D., 330
Peano, G., 68
Peirce, C. S., 89, 180, 321
Petty, R. E., 178
Piaget, J., 20
Pinch, T. J., 210, 216, 314
Poincaré, H., 92, 208, 371, 395–96
Poisson, S.-D., 37
Polanyi, K., 250, 271
Pólya, G., 103

Popper, K. R., 4, 9, 37, 58, 92, 106, 113,
 143, 180–81, 186, 217, 244, 245, 300,
 317, 322, 365, 378
Porter, M. E., 379
Portes, A., 87
Prebisch, R., 84
Ptolemy, 42, 216
Putnam, H., 354

Quine, W. V. O., 216

Rabelais, F., 58
Rachlin, H., 371
Radcliffe-Brown, A. R., 259
Raiffa, H., 223, 361
Rand, A., 230
Ranke, L., 235
Rapoport, A., 361, 384
Rawls, J., 230–31
Ray, A. J., 371
Reder, M. W., 371
Reich, R. B., 368
Reichenbach, H., 180, 216
Rescher, N., 94, 343
Restivo, S., 339
Ricardo, D., 68
Richard, J.-F., 104
Ricoeur, P., 290, 334
Robinson, J., 214
Rohatyn, F., 380
Rokeach, M., 115
Rorty, R., 310, 334
Rosenau, J. N., 40
Ross, E., 302
Rossi, P. H., 88
Rousseau, J.-J., 230, 254
Russell, B., 11
Russell, C., 247
Russett, B., 253
Ryan, A., 360, 385

Safra, Z., 347
Samuelson, P., 223, 360
Sassen-Koob, S., 87
Scherer, F., 372
Schopenhauer, A., 296
Schumpeter, J., 4, 322, 386
Schütz, A., 150, 293, 294–95, 305, 332
Scitovsky, T., 374, 380, 384, 394
Searle, J., 353
Sebreli, J. J., 343
Sen, A., 231, 380
Shapiro, I., 384
Sheldon, E. B., 172

Shepherd, L. J., 307, 330
Shoemaker, P. J. H., 225
Shubik, M., 395
Shweder, R. A., 328, 330
Siegel, H., 342
Simmel, G., 84, 248, 258, 286–87, 327
Simon, H. A., 172, 372, 375
Smart, J. J. C., 230, 238
Smelser, N. J., 243, 384
Smith, A., 383
Smoker, P., 178
Sorokin, P. A., 61, 175, 207
Sowden, L., 385
Spaulding, A. C., 86
Spiegel, G. M., 29
Spinoza, B., 232
Stacey, R. D., 40
Stack, G., 152
Stalin, J., 156
Starr, H., 253
Steiner, G. A., 192
Stigler, G. J., 233, 380
Stinchcombe, A. L., xii. 380
Suppes, P., 176
Swedberg, R., 5, 192, 243, 374

Taylor, C., 290
Thatcher, M., 243
Thom, R., 324
Tocqueville, A. de, 146, 158, 262
Tolstoy, L., 259
Tönnies, F., 258
Trigg, R., 342
Trigger, B. G., 310
Tversky, A., 224, 367, 371

Vaihinger, H., 42, 334
van der Zouwen, J., 158
van Dusen, R. A., 172
van Fraassen, B. 117, 356
Veblen, T., 258
Velikovsky, I., 209–10
Vico, G. B., 152
Vienna Circle, 10, 316
Ville, J., 225
von Mises, L., 55, 64, 113, 294, 321, 327
von Neumann, J., 223, 224, 361
von Schelting, A., 152

Wagner, R., 290
Watkins, J., 243
Weber, M., 4, 8, 58, 64, 68, 80, 84, 145,
    150–55, 219, 228, 235–36, 248, 253,
    285, 287–88, 294, 322, 327, 330, 345,
    369, 377
Whewell, W., 89
White, Harrison C., 149, 250, 271
White, Hayden, 334
Winch, P., 150, 244, 288
Wise, D. A., 178
Wittgenstein, L., 12, 117, 150, 244, 290,
    335, 354
Woolgar, S., 16, 209, 210, 291, 295, 296,
    313, 315, 318, 336, 337, 338, 341, 344
Wrong, D. 257

Zak, M., 41
Zeno, 54
Zinnes, J. L., 176

Index of Subjects ::

Absurdity, 309–10
Action, 74, 317
Activity, 369
Advancement, conceptual, 132
Agathonism, 233, 238
Agency-structure relation, 280–81
Aims: of science, 80, 188, 190; of technology, 201, 204
Analogy, 93
Analysis, causal, 140–41
Anarchism, epistemological, 338–89
Anomaly, 100
Anti-positivism, 317, 328
Anti-realism, 98–99, 328
Appearance, 41–44, 357. *See also* Phenomenon
Approach, 79–80, 265–67
Approximation, 96
Apriorism, 88, 320. *See also* Rationalism
Artifact, 121, 198
Assumption, 70–72; factual, 70; semantic, 64, 194
Attribution, 51. *See also* Predicate
Automata theory, 25
Autopoietic, 93
Axiology, 8, 220
Axiom, 69, 72
Axiomatization, 72, 114, 124–25

Background, of a research field, 187, 189, 202–3
Bayesianism, 37, 346–49. *See also* Probability, subjective
Behaviorism, 33–34, 83
Belief, 78, 217, 347, 350
BEPC model, 22, 271, 301
Biography, 154
Biologism, 129
Biology, 324–25
Black box theory, 110
Bottom-up analysis, 138, 147. *See also* Reduction
Boudon-Coleman diagram, 149, 280–81
Boundary of a system, 270–71
Business, 231

Calculation, 252
Cartesianism, 215–16
Case study, 86–87
Causation, 30–36
Cause, 139, 141, 144, 152
Cell, social, 275
CES sketch, 109, 264, 270
Ceteris paribus condition, 119–20, 168
Chance, 36–39, 140, 346–50
Change, 25, 276–77, 384. *See also* Event; History; Process

Chaos theory, 39–41, 160
Choice, 172
Choice-action gap, 381
Class, social, 68–69
Classification, 111–13
Code, moral, 226–27
Cognition, 76–77, 105
Collection, 26, 51
Collectivism. *See* Holism
Communication, 59, 94
Community, 187, 189, 200, 202, 258
Competition, 272–73
Complexity, 83
Comprehensive sociology, 151–57. *See also* Dilthey, W.; Simmel, G.; Verstehen; Weber, M.
Computationalism, 129
Computer, 65, 88
Concept, 49
Concomitance, 32
Concrete, 25
Confirmation, 89, 180–81
Confirmationism, 180–81
Connotation, 55. *See also* Sense
Consensus, 94, 97
Consequentialism, 230, 400
Consistency: external, 11, 181–82, 104, 217; internal, 11, 104
Construction, social, 336
Constructivism, 295–98, 336–37, 352–53, 335–38
Constructivism-relativism, 15–16, 96–98, 209–10, 214, 235, 312–15, 324
Contamination, ideological, 214–15, 236
Contractarianism. *See* Contractualism
Contractualism, 230–31, 254–55
Contradiction, 53, 309–10
Controversy, 5–6, 215, 341–42
Convention, 69, 119
Conventionalism, 118, 216, 323, 324, 332–35
Cooperation, 272, 273, 379
Correlation, statistical, 28–29
Correspondence principle, 118
Cost-benefit analysis, 375
Covering law model, 143
Creativity, 101
Criterion, 69
Critical theory, 214. *See also* Habermas, J.
Criticism, 81, 99–101
Crypto-systemism, 253–55
Crypto-tautology, 54
Culture, contemporary, 185

Data, 71, 84–90; data-theory translation, 394
Decision theory, 349–50
Deductivism, 89–90, 180–82
Definiendum, 68
Definiens, 68
Definition, 68–70; axiomatic, 68–69; operational, 169; persuasive, 70; reductive, 126–27
Demarcation criterion, 4
Demography, 28
Denotation, 55. *See also* Reference
Density matrix, 275, 276
Deontologism, 229–30
Description, 135–37
Descriptivism, 34, 141–42
Design, 198–200
Determinism, 299
Deviance, social, 269
Diagram, 110–11
Dialectics, 114, 301
Dimension, 65
Duty, 226, 227, 233

Economicism, 192–93. *See also* Imperialism, economic
Economics, 5, 67, 72–73, 120, 223, 286, 294, 354, 373, 382
Eddington's desks, 278
Egoism, 230
Emergence, 20, 24, 45–46, 248–49, 251, 255
Emotion, 380–81
Empathy, 307
Empiricism, 67, 76, 88, 106, 305, 311–13, 316–17, 322; logical, 10, 180, 316–17, 322. *See also* Neo-positivism
Engineering, social, 241
Endostructure, 270
Enlinghtenment, 58, 211–12
Environmentalism, 273
Epistemology, 2, 7, 104–07
Epoché, 294, 308, 331
Equality, 68
Equilibrium, 373
Equivalence 66–67, 246, 274–75
Error, 78, 85, 96, 177, 208, 341, 355, 357–58
Essence, 308, 331
Essentialism, 17
Ethics, 8, 229–34; agathonist, 233; contractualist, 230–31; rational choice, 231–33; utilitarian, 231–33
Ethnomethodology, 210

Ethos of science, 188
Event, 24–25, 31
Evidence, 90, 180–82, 322
Evolution, 24
Exactification, 11, 37, 61
Exactness, 59, 61
Excluded middle, 53
Existentialism, 9, 295. *See also* Heidegger, M.
Exostructure, 270
Expectation, 33–34, 251
Experiment, 177–80, 216
Explainability principle, 121
Explanandum, 143
Explanans, 143
Explanation, 137–42, 160; causal, 139–41, 377–78; logic of, 142–44, 156; mechanismic, 138–44; by reasons, 377–78; reductive, 138; of variables, 141; teleological, 204–5
Extension of a predicate, 52–53, 245

Fact, 15–46, 85, 297; finding, 88; social, 44–46, 130, 135
Fact-value gap, 222
Fallibilism, 23, 71, 120
Feeling, moral, 232
Fictionism, 98, 117, 334
Foraging theory, 375
Forecast, 157–65; active, 163–65; logical form, 159; passive, 163–64; probabilistic, 160; social, 162–63, 251
Formalization, 61–65
Foundationalism, 232
Frankfurt school, 214
Freedom, 1663, 227–29, 232, 234–35, 255, 256
Free will, 228
Frequency, relative, 39
Function, mathematical, 31–32, 50–51
Functionalism, 259
Futility theory, 397–98
Future design, 164–65
Futurology, 163–65
Fuzzy logic, 60

Geisteswissenschaften, 151, 288
Gemeinschaft, 258
Generalism, 196
Generalization, empirical, 71
General systems theory, 21
German historical school, 258
Gesellschaft, 258
Glue formula, 130
Gobbledygook, 58

Good, 221
Goodness of fit, 104
Graph, 88
Gray box theory, 110, 123

Hegelianism, 9
Hermeneutics, philosophical, 93, 151, 190–93, 286–88, 343–46
Hindcast, 157–58
Historicism, 142
History, 5, 24, 392
Holism, 22, 80, 258–62; methodological, 260–62; moral, 260, 262; ontological, 260–61
homo oeconomicus, 67
Humanist social studies, 67
Hyper-rationalism, 227
Hypothesis, 42, 72, 88–93, 151, 172, 333; ad hoc, 99, 115, 181; factual, 71, 292; programmatic, 2, 51
Hypothetico-deductive system 72–73. *See also* Theory

Idea, 43, 46, 47–75
Ideal: object, 26; type, 66–68, 294
Idealism, 27, 62, 282–98
Idealization, 66, 116
Identity, 68
Ideology, 184–85, 211–18, 235–36
Idiographic discipline, 3
Imperialism, economic, 94, 192–93, 243, 249. *See also* Becker, G. S., Economicism
Implication, 68
imprecision, 60
Improvement, technological, 200
Incommensurability, 118
Indicator, 167, 169–74, 176, 292; empirical, 176; hypothesis, 169–74, 393–94; social, 172–74, 292
Individholism, 253–54
Individual, 51
Individualism, 22, 80, 241–58, 312; institutionalist, 255; methodological, 45, 146–48, 245, 257; moderate, 249; moral, 245, 247; ontological, 45, 244–47; radical, 249
Individualism-holism-systemism trilemma, 3, 52, 241
Induction, 71–72, 89
Inductivism, 71, 88–89, 93–94, 180–82
Inexactness, 60
Inference, 92
Information, 59, 289
Infrastructure-superstructure relation, 299–300, 302

Inquiry, 76–107
Inscription, 337–38
Instability, 40–41
Institution, 22
Instrumentalism. *See* Pragmatism
Integration. *See* Merger of research fields
Intelligibility principle, 121
Intention, 155–56
Interdiscipline, 193
Interest, 374
Interpretation, 64, 91–92, 289, 191–92, 343–44. *See also* Verstehen
Intersubjectivity, 329
Intuition, 49, 174, 309
Intuitionism, 106, 161–62, 305–9
Invention, 161, 200
IQ test, 210
Irrationalism, 64, 227, 309, 321, 324, 362
Irrationality, 360
Isms, 242
Issue, 81, 82

Justice, 351–52
Justification, 323

Kind, natural, 66, 112
Know-how. *See* Knowledge, tacit
Knowledge, 73, 76–78, 82, 217, 234; background, 79, 181–82; fund of, 189; problem of, 104–7; tacit, 73, 77

Laboratory, 313–14, 318–20, 337–38
Language, 136
Law, 26–27, 143–44, 392–93; scientific, 74, 158–59; social, 27–28; statement, 27, 73, 118; theoretical, 119–21
Lawfulness principle, 30, 121
Learning, 91
Lebenswelt, 193–94
Levels analysis, 145–50, 277–79
Linguistics, 289–90
Logic, 2, 7, 9, 19, 39, 49, 53–55, 68, 73, 78

Macro-concept, 250, 253
Macro-data, 85–86
Macro-fact, 147
Macro-reduction, 148
Macro-variable, 148–49
Magical thinking, 330, 345
Marginality, social, 63
Market, 94
Markov chain, 38–39
Marxism, 5, 9, 147, 212, 299–300
Material, 25

Materialism, 44, 282–85, 298–303, 324; cultural, 361, 375; emergentist, 44, 299; historical, 299–301; mechanistic, 298
Mathematics, 54–55, 62–65, 95, 19, 193–94, 339–40
Matter, 25, 302
Meaning, 55–57; as purpose, 151–52
Means-end relation, 221
Measure, 176
Measurement, 176–77
Mechanism, 31, 110, 124, 137–38, 159–60; social, 138
Mechanismic, 124. *See also* Translucent box theory
Meliorism, 23, 71, 120
Membership relation, 51, 244, 246
Memory, 25, 206
Merger of research fields, 130–32
Metaphor, 93–94
Metaphysics. *See* Ontology
Meta-rule, 73
Metastatement, 125–26
Metatheory, 3, 6–12, 125–26. *See also* Philosophy of science
Method, 79, 101–4; scientific, 29–30, 102–3; technological, 199
Methodenstreit, 5
Methodics, 79–80, 188, 201
Methodology, 7, 103
Metric spaces, 394–95
Micro-concept, 250
Micro-data, 85–86
Micro-explanation, 148. *See also* Micro-reduction
Micro–macro relation, 145, 277–81
Micro-reduction, 148, 150–57
Micro-variable, 148–49
Model, 64–65, 115–17, 123–24
Modus ponens, 53
Morals, 225–27
Movement, social, 272

Naturalism, 152, 298
Needs, 221
Neo-individualism, 254. *See also* Crypto-systemism
Neo-Kantianism, 58, 327. *See also* Dilthey, W.; Simmel, G.; Weber, M.
Neo-positivism, 10, 57. *See also* Empiricism, logical
Network, social, 250, 271
Newtonianism, 215–16
Nominalism, 245–46
Nomothetic disciplines, 3

Nonrationality, 374
Norm, 2, 226
N-tuple, 51, 245

Objectivism, 329–30. *See also* Realism
Objectivity, 43, 326–32
Obscurantism, philosophical, 58–59
Observation, 175–76; participant, 314
Ontology, 2, 7. *See also* Holism, Individualism, Systemism
Operation, empirical, 166–83
Operationism, 169–70, 319–20, 393–94
Optimization, 372–73
Ordinarism, 312
Ordinary language philosophy, 11
Organicism. *See* Holism
Organization, 22, 271
Originality, 11

Paradigm, 81, 190
Parameter, 50–51
Participation, 63
Partition of a set, 66, 274–75
Part-whole relation, 279–80
Patent, 202
Pattern, 26, 42, 119
Perception, 41–43, 351–53, 355
Perverse effect, 160
Phenomenalism, 42–43, 98, 171, 356
Phenomenology, 9, 293–95, 307–08, 331–32
Phenomenon, 41, 44. *See also* Appearance
Philosophy, fertility of, 11
Philosophy of science, xi, 194–95, 218, 322
Physicalism, 128–29, 192, 315
Planning, 164–65
Policy, 29
Politology, 382
Positivism, 9, 27, 71, 283. *See also* Empiricism
Postmodernism, 294. *See also* Irrationalism
Poverty, 173
Pragmatism, 76, 98, 106, 203, 306, 317–20
Predicate, 18, 50, 52
Predictability, 157–63
Prediction, 157–65, 382. *See also* Forecast
Preference relation, 233, 400
Presupposition, 70–71,189, 223, 353
Primitive 68–69
Probability, 36–39, 140, 224, 363–64, 395; objective, 224, 346–50; subjective, 224, 346–50, 363–64
Problem, 79, 81–84; direct, 83, 124, 151, 155; inverse, 83–84, 124, 151, 155; social, 82

Problematics, 79–80, 189, 203–4
Process, 24–25, 36; social, 272, 276–77
Projection. *See* Forecast, Hindcast
Propensity, 37. *See also* Probability, objective
Property, 17–20; emergent, 19–20
Prophecy, 158; self-defeating, 158, 164; self-fulfilling, 158, 164
Proposal, 49, 198
Proposition, 49, 53, 71
Pseudo-exactness, 61
Pseudoscience, 174, 205–11
Pseudotechnology, 202
Psychoanalysis, 205–6
Psychologism, 129, 192
Psychology, 248, 206, 258, 284, 380–87
Purpose, 139

Quality, 62
Quantification. *See* Quantitation
Quantitation, 62–64
Quasilaw, 120

R&D 198–99, 202
Randomness, 36–38, 346–48
Ratio-empiricism, 322–24, 359
Rational choice theories, 223, 233, 248–53, 302, 347, 359–87
Rationalism, 76, 106, 306, 320–22, 324, 359
Rationality, 153, 233, 376–77, 359–360, 373–77; principle, 224, 366–70, 379–80
Real, 25, 41
Realism, 43, 152, 185, 203, 216, 323, 326–30, 353–58, 362; scientific, 43–44, 99, 107, 323, 355–58
Reality, 26, 43, 296, 302; check, 174–80
Reason, 380–81; as cause, 35–36, 139–40, 377–78
Reasoning, 70
Reduction, 126–29, 251–52
Reductionism, 128–32, 192–93, 365
Reference, 6, 52–53, 55, 56, 131, 277, 278
Refutationism, 89, 178, 180–81
Relation, 245–46, 274. *See also* Predicate
Relativism, 78–79, 238, 338–43
Relativity theory, 313, 344
Representation, 110, 117
Research, 82
Residue, 169
Rhetoric, 310–11, 362
Right, 226, 233
Risk, 349
Rival theories, 118
Romanticism, 58
Rule, 29, 73–74, 103, 198, 392–93

Sampling, 36–37
Sartisficing, 372
Science, 15, 84–85, 107, 184–88, 196–97; ethos of, 234–35; unity of, 191–96, 241
Scientism, 107, 323, 356
Self-reference, 93, 158
Semantics, 2, 7, 95
Semi-science, 188, 191
Sensationalism, philosophical, 316
Sense, 56–57
Set, 51, 62
Signification, 57
Simplicity, 118, 333
Simulation, 178–79
Situational logic, 378
Skepticism, 97, 99, 105, 323, 338, 339
Sketch, 109–11
Society, 241, 271
Sociologism, 129
Sociology of science, 208–11
Sociotechnology, 205, 387
State: function, 23, 391–92; space, 30, 228, 391–93; of a thing, 23–24
Statistics, 71, 86–87
Strong programme, 216–17
Structural interdependence, 254
Structuralism, 273, 289–90
Structure, 245–46, 289; social, 246, 270, 274–76
Structure-agency relation, 280
Subjectivism, 16, 25, 97, 153, 326–32
Subjectivity, 43, 351–53
Subsumption, 142–44
Subsystem, 22, 270
Success, 319
Supersystem, 23, 270
Survival, social, 155
Symbol, 47, 60–61, 345
Symbolic interactionism, 289
Systematization, 108–32
Systemicity, 132
System, 20–21, 83, 108–32, 270, 302; social, 20–22, 44–45, 59, 129, 147, 192, 246–47, 255, 261, 270–74; sociotechnical, 204; symbolic, 21, 270
Systemism, 20, 44, 132, 195–96, 241–42, 249, 264–81
Systems: analysis, 267; theory, 265, 267

Tautology, 53–54, 168
Technics, 198
Technology, 73–74, 80, 184–85, 197–205, 234–37, 319

Teleology, 121
Test, 166, 174–80, 216–17
Testability, 57, 65, 167–69, 370
Textualism, 129–30, 151, 290–93, 343–46. See also Hermeneutics, philosophical
Theoretical entity, 117
Theory, 56, 70, 113–18, 121–27, 297, 318–19, 330, 333; range, 121–22; relation to data, 324–25; underdetermination by data, 216–17, 333
Thermodynamics, 93
Thing, 17; for us, in itself, 354
Thomism, 212
Thought: collective, 48; style, 80. See also Paradigm
Top-down analysis, 138, 147. See also Microreduction
Translucent box theory, 110, 123–24
Trap, social, 368
Trend, 28, 162–63
Trial and error, 80
Truth, 15–16, 77, 94–99, 117–18, 143, 235; factual, 95, 166–67, 318, 321, 333, 357; formal, 54, 95, 321; indicator, 180–81; partial, 38, 96, 340; tests, 166–83
Turing machine, 25

Understanding, 143, 151, 154. See also Interpretation, Verstehen
Universality, 11
Universe of discourse, 187, 200. See also Reference
Unobservable, 89, 169–71
Utilitarianism, 222, 231–33
Utility, 222–25, 347; function, 223, 263–64, 394–97; maximization, 128–29, 224, 231–32, 365–68, 370–73; set-theoretic formalizations, 399–400

Value, 201, 204, 219–25, 235, 237, 388–400
Variable, 50–51, 110, 165
Verifiability theory of meaning, 57
Verstehen, 80, 83–84, 150–57, 286, 290, 307

Want, 221
Well-formedness, 103
World system, 272
World view, 217

H
61
.B793
1996

ℓ.c.a.

HUMANITIES   Philosophy

34-4402   H61   96-4399 CIP
Bunge, Mario. **Finding philosophy in social science.** Yale, 1996. 432p bibl indexes
afp ISBN 0-300-06606-6, $45.00

A prolific scholar in the areas of philosophy of science and general philosophy, Bunge (McGill Univ.) has charted an independent course, which, having weathered the passage of time far better than many of the fashionable philosophical alternatives he eschewed, leaves him today deservedly recognized as among the most eminent of living philosophers. In a projected companion volume, Bunge explores issues particular to individual social sciences. In this volume, he addresses issues pertinent to all social sciences. While focused on criticism of the "new sociology of science" and its "constructivist-relativist" view of science as a socially constructed ideology lacking any legitimate claim to universal truth, it also serves as a compendium covering a wide range of problems in the philosophy of the social sciences. The work also includes an extended criticism of rational choice models in the social sciences. Along with the sharpness and clarity of Bunge's thought, the detailed name and subject indexes make this an excellent reference work for philosophers of science and for students and scholars in the social sciences who must deal with the philosophical minefields that litter their chosen disciplines. Upper-division undergraduate; graduate; faculty.—*R. Hudelson, University of Minnesota—Duluth*

Finding Philosophy in Social Science